(Continued on back endsheets)

Sixteenth-Century British Nondramatic Writers
Second Series

Sixteenth-Century British Nondramatic Writers
Second Series

Edited by
David A. Richardson
Cleveland State University

A Bruccoli Clark Layman Book
Gale Research Inc.
Detroit, Washington, D.C., London

For Mark and Helena,

"In prime of youthly yeares"

Contents

Contents

Plan of the Series

. . . Almost the most prodigious asset of a country, and perhaps its most precious possession, is its native literary product — when that product is fine and noble and enduring.

Mark Twain*

The advisory board, the editors, and the publisher of the *Dictionary of Literary Biography* are joined in endorsing Mark Twain's declaration. The literature of a nation provides an inexhaustible resource of permanent worth. We intend to make literature and its creators better understood and more accessible to students and the reading public, while satisfying the standards of teachers and scholars.

To meet these requirements, *literary biography* has been construed in terms of the author's achievement. The most important thing about a writer is his writing. Accordingly, the entries in *DLB* are career biographies, tracing the development of the author's canon and the evolution of his reputation.

The purpose of *DLB* is not only to provide reliable information in a convenient format but also to place the figures in the larger perspective of literary history and to offer appraisals of their accomplishments by qualified scholars.

The publication plan for *DLB* resulted from two years of preparation. The project was proposed to Bruccoli Clark by Frederick C. Ruffner, president of the Gale Research Company, in November 1975. After specimen entries were prepared and typeset, an advisory board was formed to refine the entry format and develop the series rationale. In meetings held during 1976, the publisher, series editors, and advisory board approved the scheme for a comprehensive biographical dictionary of persons who contributed to North American literature. Editorial work on the first volume began in January 1977, and it was published in 1978. In order to make *DLB* more than a reference tool and to compile volumes that individually have claim to status as literary history, it was decided to organize volumes by topic, period, or genre. Each of these freestanding volumes provides a biographical-bibliographical guide and overview for a particular area of literature. We are convinced that this organization — as opposed to a single alphabet method — constitutes a valuable innovation in the presentation of reference material. The volume plan necessarily requires many decisions for the placement and treatment of authors who might properly be included in two or three volumes. In some instances a major figure will be included in separate volumes, but with different entries emphasizing the aspect of his career appropriate to each volume. Ernest Hemingway, for example, is represented in *American Writers in Paris, 1920–1939* by an entry focusing on his expatriate apprenticeship; he is also in *American Novelists, 1910–1945* with an entry surveying his entire career. Each volume includes a cumulative index of the subject authors and articles. Comprehensive indexes to the entire series are planned.

With volume ten in 1982 it was decided to enlarge the scope of *DLB*. By the end of 1986 twenty-one volumes treating British literature had been published, and volumes for Commonwealth and Modern European literature were in progress. The series has been further augmented by the *DLB Yearbooks* (since 1981) which update published entries and add new entries to keep the *DLB* current with contemporary activity. There have also been *DLB Documentary Series* volumes which provide biographical and critical source materials for figures whose work is judged to have particular interest for students. One of these companion volumes is entirely devoted to Tennessee Williams.

We define literature as the *intellectual commerce of a nation*: not merely as belles lettres but as that ample and complex process by which ideas are generated, shaped, and transmitted. *DLB* entries are not limited to "creative writers" but extend to other figures who in their time and in their way influenced the mind of a people. Thus the series encompasses historians, journalists, publishers, and screenwriters. By this means readers of *DLB* may be aided to perceive literature not as cult scripture in the keeping of intellectual high priests but firmly po-

From an unpublished section of Mark Twain's autobiography, copyright by the Mark Twain Company

sitioned at the center of a nation's life.

DLB includes the major writers appropriate to each volume and those standing in the ranks immediately behind them. Scholarly and critical counsel has been sought in deciding which minor figures to include and how full their entries should be. Wherever possible, useful references are made to figures who do not warrant separate entries.

Each DLB volume has a volume editor responsible for planning the volume, selecting the figures for inclusion, and assigning the entries. Volume editors are also responsible for preparing, where appropriate, appendices surveying the major periodicals and literary and intellectual movements for their volumes, as well as lists of further readings. Work on the series as a whole is coordinated at the Bruccoli Clark Layman editorial center in Columbia, South Carolina, where the editorial staff is responsible for accuracy of the published volumes.

One feature that distinguishes DLB is the illustration policy – its concern with the iconography of literature. Just as an author is influenced by his surroundings, so is the reader's understanding of the author enhanced by a knowledge of his environment. Therefore DLB volumes include not only drawings, paintings, and photographs of authors, often depicting them at various stages in their careers, but also illustrations of their families and places where they lived. Title pages are regularly reproduced in facsimile along with dust jackets for modern authors. The dust jackets are a special feature of DLB because they often document better than anything else the way in which an author's work was perceived in its own time. Specimens of the writers' manuscripts are included when feasible.

Samuel Johnson rightly decreed that "The chief glory of every people arises from its authors." The purpose of the *Dictionary of Literary Biography* is to compile literary history in the surest way available to us — by accurate and comprehensive treatment of the lives and work of those who contributed to it.

The *DLB* Advisory Board

Introduction

The early modern period from 1485 to 1603 is commonly referred to as "the Renaissance" in England and as "the age of the Tudors," for it can be conveniently divided into the reigns of Henry VII, Henry VIII, Edward VI, Mary, and Elizabeth I in deference to an unbroken string of idiosyncratic Tudor monarchs. There is no single theory, history, concept, or tag for sixteenth-century British nondramatic literature – none at least that inspires widespread and lasting conviction. In matters of literary history each defining term and every generation of scholarship has been succeeded by new information, interpretations, and labels.

Twentieth-century scholarship about sixteenth-century English writing is first dominated by historical, philological, and bibliographic work, with the New Criticism especially prominent after World War II. The latter half of the twentieth century – and especially the final third – has seen an explosion of scholarship influenced by Freudian and other psychologies, Marxist theories of history and economics, feminist and gender issues, and deconstructionism and a vast array of other French theories. Each has had or is having its day, as the New Historicism, for instance, is succeeded by "New New Historicism," and received studies of the British literary empire are reassessed in light of postcolonial anthropological or ethnographic criticism. Two important background studies for sixteenth-century scholarship were made by Jacob Burckhardt (1860) and E. M. W. Tillyard (1944). (For titles and publication information about these and the following works, please see the Checklist of Further Readings at the end of this volume.) Some of the most influential works of the twentieth century include studies by Douglas Bush (1939), Hallett Smith (1952), C. S. Lewis (1954), Mikhail Bakhtin (1968), Michel Foucault (1979), and Stephen Greenblatt (1980). The present state of sixteenth-century literary history is nothing less than effervescent.

For a quick overview of the scholarly status quo, see Leah S. Marcus's essay on "Renaissance / Early Modern Studies" (1992). An evolving history of sixteenth-century literature is implicit – often aggressively explicit – in "Recent Studies in the English Renaissance" (annually in *Studies in English Literature,* winter issue), and readers will quickly spot trends from articles in respected journals such as *English Literary Renaissance* and from book reviews in *Renaissance Quarterly* and the *Sixteenth Century Journal.* Although now two decades old, *The New Cambridge Bibliography of English Literature* (volume one, 1974) is an invaluable guide to primary and secondary materials, including literary history. Michael J. Marcuse's "Literature of the Renaissance and Earlier Seventeenth Century" (1990) is a more current bibliographic starting point.

This introduction does not pronounce on what is past or passing nor does it predict what is to come in the understanding of sixteenth-century literary history. Instead it highlights some of the recurrent motifs of the entries in this volume: literary innovation of several types, emphasis upon didactic and useful writing, science and medicine, a concern for the aesthetic and practical resources of vernacular English, and the popularity of works among a growing readership as well as a commitment to the principles of humanism and the Protestant Reformation. These emphases will inevitably change with the discovery of new documents, reinterpretations of standard texts, and the rise and fall of theoretical schools in the universities. For the last decade of the twentieth century, however, the entries in this volume show the following as some important traits of sixteenth-century British nondramatic literature.

Innovation. The writers discussed in this volume, like those in *DLB 132: Sixteenth-Century British Nondramatic Writers,* First Series, are conveniently labeled "Renaissance authors," but they were far more than literary discoverers and revivers, or adapters and imitators, of "reborn" classical texts. Their works are often strikingly new, even revolutionary. Collectively their literary biographies document innovation on a scale perhaps unequaled in the history of English and in a diversity that almost defies classification.

Genres. Among new genres of literature, perhaps the best-known secular title of the age is Thomas More's *Utopia* (1516), which inaugurated utopian literature in England, gave it its name, and became its chief model. At the same time, many of the epigrams in More's *Epigrammata* (1518) are the first translations of such items from Greek into Latin, while those of John Heywood may have been the first written in English. Also early in the century John Skelton, the first major Tudor poet, adapted strophic plainsong and Gregorian chant for his "Skeltonics"; his poems written against Christopher Garnesche are the first example of a "flyting" (that is, a duel of invective) in English. The object of much of Skelton's satire, Cardinal Thomas Wolsey, was responsible for introducing episcopal pluralism into England – the incentive for much outrage and further satire among Skelton's literary heirs.

John Leland was a pioneer in writing in the "topo-chrono-graphical" mode (descriptions of places, the times, and writing) in his *Cygnea cantio* (1545). The manuscript for Andrew Boorde's accounts of his journeys in Europe during the 1530s and 1540s might have become the first major travel book to be published in English if Thomas Cromwell had not lost it. Blank verse was introduced into English through the translations from Virgil's *Aeneid* by Henry Howard, Earl of Surrey, and put to early use by Nicholas Grimald in his contributions to *Tottel's Miscellany* (1557). Thomas Harman's "cony-catching" pamphlet *A Caveat for Common Cursitors* (1567) is among the earliest examples of crime writing in English. Edward Tilney's *Flower of Friendship* (1568) is the first work of English prose fiction to imitate the dialogue form of Giovanni Boccaccio and Baldassare Castiglione; building on a tradition deriving also from Geoffrey Chaucer and More, Tilney introduced to Elizabethan fiction the convention of giving the author a prominent role in the dialogue. William Painter inaugurated the fashion for translating Continental novellas into English; John Webster and William Shakespeare raided him for dramatic material, his translation in his *The Palace of Pleasure* (1566) of "Giletta of Narbonne" from Boccaccio's *Decameron* (1351–1353) being the first appearance in English of Shakespeare's source for *All's Well That Ends Well* (1623).

In *The Travayled Pilgrim* (1596), his translation of Olivier de la Marche's *Le Chevalier délibéré* (1488), Stephen Bateman wrote what contributor David Galbraith, quoting Anne Lake Prescott, calls "England's only significant nondramatic Protestant quest allegory before [Edmund] Spenser." Bateman also wrote the first mythography to be printed in England, *The Golden Book of the Leaden Gods* (1577). George Whetstone's elegies give him a good claim for being the first professional biographer in England. His collection of novellas, *An Heptameron of Civil Discourse* (1582), is the second collection in En-

glish to be structured around a frame story in imitation of Boccaccio and Chaucer; and his *Promos and Cassandra* (1578) contains one of the earliest critical statements in English about drama, rebuking English playwrights for indecorously mixing the comic with the tragic. His *Honorable Reputation of a Soldier* (1585) is the sole conduct book of its era directed specifically to military men. Also among the innovators, Geoffrey Whitney claimed that he was the first to attempt an anthology of emblems (woodcuts with accompanying mottos and verses) with full histories, applications, and expositions in English. In fact, he was drawing on European emblematists and a manuscript collection, given him by Thomas Palmer in 1560, that was apparently the first such effort in England; but his much-revised *A Choice of Emblems* (1586), an epitome, analysis, and overview of the genre, was developed beyond any other native or Continental example. Thomas Moffet wrote one of the earliest biographies of Sir Philip Sidney in 1593 (though it was not published until 1940); his *Silkworms* (1599) is the first Virgilian georgic in English.

George Gascoigne was perhaps the single most innovative author in various dramatic and nondramatic genres. His *Steel Glass* (1576) is the first attempt in English to unite the native tradition of satire exemplified by William Langland's fourteenth-century poem *Piers Plowman* with the classical modes of Horace and Juvenal. He wrote the first treatise on English prosody, "Certain Notes of Instruction" (1575), and his "Adventures of Master F. J." (1573) is, with its unique commentary by the narrator about verse romance, perhaps the first English novel to parody the Petrarchan tradition (see also the entry on William Baldwin in *DLB 132*). Gascoigne wrote the only English example of the prodigal-son play, *The Glass of Government* (1575), and coauthored the first Greek-style tragedy in English, *Jocasta* (1566); his *Supposes* (1566), based on a play by Ludovico Ariosto, is the first example of Italian-style comedy in English and is a major legacy to the theater, especially to Shakespearean comedy.

(For types of writing by other writers who were not necessarily innovators, see the entries listed under *Genres* at the end of this introduction.)

Woman authors. Women as well as men were literary inventors in sixteenth-century England. *Jane Anger Her Protection for Women* (1589) is the first defense of women to make a serious claim of female authorship, creating a new persona for articulate female anger and a new tone and writing style for woman authors. Isabella Whitney is the first Englishwoman known to have written original secular poetry for publication. Elizabeth Grymeston's posthumously published *Miscelanea* (1604), in the genre of the "mother's advice book," has been called the first autobiography of an Elizabethan woman's mind. And Catherine Parr's *Prayers or Meditations* (1545) is, according to contributor Jeanne Costello, "one of the first popular publications of courtly devotional literature in the English Protestant tradition"; her *Lamentation of a Sinner* (1547) is among the earliest Protestant spiritual autobiographies in English. George Pettie, who sought to provoke rather than simply to charm with his works, may be recognized as one of the earliest and most articulate proponents of literature for women in England. (For other woman authors or men whose writing is relevant to women in the Renaissance, see the entries on Anne Askew, Nicholas Breton, Elizabeth I, Thomas Elyot, Geoffrey Fenton, More, Barnabe Riche, Reginald Scot, and Tilney.)

Language and dictionaries. Authors are necessarily concerned with language in creating their works, and the sixteenth century brought many language-related innovations. Robert Copland's *Highway to the Spital-House* (circa 1536) and Harman's *Caveat for Common Cursitors* are two of the earliest records of English slang, specifically of the subculture dialect of beggars, thieves, and vagrants known as "Pedlar's French" or "the canting tongue." Boorde cited the first known example of Gypsy language in an English work in his *Introduction of Knowledge* (1555?). Elyot's *Doctrinal of Princes* (1533?) is the first translation of Greek directly into English rather than through Latin, and his *The Dictionary of Sir Thomas Elyot* (1538), enlarged as *Bibliotheca Eliotae* (1542), is the first English dictionary of classical Latin.

Useful innovations. Elyot is also important for introducing several new kinds of practical prose: his *Castle of Health* (1537?) is, if not the earliest to be written, certainly the first widely circulated manual of health written in English; and his *Book Named the Governor* (1531) is the first English account of the fashioning of a gentleman by a humanist educational curriculum. Copland, the second Englishman to establish a printing press in the sixteenth century – John Rastell was the first – translated and published in 1528 the first printed book on navigation, Pierre Garcie's *Rutter of the Sea*, which had originally been published in 1502. Rastell pioneered in the printing of music, designed the first permanent theater in England, and tried without success to be the first Englishman to colonize the New World. The first printed English account of colonization in the Western Hemisphere was Thomas Harriot's *Brief and True Report of the New Found Land of Virginia* (1588), which provided perhaps the most important intellectual foundation for the British Empire. John Dee is the first author known to have used the phrase *British Impire,* doing so in 1577.

Other innovative authors of various useful works include Boorde, the first writer since Hippocrates to discuss home and health together in his *Dietary of Health* (1542); his medical works of the 1540s are the first composed in English for the ordinary man and woman. Leland was acknowledged by his sixteenth-century successors as the founder of modern antiquarian studies in England; his surviving papers are prototypes for the various county histories. Scot wrote the first tract on hop farming in England (1574) as well as the first discourse in English about witchcraft (1584); in the latter work he exposes many popular illusions about witches and much of the cruelty with which alleged witches were treated. Although not strictly a "first," Edward Hake's legal treatise *Epieikeia* – written before 1603 but not published until 1953 – is a unique source of information about sixteenth-century notions of chancery and common-law equity. Thomas Digges published the first known image in an English book of the heliocentric universe and was the first modern astronomer to portray an infinite universe; his revisions of his father's *Pantometria* (1571) and *Stratioticos* (1579) are the first studies of ballistics in England. Gascoigne's *Spoil of Antwerp* (1576?) is one of the earliest examples of war correspondence in English, and his translation of Saint Augustine's *De Ebritate* as *A Delicate Diet for Dainty-mouthed Drunkards* (1576) is one of the earliest English temperance tracts.

In 1563 Richard Rainolde wrote the first English example of a "formulary" rhetoric (one that instructs by formula and example) and held political effectiveness to be the true virtue of rhetoric. Giles Fletcher the elder's contempt for Russian autocracy led him to write the first coherent study of Russian politics, *Of the Russe Commonwealth* (1591). In his sermons Hugh Latimer was the first to use a lively colloquial style to link court and country, magistrate and yeoman; his success in popularizing Reformation theology is due in large measure to the images and diction he drew from secular life.

Didacticism and usefulness. Given this abundance of innovation outside conventional forms of literature, it should not be surprising to find a large portion of sixteenth-century writing devoted to instruction or other utilitarian purposes. This is not to suggest that belles lettres was quiescent, but the majority of the authors treated in this volume implicitly and often explicitly wrote for useful ends, in both sacred and secular contexts.

Skelton created art in the service of his faith and of morality in virtually every one of his works, especially those attacking Cardinal Wolsey. His earthy *Tunning of Elinor Rumming* (circa 1521) may be a parody of the immorality and self-indulgence of Wolsey's court; and even his *Philip Sparrow* (circa 1545), sometimes considered merely an erotic catalogue of Jane Scope's physical charms, conveys profound ideas about the resurrection of the soul. Likewise, Heywood seems to have been interested in poetry not for its own sake but as a means to serve God, his monarch, and his fellow human beings. His volume of proverbs (1546) uses a traditional literary device that can teach without heavy-handed moralizing, and his parable *The Spider and the Fly* (1556) is a call for reform of sixteenth-century English society.

The first book of More's *Utopia* is only one of many outcries against exploitation and injustice. Copland's works are valuable as social history, with their analyses of the ills associated with poverty in contemporary Tudor society; his *Highway to the Spital-House* is an exposure of dishonest beggars. Arthur Golding's translations extract practical morality from literature and draw biblical parallels to classical texts. Didacticism permeates many of Gascoigne's works: in 1575 he revised his "Adventures of Master F. J." to make it much less innovative and more clearly moralistic, and his *Glass of Government* is laden with heavy-handed moralism. William Smith's manuscript "New Year's Gift" for Mary Sidney is an allegorical meditation on time, ending with the admonition to use it with care.

Whetstone was known to his contemporaries as an elegist, a patriotic author, and a moralist. He envisioned Protestant England as a world power and wanted to improve the conduct of the English in domestic affairs and in the military camps. Riche's satires make unflattering observations on both the foibles and the enormities of his time. In his role as an informer for Queen Elizabeth he wrote on Irish treachery and the corruption of English officials in Dublin. (See also the entry on Maurice Kyffin.) As Louis B. Wright observes in his *Middle-Class Culture in Elizabethan England* (1935), "the type of criticism exemplified in Riche's works was thundered from the pulpit and echoed in poems and pamphlets." Fenton loved to moralize in all genres – in the words of contributor Alison Taufer, "even where there is no moral to be drawn."

Geoffrey Whitney, by contrast, avoided explicit application to the political and religious context of the 1580s in his *A Choice of Emblems* to attract wider and longer-lasting interest. Breton's works are informed by what contributor James Nielson calls a "strong, if unpretentious . . . didactic streak," and Painter pursued a dual Horatian purpose in his fiction – instruction complemented by delight for the reader. The preface to the first volume (1566) of his *Palace of Pleasure* announces his didactic intentions, and the second volume (1567), in particular, contains both moralizing commentary and literary asides. Although Hake perhaps wrote at his best when simply reveling in the language without any strict moral intention, his *Touchstone for This Time* (1574) is more typical of his bent: it is a cranky prose polemic against misgovernment in the established Church, the miseducation of girls, the evils of face painting and intemperate dancing, and the social maladies associated by the Puritans with what they called "popery."

In addition to moralizing, however heavy or light, other authors clearly wrote for worldly and pragmatic ends. Sir Humphrey Gilbert proposed a third university, the "Queen's Academy," to train students in practical military and political analysis. His *A Discourse of a Discovery* (1576), part of an accelerating production of works about the New World and part of an emerging scientific discourse, encourages exploration for a northwest passage on theoretical grounds, drawing on previous English-language narratives touting the benefits of global exploration and trade. Richard Hakluyt was also practical in his aggressively nationalistic writings. His *Principal Navigations* (1589) has at least the ends of furthering English knowledge about lands beyond Europe, facilitating English mastery of those lands, and providing historical precedent for claiming them.

Similarly, Digges wanted to use his ideas and works to serve his country. He was like Dee in defending geometry on utilitarian grounds. He combined theory and practice, applying mathematics to military applications in *England's Defense* (written in 1588 but not published until 1680), in which he outlined a contingency plan to defend against coastal invasion. Tilney's manuscript for an enormous manual on European politics, geography, and genealogy would have been extremely useful for English diplomats had it been published. Moffet was involved with what contributor Victor Houliston calls "compendious projects aimed at public education in health and natural history"; he wrote his *Silkworms* in part to interest Queen Elizabeth in an English silk industry, and his treatise *Health's Improvement* (written circa 1596–1597 but not published until 1655) approximates the "table talk" genres of Athenaeus and Plutarch.

The most mundane concerns attracted the talents of sixteenth-century writers, including Queen Elizabeth's godson Sir John Harington. His treatise on the flush toilet, *The Metamorphosis of Ajax* (1596), used low subject matter (the jakes) to attract attention to more-serious messages; he also made a verse translation of a medical treatise, *The Englishman's Doctor* (1607). In his more literary translation of Ariosto's *Orlando Furioso* (1591) he drew many applications for English manners and government. Like so many of his contemporaries, he seems to have been what contributor D. H. Craig calls "a humorous, mildly skeptical, but always optimistic moralist."

One author in particular deserves the thanks of everyone who reads this volume: Leland spent most of his life in pursuit of two obsessions: describing the topography and antiquarian history of English counties and making lists of the books and manuscripts that were dispersed from monastic libraries when Henry VIII closed the monasteries. Without his efforts, far less would be known about the texts available to sixteenth-century English nondramatic writers.

Science and medicine. Dee was one of the most eminent scientists of his day, pursuing research and applications in mathematics, navigation, astrology and astronomy, reform of the calendar, linguistics and sacred languages, and Paracelsian medicine. He consulted Welsh authorities to help confirm the British settlement of North America, tried to find a northwest passage to the Orient, and made alchemical studies. Harriot shared Dee's interest in mathematics, astronomy, ethnography, and linguistics. His epitaph asserts that he "cultivated all the sciences / And excelled in all." Working in some of the same areas as Dee and Harriot, Digges may have been Elizabethan England's most important author and editor of scientific texts, especially in mathematics and astronomy; his command of cosmology and modern scientific method is exceptional. He was England's principal advocate of Copernican cosmology. Boorde, who wrote about medicine as well as social history, was an early advocate of laughter as the best medicine in his *Dietary of Health*. And Moffet, a distinguished physician and natural historian who wrote – chiefly in Latin – on pharmacology and entomology, was an enthusiast for Paracelsian medicine.

Vernacular and native traditions. Scholars such as Dee, Moffet, More, and Desiderius Erasmus wrote easily in Latin, the language of learned discourse throughout Europe well into the seventeenth century. At the same time, Boorde's remarks about the inadequacy of English in the first half of the sixteenth century reflect the unwillingness of the learned to write in the vernacular for a lay readership. But even early in the century the reputation of English as suitable for learned authors was being enhanced by translations of classical and Continental languages and by the increasing standardization of spelling. Obviously, translation creates vast opportunities for enriching the vernacular: Copland translated Pietro Tommai of Ravenna's *Art of Memory* around 1545 and said in the preface that he wanted all arts and sciences translated into English for the common good. Among those who joined him in promoting English as a fit medium for learned works was Elyot, a pioneer in using English for serious writing; he tried to enrich the vernacular as a translator and as an enthusiastic coiner of neologisms.

Rainolde also held English to be capable of producing eloquent expression. The surviving works and the titles of many of his lost translations show Grimald to be, in the words of contributor Seymour Baker House, a "moderate classicist who saw the English language as capable of bearing the weight of Latin rhetoric." Gascoigne was, in the words of contributor Susan C. Staub, "supremely interested in proving the English language as fit a medium for poetry as other languages." In 1581 Pettie translated Stefano Guazzo's *Civil Conversation* from a French version to show that English is as copious, compendious, choice, pithy, pleasant, and eloquent as any other language.

The conviction that English was adequate for literary and learned writing extended beyond the language itself to include forms and genres created in England or assimilated to such an extent that they seemed native. Skelton's dream visions *The Bouge of Court* (circa 1499) and *The Garland of Laurel* (1523) are native and traditional in every way. The predecessors of his persona, "Poeta Skelton," are not classical but English: Chaucer, John Gower, and John Lydgate. Heywood was an experimenter with the poetic resources of English, yet his *The Spider and the Fly* is a traditional topical allegory (to which the key for identifying the figures has been lost). Hake followed domestic medieval models such as *Piers Plowman* in his satires. In his epigrams, Harington borrowed the English tradition of jesting from Heywood and More to complement the sardonic classical model of Martial. Golding translated the works of Ovid and Aesop's fables within a moralized medieval English tradition.

Luke Shepherd used native styles in ballads, satire, and personal invective for Reformation protests. His *John Bon and Mast Parson* (1547?) uses the native conceit of the theological plowman, while *Doctor Double Ale* (1548?) champions scriptural wisdom and what contributor House calls "the simple English of the unlearned narrator." Gascoigne, who felt that English poets had neglected Chaucer and native traditions, wrote his *Hundred Sundry Flowers* (1573; revised as *The Posies*, 1575) to advance the cause of the vernacular. He recasts the Ovidian myth of Philomela into a native English dream vision set in the English countryside in his *Complaint of Philomene* (1576). Riche also used the medieval English dream motif as a framing device in his *Dialogue between Mercury and an English Soldier* (1574). In his *De literis antiquæ Britanniæ,* written before 1581 but published in 1633, Fletcher traced British intellectual endeavors and letters back to the Druids, an antedating of the dominant Roman Catholic church by a native tradition that made him popular with post-Reformation authors. Late in the century Geoffrey Whitney recognized the literary accomplishments of Sir Edward Dyer and Sidney, but he reverted to traditional poulter's measure for his own *A Choice of Emblems.*

Readership and popularity. Whether writing in Latin or English, on sacred or secular topics, in utilitarian or artistic modes, authors in sixteenth-century England found a growing reading public eager for their works. Skelton's works went through twenty-one editions between 1545 and 1563 under both Protestant and Catholic monarchs. Parr's *Prayers or Meditations* sold in ten editions during the sixteenth century – chiefly in modestly priced volumes, in keeping with her humanistic goal of making religious literature widely available. Askew's *Examinations* (1546, 1547), in John Bale's militantly Protestant edition, were reprinted four times during the short reign of Edward VI.

Thomas Becon was one of the most prolific and popular Tudor authors; *The Sick Man's Salve* (circa 1560) was his most read work. His prayers received wide circulation in the *Primer or Book of Private Prayer* (1553), and many of his tracts ran to several editions during his lifetime. He summed up his objective: "in all my sermons and writings I have not attempted matters . . . far removed from the common sense and capacity of the people, but have been content . . . to . . . edify the brethren, [rather]

than to drive them into a . . . stupor at the doctrine of so . . . unsearchable mysteries." Henry Smith's career as preacher was quite brief; but within twenty years of his death in 1591, his sermons appeared in more than eighty-five editions.

Secular works were also popular. Boorde responded to the demand for useful books for unlearned men and women. His simple verses helped to popularize poetry within a growing class of "ordinary" readers; his practical advice about such subjects as diet, construction sites, sanitation, and budgeting was widely read during his lifetime and much reprinted after his death. Some of his works were apparently read literally to pieces, for there are no surviving copies of some of his titles. Copland, too, wrote for lay readers. As both an author and a publisher he could write and select works to print and could thus guide the public in its choice of reading matter. He provided cheap books for the many instead of a few elegant books for the more discerning.

Heywood's admonitory *Dialogue of Proverbs* (1546) went through at least six editions during its author's life, and Harman's *Caveat for Common Cursitors* went through four editions during his. Scot's *Perfect Platform of a Hop Garden* (1574) went through three editions before the author's death in 1599. Digges was extraordinarily successful in making science attractive to a wide popular audience as well as to the learned; his English translations of portions of Nicolaus Copernicus's *De Revolutionibus* (1543), published in Digges's edition of his father Leonard's *A Prognostication Everlasting* (1576), were accurate and accessible to lay readers, and *Prognostication Everlasting*, printed with Thomas's own "Perfect Description of the Celestial Orbs," went through six editions in his lifetime. In fiction Pettie cultivated a female audience with his *Petite Palace of Pettie His Pleasures* (1576), which went through six editions by 1613. Tilney's *Flower of Friendship* had at least six editions within twenty years. Breton's epistolary *Post with a Mad Packet of Letters* (1602) went through many reprints and provoked several imitations.

In contrast to the wide audience of some authors, Queen Elizabeth I constituted almost the entire readership for the letters and verses of Robert Devereux, second Earl of Essex. Dyer circulated his poems in manuscript in a rather narrow courtly circle; they were quite popular and widely imitated both before and after print publication. One of Golding's translations of Ovid's *Metamorphoses* (1567) was printed in six editions during Golding's life and received many compliments from contemporaries, including borrowings by Shakespeare. Riche saw four editions of his *Farewell to Military Profession* (1581), which provided the full or partial source for at least nine plays. Erasmus's *Colloquia* (1518) went through more than a dozen editions during his life, and his *De duplici copia* (1512) – which was to prove extremely influential on English prose and verse style – was published in almost a hundred editions in the same period.

Humanism. Elyot and More were the foremost English humanists of their generation, along with the frequent visitor from the Continent, Erasmus. English Renaissance humanism has been described in many ways, but it may be epitomized in Elyot, with his broad range of interests, his attempts to combine action and contemplation, and his lifelong devotion to publishing scholarly works to improve society according to idealistic precepts based on the wisdom of the ancients. His interests encompassed education, moral and political philosophy, religion, language, and medicine. Of particular interest are his translation of Plutarch's work on educating children (circa 1530) and his syncretic *Book Named the Governor* (1531) with its hierarchical, progressive theory of education. His aim for his *Bibliotheca Eliotae* was a vast compendium of universal knowledge.

More and his circle of Rastell, John Colet, Thomas Linacre, and William Grocyn shared scholarly, educational, and literary ideals based on the study of ancient languages and cultures. In education More stressed the study of grammar, rhetoric, history, poetry, and ethics; he opposed the late-Scholastic emphasis on dialectic. He considered mastery of rhetorical modes central to a humanist program to solve moral and social problems. In epistolary essays he defended humanism while struggling with his own conflicts over a life of action versus one of contemplation. Between 1503 and 1520 he wrote his principal humanistic works: his translation of the works of Lucian (1506) and his *Utopia, Epigrammata,* "History of Richard III" (1543), and several defenses of humanism.

Although not English himself, Erasmus had a profound influence on sixteenth-century English writing. He regarded verbal fluency as the single most important skill to be gained from humanistic education, and he fostered it with his *De duplici copia,* which became a textbook for generations of students.

(For other writers whose work is associated with Renaissance humanism, see the entries on Askew, Boorde, Digges, Elizabeth I, Grimald,

Hake, Harington, Harrison, Leland, Moffet, Richard Morison, Painter, Parr, Rainolde, Rastell, and Scot.)

Reformation. Erasmus may be considered the father of modern biblical scholarship and, therefore, one of the foremost figures of the Protestant Reformation. He wanted accurate texts of the Bible to be made available to the widest possible audience. To this end he improved his rhetorical skills and mastered Greek. His text of the New Testament was a direct influence on William Tyndale's translations into English (see the Tyndale entry in *DLB 132*).

One of the best-known preachers of his day, Latimer was perhaps the single greatest popularizer and most effective proponent of early English Protestant doctrine. He was notorious even when a student at Cambridge as an outspoken Protestant of the "early evangelical" type, having been influenced by humanist, early Lutheran, and especially native Lollard convictions about corrupt and unscriptural practices within the church. Like the Lollards, he was a violent and committed iconoclast who supported Henry VIII's conservative Reformation; but he much more enthusiastically accepted appointment as an official apologist under Edward VI for Lord Protector Edward Somerset's more radical program of reform. What is most radical about Latimer is his assertion that the king is accountable to the law of God – and therefore subject to the faithful preacher.

(For other writers whose work has a bearing on the Reformation, see the entries on Askew, Bateman, Becon, Henry Constable, Golding, William Harrison, Maurice Kyffin, More, Morison, Parr, Rastell, Shepherd, and Henry Smith.)

Other. This introduction has focused on seven categories that are conspicuous in the articles in this volume: literary innovation, didactic and useful writing, science and medicine, concern for the aesthetic resources and native traditions of vernacular English, a growing readership, principles of humanism, and the Protestant Reformation. Other important topics, and the entries that deal with them, are listed here.

Biography and autobiography: Askew, Becon, Gascoigne, Grymeston, Moffet (one of the earliest biographers of Sidney), More, Parr, Whetstone (possibly the first professional biographer in England), and Isabella Whitney.

Dialogue: Askew, Becon, Breton, Elyot, Hake, More, Pettie, Shepherd, and Tilney.

Genre: Breton (character, lyric, pastoral, proverb, satire), Chettle (prose fiction, satire), Constable (lyric), Copland (rogue literature), Dee (aphorism), Devereux (epistle, lyric), Dyer (lyric), Elizabeth I (epistle, lyric, oration), Erasmus (adage, colloquy, conduct book, oration, satire), Fenton (prose fiction), Fletcher (lyric, prose treatise), Grange (prose fiction), Everard Guilpin (epigram, satire), Hake (colloquy, satire), Hakluyt ("prose epic"), Harington (epigram, epistle, satire), Harrison (social history), Heywood (ballad, debate, epigram, parable, proverb), Latimer (sermons), Riche (character, militaria, novella, pamphlet, prose fiction, romance, satire), Shepherd (satire, theological "flyting"), Henry Smith (sermon), and William Smith (lyric).

Neo-Latin literature: Becon, Dee, Erasmus, Leland, Moffet, More, Rainolde, and Henry Smith.

Style: Askew, Becon, Breton, Dyer, Elizabeth I, Elyot, Erasmus, Fenton, Gascoigne, Golding, Grange, Hakluyt, Heywood, Moffet, Painter, Pettie, Rainolde, Riche, Scot, Shepherd, Skelton, Henry Smith, Whetstone, and Isabella Whitney.

Translation: Bateman, Copland, Digges, Elizabeth I, Elyot, Fenton, Gascoigne, Grimald, Hakluyt, Golding, Harington, Harriot, Kyffin, More, Morison, Painter, Pettie, Skelton.

Note: Titles in the lists of authors' works at the beginnings of the entries have been checked against *A Short-Title Catalogue of Books Printed in England, Scotland, and Ireland and of English Books Printed Abroad 1475–1640* (1976–1991) and other sources and are given, as far as possible, with the original spellings and punctuation but modernized capitalization. Titles and quotations in the texts of the entries are modernized in capitalization, spelling, and punctuation, and the titles are generally shortened.

— David A. Richardson

ACKNOWLEDGMENTS

This book was produced by Bruccoli Clark Layman, Inc. Philip B. Dematteis and Samuel Bruce were the in-house editors.

Photography editors are Edward Scott and Timothy C. Lundy. Layout and graphics supervisor is Penney L. Haughton. Copyediting supervisor is Bill Adams. Typesetting supervisor is Kathleen M. Flanagan. Darren Harris-Fain and Julie E. Frick are editorial associates. Systems manager is George F. Dodge. The production staff includes Joseph Matthew Bruccoli, Ann M. Cheschi, Patricia Coate, Rebecca Crawford, Denise Edwards, Joyce Fowler, Robert Fowler, Laurel Gladden, Jolyon M. Helterman, Ellen McCracken, Kathy Lawler Merlette, Sean Moriarty, Pamela D. Norton, Thomas J. Pickett, Patricia Salisbury, Maxine K. Smalls, William L. Thomas, Jr., and Wilma Weant.

Walter W. Ross, Deborah M. Chasteen, and Brenda Gross did library research. They were assisted by the following librarians at the Thomas Cooper Library of the University of South Carolina: Linda Holderfield and the interlibrary-loan staff; reference librarians Gwen Baxter, Daniel Boice, Faye Chadwell, Cathy Eckman, Gary Geer, Qun "Gerry" Jiao, Jean Rhyne, Carol Tobin, Carolyn Tyler, Virginia Weathers, Elizabeth Whiznant, and Connie Widney; circulation-department head Thomas Marcil; and acquisitions-searching supervisor David Haggard.

Sixteenth-Century Nondramatic Writers

Second Series

Dictionary of Literary Biography

Jane Anger

(flourished 1589)

A. Lynne Magnusson
University of Waterloo

BOOK: *Iane Anger Her Protection for Women: To Defend Them against the Scandalovs Reportes of a Late Surfeiting Louer, and All Other Like Venerians That Complaine So to Bee Ouercloyed with Womens Kindnesse,* as Ia: A. Gent. (London: Printed by Richard Iones & Thomas Orwin, 1589).

Editions: "Jane Anger, Her Protection for Women," in *First Feminists: British Women Writers, 1578–1799,* edited by Moira Ferguson (Bloomington: Indiana University Press, 1985), pp. 58–73;

"Jane Anger, Her Protection for Women," in *Half Humankind: Contexts and Texts of the Controversy about Women in England, 1540–1640,* edited by Katherine Usher Henderson and Barbara F. McManus (Urbana & Chicago: University of Illinois Press, 1985), pp. 172–188;

"Jane Anger, Her Protection for Women," in *The Women's Sharp Revenge: Five Women's Pamphlets from the Renaissance,* edited by Simon Shepherd (London: Fourth Estate, 1985), pp. 29–51.

Jane Anger is known only as the writer of *Jane Anger Her Protection for Women* (1589). The pamphlet is a landmark in the history of English letters for it is the first extended defense of women to make a serious claim to female authorship. It brings a distinctive new voice to English writing – the voice of articulate female anger. Developing this new persona involved rhetorical innovation: Anger transformed masculine models of composition to invent a female writing style suited to her enterprise. Furthermore, she offers a perspective on Elizabethan courtship practices quite unlike any available in the amatory verse or prose romance of the time.

Whether "Jane Anger" is the writer's own name or a pseudonym remains unknown. More than one Jane (or Joan) Anger lived in England at the time, but none of them has been identified as the writer of the pamphlet. Even the female authorship of *Her Protection for Women* has been called into question, despite the writer's consistent self-identification as a woman. The case against female authorship includes the slim chance that secular writing by a woman would find its way into print in the late sixteenth century, the omission of the usual apologies by female writers for being so bold as to enter into print, the rare accomplishment for a middle-class Englishwoman of Latin learning, the fact that men sometimes wrote defenses of women, and the author's acknowledgment of female faults and male supremacy.

In favor of female authorship is the increasing frequency with which works by women writers appeared in print in the late sixteenth and early seventeenth centuries; in fact, Anger's printer, Thomas Orwin, published another work openly attributed to a woman writer in 1589: Anne Dowriche's *French History.* Also, men had nothing to gain at that time by using a female pseudonym: neither prestige nor profit attached to female authorship. Men writing in defense of women had their choice of established masculine personae: the chivalrous protector of women, the sophisticated ironist, or the former attacker turned penitent over his earlier abuse of women; they did not choose to ventriloquize female voices. Works such as Sir Thomas Elyot's *Defense of Good Women* (1540) and Nicholas Breton's "Praise of Virtuous Ladies" (1597) do not, like Anger's, offer protection to "all women in general," and they avoid generalizations like Anger's about the wicked-

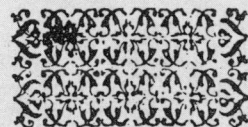

IANE ANGER
her Protection
for VVomen.

To defend them against the
SCANDALOVS RÉPORTESOE
a late Suiteiring Louer, and all other like
Vnerans that compline fo to bee
ouercloyed with womens
kindnesse.

Written by Ia: A. Gent.

At London
Printed by Richard Ione, and Thomas
Orwin. 1589.

Title page for Anger's only book, an early feminist tract

ness of "all men." Against the claim that Latin learning points to male authorship, especially if the writer is middle-class and not among the handful of noblewomen noted for such learning, one can suggest that all of the learned materials – the classical authorities cited, the lists of famous or mythical women of virtue and men of vice, the handful of Latin phrases – could be gleaned from contemporary sources: compilations such as Pierre de La Primaudaye's *The French Academy,* translated into English in 1586 by Thomas Bowes; popular writers, such as Robert Greene, who displayed their learning in precisely these forms; and earlier books that took up the controversy over women. Furthermore, if thinking is shaped even in part by one's cultural and historical situation, then Anger's acceptance in 1589 of male supremacy and female imperfections in no way marks her thinking as masculine. In short, the case that has been made against female authorship is weak.

Anger explains that she wrote *Her Protection for Women* in 1588 in response to *Boke, His Surfeit in Love,* which she describes as one of many books in which disenchanted lovers berate their own folly in love and turn to abuse of women. The printer

Orwin did enter the title *Boke, His Surfeit in Love, with a Farewell to the Follies of His Own Phantasy* in the Stationers' Register on 27 November 1588; but no copies now exist, and the author has not been identified.

Anger identifies her intended audience in two dedicatory letters, one to "the Gentlewomen of England" and the other to "all women in general, and gentle reader whatsoever." Despite the appearance on the pamphlet's title page of the signature "Ja: A. Gent.," Anger's switch from "you" in the first letter to "we" in the next suggests her closer identification with the larger group of women and her membership in the middle class. There is a marked shift in tone between the letters. To the gentlewomen she attributes the good judgment needed to consider her defense as if it were a case at law; she adopts a polite tone, apologizing for her presumption in writing and requesting their "protection" for her *Protection.* The second letter begins more passionately – "Fie on the falsehood of men" – and develops in colorful terms the wish to see them punished for their "devilish practices" against women. Her plea to the gods and goddesses for action against men's crimes goes hand in hand with her frustration that women "stand still and say nought," which makes her vow to "stretch the veins of her brains, the strings of her fingers, and the lists of her modesty" to answer men's "surfeitings." Anger believes that men continue to misrepresent women partly because they assume that women will not enter the male sphere of the printed word to challenge them: "their slanderous tongues are so short, that the time wherein they have lavished out their words freely hath been so long, and they know we cannot catch hold of them to pull them out, and they think we will not write to reprove their lying lips."

The pamphlet opens with a critique of masculine rhetorical practices, especially their overemphasis on "manner" over "matter." Anger identifies a contradiction between the high value male writers place on women as a stimulus to their creativity and the devaluation of women that their writings actually produce. She parodies the mythmaking that accompanies their claims to inspiration: "If they may once encroach so far into our presence as they may but see the lining of our outermost garment, they straight think that Apollo honors them." She details how men's ignorance and devaluation of women make them misread women's behavior, especially in regard to sex: "If we will not suffer them to smell on our smocks, they will snatch at our petticoats; but if our honest natures cannot away with that uncivil kind of jesting, then we are coy. Yet if we bear with their rudeness and be somewhat modestly familiar with them, they will straight make matter of nothing, blazing abroad that they have surfeited with love, and . . . telling the manner how." For Anger, it is above all women's "kindness" to men that gets misconstrued. She seems to be answering some general charges against the looseness of women's morals, arguing that it is men's own "filthy lust," reacting either to disappointment or a self-loathing that follows "surfeiting," that causes them to invent women's lascivious nature.

Anger proposes her own story to counter the Surfeiter's account of courtship and its aftermath. He charges that women seduce men only to make the men's lives miserable. Unmarried men who get involved with women are drawn into wickedness that they repent, and men who marry suffer extreme miseries. In Anger's version of courtship it is women who are preyed on by men. Neither women's allurements nor their immodesty can be held responsible for leading men on: "If we clothe ourselves in sackcloth, and truss up our hair in dishclouts, Venerians will nevertheless pursue their pastime. If we hide our breasts, it must be with leather, for no cloth can keep their long nails out of our bosoms." Instead, she claims, men's flattery leads women on; but the sweet talk ends when "they have their answers," and "they fall a-railing on us which never hurt them." Men complaining about the miseries of long-term female companionship fail to recognize all that women do for them: Anger emphasizes the domestic work performed by women in providing "meat, drink, clothing, or any other necessary," in keeping men's "bodies freed from diseases by our cleanliness," and in caring for men's hurts and injuries. Women sometimes make men's lives difficult, but if men treated women better they would experience more of the sweet side of women's natures. Domestic harmony requires the goodwill of both men and women.

In the spirited opening and in Anger's analysis of courtship and domesticity the reader seems to hear an independent voice adding new tones to the limited repertoire for English women writers. In the long sections where the pamphlet directly engages the Surfeiter's specific points and arguments Anger reports a great deal of what is "recited in *Boke, His Surfeit in Love*" and delivers her answers to it. *Boke, His Surfeit in Love* appears to be a conventional entry in the controversy over women with its debate form; its prolific use of historical and literary examples, usually biblical and classical in origin, of good and bad women and men; and its repertoire of abstract arguments drawing on the authority of renowned thinkers rather than on life experience. With a great deal of rhetorical ingenuity, Anger shapes her answers to meet the demands of this prefabricated dialogue. One of her strategies is to attribute to the Surfeiter a misunderstanding of his own apparently antiwoman materials and then to correct or rewrite them, as when she announces her revision of the Ninus and Semiramis story as he has told it: "of [Ninus] this shall be my censure (agreeing with the verdict of the surfeiting lover, save only that he hath misplaced and mistaken certain words) in this manner." She reinterprets the maxims he offers, claiming that "he saith more truly than he is aware of" and reconstruing what was meant as dispraise in a positive light: " 'Aut amat, aut odit; non est in tertio': she loveth good things and hateth that which is evil; she loveth justice and hateth iniquity; . . . she loveth man for his virtues and hateth him for his vices. To be short, there is no *Medium* between good and bad, and therefore she can be *In nullo tertio*." At the end of the pamphlet she offers her revision, from a female point of view, of the misogynist allegory of the Labyrinth of Love, with women now at the center as heroines who must navigate a safe path past the perils of men's lovemaking. Together with the simpler expedient of caricaturing the Surfeiter, these fairly sophisticated revisionary strategies produce an imaginative piece of writing. The attention Anger pays to style bears witness that she labored to excel in her writing. Though she blames the Surfeiter for his subject matter, she remarks on the pleasure she took in his style. Her sentences occasionally develop a euphuistic flourish; she also tries her hand at verse to summarize and to emphasize.

Anger quotes enough from *Boke, His Surfeit in Love* to establish that the Surfeiter borrowed liberally from *The French Academy* for his exempla and his authoritative sayings. Some overlaps exist between Anger's work and Breton's "Praise of Virtuous Ladies"; it is, however, unknown whether or not Breton's work, which survives in a 1597 edition of *The Will of Wit,* was in general circulation before 1589, so the direction of borrowing remains uncertain. Nonetheless, misogynist materials in Anger's day were circulating in popular prose romances, including some of Greene's and John Lyly's works. Anger objects to the Surfeiter's "discourse of love," a narrative pattern typical of prose romances in which young men's misadventures in love lead to repentance and rejection of women; and it is possible that the prose romances of her time are among the "innumerable number of books" like the Surfeiter's that she announces as her target.

Three new editions of Anger's pamphlet appeared in 1985; it is an essential work for scholars interested in developing a canon of British women writers or a history of feminist writing. Whether she should be called "feminist," "protofeminist," or "prowoman," this author opened up a new possibility for women writers beyond those of "stand[ing] still and say[ing] nought."

References:

Elaine V. Beilin, *Redeeming Eve: Women Writers of the English Renaissance* (Princeton: Princeton University Press, 1987), pp. 247–253;

Helen Andrews Kahin, "Jane Anger and John Lyly," *Modern Language Quarterly,* 8 (1947): 31–35;

A. Lynne Magnusson, "'His pen with my hande': Jane Anger's Revisionary Rhetoric," *English Studies in Canada,* 17 (1991): 269–281;

Magnusson, "*Jane Anger her Protection, Boke his Surfeit,* and *The French Academie,*" *Notes and Queries,* 234 (September 1989): 311–314;

Magnusson, "Nicholas Breton Reads Jane Anger," *Renaissance Studies,* 7 (1993): 291–300;

Betty Travitsky, "The Lady Doth Protest: Protest in the Popular Writings of Renaissance Englishwomen," *English Literary Renaissance,* 14 (Autumn 1984): 255–283;

Retha M. Warnicke, *Women of the English Renaissance and Reformation* (Westport, Conn.: Greenwood, 1983), pp. 123–126;

Linda Woodbridge, *Women and the English Renaissance: Literature and the Nature of Womankind, 1540–1620* (Urbana & Chicago: University of Illinois Press, 1984).

Anne Askew

(circa 1521 – 16 July 1546)

Elaine V. Beilin
Framingham State College

BOOKS: *The First Examinacyon of Anne Askewe, latelye Martyred in Smythfelde, by the Romyshe Popes Vpholders, wyth the Elucydacyon of Iohan Bale* (Marburg [i.e., Wesel: Printed by Derick van der Straten], 1546);

The Lattre Examinacyon of Anne Askewe, Lately Martyred in Smythfelde, by the Wycked Synagoge of Antichrist, with the Elucydacyon of Johan Bale (Marburg [i.e., Wesel: Printed by Derick van der Straten], 1547).

Editions: "The Two Examinations of the Worthy Servant of God, Mistress Anne Askew," in *Actes and Monuments of These Latter and Perillous Dayes, Touching Matters of the Church* (London: Printed by John Day, 1563);

British Reformers, volume 3: *Writings of Edward the Sixth, William Hugh, Queen Catherine Parr, Anne Askew, Lady Jane Grey, Hamilton and Balnaves* (Philadelphia: Presbyterian Board of Publication, 1842);

The Account of the Sufferings of Anne Askew, for Opposing the Gross Fictions of Transubstantiation: Written by Herself, and Re-printed by a Catholic (London: Rivington, 1849);

The Examinations of Anne Askew, edited by Elaine Beilin, Women Writers in English, 1350–1850 (New York & Oxford: Oxford University Press, forthcoming, 1994).

Anne Askew was a Reformer who became widely known through her posthumously published works, *The First Examination of Anne Askew* (1546) and *The Latter Examination of Anne Askew* (1547), in which she re-creates her interrogations for heresy. Askew's work is memorable for its dramatic first-person narrative, for its careful crafting of the dialogue between Askew and a succession of government and church officials, and for its defiance of traditional injunctions against women publicly debating religious issues. In an often gripping account she reveals her sufferings and triumphs, presenting herself as a deeply pious and quick-witted opponent of

her questioners. The *Examinations* are both spiritual autobiography and dramatic dialogue; as historical documents they offer insight into the religious and political controversies of Henry VIII's last days.

The fifth of six children, Askew was born in South Kelsey, Lincolnshire, around 1521 to Sir William Askew (also Ayscough) and Elizabeth Wrottesley Askew. The Askews were a prominent landed family, and Sir William served in the court of Henry VIII. About Askew's education one can only assume enough instruction in letters, rhetoric, and Scripture to make her capable of writing in a polemical and witty style. Perhaps like other fathers at court, Sir William Askew permitted his daughters to be educated by his sons' tutors. In his biographical sketch of Askew in *The First Examination,* John Bale records that Sir William arranged a marriage between Anne's older sister, Martha, and a neighboring Catholic landowner, Thomas Kyme of Kelsey. When Martha died before the ceremony, Anne was offered in her stead "to save the money"; she appears to have married Kyme sometime before 1540. Whether seeking an annulment of this unhappy marriage or following another northern Reformer, John Lascells, Askew eventually arrived in London and joined a circle of Reformers associated with Queen Catherine Parr. Perhaps the least protected of the queen's associates, she was arrested in 1545; tried, acquitted, and released; tried again the following year; tortured; and burned as a heretic on 16 July 1546 at Smithfield.

In November 1546 Bale, a Protestant apologist, had Askew's first *Examination* published in Wesel in the Duchy of Cleves. Presumably the manuscript was smuggled out of Newgate; according to Bale, a copy was brought to him in Wesel by Dutch merchants. Bale concealed his own whereabouts by inscribing "Marpurg" (Marburg in Hesse) as the place of publication. In his bibliography, *Illustrium majoris Britanniae scriptorum . . . summarium* (1548), he remarks that "She wrote this in her own hand and I illustrated it with prefaces and notes."

Title page for John Bale's edition of Askew's account of her interrogations for heresy, with a woodcut depicting
Askew holding the Bible and a martyr's palm and trampling the papal dragon

Bale saw the text as a valuable contribution to the Reformers' cause, and in his prefaces and interspersed "elucidation" he attempts to establish the providential nature of Askew's experience and to vilify her Catholic accusers, whom he designates "the great Antichrist's upholders." Askew's writings had an immediate audience among fellow Reformers and were reprinted four times during the reign of Edward VI.

Bale's preface also situates Askew in the tradition of the martyrs of the primitive church — Cecilia and especially Blandina — in keeping with the Reformist doctrine that the Reformed church represented a return to the purity of early Christianity. Also reflecting Bale's image of Askew is the woodcut on the title pages of the *Examinations:* she is depicted holding the Bible and a martyr's palm, trampling the crowned "Papal beast," and standing before a wall — perhaps part of the New Jerusalem the Reformers believed they were building. As John N. King has shown, the radiance around her head associates Askew with the Woman Clothed with the Sun from Revelation 12:1, a Reformation image for the true Christian woman, and the picture as a whole substitutes Askew and the Bible for traditional Catholic depictions of the dragon-slaying Saint Margaret of Antioch.

In re-creating her examinations Askew continually depicts herself as the strong, ardent, true Christian challenging and routing her powerful but erring questioners at every turn. The *Examinations* are a series of cleverly written dialogues in which a succession of male authorities confronts a woman who wishes to debate publicly the key theological issues of the day. When the bishop's chancellor "rebuked me, and said that I was much to blame for uttering the Scriptures" because Saint Paul forbade women to do so, Askew immediately quotes Saint Paul, for "I knew Paul's meaning so well as he, which is . . . that a woman ought not to speak in the congregation by the way of teaching." She then becomes the questioner, asking the bishop's chancellor "how many women he had seen go into the pulpit and preach." He admits that he never saw any. Askew concludes with a reprimand, telling the chancellor that "he ought to find no fault in poor women except they had offended the law." Here, as elsewhere in her text, Askew ironically reverses the role of examiner and examined.

It is Bale, rather than Askew herself, who provides most of the biographical information. In her second *Examination* Askew records that at Greenwich the King's Council questioned her about Master Kyme, but she refused to discuss her husband with anyone but the king. In his commentary on this passage Bale says that she was "compelled against her will, or free consent, to marry with him" but acted "like a Christian wife" and gave birth to two children. He avers that her frequent reading of the Bible brought Askew to leave the Catholic church and to embrace Reformed doctrine. The Lincolnshire priests then told Kyme to drive his wife out of the house; in turn, she sought a divorce in Lincoln and later in London but was never successful in gaining it.

Edmund Bonner, bishop of London, rebuked her, she says, because she had claimed that sixty priests of Lincoln "were bent against me." She admits making this claim, for "my friends told me, if I did come to Lincoln, the priests would assault me and put me to great trouble, as thereof they had made their boast." Undeterred, she went to Lincoln for six days "to see what would be said unto me." Almost casually, she describes herself in Lincoln minster, reading the Bible and being approached by groups of priests who said nothing to her. When questioned more closely by Bonner, Askew allows that one priest finally did speak, but that "his words were of so small effect, that I did not now remember them." This episode conveys something of Askew's method and tone in many passages of her *Examina-*

tions: she gives an account of each of her confrontations with the clergy, shaping it in such a way as to belittle and discredit every priest and bishop involved. The passage also contains the striking image of a young woman reading the Bible in English in a public place, a defiance of Parliament's act of 1543 decreeing that gentlewomen might read the English Bible in private only.

Askew everywhere seizes the opportunity to declare her Reformist beliefs and her reasons for leaving the Catholic church. Although her account is certainly subjective, it is, nevertheless, a document of an inquisition for heresy amid the complicated politics of the last two years of Henry VIII's reign. Her critical depictions of Stephen Gardiner, Bishop of Winchester; of Bonner, Bishop of London; of Lord Chancellor Thomas Wriothesley; and of the King's Council are an integral part of the role she assumes as a witness to the Reformation. She allows her antagonists to articulate their accusations and their doctrine and then presents her refutation and discomfiting of the "authorities." Bale's much more vociferous commentary increases the political implications of the text through the violence of its attack on Askew's questioners, whom Bale attacks as "tormentors and tyrants abominable." The effectiveness of Bale's attack on the bishop of Winchester is evident in Gardiner's letter of 21 May 1547 to Lord Protector Edward Seymour, Duke of Somerset, requesting that the book be repressed because Bale's "untruth appeareth evidently in setting forth the examination of Anne Askew, which is utterly misreported."

The political nature of the religious controversy is evident when Askew records the attempt of the Catholic faction to implicate the courtiers in Queen Catherine Parr's Reformist circle in her own alleged heresy. In Askew's chilling account of her questioning in the Tower of London, Sir Richard Rich and a privy councillor ask her whether Catherine Brandon, Duchess of Suffolk; Anne Radcliffe, Countess of Sussex; Anne Seymour, Countess of Hertford; Lady Joan Denny; and Lady Fitzwilliam are Reformers. Askew replies that she has no proof of their activities, nor does she respond to the request for other names of her coreligionists. Her questioners want to know what gentlewomen are sending her money in prison; Askew says that she receives money but has no proof of its source. They want to know what councillors support her; she denies that any do. And then, in words shocking for their understatement, Askew writes that "they did put me on the rack, because I confessed no ladies nor gentlewomen to be of my opinion, and thereon

Woodcut showing the preparations for the burning of Askew as a heretic at Smithfield on 16 July 1546; from Robert Crowley,
The Confutation of XIII. Articles, Whereunto Nicolas Shaxton, Late Byshop of Slisburye, Subscribed *(1548),*
which describes Askew's execution

they kept me a long time. And because I lay still and did not cry, my Lord Chancellor and Master Rich took pains to rack me [with] their own hands, till I was nigh dead."

The crucial theological issue that brought Askew to trial and that occupies much of her writing is the Protestant-Catholic controversy over the Sacrament. In the opening lines of *The First Examination* Askew records that she was asked "if I did not believe that the Sacrament hanging over the altar was the very body of Christ really." Her refutation of this doctrine and her argument for the symbolic presence of Christ in the Sacrament are conducted with passionate conviction; her many detailed scriptural references reinforce a style that echoes scriptural cadences. In her deliberately bold statements in *The Latter Examination* she tells her questioners that "that ye call your God is but a piece of bread. For a more proof thereof (mark it when you list), let it lie in the boxe but three months, and it will be mould and so turn to nothing that is good." She knew that these words alone would condemn her; after using similar phrases she declares, "And upon these words that I have now spoken will I suffer death." Askew may have meant her final writings to

document her martyrdom, for in a letter to Lascells she wrote, "I doubt it not, but God will perform his work in me, like as he hath begun."

Askew's last word in these volumes is "The Ballad which Anne Askew made and sang when she was in Newgate." Written in *abab* iambic trimeter, the ballad images Askew as the "armed knight" of Ephesians 6:11, ready to fight the world with the shield of faith. Surrounded by enemies more numerous "than hairs upon my head," she asks for God's help in the fight against Satan but ends by praying that her foes will not suffer "the hire / Of their iniquity."

Bale's rapid publication of Askew's *Examinations* suggests that he realized the usefulness of her narrative to the Protestant cause. For similar reasons, John Foxe reprinted her work in his *Actes and Monuments* (1563) without Bale's commentary, providing his own admiring comments on "this godly woman" and attacking her questioners. Foxe's text is accompanied by a woodcut, "The Execution of Anne Askew," which John N. King identifies as John Day's work and calls "a vivid, visual record of her actual death." As late as 1673 Bathsua Makin referred to Askew as "a person famous for learning and piety, who so seasoned the queen and ladies of the court, by her precepts and examples, and after sealed her profession with her blood, that the seed of reformation seemed to be sowed by her hand." Askew's story is vividly retold in a documented narrative by Derek Wilson, *A Tudor Tapestry: Men, Women, and Society in Reformation England* (1972), and in two novels, Anne Manning's *Lincolnshire Tragedy:* (1866) and Alison Macleod's *The Heretic* (1966), both of which quote extensively from the *Examinations*. Further scholarship on Askew might focus on research into her beginnings in Lincolnshire and her association with Parr's Reformist circle; on the political, religious, and literary contexts of the *Examinations*; and on her influence on other Reformers.

References:

Elaine V. Beilin, *Redeeming Eve: Women Writers of the English Renaissance* (Princeton: Princeton University Press, 1987), pp. 29–47;

Leslie P. Fairfield, *John Bale: Mythmaker for the English Reformation* (West Lafayette, Ind.: Purdue University Press, 1976);

John N. King, *English Reformation Literature: The Tudor Origins of the Protestant Tradition* (Princeton: Princeton University Press, 1982);

King, *Tudor Royal Iconography: Literature and Art in an Age of Religious Crisis* (Princeton: Princeton University Press, 1989);

Alison Macleod, *The Heretics* (London: Hodder & Stoughton, 1965); republished as *The Heretic* (Boston: Houghton Mifflin, 1966);

Bathsua Makin, *An Essay to Revive the Ancient Education of Gentlewomen in Religion, Manners, Arts and Tongues: With an Answer to the Objections against This Way of Education* (London: J. D., 1673); republished in *The Female Spectator: English Women's Writings before 1800*, edited by Mary R. Mahl and Helene Koon (Bloomington: Indiana University Press, 1977), pp. 125–135;

Anne Manning, *The Lincolnshire Tragedy* (London: Bentley, 1866); republished as *Passages in the Life of the Faire Gospeller, Mistress Anne Askew* (New York, 1867);

James Kelsey McConica, *English Humanists and Reformation Politics under Henry VIII and Edward VI* (Oxford: Clarendon Press, 1965), pp. 222–227;

Benjamin O. Sharp, *Anne Askew, Martyr, A.D. 1545* (London, 1869);

Mary E. T. Stirling, *A Short Life of Anne Askew* (London: Thynne, 1913);

Betty Travitsky, ed., *The Paradise of Women: Writings by Englishwomen of the Renaissance* (New York: Columbia University Press, 1989), pp. 167–186;

Maria Webb, *The Fells of Swarthmoor Hall and Their Friends: With an Account of Their Ancestor, Anne Askew, the Martyr* (London: Bennett, 1865);

Diane Willen, "Women and Religion in Early Modern England," in *Women in Reformation and Counter-Reformation Europe*, edited by Sherrin Marshall (Bloomington & Indianapolis: Indiana University Press, 1989), pp. 140–165;

Derek Wilson, *A Tudor Tapestry: Men, Women, and Society in Reformation England* (London: Heinemann, 1972).

Stephen Bateman

(circa 1510 – 1584)

David Galbraith
University of Toronto

BOOKS: *A Crystall Glasse of Christian Reformation, wherein the Godly Maye Beholde the Coloured Abuses Vsed in This Our Present Tyme* (London: Printed by Iohn Day, 1569);

The Golden Booke of the Leaden Goddes, wherein Is Described the Vayne Imaginations of Heathen Pagans, and Counterfaict Christians: Wyth a Decription of Their Seueral Tables, What Ech of Their Pictures Signified (London: Printed by Thomas Marshe, 1577);

The New Arival of the Three Gracis, into Anglia. Lamenting the Abusis of This Present Age (London: Printed by Thomas East for William Norton & Stephen Bateman, 1580?).

Edition: *The Golden Booke of the Leaden Gods,* edited by Stephen Orgel (New York & London: Garland, 1976).

OTHER: Olivier de la Marche, *The Trauayled Pylgrime, Bringing Newes from All Partes of the Worlde, Such like Scarce Harde of Before,* translated and adapted by Bateman (London: Printed by Henrie Denham, 1569);

John Rogers, *The Displaying of an Horrible Secte of Grosse and Wicked Heretiques, Naming Themselues the Familie of Loue. Newley Set Foorth by I. R. 1578. Whereunto Is Annexed a Confession of Articles, Made the 28. of May 1561,* preface by Bateman (London: Printed [by Henry Middleton] for George Bishop, 1578);

Conrad Lycosthenes, *The Doome Warning All Men to the Iudgemente: Wherein Are Contayned for the Most Parte All the Straunge Prodigies Hapned in the Worlde, with Diuers Secrete Figures of Reuelations Tending to Mannes Stayed Conuersion towardes God: In Maner of a Generall Chronicle, Gathered out of Sundrie Approued Authors,* translated, with additions, by Bateman (London: Printed by Ralphe Nubery, assigned by Henry Bynneman, 1581; edited by John R. McNair, Delmar, N.Y.: Scholars' Facsimiles and Reprints, 1984);

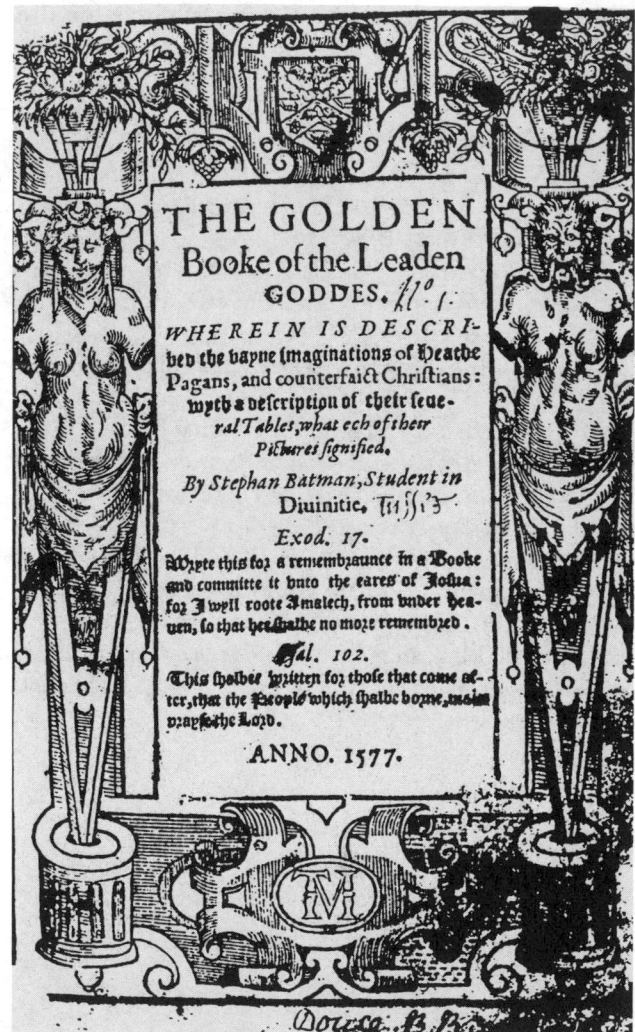

Title page for Bateman's description of the classical deities

Bartholomaeus Anglicus, *Batman vppon Bartholome, His Booke De Proprietatibus rerum, Newly Corrected, Enlarged and Amended; with Such Additions as Are Requisite, vnto Every Severall Booke,* edited by Bateman (London: Printed by Thomas East, 1582); edited by Jürgen Schäfer (Hildesheim & New York: Olms, 1976).

Stephen Bateman (or Batman) was an author, translator, and religious controversialist whose works include a widely read encyclopedia, the first mythography published in England, and an important religious allegorical poem that has been cited by some critics as an influence on Edmund Spenser's *Faerie Queene* (1590–1596). Bateman also played a significant role in the antiquarian circle that was inspired by Matthew Parker, Archbishop of Canterbury.

Biographical information on Bateman is scarce and unreliable. He was born in Bruton, Somersetshire, and attended Cambridge, from which he seems to have received his LL.B. in 1534; later he received his D.D. Bateman served in the household of Archbishop Parker and as rector of Merstham and parson of Newington Butts, both in Surrey. In 1582 he was a chaplain in the household of Henry Carey, Lord Hunsdon. In 1583 he licensed a book for the press. He died in 1584.

Bateman entered Parker's household as domestic chaplain sometime after the latter's appointment as archbishop of Canterbury in 1559. He was involved with an active group of antiquarians organized by the archbishop, which also included John Joscelyn (Parker's Latin secretary) and Alexander Neville. Bateman seems to have been employed principally as a collector of books and manuscripts for Parker's library.

In the sixteen years he was archbishop, Parker played an extremely significant role in defining the character of the Elizabethan religious settlement. He was largely responsible for the final text of the Thirty-nine Articles of the Church of England (1571) and for the production of the *Bishops' Bible* (1563–1568). He was also a student of English history. In addition to his own work, *De antiquitate Britannicae ecclesiae* (1572), on the history of the English church, he supervised the first printed editions of many of the major medieval sources, such as the works of Asser and Matthew Paris. Parker's antiquarian interests were derived in large measure from his desire to assert the authority and privileges of the English church against its Roman Catholic and radical Protestant critics.

Bateman played an important role in Parker's recovery of historical documents. Henry VIII's dissolution of the monasteries from 1535 to 1537 had led to the dispersal of some of the most important monastic libraries. Although John Bale had already listed the holdings of some of these libraries, Parker used his position and the members of his household to retrieve many manuscripts that might otherwise have been lost. Bateman seems to have been one of the most active of Parker's agents. In *The Doom Warning All Men to the Judgment* (1581) he writes in a note on Parker's death that the archbishop, "by virtue of commission from our sovereign Queen her majesty, did cause to be diligently gathered many books of antiquity . . . when the religious houses of the Popish were suppressed, their libraries were almost utterly spoiled, to the great loss and hindrance of learning. Among whose books remained . . . some worthy the view and safe-keeping, gathered within four years, of divinity, astronomy, history, physic, and others of sundry arts and sciences . . . six thousand seven hundred books, by my own travail." Although he is certainly exaggerating both his own role and the size of the collection, the claim is suggestive of the importance of the library that was left, after Parker's death in 1575, to Corpus Christi College, Cambridge, where it remains today. Bateman also seems to have collected books for himself: an eleventh-century manuscript of the Four Gospels, now in the Bodleian Library at Oxford, contains the inscription, "Stephen Batman, the true owner of this book, which cost xx [shillings?]."

Bateman seems to have been well known among his contemporaries for his learning. At the beginning of *A Learned and True Assertion* (1582), a translation of John Leland's defense of the Arthurian legends (1544), Richard Robinson thanks "Master Steven Batman, a learned preacher and friendly favorer of virtue and learning" who "gave me assured knowledge on this manner taken out of the ancient records written at Avalonia."

Bateman's literary production consists, for the most part, of translations and adaptations of late-medieval sources. Most of these works attempt to adapt the medieval literary heritage for contemporary religious and intellectual purposes, an aim they have in common with his activities on Archbishop Parker's behalf.

The Travayled Pilgrim (1569) has been described by Anne Lake Prescott as "England's only significant nondramatic Protestant quest allegory before Spenser." The poem is written in "fourteeners," the characteristic form of narrative verse in the mid sixteenth century. It is ultimately based on *Le Chevalier délibéré*, a popular poetic allegory by Olivier de la Marche, an official in the Burgundian court, which was written in 1483, published in 1488, and translated into several languages. La Marche's poem combines the conventions of the pilgrimage allegory with praise of the Burgundian dynasty. Bateman's more immediate source is the 1553 Spanish translation by Hernando de Acuña, *El*

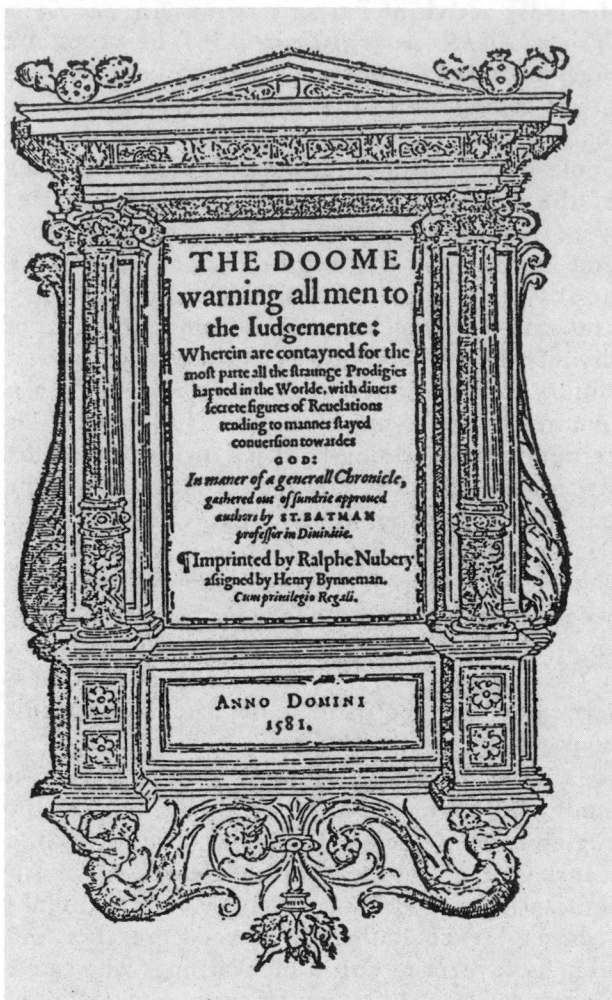

THE DOOME
warning all men to
the Iudgemente:
Wherein are contayned for the
most parte all the straunge Prodigies
hapned in the Worlde, with diuers
secrete figures of Reuelations
tending to mannes stayed
conuerfion towardes
GOD:
In maner of a generall Chronicle,
gathered out of sundrie approued
authors by ST. BATMAN
professor in Diuinitie.

¶Imprinted by Ralphe Nubery
afsigned by Henry Bynneman.
Cum priuilegio Regali.

ANNO DOMINI
1581.

Title page for Bateman's translation of Conrad Lycosthenes' history of the world from creation to 1557, with additions by Bateman extending the chronicle to 1580

Cavallero determinado, in which the Hapsburgs supplant the Burgundian dukes as objects of praise; Bateman's illustrations are also based principally on this source. In his work the Tudors replace the Hapsburgs.

In his note to his readers Bateman says that the poem describes "the state of man, and the innumerable assaults that he is daily and hourly environed withall." The pilgrim-knight embarks on the journey of life, riding the horse of Will and armed with the sword of Courage and the shield of Hope. After a series of allegorical encounters and contests he is joined by Memory. She explains the significance of a contest they witness pitting Debility and Dolor against the members of the Tudor dynasty. Her explanations emphasize the religious dimensions of the Tudor achievement, beginning with Henry VIII, who "brake the neck of Papistry, and gave a deadly

wound / Unto the mass that Romish hell, that did our souls confound." He is followed by Edward, in whose brief life "All false idolatry was quite out of his region rent," and by Mary, for whose reign the pilgrim-knight is advised to consult John Foxe's martyrology: "If thou wilt more, said Memory to me, of Mary's reign, / The Acts and Monuments put forth, of that time show thee plain." The sequence ends with Elizabeth, who is shown in the accompanying woodcut in a Triumph of Fame, "neither Dolor nor Debility as yet not able to resist."

Critics have detected parallels between Bateman's poem and *The Faerie Queene,* particularly book 1, Spenser's legend of holiness. It seems unlikely, however, that Spenser was specifically indebted to Bateman; the parallels between the two works seem to be derived from the similarity of the allegorical conventions on which they draw. Prescott is almost certainly correct in seeing *The Travayled Pilgrim* as a "precedent" of Spenser's text in which some of the explicitly Protestant dimensions of *The Faerie Queene* are anticipated.

Also in 1569 Bateman's *A Crystal Glass of Christian Reformation* was printed by John Day, who was closely associated with Archbishop Parker. This profusely illustrated work has been described by Samuel Chew as "the most ambitious of all English treatments" of the popular theme of the Seven Deadly Sins. Each sin is illustrated by four woodcuts, many of them anti-Catholic, accompanied by elaborate explanations and commentaries. The book also contains a commentary on some of the virtues and a criticism of the Catholic doctrine of Purgatory.

Bateman's *The Golden Book of the Leaden Gods* (1577), dedicated to Lord Hunsdon, is the first mythography to be printed in England. It is derived principally from Georg Pictorius's *Apotheoseos* (1558), an important description of the classical deities. Bateman explains the attributes of the classical gods and juxtaposes them to the truth of Christianity, which he sets, in turn, against the "heresies" of contemporary Roman Catholicism and Protestant radicalism and those of the early church, such as the Arians and the Pelagians.

The Doom Warning All Men to the Judgment is a translation of Conrad Lycosthenes' *Prodigiorum ac ostentorum Chronicon* (1557) with additions by Bateman. A lengthy chronicle extending from the creation of the world (dated 3959 B.C.) to 1580, the book describes "those true prodigies which are most assured tokens of God's wrath and vengeance." It is a catalogue of historical events, natural disasters, and freaks of nature, all intended to warn of the impending day of judgment, and it concludes with a de-

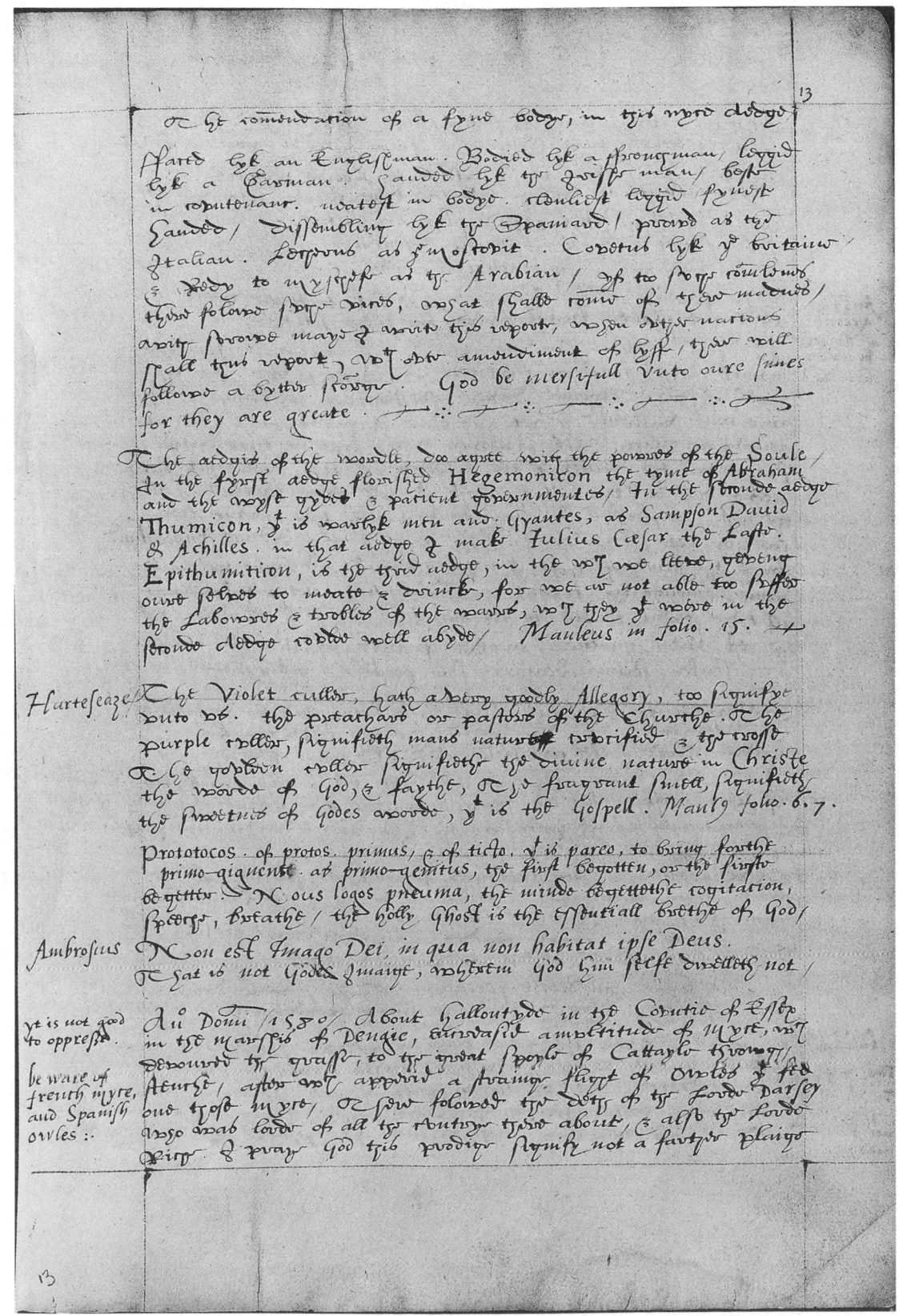

Page from Bateman's commonplace book for 1580, including material he used in The Doom Warning All Men to the Judgment *(Houghton Library, Harvard University)*

scription of a series of recent omens in various parts of England. Bateman's purpose in translating and augmenting Lycosthenes' work may have been the political one of opposing the proposed marriage between Elizabeth and François, Duc d'Alençon, of France; as John R. McNair argues, the concluding omens may have been intended to suggest divine support for the opponents of the match.

The work that seems to have been most widely read by Bateman's contemporaries, *Batman upon Bartholome* (1582), is a translation and adaptation of *De Proprietatibus rerum,* compiled in the first half of the thirteenth century by the Franciscan Bartholomaeus Anglicus. The most influential encyclopedia of the later Middle Ages, Bartholomaeus's work survives in many manuscripts and was widely translated; it was printed on more than twenty occasions before 1500 and frequently afterward, in Latin and in several modern European languages. In nineteen books and twelve hundred chapters Bartholomaeus attempts to present comprehensively the orders of creation, from the hierarchies of angels through geography, botany, and biology. His sources include the classical authorities accessible in the Middle Ages, including Aristotle, Pliny, and a wide variety of medieval authors.

An English translation of *De Proprietatibus rerum* prepared by John Trevisa at the end of the fourteenth century was printed by Wynkyn de Worde in 1495 and reprinted by Thomas Berthelet in 1535. Bateman's version is an adaptation of Trevisa's translation, with "additions answerable to the time present, using new titles." His new authorities include Conrad Gesner on the natural sciences and Sebastian Munster and Abraham Ortelius on geography. Bateman's additions take the form of marginal annotations or of notes, printed in a different typeface, at the conclusion of Bartholomaeus's chapters. The longest single addition is taken from Cornelius Agrippa's *De occulta philosophia* (1533), an important work of Renaissance occult theory.

Batman upon Bartholome was probably the most influential English encyclopedia of the late sixteenth century. It is particularly useful today in glossing references to the natural sciences in the works of Bateman's contemporaries. The book is also an important reminder of the intellectual continuities between the Middle Ages and the Renaissance and of the influence of medieval sources and authorities as late as the end of the sixteenth century, even on authors as committed to the Reformation as Bateman.

The New Arrival of the Three Graces into Anglia (1580?) is a dream vision with sections in verse and prose that, like *The Doom Warning All Men to the Judgment,* emphasizes the omens of divine judgment. Bateman also provided a preface to John Rogers's *The Displaying of a Horrible Sect of Gross and Wicked Heretics* (1578), an attack on a Protestant sect called the Family of Love.

Although none of his works has been widely discussed by modern critics, Bateman's career is worthy of attention principally because of his role in preserving significant material from the medieval period and in making it available to sixteenth-century readers, albeit largely in the service of Reformation controversy. In this respect there is an underlying continuity between his work on Parker's behalf, which was of considerable significance in the emergence of English antiquarianism, and his literary activity, which contributed to the Protestant reappropriation of this heritage. Bateman's work merits more attention than it has yet received and ought to be made available in modern editions.

References:

Samuel Chew, *The Pilgrimage of Life* (New Haven: Yale University Press, 1962);

Anne Lake Prescott, "Spenser's Chivalric Restoration: From Bateman's *Travayled Pylgrime* to the Redcrosse Knight," *Studies in Philology,* 86 (Spring 1989): 166–197;

Susie Speakman Sutch and Prescott, "Translation as Transformation: Olivier de la Marche's *Le Chevalier délibéré* and Its Hapsburg and Elizabethan Permutations," *Comparative Literature Studies,* 25, no. 4 (1988): 281–317.

Papers:

Stephen Bateman's commonplace book is in the Houghton Library, Harvard University.

Thomas Becon
(Theodore Basille)

(circa 1512 – 30 June 1567)

Seymour Baker House
University of Otago

BOOKS: *Newes out of Heauen Both Pleasaunt & Ioyfull,*
as Theodore Basille (London: Printed by
John Mayler for John Gough, 1541?);

*A Christmas Bankette Garnyshed with Many Disshes,
Newly Prepared,* as Basille (London: Printed by
John Mayler for John Gough, 1542);

A Potaciõ or Driikynge for This Holi Time of Lent, as
Basille (London: Printed by John Mayler for
John Gough, 1542);

A Newe Pathwaye vnto Praier, as Basille (London:
Printed by John Mayler for John Gough,
1542); enlarged as *The Right Path Waye vnto
Prayer, wyth a Table Lately Made* (London:
Printed by John Mayler for John Gough,
1543);

A Pleasaunt Newe Nosegaye, as Basille (London:
Printed by John Maylerre for John Gough,
1542);

The New Pollecye of Warre, as Basille (London:
Printed by John Maylerre for John Gough,
1542); enlarged as *The True Defence of Peace*
(London: Printed by John Mayler for John
Gough, 1543); enlarged as *The True Defence of
Peace, Called Before the Pollecye of Warre, Lately
Recognised* (London: Printed by John Mayler
for John Gough, 1543);

Dauids Harpe Ful of Moost Delectable Armony, as
Basille (London: Printed by John Mayler for
John Gough, 1542);

*A New Yeares Gyfte More Precious than Golde, Newly
Published,* as Basille (London: Printed by John
Mayler for John Gough, 1543);

An Inuectyue agenst the Mooste Wicked Vyce of Swearing,
as Basille (London: Printed by John Mayler
for John Gough, 1543);

*The Gouernans of Vertue, Teachyng a Christen Man,
Howe He Oughte Dayely to Lede His Life. Also
Many Godly Prayers. With a Table in Thende,*
anonymous (Southwark: Printed by James
Nicholson, 1538 [i.e., circa 1548–1550]; re-

Portrait of Thomas Becon published as the frontispiece to The Sick
Man's Salve Newly Made *(courtesy of the Folger
Shakespeare Library)*

vised and enlarged edition, London: Printed
by John Daye, 1560?);

*A Newe Dialog betwene Thangell of God, & the Shepherdes in
the Felde,* as T. B. (London: Printed by Richard
Wyer for John Daye, 1547?);

The Physyke of the Soule (London: Printed by Thomas Raynald & William Hill, sold by William Hill, 1549);

The Castell of Comforte, in the Whiche It Is Proued, yt God Alone Absolueth (London: Printed by John Daye & William Seres, 1549?);

The Fortresse of the Faythfull agaynst ye Cruel Assautes of Pouertie (London: Printed by John Daye & William Seres, 1550);

The Iewell of Ioye (London: Printed by John Daye & William Seres, 1550?);

The Flower of Godlye Prayers (London: Printed by John Daye, circa 1550);

The Principles of Christen Religion (London: Printed & sold by John Daye, 1550?);

A Fruitful Treatise of Fasting (London: Printed & sold by John Daye, 1551?);

A Confortable Epistle, too Goddes Faythfull People in Englande (Strasbourg [i.e., Wesel?]: At the signe of the Golden Bibel [i.e., Joos Lambrecht?], 1554);

An Humble Supplicacion vnto God, for the Restoringe of Hys Holye Woorde, vnto the Churche of Englande, anonymous (Strasbourg [i.e., Wesel?]: At the signe of the golden Bibell [i.e., Joos Lambrecht?], 1554);

The Pomander of Prayer: Whereunto Are Added Meditations Called S. Augustins, anonymous (London: Printed by John Daye, 1558); revised as *The Pomaynder of Prayer, Newly Made* (London: Printed by John Day, 1561);

Coenae sacrosanctae domini nostri et missae papisticae comparatio (Basel: John Oporinus, 1559);

The Sycke Mans Salue: Newly Made (London: Printed by John Daye, circa 1560);

The Relikes of Rome, concernynge Church Ware and Matters of Religion (London: Printed by John Day, circa 1560);

The Worckes of Thomas Becon, Whiche He Hath Hytherto Made and Published, with Diuerse Other Newe Bookes Added, 3 volumes (London: Printed by John Day, 1560–1563);

A New Postil Conteinyng Most Godly Sermons vpon the Sonday Gospelles, 2 volumes (London: Printed by Thomas Marshe & John Kingston, 1566).

Editions and Collections: *Writings of the Rev. Thomas Becon, Chaplain to Archbishop Cranmer, and Prebendary of Canterbury* (London: Printed for the Religious Tract Society, 1830?; Philadelphia: Presbyterian Board of Publication, 1843);

Works, 3 volumes, edited by John Ayre (Cambridge: Cambridge University Press, 1843–1844).

OTHER: Heinrich Bullinger, *The Christen State of Matrimonye,* translated by Miles Coverdale, preface by Becon (Antwerp: Printed by Matthias Crom, 1541); republished as *The Golden Boke of Christen Matrimonye* (London: Printed by John Mayler for John Gough, 1542);

"Homely agaynst Whordome," in *Certain Sermons, or Homilies, Appoynted by the Kynges Maiestie, to be Declared and Redde, by all Parsons, Vicars, or Curates, Euery Sōday in Their Churches, Where Thei Have Cure,* by Becon, Thomas Cranmer, and others (London: Printed by Richard Grafton, 1547);

The Solace of the Soule agaynst the Bytter Stormes of Sycknes and Deathe, Greatly Encouragynge the Faythfull, Paciently to Suffer the Good Pleasure of God in All Kynde of Aduersite, Newly Setforth in Englysshe, translated by Becon (London: Printed by William Hill for John Casse, 1548);

The Shelde of Saluacion: Newly Sette Forthe in Englysshe, translated by Becon (London: Printed & sold by Richard Wyer, 1548?);

Christen Prayers & Godly Meditacions vpon the Epistles to the Romains, Newly Translated out of Italian, translated by Becon (London: Printed by John Wyer, 1550);

Otto Werdmueller, *A Spyrytuall and Moost Precyouse Pearle: Teachyng All Men Howe, Consolacyon in Afflyccyons Is to Be Soughte,* translated by Coverdale, contributions by Becon (London: Printed by Steven Mierdman for Gualter Lynne, 1550);

Martin Luther, *A Very Comfortable, and Necessary Sermon, Concerning the Comming of Christ,* translated by Becon (London: Printed by John Daye, 1570).

Thomas Becon was one of the most prolific and popular Tudor writers; he composed dozens of works and produced several translations, and his popularity is reflected by the fact that a translation of Heinrich Bullinger's *The Golden Book of Christian Matrimony* (1542) was, as he said, "for the more ready sale set forth in my name by the hungry printer with my preface." In his life and works one can track the progress of the English Reformation from its early days under Henry VIII, through the consolidation of Protestantism under Edward VI and the reassertion of Catholicism under Mary, until the years after the Elizabethan Settlement. Many of his tracts ran to several editions during his lifetime and continued to inform the spiritual lives of English men and women long after his death. In the confusion of the early Reformation, Becon's first publisher claimed that his pen name on the cover made a book "the more plausible to the readers." Intended as Protestant guides for lay worship, Becon's most popular works were hortatory and devotional, presenting none of the historiographical and theological complexity found in the works of his contemporaries John Foxe and John Bale. Using the newly available English Bible as his source and model, Becon expounded the Protestant message for a population that until recently had been deprived of both access and guides to Scripture. Forced to recant his views twice under Henry VIII, he found protection during the reign of Edward VI under Archbishop of Canterbury Thomas Cranmer and the Lord Protector Edward Seymour, Duke of Somerset, but was exiled under Mary I. During his exile his theological convictions were hardened through exposure to England's leading Protestant theologians — men who would later form the core of the Elizabethan episcopate. In *The Works of Thomas Becon* (1560–1563) can be seen the teachings of a popular Protestant divine in the mainstream of the official Tudor church. Through their moderate language, exemplary piety, and congenial tone, his writings appealed to the growing numbers of English readers in search of a trustworthy guide to the changing face of public and private worship.

Despite frequent autobiographical revelations in his works, little is known of Becon's birth and parentage. He appears to have been born around 1512 in Norfolk. His father died when Becon was young, and his mother remarried. By the time Becon entered Cambridge, around 1527, the university was known for its Lutheran leanings. He was introduced to reformed theology through the sermons of Hugh Latimer, on whose direct and engaging style he would model his own successful preaching. In 1531 he left Cambridge with his B.A.; the following year he entered the community of religious scholars at the College of Saint John Evangelist in Rushworth near Thetford, where he was ordained priest on 12 April 1533. He did not remain there long — Becon's signature is not among those on the 1534 list of Rushworth members acknowledging the royal supremacy. By 1538 he had secured the patronage of Thomas, Lord Wentworth of Nettlestead, a supporter of reformed preachers. Wentworth presented Becon to the chantry of Saint Lawrence in Ipswich, but the appointment may have fallen through. What is certain is that Becon toured as an itinerant preacher — the sine qua non of the reformed clergy — from Norwich to London. The conservative backlash that culminated in the

Act of Six Articles in 1539 and the executions of Thomas Cromwell and Robert Barnes in 1540 forced him to recant his views in Norwich in June 1541; his sermons had challenged the act's teaching on clerical celibacy and the real presence. Rejecting exile, Becon retired to Kent under the assumed identity of the layman Theodore Basil and, as he put it, "changed the form of teaching the people from preaching to writing."

From the relative security of sympathetic gentry households between 1541 and 1543 Becon wrote at least nine works expounding Lutheran reform. They range in style from a simple arrangement of scriptural passages explaining Protestant theology, *News out of Heaven* (1541?), and the psalmodic exegesis of *David's Harp* (1542) to the more formally didactic *A New Pathway unto Prayer* (1542) and the patriotic exhortation against England's Catholic enemies in the person of Cardinal Reginald Pole in *The New Policy of War* (1542). Becon also began a series of Socratic dialogues that drew on his experience as theological tutor to the Protestant gentry: *A Christmas Banquet* (1542), *A Potation or Drinking for This Holy Time of Lent* (1542), *A Pleasant New Nosegay* (1542), and *A New Year's Gift* (1543). While outwardly resembling the popular colloquia of Desiderius Erasmus, these works lack the classical allusion and rhetorical refinement of the humanist models Becon eschewed. Sequentially linked and seasonally adjusted, they provide the lay reader with a catechetical exploration and explanation of Scripture aimed at increasing both biblical literacy and Protestant devotion. They also contain much autobiographical material, with Becon himself centrally placed as Philemon. Becon's other form of prose composition, the moral exhortation or invective necessitated by the apparent arrest of the reform movement, employs the rhetorical features of his homilies while shifting the emphasis from exegesis to denunciation. In *An Invective against the Most Wicked Vice of Swearing* (1543) he marshals an exhaustive array of scriptural verses to chastise sinners for their failure to embody the ethical standards of the Gospel. Both the devotional dialogue and the polemical diatribe would become mainstays in his later literary works, which draw from a common Protestant stock of anti-Catholic concepts and phrases.

Despite his pseudonym and layman's garb, Becon's links to the most radical members of the London book trade attracted the attention of the authorities. Following publication in 1543 of the final Henrician formulary, *A Necessary Doctrine,* which stiffened the government's anti-Protestant posture while affirming royal supremacy, he was forced into his second recantation on 8 July 1543 at a public ceremony at Paul's Cross in London. There he cut up his works and denounced the pride that had led him to oppose the king's learned bishops. Avowedly Lutheran, his works had been circumspect when dealing with the Eucharist, which saved him from accusations of sacramentarianism. Becon left London shortly after his humiliation and went north. He linked up with groups of Protestants in Derbyshire, Staffordshire, and finally Warwickshire, where he seems to have settled as a schoolmaster. In 1546 his works fell under the royal ban on Protestant literature.

After the accession of Edward VI in 1547 Becon became rector of Saint Stephen's, Walbrook; became chaplain in the flourishing intellectual household of the king's uncle, Seymour, the lord protector; and was appointed by Archbishop Cranmer as one of the six preachers at Canterbury and shortly thereafter as one of Cranmer's chaplains. Save for a short quasi-dramatic dialogue written possibly for a Christmas recitation at Seymour's house — *A New Dialogue between the Angel of God and the Shepherds in the Field* (1547?) — and published under his pseudonym for purely commercial reasons, the works he wrote during Edward's reign appeared under his own name and employ familiar techniques: they are Socratic dialogues — *The Jewel of Joy* (1550?) and *The Fortress of the Faithful* (1550) — in which he exults in the triumph of the Reformation but urges further consolidation and catechetical expositions that instruct his readers in the tenets of Protestant Christianity, such as *The Castle of Comfort* (1549?) and *The Principles of Christian Religion* (1550?).

Under Edward VI, Becon seems to have married; clerical celibacy was no longer mandatory after 1549. The name of his wife is not known, although he mentions his children — two sons named Theodore (the first one died), Christophile, Basil, and Rachel — from time to time and writes warmly of the happiness of marriage and domestic life. Becon's works written during Edward's reign, reflecting his pastoral responsibilities, show a marked shift from Lutheran to Zwinglian theology and clearly demonstrate his ability as a preacher. His concern with current social and economic problems, stemming from the belief that Christian charity must follow pure doctrine, is everywhere apparent; rural decay and the decline of hospitality are themes to which he warms. In *The Jewel of Joy,* using an image of men-devouring sheep drawn perhaps from Thomas More's *Utopia* (1516), he laments:

here many men had good livings and maintained hospitality, able at all times to help the king in his wars and to sustain other charges, able also to help their poor neighbors and virtuously to bring up their children in godly letters and good sciences, now sheep and coneys devour altogether, no man inhabiting the aforesaid places. Those beasts which were created of God for the nourishment of man do now devour man. The Scripture saith that God made "both sheep and oxen with all the beasts of the field" subject unto man; but now man is subject unto them. Where man was wont to bear rule, there they now bear rule. Where man was wont to have his living, there they now only live. Where man was wont to inhabit, there they now range and graze.

And the cause of all this wretchedness and beggary in the commonweal are the greedy gentlemen, which are sheepmongers and graziers. While they study for their own private commodity, the commonweal is likely to decay. Since they began to be sheep-masters and feeders of cattle, we neither had victual nor cloth of any reasonable price. No marvel, for these forestallers of the market, as they use to say, have gotten all things so into their hands that the poor man must either buy it at their price or else miserably starve for hunger and wretchedly die for cold: for they are touched with no pity for the poor. It is found true in them that St. Paul writeth: "All seek their own advantage, and not those things which belong unto Jesus Christ."

Along the same lines, *The Fortress of the Faithful,* published in two simultaneous editions, expresses guarded sympathy for the oppressed poor who rebelled in Devonshire and Norfolk in 1549.

Becon exploits his ability as a devotional writer in *The Flower of Godly Prayers* (circa 1550), dedicated to the lord protector's wife. Written as a Protestant prayer manual and showing a marked shift from Lutheran to Zwinglian theology, it contains many pieces he would reuse in *The Pomander of Prayer,* an enormously successful book published in 1558 but composed before 1553 and dedicated to Anne of Cleves. That many of the prayers from these two works found their way into the official manual, *A Primer or Book of Private Prayer* (1553), attests to Becon's reputation and skill.

Sometime before Edward's death Becon wrote the last of his seven dialogues, *The Sick Man's Salve* (circa 1560). It remained unprinted until well into Elizabeth's reign and may have undergone considerable revision during Becon's exile, but it proved to be his most popular work. Four interlocutors, familiar to readers of his earlier dialogues, instruct a dying companion in a Protestant meditation on death similar to that in Becon's short translation *The Solace of the Soul* (1548). His place among the elect assured by his faith, the sick man dies while Philemon recites prayers from *The Flower of Godly*

Prayers. As in the other dialogues, *The Sick Man's Salve* presents the Protestant creed in confident and sober, if somewhat rigorous, terms. It also sets out sound advice in the form of the dying man's final words to his family and servants, each in turn. Addressing his daughters, he says: "What shall I say to you, my little daughters? I pray God bless you and make you joyful mothers of many children. Serve God. Obey your mother. Be diligent to please her. Give ear to her wholesome admonitions and follow them. Do nothing without her counsel and advisement. When your age shall require you to be married, follow the counsel of your mother and other of your faithful friends, which wish you to do well, in choosing your husbands. Take heed you be not corrupted with the gifts of naughty packs, nor deceived with the flattering tongues of wicked and unthrifty persons. For many in our days seek not the woman but the woman's substance. Couple yourselves with such as fear God, love his word, and be of honest repute. And when you be once married, reverence your husbands, know them to be your heads and governors appointed of God, obey them, and submit yourselves unto them. Suffer not your love to depart from your husbands, neither know any man besides them; but keep the bed undefiled, that your matrimony may be honorable and pure in the sight of God and his holy congregation. And if God blesses you with children, look that you bring them up in the glory of God, in his fear and doctrine. Ingraft in their young breasts, even from their tender age, virtue, godliness, and good manners: look well unto your household, and be an example to your maids of godliness and honesty." Disdaining trivial or ungodly occupations, the life of scriptural study Becon prescribes for the true Christian has prompted some to see him as a proto-Puritan, a view supported by his frequent lamentations on the secular quality and focus of English education and his sporadic denunciations of popular amusements such as parish ales, folk drama, and traditional games.

On Mary's accession Becon was sent to the Tower as a seditious preacher, along with many other notable Protestant divines, and deprived of his livings. Released on 22 March 1554, he fled first to Strasbourg and then to the congregation of English exiles in Frankfurt am Main, where he sided with Richard Cox and the more conservative members favoring the second *Book of Common Prayer* (1549) as their liturgical guide against John Knox and those with more radical, Calvinist leanings. Becon continued to write in English for his countrymen; he also wrote in Latin for an international audience. His exile works include *A Comfortable Epistle*

Title page for the first volume of Becon's collected works (courtesy of the British Library)

to God's Faithful People in England (1554) and *An Humble Supplication unto God for the Restoring of His Holy Word unto the Church of England* (1554). Many of his Continental works in Latin no longer survive. In the summer of 1556 he moved to Marburg, where he was patronized by Philip, Landgrave of Hesse, to whose son he dedicated one of his Latin works, *Coenae sacrosanctae domini nostri et missae papisticae comparatio* (1559), a work he later translated into English as "A comparison betwene the Lordes supper, and the Popes Masse" for his collected works. By January 1559 Elizabeth was on the throne and Becon was back in England, where his son Basil was baptized in Becon's old rectory of Saint Stephen's, Walbrook. His five-year exile among more radical Protestants had produced a more strident polemical tone in his invectives as they set about to interpret the events they had helped to bring about. Influenced by the scriptural historiography of his fellow exiles Foxe and Bale, Becon saw the temporary reversal of the Reformation under Mary as proof of divine anger at the Protestant failure to adhere rigidly to the Word of God.

Shortly after his return Becon set about collecting and revising his earlier works in preparation for the massive three-volume *Works of Thomas Becon*. The collection also includes more than a dozen new works, written either during his exile or shortly after his return to England. Some additions, such as "The Monstrous Merchandise of the Romish Bishops" and "The Displaying of the Popish Mass," are unrestrained polemics that demonstrate clearly that Becon was true to his claim to have "somewhat more sharpened my pen . . . against Antichrist and his Babylonical brood." No longer circumspect in their denial of the real presence and other sacramental teachings of the Catholic church, many of his later works include a concern with chiliastic theology that was popular among returning exiles. Yet Becon remained a popularizer of official Elizabethan piety and continued to write manuals of devotion. His collected works contain many new compositions in the form of scriptural aids for laymen and pastors alike such as the "New Catechism," "The Commonplaces of the Holy Scriptures," "The Summary of the New Testament," "The Demands of Holy Scripture with Answers to the Same," and the appealing synoptic account of Jesus' life and ministry, "Christ's Chronicle." Patronized by Matthew Parker, Archbishop of Canterbury, to whom he dedicated his collected works, and other notables throughout England, Becon served the state church in a variety of ways after his return: in addition to his prebendal stall in Canterbury, Becon held several livings in plurality, including the rectory of Saint Dionis Backchurch in London and the vicarages of Sturry, near Canterbury, and of Christ Church, Newgate, in London. He was probably not resident in any of these cures. He also performed ecclesiastical visitations for Archbishop Parker in 1559 and 1561. He died on 30 June 1567. His homilies, perhaps his most attractive works, appeared in two volumes as *A New Postil Containing Most Godly Sermons upon the Sunday Gospels* (1566).

Becon's writings bridge the distance between Protestant sermon and Reformation tract. Ever conscious of his limits as a theologian and his ability as a pastor, Becon summed up his career to Parker: "in all my sermons and writings I have not attempted matters of high knowledge and far removed from the common sense and capacity of the people, but have been content . . . to handle such matters as might edify the brethren, than to drive them into an admiration or stupor at the doctrine of so rare, unwonted, high, and unsearchable mysteries." Retaining their focus on Scripture as their source and validation, his writings ignore Renaissance literary preoccupations with classical forms and models while employing many patristic authors (notably Chrysostom and Augustine) and, more rarely, those of classical antiquity. As the second generation of Protestants began to review their theological roots, Becon adapted his direct and homiletic style to reach this larger and increasingly more sophisticated audience. Famous in his time as a stirring preacher along the lines of Latimer and as a highly regarded composer of prayers, he blended pastoral and polemic concerns, and his works remain important sources for understanding popular piety in the English Reformation. Little attention has been paid to him since John Ayre's edition of his works in 1843–1844. The few recent commentators who discuss Becon at any length see him as representative of popular theology in mid-Tudor England.

Bibliographies:

John Bale, *Scriptorum Illustrium Majoris Britanniae Catalogus,* 2 volumes (Basel: Printed by John Oporinus, 1557–1559; reprinted, Farnborough: Gregg International, 1971), I: 756–757;

Thomas Tanner, *Bibliotheca Britannico-hibernica,* edited by D. Wilkins (London: Bowyer, 1748);

Bale, *Index Britanniae Scriptorum,* edited by Reginald Poole and Mary Bateson (Oxford: Clarendon Press, 1902), pp. 430–431;

Derek Bailey, *Thomas Becon and the Reformation of the Church in England* (Edinburgh: Boyd, 1952), pp. 140–147.

Biography:

Christian Garrett, *The Marian Exiles* (Cambridge: Cambridge University Press, 1938), pp. 84–85.

References:

Derek Bailey, *Thomas Becon and the Reformation of the Church in England* (Edinburgh: Boyd, 1952);

Susan Brigden, *London and the Reformation* (Oxford: Clarendon Press, 1989), pp. 345, 348–351, 458, 530, 570n;

John King, *English Reformation Literature* (Princeton: Princeton University Press, 1982), pp. 27–28, 117–118, 290–297;

Ranier Pineas, "Polemical Technique in the Works of Thomas Becon," *Moreana,* 5 (1968): 49–55;

Pineas, "Thomas Becon as a Religious Controversialist," *Nederlands Archief voor Kerkgeschiedenis,* 46 (1965): 206–220.

Andrew Boorde

(circa 1490 – April 1549)

Sheila Ahern
Victoria University of Wellington

BOOKS: *Here Is a Mery Iest of the Mylner of Abyngton with His Wyfe and Doughter,* sometimes attributed to Boorde (London: Printed by Wynkyn de Worde, 1532–1534?);

Hereafter Foloweth a Compendyous Regiment or a Dyetary of Helth, Made in Mounpyllier (London: Printed by Robert Wyer for John Gowghe, 1542; enlarged edition, London: Printed by Wyllyam Myddylton, 1564 [i.e., 1544]); revised and enlarged as *A Compendyous Regiment or a Dyetary of Healthe Made in Mountpyllyer: Newly Corrected with Dyuers Addycyons* (London: Printed by Wyllyam Powell, 1567 [i.e., 1547]); excerpts published as *The Boke for to Lerne a Man to Be Wyse in Buyldyng of His Howse for the Helth of Body & to Holde Quyetnes for the Helth of His Soule, and Body. The Boke for a Good Husbande to Lerne,* anonymous (London: Printed and sold by Robert Wyer, 1550?);

A Prognostycacyon or an Almanacke (London, 1545);

The Breuiary of Helthe, for All Maner of Syckenesses and Diseases the Which May Be in Man, or Woman Doth Folowe. Expressynge the Obscure Termes of Greke, Araby, Latyn, and Barbary in to Englysh Concerning Phisicke and Chierurgye (London: Printed by Wyllyam Myddelton, 1547; enlarged edition, London: Printed by Thomas East, 1587);

The Pryncyples of Astronamye the Whiche Diligently Perscrutyd Is in Maner a Prognosticacyon to the Worldes End (London: Printed by Robert Coplande, 1547?);

The Fyrst Boke of the Introduction of Knowledge (London: Printed at the Signe of the Rose Garland, William Copland, 1555?);

Merie Tales of the Mad Men of Gotham, attributed to Boorde (London: Printed by Thomas Colwell, circa 1565);

The First and Best Part of Scoggins Jests: Full of Witty Mirth and Pleasant Shifts, Done by Him in France. Gathered by A. Boord, attributed to Boorde (London: Printed by Miles Flesher for Francis Williams, 1626);

Woodcut purportedly depicting Andrew Boorde (from Boorde's Introduction of Knowledge*)*

"The Peregrination of Doctor Boarde," in Benedict, Abbot of Peterborough, *De vita et gestis Henrici II. et Ricardi I.,* edited by Thomas Hearne, volume 2 (Oxford: Sheldonian Theatre, 1735), pp. 764–804.

Editions: *The Fyrst Boke of the Introduction of Knowledge. The Which Doth Teache a Man to Speake Parte of All Languages, and to Knowe the Vsage and Fashion of All Maner of Coynes of Money, ye Which Is Currant in Euery Region,* edited by William Upcott (London: Reprinted by R. and A. Taylor, 1814);

The First Boke of the Introduction of Knowledge Made by Andrew Borde of Physycke Doctor; A Compendyous Regyment or A Dyetary of Helth Made in Mountpyllier, Compyled by Andrewe Boorde of Physycke Doctour; Barnes in the Defence of the Berde: A Treatyse

Frontispiece for Boorde's Breviary of Health

Made, Answerynge the Treatyse of Doctor Borde upon Berdes, edited by F. J. Furnivall (London: Published for the Early English Text Society by Kegan Paul, Trench, Trübner, 1870);

The Wisdom of Andrew Boorde, edited by H. Edmund Poole (Leicester: Backus, 1936);

The Breuiary of Helthe (Amsterdam & New York: Da Capo, 1971).

Andrew Boorde was an author, physician, traveler, and scholar. He is now a neglected writer, but his works were popular during his lifetime and were reprinted frequently in the first few decades after his death. For modern scholars he is useful mainly as a source for medical and social history, but his verse and prose compositions are of interest to students of literature. His remarks on the inadequacies of the English language in his day explain in part the unwillingness of learned authors to write in the vernacular for a lay readership. Boorde, however, chose to write in English for the common good, displaying the spirit of the new humanism that saw virtue in educating the populace. His *Dietary of Health* (1542) and *Breviary of Health* (1547) were the first medical works composed in English for the ordinary man and woman.

Personal passages in all of Boorde's works, together with his will and few remaining letters, form the basis of what is known about his life. He was born at Boord's Hill in Holmsdale near Cuckfield, Sussex, around 1490; attended Oxford University; and became a Carthusian monk while underage. His approximate date of birth can be calculated because in 1521 he was appointed suffragan bishop of Chichester for the aged Bishop Robert Sherborne; for this position he would have had to be at least thirty. In an account of his early years in a letter to Thomas Cromwell he explains that because he was a monk he was given a special papal dispensation to take up the post but did not act in Sherborne's place after all. It is likely that his family was behind this attempt to extricate him from London and from the rigors of the strict Carthusian order, which he disliked. By 1529 he had obtained a dispensation from the Carthusians to go abroad to study medicine at Montpellier, which he described as "the most noblest university of the world for physicians and surgeons."

On his return to England in 1530 he became physician to Sir Robert Drury, who brought him to the attention of Thomas Howard, third Duke of Norfolk. It has been wrongly claimed that he was physician to Sir Robert Dudley and that he treated Henry VIII, but as Norfolk's doctor he began to move in court circles and met the king. About 1532 he went abroad again, visiting the major universities of Europe and hazarding a dangerous journey across Spain during which his nine companions died from eating the fruit – against his advice – and drinking the water. He later wrote in *The Introduction of Knowledge* (1555?) that "for all the craft of physic that I could do, they died" and that when he returned to France he kissed the ground for joy and thanked God for delivering him out of great danger.

By May 1534 he was back with the Carthusians at the London Charterhouse, where he took the Oath of Supremacy but was for some unstated reason confined by the prior. Cromwell, acting as Henry VIII's vicar-general, secured his release and sent him on a mission to Europe. At Chartreux he visited the head of the Carthusian order, who released him from his vows. He wrote to Cromwell for approval of the discharge, then spent a year in Scotland studying and practicing medicine.

His third visit to Europe was as Cromwell's emissary to report on the depth of feeling aroused by Henry VIII's quarrel with the pope. It provided him with another opportunity to visit France, Spain, and Portugal and the Universities of Paris, Orleans, Poitiers, Toulouse, and Montpellier. A letter to Cromwell dated 20 June 1535 reports bad news: "few friends England hath in these parts of Europe."

A letter to Cromwell from Cambridge in August 1537 gives the first hint of the scandal that would subsequently attach to Boorde's name. On his way down from Scotland, he writes, he had been robbed of two horses, and he asks Cromwell to secure their restitution. He also asks Cromwell to help him recover more than forty pounds owed him by certain people in London who were slandering him with accusations that twenty years previously he had been "conversant with women." Soon after writing this letter he left England on his fourth and last journey, traveling far and wide before settling to work in Montpellier for about a year.

On his journeys Boorde had visited almost every European country and had traveled as far afield as Jerusalem, Turkey, Egypt, and North Africa. It was his practice to record his observations of the landscapes, people, and customs he encountered, paying special interest to vernacular languages; words and phrases from each country are included in *The Introduction of Knowledge*. The book contains the earliest known example of the Gypsy language: *Maysta ves barforas* (You are welcome in town) and *Mole pis lauena?* (Will you drink some wine?). These observations were also the basis of a book he wrote on Europe, the manuscript for which Cromwell borrowed and lost. An itinerary of England published under the title "The Peregrination of Doctor Boarde" (1735) was probably part of the missing book. Had this major travel book survived, it would have been the first of its kind in English.

At Montpellier he wrote his three main works, the *Dietary of Health, The Breviary of Health,* and *The Introduction of Knowledge,* which were published when he returned to England. He is probably best known for the humorous verse that introduces chapter 1 of *The Introduction of Knowledge:*

I am an Englishman, and naked I stand here,
Musing in my mind what raiment I shall wear;
For now I will wear this, and now I will wear that;
Now I will wear I cannot tell what.

The *Dietary of Health,* dedicated to the duke of Norfolk, quickly went through several editions. Its opening chapters, on how to build a house, were also printed as a separate tract. The work contains a good deal of sound advice on building and sanitation, on budgeting and spending income, and on maintaining physical well-being; it also tells which fruits, vegetables, meat, and fish are good to eat. Boorde recommends a good diet, mirth, temperance, and moderate sleep as the best aids to good health. Works of infor-

Title page for the book in which Boorde claims to impart knowledge of all regions and countries of the world

mation and self-knowledge were then much in demand.

In the preface to the *Breviary of Health,* also dedicated to Norfolk, Boorde says, "I do not write these books for learned men, but for simple and unlearned men that they may have some knowledge," and the text concludes: "Thus endeth these books . . . to the profit of all poor men and women." The book lists diseases alphabetically by their Latin names and describes their symptoms, remedies, and treatments. In the chapter on mirth Boorde declares: "The principal mirth is when a man lives out of deadly sin . . . without swearing and slandering and ribald speaking. Mirth is in musical instruments, and spiritual and godly singing; mirth is when a man lives out of debt, and may have meat and drink and clothes, although he has never a penny in his purse; but nowadays, he is merry that has gold and silver, and riches with lechery; and all is not worth a blue point." It is a serious

Woodcut depicting the Englishman who is a slave to fashion in clothing (from The Introduction of Knowledge)

work but is lightened by some strange remedies and by Boorde's humorous asides (for example, "for when the drink is in, the wit is out").

The Introduction of Knowledge has been called the most curious and interesting volume ever printed by William Copland. It is dedicated to Henry VIII's daughter, Princess Mary, and claims to teach of all regions, countries, customs, and languages. Each chapter begins with an amusing satirical verse on the follies of the nation discussed, followed by a prose account of the country and its people. Boorde gently ridicules the weaknesses of his countrymen and even acknowledges that they are prone to treason and deceit, yet he is full of nationalistic pride; in this respect, he shares a common trait of sixteenth-century English poets, dramatists, and historians. Englishmen, he writes, are "bold, strong, and mighty; the women are full of beauty . . . Constantinople, Venice, Rome, Florence, Paris, Cologne cannot be compared to London." The English nation, he asserts, is not just the equal of any other in the world "but superior in courage and good manners." He marvels that the Saxons ever conquered England, because "I think, if all the world were set

against England, it might never be conquered, they being true to themselves." The Scots, on the other hand, "be hardy men, and strong men, and well favored, and good musicians; in these four qualities they be most like, above all other nations, to an English man; but of all nations they will . . . boast themselves, their friends, and their country, above reason; for many will make strong lies." He asserts that his work would have been easier to write had he possessed his lost *Itinerary of Europe.*

Most of Boorde's verse is satirical, and in his prose writings he admits that his purpose is to make merry; he was an early advocate of laughter as the best medicine. "I do write words of mirth," he writes in the preface to the *Dietary of Health,* "for mirth is one of the chiefest things in physic." His dietary advice is entertainingly written, with witticisms that modern readers can appreciate; for example, "A good cook is half a physician." Yet the book is best known for its advice on how to site a house and establish proper sanitary arrangements; it made Boorde the first writer since Hippocrates to discuss health and home together. He observes that if "the eye be not satisfied, the mind cannot be contented." In almost all that he wrote there is this intermingling of wisdom and wit, which has led to the jestbooks *A Merry Jest of the Miller of Abington* (1532–1534?), *Merry Tales of the Mad Men of Gotham* (circa 1565), and *Scoggin's Jests* (1626) being ascribed to him. A similar work of his own composition was the lost *Book of Beards,* known from the answer to it by a man named Barnes (1541?); Barnes claims to have known Boorde when the latter was practicing medicine at Montpellier in 1542.

In April 1549 Boorde died in the Fleet Prison, where he may have been confined for lechery or for debt. His memory has been tarnished by accusations of loose living and, since his writings contain much sound advice on how to live a wise and healthy life, of hypocrisy. The 1924 edition of *Chambers' Biographical Dictionary* branded him "the fantastic old reprobate," but later editions removed this condemnation. Boorde's will, proved at Canterbury on 25 April 1549, left a considerable amount of property, some of which he had inherited from his brother, Richard, and some that had been given to him by William Conynsby, a judge and member of Parliament. Unquestionably, he did not die in debt, and it may be that his connections with disgraced political figures such as Cromwell and the duke of Norfolk led to his fall.

That Boorde was esteemed in his lifetime as a physician and scholar is confirmed by Barnes in the preface to *The Treatise Answering the Book of Beards.* Books by Boorde were sought after and, presumably, literally read to pieces, since no copies can be found of some of the early editions of his work. Popular sixteenth-century writers such as Thomas Wilson and William Harrison quoted from Boorde's works, in particular from *The Introduction of Knowledge.* What destroyed his good name were the disclosures made by Bishop John Ponet in 1555 in a book attacking Stephen Gardiner, Bishop of Winchester. Ponet asserted that Boorde, who had settled in Winchester sometime before 1548, had been arrested for keeping three whores in his chamber. His evidence was hearsay, but it was repeated by John Bale in the second volume of the second edition of his *Scriptorum illustrium maioris Britanniae scriptorum* (1557, 1559) and embellished with an assertion that Boorde committed suicide in the Fleet Prison out of shame. William Harrison and John Strype repeated the charges, although in 1813 Anthony à Wood claimed to have seen evidence that the three women were Boorde's patients. Ponet's controversy with Gardiner arose over the issue of priests' marriages, an issue addressed by Boorde in *The Introduction of Knowledge,* where he condemns the practice along with Martin Luther's heretical beliefs. These views would have been totally unacceptable to Protestant writers such as Ponet, Bale, and Harrison. In 1587 Harrison called Boorde "a lewd popish hypocrite and ungracious priest," even though when Boorde was arrested – for whatever reason – in 1548, he was no longer in holy orders. Harrison's comment, however, serves to confirm that the Catholic sentiments expressed in Boorde's writings were a cause of his censure. It was also Boorde's misfortune that his patrons were disgraced: in 1540 Cromwell fell from power; in 1546 the duke of Norfolk was arrested; in 1548 Gardiner was imprisoned in the Tower.

Boorde was a scholar who wrote of serious matters with wit and good-natured chaff for the benefit of the unlearned. His writing augmented the English language, which he readily acknowledges "is a base speech" compared to Italian, Spanish, and French but which "of late days is amended." As a humanist scholar, he hopes for a similar improvement in the populace urging: "Oh good English man, hear what I shall say / Study to have learning with virtue, night and day / Leave thy swearing, and set pride aside / And call thou for grace, that with thee it may bide." His simple verses helped to popularize poetry to the new class of readers with whom his work was popular. He is satirical but not unkind, reproving but not condemnatory, sensible and with a shrewd insight into human nature. Boorde's writings reflect the new spirit of the Tudor age and are therefore useful for modern social historians. In the nineteenth century scholars such as F. J. Furnivall regarded his literary talent quite highly, but today he ranks among the lesser-known literary figures of the sixteenth century. A reconsideration of Boorde would bring to an end a period of undeserved neglect and at the same time add greatly to modern understanding of the early English Renaissance.

Letters:

Henry Ellis, ed., *Original Letters, Illustrative of English History,* volume 2 (London: Bentley, 1846), pp. 295–305.

References:

Joseph Ames, *Typographical Antiquities* (London: Printed by W. Faden and sold by J. Robinson, 1749);

William Harrison, *The Description of England,* edited by Georges Edelen (Ithaca, N.Y.: Cornell University Press, 1968);

John Strype, *Ecclesiastical Memorials* (London: Wyatt, 1721);

Anthony à Wood, *Athenae Oxoniensis,* edited by Philip Bliss (London: Rivington, 1813).

Nicholas Breton

(circa 1555 – circa 1626)

James Nielson
University of British Columbia

BOOKS: *A Smale Handfull of Fragrant Flowers,* as N. B., attributed to Breton (London: Printed by Richard Jones, 1575);

A Floorish vpon Fancie, as N. B. Gent. (London: Printed by William How for Richard Jhones, 1577);

The Workes of a Young Wyt, Trust vp with a Fardell of Pretie Fancies, as N. B. Gent. (London: Printed by Thomas Dawson & Thomas Gardyner, 1577);

A Discourse in Commendation of the Valiant Gentleman, Maister Frauncis Drake (London: Printed by John Charlewood, 1581);

The Historie of the Life and Fortune of Don Frederigo di Terra Nuova (London: Printed by John Charlewood for Rice Johnes, 1590);

Brittons Bowre of Delights: Contayning Many, Most Delectable and Fine Devices, of Rare Epitaphes, Pleasant Poems, Pastorals and Sonets, as N. B. Gent., by Breton and others (London: Printed by Richard Jhones, 1591);

The Pilgrimage to Paradise, Ioyned with the Countesse of Penbrokes Loue (Oxford: Printed by Joseph Barnes, to be sold by Toby Cooke, London, 1592);

The Passions of the Spirit, anonymous (London: Printed by Thomas Este, 1594);

Marie Magdalens Loue, anonymous, attributed to Breton (London: Printed by John Danter, sold by William Barley, 1595);

The Wil of Wit, Wits Will, or Wils Wit, Chuse You Whether: Containing Fiue Discourses (London: Printed by Thomas Creede, 1597; revised, 1606);

The Arbor of Amorous Deuises. Wherein, Young Gentlemen May Reade Many Plesant Fancies, and Fine Deuises. And Thereon, Meditate Divers Sweete Conceites to Court the Love of Faire Ladies and Gentlewomen, as N. B. Gent., by Breton and others (London: Printed by Richard Johnes, 1597);

Title page for the allegory that began Breton's fifteen-year period of religious writing

Wits Trenchmour, in a Conference Had betwixt a Scholler and an Angler (London: Printed by James Roberts for Nicholas Ling, 1597);

Auspicante Jehoua: Maries Exercise (London: Printed by Thomas Este, 1597);

A Solemne Passion of the Soules Loue (London: Printed by Simon Stafford in the shop of Valentine Simmes for William Barley, 1598);

Pasqvils Mad-Cap. And His Message, anonymous (London: Printed by Valentine Simmes for Thomas Bushell, 1600); republished as *Pasqvils Mad-Cappe, Throwne at the Corruptions of These Times* (London: Printed by Augustine

Mathewes for Francis Falkner, Southwarke, 1626);

The Strange Fortunes of Two Excellent Princes, anonymous (London: Printed by Peter Short for Nicholas Ling, 1600);

The Second Part of Pasqvils Mad-Cap Intituled: The Fooles-Cap, as N. B. (London: Printed [by Gabriel Simson?] for Thomas Johnes, 1600); republished as *Pasqvils Fooles-Cap Sent to Svch as Are Not Able to Conceiue Aright of His Mad-Cap* (London: Printed by Richard Bradock for Thomas Johnes, 1600);

Pasqvils Passe, and Passeth Not: Set down in Three Pees, as N. B. (London: Printed by Valentine Simmes for John Smithicke, 1600);

Melancholike Humours, in Verses of Diuerse Natures (London: Printed by Richard Bradocke, 1600);

Pasquils Mistresse: Or the Worthie and Unworthie Woman, as Salohcin Treboun (London: Printed [by Richard Bradock?] for Thomas Fisher, 1600);

The Soulles Heauenly Exercise Set downe in Diuerse Godly Meditations, Both Prose and Verse (London: Printed by Richard Bradock for William Leake, 1601);

The Passion of a Discontented Minde, anonymous, attributed to Breton (London: Printed by Valentine Simmes for John Bailey, 1601);

A Diuine Poeme, Diuided into Two Partes: The Rauisht Soule, and the Blessed Weeper (London: Printed by Richard Bradock for John Browne & John Deane, 1601);

An Excellent Poeme, vpon the Longing of a Blessed Heart (London: Printed [by Richard Bradock] for John Browne & John Deane, 1601);

No Whippinge, Nor Trippinge: But a Kinde Friendly Snippinge, anonymous (London: Printed [by Richard Bradock?] for John Browne & John Deane, 1601);

The Mothers Blessing, anonymous (London: Printed by Thomas Creede for John Smethick, 1602);

A True Description of Unthankfulnesse (London: Printed by Thomas Este, 1602);

A Poste with a Madde Packet of Letters, anonymous (London: Printed by Thomas Creede for John Smethicke, 1602); enlarged as *A Poste with a Packet of Madde Letters* (London: Printed by Thomas Creede for John Smethicke, 1603; enlarged edition, printed by John Windet for John Smethicke & John Browne, 1607);

A Poste with a Packet of Mad Letters: The Second Part, anonymous (London: Printed by Thomas Creede for John Browne & John Smethicke, 1602);

Old Mad-Cappes New Gally-mawfrey (London: Printed by William White for Richard Johnes, 1602);

Wonders Worth the Hearing: Which Being Read May Serve to Purge Melancholy (London: Printed by Edward Allde for John Tappe, 1602);

A Dialogue Full of Pithe and Pleasure: Between Three Phylosophers: Vpon the Dignitie, or Indignitie of Man. Partly Translated out of Italian, and Partly Set downe by Way of Obseruation (London: Published by Thomas Creede for John Browne, 1603);

A Merrie Dialogue betwixt the Taker and Mistaker (London: Printed by Richard Field for James Shaw, 1603); republished as *A Mad World My Masters, Mistake Me Not; or, A Merry Dialogue betweene the Taker, and Mistaker* (London: Printed by Robert Raworth for John Spencer, 1635);

The Passionate Shepheard, or the Shepheardes Love: With Many Poems and Sonnets, as Bonerto (London: Printed by Edward Allde for John Tappe, 1604);

Grimellos Fortunes, with His Entertainment in His Travaile: A Discourse Full of Pleasure, as B. N. (London: Printed by Edward Allde for Edward White, 1604);

The Case Is Altered. How? Ask Dalio, and Millo, attributed to Breton (London: Printed by Thomas Creede for John Smethicke, 1604);

A Piece of Friar Bacons Brazen-heads Prophesie, as William Terilo, attributed to Breton (London: Printed by Thomas Creede for Arthur Johnson, 1604);

I Pray You Be Not Angrie: A Pleasant and Merrie Dialogue, betweene Two Travellers, as N. B. (London: Printed by William White for William Jones, 1605);

An Olde Mans Lesson, and a Young Mans Love (London: Printed by Edward Allde for Edward White, 1605);

The Soules Immortall Crowne Consisting of Seaven Glorious Graces, as Ber. N. Gent. (London: Printed by Humphrey Lownes, sold by Jeffrey Charlton & Francis Burton, 1605);

Honest Counsaile: A Merrie Fitte of a Poeticall Furie, as N. B. (London: Printed by William White for William Jones, 1605);

The Honour of Valour (London: Printed for Christopher Purset, 1605);

Choice, Chance, and Change: Or, Conceites in Their Colours, anonymous, attributed to Breton (London: Printed by Richard Bradock for Nathaniel Fosbrooke, 1606);

A Murmurer, anonymous (London: Printed by Robert Raworth, sold by John Wright, 1607);

Wits Private Wealth: Stored with Choise Commodities to Content the Minde (London: Printed by Edward Allde for John Tappe, 1607);

Divine Considerations of the Soule, Concerning the Excellencie of God, and the Vilenesse of Man (London: Printed by Edward Allde for John Tappe, 1608);

The Uncasing of Machivils Instructions to His Sonne, anonymous (London: Printed by John Beale for Thomas Bushell, 1613); abridged as *Grandsire Graybeard: Or Machiavell Displayed* (Printed by William Stansby for Richard Higgenbotham, 1635);

I Would, and Would Not, as B. N. (London: Printed by Thomas Creede for Thomas Bushell, 1614);

Characters upon Essais Morall, and Divine (London: Printed by Edward Griffin for John Gwillim, 1615);

The Good and the Badde, or Descriptions of the Worthies, and Unworthies of This Age (London: Printed by George Purslowe for John Budge, 1616);

Crossing of Proverbs. Crosse-Answeres. And Crosse-Humours, as B. N. Gent (London: Printed by George Eld for John Wright, 1616);

Crossing of Proverbs: The Second Part, as B. N. Gent (London: Printed by George Eld for John Wright, 1616);

The Hate of Treason, with a Touch of the Late Treason, as N. B. (London: [Printed by George Eld?], 1616);

Machivells Dogge, anonymous (London: Printed by Bernard Alsop for Richard Higgenbotham, 1617);

The Court and Country, or a Briefe Discourse betweene the Courtier and Country-man (London: Printed by George Eld for John Wright, 1618);

Strange Newes out of Divers Countries, as B. N. (London: Printed by William Jones for George Fayerbeard, 1622);

Fantasticks: Serving for a Perpetuall Prognostication, as N. B. (London: Printed by Miles Flesher for Francis Williams, 1626);

The Figure of Foure: The Second Part, as N. B. (London: Printed by the Eliot's Court Press for John Wright, 1626);

Soothing of Proverbs: With Only True Forsooth. In Two Parts, as B. N. Gent. (London: Printed by Eliot's Court Press for John Wright, 1626);

The Figure of Foure, or a Handfull of Sweet Flowers (London: Printed by the Eliot's Court Press for John Wright, 1631);

Conceyted Letters, Newly Layde Open, as I. M. (London: Printed by Bernard Alsop for Samuel Rand, 1632).

Editions: *The Works in Verse and Prose of Nicholas Breton,* 2 volumes, edited by Alexander B. Grosart (Edinburgh: Constable, 1879; reprinted, New York: AMS, 1966);

"Choice, Chance and Change" (1606) or, Glimpses of "Merry England" in the Olden Time, edited by Grosart (Blackburn, U.K.: Printed by C. Simms, Manchester, 1881);

A Mad World My Masters, and Other Prose Works, edited by Ursula Kentish-Wright (London: Cresset, 1929; reprinted, Grosse Pointe, Mich.: Scholarly Press, 1968);

Melancholike Humours, edited by G. B. Harrison (London: Scholartis, 1929);

Two Pamphlets of Nicholas Breton: Grimellos Fortunes (1604), An Olde Mans Lesson (1605), edited by E. G. Morice (Bristol, U.K.: Published for the University of Bristol by J. W. Arrowsmith, 1936);

The Arbor of Amorous Devices, edited by Hyder Edward Rollins (Cambridge, Mass.: Harvard University Press, 1936);

Brittons Bowre of Delights, edited by Rollins (Cambridge, Mass.: Harvard University Press, 1936);

Poems (Not Hitherto Reprinted), edited by Jean Robertson (Liverpool, U.K.: Liverpool University Press, 1952).

OTHER: "Phillida and Corydon," in *The Honorable Entertainment Giuen to the Queenes Maiestie at Eluetham* (London: Printed and sold by John Wolfe, 1591);

"The Preamble to N. B. His Garden Plot," "A Strange Description of a Rare Garden Plot," "An Excellent Dream of Ladies and Their Riddles," "The Chess Play," and "A Most Excellent Passion," in R. S., *The Phoenix Nest* (London: Printed by John Jackson, 1593);

"Astrophell His Song of Phillida and Coridon," "A Report Song in a Dream," and "Another of the Same," in *Englands Helicon,* edited by Nicholas Ling (London: Printed by James Roberts for John Flasket, 1600);

"In laudem Authoris," in John Taylor, *The Sculler, Rowing from Tiber to Thames* (London: Printed by Edward Allde, sold by Nathaniel Butter, 1612).

Nicholas Breton was one of the most prolific writers of the English Renaissance. He wrote in an impressive variety of genres and styles, sometimes with considerable originality. Apparently without academic credentials or social standing, he presumed to educate the powerful and explore issues of theological, philosophical, social, and political importance while also writing popular fiction and poetry. His works are sensible and sensitive; indeed, his homeliness and basic sanity may have been as great a barrier to critical analysis as the sheer quantity of his output and its lack of thematic coherence. His books are about all sorts of things, but it is easy at times to feel that they are about nothing much at all.

Breton was born into an old, established Essex family, probably in the early 1550s. His father, William Breton, died in 1559; his mother, Elizabeth Bacon Breton, seems almost immediately thereafter to have married a man named Edward Boyes. In 1561 she married the poet and ill-starred courtier George Gascoigne; as she was not yet legally divorced from her second husband, and since property was involved, a legal battle ensued. There was a divorce from Boyes and a second wedding to Gascoigne, and in the end he and Elizabeth won the suit.

There is no record of Breton's schooling; there is some evidence to indicate that he may have attended Oxford, but his vocabulary and the way he presents himself in his works make it improbable that he did so. In the dedication to Sir Francis Bacon (to whom he was distantly related) in *Characters upon Essays* (1615) Breton asks that he be allowed to write like a scholar even though he is not one.

By 1577 he was establishing himself in London as a fledgling poet. His earliest books are collections of poems apparently intended to introduce a budding talent into the courtly milieu. The first may be *A Small Handful of Fragrant Flowers* (1575), which was published under the initials "N. B."; Breton's authorship has been disputed. It is a slight volume, dedicated to Lady Douglas Sheffield and offering a poetic bouquet of virtues to the ladies of the court. A connection with Gascoigne's ill-fated *A Hundred Sundry Flowers* (1573) — republished as *The Posies* (1575) — is to be discerned not just in the floral metaphor but also in the use of personae, including Gascoigne's own "G. T." The book could have been one of Gascoigne's schemes, in which he involved his stepson — or at least his stepson's initials.

In 1577 appeared two collections, more substantial than *A Small Handful of Fragrant Flowers*, whose authorship has never been disputed: *A Flourish upon Fancy* and *The Works of a Young Wit. The*

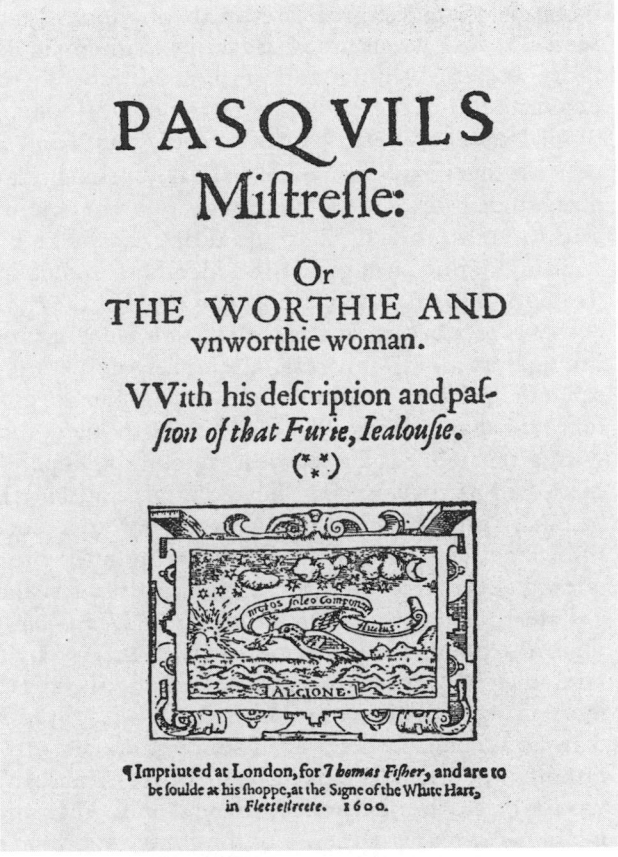

Title page for Breton's satirical essay on women

Works of a Young Wit claims to contain Breton's earliest efforts; *A Flourish upon Fancy,* though published first, is certainly the more mature of the two. It begins with a farewell to Fancy and a "dissuasion" from it that ends up almost as a celebration of it. No doubt the personified "Fancy," with her pervasive involvement in worldly affairs, owes something to the "Folly" of Desiderius Erasmus; but Breton, typically, displays less irony and more deliberation in his reflections on his subject. The rest of *A Flourish upon Fancy* is taken up with "The Toys of an Idle Head," a miscellany that includes lovers' complaints, Christmas songs, philosophical quiddities, a dream vision, and many other occasional poems. Most of these, like most of the poems in *The Works of a Young Wit,* are strung together with artificial semi-narrative frameworks reminiscent of, but less inspired than, those in Gascoigne's book.

In *The Works of a Young Wit* one can particularly see Gascoigne's influence in the attempt to adopt a world-weary attitude, the narrative links, and the pretended multiplicity of provenance; even some of the subject matter seems derivative. The most frequent theme of *The Works of a Young Wit* — misery — would engage Breton throughout his career. But his overall sunniness tends to undercut his more pathetic writing, and perhaps his most fluent performance in the early poetry is a playful romantic dialogue between a pair of country bumpkins.

In this largely conventional early verse Breton already displays his trademarks: gentle moderation and thoughtfulness. These qualities can make his writing bland; but against the idealistic and melodramatic musings of his contemporaries they are sometimes a breath of fresh air. Even when crying out against a hard mistress, attempting desperately sardonic nihilism, or constructing a somber allegorical landscape, Breton's verse tends to leave one with a sense of reasonableness, openness, hopefulness, and mature, uncomplicated appreciation. His basically philosophical nature leads him to a more than technical interest in enumerating and entertaining alternative interpretations and attitudes, and a dialogic balance is often struck (in *A Flourish upon Fancy* the poem against gambling is countered by a "defense of cards and dice" — when played in moderation). These tendencies stay with Breton throughout his career; and if some of his most frequently recurring themes are misfortune and the vanity of earthly existence, there is still what one might call a repressed sense of the sunny in Breton's writing. There is also a craftsmanlike pleasure in his task and in his subject matter.

In the 1580s only one or two pamphlets by Breton seem to have been published; it has been speculated that he was traveling abroad — possibly to Italy, since he seems to have been proficient in the Italian tongue. *A Flourish upon Fancy* is dedicated to "all the young gentlemen that delight to travel in foreign countries," suggesting that Breton's initial foray into poetic production may have been followed by a stint of diplomatic work. His last extant publication before 1590 was a pamphlet of 1581 in praise of the newly returned expedition of Francis Drake. He laments not having been part of the voyage and insists so interminably on "the treasure found in travel, and the want thereof at home" that one can imagine the sentiments to be more than conventional. Nothing more is known of his affairs until he married Ann Sutton in 1593. During the first decade of the new century they were to have at least four children, at least three of whom would die in infancy or adolescence.

Although the Drake pamphlet had inaugurated almost a decade of silence, it has usually been assumed that before Breton disappeared from the literary scene in the 1580s he had followed up his youthful poetry collections with a surprisingly mature work: *The Will of Wit*. The earliest surviving edition, published in 1597, takes the form of a five-part prose tract. It has been assumed that this edition was a reprint of a now-lost book of that title that was entered in the Stationers' Register in 1580 and was supposedly well known by 1583. If so, Breton had certainly developed a personal flair before turning from poetry to prose; the book is almost vintage Breton. Its fifth part, "The Praise of Virtuous Ladies," a relatively outspoken rejoinder to women's detractors, is especially promising. Although Breton feels compelled to apologize for his opinions, and although the piece gives in to some of the usual qualifications of the period, it is surprisingly sensible compared to other Elizabethan writings on women; one feels that Breton would like to be able to say even more. One critic sees a parody in this defense of women, and it is usual to emphasize its ironic tone; but Breton seems to have been too sincere and thoughtful to have intended sarcasm. He seems serious when he counters accusations that he is a "ladies' man" by saying that a fellow is "little wise that would not rather choose the favor of one woman than the friendship of any man," and he earnestly argues for the equality of the feminine sex: "what man was ever so good, so just, so pitiful, so liberal, so learned, so famous for rare excellencies, but there may be found a woman every way his match?" Even in the more equivocal passages, as when he insists on the lack of wisdom in pursuing a wise woman, his sardonic tone seems to be more at the expense of the man and the fragile male ego than sincerely antifeminist: "let it suffice that it is wisdom for a man to take heed that a woman be not wiser than himself; and how wise soever he be, to count them no fools. For indeed, as the common proverb is, the wit of a woman is a great matter; and true, when a man with all his wisdom is sometime to learn from her." Elsewhere Breton occasionally parrots some of the misogynistic platitudes of his day, but his protracted treatments of women seem unusually progressive.

In evidence in *The Will of Wit* is a rhetorical resourcefulness that became one of Breton's standards: he rings all the changes on a set of terms, such as *Will* and *Wit* in the title section or *Something* and *Nothing* in a dialogue between a scholar and a soldier. Although the scholar's musings in the latter piece might be parodic, they are not unlike the verbiage in some of Breton's other dialogues or even his own authorial style on certain occasions: "Why? Nothing is nothing, so what so disturbs me? That what must be nothing, for some thing it cannot be, yet some thing it is. And what is it, trow I? It is *Aliquid nihil,* that some nothing know I. What! do I know nothing?" At times Breton goes on in this way for pages. While he might seem to be exploring the paradoxical nature of language or thought or, as in the dialogue "Will and Wit," allegorically delineating psychological relationships of a Blakean complexity, the result, at least for the modern reader, is likely to be nonsense. Breton's wordplay is too inventive to be merely mechanical and too serious to be merely fanciful, but it still tries the patience of anyone attempting to read for content. Such writing seems to be an exuberant textual hemorrhaging for its own (or pecuniary) ends rather than the epistemological critique of humanist letters or thought that one might initially see in it. Breton lists proverbs only to gainsay them, forces every configuration out of a figure of speech, and considers a topic from every point of view he can; but this play generates neither drama nor parody. Although there are some of the mild satiric inflections of the anatomy genre, there is neither the serene irony of a thinker such as Erasmus nor the fierce, carnivalesque funniness of a verbal acrobat such as Thomas Nashe. Breton's more philosophical writing could perhaps charitably be seen as the true precursor of the styles of Robert Burton or Sir Thomas Browne; but his convolutions finally lack the learning, depth, and dark pensiveness of such writers and share only their verbal profligacy and nervous energy. To use a formula that Breton himself might have enjoyed exploring: his sentences often lead everywhere and nowhere.

Breton's experiments with the dialogue form are, nevertheless, varied and reasonably entertaining. The dialogue was his most frequently used framework for fiction, and he also used it for didactic material and for exploratory essays. Clearly he saw it as an unusually flexible vehicle. A piece such as *Wit's Trenchmore* (1597) starts out as a philosophical conversation, moves into colloquial speech, briefly modulates into snappy "cross answers," and then makes room for an extended set piece as one interlocutor tells a short story or perorates on a philosophical theme. For most modern readers much of this material will be tedious; innuendo and witticisms are now often lost, and there is only sporadic dramatic or conversational realism. Read patiently, however, the dialogues can provide both pleasure and information; and a pamphlet such as *Wonders Worth the Hearing* (1602) is not only entertaining but also precious for the glimpses it offers into Elizabethan society and mores.

Breton's more formal writing is either artificially patterned or somewhat gawky. When he returned to London to resume a writing career in which he would be involved for the next fifteen years, his first effort was *The History of the Life and Fortune of Don Frederigo di Terra Nuova* (1590), an attempt at a typical Elizabethan novel with shipwrecks and pirates, wrongful imprisonment and estranged lovers, erotic dalliances, euphuistic lectures, and interspersed songs. The romance is relatively successful (it may be a translation), but one senses even here that, heterogeneous as the Elizabethan novel form was, it was too structured for Breton's plotless mentality.

The lyric was more suited to his talents. His contemporaries seem to have respected him as a poet more than anything else, and he was quick to take advantage of the craze for lyric poetry in the 1590s. It is possible that from his handful of published works Breton had gained by 1591 enough of a reputation for his name to be a selling point. At least it has been assumed that *Britton's Bower of Delights,* published that year, was given that ambiguous title by the unscrupulous publisher Richard Jones to make it more salable, and that Breton was sincere when he vehemently disclaimed authorship of most of the poems in the miscellany. Given Breton's earlier and subsequent collaboration with Jones, however, it is possible that the work is an example of the common pretense whereby authorship was both affirmed and denied and responsibility was discharged onto the printer. In any case, Breton took his place — neither foremost nor last — among the semicourtly sonneteers and pastoralists who burst into print during the 1590s. New poems and reprints appeared in *The Phoenix Nest* (1593), *The Arbor of Amorous Devices* (1597), and *England's Helicon* (1600). *Britton's Bower of Delights* and *The Arbor of Amorous Devices* are something between miscellanies and personal collections; most of the poems in *Britton's Bower of Delights* seem to be by Breton, and probably many in *The Arbor of Amorous Devices* are as well. These poems include elegies on Sir Philip Sidney, acrostics dedicated to ladies of the court, pastoral and courtly lyrics, complaints, and an allegorical dream vision or two.

In his mature poems Breton is sometimes enjoyable or even mildly original, but he is rarely exciting as a versifier. At his best he is fresh and gracefully naturalistic, as when, in *The Phoenix Nest,* he introduces one of his night visions with the details of his tossing and turning in bed, looking for a side on which he could fall asleep:

> On loathèd bed I lay, my lustless limbs to rest,
> Where still I tumble to and fro, to seek which side were
>   best.
> At last I catch a place, where long I cannot lie,
> But strange conceits from quiet sleeps do keep awake
>   mine eye.

He rarely accomplishes anything like compression, but many of his lines are padded with colloquial and proverbial expressions that add life and humanity to them and give some of his poetry a conversational feel. There is not a great deal of convincing personal involvement, linguistic ingenuity, or tonal subtlety to his work, though he periodically surprises one with a sudden surge in depth or deftness. He was well regarded by the critics of his day and was sometimes grouped with such writers as Edmund Spenser and William Shakespeare.

His last gasp in the purely lyrical vein was *The Passionate Shepherd* (1604), a rather late entry in the craze for pastoral Petrarchism ("Bonerto" here beseeches "Aglaia"). The pastorals are among his most satisfying pieces. His natural delicacy, sense of the country, and homely, sunny style are refreshingly suited to the mode.

Pastoral escapism was only one of his responses to a world of misery and vanity — a world that was partly a literary convention. In 1592 he began a series of religious writings that were to occupy him throughout the next fifteen years. The authorship of a few of these works is in question, and the exact nature of his religious belief is not well established; but he clearly warmed to the themes of worldly vanity and heavenly love, and he seems to have suffered along with many others at the beginning of the new century from a malaise from which he found solace in religiosity. *The Pilgrimage to Paradise* (1592) is an allegory in the late medieval — or perhaps, modified Spenserian romantic — manner, but "The Countess of Pembroke's Love," appended to it, sets the tone for his subsequent religious writing: sonorous yet humble, litanylike, and written for someone else's vicarious devotion.

"The Countess of Pembroke's Love" is a long apostrophe to love, fundamentally in its holy aspect, put into the mouth of "Love's saint" — that is, the countess, who was Sidney's sister, the influential Mary Herbert. She was, apparently, Breton's patroness for a time, or was at least willing to have a few of his more spiritual pieces dedicated to her; there seems to have been a brief falling out between them in the mid 1590s. Apart from the pieces written for her — some of them supposedly from her point of view — he may have had her in mind when he wrote *Mary Magdalen's Love* (1595), since, as Jean Robertson has put it, Breton was "inclined to confuse the two Marys." (Perhaps it was this work, and not some courtly contretemps, that resulted in her temporary displeasure.)

In large part Breton's spiritual poems deal with "love" and "passion" as religions themes; like Spenser's *Fowre Hymnes* (1596), they explore the conflation of Platonic, erotic, and Christian love. For Breton, the emphasis is on the erotic aspects of religious passion; and while he indulges in expansive paeans to the power of love as an ideal and transcendent force, his poems try to convey the emotional and visceral realities of religious longing or loss or the ecstatic cries of a "ravished soul." The theme of love becomes less central in his later spiritual verse. *The Soul's Immortal Crown* (1605), dedicated to James I, provides a week of devotionals in poems on the themes of virtue, wisdom, love, constancy, patience, humility, and "the infinite praise to the infinite glory of the infinite goodness of the infinite God." *The Mother's Blessing* (1602) and *Honest Counsel* (1605) offer pious advice from a mother and a father, respectively.

Breton's three prose religious tracts are similarly more practical in nature. He seems to have thought himself a fit tutor for the high and mighty; his *Auspicante Jehova* (1597), subtitled *Mary's Exercise,* features a series of prayers based sermon-style on biblical texts and was apparently meant for the edification of the countess of Pembroke. *The Soul's Heavenly Exercise* (1601) contains a similar set of ready-made prayers, dedicated to and intended for the use of the lord mayor of London. *Divine Considerations of the Soul* (1608) shows Breton moving out of his period of religious fervor toward the more moralizing mood of his late style; it is a theological analysis of God's goodness and humanity's inadequacy.

During this period of intense religiosity, which lasted roughly from 1595 to 1605, Breton also turned his hand to the writing of satires. Many of his spiritual works seem to spring from frustration at the ways of the world and from depression, and this dissatisfaction also expresses itself in the early 1600s in the fashionable tendency to carp. The extent to which this satirical bent overlapped with religious consolation can be seen clearly in *The Passion of a Discontented Mind* (1601) and in the part-lyrical, part-religious, part-philosophical, and part-satirical oddity *Melancholic Humors* (1600). The latter is probably Breton's most intriguing volume of poetry. Here, for once, he achieves a cynicism that is hauntingly convincing as well as occasionally sophisticated. The style is often enigmatic, almost "metaphysical" (the play on *patience* and *passion,* for instance, is refined without being artificial), and the cadences and tonalities are unusually rich:

To learn the babies' A, B, C,
Is fit for children, not for me.

I know the letters all so well,
I need not learn the way to spell;
    And for the cross before the row,
    I learned it all too long ago.

Then let them go to school that list,
To hang the lip at − − − *Had I wist*;
I never loved a book of horn,
Nor leaves that have their letters worn;
    Nor with a fescue to direct me,
    Where every puny shall correct me.

I will the truant play awhile,
And with mine ear mine eye beguile;
And only hear what others see,
What mocketh them as well as me;
    And laugh at him that goes to school,
    To learn with me to play the fool.

But soft awhile: I have mistook,
This is but some imagined book
That wilful hearts in wanton eyes
Do only by conceits devise;
    Where spell and put together prove
    The reading of the rules of love.

But if it be so, let it be;
It shall no lesson be for me.
Let them go spell that cannot read
And know the cross unto their speed;
    While I am taught but to discern
    How to forget the thing I learn.

Bearing a seal of approval in commendatory verses by no less a "humorist" than Ben Jonson, *Melancholic Humors* seems to offer itself as the last will and testament in a series of more pedestrian tracts brought out the same year in the gadfly persona of "Pasquil." These satires are more industrious than inspired; there are catalogues of fools and madmen, and Breton typically ends up calling for condescension in the face of their folly. *Pasquil's Mistress* is a somewhat derivative rundown of what to watch out for in a wife. Nevertheless, even this pamphlet is less objectifying and demonizing than one might expect. All of his praise is for the intelligence and inner nobility of a woman − without these qualities, he says, beauty, birth, and money are valueless − although it is true that the description of his own difficult mistress offers the standard blazon of her physical attributes. (The seeming echoes of a romantic disappointment in many writings from this period are alarming coming from a married man and expectant father.)

In general Breton's satire, especially in the overtly satirical Pasquil pamphlets, lacks pith and direction. Although once in a while he surprises his readers with something that has a bit more "edge,"

his forte is the indulgent humor that punctuates so much of his writing. That he was too reasonable and positive to excel at an essentially critical mode is suggested by his unwillingness to engage in personal invective and by *No Whipping, Nor Tripping; But a Kind Friendly Snipping* (1601), his essentially conciliatory contribution to a pamphlet war.

If Breton's good-naturedness leads to weakness in most of his satire and a lack of drama in his dialogues, it turns some of his more straightforward political pieces into banal accommodations. In his response to the Gunpowder Plot, *The Hate of Treason* (1616), for example, he is aghast at such seditious behavior; and *A Murmurer* (1607) advises not merely conformity to the status quo but a deeper appreciation of the blessings of bourgeois society in a United Kingdom under James I, the supposed harmony of which reflects that of all Christians under God in an ideal order.

A strong if unpretentious (and not always so conservative) didactic streak runs through Breton's writings, especially after 1600. In his later career even his dialogues, such as *Grimello's Fortunes* (1604) and *An Old Man's Lesson* (1605), tend to have pointed morals that are unqualified by dialogic interplay. Only rarely does Breton set up contradictions with real ideological tension or without a conservative resolution. *The Uncasing of Machiavelli's Instructions to His Son* (1613) probably contains his most biting passages of countercultural cynicism in the form of ironic advice from Niccolò Machiavelli to his son. But Breton cannot sustain this negativity even long enough to establish a strong position to be controverted. Interspersed with an unusually saucy immoralism are bits of sound humanistic counsel genteel enough to be found in Baldassare Castiglione's *Book of the Courtier* (1518), and the whole is, in any case, annulled by a lengthy retraction. *I Would, and Would Not* (1614) is a fairly lively 154 stanzas in which Breton considers the advantages and disadvantages of trading his present situation for various alternative lifestyles, from king to courtesan to gardener. The brief characterizations are handled with zest, and the undercutting considerations are neatly pointed, but the collection ends with an admonition to be happy with what one has. *Crossing of Proverbs* (1616) consists of a list of established saws, each of which is contradicted by a cynical cavil. There is a rare bit of dark realism to many of these ("Nothing breaks the heart more than thought." − "Yes, a bullet"); yet the second installment concludes with the section "Brief Questions and Answers," which forms a catechism of conformity ("What is most troublesome in a commonwealth?" − "Sects"). Indeed, the earlier *Wit's Private Wealth* (1607) and the later *Soothing of Proverbs* (1626) are compendiums of proverbial wisdom *without* objections. There is, in fact, something proverbial about Breton's overall manner — it is homely and thoughtful but rather conservative and unself-conscious. He was so excessively fond of proverbial phrases that Jean Robertson believes that he may be parodied in the character "Nicholas Proverbs" in Henry Porter's play *The Two Angry Women of Abingdon* (1599).

Breton's wit and thoughtfulness shine out above his conventionality when he is allowed to exploit his sensitivity to voices and his gentle joy in orchestrating words and ideas in a situation where no moral is called for. One of his most innovative books is *A Post with a Mad Packet of Letters* (1602), whose popularity led to at least one sequel, many reprints, and several imitations. It is a collection of letters that resemble the models in correspondence manuals or the made-up epistles in novels but are divorced from any educational or narrative framework; the letters are simply given. Sometimes there are pairs — the letter and its answer — and, rarely, longer sequences of correspondence, but in general there is no relationship between one letter and the others in the collection. Included are letters of advice from fathers and friends, lovers' supplications and mistresses' rebuffs, notes to creditors and other business correspondence, and news letters. Breton shows his ability to write in different styles and to create — if only briefly — a dramatic exchange; but the collection demonstrates what is most provocative and most frustrating about his prose: any meaning, intrigue, or argument is short-lived and, rather than being integrated into a larger whole, is simply included. It is possible to adjust to this sense of local and transient meaning, and one could even argue that it conveys a kind of realism, but it makes Breton's work seem trivial and pointless.

Though Breton may have "nothing to say," his later works could be described as predominantly philosophical. After 1605 his productivity waned somewhat, to revive briefly around the middle of the next decade. With the approach of old age he seems to have developed a more meditative mood. *Characters upon Essays* and *The Good and the Bad* (1616) are collections of brief characterizations of abstract concepts and ideal types; they are something between character writing and essays. The hybrid results in rather insipid and overly sanctimonious vignettes: "Honor is a title or grace given by the spirit of virtue to the desert of valor, in the defense of truth, etc." They lack the lively detail of

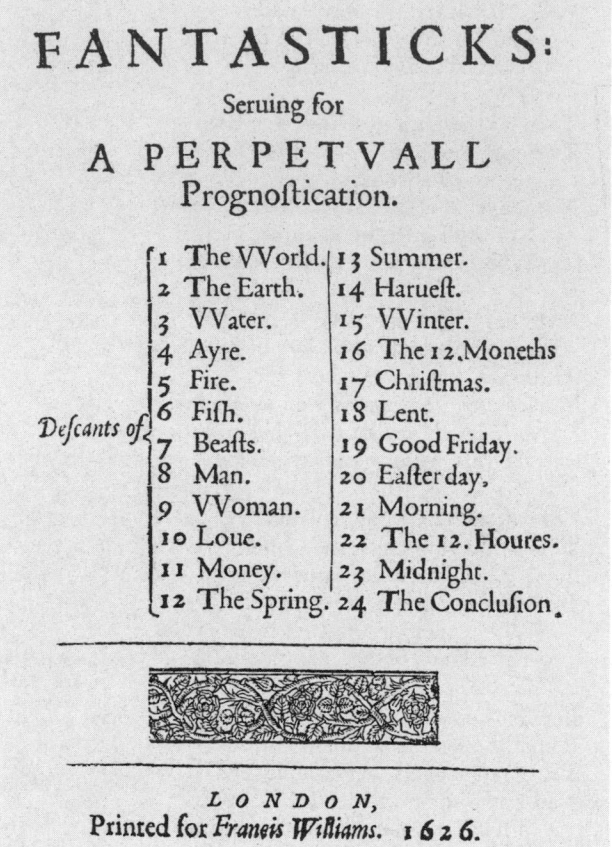

Title page for Breton's most widely appreciated book, poems on topics including the seasons, the months, the hours of the day, and various festivals

much character writing and certainly the analytical unsqueamishness or political savvy of essays by Michel de Montaigne or Bacon.

The book that was perhaps the last one Breton saw through the press was a new departure for him: the genuinely satirical fantasy *Strange News out of Divers Countries* (1622), a bizarre miscellany in which the foreign realms described are presumably, as in Jonathan Swift's *Gulliver's Travels* (1726), half-affectionate, half-scathing fantasias on the author's homeland. There are rude puns ("ass-bands" for "husbands"), absurd bits of humor and fancy, and some unusually trenchant witticisms.

Fantastics (1626) has probably been Breton's most widely appreciated book; it would be gratifying to be able to take it as the culmination of his career, but since it was entered in the Stationers' Register in 1604 there was probably an earlier edition that is now lost. It is a lovely set of prose poems on the seasons, the months, a few holidays, and the hours of the clock. Brimming over with rural detail and deftly captured moods, these "descants" are truly, as Alexander B. Grosart insisted, "of his finest warbled prose."

Perhaps this book actually was the last that was published during Breton's life. If not, his career had ended on a rather enigmatic note with entries in the 1622 Stationers' Register for three nonexistent books whose titles suggest a mounting negativity: "Nay then," "Nothing," and "Odds; or, All the World to Nothing." Nothing more is heard of Breton after these entries unless he did see the extant edition of *Fantastics* through the press in 1626. He appears to have been alive when his daughter Matilda died in 1625; the date of his own death, like that of his birth, is a mystery.

It is probably just as well that these late negative pieces, if they were ever published, are lost. Breton's strength lay in a warm and optimistic sensibility, a simple appreciativeness, and the modest pretensions that have made him seem naive and unoriginal to most readers. It is possible that the thematic incoherence and triviality that made him relatively uninteresting to those who established the Elizabethan canon, and the lack of philosophical or political unease that have caused him to remain of little interest to more recent students of the period, call for reevaluation. He shares with Robert Greene the distinction of being the first professional writers in English, and his mundane and unfocused pamphleteering could be considered more characteristic of the English Renaissance than is the work of any of its more imposing literary figures. Of his best works one might at least claim what he claims for the last of his dialogues, *The Court and Country*

(1618): "Matter of state is not here meddled with; scurrility here is none: no taxing of any person nor offense justly to any whatsoever. But passages of wit, without malice of any evil mind. And in sum, matter of good substance, and mirth enough to drive away a great deal of melancholy."

Bibliography:
Samuel A. and Dorothy R. Tannenbaum, *Nicholas Breton (A Concise Bibliography),* Elizabethan Bibliographies, no. 39 (New York: Tannenbaum, 1946).

References:
C. N. Greenough, "Nicholas Breton, Character-Writer and Quadrumaniac," in *Anniversary Papers by Colleagues and Pupils of George Lyman Kittredge* (Boston: Ginn, 1913), pp. 351–357;

Nellie Elizabeth Monroe, "Nicholas Breton as a Pamphleteer," Ph.D. dissertation, University of Pennsylvania, 1929;

H. E. Rollins, "Nicholas Breton's *The Works of a Young Wit,*" *Studies in Philology,* 33 (April 1936): 119–133;

Rollins, "*A Small Handful of Fragrant Flowers,*" *Huntington Library Bulletin,* 9 (April 1936): 27–35.

Papers:
The British Museum has the manuscripts for Nicholas Breton's *The Hate of Treason* and "Elegy of Queen Elizabeth" as well as some poems. Five poems in the commonplace book of Sir Stephen Powle are in the Bodleian Library.

Henry Chettle

(circa 1560 – circa 1607)

John Jowett
University of Birmingham

BOOKS: *A Dolefull Ditty, or Sorowfull Sonet of the Lord Darly* [sic], *Sometime King of Scots,* as H. C. (London: Printed for Thomas Gosson, 1579?);

The Forrest of Fancy. Wherein Is Conteined Very Prety Apothegmes, and Pleasaunt Histories, Both in Meeter and Prose, Songes, Sonets, Epigrams and Epistles, of Diuerse Matter and in Diuerse Manner. With Sundry Other Deuises, No Lesse Pithye Then Pleasaunt and Profytable, as H. C. (London: Printed by Thomas Purfoote, 1579);

Greenes, Groats-worth of Witte, Bought with a Million of Repentance. Describing the Follie of Youth, the Falshood of Makeshifte Flatterers, the Miserie of the Negligent, and Mischiefes of Deceiuing Courtezans. Written before His Death and Published at His Dyeing Request, purportedly by Robert Greene, but more probably by Chettle (London: Printed by John Wolfe and John Danter for William Wright, 1592);

Kind-harts Dreame. Conteining Fiue Apparitions, with Their Inuectiues against Abuses Raigning. Deliuered by Seuerall Ghosts vnto Him to Be Publisht, after Piers Penilesse Post Had Refused the Carriage, as H. C. (London: Printed by John Wolfe and John Danter for William Wright, 1592);

Piers Plainnes Seauen Yeres Prentiship, as H. C. (London: Printed by John Danter for Thomas Gosson, 1595);

The Death of Robert, Earle of Huntington: Otherwise Called Robin Hood of Merrie Sherwode: With the Lamentable Tragedie of Chaste Matilda, His Faire Maid Marian, Poysoned at Dunmowe by King Iohn, anonymous, by Chettle and Munday (London: Printed by Richard Bradocke for William Leake, 1601);

The Pleasant Comodie of Patient Grissill. As It Hath Beene Sundrie Times Lately Plaid by the Right Honorable the Earle of Nottingham (Lord High Admirall) His Seruants, anonymous, by Chettle, Thomas Dekker, and William Haughton (London: Printed by Edward Allde for Henry Rocket, 1603);

Englandes Mourning Garment: Worne Here by Plaine Shepheardes; in Memorie of Their Sacred Mistresse, Elizabeth, Queene of Vertue while Shee Liued and Theame of Sorrow, Being Dead. To Which Is Added the True Manner of Her Emperiall Funerall. After Which Foloweth the Shepheards Spring-Song, for Entertainement of King Iames Our Most Potent Soueraigne (London: Printed by Valentine Simmes for Thomas Millington, 1603; enlarged edition, anonymous, London: Printed by Emma Short for Thomas Millington, to be sold by Walter Burre, 1603);

A True Bill of the Whole Number That Hath Died . . . since the Time That This Last Sicknes of the Plague Began to October the Sixt Day, 1603 (London: Printed by James Roberts for John Trundle, 1603);

The Tragedy of Hoffman or A Reuenge for a Father, As It Hath Bin Diuers Times Acted with Great Applause, at the Phenix in Druery-Lane, anonymous (London: Printed by John Norton for Hugh Perry, 1631);

The Blind-Beggar of Bednal-Green, with the Merry Humor of Tom Strowd the Norfolk Yeoman, as It Was Divers Times Publickly Acted by the Princes Servants, by Chettle and John Day (London: Printed for R. Pollard and Thomas Dring, 1659).

Editions: H. C., "Doleful Ditty of the Lord Darnley" (1579), in *The Harleian Miscellany,* edited by William Oldys and Thomas Park, volume 10 (London: Printed for J. White & J. Murray, 1813), pp. 264–265;

"England's Mourning Garment (1603)," in *Shakspere Allusion-Books,* edited by C. M. Ingleby, volume 1 (London: Published for the New Shakespeare Society by N. Trubner, 1874), pp. 77–112;

The Blind Beggar of Bethnal Green, by Chettle and John Day, edited by Willy Bang-Kaup, Materialien zur Kunde der Älteren Englischen Dramas, volume 1 (Louvain: Uystpruyst, 1902);

The Book of Sir Thomas More, by Chettle, Anthony Munday, Thomas Dekker, probably William Shakespeare, and perhaps Thomas Heywood, edited by W. W. Greg (London: Printed for the Malone Society at Oxford University Press, 1911; reprinted with a supplement by Harold Jenkins, 1961);

Groats-worth of Witte, Bought with a Million of Repentance, The Repentance of Robert Greene, 1592, edited by George Bagshawe Harrison (London: Lane, 1923; New York: Dutton, 1923);

Henry Chettle: Kind-Hartes Dreame, 1592; William Kemp: Nine Daies Wonder, 1600, edited by Harrison (London: Lane, Bodley Head, 1923; New York: Dutton, 1923);

John of Bordeaux, or The Second Part of Friar Bacon, by Chettle and Robert Greene, edited by William Lindsay Renwick (Oxford: Malone Society Reprints, 1936 [i.e., 1935]);

The Tragedy of Hoffman, edited by Harold Jenkins (Oxford: Malone Society Reprints, 1951 [i.e., 1950]);

Patient Grissil, by Chettle, Dekker, and William Haughton, in *The Dramatic Works of Thomas Dekker,* edited by Fredson Bowers, volume 1 (Cambridge: Cambridge University Press, 1953), pp. 207–298;

"Piers Plainness: Seven Years' Prenticeship," in *The Descent of Euphues, Three Elizabethan Romance Stories: Euphues, Pandosto, Piers Plainness,* edited by James Winny (Cambridge: Cambridge University Press, 1957), pp. 122–174;

The Death of Robert, Earl of Huntingdon, by Chettle and Munday, edited by John C. Meagher (Oxford: Malone Society Reprints, 1967 [i.e., 1965]);

William Shakespeare, *Romeo and Juliet,* probably augmented by Chettle, in *Shakespeare's Plays in Quarto: A Facsimile Edition of Copies Primarily from the Henry E. Huntington Library,* edited by Michael J. B. Allen and Kenneth Muir (Berkeley: University of California Press, 1981), pp. 117–155.

PLAY PRODUCTIONS: *The Death of Robert, Earl of Huntingdon,* by Chettle and Anthony Munday, London, Rose theater, licensed 28 March 1598;

The Famous Wars of Henry I and the Prince of Wales (also known as *The Welshman's Prize*), by Chettle, Thomas Dekker, and Michael Drayton, London, Rose theater, March 1598;

Earl Godwin and His Three Sons, part 1, by Chettle, Dekker, Drayton, and Robert Wilson, London, Rose theater, March 1598;

Black Bateman of the North, part 1, by Chettle, Dekker, Drayton, and Wilson, London, Rose theater, May 1598;

Earl Godwin and His Three Sons, part 2, by Chettle, Dekker, Drayton, and Wilson, London, Rose theater, June 1598;

The Funeral of Richard, Coeur de Lion, by Chettle, Drayton, Munday, and Wilson, London, Rose theater, June 1598;

Black Bateman of the North, part 2, by Chettle, Wilson, and possibly Henry Porter, London, Rose theater, July 1598;

Hot Anger Soon Cold, by Chettle, Porter, and Ben Jonson, London, Rose theater, August 1598;

Chance Medley, by Chettle or Dekker and Drayton, Munday, and Wilson, London, Rose theater, August 1598;

Vayvode, probably an old play revised by Chettle, London, Rose theater, August 1598;

The Conquest of Brute, part 1, by Chettle and John Day, London, Rose theater, September 1598;

The Conquest of Brute, part 2, London, Rose theater, October 1598;

The Downfall of Robert, Earl of Huntington, by Munday, and *The Death of Richard, Earl of Huntington,* by Chettle and Munday, both revised by Chettle, Whitehall Palace, November–December 1598;

The Spencers, by Chettle and Porter, London, Rose theater, March 1599;

Troilus and Cressida, by Chettle and Dekker, London, Rose theater, April 1599;

Agamemnon, by Chettle and Dekker, London, Rose theater, summer 1599;

Robert II; or, The Scot's Tragedy, by Chettle, Dekker, Jonson, and perhaps John Marston, London, Rose theater, September 1599;

The Stepmother's Tragedy, by Chettle and Dekker(?), London, Rose theater, October 1599;

Polyphemus; or, Troy's Revenge, London, Rose theater, October 1599;

Patient Grissell, by Chettle, Dekker, and William Haughton, London, Rose theater, January 1600;

The Seven Wise Masters, by Chettle, Day, Dekker, and Haughton, London, Rose Theater, March 1600;

Damon and Pythias, London, Rose theater, May 1600;

The Golden Ass; or, Cupid and Psyche, by Chettle, Day, and Dekker, London, Rose theater, May 1600;

The Blind Beggar of Bethnal Green, part 1, by Chettle and Day, London, Rose theater, May 1600;

All Is Not Gold That Glisters, London, Fortune theater, April 1601;

King Sebastian of Portugal, by Chettle and Dekker, London, Fortune theater, May 1601;

The Life of Cardinal Wolsey, London, Rose theater, August 1601;

The Rising of Cardinal Wolsey, by Chettle, Drayton, Munday, and Wentworth Smith, London, Fortune theater, November 1601;

Too Good to Be True, by Chettle, Smith, and Richard Hathaway, London, Fortune theater, January 1602;

Friar Rush and the Proud Woman of Antwerp, by Day and Haughton, revised by Chettle, London, Fortune theater, January 1602;

Love Parts Friendship, by Chettle and Smith, London, Fortune theater, May 1602;

Tobias, London, Fortune theater, 1602;

Felmelanco, by Chettle and a Mr. Robinson, London, Fortune theater, September 1602;

Lady Jane, part 1, by Chettle, Dekker, Heywood, Smith, and John Webster, London, Boar's Head or Rose theater, October 1602;

Christmas Comes but Once a Year, by Chettle, Dekker, Heywood, and Webster, London, Boar's Head or Rose theater, November 1602;

The London Florentine, part 1, by Chettle and Heywood, London, Fortune theater, January 1603;

The Tragedy of Hoffman, London, Fortune theater, early 1603;

The London Florentine, part 2, Fortune theater, March 1603;

Shore, by Chettle and Day, London, Rose theater, May 1603.

OTHER: Pope Gregory XIII, *The Popes Pittiful Lamentation, for the Death of His Deere Darling Don Joan of Austria,* possibly translated by Chettle as H. C. (London: Printed by John Charlewood, 1578);

"To his good friend Master A.M.," in *Gerileon of England: The Second Part,* by Etienne de Maisonneuve, translated by Anthony Munday (London: Printed by Thomas Scarlet? for Cuthbert Burby, 1592);

Robert Greene, *The Repentance of Robert Greene, Master of Arts,* edited by Chettle (London: Printed by John Danter for Cuthbert Burby, 1592);

"To his good friend Master Anthony Munday" and "Of the Translation, against a Carper," in *The Second Booke of Primaleon of Greece,* translated by Munday (London: Printed by John Danter for Cuthbert Burby, 1596);

William Shakespeare, *An Excellent Conceited Tragedie of Romeo and Juliet,* corrupt text, probably augmented by Chettle (London: Printed by John Danter [and Edward Allde?], 1597);

"To His Flocks," "Damelus' Song to His Diaphanta," and "A Pastoral Song between Phyllis and Amarylis, Two Nymphs, Each Answering Other Line for Line," as "H. C.," in *Englands Helicon,* edited by Nicholas Ling (London: Printed by James Roberts for John Flasket, 1600).

Henry Chettle existed on the insecure fringes of sixteenth-century literary culture. He followed a career that embraced printing, editing, pamphleteering, and playwriting. His prose works reflect a sense of modesty and decorum combined with the brashly opportunistic manner of a literary journalist.

The son of Robert Chettle, a London dyer, Chettle was apprenticed to the stationer Thomas East from 1577 to 1584. He must have encountered John Lyly's *Euphues,* which East printed in 1578. His first literary endeavors belong to about this time if, as is likely, he is the "H. C." who in 1579 translated a tract by Pope Gregory XIII on the death of John of Austria and wrote both a broadside ballad on the murder of Henry Stewart, Lord Darnley, "to be sung to the tune of 'Black and Yellow,'" and a miscellany called *The Forest of Fancy.* The latter work confesses its author's "young years and small experience." Its fictional letters, prose narratives, and poems are Chettle's apprenticeship in writing. The epistolary sections anticipate the invectives in *Kindheart's Dream* (1592) and, by giving distinct voices to various fictional speakers, prepare the way for his dramatic writings.

After 1584 Chettle probably remained active as a printer. He went into a short-lived partnership with the stationers John Danter and William Hoskins in 1591, during which year they brought out Thomas Lodge's *Catharos* and a sermon by Henry Smith that was supposedly recorded by "charactery" (that is, shorthand). Despite an altercation in 1593 Chettle's association with Danter continued for several years. He evidently acted as intermediary between Danter and authors such as Lodge, Anthony Munday, and Thomas Nashe and also as compositor, repairer of incomplete texts, and epistle writer. Danter favored works that were short and popular, and he was prepared to risk controversy. He printed part of *Greene's Groatsworth of Wit* (1592), a work purportedly written by Robert Greene but which Chettle at least edited and may have written. In his own *Kindheart's Dream* Chettle publicized Nashe's *Strange News* (1592), urging Nashe to attack Gabriel Harvey even as Nashe's attack was being printed in Danter's shop. In 1596 Chettle claimed to have "done all my diligence to further the edition" of Munday's translation of *The Second Book of Primaleon of Greece,* which Danter printed. And it was probably Chettle who, a year later, had a hand in preparing Danter's copy for the "bad" quarto of William Shakespeare's *Romeo and Juliet.* The pirated text evidently had gaps, which were filled in by someone writing in a non-Shakespearean style. That style resembles Chettle's, and some of the stage directions are similar to those in his plays.

Chettle first crossed Shakespeare's path in connection with *Greene's Groatsworth of Wit.* This repentance pamphlet, supposedly written by Greene on his deathbed, includes notorious attacks on Christopher Marlowe as an atheistic Machiavellian and on the actor-turned-dramatist Shakespeare as an "upstart crow" beautified with the feathers of Greene and his fellow professional dramatists; Shakespeare is called a *"Johannes Factotum"* (jack-of-all-trades) and, it seems, is accused of being a plagiarist. The extent of Chettle's role in preparing this pamphlet is disputed: it was entered in the Stationers' Register "upon the peril of Henry Chettle" on 20 September 1592, a few weeks after Greene's death, and in an epistle prefixed to *Kindheart's Dream* Chettle admits having transcribed Greene's almost illegible scrawl. He is answering those – evidently Shakespeare and Marlowe – who accused Chettle of writing the work himself. He denies having written a word of it, but strong stylistic evidence suggests that the work is indeed Chettle's. His first mature work may, therefore, be a skillful if unprincipled literary pastiche, and *Kindheart's Dream,* written the same year, has similar qualities of literary imitation. In the epistle to *Kindheart's Dream* Chettle affirms his own hostility to Marlowe but offers an apology to Shakespeare "as if the original fault had been my fault." Apparently having met Shakespeare in the intervening months, Chettle now praises "his uprightness of dealing, which argues his honesty, and his facetious grace in writing, that approves his art." Chettle probably had dealings with the acting company Strange's Men, for his hand is found patching *John of Bordeaux* (1593), which was probably written by Green and was performed by the company in the early 1590s. Thus, in the wake of Greene's death

Title page for the satirical work in which Henry Chettle expresses his thoughts on authors and the theater of his day

Chettle made contact with a widening circle of pamphleteers and dramatists, published his own prose tract, and began his association with the theater. The boundaries between his work for Danter and his literary work are indistinct, and some of his writings are mere shreds and patches.

Two prose works – *Kindheart's Dream* and *Pierce Plainness* (1595) – are more substantial, though the former is itself a piecemeal composition. After the epistle *Kindheart's Dream* takes Kindheart the tooth drawer as its authorial persona. Whereas satirists exacerbate pain, Kindheart aims to relieve it. Chettle uses the convention of the dream to allow a succession of dead figures to address the world they have left behind. He may have been influenced by the posthumously published *Greene's Vision* (1592), in which Greene is visited by Geoffrey Chaucer and

PIERS
Plainnes feauen
yeres Prentiſhip.

By H. C.

Nuda Veritas.

Printed at London by I. Danter
for Thomas Gosson, and are to be ſold at his
ſhop by London bridge Gate.
· 1 5 9 5 ·

*Title page for Chettle's story about the adventures of a
Greek apprentice*

Nashe's irregular style. The final ghost, the juggler William Cuckoo, inveighs against false juggling. Thus the potentially disreputable activities of balladry, quackery, playwriting, pamphleteering, clowning, and juggling are brought into loose association as the objects of Chettle's restrained satire. But the tract has a double function: it also orients its author in relation to Shakespeare, Marlowe, Nashe, Harvey, and the institution of the theater, making peace and waging war as appropriate. Chettle reaches for a place through literary allusion and for a voice through literary pastiche.

Pierce Plainness is a sustained prose fiction that alternates its passages satirizing Nashe's *Pierce Penniless* (1592) written in a predominately euphuistic style. The narrator's name implies a plainspoken country fellow. Pierce has frequented city and court but is now a hired hand to a Thracian shepherd. From a secure and idealized pastoral vantage he surveys his fortunes as "prentice" to a succession of masters. This narrative frame is borrowed from the picaresque novel *La vida de Lazarillo de Tormes* (The Life of Lazarillo de Tormes, 1554; sometimes attributed to Diego Hurtado de Mendoza), though Pierce is an observer and passive participant rather than a rogue. The villainy lies with his masters and the nobility.

The plots are tenuously connected through the theme of master and subordinate: "one of his men's men was my master." Pierce is conveyed to Crete for the final resolution, but the stories mostly follow separate courses. Chettle repeatedly draws wry attention to the arbitrary nature of the narrator's shifts from plot to plot: "Of her, him, and myself, *plura sequuntur;* but in this place lay a straw, all being scant worth a straw, and, passing our estates, deal we with state matters." The story often seems in danger of eluding its teller, and Pierce's determination to finish his tale by sundown puts the narrative under further pressure.

Pierce's masters include a spendthrift courtier and a usurer; their degeneracy echoes that in higher places. In Thrace, Celinus deposes his brother, King Hylenus. In Crete, Rhegius has incestuous designs on his niece, the ruling princess Aeliana. Hylenus and his children, put out to sea like Shakespeare's Prospero, arrive in Crete just in time for Hylenus's son, Aemilius, to rescue Aeliana from rape in the forest. After further adventures, Aemelius and Aeliana marry. Aemelius becomes king of Crete; the throne of Thrace, restored to Hylenus, can be inherited by the reformed Celinus. Rhegius is redeemed by falling in love with Hylenus's daughter, Rhodope.

John Gower. In Chettle's work one of the shades is Greene.

The first apparition, Anthony Now-now, is an old singer who garrulously reproves those who deal in bawdy ballads. Now-now probably speaks for, and gently mocks, Munday. An oration against medical quackery is delivered by Dr. Burcot. The next two apparitions are Greene and the clown-actor Richard Tarleton. Chettle revises Greene's advice to Nashe in the *Groatsworth* against making enemies "by bitter words": evidently Gabriel Harvey's onslaught against Greene and Nashe in his *Four Letters* (1592) now requires Nashe, addressed as Pierce Penniless, to "awake, secure boy, revenge thy wrongs." Tarleton mounts a mock attack on the theater, followed by a genuine defense that claims that plays are as moral as books. Chettle may be picking up on Harvey's characterization of Nashe as Tarleton in *Four Letters,* and he imitates

PLATE XX.

Englandes Mourning Garment:

Worne here by plaine Shepheardes;
in memorie of their ſacred Miſtreſſe,
ELIZABETH, Queene of Vertue while ſhee
liued, and Theame of Sorrow,
being dead.

To which is added the true manner of her
Emperiall Funerall.

After which foloweth the Shepheards Spring-Song.
for entertainement of King IAMES our
moſt potent Soueraigne.

Dedicated to all that loued the deceaſed Queene,
and honor the liuing King.

Non Verbis ſed Virtute.

*Title page for Chettle's commemoration in prose and verse of the
death of Queen Elizabeth I*

The structure of *Pierce Plainness,* with its multiple plots and sudden shifts from scene to scene, resembles that of a play, and Chettle was probably already an experienced dramatist. About 1593 he had probably collaborated with Munday on the first version of *Sir Thomas More.* The play is extant in a manuscript prepared by Munday, supplemented by revisions in several hands made perhaps ten years later. The writing of Shakespeare, Dekker, Heywood, and Chettle has been identified with reasonable certitude. In 1598 Francis Meres applauded Chettle as among "the best for comedy"; between 1598 and 1603 there are detailed records in Philip Henslowe's diary of Chettle's work for the acting company Admiral's Men and, in 1602–1603, Worcester's Men. Chettle was prolific, though most of his plays were written in collaboration. Only a small portion of his output remains. The part of *The Death of Robert, Earl of Huntingdon* (1601) that deals with the tragedy of Matilda is likely to be Chettle's work, though this contention has been disputed. In *Patient Grissel* (1603) Chettle probably concentrated on the marquis's heartless testing of his lowly wife, Grissel. To the otherwise ballad-based *Blind Beggar of Bethnal Green* (1659) he evidently added the play's quasihistorical material. *The Tragedy of Hoffman* (1631), written, as far as is known, by Chettle alone, is a sometimes lurid revenge tragedy that supplies a conservative critique of the stage Machiavellian, answering overhasty slaughter with the duchess of Lüneberg's dignified restraint.

Chettle's dramatic work repeatedly shows the fate of strong, stoical women at the hands of cruel men. His style varies from the melodramatic to the pleasantly lyrical, and his plays are more moralistic than moral. He is a representative figure: no great drama was written for Henslowe's literary assembly line, to which, as the diary shows, Chettle was chained by poverty. But one suspects that Chettle would never have proved to be another Ben Jonson or Thomas Middleton, and he evidently recognized his modest talents for what they were: in his last known literary composition, *England's Mourning Garment* (1603) – a pastoral tract in prose and verse written to commemorate Queen Elizabeth's death, in which the fictional persona is Spenserian but the title echoes *Greene's Mourning Garment* (1590) – Chettle asks his fellow writers why they, who are better able than he, neglect to sing Elizabeth's praise. So Chettle vanishes from the literary scene still appropriating others' voices and lamenting his ownmarginality.

John Fenton praised *England's Mourning Garment* in 1603. After Chettle's death his former collaborator Dekker made a detailed and happily inclusive allusion to this allusion maker: In *A Knight's Conjuring* (1607) he describes Chettle's arrival in the Elysian Fields, "sweating and blowing by reason of his fatness . . . to welcome whom, because he was of old acquaintance, all rose up and fell presently on their knees, to drink a health to all the lovers of Helicon." Chettle has subsequently been largely neglected, except in surveys of Elizabethan prose – notably Walter R. Davis's *Idea and Act in Elizabethan Fiction* (1969) – and in Harold Jenkins's indispensable 1934 biography.

Bibliographies:

Terence P. Logan and Denzell S. Smith, "Other Dramatists," in *The Popular School: A Survey and Bibliography of Recent Studies in English Renaissance Dramatists,* edited by Logan and Smith (Lincoln: University of Nebraska Press, 1975), pp. 251–255;

James L. Harner, *English Renaissance Prose Fiction: An Annotated Bibliography of Criticism* (Boston: Hall, 1978), pp. 107–111;

Biography:

Harold Jenkins, *The Life and Work of Henry Chettle* (London: Sidgwick & Jackson, 1934).

References:

Warren B. Austin, *A Computer-Aided Technique for Stylistic Discrimination: The Authorship of "Greene's Groatsworth of Wit"* (Washington, D.C.: U.S. Office of Education, Bureau of Research, 1969);

Austin, "Technique of the Chettle-Greene Forgery: Supplementary Material on the Authorship of the *Groatsworth of Wit*," *Shakespeare Newsletter,* 20 (December 1970): 43;

Peter W. M. Blayney, "*The Book of Sir Thomas More* Re-examined," *Studies in Philology,* 69 (April 1972): 167–191;

Neil Carson, *A Companion to Henslowe's Diary* (Cambridge: Cambridge University Press, 1988), pp. 61–63;

Walter R. Davis, *Idea and Act in Elizabethan Fiction* (Princeton: Princeton University Press, 1969), pp. 202–210;

Thomas Dekker, *A Knights Conjuring. Done in Earnest: Discovered in Jest,* edited by Edward F. Rimbault (London: Percy Society, 1842);

Mark Eccles, *Brief Lives: Tudor and Stuart Authors,* supplement to *Studies in Philology,* 79 (Fall 1982): 22–23;

Gabriel Harvey, *Foure Letters, and Certaine Sonnets,* edited by G. B. Harrison (London: Lane, 1922);

H. R. Hoppe, *The Bad Quarto of "Romeo and Juliet"* (Ithaca, N.Y.: Cornell University Press, 1948), p. 220;

John Jowett, "Henry Chettle and the Original Text of *Sir Thomas More,*" in *Shakespeare and "Sir Thomas More": Essays on the Play and Its Shakespearean Interest,* edited by T. H. Howard Hill (Cambridge: Cambridge University Press, 1989), pp. 131–150;

J. J. Jusserand, *The English Novel in the Time of Shakespeare* (London: Unwin, 1890), pp. 328–330;

Francis Meres, *Palladis Tamia; Wits Treasury,* edited by Arthur Freeman (New York & London: Garland, 1973), p. 283;

Charles Nicholl, *A Cup of News: The Life of Thomas Nashe* (London: Routledge & Kegan Paul, 1984), pp. 140–141;

Paul Salzman, *English Prose Fiction 1558–1700: A Critical History* (Oxford: Clarendon Press, 1985), pp. 86–87, 184–185;

Chauncey Elwood Sanders, "Robert Greene and His 'Editors,'" *PMLA,* 48 (June 1933): 392–417;

Margaret Schlauch, *Antecedents of the English Novel, 1400–1600 (from Chaucer to Deloney)* (Warsaw: PWN–Polish Scientific Publications, 1963);

Sidney Thomas, "Henry Chettle and the First Quarto of *Romeo and Juliet,*" *Review of English Studies,* new series 1 (January 1950): 8–16;

C. T. Wright, "Mundy and Chettle in Grub Street," *Boston University Studies in English,* 5 (Autumn 1961): 129–138;

Wright, "Young Anthony Mundy Again," *Studies in Philology,* 56 (January 1959): 150–168.

Papers:

The manuscript for *The Book of Sir Thomas More* is in the British Library (Harley 7368); the manuscript for *John of Bordeaux* is at the University of Durham (Alnwick collection).

Henry Constable

(1562 – 9 October 1613)

Emily E. Stockard
Florida Atlantic University

BOOKS: *Examen pacifique de la Doctrine des Huguenots. Prouuant contre les Catholiques rigoureux de nostre temps & particulierement contre les obiections de la response faicte a l'apologie Catholique, que nous qui sommes membres de l'Eglise Catholique apostolique & Romaine ne deurions pas condemner les Huguenots pour heretiques iusques a ce qu'on ait faict nouuelle preuue,* anonymous (Paris [*i.e.,* London: Printed by John Wolfe], 1589); translated by W. W. as *The Catholike Moderator: Or A Moderate Examination of the Doctrine of the Protestants. Proving against the Too Rigid Catholikes of These Times, and against the Arguments Especially, of That Booke Called, The Anser to the Catholike Apologie, That We, Who are members of the Catholike, Apostolike, & Roman Church, Ought Not to Condeme the Protestants for Heretikes, vntill Further Proofes Be Made. First Written in French by a Catholike Gentleman, and Now Faithfully Translated* (London: Printed by Eliot's Court Press for Nathan Bvtter, 1623);

Diana: The Praises of His Mistres, in Certaine Sweete Sonnets, as H. C. (London: Printed by John Charlewood for Richard Smith, 1592); enlarged as *Diana; or, The Excellent Conceitful Sonnets of H. C. Augmented with Diuers Quatorzains of Honorable and Lerned Personages. Deuided into viij. Decads* (London: Printed by Iames Roberts for Richard Smith, 1584 [*i.e.,* 1594]);

A Discoverye of a Counterfecte Conference Helde at a Counterfecte Place, by Counterfecte Travellers, for Thadvancement of a Counterfeit Tytle, and Invented, Printed, and Published by One (Person) That Dare Not Avowe His Name, anonymous (Collen [*i.e.,* Paris?], 1600);

Spirituall Sonnettes to the Honour of God, and Hys Sayntes. By H. C. From a Manuscript in the Harleian Collection, No. 7553. Now First Printed, edited by Thomas Park (London: Longman, Hurst, Rees, Orme & Brown, 1815).

Editions: *The Harleian Miscellany,* edited by Thomas Park, revised edition, volume 2 (London: Printed for Robert Dutton, 1812), pp. 489–517;

Diana: The Sonnets and Other Poems of Henry Constable, B. A. of St. John's College, Cambridge. Now First collected, and Edited, with Some Account of the Author, edited by William Carew Hazlitt (London: Pickering, 1859);

"Diana, or, The excellent conceitful sonnets of H. C. Augmented with divers Quatorzains of honourable and learned personages," in *An English Garner: Elizabethan Sonnets,* volume 2, edited by Sir Sidney Lee (New York: Dutton, 1904), pp. 75–114;

The Poems of Henry Constable, edited by Joan Grundy (Liverpool, U.K.: Liverpool University Press, 1960);

"A Discovery of a Counterfeit Conference (1600)," in *English Recusant Literature, 1558–1640,* volume 6, edited by D. M. Rogers (Menston, U.K.: Scolar, 1969);

Diana, edited by Donald Cheney (Menston, U.K.: Scolar, 1973);

Resolved to Love: The 1592 Edition of Henry Constable's "Diana" Critically Considered, edited by Robert F. Fleissner (Salzburg: Institut für Anglistik und Amerikanistik, 1980).

Author of one of the earliest Elizabethan sonnet sequences, Henry Constable embodied, though at different times in his life, two types of the Renaissance artist: the court poet and the religious poet. His court verse, written while he was engaged in his diplomatic career as a crusader for Anglican Protestantism, sounds the notes of the occasional and Petrarchan sonnets appreciated by his audience: the religious poetry, unread by his countrymen, is that of an exiled Catholic determined to use his diplomatic skills and contacts to convert the king and his

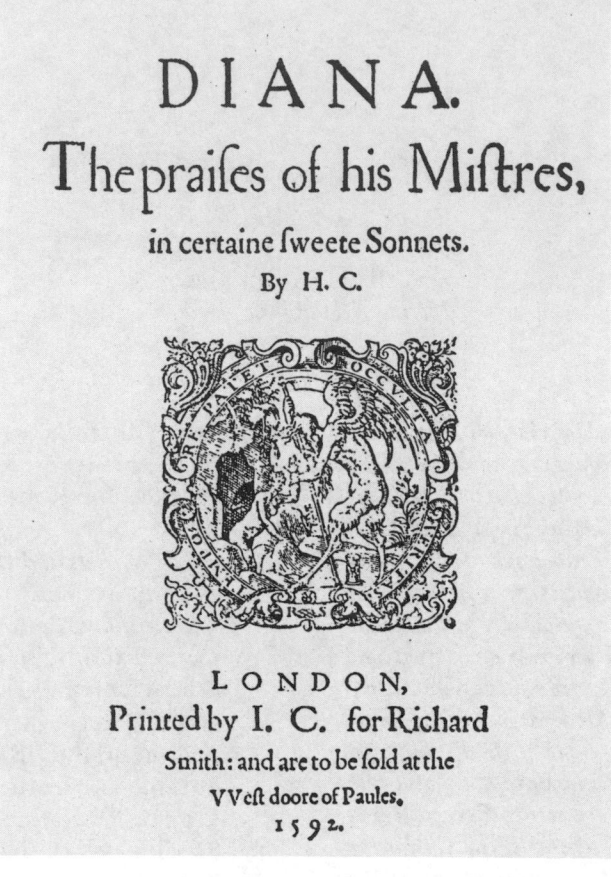

DIANA.

The praises of his Mistres,

in certaine sweete Sonnets.
By H. C.

LONDON,
Printed by I. C. for Richard
Smith: and are to be sold at the
VVest doore of Paules.
1592.

*Title page for Constable's sonnet sequence, one of the earliest
such works in English*

court. In his poetry, passionately held religious and political convictions are represented in the most conventional of poetic forms.

Constable was born in 1562 into a family distinguished by its connections to nobility and by military and public service to a series of monarchs. His grandmother was Catherine Manners, sister of Thomas Manners, first Earl of Rutland, and great-granddaughter of Richard Plantagenet, Duke of York. Through her Constable was related also to the earls of Shrewsbury and Westmoreland. His father, Sir Robert Constable, knighted on a Scottish battlefield in 1570 and evidently a resolute Protestant, was appointed in 1588 as lieutenant of the Queen's Ordnance. Sir Robert's acquisition of the Spittal in Newark, Nottinghamshire, probably resulted from his marriage (after the death of her first husband) to Christiana Forster, daughter of John Dabridgecourt and also a member of a distinguished family.

Constable attended Saint John's College, Cambridge, matriculating in 1578 as a fellow-commoner and receiving a bachelor's degree in 1580. After spending a few months at Lincoln's Inn, he embarked on a trip to the Scottish court – the first of the diplomatic missions to which he would devote his life. He arrived in Saint Johnston's (today, Perth) by September 1583, probably accompanied by Francis Walsingham, his patron and his father's longtime friend. The two hoped to persuade James VI to desist from his anti-English inclinations. Presumably again serving the Protestant cause, Constable turned up in Paris later that year with a recommendation from Walsingham to Sir Edward Stafford, the English ambassador. There he spent time at court, and in a letter to Walsingham, Stafford suggested that Constable might be able to bolster Henry of Navarre's Protestanism: "Either Mr. [Anthony] Bacon at Bordeaux or my cousin Constable here would discharge it well and with little cost, and I think it might do a great deal of good." In 1585 Constable traveled to Germany, Italy, and Poland, again under Walsingham's auspices. Constable wrote sonnets that refer to these journeys and defend Queen Elizabeth against the papists. A pamphlet, *A Short View of a Large Examination of Cardinal Allen His Traitorous Justification of Sir William Stanley and York, Written by Mr. Henry Constable, and This Gathered* out of His Own Draught, probably written in 1588 and existent today only in an extract in a commonplace book in the Marsh Library, displays Constable's knowledge of the war in the Low Countries as well as his interest in militant English Protestantism. In it he replies to a Catholic attack on Elizabeth by defending Leicester's military conduct, the queen's foreign policy, and Protestant theology.

Back at the English court in 1588-1589, Constable continued to establish himself as a courtier in the mold of Sir Philip Sidney, writing sonnets to Penelope Rich and Arabella Stuart. At the same time, he strengthened his relationships with others keenly interested in religion and politics, becoming friends with Continental Protestants and followers of Henry of Navarre. During this period he formed an alliance with Jean Hotman, son of the Huguenot jurist François Hotman, a friendship that, ironically, would prove instrumental in his religious conversion. In Edinburgh in the fall of 1589, seeking to curry favor for Robert Devereux, second Earl of Essex, Constable was admitted to the literary circle of the king, with whom he shared interests in matters literary and religious. He addressed sonnets to both the king and to his bride, Queen Anne.

Published in 1592 and enlarged in 1594, Constable's Diana is one of the earliest English sonnet sequences. Manuscript evidence that all the sonnets in it were written before 1591, the year Sidney's Astrophil and Stella was published, strengthens Constable's solid claim to have set literary precedent. Unfortunately for literary historians, he almost certainly did not oversee publication of either edition of Diana, having left the country by 1592. The two versions of the sequence differ considerably, and the existence of additional manuscripts makes establishing the Constable canon a difficult matter. Modern editors of the sequence claim fidelity to Constable's intentions. During the period in question, however, he held different intentions at different times.

The 1592 edition of Diana may reflect, as Robert F. Fleissner says, "Constable at his spontaneous best" — a court poet writing love poetry to an unattainable mistress. The work opens with the sonnet "To his absent Diana," followed by a note "To the Gentlemen Readers" urging them to accept "these ensuing sonnets . . . now by misfortune left as orphans." Twenty sonnets, written in Italian form, follow. The sequence concludes with "Ultimo Sonnetto." The 1594 version, described on the title page as "Augmented with divers quatorzains of honorable and learned person-

ages," is divided into eight decades — with only five sonnets in the last section — plus a final sonnet. This edition includes eight sonnets now attributed to Sidney.

For the standard edition (1960) Joan Grundy has rejected the published versions and chosen the Todd manuscript in the Victoria and Albert Museum, which contains the largest number of Constable's sonnets and which, she argues, "probably represents the author's own recension." The plan of the sequence prepares the reader for Constable's later rejection of secular poetry and worldly concerns. Chronicling the rise and demise of love, the sequence is divided into three parts, each of which is further divided into three groups of seven sonnets. Part 1 is devoted to praising Diana and recording the poet's pursuit of her; part 2 praises by turn the king and queen of Scots and specific women of the court and commemorates births and deaths. Part 3 combines these concerns, finding in heaven consolation for Sidney's death and describing the death of Constable's love for Diana, his rejection of all earthly love, and his determination to "employ the remnant of [my] wit to other calmer thoughts less sweet and less bitter." This rejection may reflect the religious conversion Constable was either contemplating or had already undergone.

However vexed the question of texts may be, individual sonnets are not so difficult to characterize. As a love poet, Constable employs figures common to the Petrarchan sonneteer's arsenal: darts, eyes, flames, water, blood, and sun are among his favorite images. He uses the images of fire and sun to express the Neoplatonic conception that love elates the lover:

In thee doth shine, in me doth burn a fire;
Fire draws up others and it self ascends.
    Thine eye a fire and so draws up my love;
    My love a fire and so ascends above.

The inherently erotic imagery shows Constable beset by a problem common to Elizabethan sonneteers: he aspires to the diviner qualities of love but is tortured by carnal desire. Although descriptions of Diana emphasize her angelic qualities, Constable is also capable of expressing physical desire directly:

To fight thou needst no weapons but thine eyes.
Thy hair hath gold enough to pay thy men
And for their food thy beauty will suffice.
For men and armor (Lady) care have none,
    For one will soonest yield unto thee then,
    When he shall meet thee naked and alone.

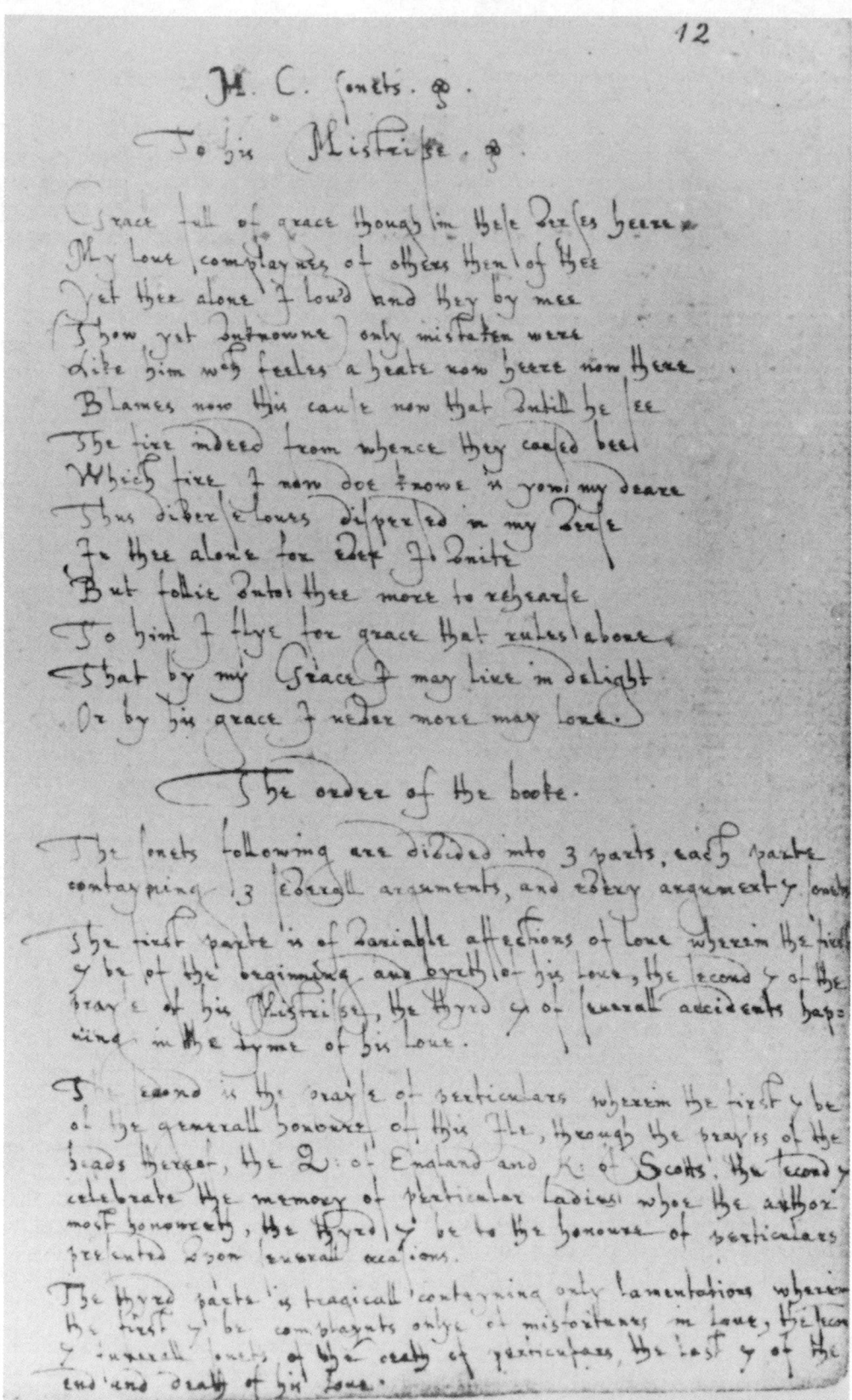

Constable's plan for Diana, *in the Todd Manuscript, a scribal copy of poems by various poets, dating from the early seventeenth century. Neither of the works published in Constable's lifetime followed this plan (Ms. Dyce 44, Victoria and Albert Museum).*

These lines typify the smooth versification praised by Constable's contemporaries.

Constable's occasional sonnets demonstrate the connection between his love poetry and political poetry. He uses Petrarchan conventions to praise King James and Queen Anne. He also uses the conceit of the weeping lover's tears to describe both the effects of military strength and the seas surrounding the British Isles:

> So if the sea by miracle were dry,
> Easy thy foes thy kingdom might invade –
> Fools which know not the power of thine eye.
> Thine eye hath made a thousand eyes to weep
> And every eye [a] thousand seas hath made
> And each sea shall thine Isle in safety keep.

Constable also praises the Scottish queen in the same religious terms that he uses to praise his mistress.

In contrast to these sonnets and to the more ardent tone of the poems addressed to his mistress, those written for various aristocratic women offer general praise by solving some puzzle with a slight piece of diplomatic wit. For example, he explains that Louise, Princess of Orange, is not queen only because "God on earth full bliss will not permit"; incapable of sufficiently praising two sisters, Margaret Clifford and Anne Dudley – the countesses of Cumberland and of Warwick, respectively – he concludes by saying "that one of you like to the other is"; he praises Lady Arabella by comparing her to a woman rather than a goddess, because when

> We speak of Gods we liken them to men:
> Not them to praise, but only them to know.
> Not able thee to praise, my drift was this:
> Some earthly shadow of thy worth to show,
> Whose heavenly self above world's reason is.

This light wit does not serve Constable well when he reflects on the more weighty problem of death. In his sonnet to the princess of Orange "upon occasion of the murder of her father and husband," the use of sonnet conventions to describe literal deaths seems especially inappropriate. The sonnet begins

> When murdering hands, to quench the thirst of tyranny,
> The world's most worthy, thy spouse, and father slew:
> Wounding thy heart through theirs, a double well they drew
> A well of blood from them, a well of tears from thee.

A sonnet to Walsingham's daughter, Frances Devereux, Countess of Essex, "upon occasion of the death of her first husband Sir Philip Sidney," strangely combines expressions of praise and suggestions for revenge:

> Sweetest of ladies if thy pleasure be
> To murder hearts, stay not in England still,
> Revenge on Spain thy husband's death, and kill
> His foes, not them that love both him and thee.

The sonnets about death underscore the triviality of the figurative loss of life the love sonneteer writes of; they can be seen as leading up to Constable's rejection of earthly love and his attention to preparing the soul for the life to come in heaven.

The difficulty of dating Constable's sonnets and the more general difficulty of tracing connections among sonneteers make arguments about influence futile. It is uncertain, for instance, whether Constable owes a debt to Samuel Daniel's *Delia,* also published in 1592, or vice versa. Other sonneteers whose work may display familiarity with Constable's include Barnabe Barnes, Richard Barnfield, Bartholomew Griffin, Michael Drayton, and William Shakespeare. Questions of influence aside, however, Constable's secular verse won him a reputation among his contemporaries as a major poet worthy of high praise. Both Drayton and Ben Jonson link the names Constable and Sidney as poets to be celebrated, and Sir Walter Ralegh and Gabriel Harvey include him in their lists of notable poets. Among his poetic contemporaries, his verse is noted chiefly for its purity and sweetness: he is "well-languaged," a quality that Edmund Bolton found lacking in Edmund Spenser; his muse, according to Jonson, is "ambrosiack"; he is "Sweet Constable": and, in an anonymous poem lamenting his exile, he is "England's sweet nightingale." Later, Constable appeared to reject the sonnets that his countrymen praised when he gave up his life in the courtly milieu that fostered them. The religious sequence *Spiritual Sonnets to the Honor of God and His Saints* (1815) proves that poetry was not for him simply a courtly pursuit.

Constable's conversion to Catholicism and the accompanying literary conversion from secular and occasional to religious verse were, perhaps, in a curious way both occasioned and signaled by his anonymous authorship of *Examen pacifique de la Doctrine des Huguenots* (1589), a book sometimes attributed to his friend and fellow convert, Cardinal Davy Du Perron. The book was popular enough to have a second edition in 1590 and to be translated into English in 1623 as *The Catholic Moderator.* Constable uses a Catholic persona in an effort to persuade French Catholics to accept the Protestant Henry IV as their king. Though pro-Huguenot and circulated on the Continent by his Huguenot friend Hotman, who perhaps influenced his decision to

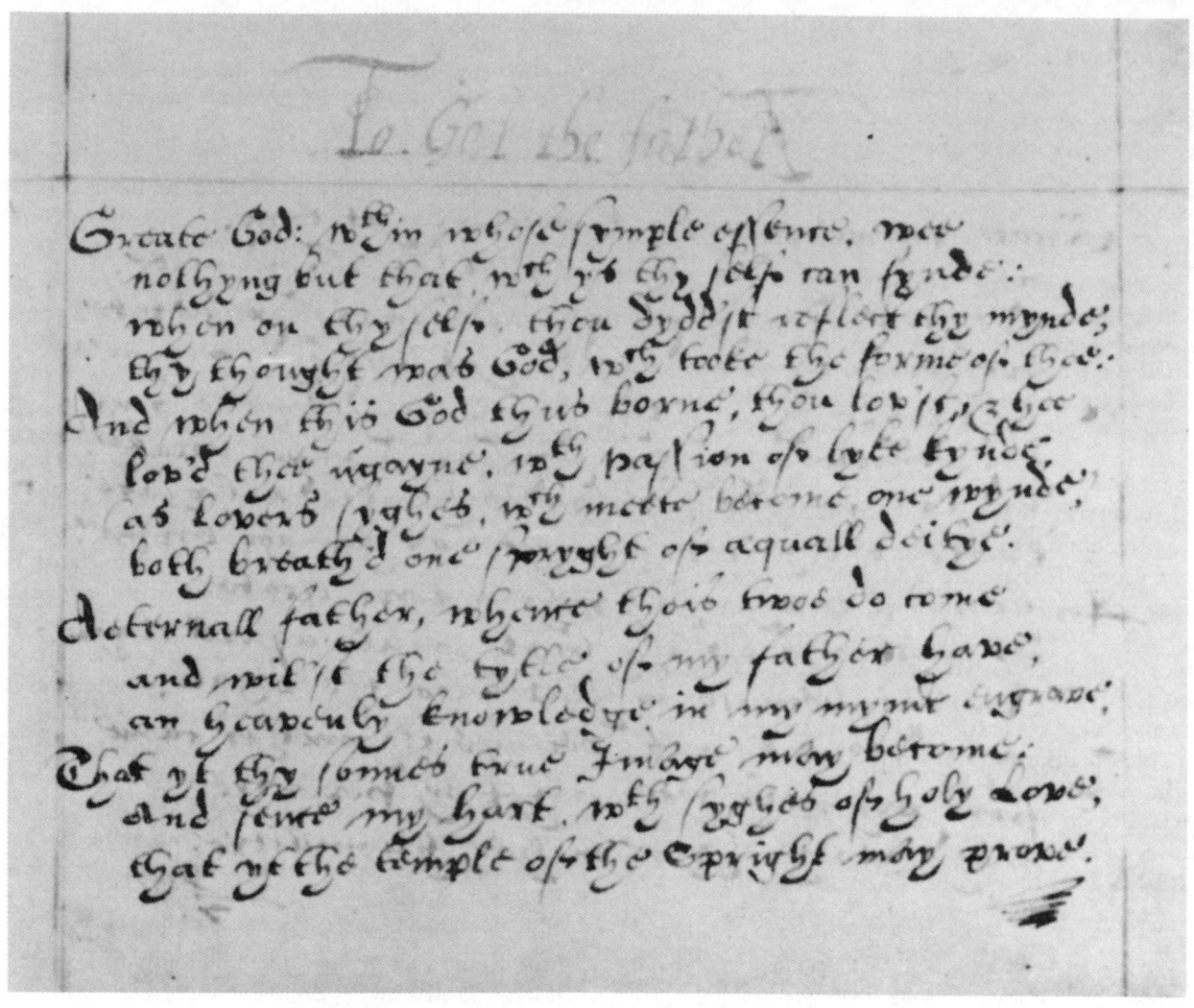

First page of the only extant transcription of Constable's Spiritual Sonnets *(Harleian Ms. 7553, British Library)*

write it, the book apparently provided Protestants an occasion for suspecting Constable to be Catholic.

Although it is possible to infer from the book that Constable's conversion had already taken place, his conversion became manifest in the late summer of 1591 when he left Essex's French expedition in support of Henry IV to join the Catholics. Separated from family (his father died in November 1591, reportedly heartbroken over his son's conversion) and denied his inheritance, Constable depended for his livelihood on an apparently unreliable pension from Henry IV and contributions from relatives in England. He wrote to Mary Talbot, Countess of Shrewsbury, who was also a Catholic, that he remained determined to "live contented with how little soever I shall have, serving no other mistress but God Almighty, who I know will love me if I love him, and in whose company I can be when I will." He also remained determined to serve

his country, though in his own way: by seeking religious toleration for English Catholics and by aiming ultimately for religious unification, the primary step toward which would be the conversion of James IV. To this futile effort Constable devoted the rest of his life.

During his exile Constable wrote religious sonnets which, like his court poetry, show him in tune with the literary movements of the time. Although the *Spiritual Sonnets* sequence resists precise dating, a probable date is 1593. Apparently unknown to his contemporaries, this sequence exhibits characteristics of Counter-Reformation devotional poetry, perhaps the result of a visit to Rome. Variously addressing these seventeen sonnets to God and his saints, in particular to Mary Magdalen, Constable uses the language of the Petrarchan lover to express the soul's love for the divine. Like their Italian models, his poems take the form either of prayer or of narrative and represent the poet repenting sins and begging forgiveness. The final sonnet, addressed to Mary Magdalen, describes his soul, "whom sinful passions once to lust did move," and prays that

> When death shall bring the night of my delight
> My soul uncloth'd, shall rest from labors past:
> And clasped in the arms of God, enjoy
> By sweet conjunction, everlasting joy.

The sonnet repeats the rejection of earthly love already announced in *Diana*.

Throughout his exile Constable avowed his patriotism, keeping up correspondence with Essex and Bacon and vigorously seeking papal support of the Scottish rather than the Spanish claim to the English throne. As a Catholic he continued to write theological tracts, now known only by references in letters. He is also assumed, though the claim is uncertain, to be the author of a book defending James's title to the English throne, *A Discovery of a Counterfeit Conference Held at a Counterfeit Place, by Counterfeit Travellers, for the Advancement of a Counterfeit Title, and Invented, Printed, and Published by One (Person) That Dare Not Avow His Name* (1600). Although the pope refused official support of Constable's efforts to convert James, Constable remained confident of success. James reported that "he has undertaken to convert me saying he had conferred with me long since and found me not so grounded in religion but I might be persuaded to become a Catholic." During a visit to Leith in 1599 Constable appears to have gained the king's ear, but subsequent failures to capture it rendered him, in the eyes of the queen, "but simple." His persistence led to his eventual ruin.

When James VI took the English throne in 1603 as James I, Constable, aided by Scottish connections and powerful English friends, was welcomed home and allowed to resume possession of his land. Despite his promise to Robert Cecil, who had sued in his behalf, "to behave myself according to [James's] liking in all actions that he can with reason require of one of my religion," he remained unswerving in his mission to convert the king. Constable's fortunes changed when his letters to Del Buffalo, the papal nuncio in Paris, were intercepted and turned over to the English crown by Henry IV. The plans outlined there to win James over to Catholicism were judged as near-treason. Constable's conviction that the king could not continue blind to the truth of Catholicism, as well as his cynical insight into the opportunism of English politicians, landed him in the Tower in April 1604; he

was released in a few months. After spending six years under parole to the archbishop of Canterbury, during which he served a brief sentence in Fleet Prison, Constable was either exiled or allowed to leave England for Paris in 1610. He died three years later in Liège, Belgium, where he was attending to the conversion of a Protestant divine.

Although admired in his own day as a first-rate poet, Constable's reputation faltered in the next century. His verse and reputation were revived chiefly owing to the biographical interests of mid-eighteenth-century literary antiquarians. *Spiritual Sonnets* first appeared in 1815 with a note by the editor, Thomas Park, that "several are marked . . . with a latitude of expression which some pious minds would deem indecorous." Although republished in several editions, Constable's poetry was first reconsidered critically in 1859 by William Carew Hazlitt, who judged the secular sonnets to surpass the religious ones. Until recently, subsequent critics have agreed; this evaluation perhaps explains Constable's reputation primarily as the author of a minor sonnet sequence, chiefly interesting in the evidence he provides of the Elizabethan rage for such verse. Lisle C. John includes *Diana* in his *Elizabethan Sonnet Sequences* (1938), generally limiting his commentary to detrimental remarks on Constable's use of particular conventions. The sonnets have also provided grist for scholars studying foreign influences on Elizabethan sonneteers – particularly, in the case of Constable, the French poet Philippe Desportes. Recent critical appreciation of the *Spiritual Sonnets* has tended to reverse Hazlitt's negative estimation of them. Grundy describes them as approaching the metaphysical style; though finding in the secular sonnets evidence "of a finically tidy mind," she sees in the religious verse "that pressure of thought and emotion which constitutes poetic inspiration." J. de Oliveira e Silva prizes in Constable the "plain style" that marks a sincerity found more often in the religious than the secular verse. The study of Constable's life and work calls into question the frequent objection to Renaissance poetry, made even while it was being written, that conventions substitute of sincere expression of emotion. In Constable's case, although the quality of the religious verse can be questioned, the sincerity of the beliefs expressed can hardly be exaggerated.

Biographies:

Louise Imogen Guiney, "Henry Constable," in her *Recusant Poets* (New York: Sheed & Ward, 1939), pp. 303–318;

George Wickes, "Henry Constable, Poet and Courtier (1562–1613)," *Biographical Studies 1534–1829,* 2, no. 4 (1954): 272–300.

References:

John Bossy, "A Propos of Henry Constable," *Recusant History,* 6 (April 1962): 228–237;

Edward Dowden, "An Elizabethan MS. Collection: Henry Constable," *Modern Quarterly of Language and Literature,* 2 (1898–1899): 3–4;

Ruth Hughey, *The Arundel Harington Manuscript of Tudor Poetry,* volume 2 (Columbus: Ohio State University Press, 1960), pp. 327–349;

Hughey, "The Harington MS. at Arundel Castle and Related Documents," *Library,* fourth series, 15 (March 1935): 388–444;

Lisle C. John, *Elizabethan Sonnet Sequences: Studies in Conventional Conceits* (New York: Columbia University Press, 1938);

Kenneth Muir, "The Order of Constable's Sonnets," *Notes and Queries,* 199 (October 1954): 424–425;

J. de Oliveira e Silva, "'Plainness and Truth': The Secular and Spiritual Sonnets of Henry Constable," *University of Hartford Studies in Literature,* 15–16 (1983–1984): 33–42;

David Rogers, "'The Catholic Moderator': A French Reply to Bellarmine and Its English Author, Henry Constable," *Recusant History,* 5 (October 1960): 224–235;

Janet G. Scott, *Les Sonnets Elizabéthains* (Paris: Librarie Ancienne Honoré Champion, 1929), pp. 129–142;

George Wickes, "Henry Constable's Spiritual Sonnets," *Month,* 18 (July 1957): 30–40.

Papers:

Henry Constable's manuscripts are in the Henry E. Huntington Library and Art Museum, San Marino, California; the Victoria and Albert Museum and the British Museum, London; the Bodleian Library, Oxford; Corpus Christi College, Oxford University; the Marsh Library; and Arundel Castle. His correspondence, which is largely unpublished, is scattered in a variety of locations, including the Hatfield Collection and the Roman Transcripts in the Public Record Office, London.

Robert Copland
(1470? – 1548)

Sheila Ahern
Victoria University of Wellington

BOOKS: *The Hye Way to the Spyttel Hous* (London: Printed by Robert Copland, circa 1536);

Jyl of Breyntfords Testament, Newly Compiled (London: Printed by William Copland, circa 1563);

The Seuen Sorowes That Women Haue When Theyr Husbandes Be Deade (London: Printed by William Copland, circa 1565).

Editions: *Jill of Brentford's Testament*, edited by Frederick J. Furnivall (London: Early English Text Society, 1871);

The Highway to the Spital-House, in *Elizabethan Underworld*, edited by Arthur Valentine Judges (London: Routledge, 1930; reprinted, London: Routledge & Kegan Paul, 1965), pp. 1–25;

Poems, edited by Mary Carpenter Erler (Toronto: University of Toronto Press, 1993).

OTHER: William Nevill, *Castell of Pleasure,* includes verse prologue by Copland (London: Printed by W. de Worde, 1518);

William Walter, *Spectacle of Lovers,* includes verse prologue by Copland (London: Printed by W. de Worde, 1520);

Saint Edmund Rich, Archbishop of Canterbury, *The Myrrour of the Chyrche,* edited by Copland (London: Printed by W. de Worde, 1521);

Geoffrey Chaucer, *The Assemble of Foules,* includes verse prologue by Copland (London: Printed by W. de Worde, 1530);

Giovanni Boccaccio, *Guystarde and Sygysmonde,* translated by William Walter, includes verse prologue by Copland (London: Printed by W. de Worde, 1532).

TRANSLATIONS: Anonymous, *Kalendar & Compost of Shepherds* (London: Printed by Wynkyn de Worde, 1508);

Anonymous, *Kynge Appolyn of Thyre* (London: Wynkyn de Worde, 1510);

Anonymous, *The Knyght of the Swanne. Here Begynneth the Hystory of the Noble Helyas* (London: Printed by Wynkyn de Worde, 1512);

Pierre Gringore, *Here Begynneth the Complaynte of Them that Ben to Late Maryed* (London: Printed by Wynkyn de Worde, circa 1518);

Anonymous, "The Manner to Dance Bace Dances after the Use of the French," in *Here Begynneth the Introductory to Wryte, and to Pronounce Frenche,* by Alexander Barclay (London: Printed by Robert Copland, 1521);

Pierre Garcie, *Thus Endeth the Rutter of ye See* (London: Printed by Robert Copland for Richard Bankes, 1528);

Thus Endeth the Secrete of Secretes of Arystotle (London: Printed by Robert Copland, 1528);

The Tryumphant Vyctory of the Imperyall Mageste Agaynst the Turkes: The XXVI Day of Septembre in Steumarke by a Captayne Named Michael Meschsaer (London: Printed by Robert Copland for Richard Bankes, 1532);

Pierre Gringore, *A Complaynt of Them that Be To Soone Maryed* (London: Printed by Wynkyn de Worde, 1535);

Guy de Chauliac, *The Questyonary of Cyrurgyens, with the Formulary of Lytell Guydo . . . with the Fourth Boke of the Terapentyke of Galyen* (London: Printed by Robert Wyer for Henry Dabbe & Richard Bankes, 1542);

Pietro Tommai, *The Art of Memory* (London: Printed by William Middleton, circa 1545).

Robert Copland, author and printer, was associated with the London printing trade for almost fifty years in the varied capacities of printer, editor, writer, translator, and bookseller. He was one of the

*Title page for Copland's 1536 book, depicting the author
flanked by two of the book's subjects*

minor printers of the sixteenth century and, as far as we know, printed about thirty books. His various ballads, practical treatises, law books, and romances attest to his broad humanist interests. Copland's work provides important evidence of an early French influence in Tudor literature, and his interest in secular learning is demonstrated by his printing the first French grammar book, as well as the works he selected to translate from Latin and French. He also wrote original works of popular literature for English readers. The intensely personal approach of these writings provides considerable insight into contemporary printing, publishing, and bookselling practices. His significance as a literary figure lies in three major compositions: *The Highway to the Spital-House* (circa 1536); *Jill of Brentford's Testament* (circa 1563); and *The Seven Sorrows That Women Have When Their Husbands Be Dead* (circa 1565). Through his numerous translations, his use and advocacy of English as a suitable language for learned writers, and his declared intention to improve the vulgar tongue and to standardize the diversity of English spelling, he enhanced the repute of the English language.

Details of Robert Copland's personal life are extremely scarce. He was probably born around 1470, but lack of precise information has led to dis-

agreement concerning his age, his association with William Caxton, and even his country of origin. His own writings, from which a partial picture of his background emerges, are the principal source of available data. It has been suggested from the fact that he wrote some verses in French and translated books from French into English that he was a Frenchman. He was, in fact, an Englishman, describing himself as "of the north" in *The Highway to the Spital-House* and referring to the English language as his "maternal tongue" in several prologues. It seems that he came to London to work as Caxton's apprentice and remained at the Westminster Press working for Caxton's successor, Wynkyn de Worde, a foreigner from Alsace who was previously employed by Caxton. By 1508 Copland was sufficiently established to have accumulated a small library of books and pamphlets of his own and to be in a position where he could suggest publications to his employer. In a prologue to his translation of *King Appolyn of Tyre* (1510) Copland writes of Caxton as his "master." The prologue describes how he had followed Caxton's example or possibly advice: "Gladly following the trace of my master Caxton beginning with small stories and pamphlets and so to other." To have been employed by Caxton, who died in 1491, would have made Copland a veteran printer by the

Title page for Copland's 1528 translation of a work then attributed to Aristotle. The printer's device is one of several monograms that Copland designed for himself.

middle of the sixteenth century, a fact confirmed by Dr. Andrew Boorde in his *The Principles of Astronomy* (published by Copland in 1547), where he refers to Copland as "the eldest printer of England."

Robert Copland began his independent career as a printer in 1514, but he continued to work on joint ventures with de Worde to mutual advantage. He was apparently the directing spirit and mastermind behind de Worde's long and successful printing career, and when de Worde died in 1535, he showed his gratitude for Copland's continued collaboration as editor and translator by leaving him a large bequest of ten marks. It is possible that de Worde had very little literary judgment and had to rely heavily throughout his career on his English workman Copland. One of de Worde's most successful productions was a verse translation by Copland of a contemporary work of French literature, *The Calendar & Compost of Shepherds* (1508). In the prologue Copland explains how he had read the French version and then had drawn de Worde's attention to its potential. The following year de Worde published, again presumably on Copland's recommendation, another commercial success, Henry Watson's prose translation of Sebastian

Brant's popular *Narrenschiff* (1494), a work preeminent in jest literature.

For some time after Caxton's death there were no English printers at work in England; and although the number of printers had reached six by 1500, they were all foreigners and monopolized the trade. De Worde and Richard Pynson (who came from Normandy) printed between them over seventy percent of the total book production for the first twenty years of the sixteenth century, leaving little scope for English-born printers. In 1513 John Rastell had begun printing law books at his premises in Saint Paul's Churchyard. Thus when Copland began to work independently in 1514 from his premises known as the Rose Garland in Fleet Street, he was only the second Englishman to establish a press in the sixteenth century.

Copland's own work was varied, including law books, devotional works, and a collection of translations. Throughout his working life he undertook translation work for de Worde and other printers, and he referred to his acquaintance with other contemporary translators such as Andrew Chertsey, Henry Watson, and Richard Whitford. By the 1530s, when he wrote his major literary work, he appeared to be mainly concerned with translating French poetry, publicizing writers such as Boccaccio and Chaucer, and promoting works of literary merit. Without doubt, he was aware of the mainstream of contemporary European literature, and his main work, *The Highway to the Spital-House,* took its theme and title from a recent, rather dull prose work in French, *Le Chemin de l'ospital* (1502) by Robert de Balzac. De Balzac's account was a brief catalogue of character types, but Copland, in verse, achieved contemporary color and realism in his descriptive cameos. For some scholars his descriptions of sixteenth-century rogues and vagabonds make up the sole attraction of the poem:

> Scabby and scurvy, pock-eaten flesh and rind,
> Lousy and scaled, and peeled like as apes,
> With scarcely a rag for to cover their shapes,
> Breechless, barefooted, all stinking with dirt,
> With thousands of tatters, drabbling to the skirt,
> Boys, girls, and luskish [lusty] strong knaves.

Notable among Copland's many translations is Pietro Tommai of Ravenna's *Art of Memory* (circa 1545), a book of rhetoric which furthered the development of the English language. He also translated three difficult technical works by French authors. Two of these, translated in 1542, were medical works, a French version of Galen's *Fourth Book* and Guy de Chauliac's *Questionary of Surgeons.* The third, translated in 1528, was a new work, Pierre Garcie's *Rutter of the Sea* (1502), the very first printed book on navigation. It is greatly to Copland's credit that he was the first English printer to recognize this work's worth. Books such as these were of little general interest and so not likely to be very profitable productions. Copland states in his prefaces, however, that he works for the common good by increasing the store of knowledge available in the English language. His desire to see every known science and art translated into the vernacular is clearly illustrated by his declaration, following Renaissance traditions, in the prologue to Galen's *Fourth Book* that "every science, art, and faculty [would find] a perpetual benefit to be set forth by writings vulgarly in every tongue."

In 1896 Henry R. Plomer declared that Copland deserved a place "in the ranks of literature," yet he has remained a much-neglected writer. He is best remembered for two of his original works, *Jill of Brentford's Testament* and *The Highway to the Spital-House.* In describing beggarly folk, dishonest knaves and vagabonds, and the corruption in society, both works helped to form the new genres of rogue and

"cony catching" literature, which aimed at the exposure of dishonest practices.

Jill of Brentford's Testament, with its "widow of a homely sort / Honest in substance and full of sport," is a verse satire in the form of a will which lists the foolish qualities of its beneficiaries; but the poem has little claim to literary distinction. Conversely, *The Highway* has real merit, containing lines that rank among the best that Tudor poetry has produced. However, part of the interest of this poem lies in its exposure of astonishingly complex frauds and deceits practiced by dishonest beggars on unwary citizens. In one example a rogue tricks an unwary housewife into providing him and his companions with board and lodgings for the space of several weeks. The man of the house is ill, and the rogue pretends to be a mysterious foreign physician who takes no payment for his cures. The wife is most grateful when the interpreter translates:

> For my labor I shall ask nothing at all,
> But for the drugs that occupy he shall,
> The which be dear and very precious.
> And surely I will never out of your house
> Till he be whole . . .[.]

The poem reveals how people bring about their own ruin through unscrupulous dealings, extravagance, and worldly stupidity. It also treats such traditional comic themes as that of the shrewish wife and foolish husband with amusing irony:

> Come hither any of these woeful creatures,
> That be sore wounded and much woe endures
> With a shrewd wife, and is never quiet,
> Because that she would have all her diet,
> But brawl and chide, babble, cry, and fight
> Ever uncontented both day and night?

The Highway is essentially a satirical and entertaining poem with a deep social significance. For social historians it makes a contribution toward an analysis of contemporary Tudor society by highlighting the ills associated with poverty. It alerts its readers to a new and growing menace, the formation of organized bands of beggars. Further, Copland is the first in England to identify the language of a subculture, in this instance the speech that beggars had devised for themselves termed "canting" or "Pedlars French." Thomas Harman has been credited with identifying and writing down the first glossary of this thieves' slang in his *Caveat for Common Cursitors* (1567), but the language was first quoted by Copland in this poem:

Tour [see] the patrico [priest] in the darkman's case
  [night-time] . . .
 . . . for my watch [myself] it is [I am] nace [drinking]
  gear [equipment];
For the bene [good] bouse [drink] my watch [I] hath
 [have] a wyn [a penny].
And thus they babble, till their thrift [money] is thin,
I wot not what, with their babbling French.

Almost every book with which Copland was connected as printer or translator revealed something of his personality, for he invariably added preambles, postscripts, and insertions to the texts. By contrast, relatively little is known about his family and personal life. Boorde's reference to Copland in 1547 is the last available mention of the author, who probably died early in 1548. His technical inadequacies have been deplored as "mediocre," "mean and unattractive," but this condemnation needs to be qualified. Copland saw in printing an opportunity to guide the public in its choice of reading matter. He recognized an opportunity to enrich the vernacular language through his selection of texts. His ideals created a dilemma, for he was in business to make a living. In writing *The Seven Sorrows,* a tale of a widow's antics and her doubts about taking another husband, he acknowledges that his purpose was to "get a penny as well as I can." The poem itself is mundane, but it has an interesting verse prologue which describes contemporary printing, publishing, and bookselling practices. Copland's real concern was with the rapid provision of cheap books in the English language to benefit readers rather than in the achievement of a few carefully crafted books for a more discerning public.

As printer and author his achievement in promoting the English language as a medium for scholarly works deserves greater recognition by modern critics. For his own literary compositions he unquestionably deserves a place in the history of English literature. His editorial efforts, designed to inspire a love of literature in readers and under-taken as a service to the literate public, have been much neglected. A reconsideration of Copland's work would establish his great contribution to the development of English humanism and his well-deserved place in the English Renaissance.

References:

Henry Stanley Bennett, *English Books and Readers 1475–1557* (Cambridge: Cambridge University Press, 1952);

John Milton Berdan, *Early Tudor Poetry* (New York: Macmillan, 1931);

Edward Gordon Duff, *A Century of the English Book Trade* (Philadelphia: Folcroft Library Edition, 1972);

Frank Charles Francis, *Robert Copland, Sixteenth-Century Printer and Translator* (Glasgow: Jackson, Son & Company, 1961);

Charles Harold Herford, *Studies in the Literary Relations of England and Germany in the Sixteenth Century* (Cambridge: Cambridge University Press, 1886), pp. 357–362;

Arthur Valentine Judges, *Elizabethan Underworld* (London: Routledge, 1930);

W. G. Moore, "Robert Copland and His Hye Way," *Review of English Studies,* 7 (October 1931): 406–418;

George Duncan Painter, *William Caxton* (London: Chatto & Windus, 1976);

Henry R. Plomer, "Robert Copland," in *Transactions of the Bibliographical Society,* 3 (London: Bibliographical Society, 1896), pp. 211–225;

Plomer, *Wynkyn de Worde and His Contemporaries* (London: Grafton & Company, 1925), pp. 52–53, 191–193;

"Two References to the English Book Trade, Circa 1525," *Bibliographica,* 1, no. 2 (London: Kegan Paul, Trench, Trübner, 1895): 252–256.

John Dee

(13 July 1527 – 26 March 1609)

Julian Roberts
Bodleian Library, Oxford University

BOOKS: Προπαιδεύματα ἀφοριστικὰ *Joannis Dee Londinensis, de præstantioribus quibusdam naturæ virtutibus* (London: Printed by Henry Sutton, 1558; revised edition, London: Printed by Reyner Wolfe, 1568);

Monas hieroglyphica (Antwerp: Printed by G. Sylvius, 1564; Frankfurt am Main: Printed by Johann Wechel and Peter Fischer, 1591);

Parallaticæ commentationis praxewsq; nucleus quidam (London: Printed by John Day, 1573);

General and Rare Memorials Pertayning to the Perfect Arte of Nauigation: Now First Published: 24. Yeres, After the First Inuention Thereof (London: John Daye, 1577);

A Letter, Containing a Most Briefe Discourse Apologeticall, with a Protestation, for the Lawfull, and Christian Course, of the Philosophicall Studies and Exercises, of a Certaine Gentleman: An Ancient Seruant to Her Maiesty (London: Printed by Peter Short, 1599); enlarged as *A Letter, Nine Yeeres Since, Written and First Published: Containing . . . Gentleman: A Faithfull Seruant to Our Late Queene and (Anno 1603. Aug. 9.) Sworne Seruant to the King* (London: Printed by Emma Short, 1603 [1604?]);

A True & Faithful Relation of What Passed for Many Yeers Between Dr. John Dee . . . and Some Spirits: Tending (Had it Succeeded) to a General Alteration of Most States and Kingdomes of the World, edited by Meric Casaubon (London: Printed by David Maxwell for Timothy Garthwait, 1659);

The Private Diary of Dr. John Dee, and the Catalogue of His Library of Manuscripts, edited by James Orchard Halliwell (London: Camden Society, 1842);

Diary for the Years 1595–1601, of Dr. John Dee, Warden of Manchester from 1595 to 1608, edited by John Eglinton Bailey (N.p., 1880).

Editions: *Monas hieroglyphica* (1564), translated into English by Conrad Hermann Josten in *Ambix,* 12 (June/October 1964): 84–221;

John Dee (Ashmolean Museum, Oxford)

General and rare memorials pertayning to the perfect arte of navigation, English Experience (Amsterdam & New York: Da Capo, 1968);

A True & Faithful Relation of What Passed for Many Yeers Between Dr. John Dee . . . and Some Spirits (London: Askin, 1974);

John Dee on Astronomy, edited by Wayne Shumaker (Berkeley: University of California Press, 1978).

OTHER: John Feild, *Ephemeris anni .1557. currentis iuxta Copernici et Reinhaldi canones. Supputata ac examinata ad meridianum Londinensem,* preface by Dee (London: Printed by Thomas Marshe, 1556);

Robert Record, *The Ground of Artes Teachyng the Worke and Practise of Arithmetike. Now of Late Ouerseen & Augmented,* revised and enlarged by Dee (London: Printed by Reyner Wolfe, 1561);

"Mathematicall Praeface," in Euclid, *The Elements of Geometrie . . . Faithfully translated by H. Billingsley. Whereunto Are Annexed Scholies, Annotations, and Inuentions, Both of Time Past, and in This Our Age. With a Præface by J. Dee* (London: Printed by John Daye, 1570);

Machometus Bagdedinus, *De superficierum divisionibus,* edited by Dee and Federigo Commandino (Pesaro: Printed by H. Concordia, 1570);

"In Praise of the author," in George Ripley, *The compound of alchymy* (London: Printed by Thomas Orwin, 1591);

Henry Perry, *Eglvryn Phraethineb. Sebh, Dosparth ar Retoreg* (London: Printed by John Danter, 1595) – includes a six-line Latin elegiac poem by Dee;

John of Glastonbury, *Chronica,* edited by Thomas Hearne (Oxonii: e Theatro Sheldoniano, 1726) – includes Dee's "Compendious rehearsal" and "Supplication."

John Dee was best known as a mathematician to his contemporaries, and it is in this capacity that Dee is most frequently mentioned for fifty years after his death. From mathematics he branched out into the study of astrology and, more profitably for his compatriots, into instruction in navigation, so that his influence is apparent in the early voyages of the Muscovy Company and is believed to have contributed to Sir Francis Drake's world voyage of 1577–1580. There can be no doubt of the extent of his learning and of his influence in many areas, including the British expansion into the New World. Dee's learning was based on the possession of one of the three largest English libraries of the sixteenth century. Unlike his rivals in collecting, John, Lord Lumley, and Andrew Perne, Dee played a major part in saving and encouraging others to save manuscripts from the recently dissolved monastic libraries. The publication of Dee's *Library Catalogue* in 1990 has revealed how intensively this polymathic scholar used his books, and has provided evidence for his pursuit of other significant strands of learning such as hermeticism and cabala and for his obsession with alchemy and the quest for the philosopher's stone. Particularly significant for Dee's current reputation has been the advocacy of literary historian Frances A. Yates, who emphasizes – and, some may think, exaggerates – Dee's role as an intellectual influence in the English Renaissance.

Dee was born in London on 13 July 1527, the son (and apparently only child) of Rowland Dee and Jane Wild. Rowland is described by his son as "antesignanus dapiferorum" (gentleman sewer, a household officer) to Henry VIII but was a merchant in later life; the date of his death is unknown. The Dee family was of Welsh origin, and John possessed two elaborate pedigrees tracing his descent through princely lines to the legendary Coel Hen ("Old King Cole"). The Welsh connection was evidently of little importance to him in early life, though after about 1570 it assumed considerable significance. He was educated at Chelmsford Grammar School and Saint John's College, Cambridge (from 1542). In 1546 he was made a fellow of the new foundation of Trinity College. Granted his M.A. in 1548, he enrolled at the University of Louvain in the same year; after a brief return to England he remained there for two years. That was the end of his formal education.

Most of the details of Dee's life known to current scholarship are drawn from his autobiographical "Compendious Rehearsal," which he wrote in 1592. There is abundant, if patchy, documentation from 1577 to 1600 derived from Dee's manuscript notes in two sets of printed ephemerides ("Joannes Stadius," 1570, and "Joannes Maginus," 1582), and this can be supplemented from 1583 to 1587, and, briefly, 1607, by similar notes taken from Dee's records of "angelic conversations" preserved in *A True and Faithful Relation* (1659). Dee's gathering together of a great library is one unifying theme in his life, and the surviving books and manuscripts are, particularly before the mid 1560s, valuable in preserving both autobiographical notes and the whereabouts of their owner at the time of purchase.

Dee's published works, however, are relatively slight and few in number, in view of the length of his life and the evident intensity of his intellectual activity. Dee lists in the "Compendious Rehearsal" many works which then remained in manuscript, though most of these have not survived. Dee also apparently experienced serious difficulty in the very act of publication, evidenced not only by the paucity of his published work, but by his prefatory references to illness, haste, and even self-censorship. He frequently tampered with his own published texts by making minute written and, with the aid of tiny cancel slips, printed alterations to much of his work.

Dee made two visits to Louvain to confer with such mathematicians and geographers as Gerard Mercator and Gemma Frisius, and records of book purchases attest to his movement between Louvain

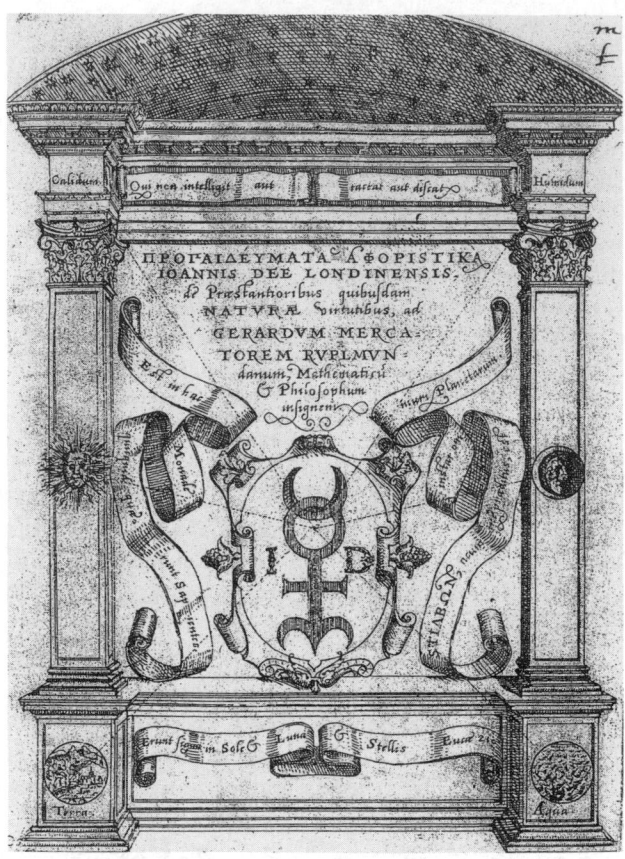

Title page of Dee's influential collection of aphorisms

and the port of Antwerp. In July 1550, as Dee records in the "Compendious Rehearsal," he set out for Paris, "where, within a few days after at the request of some English gentlemen . . . I did undertake to read freely and publicly Euclid's elements geometrical, *Mathematicè, Physicè, et Pythagoricè,* a thing never done publicly in any university of Christendom." Several extant items from Dee's library prove that even before this he had bought a great quantity of books. Again he lists among his acquaintances leading scholars and scientists of Paris – Oronce Finé, Antoine Mizauld, Jacques Goupyl, Pierre de la Ramée, Guillaume Postel, and Jean Fernel. He was back in England by December 1551, when on the recommendation of classical scholar Sir John Cheke he was sent for by Secretary of State William Cecil and awarded by King Edward VI a pension of one hundred crowns, later replaced by the rectory of Upton-on-Severn.

Thus provided with a basic income, Dee became a tutor in noble households, first in that of William Herbert, Earl of Pembroke, and later in that of John Dudley, Duke of Northumberland. He seems to have been particularly close, to judge

from the glowing tribute in his preface to Henry Billingsley's translation of Euclid's *Elements of Geometry* (1570), to the third, but eldest surviving, son, John, Earl of Warwick. But the Dudleys fell from power in 1553, with the death in July of Edward VI and the duke's support for the ill-fated Lady Jane Grey as queen. The young earl of Warwick died the following year, but neither books nor records survive to show the immediate effect of the catastrophe on the family's tutor.

By Dee's own account he was offered the chance to lecture in mathematics at Oxford in 1554; a book and a manuscript survive to show that he was there, and he had a pupil, Christopher Carye, who was in Oxford during 1554. More probably, Dee was establishing himself as a teacher of mathematics and of navigation in London and as an adviser to those who founded the Muscovy Company. Such a role, as a London-based rather than a university-based teacher, was by this time the one he had no doubt chosen for himself, and the position with a noble family, even if temporary, is consistent with the interdisciplinary nature of his early writings and his later vision of himself as a Christian Aristotle, whether his "Alexander" was to be English, imperial, or even Russian royalty. Insofar as can be judged from his acquisition of books at this time, Dee's thought was dominated by Aristotle, but he was also buying and annotating the works of the classical scientists and of the Neoplatonist writers. He was aware of the work of Polish astronomer Nicolaus Copernicus, as his first published work, the preface to John Feild's *Ephemeris anni 1557* (1556), shows. His ownership of two copies of Copernicus's *De revolutionibus orbium coelestium* (1543) suggests that Dee taught heliocentricity – but only as a hypothesis.

But Dee's scholarly career was interrupted in 1555 by his arrest and that of his associates Feild, Carye, and Sir Thomas Benger, on charges which can perhaps best be summed up (as Dee did later) as "magic." His companions were released, but Dee found himself in the custody of Edmund Bonner, the Catholic bishop of London – by this time Mary was on the throne – a dangerous situation for someone whose religious position had probably been that of "Protestant humanist." Remarkably, Dee satisfied Bonner on the subject of his orthodoxy and was shortly a member of the bishop's household, even, according to the martyrologist John Foxe, acting as his chaplain.

This conformity with Marian Catholicism seems to have bred in Dee an awareness of the damage to English learning wrought by the dissolution of the monasteries and the destruction of their libraries. He was the first to lament publicly the dispersal and to attempt to remedy the loss. In January 1556 he drew up a "Supplication" to Queen Mary in which he proposed the setting up of a national library to house either the surviving manuscripts or copies which would be made of them where the English books would be joined by copies made from the great libraries of Europe and by printed books "in wonderful abundance." Although Bonner supported him, it was ultimately Dee alone who did the borrowing and copying; the great library he envisaged was to be his own, though his "Supplication" influenced the collecting initiative of Archbishop Matthew Parker in Elizabeth's reign. The "Supplication" and its results are perhaps Dee's most important legacy. Some of his borrowing activities are recorded in his notebooks as taking place in Oxford and Cambridge, where the university libraries were being eroded and the colleges were discarding manuscripts in favor of printed books.

It is clear from the documents that survive on his book-collecting activities that unlike his contemporaries Dee was interested in scientific, and particularly in English scientific, works. There remain lists of the manuscripts that he owned at this time, a list of alchemical books that he read, and a partial list of his books and manuscripts made between 1557 and 1559. Among the branches of classical and medieval science which Dee had been cultivating most keenly was astronomy; and from the movement and position of the stars flowed their influence, the province of the astrologer.

Roger Bacon was an important influence on Dee's first book, Προπαιδεύματα ἀφοριστικὰ (*Propaideumata aphoristica*) of 1558. It was conceived, written, and published before the collapse of Queen Mary's Catholic regime at her death in November 1558 and the subsequent removal of Dee's patron Bonner from office. The Προπαιδεύματα is a series of 120 aphorisms written in Latin, a fact that, with the dedication to Flemish geographer Mercator, indicates Dee's confidence in his international status. The handsome engraved title page carries an early version of Dee's Monas symbol, the elaboration of which is the subject of his next published work, the *Monas hieroglyphica* (1564). When the second edition of Προπαιδεύματα appeared in 1568, the Monas, this time a woodcut, and the text were altered to agree with the intervening work.

The cosmology of the *Propaideumata* is Ptolemaic and geocentric, and Dee brings the skills of the mathematician to astrology. His thesis is that the influence of the stars is conveyed by certain rays which emanate from them, analogous to light; that the conjunction of these rays at a particular spot and at one time is unique; and that they can be measured. Historian Nicholas H. Clulee notes that, like most of Dee's work, this one does not observe the accepted boundaries of the sciences and that this fact is related to Dee's deliberate standing away from academic life.

The three years immediately after the accession of Queen Elizabeth I in 1558 are, with the exception of those at the very end of Dee's life, the most obscure. To counteract the odium of his association with Bonner, Dee had an advantage in that the most influential men in the state were his Cambridge contemporaries; he had also been close to the Dudleys, and Robert Dudley, Earl of Leicester, the queen's favorite, used Dee's astrological advice in settling the date of the coronation. During this period Dee was also actively looking for and copying manuscripts, as several extant examples reveal, though this does not seem to have brought him into contact with Archbishop Parker's circle.

By early 1562 Dee was in the Netherlands. Enough books survive to suggest that he spent most of 1562 in Louvain but began to travel in the spring of 1563, meeting Conrad Gesner in Zurich and crossing the Alps to Chiavenna, Venice, and Padua. From Italy he moved north to witness the coronation of Maximilian II as king of Hungary at Bratislava. Back in the Netherlands in early 1564, Dee wrote (in haste) and published his *Monas hieroglyphica,* dedicated to Maximilian, at Antwerp, and he returned to England in June.

From his contacts, his purchases, and a letter to Sir William Cecil, it is possible to build up a picture of Dee's activities and interests in this period. Mathematics was one; but new preoccupations included Hebrew and related languages and the works of the Swiss alchemist and physician Paracelsus. (Dee was a superb linguist and read Paracelsus in Latin and German.) Dee's Hebrew library was the largest in England, but the paucity of Dee's notes in extant examples of this collection suggests that here at least he was not fluent. His interest is generally linked to the cabala, but it may plausibly be connected to the concerns shown in the *Monas hieroglyphica* with languages in general and the sacred language in particular.

The *Monas hieroglyphica* is Dee's least approachable book, though it achieved a second edition at Frankfurt in 1591 and was twice reprinted in alchemical compendiums in the following century. It is a series of theorems expounding the Monas symbol, which had first appeared in the *Propaideumata*

Title page for Dee's 1564 work, an explication of his mystical "Monas" symbol, depicted in the center of the page

aphoristica in 1558. Dee based the Monas on the astronomical sign for Mercury, combining with it those of the other planets (those for the Sun and Moon being most obvious), the cross (which could represent the four qualities of hot, cold, moist, and dry and the four elements of earth, fire, water, and air), and, at the base, the sign of the constellation Aries. In the Monas, Dee believed he had created a symbol of enormous power, which not only represented the alchemical process of transmutation of metals, but also the transmutation of the soul in its progress toward God.

After his return in 1564, Dee married Katherine, the widow of Thomas Constable, a prominent London merchant with whom he had been associated in 1558. This no doubt occasioned the move to the property at Mortlake in Surrey, which he occupied for the rest of his life. Mortlake was also very close to the royal residence at Richmond, and its spaciousness and proximity to the Thames enabled Dee to set up alchemical laboratories.

Meanwhile he continued, with the encouragement and perhaps the aid of Cecil, the program of

copying and collecting books he had developed in 1556. There was now more competition from Parker and other antiquaries for the manuscripts from the dissolved monasteries; thus the continuing growth in Dee's library was on the printed side, and he is known to have frequented the shop of Arnold Birckmann, the London representative of the Cologne firm who was the principal importer of books at this time. Many of the mathematical, alchemical, and Paracelsian works from Dee's library are present in multiple copies, no doubt for the use of pupils attracted to Mortlake by Dee's reputation as a teacher of mathematics and alchemy. The names of Dee's pupils are not known, but one strong candidate is the navigator John Davis.

In 1570 Dee coedited, with his friend Federigo Commandino, and wrote the preface to Machometus Bagdedinus's mathematical work, *De superficierum divisionibus*. But his reputation as a mathematician was assured with the publication of another work in that same year, his "Mathematical Preface" to Henry Billingsley's English translation of Euclid's *Elements of Geometry*. Many of the books Dee cites had been in his library for some time, and there are, with one exception, none of the mystical and magical elements in the natural philosophy expressed in the *Monas hieroglyphica*.

The "Mathematical Preface" may thus be seen as a retrospective statement of his philosophy as a teacher for the previous twenty years. His statement of the dignity and role of mathematics at the outset is strongly influenced by Neoplatonism, particularly that of the fifth-century Greek philosopher Proclus. But this is also a statement in English rather than the scholarly language of Latin, by someone who has distanced himself from the university world, and a large part of the "Mathematical Preface" is devoted to setting out the importance of mathematical studies to "mechanicians," those who practice a variety of arts and technologies. Dee gives these arts a series of Greek-derived names which have not lasted, though his eloquent championing of the value of mathematics to mechanicians may well be his abiding contribution to the scientific revolution. Beyond this there is a major difference of opinion as to whether his scientific "method" was either equally far-reaching or anticipatory of Francis Bacon. One of Dee's outlandishly named disciplines, for example, is "thaumaturgike," literally "wonder-working"; and since this is followed by a passionate defense of himself from the charge of "conjuring," one may reasonably suppose that this "thaumaturgic" practice, perhaps in conjunction with dramatic presentation, had been the source of his troubles with the law in 1555.

It is also a matter of dispute as to how far the magical elements in the *Monas hieroglyphica* and Dee's claims for mathematical science in the preface were influenced by his reading of the Hermetic corpus (a body of works supposedly by Hermes Trismegistus, then believed to have influenced Moses). He possessed many editions, but the only surviving copy so far identified is a 1516 printing of the Italian philosopher Marsilio Ficino's collection of the texts. This was an early purchase by Dee and is well annotated.

In the 1570s Dee was at the height of his prosperity and reputation. The alchemical work at Mortlake required a brief trip in 1571 to the Continent in search of equipment. The appearance of a nova in the constellation Cassiopeia in 1572 was a major event for astronomers, since a new star in the supposedly unchangeable sphere of the fixed stars was contrary to the Aristotelian cosmology. The occurrence prompted Dee to write *Parallaticæ commentationis praxeosque nucleus quidam* (1573); notes he made at the time show that he also attached enormous astrological significance to it.

His domestic settlement and growing reputation perhaps stimulated antiquarian interests. One of his Welsh cousins had already given him a copy of his pedigree, and this gift along with the publishing activities of Archbishop Matthew Parker and his circle in Anglo-Saxon and medieval English history awoke Dee's Welsh, or "British," pride. Dee seems to have resumed the collecting and copying of manuscripts, concentrating now on those in Welsh and relating to Welsh history; his journey in August 1574 from Chester into northeastern Wales and back into Herefordshire clearly had this as one of its aims. A modest competence in the Welsh language and a fervent belief in Geoffrey of Monmouth's twelfth-century *Historia Britonum* (History of the Britons) led Dee to regard the conquests of King Arthur and the supposed voyage of Prince Madog ab Owain Gwynedd to America as historical warrant for British settlement in North America.

Thus three of Dee's concerns — his undoubted navigational knowledge, his alchemical and metallurgical interest in the ores that Sir Martin Frobisher brought back from the New World, and an uncritical zeal for British history — came together in the 1570s to involve him in several plans for settlement and exploration. These plans drew their inspiration from various sources, the first of which was economic, the desire for riches. This found expression in the formation of mining companies in England (in which Dee was involved) and the impulse to emulate Spain in tapping the riches of the New World. Dee was involved in Frobisher's, and probably Sir Francis Drake's, voyages, and his teaching of "chemistry" to Philip Sidney is doubtless linked to these motives. Whatever his own religious stance, he was also associated politically with the more aggressively Protestant grouping at court of Sir Francis Walsingham, Robert Dudley, Earl of Leicester, and Sidney, who seem to have used his astrological advice to dissuade the queen from marriage with the French king's brother, François, Duc d'Alençon. The group's policy was also anti-Spanish to the point of annoying the king of Spain, by raiding Spanish colonies in Central and South America in association with Sir Humphrey Gilbert. Settlement in North America was preferably sanctioned by titles the queen might have to that land, and Dee was ready to provide them. Colonies in North America would also protect an English sea route to the markets of India and China, if a passage could be found, and Dee's help was thus enlisted in the quest for a northwest passage.

In addition to his involvement with British efforts at exploration and colonization, Dee's library also indicates a strong and growing interest in Paracelsian medicine at the same time, but the only evidence for any medical practice by Dee is a series of consultations with the queen recorded in his ephemera at the end of 1578. She was suffering from a mysterious illness, and Leicester and Walsingham sent Dee to Germany to confer with the physician Leonhard Thurneysser von Thurn.

Dee's interests in navigation and British and English history bore fruit in 1577 with his *General and Rare Memorials Pertaining to the Perfect Art of Navigation*. This was a "private" printing by John Day in an edition of one hundred copies, characteristically written in haste and purporting to be part of a larger work which was either destroyed or remained in manuscript. Its principal aim was to urge the queen to build up a powerful navy, both for economic and imperial purposes — Dee uses the term "British Impire" for the first time in this work — but he also introduces much antiquarian and other, even personal, matter. The great exemplar in the work is for once not Arthur but the Saxon king Edgar.

Dee's wife (presumably Katherine, though he does not name her) died in 1576. In February 1578 he married Jane Fromond. She was already pregnant when Dee was sent to Germany in 1579, and their first son, significantly christened Arthur, was born on 13 July of that year. Altogether the couple had eight children, but only Arthur and their sec-

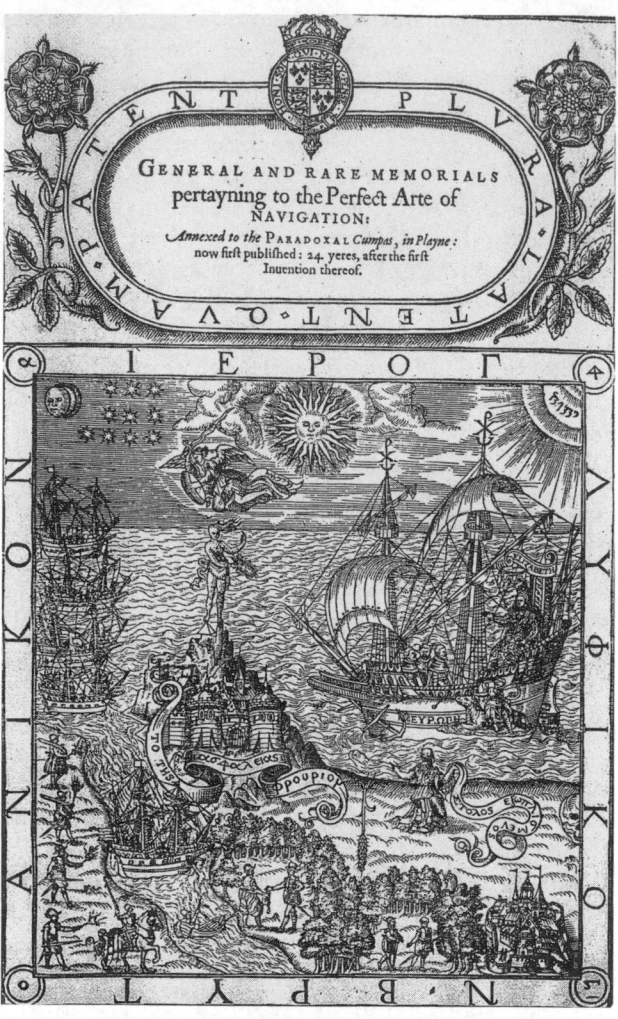

Title page for Dee's 1577 book on navigation, aimed at convincing Queen Elizabeth to strengthen the English navy

ond child, Katherine (born 1581), survived their father.

Dee began "scrying" (apparently some form of cristallomancy) at about this time; Clulee believes that Dee alludes to the practice when he mentions the "Ars sintrillia" in the "Mathematical Preface" of 1570. Dee usually was unable to see visions in his crystals or mirrors and employed mediums, of whom William Emery was probably the first and Barnabas Saul the second. Saul left Dee in March 1582, but his place was quickly taken by the man Dee first knew as Edward Talbot and later as Edward Kelley. Dee began a series of séancelike "angelic conferences" on 10 March. Among the questions asked of the angels, in the presence of Adrian Gilbert, Sir Humphrey's brother, were some about the northwest passage, a topic which, in discussion with Gilbert, the explorer John Davis, Walsingham, and Robert Beale, consumed much of Dee's atten-

tion in January 1583. Dee was also working on a book on the reform of the calendar, which he delivered to Lord Burghley in February. He advocated the adoption of the Gregorian system, but this was opposed by the bishops, and the Julian system was retained in England until 1752.

In March 1583 Dee learned of the impending arrival of the Polish count Albrecht Laski. The motives for Laski's visit to England remain unknown, but visiting Dee, of whom he may have learned from Sidney, was certainly one. Dee met him first in Leicester's quarters at Greenwich, and Laski later came to Mortlake and participated in "angelic conferences." Dee, Kelley, and their families left for Poland with Laski on 21 September.

One of his last actions before leaving was to make two fair copies of the catalogue of his library. The work of cataloguing had been done by Andreas Fremonsheim, the London factor for the Birckmanns of Cologne, and it is fairly clear that Dee's recent accessions, as well as many manuscripts, were omitted through haste.

The reasons for Dee's precipitate departure are almost as obscure as those for Laski's coming. The connection was evidently blessed by Leicester and Sidney, which suggests a political motive, perhaps the reconversion of Laski to Protestantism, in the hope that with financial backing he might be elected to the throne of Poland. Dee originally intended an absence of twenty months. The books he took with him are notably connected with alchemy and Paracelsian medicine. These were known interests of Laski, and the quest for the philosopher's stone was carried out with angelic assistance in Poland and Bohemia, as the sessions so painstakingly recorded in *A True and Faithful Relation* reveal. This work also chronicles Dee's movements from Kraców to Prague and thence to Trebona, as he passed from the patronage of Laski to that, briefly, of Emperor Rudolf, and finally to that of Vilém Rožmberk.

Not long after his departure his house and library, left in the care of his brother-in-law Nicholas Fromond, were raided, many of his instruments broken, and a great many books stolen. The culprits were John Davis and Nicholas Saunder (probably a pupil of Dee and an associate of Davis), and Adrian Gilbert may well have been involved. They were no doubt angry at Dee's defection from the cause of the northwest passage.

In the association between Dee and Kelley there was a strong degree of mutual dependence. Kelley was a fraud, but he was encouraged in his fraud by a knowledge of what Dee needed and by a wide if superficial learning derived from Dee and his library. Ultimately they parted as Kelley began

Platonis opera lat. à Marsilio Ficino
     commentarijs illustrata f° Bas.

Etymologicon magnū græcū f° Ven. Ald. 1549.

Ovidij metamorphosis cū commentarijs
     Raphaëlis Regij f° Ven. 1565.

Dubravij historia Bohemica f° Basil.

Lud. Lavaterus in paralipomena f° Tig. 1573.

Arriani Alexāder Magnus græcolat. f°
     Henric. Stephani 1575.

Δ Joh. Forsteri Lexicon hebraicū f° Basil. 1564.

Δ Alberti Krantzij Chronica regnorū
     Aquilonariū Daniæ, Sueciæ &c f° 1561.

Euclides cū commentarijs Theonis græce f° Basil. 2 vol.
Δ Euclides cū commentarijs Theonis græce f° Bas. 1533. uno vol.

Δ Euclides cū commentarijs Theonis & Capani lat. f° Bas. 1537.

Δ Orontij de rebus Mathematicis, libri quatuor f°
     paris. 1556.

Leonardi Thurnisseri Archidoxa germanice f°

Alberti Magnus de animalibg f° Ven. 1519.

Arriani Periplus ponti Euxini & maris
     Erythræi cū doctissimis commentarijs
     Stuckij f° Genevæ 1577.

Ptolomæi quadripartitū f° Ven. 1519.

Alberti Dureri Geometria f° lat. parisijs.

Theodosij sphærica lat. f° Messanæ 1558.

Bonifacius Simoneta f° Basileæ 1509.

Vitruvij Architectura cū commentarijs
     Danielis Barbari f° Ven. 1567.

Diodorus siculus lat. f° Basil. 1548.

Petri Apiani introductio Geographica
     &c f° Ingolstadij 1533.

A page from the catalogue of Dee's library. Dee made the "Δ" notation next to books he considered especially important (Ms. Harley 1879, British Library).

to dominate the alchemical work and Dee began his long journey back to England in February 1589. His progress through Europe was steady and almost triumphal; but his arrival in England in December was not, and the first months were spent in the effort to recover his half-ruined house from Fromond and his books from Davis (who returned them) and Saunder (who kept them).

Dee's family was still growing, and his ambitions had not decreased, so he began a new struggle for patronage. Some money came from the queen and from pupils, but his calls for preferment were ignored until the wardenship of the Collegiate Church at Manchester was granted to him in 1596. Some of his stay there is documented in his ephemerides, but there are long gaps, when he was probably at Mortlake, and there are hardly any entries after 1600. Contemporaries speak of his growing poverty, which was only partly alleviated by gifts of food from his Welsh cousins and from a friend, John Pontois, and by the disposal of some of his books. Jane Dee and perhaps several of the Dee children died of plague in Manchester in 1605, after which Dee left the wardenship and returned to Mortlake. Fragments of further "angelic conferences" appear in *A True and Faithful Relation;* they seem to be of 1607, and the medium was Bartholomew Hickman. They hint of an intended journey in the company of his daughter Katherine; a young servant, Patrick Saunders; and Pontois. The angels also instructed Dee to dispose of his library to Pontois. Dee is traditionally said to have died at Mortlake in December 1608. However, Pontois, who as heir did receive Dee's library and ephemerides, added to the Maginus' Ephemeris for the date 26 March 1609 a death's head (a sign he used for other obituaries) and "Jno Δ." It is therefore likely that Dee died then, in Pontois's house in Bishopsgate Street in the city of London.

The epithet Dee most cherished for himself was that of "philosopher," though an epithet which he attracted — and detested — during his life was that of "conjurer." This latter was to prove durable, helped no doubt by Meric Casaubon's publication in 1659 of Dee's notes on the angelic conferences under the title *A True and Faithful Relation of What Passed for Many Years between Dr. John Dee (a Mathematician of Great Fame in Queen Elizabeth and King James Their Reigns) and Some Spirits.* The degradation of his reputation was perhaps completed in William Godwin's *Lives of the Necromancers* (1834) and only partially restored by the *Dictionary of National Biography* and with Charlotte Fell-Smith's 1909 biography. Both James Orchard Halliwell and Montague

Rhodes James perceived his significance as a collector of manuscripts; but his rehabilitation began in earnest with Eva Germaine Rimington Taylor, who in 1930 recognized Dee's importance as a teacher of navigation. While Dee is still, unfortunately, prey to the enthusiasm and ignorance of occultists, his stature as a Renaissance scholar has grown with the publication of several full-length books and numerous articles.

Biographies:

Charlotte Fell-Smith, *John Dee (1527–1608)* (London: Constable, 1909);

Peter J. French, *John Dee: The World of an Elizabethan Magus* (London: Routledge & Kegan Paul, 1972).

References:

Nicholas H. Clulee, "At the Crossroads of Magic and Science: John Dee's Archemastrie," in *Occult and Scientific Mentalities in the Renaissance,* edited by Brian Vickers (Cambridge: Cambridge University Press, 1984), pp. 57–71;

Clulee, *John Dee's Natural Philosophy: Between Science and Religion* (London & New York: Routledge, 1988);

Montague Rhodes James, ed., *List of Manuscripts Formerly Owned by Dr. John Dee* (London: Bibliographical Society, 1921);

John D. North, "The Western Calendar; 12. John Dee as an Historian," in *Gregorian Reform of the Calendar,* edited by George V. Coyne, M. A. Hoskins, and Olaf Pedersen (Vatican City, 1983), pp. 102–104;

Julian Roberts, "John Dee and the Matter of Britain," *Transactions of the Honourable Society of Cymmrodorion* (1991): 129–143;

Roberts and Andrew G. Watson, eds., *John Dee's Library Catalogue* (London: Bibliographical Society, 1990);

Eva Germaine Rimington Taylor, *Tudor Geography, 1485–1583* (London: Methuen, 1930), pp. 75–139;

Gwyn A. Williams, *Madoc: The Making of a Myth* (London: Eyre Methuen, 1979), pp. 31–67;

Williams, *Welsh Wizard and British Empire: Dr. John Dee and a Welsh Identity* (Cardiff: University College Cardiff Press, 1980);

Frances A. Yates, *The Occult Philosophy in the Elizabethan Age* (London: Routledge & Kegan Paul, 1979), pp. 79–108;

Yates, *The Rosicrucian Enlightenment* (London & Boston: Routledge & Kegan Paul, 1972), pp. 30–40;

Yates, *Theatre of the World* (London: Routledge & Kegan Paul, 1969), pp. 1–41.

Robert Devereux,
Second Earl of Essex

(10 November 1565 – 25 February 1601)

Edward Doughtie
Rice University

BOOKS: *To Maister Anthonie Bacon: An Apologie of the Earle of Essex, Against Those which Falsly Taxe Him to Be the Onely Hinderer of the Peace, of His Countrey* (N.p., n.d. [London?: Printed for John Smethwick?, 1600?]);

The Passion of a Discontented Minde, anonymous (London: Printed by V[alentine] S[ims] for John Smethwick, 1601);

Profitable Instructions; Describing What Speciall Observations Are to Be Taken by Travellers in All Nations, by Robert, Late Earle of Essex. Sir Philip Sidney. And, Secretary [William] Davison (London: Printed [by John Beale?] for Benjamin Fisher, 1633);

The Earle of Essex His Letter to the Earle of Sovthampton in the Time of His Troubles (London: Printed by Luke Norton for T. Thomson, 1642).

Edition: *The Poems of Edward DeVere, Seventeenth Earl of Oxford, and of Robert Devereux, Second Earl of Essex,* edited by Steven W. May, in *Studies in Philology,* Texts and Studies, 77 (Winter 1980): 43–64.

Robert Devereux, Earl of Essex (National Portrait Gallery, London)

Although Robert Devereux, second Earl of Essex, did not write a tragedy, he lived one. Born with little wealth but with great gifts and opportunities, he lost all when his faults conspired with his fortunes and his enemies. Before his abortive rebellion against Queen Elizabeth, his followers arranged for William Shakespeare's company to inspire them with a performance of *Richard II;* later writers perceived the tragic potential of Essex's own story and told it in fiction, in drama, and in opera. During his life Essex cast himself in several roles, one being a poet; but, like the roles, his writing always had a practical intent. The dozen or so poems attributed to him were occasional and written for a small courtly coterie. His other writings include propaganda, strategy papers, and letters, including many to the queen. Essex not only wrote himself but was also the cause of writing by others: some made flattering allusions to Essex before his troubles, several sought him as a patron, and many mourned his death.

Essex was born on 10 November 1565 to Walter Devereux and Lettice Knollys Devereux. Walter was created first earl of Essex in 1572, but despite the title he had little land and many debts. He died in Dublin in 1576 during an unsuccessful campaign to control land granted to him, leaving even more debts to his son, who would later find Ireland to be uncooperative with his own ambitions. In 1578 Essex's mother married the powerful Robert Dudley, Earl of Leicester, provoking a fit of rage in the queen. In the meantime young Essex had been attending Trinity College, Cambridge, receiving his M.A. in 1581. He had grown into a tall, handsome, and charming young man. Leicester took him to court in 1584 to help repair his fading influence, though he had little success; he then gave Essex a taste of military life in a campaign against the Spanish in the Netherlands in 1585. Essex went further into debt to equip a private troop of over two thousand followers for this campaign. In 1586 he fought bravely at Zutphen with Sir Philip Sidney, who had celebrated Essex's sister Penelope as the "Stella" of his sonnets, and who, on his deathbed, gave Essex his sword. A few years later, in 1590, Essex was to complete this symbolic assumption of Sidney's role as Protestant hero by marrying his widow, Frances Walsingham.

When Essex returned from the Netherlands, he found the court agog over the plot of Sir Anthony Babington to kill the queen and enthrone Mary, Queen of Scots. After much ambivalence Queen Elizabeth acquiesced to the execution of Mary in February 1587. Perhaps as relief from the stress of this episode, the queen allowed herself to be amused and then captivated by the lively Essex. They spent much time together all that spring, and in June she gave him the first of many offices and favors, mastership of the queen's horse. They also had the first of many quarrels over Essex's real or perceived rivals, in this case Sir Walter Ralegh. Essex reacted in a manner which was to become typical: he fled the court. The queen's messenger caught him as he was about to take ship for the Netherlands and a possible romantic death in battle.

The armada threat of the next year was more serious, but when the defense forces assembled at Tilbury, Essex provided an extravagant display of a personal troop uniformed in orange and white. Since the armada was destroyed at sea, Essex saw no action; but he was soon admitted to the Order of the Garter, wearing the insignia left him by Leicester, who died a month after the Spanish defeat. The weakness of the Spaniards encouraged the English to mount an expedition in support of Don Antonio, pretender to the throne of Portugal, in the spring of 1589. Essex infuriated the queen by joining this force without her permission. One of the first to land, he later issued a challenge to single combat to any Spaniard in Lisbon. This chivalrous gesture got no response, but it stuck in the popular memory. His return was celebrated in a poem by George Peele, *An Eclogue Gratulatory . . . to the Right Honorable and Renowned Shepheard of Albion's Arcadia: Robert, Earl of Essex and Ewe, for His Welcome into England from Portugal* (1589). (Peele went on to celebrate Essex's participation in the Accession Day tilts of 1590 and 1595 in *Polyhymn* and "Anglorum Feriae.")

Essex survived the queen's displeasure over the Portuguese escapade and over his marriage, and he even won from her a lucrative monopoly for the duties on sweet wines. The rivalry with Ralegh around this time seems to have produced the first of Essex's surviving poems. Ralegh had written some verses commending Edmund Spenser's *Faerie Queene*, the latter being published in 1590 and including a dedicatory sonnet to Essex. Essex seems to allude to Ralegh's verses in his obscure "Muses no more," in which he attacks their author as "filthy water" (with a pun on "Walter"). Another occasion about a year later reveals how Essex presented his verses to the queen: his secretary, Sir Henry Wotton, recalled that when Essex feared that the earl of Southampton was ascending to favor, he "chose to evaporate his thoughts in a sonnet (being his common way) to be sung before the queen . . . by one Hales, in whose voice she took some pleasure." Robert Hales was a royal musician for many years and published a song in Robert Dowland's *Musical Banquet* (1610). Two other poems by Essex were published with musical settings in this collection; moreover, John Dowland set to music two poems probably by Essex, plus part of another ascribed on good evidence to him, which suggests that Essex may be the author of some of the other anonymous texts in the songbooks of the period.

The next favor Essex begged and obtained from the queen was his first command, as leader of an English army on an expedition to help the then-Protestant king Henry IV of France. In August 1591 he set off with a force that included the poets Thomas Campion and Barnabe Barnes among its "gentleman adventurers." Essex was soon frustrated by the cagey manipulations of the French king while his own army dwindled from disease, his brother Walter was killed, and the queen complained. He was recalled to England in early October, but not before knighting two dozen of his followers despite instructions to give few honors. He responded to the queen's criticism with sulking withdrawal and depression. Essex was sent back to France by 18 October, where he participated in the siege of Rouen; he was recalled again in November and finally sent back once more. Once, when action was slow, he sent a challenge to single combat to the

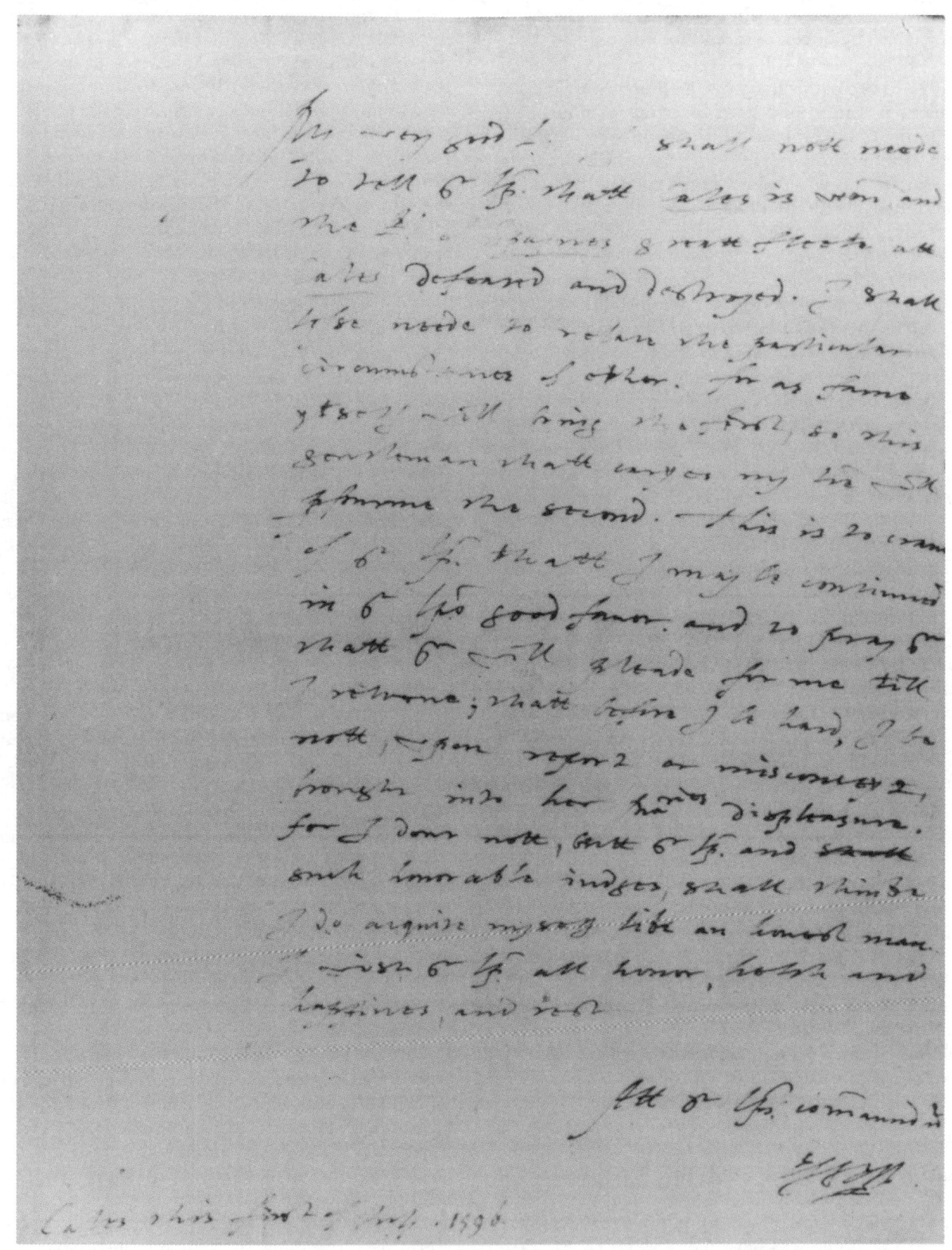

Letter from Essex to William Cecil, Lord Burghley, after Essex's military success at Cadiz (British Library)

governor of Rouen; again his chivalry was declined, and again the queen ordered him home.

Soon after he returned from France in January 1592, Essex came to know Anthony and Francis Bacon. Anthony had been living abroad and contributing to Sir Francis Walsingham's spy network; he was recruited by Essex to organize foreign intelligence. Francis was trained in the law and had sat in Parliament. With their help Essex began to cultivate the civilian side of his political career, though he preferred the military. Essex lacked some of the guile thought necessary to be an effective courtier: he had the reputation for wearing his hate and love on his brow. But he began to show seriousness and industry, his reports were valuable, and he had influence in the new Parliament. The queen soon recognized these developments and named him to the Privy Council. Moreover, the recent disgrace of Ralegh over his marriage to the queen's maid of honor, Elizabeth Throgmorton, had caused a shift in factional power, and Elizabeth may have wanted to raise Essex to balance the power of William Cecil, Baron Burghley, her lord treasurer and longtime adviser, and his ambitious son, Robert Cecil. Around this time Essex showed that he could be a generous friend in his persistent (but ineffective) efforts to get a post for Francis Bacon and that he could be a cruel and paranoid enemy in his persecution of the queen's Jewish physician, Dr. Lopez, whom Essex suspected of plotting to poison her.

Francis Bacon continued to help Essex with courtiership, as in a 1595 entertainment, or "device," for the celebration of Elizabeth's accession. Bacon is credited with the first part, in which a hermit, a secretary, and a soldier – representing the attractions of contemplation, statecraft, and the military – are shown to vie for the earl's attention. Essex is the author of another device for the occasion, in which the queen is presented with a blind Indian prince who, according to a verse prophecy beginning "Seated between the old world and the new," can be healed only by the queen. The prince recovers his sight – possibly to the accompaniment of John Dowland's song "Behold a wonder here" – and turns out to be Cupid, who now can cause his followers to "love and be wise."

But Cupid had soon to give way to Mars. To forestall another armada, the English, with one squadron under Essex, attacked the Spanish port of Cadiz on 22 June 1596. Ralegh led another squadron, and John Donne was among the gentleman adventurers. Luck was with the raiders; Essex acted with his usual flair and gallantry, personally leading his troops in dangerous but effective sallies. The English captured and sacked the city, showing remarkable mercy to the inhabitants, but the Spanish deprived them of considerable plunder by setting fire to their own ships. Essex created sixty-eight new knights, which would displease the queen, as would the relative lack of booty. Essex wanted to remain in Cadiz but was overruled; he then suggested intercepting the Spanish treasure fleet, but the other commanders insisted on returning to England. He was vindicated when it was learned that the English sailed by Lisbon two days before the treasure fleet arrived.

In the meantime Essex had written an account of the capture of Cadiz which he sent to England to be printed under a pseudonym. But his messenger betrayed him to the queen, who prohibited the account's publication, though Anthony Bacon managed to circulate a few copies in manuscript, none of which seem to have survived. Another document from this time that did survive, thirty-two pages in Essex's own hand, presents a larger view of his strategy for dealing with Spain; it is thoughtful and original, but it seems not to have been finished. In January 1597 Essex wrote on more general matters in a letter of advice on manners, education, and conduct addressed to the young earl of Rutland; it was printed in 1633 as *Profitable Instructions*.

The Cadiz expedition was a popular success, as Spenser's allusion to Essex in his *Prothalamion* (1596) testifies, but during Essex's absence Cecil was made principal secretary. Essex's next expedition was a disaster. The "Islands Voyage" of 1597 to strike at the second armada and intercept the treasure fleet in the Azores was doomed by bad weather, quarrels between Essex and Ralegh, and missed opportunities. (John Donne, present on this voyage too, recorded some of his impressions in "The Storm" and "The Calm.") They returned after much expense and little profit. When they reached Plymouth on 26 October 1597, they found the country in fear of Spanish invasion. Fortunately, the Spanish fleet was destroyed by a storm, but the queen was still highly critical of Essex's conduct. He returned from the trials of the voyage to face not only criticism, but worse: the elevation of Adm. Charles Howard of Effingham, who had stayed home, to the earldom of Nottingham and hence to a step ahead of Essex in precedence. Once again Essex withdrew from court to sulk. Eventually he was persuaded to return to see to his interests, and the queen heard a more favorable account of the voyage from Sir Francis Vere. Essex was then appointed earl marshal, both as a reward for leading the Islands Voyage and to placate him for losing precedence to Howard.

HIC TVVS ILLE COMES CENEROSA ESSEXIA NOSTRIS
QVEM QVAM GAVDEMVS REBVS ADESSE DVCEM

Essex in 1600 (engraving by Robert Boissard)

Essex's poem "Change thy mind since she doth change," which dates from this time, may refer to his unhappiness with the queen over these issues.

Around this time Essex composed a long discourse in the form of a letter to Anthony Bacon. It was circulated in manuscript and printed in 1600 – to his embarrassment at the time – as *An Apology of the Earl of Essex*. In it Essex defended his previous military expeditions and answered anonymous charges that he preferred war to peace. The problem was not that he liked war – he reminded his reader that he had lost a brother and spent much of his substance in the service of his country – but that the Spanish could not be trusted to keep the peace. He praised men of action, perhaps implying criticism of civilians such as the Cecils. That Essex was still popular as a military hero is suggested by the publication of a selection from George Chapman's translation of the *Iliad* in the spring of 1598 dedicated to him; the portions translated clearly reinforced a favorable parallel between Essex and Achilles.

In the meantime the situation in Ireland was deteriorating. At a Privy Council meeting on 1 July 1598 Essex proposed Sir George Carew, one of the Cecil faction, to be lord deputy of Ireland. It was so transparent a ruse to get an opponent into a difficult spot that the queen dismissed the suggestion. In the heat of argument Essex turned his back on the queen, who gave him a box on the ear. Essex protested with his hand on his sword. This was a serious breach. In answering Sir Thomas Egerton's attempt at reconciliation, Essex made further difficulties by writing "What, cannot princes err? Cannot subjects receive wrong? Is an earthly power or authority infinite?" This challenge to the queen's divine authority would be remembered at his later trials.

While various efforts were being made to reconcile Essex and the queen, a massacre of English forces in Ireland on 14 August loosed a rash of attacks on the English colonials, including Spenser. Military action was needed, and Essex, unsatisfied with those proposed to lead the English forces, felt

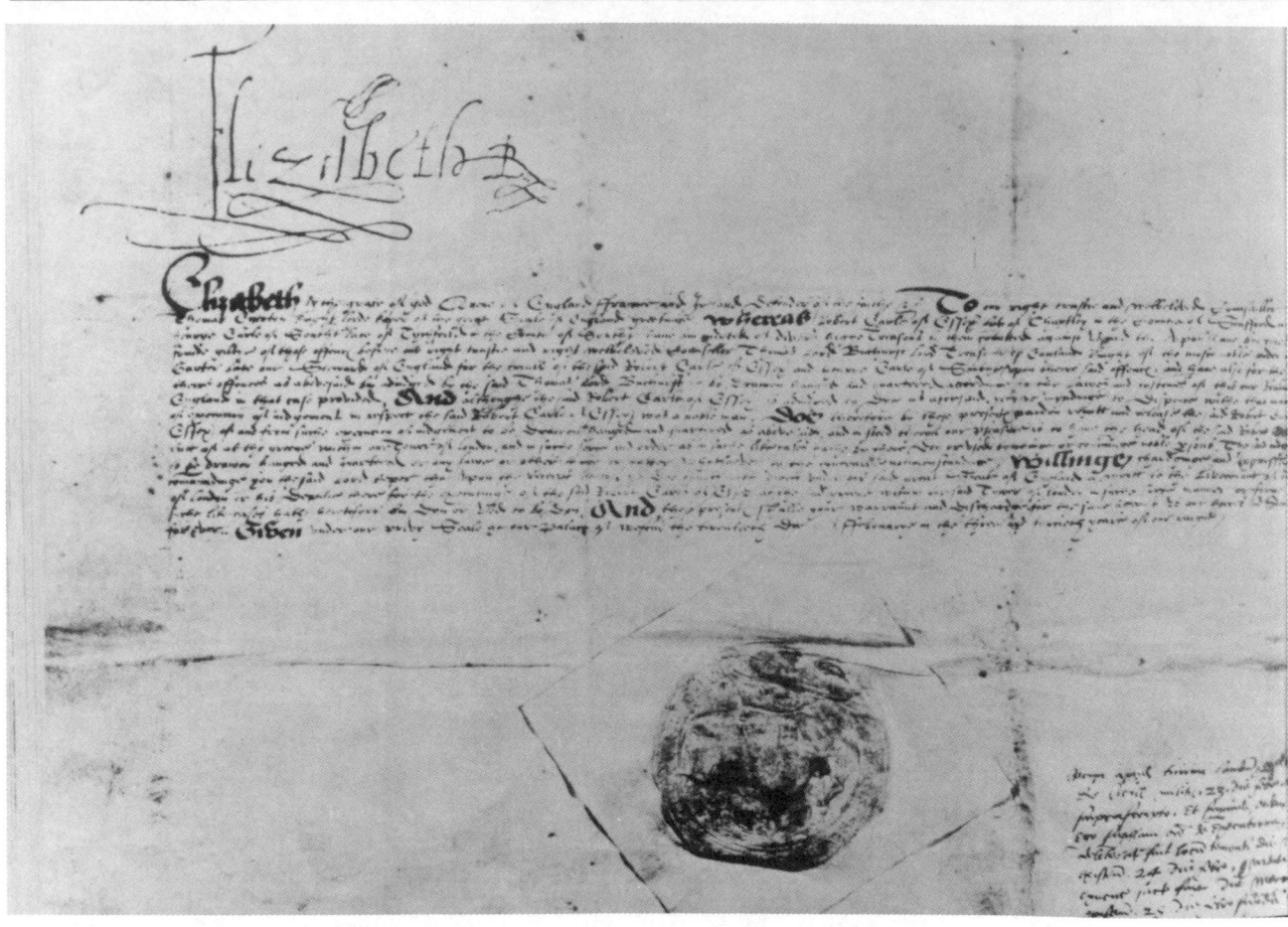

Essex's death warrant (Collection of the Duke of Sutherland)

constrained to take the job. Although he realized the dangers of such an expedition, he saw no alternative and set out accompanied by popular acclaim like that voiced by Shakespeare in *Henry V* (V.i.30–34). He landed his force in Dublin in April 1599. The campaign which followed was frustrating: the Irish were shrewd guerrilla fighters, and Essex wandered over Ireland to little effect while his army suffered as much from sickness as from combat. He created over eighty knights, once more against instructions. Finally, on 3 September 1599 he confronted the rebel leader, Hugh O'Neil, Earl of Tyrone, and his army, now twice the size of Essex's. After some bravery and challenges a parley was arranged, Essex and Tyrone met alone, and a truce was concluded on 8 September. But the queen refused the terms.

Essex felt he was being undermined at home, so he abandoned his command and made a desperate ride for England. He burst in on the queen unannounced on 28 September. The surprised queen received him cordially — and perhaps a bit fearfully — but the next day she questioned him

more critically and dismissed him. After conferring with the council, she placed him in the custody of the lord keeper, Sir Thomas Egerton. She eventually freed him but banished him from court. Although Essex received word that the queen wanted to correct but not ruin him, she let his monopoly on the duties for sweet wines lapse on 30 October 1600. For Essex, who despite having received nearly half of all the queen's patronage since 1591 was in debt at least forty thousand pounds, this was ruin. Retirement to rural poverty sometimes seemed attractive to Essex: a poem beginning "Happy were he could finish forth his fate / In some unhaunted desert most obscure" was written either at this time or possibly during one of the Irish campaign's many low points. But there were too many others with interest in his fortunes to allow him the luxury of retirement.

Essex's desperate situation; his natural tendency to look for the malice of others instead of mistakes of his own; and the support of his worst instincts by the hotheaded partisans around him such as Sir Gelly Meyrick and Henry Wriothesley, Earl

The execution of Essex, as depicted in a woodcut illustrating a popular ballad

of Southampton, eventually led him to attempt an insane coup. He imagined that his old enemies Ralegh and Henry Brooke, Baron Cobham, were going to murder him; he feared that Cecil was plotting to bring in Philip II's daughter Isabel, the infanta of Spain, as Elizabeth's successor. After much talk but little realistic planning, Essex and his followers, the earls of Southampton, Rutland, and Bedford, the lords Mounteagle and Cromwell, Sir Christopher Blount, Sir Charles Danvers, and some two hundred others set out on 8 February 1601 to raze the city and take over the court. Essex professed he never intended harm to the queen but wished to purge the court of her evil counselors and force recognition of James VI's claim to the succession. The popular rising upon which Essex was counting never materialized, and the rebels were soon forced to surrender. Essex defiantly maintained the justice of his cause through his trial. But then his chaplain, Abdie Ashton, managed to make him see his offenses in a new light, throwing him into an orgy of repentance. Essex wrote Southampton to be warned by his example and look to his soul. (This letter was printed several times in the 1640s.)

Between 21 and 24 February Essex also wrote a long penitential poem. It was printed anonymously in 1601 as *The Passion of a Discontented Mind* but is convincingly ascribed to Essex in two manuscript copies. It is conventional in many ways, but it indirectly reflects Essex's situation. Curiously, the speaker in the poem does not seem to expect to die immediately, though Essex had been sentenced to death. Ashton later wrote that the earl had thought he might be spared as Southampton was. Perhaps in this last work, as in his others, he hoped to persuade the queen that he was worthy of yet one more favor. This attitude may have given rise to the legend that Elizabeth had given Essex a ring which he need only show her to be saved from any trouble. Supposedly Essex sent the ring to the queen, but it was intercepted by a cast-off mistress, who also told the queen that Essex was defiant and unrepentant. This story seems to have arisen a generation after the event and is not supported by any contemporary account. In any event, Essex lay piously before the block on 25 February 1601.

Essex's death produced a variety of reactions. Preachers of course took the official line and celebrated the deliverance of the queen from treason and rebellion. While some of the populace applauded these sentiments, others tried to murder the executioner. Still others mourned the loss of their hero from the safety of private manuscripts and in anonymous ballads such as "Essex's Last Good Night." A German visitor found people singing this ballad even at Elizabeth's court a year and a half after the execution and was shown significant places and trophies connected with the hero. Harleian MS 6910 contains a laudatory pastoral elegy of nearly eight hundred lines, "Verses upon the report of the death of the right Honorable the Lord of Essex," and Additional MS 15226 contains two poems put in the mouth of Ralegh, supposedly confessing his treachery toward Essex in the manner of *A Mirror for Magistrates*. John Ramsey, in his commonplace book, refers to Essex as "Of famous memory being the very Hercules, Achilles, or Julius Caesar of his time but most unfortunate."

After the succession of James admiration of Essex could be more open; Richard Williams addressed his poem "A Lamentable Motion or Mournful Remembrance for the Death of Robert Lord Devereux, Late Earl of Essex" to the king. Robert Prickett's poem *Honor's Fame in Triumph Riding; or, The Life and Death of the Late Honorable Earl of Essex* appeared in 1604 dedicated to Southampton and Mountjoy. Chapman, who had dedicated his *Iliad* to Essex, has the title character of *The Tragedy of Charles, Duke of Byron* (1608) compare his own "life and fortune" with that of Essex. But Samuel Daniel got in trouble over his *Tragedy of Philotas* (1605), which was read as an allegory of the Essex affair, and he later thought it wise to omit passages praising Essex from the 1609 edition of his *Civil Wars,* first published in 1595. Sir John Harington, the queen's godson and one of Essex's Irish knights, wrote epigrams boasting of Essex's approval of his translation of Ariosto and complaining that his execution showed a lack of pity; these were not published until after Harington's death in 1612.

Essex's story, without protective cover, became matter for fiction and drama in the later seventeenth century. Two French plays entitled *Le comte d'Essex*, one by La Calprenède (1639) and the other by Thomas Corneille (1678), adapted the material to suit the demands of heroic drama. A later French play, François Ancelot's *Elisabeth d'Angleterre* (1832), was the main source for Gaetano Donizetti's opera *Roberto Devereux* (1837). An anonymous novel, *The Secret History of the Most Renowned Queen Elizabeth and the Earl of Essex* (1680), was the source of John Banks's tragedy *The Unhappy Favourite* (1682), which in turn inspired James Ralph's *The Fall of the Earl of Essex* (1731) and plays by Henry Jones (1753) and Henry Brooke (1761), both tragedies titled *The Earl of Essex*. Lytton Strachey's *Elizabeth and Essex* (1928), a biography which uses fictional techniques

and is strongly colored by Freudian ideas, was the source of the most recent operatic treatment of the story, William Plomer's libretto for Benjamin Britten's *Gloriana* (1953).

Besides providing material for art, Essex supported the arts as a patron. He gave a group of players permission to use his name; they toured the provinces from 1581 until 1596. Over eighty books were dedicated to him, including the works by Peele, Chapman, and Spenser already mentioned and verse by Thomas Middleton and Joshua Sylvester and by such lesser lights as Thomas Churchyard, Henry Lok, John Phillips, and Maurice Kyffin. Robert Greene and Anthony Munday dedicated both original and translated fiction to Essex; Thomas Watson, his *Italian Madrigals Englished* (1590); and John Mundy, his *Songs and Psalms* (1594). Other books dedicated to Essex include Latin verse and prose, divinity, history, chivalry, several titles on warfare and fencing, agriculture, medicine, and navigation.

Essex's own writings were by-products of a busy life. As a poet, he did not have the originality and virtuosity of Sidney or the distinctive voice of Ralegh. He used the materials available to him — the sonnet, common lyric stanzas, familiar rhetorical structures such as anaphora and anadiplosis — to find a style that was fluent and unornamented but free from the rigidity and intrusive alliteration of his older contemporaries. His voice is heard most distinctly in his letters. Essex can be brusque and businesslike or gracious and graceful, with an easy command of the balance and rhythm of rhetorically sophisticated Elizabethan prose. In letters to the queen he can be flattering, whining, and occasionally eloquent. Before setting out to face Tyrone, he wrote on 30 August 1599, "From a mind delighting in sorrow; from spirits wasted with travail, care, and grief; from a heart torn in pieces with passion; from a man that hates himself and all things that keep him alive; what service can your majesty reap?" In his final disgrace Essex wrote bitterly and prophetically: "The prating tavern haunter speaks of me what he lists; they print me and make me speak to the world, and shortly they will play me upon the stage."

Letters:

Walter B. Devereux, *Lives and Letters of the Devereux, Earls of Essex,* 2 volumes (London: John Murray, 1853).

Biographies:

Lytton Strachey, *Elizabeth and Essex* (New York: Harcourt, Brace, 1928);

George Bagshaw Harrison, *The Life and Death of Robert Devereux, Earl of Essex* (New York: Holt, 1937);

Robert Lacey, *Robert, Earl of Essex* (New York: Atheneum, 1971).

References:

John Banks, *The Unhappy Favourite; or, The Earl of Essex,* edited by Thomas Marshall Howe Blair (New York: Columbia University Press, 1939);

Thomas Birch, *Memoirs of the Reign of Queen Elizabeth,* 2 volumes (London: Printed for A. Millar, 1754; facsimile, New York: AMS Press, 1970);

John Channing Briggs, "Chapman's *Seaven Bookes of the Iliades:* Mirror for Essex," *Studies in English Literature,* 21 (Winter 1981): 59–73;

Samuel Daniel, *The Tragedy of Philotas,* edited by Laurence Michel (New Haven: Yale University Press, 1949);

Edward Doughtie, "The Earl of Essex and Occasions for Contemplative Verse," *English Literary Renaissance,* 9 (Autumn 1979): 355–363;

Frederick James Furnivall and William Richard Morfill, eds., *Ballads from Manuscripts,* volume 2 (Hertford: Stephen Austin for the Ballad Society, 1873), pp. 217–259;

Ray Heffner, "Essex the Ideal Courtier," *English Literary History,* 1 (April 1934): 7–36;

L. W. Henry, "The Earl of Essex as Strategist and Military Organizer (1596-7)," *English Historical Review,* 68 (July 1953): 363–392;

Charles Hindley, ed., *The Roxburghe Ballads,* 2 volumes (London: Reeves & Turner, 1873), 1: 394–398, 2: 202–211;

Historical Manuscripts Commission, *Calendar of the Most Hon. the Manuscripts of the Marquis of Salisbury K.G. . . . Preserved at Hatfield House,* parts 1–24 (London, 1883–1976).

David H. Horne, *The Life and Minor Works of George Peele* (New Haven: Yale University Press, 1952), pp. 163–181, 224–275;

Mervyn James, *Society, Politics and Culture* (Cambridge: Cambridge University Press, 1986), pp. 416–465;

Beach Langston, "Essex and the Art of Dying," *Huntington Library Quarterly,* 13 (February 1950): 109–129;

Steven W. May, *The Elizabethan Courtier Poets* (Columbia: University of Missouri Press, 1991), pp. 103–139, 250–269;

Richard C. McCoy, *The Rites of Knighthood: The Literature and Politics of Elizabethan Chivalry* (Berkeley: University of California Press, 1989), pp. 79–102;

John Ernest Neale, *Queen Elizabeth I* (N.p., 1934; Garden City, N.Y.: Doubleday, 1957);

Lacey Baldwin Smith, *Treason in Tudor England* (London: Cape, 1986), pp. 192–276;

Lawrence Stone, *The Crisis of the Aristocracy, 1558–1641* (Oxford: Clarendon, 1965), pp. 481–488.

Papers:

A large collection of Robert Devereux's letters is at Hatfield House, Hertfordshire; other papers are among the Hulton Papers on loan to the British Library; at Longleat House, Wiltshire; in the Public Record Office in London, and in the Folger Shakespeare Library in Washington, D.C.

Thomas Digges

(circa 1546 – 24 August 1595)

William H. Sherman
University of Maryland at College Park

BOOKS: *Alæ seu scalæ mathematicæ, quibus visibilium remotissima cœlorum theatra conscendi, & planetarum omnium itinera nouis & inauditis methodis explorari: Tùm huius portentosi syderis in mundi boreali plaga insolito fulgore coruscantis, distantia, & magnitudo immensa, Situsque: Protinùs tremendus indagari, Deique: Stupendum ostentum, Terricolis expositum cognosci liquidissimè prossit* (London: Printed by Thomas Marsh, 1573) – includes "Parallaticae commentationis praxeosq; nucleus quidam," by John Dee (London: Printed by John Day, 1573);

A Briefe Report of the Militarie Services Done in the Low Covntries, by the Erle of Leicester: Written by One That Serued in Good Place There in a Letter to a Friend of His (London: Printed by Arnold Hatfield for Gregorie Seton, 1587);

Instruction of the Officers of the Musters of the Men of Warre: Practised in the Englishe Army, sinse the First of Februarij. anno Elizabethae. 27 (Leyden: Printed [by Andries Verschout?] for Thomas Basson, 1587);

A Briefe and True Report of the Proceedings of the Earle of Leycester for the Reliefe of the Towne of Sluce, from His Arriuall at Vlisshing, about the End of Iune 1587. vntill the Surrendrie There of 26 Iulij Next Ensuing. Whereby It Shall Plainelie Appeare His Excellencie Was Not in Anie Fault for the Losse of That Towne (London: Printed by Thomas Orwin, 1590);

Hvmble Motives for Association to Maintaine Religion Established: Published as an Antidote against the Pestilent Treatises of Secular Priests, attributed to Digges (London, 1601);

Foure Paradoxes, or Politique Discourses: 2 Concerning Militarie Discipline, Written Long Since by Thomas Digges, 2 of the Worthinesse of Warre and Warriors, by Dudley Digges, His Sonne (London: Printed by Humphrey Lownes for Clement Knight, 1604);

Nova corpora regvlaria: Sev, quinqve corporvm regvlarium simplicium, in quinque alia regularia composita, metamorphosis. Inventa ante annos 60 à Thoma Diggseio armigero, jam, problematibus additis nonnuillis, demonstrata à nepote (London: Printed by Thomas Harper, 1634);

Englands Defence: A Treatise Concerning Invasion; or, A Brief Discourse of What Orders Were Best for Repulsing of Forraine Forces, If at Any Time They Should Invade Us by Sea in Kent, or Elsewhere. Exhibited in Writing to the Right Honourable Robert Dudley Earl of Leicester, a Little before the Spanish Invasion, in the Year 1588 (London: Printed for F. Haley, 1680).

OTHER: Leonard Digges, *A Geometrical Practise, Named Pantometria, Diuided into Three Bookes, Longimetra, Planimetra, and Stereometria, Containing Rules Manifolde for Mensuration of All Lines, Superficies and Solides: With Sundrie Straunge Conculsions Both by Instrument and without, and also by Perspectiue Glasses, to Set Forth the True Description or Exact Plat of an Whole Region: Framed by Leonard Digges . . . Lately Finished by Thomas Digges His Sonne. Who Hathe also Thereunto Adioyned a Mathematicall Treatise of the Five Regulare Platonicall Bodies, and Their Metmorphosis of Transformation into Five Other Equilater vniforme Solides Geometricall,* edited by Thomas Digges (London: Printed by Henry Bynneman, 1571); revised as *A Geometrical Practical Treatise Named Pantometria, Diuided into Three Bookes, Longimetra, Planimetra, and Stereometria, Containing Rules Manifolde for Mensuration of All Lines, Superficies and Solides: With Sundrie Strange Conclusions Both by Instrument and without, and also by Glasses to Set Forth the True Description or Exact Platte of an Whole Region. First Published by Thomas Digges . . . With a Mathematicall Discourse of the Fiue Regular Platonicall Solides, and Their Metamorphosis into Other Fiue Compound Rare Geometricall Bodyes, Conteyning an Hundred Newe Theorems at Least of His Owne Inuention, Neuer Mentioned Before by Anye Other Geometrician. Lately Reviewed by the Avthor Himselfe, and Augmented with Sundrie Addi-*

tions, Diffinitions, Problemes and Rare Theoremes (London: Printed by Abel Jeffes, 1591);

"A Perfit Description of the Caelestiall Orbes according to the Most Aunciente Doctrine of the Phythagoreans, Latelye Reuiued by Copernicus and by Geometricall Demonstrations Approued," in *A Prognostication Euerlasting,* by Leonard Digges, edited by Thomas Digges (London: Printed by Thomas Marsh, 1576; facsimile, Amsterdam: Theatrum Orbis Terrarum / New York: Da Capo, 1975);

Leonard Digges, *An Arithmeticall Militare Treatise, Named Stratioticos: Compendiously Teaching the Science of Numbers, as Well in Fractions as Integers, and so Much of the Rules and Equations Algebricall and Arte of Numbers Cossicall, as Are Requisite for the Profession of a Soldiour. Together with the Moderne Militare Discipline, Offices, Lawes and Dueties in Euery Wel Gouerned Campe and Armie to Be Obserued: Long since Attempted by Leonard Digges Gentleman, Augmented, Digested, and Lately Finished,* edited by Thomas Digges (London: Printed by Henry Bynneman, 1579; revised edition, London: Printed by Richard Field, 1590; facsimile, Amsterdam: Theatrum Orbis Terrarum / New York: Da Capo, 1968).

Thomas Digges was, perhaps, Elizabethan England's most important producer of scientific texts. For his mathematical and astronomical learning, he deserves to be set alongside John Dee and Thomas Harriot. But in terms of his success in reaching popular as well as learned audiences and in preaching a modernized cosmology and scientific method, he is in a class of his own. Above all, his multifaceted career exemplifies the humanist belief that scholarly theory must be applied in civic practice: his educational preparations were followed by activities in the world of print as an editor and author, and in the government as an engineer, member of Parliament, and military officer.

Digges was born in Kent around 1546, the only child of Leonard Digges – whose ancestors included judges, members of Parliament, and justices of the peace – and Bridget Wilford Digges. He later recalled that his earliest years, "even from my cradle," were devoted to "the sciences liberal, and especially in searching the most difficult and curious demonstrations mathematical." When his father died in 1559, the responsibility for Digges's upbringing fell into the capable hands of Dee, whom Digges called his "parente altero" (second parent) in science. For his part, Dee considered Digges "carissimus mihi juvenis, mathematicusque meus dig-

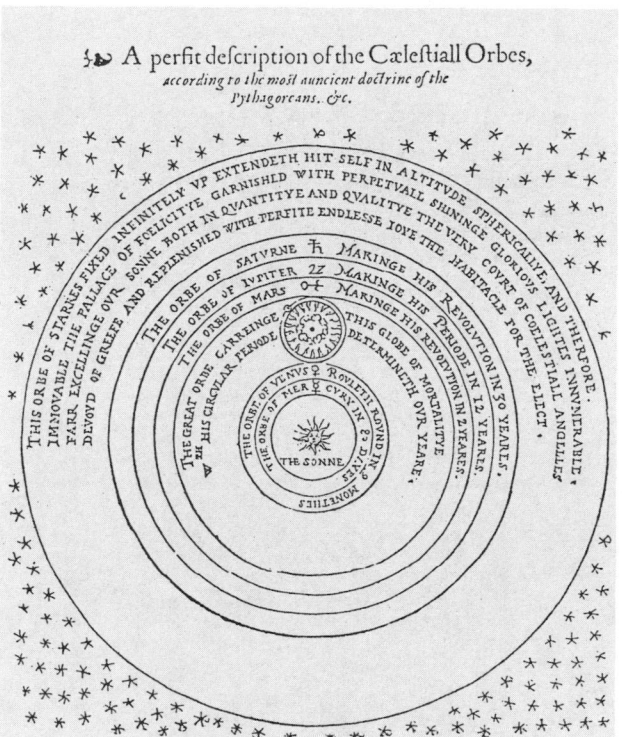

Thomas Digges's diagram of the Copernican conception of the universe, from Digges's edition of his father's A Prognostication Everlasting

nissimus haeres" (a young man very dear to me, and my most worthy mathematical heir). These "filial" experiences, which are all that is known of Digges's formal education, shaped his career in two significant ways. First, his entry into the world of publishing came by way of editions of the works of his mentors. Second, the pragmatism that distinguished his own writings and actions was something of a reaction against his theoretical apprenticeship: "After I grew to years of riper judgment, I have wholly bent myself to reduce those imaginative contemplations to sensible practical conclusions . . . [so] to be able, when time is, to employ them to the service of my prince and country."

In 1571 Digges published Leonard Digges's *Pantometria,* an introductory geometry textbook. In the dedicatory epistle he claims only a modest editorial role. Before his death, his father had prepared the text and dedicated it to his friend, Lord Keeper of the Great Seal Nicholas Bacon; it was left to Thomas to rediscover the volume and to bring it before Bacon and a wider audience. Yet in his emendations his own practical program is already in evidence. He asks Bacon to accept the discourses as "profitable fruits serving most commodiously to sundry necessary uses in a public weal," and his

¶ An Arithmeticall Militare Treatife, named
STRATIOTICOS:
Compendioufly teaching the Science of Nūbers,
as vvell in Fractions as Integers, and fo much of the Ru-
les and Æquations Algebraicall and Arte of Numbers
Cofsicall, as are requifite for the Profeffion of a Soldiour.

Together with the Moderne Militare Difcipline, Offices, Lawes and
Dueties in euery wel gouerned Campe and Armie to be obferued :
Long fince attēpted by LEONARD DIGGES Gentleman,
Augmented, digefted, and lately finifhed, by
THOMAS DIGGES, his Sonne.

VVhereto he hath alfo adioyned certaine Queftions of great Ordinaunce,
refolued in his other Treatize of Pyrotechny *and great*
Artillerie, hereafter to bee publifhed.

VIVET POST FVNERA VIRTVS.

AT LONDON:
Printed by Henrie Bynneman.
Anno Domini. 1579.

Title page for Digges's revised and enlarged edition of his
father's work on the use of mathematics in warfare

preface – like Dee's preface to the English translation of Euclid's work of 1570 – defends geometry
on the grounds of its utility in disciplines such as architecture and topography.

In Agnes St. Leger, Digges found a wife whose
family had considerable power in Ireland and Wales.
Aside from two children who died young, she bore
two daughters and two sons, the eldest of whom –
Dudley – achieved a scholarly and political prominence to rival his father's. By 1572 the time had come
for Digges to employ his skills in the service of the
state: that year, under the patronage of Robert Dudley, Earl of Leicester, he represented Wallingford in
Parliament. Although he was only twenty-six he took
an active role, participating in the debates concerning
Mary, Queen of Scots, and supporting a bill to reform
the apparel of ministers.

The year 1572 also presented an opportunity
for a collaborative publication with his other "father." In November a supernova appeared in the
constellation Cassiopeia, generating speculation
and interpretation throughout the courts of Europe. Digges sent a letter to William Cecil, Lord
Burghley, explaining the significance of the star for
the government's fortunes, and in 1573 he brought
out a volume outlining the impact of the phenome-
non on the old Aristotelian cosmology. This work,
Alae seu Scalae Mathematicae, contained Digges's text
of that title and Dee's brief treatise on stellar paral-
lax. The book brought both mathematicians international renown, and Digges's ideas, in particular,
made a deep impression on the leading astronomer
Tycho Brahe.

In 1576 Digges brought out a new edition of
his father's *A Prognostication Everlasting,* originally
published in 1555. The title page declares that this
almanac, which would aid prediction not only of
the weather but also of "plenty, lack, sickness,
dearth, wars, etc.," was finished by Leonard Digges
and "lately corrected and augmented by Thomas
Digges, his son." This augmentation includes an
epistle to the lord high admiral and another defense
"against the reprovers of astronomy and science
mathematical." More important, Digges added his
own "Perfect Description of the Celestial Orbs."
This short appendix established him as England's
principal advocate of the Copernican cosmology. Its
centerpiece, a diagram deceptive in its simplicity, is
the first known image in an English book of the heliocentric universe, and it reveals Digges as the first
modern astronomer to portray an infinite universe.
According to Francis R. Johnson, it is a graphic
illustration of how Digges "broke completely with
the older cosmologies by shattering the finite outer
wall of the universe." *A Prognostication Everlasting* was
extremely popular, going through six editions – all
of which contained "A Perfect Description of the
Celestial Orbs" – in Digges's lifetime.

Digges knew that his conclusions would meet
with both resistance and incomprehension. Therefore, he not only backed them up with a translation
of the relevant sections of Nicolaus Copernicus's *De
Revolutionibus* (1543) but also carefully introduced
them with some masterful rhetoric: "because the
world hath so long a time been carried with an opinion of the earth's stability, as the contrary cannot but
be now very impersuasible, I have thought good out
of Copernicus also to give a taste of the reasons philosophical alleged for the earth's instability, and their
solutions, that such as are not able with geometrical
eyes to behold the secret perfection of Copernicus'
theory, may yet by these familiar, natural reasons be
induced to search farther and not rashly to condemn
for fantastical, so ancient doctrine revived, and by Copernicus so demonstratively approved." The ensuing
renditions are quite liberal but are generally admired
both for their accuracy and for their accessibility to
England's less learned readers.

After a brief stint as a consultant engineer on the works at Winchelsea Harbor, Digges published in 1579 the last of his filial editions. *Stratioticos,* which aimed to teach the "science of numbers," was, according to the title page, "long since attempted by Leonard Digges" and "augmented, digested, and lately finished" by Thomas. The military inflection of the whole work, not just of the additional material, suggests that the younger Digges actively shaped, rather than merely edited, the text. The title advertises "an arithmetical military treatise," but the military all but overwhelms the arithmetical. While the first book is a straightforward introduction to integers and fractions, the second moves steadily into military questions, and the third deals exclusively with "military offices, laws, stratagems, etc." *Stratioticos* is, then, Thomas Digges's work. Accordingly, it begins with a dedication to his patron, the earl of Leicester, and a rehearsal of his other writings, both finished and unfinished.

The most striking feature of *Stratioticos* is what might be called Digges's military humanism. He constantly refers to classical texts and expresses his preference for the "ancient Roman discipline for the wars." This preference is the subject of one of the "paradoxes" published in 1604 by his son Dudley: "that the antique Roman and Grecian discipline martial doth far exceed in excellency our modern." The margins of *Stratioticos* are littered with classical examples supporting his precepts, such as "Scipio against Hannibal" or "Jugurtha in Africa against the Romans." At the beginning of the text he provides an unequivocal statement of his humanist imperative: "as in all other arts and sciences we aid ourselves with precedents from antiquity, so in this art of discipline military, so corrupted, or rather utterly extinguished, we should repair to those fountains of perfection and accommodate them to the service of our time." He remained at this stage in his career what those with more experience called a "book soldier."

After serving as supervisor of the works at Dover Harbor during the early 1580s Digges returned to the House of Commons in 1584–1585, when he sat for Southampton and delivered strong speeches on the Oath of Association and the bill against the Jesuits. For almost a decade following 1586 he acted as muster-master general of the forces in the Low Countries under the command of the earl of Leicester. This experience generated a series of works in the late 1580s and early 1590s. In 1587 a press in Leiden published a set of his instructions for his subordinate mustermasters. In the same year appeared his apology for Leicester's leadership, which was to be the subject of another tract in 1590. In 1588 Digges's focus shifted to the coasts of England and the threat posed by the Spanish Armada. That year he presented Leicester with a contingency plan to deal with a coastal invasion; it was published in 1680 as *England's Defence.* In 1590 and 1591 his final works, revised editions of *Stratioticos* and *Pantometria,* appeared. They are clearly the products of years in the field, and they incorporate the first serious studies of ballistics in England.

Digges's career wove together scholarly and political strands and progressed from mathematical theory to military practice. In the extent to which he combined scientific innovation, political commitment, and military service, Digges had no Elizabethan peer. His flexible and forceful voice, which can be heard in so many important contexts, deserves more modern auditors.

References:

Patrick Collinson, "The Monarchical Republic of Queen Elizabeth I," *Bulletin of the John Rylands Library,* 69 (Spring 1987): 394–424;

Collinson, "Puritans, Men of Business and Elizabethan Parliaments," *Parliamentary History,* 7 (1988): 187–211;

C. G. Cruickshank, *Elizabeth's Army,* second edition (Oxford: Clarendon Press, 1966);

S. K. Heninger, Jr., *The Cosmographical Glass: Renaissance Diagrams of the Universe* (San Marino, Cal.: Huntington Library, 1977);

Francis R. Johnson, *Astronomical Thought in Renaissance England: A Study of the English Scientific Writings from 1500 to 1645* (Baltimore: Johns Hopkins University Press, 1937);

Johnson and Sanford V. Larkey, "Thomas Digges, the Copernican System, and the Idea of the Infinity of the Universe in 1576," *Huntington Library Bulletin,* no. 5 (April 1934): 69–117;

A. Koyre, *From Closed World to Infinite Universe* (Baltimore: Johns Hopkins University Press, 1957);

Eleanor Rosenberg, *Leicester, Patron of Letters* (New York: Columbia University Press, 1955);

E. G. R. Taylor, *Mathematical Practitioners of Tudor and Stuart England* (Cambridge: Cambridge University Press, 1954);

Henry J. Webb, *Elizabethan Military Science: The Books and the Practice* (Madison: University of Wisconsin Press, 1965).

Papers:

Many of Thomas Digges's manuscript letters, speeches, and treatises are in the British Library and in the State Papers (Domestic and Foreign) at the Public Record Office, London.

Sir Edward Dyer

(October 1543 – May 1607)

Steven W. May
Georgetown College

WORKS: "The Songe in the Oke," in *The Queenes Maiesties Entertainment at Woodstocke* (London: Printed for Thomas Cadman, 1585), sig. C2–C3;

"Another of the Same. Excellently written by a most woorthy Gentleman [elegy on the death of Sir Philip Sidney]," "Alas, my hart," "As rare to heare," "Divide my times," in *The Phoenix Nest*, edited by R. S. (London: Printed by John Jackson, 1593), pp. 10–11, 61, 75, 88;

"Prometheus," "Alas, my hart," in *Englands Helicon*, edited by Nicholas Ling (London: Printed by James Roberts, 1600), sig. Bb 2a, L2 ab;

"The lowest trees haue topps," in *A Poetical Rapsody*, edited by Francis Davison (London: Printed by Valentine Simmes for John Baily, 1602);

"Hee that his mirth hath loste," in *Poems, Written by the Right Honorable William Earl of Pembroke ... Many of Which Are Answered by Way of Repartee, by Sir Benjamin Ruddier, Knight: With Several Distinct Poems, Written by Them Occasionally, and Apart,* edited by John Donne the Younger (London: Printed by Matthew Inman, to be sold by James Magnes, 1660), pp. 29–31;

"The Writings in Verse and Prose of Sir Edward Dyer, Knt. (1540[?] – 1607). Now First Collected. Edited with Memorial-Introduction and Notes," in *Miscellanies of the Fuller Worthies' Library,* volume 4, edited by Alexander B. Grosart (Blackburn, U.K.: Privately printed, 1872), pp. 235–348;

Steven W. May, ed., *The Elizabethan Courtier Poets* (Columbia: University of Missouri Press, 1991), includes all of Dyer's poems on pp. 287–316.

Sir Edward Dyer wrote some of the most widely circulated and influential English verse of Elizabeth I's reign. His twelve canonical poems, with the four lyrics he may have written, rank among the finest love poems in what C. S. Lewis has called the "drab" or "plain" style that characterized English verse of the mid sixteenth century. But he, along with his friend Sir Philip Sidney, also cultivated what Lewis calls the "golden" style. Dyer's works were imitated or answered by such contemporary poets as Fulke Greville, King James VI of Scotland, Sir Francis Drake, and Robert Southwell. In addition to his close friendship with his fellow courtier poets Greville and Sidney, Dyer was well acquainted with such writers as Sir John Harington; Mary Herbert, Countess of Pembroke; Sir Robert Sidney; and Robert Devereux, second Earl of Essex.

Born in October 1543 to Sir Thomas Dyer and his second wife, Frances Darcy Dyer, Edward Dyer inherited substantial properties in Somersetshire. Nothing is known of his upbringing or education: his matriculation at Broadgates Hall, Oxford, in 1558 and Continental travels in the early 1560s are largely conjectural. Even his admission to the Inner Temple in 1560 does not prove that he was in London to study law, for the Inns of Court were fashionable addresses for young gentlemen in search of preferment at court and in the government.

Dyer's learning, nevertheless, was acknowledged by many contemporaries. Robert Dudley, Earl of Leicester, praised his command of Italian, while those who dedicated books to him described Dyer as "acquainted in the languages," skilled in the "art and ability of writing," and "a special favorer of all good knowledges." He was an early advocate of English colonization in the New World, and he cultivated a lifelong interest in alchemy.

While still a young man, Dyer was sufficiently educated to move in court circles. By 1565 he belonged to the retinue of the queen's powerful favorite, the earl of Leicester. He must have quickly gained an independent claim to Elizabeth's favor, for in 1568 he was styled the queen's servant in a patent to export wheat and beans from his native Somersetshire. In 1570 Elizabeth granted him the stewardship of the manor and rangership of the

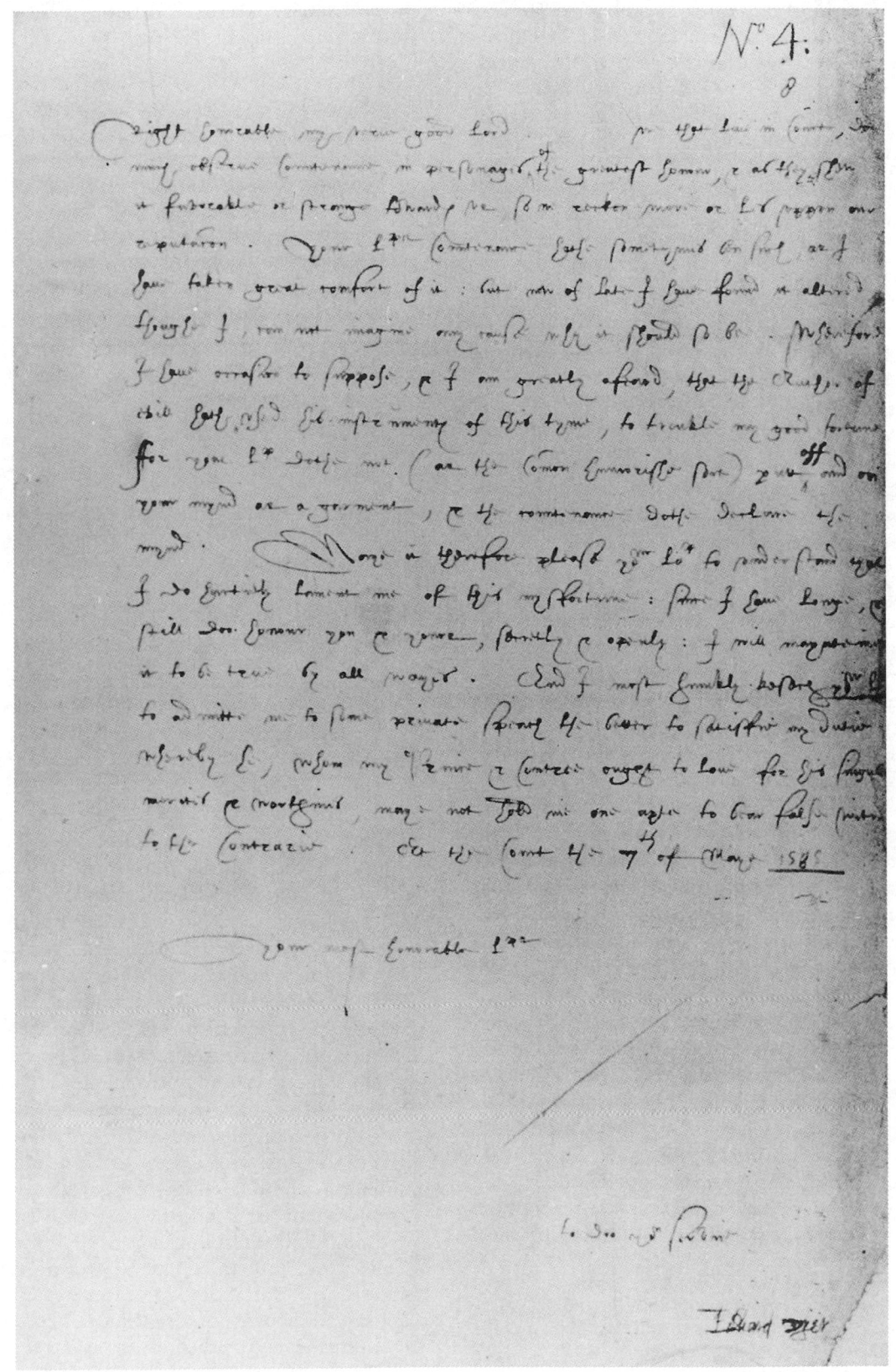

Letter from Dyer to William Cecil, Lord Burghley, 7 May 1585 (MS. Lansdowne 46, British Library)

woods of the royal palace of Woodstock. He was out of the queen's favor from 1571 to 1573, but his service in the latter year at the siege of Edinburgh was no doubt instrumental in his return to favor by 1574. He received a monopoly to license tanners in 1576, a three-thousand-pound loan in 1579, and a patent to find "concealed lands" – that is, lands properly belonging to the Crown – in 1588. Elizabeth sent him on diplomatic missions to the Netherlands in 1584 and to the court of Holy Roman Emperor Rudolph II in Prague in 1588.

Dyer was among the earliest of Elizabeth's courtiers to write and circulate vernacular love poetry. Although he may have written verse as early as the 1560s, his song for the Woodstock entertainment for the queen in September 1575 is his earliest datable lyric. The pastime of writing verse earned him a considerable contemporary reputation. Sidney deferred to Dyer as the reviver of sound English poetry; George Puttenham praised his verse as "sweet, solemn and of high conceit." Thomas Nashe alleged that Dyer "repurified poetry" and "instructed it to speak courtly." Except for his elegy for Sidney, all of the extant poems definitely written by Dyer concern love, as do three of the four works tentatively ascribed to him.

Dyer was a master of the midcentury poetic style characterized by alliterative phrasing, often in such long-line meters as the poulter's measure of "He that his mirth hath lost" or the fourteen-syllable couplets of "Before I die, fair dame." Verse in this tradition was ordinarily image-starved instead of concrete, aphoristic, and sprinkled with classical allusions. It can be pleasing to the ear as well as rhetorically sophisticated, yet the efforts of many early Elizabethan poets were long-winded as well as emotionally and psychologically sterile. The "energia," or moving emotional force, that Sidney wished to infuse once more into English verse was, however, discoverable in the work of his friend Dyer, whose love laments often achieve a technical grace and plaintive intensity seldom equaled by poets of the 1570s and 1580s. The "Song in the Oak" from the Woodstock entertainment, for example, shows Dyer breaking the habit of unrelieved end-stopped lines. He employs enjambment in each of its four stanzas, and the alliteration does not detract from the tone of the lines:

> I am most sure that I shall not attain
> The only good wherein my joy doth lie.
> I have no power my passions to refrain,
> But wail the want which nought else may supply.

Dyer injects recognizable human emotion into many passages, despite their alliteration, by writing in colloquial, almost informal syntax and diction – as in the first four lines of "Divide my times":

> Divide my times and rate my wretched hours,
>   From days to months, from months to many years,
> And then compare my sweetest with my sours
>   To see which more in equal view appears.

The reader is challenged to compare the speaker's good times with his bad ones as proof that the complaint that follows is justified. And Dyer's laments make competent use of allusions and figurative language, as in "He that his mirth hath lost" and "I would it were not as it is":

> My walk the path of plaints, my prospect into hell
> Where Sisyphus, that wretched wight, in endless pain
>   doth dwell.

> Behold my tired shoulders bear Desire's weary baiting
>   wings,
> And at my heel a clog I wear tied on with self-
>   disdaining strings;
> My wings to get at gate do haste, my clog doth sink me
>   down as fast.

Dyer clings to the traditional Petrarchan stance of unrequited, hopeless love but enlivens the pose with both a technical and an imaginative freshness that sets him apart from most of his contemporaries.

The extent to which Dyer "published" his verse or used it to advance his career as a courtier is difficult to determine. Although he did not gather his poetry for publication in print, lyrics attributed to him circulated widely in manuscript. From the mid 1580s, moreover, he was identified as a poet by such contemporaries as Puttenham, Harington, Geoffrey Whitney, and Gabriel Harvey, as well as in *England's Helicon* and *Belvedere;* both of these anthologies, which appeared in 1600, attributed poems to Dyer. He clearly released most of his poems for manuscript circulation under his name and, thus, consciously nurtured his reputation as a poet.

Presumably Dyer's early, long-line love complaints antedated his association with Sidney, who influenced him to attempt new genres while enhancing his talent for a sincere, expressive style. "Prometheus" is framed in the concise limits of an English sonnet and elicited an answering sonnet from Sidney. Dyer's first two quatrains explain the plight of a satyr who tries to kiss the fire brought to earth by Prometheus, "ere then on earth not seen": "Wood [mad] with the smart, with shouts and shrieking shrill, / He sought his ease in river, field, and bower." In the third quatrain Dyer applies the satyr's frenzied panic

Dyer (second from right) as a pallbearer at the funeral of his friend Sir Philip Sidney, 17 February 1587 (engraving by Derick Theodor de Bris after a drawing by Thomas Lant)

to his own distress at being stricken with the angelic sight of his beloved. The difference, he concludes, between the satyr's pain and his own is that "He for a while, I evermore have smart." The succinct final couplet encapsulates the dramatic dissimilarity of these comparable experiences. Dyer's concise, structured lyric anticipates the flood of polished sonnets of the 1590s inspired by Sidney's *Astrophil and Stella* (1591).

Two of Dyer's later poems also reveal Sidney's influence: "Amaryllis," a mythological and allegorical pastoral narrative, is couched in the trochaic rhythm Sidney introduced into English verse in about 1581, while "Amidst the fairest mountain tops" echoes a line from a poem by Sidney. "Amaryllis" tells of Charimell and Coridon, friends who become rivals for a woman who is utterly devoted to Diana, goddess of chastity. The friends pine and die of unrequited love for Amaryllis, who is so moved by their devotion to her that she persuades Diana to effect Ovidian metamorphoses for her unfortunate suitors: Charimell is resurrected as the yellow flower heartsease, which becomes Amaryllis's favorite; Coridon is transformed into an owl, whose despairing song Amaryllis "delights to hear" as she walks in the forest. The poem's conclusion assures the reader

that this myth is but a shadow of real events, presumably some love triangle at court whose protagonists have not been identified.

"Amidst the fairest mountain tops" is also thoroughly pastoral but quite different in tone from "Amaryllis." The inefficient opening of the poem establishes the shepherd's love for Cynthia with much backtracking and many needless parenthetical asides:

One day (I need not name the day
To lovers of their sorrows,
But say as once a shepherd said
Their moan nights have no morrows) . . .[.]

The shepherd is Sidney, who complained of "my night of evils, which hath no morrow" in "Certain Sonnets" number three in the third edition of his *The Countess of Pembroke's Arcadia* (1598). The narrator returns to his lovelorn shepherd, dreaming "all alone (if he remain / Alone that is in love)" before quoting his lament, which leads nowhere – in contrast to the definite if rather depressing resolution of "Amaryllis." Dyer's shepherd merely concludes that his beloved "hast Angel's eyes / But yet a woman's heart," and on this note the poems ends.

The poem's exaggerated, redundant rhetoric makes it a mockery of a shepherd's complaint; it is a courtier's tongue-in-cheek satire of the lowly pastoral style. Thus, Dyer attempted a wide range of styles and tones within the genre of the lover's lament. His concern with rural love and courtship in both of his pastorals as well as in the sonnet to which Sidney wrote a reply reveals his interest in the Italian motifs and forms cultivated by both Sidney and their friend Greville. The trochaic meter of "Amaryllis" marks a further departure from the conventions of midcentury poetics.

Dyer's most innovative work is his elegy for Sidney. This unrhymed sonnet is cast in uneven pentameters that perhaps were meant to approximate in English the effect of the classical, quantitative verse Sidney had cultivated. In the poem's conclusion Dyer's grief for the loss of his friend tempts him to commit suicide:

> And by my will my life itself would yield
> If heathen blame ne might my faith distain [sully];
> O heavy time! that my days draw behind thee;
> Thou dead dost live, thy Dyer, living, dieth.

Dyer's wordplay on his name in the last line resembles his punning signature to "He that his mirth hath lost": "My song, if any ask, whose grievous case is such / *Die ere* thou let his name be known, his folly shows too much."

If Dyer wrote verse after his elegy for Sidney, it has not come to light. His service to his country and his hold on royal favor, however, continued until the end of Elizabeth's reign. He served in the Parliament of 1589 and was dispatched on further missions to the imperial court at Prague in 1590 and 1591. There he was placed under house arrest in June 1591 for his efforts to persuade a countryman, Edward Kelley, who had convinced the emperor that he could change base metals into gold, to return to England. Dyer was returned to Parliament in 1593. In 1596 he received his most prestigious gift from the queen when she appointed him chancellor of the order of the garter, the chief administrative officer of Europe's oldest order of chivalry. The post required of its holder the knighthood he received that same year.

Dyer did not fare well after King James I's accession in 1603. He lost his offices at Woodstock and appears not to have attended court. He died unmarried in May 1607, with the administration of his estate passing to his sister, Margaret.

Even if Dyer did not write "My mind to me a kingdom is," to which Edward de Vere, seventeenth Earl of Oxford, has a slightly better claim, his poetry remains among the most popular and widely imitated of that of all the Elizabethan lyricists. "He that his mirth hath lost" survives in nine contemporary manuscripts. It became the model Elizabethan lover's lament, copied by Drake, James VI, Southwell, and Greville, in addition to several anonymous imitators. "The lowest trees have tops," a subtle, finely structured lover's complaint, is known in at least twenty manuscript copies dating well into the seventeenth century. It, too, attracted many replies and imitations. "Prometheus" and "I would it were not" also circulated widely. Thus, Dyer significantly influenced Jacobean as well as late Elizabethan writers.

Dyer's place in English Renaissance poetry has yet to be clearly defined, although the task has been simplified by Ralph Sargent's biography (1935) with its outdated but competent edition of the poems. Scholarly attention to Dyer has been almost exclusively confined to his relationships with Sidney and Edmund Spenser. Further consideration of his poetry would reveal that it exemplified the best of the midcentury style, onto which he grafted in his later lyrics the innovations in tone and form he had practiced with his friends Sidney and Greville. Above all, Dyer's influence on contemporary poets and on those of the next generation deserves further study.

Biography:

Ralph Sargent, *At the Court of Queen Elizabeth: The Life and Lyrics of Sir Edward Dyer* (London & New York: Oxford University Press, 1935); republished as *The Life and Lyrics of Sir Edward Dyer* (Oxford: Clarendon, 1968).

References:

Calendar of the Patent Rolls Preserved in the Public Record Office, volume 5 (London: Her Majesty's Stationery Office, 1964);

C. S. Lewis, *English Literature in the Sixteenth Century, Excluding Drama* (Oxford: Clarendon, 1954);

Steven W. May, "The Authorship of 'My Mind to Me a Kingdom Is,' " *Review of English Studies,* 26 (November 1975): 385–394;

May, *The Elizabethan Courtier Poets* (Columbia: University of Missouri Press, 1991);

George Puttenham, *The Arte of English Poesie,* edited by Gladys Doidge Willock and Alice Walker (Cambridge: Cambridge University Press, 1936);

Bernard M. Wagner, "New Poems by Sir Edward Dyer," *Review of English Studies,* 11 (October 1935): 466–471.

Elizabeth I

(7 September 1533 – 24 March 1603)

Mary Thomas Crane
Boston College

BOOKS: *The Public Speaking of Queen Elizabeth: Selections from Her Official Addresses,* edited by George P. Rice, Jr. (New York: Columbia University Press, 1951);

The Poems of Queen Elizabeth I, edited by Leicester Bradner (Providence, R.I.: Brown University Press, 1964);

A Book of Devotions Composed by Her Majesty Elizabeth R, translated by Adam Fox (Gerrards Cross, U.K.: Smythe, 1970).

OTHER: John Nichols, *The Progresses and Public Processions of Queen Elizabeth,* 4 volumes (London: Printed by John Nichols, 1788–1821) – includes speeches made by Elizabeth on royal progresses;

John E. Neale, *Elizabeth I and Her Parliaments, 1559–1581* (London: Cape, 1953) – includes complete transcripts of Elizabeth's speeches to Parliament.

TRANSLATIONS: Margaret of Navarre, *A Godly Meditacyon of the Christen Sowle, Concerninge a Love towardes God and Hys Christe,* edited by John Bale (Wesel: Printed by Derick van der Straten, 1548);

Margaret of Navarre, *The Mirror of the Sinful Soul: A Prose Translation from the French of a Poem by Queen Margaret of Navarre, Made in 1544 by the Princess (Afterwards Queen) Elizabeth,* edited by Percy Willoughby Ames (London: Royal Society of Literature, 1897); republished as "The Glass of the Sinful Soul," in Marc Shell, *Elizabeth's Glass* (Lincoln & London: University of Nebraska Press, 1993);

Queen Elizabeth's Englishings of Boethius, De consolatione philosophiae, A.D. 1593; Plutarch, De Curiositate; Horace, De arte poetica (Part) A.D. 1598: Edited from the Unique Manuscript, Partly in the Queen's Hand, in the Public Record Office, London, edited by Caroline Pemberton (London: Published for the Early English Text Society by

Elizabeth I in her coronation robes; portrait by an unknown artist (National Portrait Gallery, London)

Kegan Paul, Trench, Trubner, 1899, reprinted, 1975).

Although the influence of Queen Elizabeth I on the literature of the period that bears her name has been much discussed, her own status as an author has been less recognized. Critics have traced her role as subject of or inspiration for such works as Edmund Spenser's *The Faerie Queene* (1590–1596), William Shakespeare's *A Midsummer Night's Dream* (1600), and some Petrarchan sonnets but have generally considered her as the author of only a few mediocre poems and translations. A full sense of

Princess Elizabeth, circa 1546–1547; portrait by an unknown artist (Windsor Castle Collection)

Elizabeth's literary role in the Elizabethan period, however, must include not just the works by men who shaped and were shaped by her image but also the speeches and letters that she carefully crafted with great rhetorical skill and, in some cases, revised for publication. In a period when the oration and the epistle were highly valued literary genres, her command of those forms – through which she established her image and wielded her power – provides the basis for considering Elizabeth I as a significant author in her own right.

Elizabeth's early years were marked by constant fluctuations of fortune. Her birth at Greenwich Palace on 7 September 1533 to King Henry VIII and his new queen, Anne Boleyn, was a grave disappointment, since she was not the longed-for male heir. Although she was at first treated as a princess and given precedence over her older half sister Mary – Henry's daughter by his first wife, Catherine of Aragon – her status fell with the execution of her mother on charges of adultery and treason on 19 May 1536 and, to a lesser extent, with the birth of a male heir, Edward, to Henry and his third wife, Jane Seymour, in 1537. Although Mary

and Elizabeth were both officially declared illegitimate, they nevertheless continued to appear at court and were placed after Edward in the line of succession.

Her education provided perhaps the one constant in her early life. Princess Elizabeth was one of the few Englishwomen to benefit from humanist support for the education of females: she received a complete education in Latin, Greek, French, Italian, and rhetoric from the prominent humanists John Cheke, William Grindal, and Roger Ascham; Ascham applied to her his program of double translation from Latin or Greek to English and back again. She continued to translate classical works throughout her life, completing translations of Psalm 13 and the meditations of Margaret of Navarre as a New Year's gift for her stepmother, Queen Catherine Parr (Henry's sixth wife), in 1545 – the latter work was published in 1548 as *A Godly Meditation of the Christian Soul* – and later rendering the first ninety lines of Petrarch's "Trionfo dell' Eternita" (Triumph of Eternity), the second chorus of Seneca's *Hercules Oetaeus,* some sections of Boethius's *De Consolatione philosophiae* (The Consolation of Philosophy), lines 1 to 178 of Horace's *Ars Poetica,* and Plutarch's "On Curiosity." The translations from Boethius and Horace survive in her own hand, and the handwriting, awkward English, and many errors reveal that they were done quickly. She also delivered brief and rather conventional speeches in Latin at Cambridge University on 7 August 1564 and at Oxford in August 1566 and September 1592, daring to address learned men in the preeminent language of male authority. Such manifestations of her education played an important role in establishing her image as an effective monarch, as did the mastery of English rhetoric displayed in her speeches.

Some of her earliest letters resemble school exercises in their rather stilted and convoluted style, but they respond quite subtly to various political crises during the reign of her brother, Edward VI. These letters demonstrate her growing ability to use language to conceal as much as it reveals and to tread a fine line between self-assertion and self-abnegation. An early but undated letter to her brother subtly reminds him of their shared humanist and Protestant background, citing commonplaces and using the techniques of parallelism and copious variation that both had been taught: "For though from the grace of the picture [a portrait of herself enclosed with the letter] the colors may fade by time, may give by weather, may be spotted by chance; yet the other [her mind] nor time with her swift wings shall overtake, nor the misty clouds with their lowerings may darken, nor chance with her slippery foot may overthrow."

In 1548 she was forced to defend herself in a more serious situation. Thomas Seymour, brother of the child king's protector, Edward Seymour, had married Henry's widow, Catherine Parr, in whose household Princess Elizabeth lived. Thomas Seymour evidently made some sort of sexual advances to the princess, and she was sent away. A letter of June 1548 to Parr is, on one level, a conventional thank-you note, but it also subtly pleads the writer's innocence and seeks to enlist Parr as an ally. Elizabeth assures Parr that she is "replete with sorrow to depart from your Highness, especially seeing you undoubtful of health; and albeit I answered little, I weighed it more deeper when you said you would warn me of all evilness that you should hear of me; for if your Grace had not a good opinion of me, you would not have offered friendship to me that way at all, meaning the contrary." After Parr's death in 1548 Thomas Seymour, with his eye on the throne, sought to marry Elizabeth. He was arrested in the midst of these schemes and was beheaded. Elizabeth and her servants were questioned, but no evidence of her complicity could be established. Two letters to Edward Seymour on 28 January and 6 February 1549 use conventional protestations of innocence and expressions of gratitude to place her accusers in the wrong.

In 1553 Edward VI was succeeded by Mary. As a Protestant, Elizabeth was a popular alternative to the Roman Catholic Mary and a focal point for Protestant rebellion. Although, as far as is known, Elizabeth never took part in any treasonous plots, Mary suspected her of involvement in the rebellion of Sir Thomas Wyatt the Younger on 25 January 1554. Elizabeth's letters to her sister during this period protest her own innocence and gently complain about the queen's unfairness to her; nevertheless, Elizabeth was placed under house arrest at Woodstock. Two poems probably date from her confinement. One of them, a distich scratched on a window, succinctly states her position: "Much suspected by me, / Nothing proved can be." Typically, the poem fails to address the issue of her actual guilt or innocence. The other poem, "On Fortune and Injustice," was supposedly written on the wall of the house. In this iambic tetrameter stanza, which expresses anticourt sentiments using the frequent alliteration common to moralizing poems in the period, she blames her troubles on fortune, whose "wresting wavering state / Hath fraught with cares my troubled wit."

Page from Elizabeth's translation of Margaret of Navarre's A Godly Meditation of the Christian Soul, *with a woodcut depicting Elizabeth kneeling before Jesus*

On Mary's death on 17 November 1558 the twenty-five year old Elizabeth moved from incarceration to the throne of England. Her speeches and other writings reflect her deeply felt sense of the tenuousness of her position. The dangers of proximity to power had been all too apparent to her during the violent and chaotic years of Mary's reign. Many of her subjects agreed with John Knox, whose *First Blast of the Trumpet against the Monstrous Regiment of Women* was published in 1558: in an age when women had few rights and little power, the idea of a reigning queen was difficult for some to accept. Also, as a committed, if moderate, Protestant, Elizabeth was the object of Catholic hatred and distrust both at home and abroad. Critics have emphasized that the Petrarchan language of love was used by Elizabeth and her courtiers to make a woman's power tolerable. It is true that male courtiers celebrated her beauty and professed their love for her in poems that praise her as Gloriana, Cynthia, or the Fairy Queen; in her own writings, however, Elizabeth's language is complex and multilayered. She represents herself both as loving mother and brave prince, as bride and stern counselor, as decisive and ambivalent, as clear and ambiguous. Her sophisticated political rhetoric in speeches, letters, and poems played a crucial role in maintaining her power and her popularity.

A central issue through most of her reign centered on her refusal either to marry or, more important, to name an heir. Whether or not she intended from the beginning of her reign to remain celibate has been much debated. Certainly, she used the image of herself as the Virgin Queen to provide a Protestant replacement for worship of the Virgin Mary, and she frequently repeated that she was either in love with or the mother of her people: "though after my death you may have many stepdames, yet shall you never have a more natural mother than I mean to be unto you all." It seems clear that she realized early on that marriage presented special problems for a reigning queen. Were she to marry one of her own subjects – such as her close friend and favorite Robert Dudley, Earl of Leicester – she would upset the delicate balance of power among competing factions of the nobility at her court. And if she chose a foreign husband – if one of appropriate religious affiliation could be found – she would upset the equally delicate balance of alliances among European states and probably precipitate a war. As it was, she used the prospect of marriage to manipulate her nobles at home and foreign princes abroad. On several occasions she managed to forestall a war by seeming to contemplate marriage with a relative of some particularly belligerent prince. Probably she realized that she could rule more effectively if she could offer herself perpetually as a rich but never quite attainable prize. She also may have feared the loss of independence that would come with marriage, even to a queen. She is said to have remarked that she would have but one mistress and no master.

Parliament repeatedly petitioned her either to marry or name a successor, and the queen wrote a series of speeches in response to those demands. She revised several of the speeches after delivering them and had printed copies disseminated to make her position more widely known; no copies of these printed versions survive, however. In a 1559 speech to the House of Commons she says unequivocally that she has decided to remain single. She does not seem particularly angry at receiving advice to marry, although she warns Parliament not to try to tell her *whom* to marry. She concludes with a prediction: "and in the end, this shall be for me sufficient, that a marble stone shall declare that a queen, having reigned such a time, lived and died a virgin."

Nevertheless, in the first several years of her reign many of her subjects felt that she intended to marry the earl of Leicester – even though he was already married. Despite the disapproval of William Cecil, her chief adviser, she made Leicester her master of the horse and spent much time with him. Rumors spread that she had either married him secretly or given birth to an illegitimate child by him. In September 1560 Leicester's wife was found dead under suspicious circumstances, and Elizabeth seems to have realized that the scandal prohibited marriage to him – if, in fact, she had ever seriously considered it. She also, around the same time, either contemplated or seemed to contemplate marriage to the Hapsburg archduke Charles of Austria, but the negotiations were inconclusive. In October 1562 Elizabeth almost died of smallpox, and Parliament felt justified in renewing its demands. Her two speeches to Parliament in 1563 are perhaps her most tentative and are couched in the most ambiguous language of all her speeches on the issue of marriage. In the first she says that she will "touch, but not presently . . . answer" Parliament's demands. She alludes to her recent illness, assuring Parliament that "there needs no boding of my bane. I know now as well as I did before that I am mortal." In the second speech she yields so far as to admit that celibacy is "best for a private woman" but "not meet for a prince." Although her speeches often employ long, complex sentences and a convoluted syntax – using passive voice to make it appear that events simply happen rather than being actively carried out by her – she can, especially when angry, be extremely direct, using short declarative sentences and homely metaphors. When in 1566 Parliament again pressed her to marry, she delivered a much stronger reply, concluding with an affirmation of her ability to rule: "And though I be a woman, yet I have as good a courage, answerable to my place, as ever my father had. I am your anointed queen. I will never be by violence constrained to do anything. I thank God I am endued with such qualities that if I were turned out of the realm in my petticoat, I were able to live in any place in Christendom."

Miniature of Elizabeth by Nicholas Hilliard (National Portrait Gallery, London)

In the early 1570s Queen Catherine de Médicis of France was eager for an alliance with England against Spain and offered François of Valois, Duke of Alençon, as a potential husband for Elizabeth (despite his being short, ugly, and twenty years younger than Elizabeth). Nothing came of the proposal at this point, and in 1576 Parliament was again harping on Elizabeth's unmarried state. She replied, in a speech that she proudly copied for her godson Sir John Harrington, that "if I were a milkmaid with a pail on my arm, whereby my private person might be little set by, I would not forsake that poor and single state to match with the greatest monarch." Nevertheless, the possibility of a match with the duke was revived in 1579, when Elizabeth was forty-five. Alençon came to England, and despite strong Protestant opposition and the vehement protestations of some of her advisers, Elizabeth seemed for a time to consider the match seriously. In 1582 she decided against it, precluding the possibility of bearing an heir.

A poem, "On Monsieur's Departure," perhaps written about this time, uses conventional Petrarchan language to express sorrow at disappointed love. The poem, in three rhyme-royal stanzas, complains that "I grieve and dare not show my discontent . . . I am and not, I freeze and yet am burned," concluding: "or let me live with some more sweet content, / Or die and so forget what love ere meant."

Most of Elizabeth's speeches center on the issues of marriage and succession, perhaps because they seemed most suited for a personal response. Also, marriage and succession were powerfully emotional topics, so it was important for her to shape public opinion on them if she could. But some of her letters, speeches, and poems touch on other pressing issues of her reign: the long crisis involving Mary, Queen of Scots; Elizabeth's attempts to forge and enforce an Anglican middle way between Roman Catholicism and extreme Protestantism; and, in foreign policy, efforts to play off opposing

Portrait of Elizabeth attributed to Cornelius Ketel, circa 1580–1583. The sieve in her hand is a symbol of virginity derived from the story of the Vestal Virgin Tuccia, who, to prove her chastity, carried a sieve full of water from the Tiber to the temple without spilling a drop (Pinoteca Nazionale, Siena, Italy).

European factions against each other and to champion Protestantism abroad without engaging in expensive wars.

Mary Stuart, the queen of Scotland and a Roman Catholic, was the granddaughter of Margaret Tudor, the sister of Henry VIII; as such, she was next in the Tudor line of succession to the English throne, although some factions in England championed an English and Protestant line of succession through Lady Catherine Grey. When Elizabeth became queen, Mary was married to the French dauphin, who became King Francis II of France in 1559 but died in 1560. Catholic powers in Europe hoped that Mary would become queen of England, either at Elizabeth's death or through a Catholic rebellion. Mary's hopes of gaining the English throne were hampered, however, by Elizabeth's refusal to name either her or her son James as heir, and also by domestic problems in Scotland, where the power of a strong Protestant faction was strengthened by a series of scandals involving Mary's private life. She had married her cousin, Henry Stuart, Lord Darnley, in 1565, but by 1566 she had grown to dislike her husband and was enjoying the company of her French secretary, David Rizzio. Darnley and a group of Protestant lords murdered Rizzio. In turn, Mary and her new lover, James Hepburn, Earl of Bothwell, had Darnley killed in 1567; that same year Mary and Bothwell were married. Mary was imprisoned in 1568 but soon escaped and fled to England, where she plotted Elizabeth's overthrow with Catholic factions both within and outside of England. Despite the urging of her advisers and Parliament, Elizabeth was reluctant to set the dangerous precedent of executing an anointed queen. Although she realized the threat that Mary posed both to her own safety and to the stability of the realm, she did not want to act directly to bring about her death. She vacillated, equivocated, and procrastinated until the execution could be carried out without seeming to be ordered by her. Several speeches seek to explain – or perhaps to conceal and confuse – her attitude toward Mary and her failure to act decisively against her. In a well-known phrase she assures Parliament that "your judgment [that she should execute Mary] I condemn not, neither do I mistake your reasons, but pray you to accept my thankfulness, excuse my doubtfulness, and take in good part my answer-answerless." A poem in fourteeners, "Doubt of Future Foes," comments on Mary's conspiracies using commonplaces and alliteration familiar from collections such as *Tottel's Miscellany* (1557): "For falsehood now doth flow, and subjects' faith doth ebb / Which should not be, if reason ruled or wisdom weaved the web." It concludes with more certainty and boldness than she expresses in her speeches on this subject: "My rusty sword through rest shall first his edge employ / To poll their tops that seek such change or gape for future joy." In a speech Elizabeth argued against Parliament's demand that Mary be "arraigned at the bar" and "tried by a jury" because her position as queen prohibited it: "we princes, I tell you, are set on stages, in the sight and view of all the world duly observed." A second speech, delivered on 24 November 1586, argued against Mary's execution: "neither hath my care been so much bent how to prolong [my life], as how to preserve both." This speech was published after the execution, which was carried out on 7 February 1587, evidently to publicize Elizabeth's reluctance to take such a step.

Religion was an important factor in all of the issues of Elizabeth's reign, including marriage, succession, the crisis over Mary, and foreign policy.

POSVI DEVM ADIVTOREM MEVM

SEMPER EADEM

ELISABET D·G·ANGLIAE, FRANCIAE, HIBERNIAE, ET VERGINIAE REGINA.
FIDEI CHRISTIANAE PROPVGNATRIX ACERRIMA. NVNC IN DNO REQVIESCENS.

*Engraving of Elizabeth by Crispin van de Passe after a drawing
by Isaac Oliver, one of the many portraits produced shortly
after her death*

The nature of Elizabeth's personal religious beliefs is impossible to determine with certainty, although she seems to have leaned more toward Rome than her public policies would indicate. Two guiding principles shaped her stance on religion throughout her reign: to establish the Church of England as a mean between the extremes of Catholic and Puritan belief; and to eliminate, as far as possible, persecution for private belief. She had herself experienced religious persecution under Mary Tudor and perhaps for that reason decided to allow a certain amount of private nonconformity if a show of outward orthodoxy were maintained. She is supposed to have said that she intended to make no windows into men's souls.

Thus, despite the hopes of her strongly Protestant counselors and Parliament that she would complete the reformation of the English church, she held a middle course and assured Parliament in a speech of 1585 that "if I were not persuaded that mine were the true way of God's will, God forbid I should live to prescribe it to you." Using parallel construction to emphasize her point, she assures Parliament that she will neither "animate Romanists" nor "tolerate new-fangleness" but means instead "to guide them both by God's holy true rule."

In foreign affairs her policy was similarly cautious. In contrast to her male predecessors she sought to avoid foreign wars. Such wars were expensive, and her frugality was legendary; then, too, whenever she sent an army out of the country its leaders tended to act on their own initiative and ignore her moderating orders. Although she was persuaded to send troops to help Scottish Protestant rebels in 1560, she refused to send similar help to the Netherlands in the mid 1570s. When she did send Leicester there with an army in 1585, he immediately disobeyed her orders and accepted the governorship of the region. Incensed, Elizabeth wrote a letter that is typical of her forceful and plain style when she was angry: "Jesus! what availeth wit when it fails the owner at greatest need. . . . I am utterly at squares with this childish dealing." In a speech to Parliament in 1593 she summed up her policy of nonintervention abroad using the Latinate diction, parallel constructions, and frequent subordination that characterize her more formal and considered style: "for in ambition of glory I have never sought to enlarge the territories of my land, nor thereby to advance you. If I have used my forces to keep the enemy far from you, I have thereby thought your safety the greater, and your danger the less."

Her greatest triumph in warding off danger was the defeat of the Spanish Armada in 1588. Spain, as the most powerful Catholic country in Europe, was the chief threat to England for most of her reign. She sought to forestall that threat by supporting European Protestant movements – indirectly, for the most part – and by using the promise of marriage to prevent an alliance of France and Spain against England. She eventually precipitated war with Spain, however, by sending Leicester and his army to aid the rebellion against Spanish rule in the Netherlands and by sending Sir Francis Drake to capture and rob Spanish ships and ports. Spain sent a fleet – the great Armada – to attack England, but it was defeated by the English navy and destroyed on the way home by bad weather.

Elizabeth has traditionally been credited with a stirring speech to troops gathered at Tilbury to repel the expected Spanish invasion. Although the text is not as certain as those of the parliamentary speeches, it has long been famous for its defiant language: "I know I have the body of a weak and feeble woman, but I have the heart and stomach of a king, and of a king of England too, and think foul scorn that Parma or Spain, or any prince of Europe should dare to invade the borders of my realm." The speech effectively applies the legal theory of "the king's two bodies" – the mortal "body natural" and the immortal "body politic" – to the queen's female body and suggests that the realm itself is another version of her body, vulnerable to rape by foreign powers unless she protects it. In addition to these ringing phrases, the speech includes a more practical assurance to the troops that they will be paid for their services.

The defeat of the Armada marked the high point of Elizabeth's popularity and power. As she grew older, still unmarried and still without a designated heir, there was growing fear and discontent in England. Robert Devereux, Earl of Essex, was the great favorite of her later years. She sent him on an expedition against Cadiz in 1595 and against the Irish rebel Hugh O'Neill, Earl of Tyrone, in 1598. In Ireland he ignored Elizabeth's orders, and he returned to England in defiance of her. He plotted to overthrow her in 1600 and was executed in 1601. That year she delivered her famous "Golden Speech" to Parliament, defending her practice of granting monopolies to favorites such as Essex but mostly reiterating, in that language of love and gratitude and in a style shaped by careful use of balance and antithesis that had served so well to maintain her popularity in earlier years, that her people may have had princes who were "more mighty and wise" but never "more careful and loving" than she. One can also hear a hint of weariness in this speech when she says that "to be a king and wear a crown is a thing more glorious to them that see it, than to them that bear it." She died on 24 March 1603 and was succeeded by James VI of Scotland, who became James I of England.

The unpopularity of the Stuart monarchs who succeeded Elizabeth and the civil and political upheavals during their reigns quickly caused English subjects to look back with nostalgia to the days of "good Queen Bess." The remarkable literary flowering that took place during her rule, when Shakespeare, Spenser, Sir Philip Sidney, and Christopher Marlowe were all writing, has kept alive the idea that Elizabethan England enjoyed a golden age. Certainly Elizabeth was successful at maintaining peace at home and abroad and also at establishing her own image as a loving and able ruler. Although her own writings do not begin to equal the greatest of her age, they were nevertheless important in creating and sustaining that age.

Letters:

The Letters of Queen Elizabeth and King James VI of Scotland, edited by John Bruce (London: Camden Society, 1849);

The Letters of Queen Elizabeth I, edited by G. B. Harrison (New York: Funk & Wagnalls, 1968).

Bibliography:

Steven W. May, "Recent Studies in Elizabeth I," *English Literary Renaissance,* 23 (Spring 1993): 345–354.

Biographies:

J. E. Neale, *Queen Elizabeth* (New York: Harcourt, Brace, 1934; London: Cape, 1950);

Neale, *Elizabeth I and Her Parliaments, 1559–1581* (London: Cape, 1953);

Neale, *Elizabeth I and Her Parliaments, 1584–1601* (London: Cape, 1957);

Wallace T. MacCaffrey, *The Shaping of the Elizabethan Regime* (Princeton: Princeton University Press, 1968);

Joseph M. Levine, ed., *Elizabeth I* (Englewood Cliffs, N.J.: Prentice-Hall, 1969);

Alison Plowden, *The Young Elizabeth* (London: Macmillan, 1971; New York: Stein & Day, 1971);

Richard L. Greaves, ed., *Elizabeth I, Queen of England* (Lexington, Mass.: Heath, 1974);

Paul Johnson, *Elizabeth I: A Biography* (New York: Holt, Rinehart & Winston, 1974); republished as *Elizabeth I: A Study in Power and Intellect* (London: Weidenfeld & Nicolson, 1974);

Plowden, *Elizabeth Regina: The Age of Triumph, 1588–1603* (New York: Times Books, 1980);

Lacey Baldwin Smith, ed., *Elizabeth I* (Saint Louis: Forum, 1980);

MacCaffrey, *Queen Elizabeth and the Making of Policy, 1572–1588* (Princeton: Princeton University Press, 1981);

Carolly Erickson, *The First Elizabeth* (New York: Summit, 1983);

Jasper Ridley, *Elizabeth I* (London: Constable, 1987); republished as *Elizabeth I: The Shrewdness of Virtue* (New York: Viking, 1988).

References:

Marie Axton, *The Queen's Two Bodies: Drama and the Elizabethan Succession* (London: Royal Historical Society, 1977);

Mary Thomas Crane, " 'Video et Taceo': Elizabeth I and the Rhetoric of Counsel," *Studies in English Literature,* 28 (Winter 1988): 1–15;

Susan Frye, "The Myth of Elizabeth at Tilbury," *Sixteenth Century Journal,* 23 (Spring 1992): 95–114;

Allison Heisch, "Queen Elizabeth I: Parliamentary Rhetoric and the Exercise of Power," *Signs,* 1 (Autumn 1975): 31–55;

Heisch, "Queen Elizabeth I and the Persistence of Patriarchy," *Feminist Review,* 4 (1980): 45–54;

John N. King, "Queen Elizabeth I: Representations of the Virgin Queen," *Renaissance Quarterly,* 43 (Spring 1980): 30–74;

Leah Marcus, "Shakespeare's Comic Heroines, Elizabeth I, and the Political Uses of Androgyny," in *Women in the Middle Ages and the Renaissance,* edited by Mary Beth Rose (Syracuse: Syracuse University Press, 1986), pp. 135–154;

Louis Adrian Montrose, " 'Eliza, Queene of Sheapheardes' and the Pastoral of Power," *English Literary Renaissance,* 10 (Spring 1980): 153–182;

Montrose, " 'Shaping Fantasies': Figurations of Gender and Power in Elizabethan Culture," *Representations,* 1 (1983): 61–94;

John Nichols, *The Progresses and Public Processions of Queen Elizabeth,* 4 volumes (London: Printed by John Nichols, 1788–1821);

Roy Strong, *The Cult of Elizabeth: Elizabethan Portraiture and Pageantry* (London: Thames & Hudson, 1977);

Frances Yates, *The Imperial Theme in the Sixteenth Century* (London: Routledge & Kegan Paul, 1975).

Papers:

Manuscripts of Elizabeth's letters, speeches, and poems are in the Public Records Office, London; the British Library, London; the Bodleian Library, Oxford; the Cambridge University Library; and Hatfield House, Hatfield, Hertfordshire. Most of these manuscripts are copies by other hands, but holograph versions or copies with corrections in her own hand can be found among the state papers and in the British Library.

Thomas Elyot
(1490? – 26 March 1546)

Alistair Fox
University of Otago

BOOKS: *The Boke Named the Gouernour* (London: Thomas Berthelet, 1531);

Pasquil the Playne, anonymous (London: Thomas Berthelet, 1533; revised and signed, 1540);

Of the Knowledge Whiche Maketh a Wise Man (London: Thomas Berthelet, 1533);

The Castell of Helthe, Gathered oute of the Chyefe Authors of Phisyke (London: Thomas Berthelet, 1537?; revised and enlarged, 1541);

The Dictionary of Syr Thomas Eliot (London: Thomas Berthelet, 1538); revised and enlarged as *Bibliotheca Eliotae: Eliotis Librarie* (London: 1542);

The Bankette of Sapience, . . . Newely Augmented with Dyuerse Tytles and Sentences (London: Thomas Berthelet, 1539);

The Defence of Good Women (London: Thomas Berthelet, 1540);

The Image of Gouernance Compiled out of the Actes of Alexander Seuerus, Late Translated out of Greke by Syr T. Eliot (London: Thomas Berthelet, 1541 [1540]);

A Preseruatiue agaynste Deth (London: Thomas Berthelet, 1545).

Editions: *The Boke Named the Gouernour Deuised by Sir Thomas Elyot, Knight,* 2 volumes, edited by Henry Herbert Stephen Croft (London: K. Paul, Trench & Co., 1883; New York: Burt Franklin, 1967);

The Boke of the Governor, Devised by Sir Thomas Elyot, Knight, edited by Foster Watson (London: Dent, 1907);

The Castel of Helthe (1541) . . . Together with the Title-Page and Preface of the Edition of 1539 (New York: Scholars' Facsimiles & Reprints, 1937);

Sir Thomas Elyot's The Defence of Good Women, edited by Edwin Johnston Howard (Oxford, Ohio: Anchor Press, 1940);

Of the Knowledge Which Maketh a Wise Man, edited by Howard (Oxford, Ohio: Anchor Press, 1946);

Four Political Treatises: The Doctrinal of Princes (1533), Pasquil the Playne (1533), The Banquette of Sapi-

Thomas Elyot, circa 1532 (drawing by Hans Holbein the Younger; Collection Her Majesty the Queen, Windsor Castle)

ence (1534), The Image of Governance (1541), by Sir Thomas Elyot (Gainesville, Fla.: Scholars' Facsimiles & Reprints, 1967);

Bibliotheca Eliotae (1548), Augmented by Thomas Cooper (Delmar, N.Y.: Scholars' Facsimiles & Reprints, 1975);

"The Defence of Good Women (1545)," in *The Feminist Controversy of the Renaissance,* Scholars' Facsimiles and Reprints, no. 343 (Delmar, N.Y.: Scholars' Facsimiles & Reprints, 1980).

94

TRANSLATIONS: Plutarch, *The Educacion or Bringinge vp of Children, Translated by T. Eliot Esquier, One of ye Kingis Most Honorable Counsayle* (London: Thomas Berthelet, [before June 1530]);

Lucian of Samosata, *A Dialogue. Betwene Lucian and Diogenes of . . . Life* (London: Thomas Berthelet, [1532?]);

Isocrates, *The Doctrinall of Princis* (London: Thomas Berthelet, [1533?]);

Saint Cyprian, *A Swete and Deuoute Sermon of Mortalitie of Man* (London: Thomas Berthelet, 1534); includes Pico della Mirandola, *The Rules of a Christian Lyfe by Picus Erle of Mirandula*, translated by Elyot.

Together with Sir Thomas More, Sir Thomas Elyot was the most outstanding English humanist of his generation. He was the first writer in English to fashion the idea of a gentleman educated according to a humanist curriculum; he wrote the earliest important manual of health in English; he compiled the first English dictionary of classical Latin; he was the first to translate directly from Greek into English; and he was a pioneer in the use of the vernacular for serious writing, consciously seeking to enrich and augment the English language. Generally, he was the most important English exemplar in the early sixteenth century of Erasmian humanism – in the range of his interests, in his attempts to combine contemplation with action, and in his lifelong devotion to the publication of scholarly works aimed at improving society through the dissemination of idealistic humanist precepts founded in the wisdom of the ancients.

Elyot's father was Sir Richard Elyot, a distinguished jurist and member of the Middle Temple, a judge of assize on the Western Circuit, and (after 1513) a judge of the Common Pleas. His mother was Alice Delamere Elyot, descended from the Finderns, a family owning extensive lands that Elyot would eventually inherit. Little is known of Elyot's early years, the earliest surviving record of him dating from 1510, when he was admitted to the Middle Temple. It is probable that he was born in Wiltshire, where his father held the Manors of Chalk and Winterslow. If one assumes that he was of age when he was admitted to the Middle Temple, his birth must have occurred about 1490.

Elyot records that he was educated at home until his twelfth year, and that he was not instructed by any other teacher after that, but led himself into liberal studies and both natural and moral philosophy. He also records that "a worshipfull physician"

(most probably Thomas Linacre) read him the works of Galen, Johannicius (Hunayn ibn-Ishaq), and Hippocrates. Beyond this, Elyot was largely self-taught. One "Thomas Eliett" did enter Oxford University in 1516, taking the degrees of bachelor of arts in 1519 and bachelor of civil law in 1524, but the name is common in this period, and Elyot's own testimony flatly contradicts the likelihood that this graduate is to be identified with him.

Although there is no evidence that Elyot was ever called to the bar, he was assisting his father by 1510 as clerk to the justices of assize on the Western Circuit, a position he occupied until 1526. Between 1515 and 1529 he also served intermittently as a justice of the peace for Oxfordshire, and as sheriff of Oxfordshire and Berkshire in 1527 and 1529, offices he would hold again in Cambridgeshire and Huntingdonshire in the 1530s and 1540s. Sometime after 1522 he married Margaret, daughter of John à Barrow, of North Charford, Hampshire. The couple was to remain childless, to Elyot's sadness, as he acknowledged in the dedication to his translation of Plutarch's *The Education or Bringing up of Children* (circa 1530).

All of Elyot's works are preoccupied in one way or another with humanist ideals, both practical and theoretical. They fall into several categories. One group is concerned with the promotion of a humanist system of education: *The Education or Bringing up of Children,* and *The Book Named the Governor* (1531). Another group is involved with the assertion of a humanist moral and political philosophy that is variously Platonic and neo-Stoic: *Pasquil the Plain* (1533), *Of the Knowledge Which Maketh a Wise Man* (1533?), *The Banquet of Sapience* (1539), *The Doctrinal of Princes* (1533?), and *The Image of Governance* (1541). A third group, consisting of two devotional translations and a biblical compilation, reflects the religious aspect of Elyot's Christian humanism: Saint Cyprian's *A Sweet and Devout Sermon of Mortality* (1534), Giovanni Pico della Mirandola's *The Rules of a Christian Life* (1534), and *A Preservative against Death* (1545). A final pair of works, *The Castle of Health* (circa 1537) and *The Dictionary* (1538), present humanist lexical and medical knowledge not hitherto available in English. While most of Elyot's books are cast as expositional treatises, like other humanists of his generation he occasionally attempted to exploit the fictive potential of the dialogue form, particularly to dramatize the moral and political dilemma in which he found himself in the 1530s.

Many of Elyot's writings are concerned with the proper duties of a counselor and with gaining preferment for himself. The first of them, the Latin

Lady Margaret Elyot, circa 1532 (drawing by Hans Holbein the Younger; Collection Her Majesty the Queen, Windsor Castle)

Hermathena by one "Papyrius Geminus Eleates," cannot definitely be ascribed to Elyot but in all likelihood is his because of the suggestions encoded in the fictive name of its author (*Papyrius* "clerk," *Geminus* "Thomas," and *Eleates* "Elyot") and the thematic similarity with other works by Elyot. Dedicated to the influential diplomat Richard Pace, it is a dialogue praising the liberal arts, in imitation of the Lucianic dialogues translated by More and Desiderius Erasmus a decade earlier. Given that Pace had written his own tract *On the Benefit of a Liberal Education* in 1517, and that in 1522 he was secretary to Cardinal Wolsey, the lord chancellor, it is likely that the *Hermathena* was the means by which Elyot was drawn to Wolsey's attention. In any case, as Elyot subsequently recalled in a letter to privy councillor Thomas Cromwell (8 December 1532), Wolsey advanced him to the position of junior clerk of the King's Council, a position he held for over six years, until 1530.

While serving as clerk to the council, Elyot continued to display his scholarly credentials by publishing *The Education or Bringing up of Children,* a translation of Plutarch's *De educatione puerorum,* upon which he was later to draw extensively for the system of education outlined in *The Book Named the Governor.* Elyot claimed to be working from both the Greek and Latin versions of Plutarch's work, and as

a translator he is fairly free. By his own admission, he has not simply translated literally, but has "declared at length divers histories, only touched by Plutarch," and has omitted material that is "strange from the experience or usage of this present time, partly that some vices be in those tongues reproved, which ought rather to be unknown, than in a vulgar tongue to be expressed." He suppresses, for example, Plutarch's consideration of whether homosexual suitors should be encouraged to associate with boys, or deterred from doing so. Already in this early work, therefore, one sees both Elyot's characteristic habit of including exemplary stories to illustrate his moral concerns, and also the bowdlerizing inclination that would later prompt him to declare in *The Governor* that "it were better that a child should never read any part of Lucian than all Lucian." Any hopes Elyot may have had of advancing to a more senior position on the council were dashed, however, when Wolsey fell into disgrace, forcing Elyot to relinquish his clerkship.

The circumstances leading up to this setback are complex. When originally appointed to his position attending the council, Elyot had resigned his clerkship of the assizes at the request of Wolsey, who had promised him that the king would soon promote him "both to more worship and profit." Neither advancement nor profit was forthcoming, however, and Elyot found himself, as junior clerk, doing most of the work of recording the statements of defendants and witnesses during examinations in the Star Chamber while the senior clerk, Richard Eden, collected the stipend. Wolsey finally devised a patent in 1528 granting the senior clerkship to Elyot, but only conditionally upon Eden's relinquishing one granted to him in 1512, which the latter refused to do. On Wolsey's fall, a new patent was issued to Richard Eden and his nephew on 20 April 1530, and Elyot was discharged, being rewarded, as he complained, "only with the order of knighthood" and the further financial obligations required to maintain the dignity of that title. Having lost his patron, Elyot thus found himself out of pocket and without his former position in Henry VIII's administration.

The Governor was published partly as an attempt to resuscitate Elyot's expectations in the world of Tudor politics. In addition to serving as a manifesto of humanist political and pedagogical ideals, *The Governor* is also a declaration of Elyot's worthiness to be a counselor. By articulating a strikingly absolutist doctrine of regal power, it proclaimed Elyot's willingness to serve the royal cause, while its humanistic content was designed to establish his suitability as a candidate for royal service.

The Governor is divided into three complementary books that together present what the introductory "Proheme" calls "the form of a just public weal." Book 1 expounds Elyot's theory of the state and the education that is appropriate to those in authority. Book 2 describes the ideal qualities of a governor, while book 3 deals principally with the cardinal virtues and their importance to a polity. The ideas expressed in The Governor are by no means original, but the way that Elyot combines them invests the book with the quality of a personal vision.

Elyot's political theory in book 1, drawn largely from Plato's Republic, Aristotle's Politics, and Thomas Aquinas's De regimine principium, centers upon his belief in the necessity for a hierarchy reflecting the scale of being he accepts as self-evident in nature. The state, Elyot asserts, depends upon order and degree as safeguards against chaos and conflict, and order itself is dependent upon the presence of "one sovereign governor" who rules as "one sun ruleth over the day, and one moon over the night." Next in the hierarchy should be a ruling elite of "magistrates" or "inferior governors" appointed by the prince, who should function as "his eyes, ears, hands, and legs." In Elyot's view, where such an elite, or aristocracy, exists, "it seemeth impossible [for] a country not to be well governed by good laws." It is with the education of this class that the rest of the book is principally concerned. Elyot's political theory in many respects is strikingly similar to the theory of imperial sovereignty devised by Edward Foxe and Thomas Cranmer in a document called the Collectanea satis copiosa, presented to Henry VIII in September 1530. Through his long-standing friendship with Thomas Cromwell, who had been promoted to the King's Council in 1530, Elyot is likely to have known of this document, and the opening chapters of The Governor appear to have been contrived to appeal to Henry's growing sense of his own power.

Elyot's educational theory in The Governor is drawn primarily from Plutarch's De educatione puerorum, Quintilian's Institutio oratoria, and Erasmus's De ratione studii (1511) and De pueris (1529). Following his sources, Elyot outlines a curriculum constructed according to an ascending hierarchy of progressively more difficult disciplines. A child studies Greek and Latin, together with some simple poets, until the age of fourteen, after which he studies logic, rhetoric, history, and cosmography until the age of seventeen. Thereafter he proceeds to moral

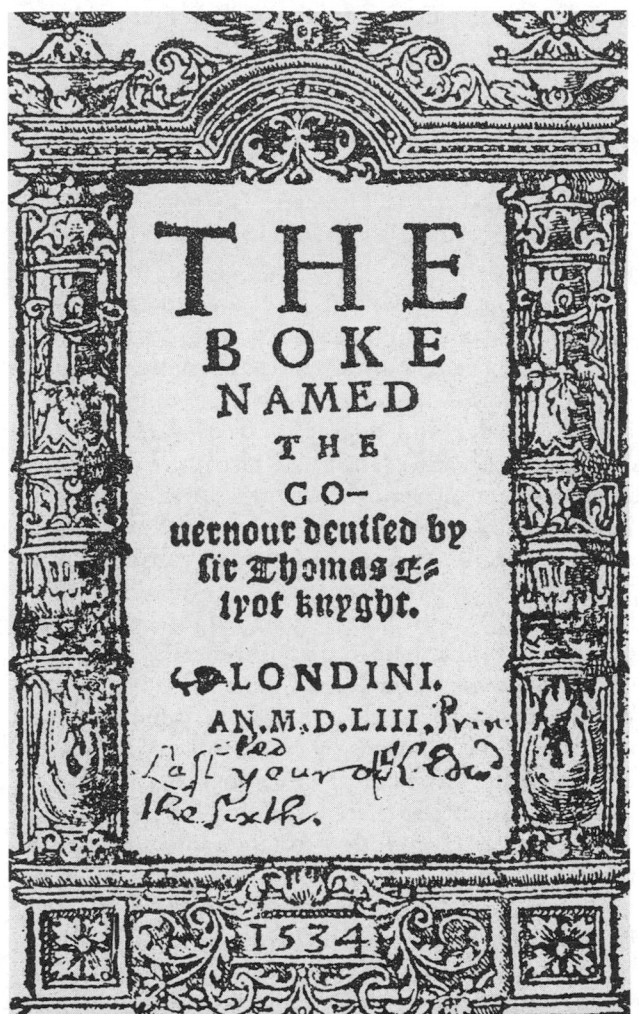

Title page for a 1553 edition of Elyot's best-known work, a major document of the early Tudor humanist movement

philosophy, the Bible, and the works of Erasmus. These academic studies are to be complemented by a variety of recreations and exercises. From Baldassare Castiglione's Courtier (1528), Elyot draws the idea that youths should study painting, sculpture, and music, while from Galen, Lucian, and Plato he adopts the view that exercises such as wrestling, running, swimming, riding, and the handling of various weapons are necessary for the preservation of health and to "make the spirits of a man more strong and valiant, so that, by the hardness of the members, all labors be more tolerable." Archery, Elyot concludes, is especially important – a view that Roger Ascham would later reiterate in Toxophilus (1545).

The most important influences on books 2 and 3, dealing with the political virtues, are Plato's Republic, Aristotle's Nichomachaean Ethics, Cicero's De of-

ficiis, Erasmus's *Education of a Christian Prince* (1516), and several treatises by the Italian humanists Giovanni Pontano and Francesco Patrizi. Elyot's definitions of the virtues are entirely derivative and commonplace, but they are enlivened by a multitude of exemplary anecdotes, the most famous of which is the story of Titus and Gisippus, which he drew from the *Decameron* (1353) of Giovanni Boccaccio.

The Governor served as a convenient source book for ideas and exempla for most English writers through the rest of the sixteenth century, including William Shakespeare, who drew upon Elyot's ideas on order and degree in *Henry V* (1599) and *Troilus and Cressida* (1601). It also gave humanist ideas a wider currency than they otherwise would have had and introduced a whole raft of new words into the English language. Latinate words such as "adumbration," "congruent," "context," "edify," "fastidious," "mutilate," "personage," and "surmount" all made their first appearance in *The Governor.* In contrast to Sir John Cheke, who urged that English be written "clean and pure, unmixed and unmangled with borrowing of other tongues," Elyot was an enthusiastic coiner of neologisms, as he later candidly admitted when describing his purposes in *The Governor:* "I intended to augment our English tongue, whereby men should as well express more abundantly the thing that they conceived in their hearts (wherefore language was ordained) having words apt for the purpose: as also interpret out of Greek, Latin, or any other tongue into English, as sufficiently as out of any one of the said tongues into another."

To match his concern with amplifying the language, Elyot chose a much more elaborate prose style for *The Governor* than he had chosen for his translation of Plutarch's *De educatione puerorum,* as befitted the more elevated status of the person to whom it was addressed, the king. Whereas the earlier work had been comparatively simple in style, containing few inkhorn words and relying largely upon a paratactic or coordinate sentence structure native to English, *The Governor* displays many features of the new "Ciceronian" style invented by the humanists in imitation of classical Latin: rhythmical intricacy, clauses arranged into complex patterns of subordination, and main verbs artfully delayed so that the sense is not complete until the last word. While for the most part Elyot handles this new style with grace and clarity, occasionally he falls victim to its pitfalls, as in the following extract from his discussion of beneficence and liberality: "Although philosophers in the description of virtues have de-

vised to set them as it were in degrees, having respect to the quality and condition of the person which is with them adorned; as applying magnificence to the substance and estate of princes, and to private persons beneficence and liberality, yet be not these in any part defalcate of their condigne praises." Here Elyot duplicates the form of a Latinate sentence without relegating the ideas contained in it into an appropriate hierarchy of subordination, so that the match between form and content is less than ideal. On a larger scale, the same is true of the rhetorical structure of the work, with the division into three books being fairly arbitrary rather than necessitated by any inherent principle of thematic organization. Book 1, for instance, switches abruptly from a philosophical speculation on the nature of a just public weal to a description of Elyot's ideal educational curriculum, which then mutates into a discussion of desirable moral qualities that crosses the divide into book 2. Unlike greater writers such as Edmund Spenser, whom he would influence, Elyot had very little sense of architectonic control, which limits the success of his books as works of art.

Despite any aesthetic limitations it may have had, *The Governor* did help Elyot gain the opportunity he desired, to enter the king's service. In early September 1531 he was appointed ambassador to the Holy Roman Emperor Charles V. The impact of *The Governor,* together with the good offices of Cromwell, had impressed Henry VIII to the extent that he believed Elyot could be useful in representing his desire for a divorce from Catherine of Aragon – a mission that was delicate, if not doomed, because Charles was Catherine's nephew. Elyot's brief was to "fish out" the emperor's opinion of Henry's efforts to procure a divorce and to ascertain whether Charles was preparing hostilities against England, reminding him not to "meddle" in the king's "great cause." Elyot was also given the task of apprehending William Tyndale in the Netherlands, whose opposition to the divorce the king wished to silence.

Within several months Henry had grown dissatisfied with Elyot, who was recalled to England in January 1532, to be replaced by Thomas Cranmer. Neither Elyot nor Eustace Chapuys, the imperial ambassador to London, could understand the reasons for Elyot's recall. Though Henry told Chapuys that Elyot had been recalled at the request of Queen Catherine, Elyot noted that the king's opinion of him had lessened, and that he was held "in less estimation" than when he first served the king as clerk to the council. It is probable that Henry and Cromwell had grown dissatisfied at Elyot's lack of progress in furthering the king's cause, which can be partly explained by the conflict between Elyot's brief and his personal beliefs regarding the matter. In reality, Elyot strongly opposed the divorce, causing him to play a double game in ways that were highly dangerous, if not downright treasonous. On his return to England in June 1532, he had not only briefed Chapuys on the conversation he had had with Henry upon his arrival, but also sent a detailed report in cipher to Gonsalvo de Pueblo, the emperor's chaplain, whose father had helped to arrange Henry's marriage to Catherine. Elyot's actions thus appear as those of one who was covertly serving the queen's interest against the orders of his royal master. In such circumstances it was impossible for him to represent the king's interests effectively, and Henry appears to have sensed this.

The next group of Elyot's writings responded to his frustration at being dispossessed of his office a second time. Despite the brave face he put on it, he felt bitterly aggrieved at his fall from favor and resented the elevation of others to the positions of confidence and counsel to which he aspired. His letters at this time show him to have nursed a sense of grievance at the failure of the king to acknowledge his true worth on one hand and his willingness to promote less-qualified men on the other. In a letter of 18 November 1532 he complained that "I perceive other men advanced openly to the place of councillors which neither in the importance of service neither in charges have served the king as I have done." Moreover, he attributed their advancement to a willingness on their part to tell the king what he wanted to hear. Indeed, by 1533 Elyot was convinced that his own dismissal had occurred because he had been unwilling to dissemble the truth, given that, upon returning from his embassy, he had remonstrated with the king against the latter's desire for a divorce. Although Elyot adopted a pose of absolute stoic integrity in response to his fall from favor, there are signs that he had felt tempted to imitate his rivals by dissembling his true opinions in order to gain promotion. Writing to John Hackett on 6 April 1533, he affirms that he is "finally determined to live and die" in the truth, and that "neither mine importable expenses unrecompensed shall so much fear me, nor the advancement of my successor the Bishop of Canterbury so much allure me that I shall ever decline from truth or abuse my sovereign lord unto whom I am sworn." The mere fact that he felt moved to make these assertions suggests that Elyot had felt a strong temptation to play the game that he knew was required.

The complex emotions aroused in Elyot by his dismissal from office produced two of his most interesting and original works. In *Pasquil the Plain* and *Of the Knowledge Which Maketh a Wise Man,* both published in 1533, he chose to dramatize his stance in order to justify it, while at the same time reproving his rivals for their encouragement of what he saw as the king's willfulness. Abandoning straightforward philosophical exposition, Elyot chose as his vehicle the dramatized dialogue, a form earlier used by Sir Thomas More in *Utopia* (1516) to explore the conflict in politics between what is honest and what is expedient.

In the earlier of the two works, Pasquil, a stone statue in Rome, and two cousins, Gnatho, a courtier, and Harpocrates, a priest-confessor, both of whom have been called to council, are brought into conflict. The encounter dramatizes three different forms of political conduct: plainspokeness, represented by Pasquil; obsequious flattery, represented by Gnatho; and hypocritical dissembling, represented by Harpocrates. In the course of the dialogue, both Gnatho's sycophancy and Harpocrates' willingness to have it seem as if his silence gives consent are rejected as modes of political conduct. Nevertheless, even though he wins the argument, Pasquil is left none the happier, for the dialogue also dramatizes the ironic position in which his moral absolutism traps him as one (as Gnatho declares) uses "unprofitable taunts and rebukes ... whereby nothing that thou blamest is of one jot amended, and thou losest thereby preferment which thine excellent wit doth require." Elyot claims in the "Proheme" to *Of the Knowledge Which Maketh a Wise Man* that *Pasquil the Plain* was not intended to touch one man more than another; but in spite of this protestation, one can detect in Harpocrates a thinly disguised caricature of his rival and successor, Cranmer, while Pasquil is an idealized projection of Elyot himself.

Of the Knowledge Which Maketh a Wise Man presents the same insoluble dilemma in dialogue form, but utilizes a historical rather than a symbolic scenario. The tale Elyot adopts is that of Plato's fall from grace at the court of Dionysius, King of Sicily, as told by Diogenes Laertius in his biographies of the Greek philosophers. When the dialogue opens Plato, dressed in rags, is traveling along the road with Aristippus, a voluptuary, and recounts to him how he was sold into slavery for having told Dionysius that he was turning into a tyrant. Although the rest of the dialogue proves that Plato could not have behaved in any other way if he were to remain true to the ideals he was proclaiming, it acknowledges the existence of the same tragic paradox that had been admitted in *Pasquil the Plain:* that any attempt to act according to the idealistic principles of humanistic doctrine was likely to disqualify a man from office, because those very principles would prevent him from acting with the degree of hypocritical sycophancy that a prince usually required. In effect, Elyot's literary response to his own political misfortunes led him to uncover the same paradoxical dilemma at the heart of Renaissance humanism that More had explored in book 1 of *Utopia* a decade earlier.

Neither of Elyot's 1533 dialogues is entirely successful as fiction, as the situations they present are exploited chiefly as pretexts for philosophical reflection rather than as the means for creating a fully imagined world. The speakers remain stereotypes because Elyot shows neither much character in action, nor much action in character. Instead, the characters express their respective philosophical positions in speech that does not strongly differentiate the one from the other. Elyot's dialogues can therefore be described as "incomplete fictions," a phrase that Kenneth Jay Wilson uses to characterize the dialogue genre as a whole in the English Renaissance.

Perhaps realizing the futility of the position his dialogues espoused, especially in the light of a friendly warning from Cromwell that he could not compel men to esteem him as he wished they would, Elyot decided to withdraw from involvement with politics into the world of scholarship. In a letter which acknowledges Cromwell's warning, Elyot affirms that *Of the Knowledge Which Maketh a Wise Man* is "the last English book which I purpose ever to make, unless the desire of some special friend compel me." Fortunately, Elyot did not abide by his decision, for the next decade saw a string of important translations and compilations, all written in English.

The first of them, *The Doctrinal of Princes* (circa 1533), is a translation from the Greek of the oration that Isocrates made to his former pupil Nicocles when the latter became king of Salamis. The oration itself is a fairly conventional "mirror" for princes, with its catalogue of virtues to be cultivated, injuries to be avoided, and duties to be performed. It is, however, chiefly interesting for Elyot's claim that he has chosen to translate it directly out of Greek "to the intent only that I would assay, if our English tongue might receive the quick and proper sentences pronounced by the Greeks." To his satisfaction, Elyot found that Greek phrasing "much nearer approacheth to that which at this day we use than the order of the Latin tongue: I mean in the senten-

ces, and not in the words." The treatise thus shows Elyot trying to bring the essence of this classical work to a wider English readership by taking a fresh approach to the original, and by showing the capacity of the vernacular to serve as a vehicle for serious political and intellectual discussion.

The next works from this period are translations: *A Sweet and Devout Sermon of the Mortality of Man,* and Pico della Mirandola's *Rules of a Christian Life,* the two being published together in a volume dedicated to Elyot's stepsister, Susan Fetiplace (a nun), probably in 1534. Both translations share a common theme: the means of avoiding vice, or "how we may be always prepared against those natural and worldly affections."

In *A Sweet and Devout Sermon* Elyot chose yet again to imitate in English the complex patterns of subordination and massive length of the Latinate periodic sentence:

> Right well-beloved friends, all be it that many of you have your minds entire and perfect, the faith stable, and the soul devout, not being moved with the hugeness of this present mortality, but like to a puissant and steadfast rock rather do break the troublous assaults of this world, and the violent floods of this present time, the soul herself not being broken nor overcome with any temptations, but only proved, nevertheless, for as much as I do consider to be in the multitude divers which either by weakness of courage, or by smallness of faith, or by sweetness of the life of this world, or by the delicateness of their kind, or (that which is a more heavy thing) being deceived in the opinion of truth, do not stand fast nor set forth the divine and invincible might of their stomachs, I might no longer dissemble that matter, nor retain it in silence, but that as far forth as the meaness of my learning or wit might extend, I would declare the doctrine of Christ by a sermon conceived and lively expressed, to the intent that the sloth and dullness of delicate mindes might be reformed.

Despite the difficulty of sustaining such elaborate syntactical structures in English, Elyot is reasonably successful in *A Sweet and Devout Sermon* in finding a sufficiently elevated style to do justice to the impassioned homiletical manner of Saint Cyprian's original.

The stylistic contrast with the *Rules of a Christian Life,* which supplements Cyprian's sermon, is striking. Whereas for *A Sweet and Devout Sermon* Elyot opted for an aureate style, for the *Rules of a Christian Life* he chose one that is comparatively plain and straightforward: "In all temptations resist the beginning, and beat the children of Babylon against the stone, which stone is Christ, and the children be evil thoughts and imaginations. For in long continuing of sin, seldom worketh any medicine or remedy." As More had earlier found when translating Pico's *Twelve Rules* into verse, Elyot discovered that the simplicity and directness of the native English plain style was the best vehicle for inculcating the lessons of practical piety that Pico had propounded.

Also in 1534 appeared the first edition of *The Banquet of Sapience* (which has survived only in a later edition), a collection of adages offered to Henry VIII for his recreation and nourishment as if they were dishes at a feast — some sweet, some poignant, and some *aigre douce* (sweet and sour). There is nothing at all original about this compilation, the entries being drawn chiefly from Seneca, Cicero, Solomon, Saint Augustine, and the Bible, but in its alphabetical arrangement it anticipates Elyot's penchant for dictionary making.

During this time Elyot must also have been assembling the entries for *The Castle of Health* (circa 1537), a manual for preserving health and treating common ailments. His interest in medicine had dated from his early years, and it had already resurfaced in book 1 of *The Governor,* in which he draws on Galen's views on the utility of exercise. By writing a manual on health, in fact, Elyot was following in an established tradition of medical humanism that had developed in Italy and begun to spread into northern Europe during the sixteenth century. Linacre had taken the degree of doctor of medicine at Padua with great distinction, and on his return to England he had translated the works of Galen from Greek into Latin, and had founded the Royal College of Physicians. *The Castle of Health* represents Elyot's attempt, in his typical fashion, to render the knowledge of medical humanism into a popular form. His compilation is not the earliest health manual to appear in English, but it is certainly the first to achieve a widespread circulation, being printed at least fourteen times before 1610 — even though, from the time it first appeared, it provoked the hostility of the Royal College of Physicians.

The Castle of Health is divided into four books. Book 1 expounds the classical theory of the humors and complexions; book 2 appraises different foods and forms of exercise; book 3, after examining methods of keeping the humors in balance, discusses "the affects of the mind" (that is, the emotions); book 4 examines "crudity," or faulty digestion, and looks at other symptoms of disease. Predictably, most of the material is drawn from Galen and Hippocrates, supplemented by information from other classical writers such as Celsus, Pedanius Dioscori-

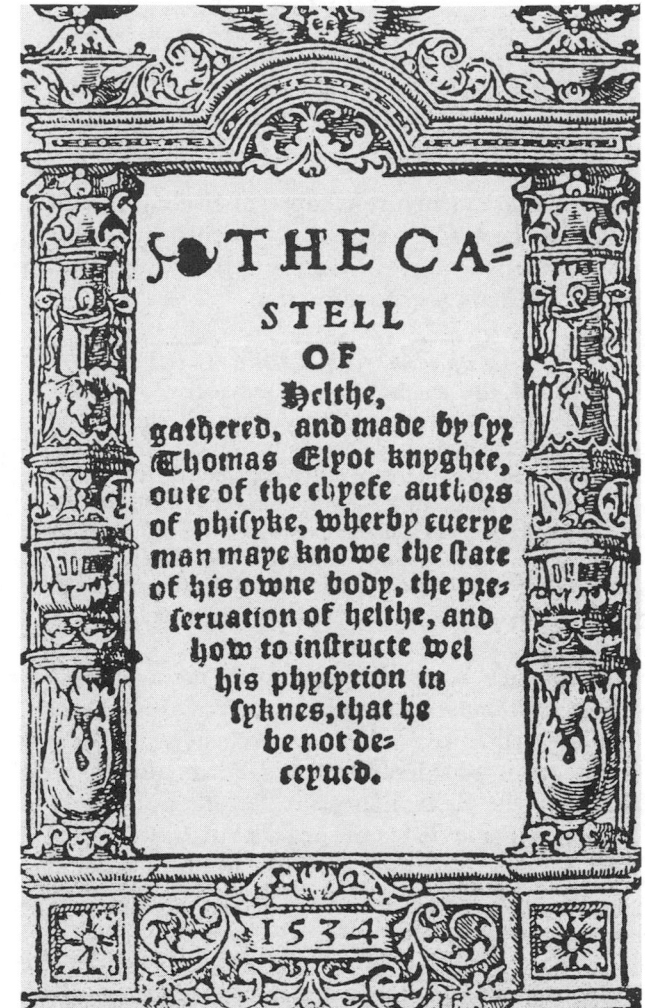

Title page for Elyot's health manual, one of the last medical works to rely on Galen's theory of bodily humors

des, Oribasius, and Aëtios of Amida, and from the Arab writers Rhazes and Damascenus (Yuhanna ibn-Masawayh). The intent of the book is to provide practical recommendations for a diet to remedy any imbalance of humors. It is ironic that *The Castle of Health* was to be the swan song of the humoral theory that had dominated medical lore from classical times, through the Middle Ages, into the Renaissance. Elyot could hardly have known that within a century William Harvey's discovery of the circulation of the blood would render obsolete most of the medical knowledge he was disseminating.

The style of *The Castle of Health* is, for the most part, simple and direct, as befits a prose of exposition, even though Elyot was still concerned to introduce Latinate neologisms where necessary, as in the word *extenuate* in the following extract:

Leeks,
Be of ill juice, and do make troublous dreams, but they do extenuate [that is, make lean] and clense the body, and also make it soluble, and provoketh urine. Moreover it causeth one to spit out easily the phlegm, which is in the breast.

His sentence structure is more often than not modeled on the trailing sentence (which in turn shows the influence of French originals) to be found in medieval manuals of instruction:

Of Bloodsuckers or Leeches. Cap. 9.
There is also another form of evacuation by worms found in waters, called bloodsuckers or leeches, which being put unto the body or member, do draw out blood. And their drawing is more convenient for fullness of blood than scarifying is, for as much as they fetch blood more deeper, and is more of the substance of blood. Yet the opinion of some men is that they do draw no blood but that which is corrupted and not proportionable unto our body.

Sentences such as these accumulate main and subordinate statements linked by connectives into a long, trailing sequence, rather than reproducing the artfully arranged hierarchy of subordinations to be found in the Ciceronian style. Elyot's willingness to adopt such a style for purposes of instruction shows that he was highly attuned to the needs of his intended lay audience, as against the courtiers to whom his political treatises were addressed.

In spite of his desire to withdraw from the political hurly-burly into scholarship, Elyot's difficulties did not end when he retreated from active political life in the mid 1530s. He remained very much under suspicion as one who harbored papist sympathies. Much of his trouble arose from his friendship with More. When, in mid 1534, Henry and Cromwell became incensed at the refusal of More and John Fisher to take the oath upholding the Act of Succession (which would have meant acknowledging the validity of Henry's divorce from Catherine of Aragon and marriage to Anne Boleyn), Elyot became tainted by association. His earlier disapproval of the king's plans for a divorce in 1532 also undoubtedly counted against him. In any case, Elyot found it necessary to exculpate himself on several occasions.

The first occurred in late 1534 in response to a royal proclamation calling for the surrender of seditious books. In a letter to Cromwell, Elyot, nervously appealing to their old friendship, begs Cromwell to advise him how he can best comply with the proclamation. Professing to own only one of the proscribed books by Fisher, he affirms that he has never been greatly interested in doctrinal matters, that he is an ardent supporter of the reform of clerical abuses, and that his reformist sympathies have led him into contention with "such persons as ye have thought that I have specially favored," which "relented the great affection between us and withdrew our familiar repair." While Elyot does not mention More by name, it is practically certain that More is the chief among those to whom he refers.

On another occasion Elyot does mention More by name. In a letter written either in late 1536 or early 1537, in which he begs Cromwell to "bring [him] into the king's most noble remembrance" so that he might be rewarded with "some convenient portion" of the suppressed monastic lands, he goes to great lengths once again to distance himself from More. He beseeches Cromwell "now to lay apart the remembrance of the amity between me and Sir Thomas More which was but *usque ad aras*" (as far as the altars – in other words, to the point at which conscience must take preeminence over friendship in dictating decisions). In the same letter Elyot acknowledges to Cromwell that "I perceive that ye suspect that I savor not truly holy scripture." He responds simply by wishing that the king and Cromwell "might see the most secret thoughts of [his] heart."

Cromwell was not the only one to suspect Elyot of being a papist. On 21 January 1537 one John Parkyns denounced him to Cromwell as being in collusion with the abbots of Reading and Eynsham in support of the monasteries. A commission of inquiry appointed by the king found Parkyns's accusations to be malicious, but the episode indicates that a belief that Elyot was a papist was widespread in the mid 1530s.

That Elyot survived the political turmoil surrounding the royal supremacy, given his known sympathy with the Catholic side, is a testimony either to his astuteness, luck, the good offices of Cromwell, or all three. Having survived these crises, he appears gradually to have regained some of the royal trust and favor that had been withdrawn from him after his ill-fated embassy of 1531. The works Elyot wrote in the last decade of his life show him once again seeking to gain court patronage and a position as councillor that he believed to be commensurate with his abilities and knowledge.

One sign of Elyot's renewed campaign to regain court patronage is the dedication to Cromwell he supplied for the second edition of *The Castle of Health* in 1539. "Friendship," he reminds Cromwell, "should be requited," but he adds disingenuously that he craves "none other thing, but only equal benevolence and faith without any suspicion." By the time the third edition of *The Castle of Health* appeared in 1541, Cromwell had been beheaded for treason, and Elyot wisely removed this dedication.

At the same time that Elyot was trying to cultivate Cromwell, he renewed his attempts to capture the attention of the king, this time by dedicating to Henry the dictionary he had compiled. As always, he drew heavily on the work of others for his *The Dictionary of Sir Thomas Elyot* (1538), notably the Latin *Dictionarium* of Ambrose Calepine of Bergamo (1502); but it was, nevertheless, an impressive accomplishment, being the first Latin-English dictionary, as distinct from a Latin-English wordbook, such as the *Promptorium parvulorum* (circa 1440). Elyot's achievement has been praised by DeWitt T. Starnes who asserts that Elyot "laid the foundation for a system of lexicography in England, a foundation on which his successors continued to build during the sixteenth century." Elyot's system, influenced by Continental predecessors, involved the alphabetical arrangement of entries and the inclusion of grammatical and etymological information as well as definition.

In the dedicatory epistle to the king, Elyot records how he had "received a new spirit" when he heard that Henry, having been alerted by Cromwell to this lexicographical endeavor, commended his enterprise and offered the assistance of his counsel and books. Thus encouraged, Elyot set about thoroughly revising and augmenting his work, which resulted in the much grander *Bibliotheca Eliotae* of 1542, again dedicated to the king.

The expanded *Bibliotheca,* incorporating material drawn from Robert Estienne's *Dictionarium Latino-Gallicum* (1538), Erasmus's *Adagia* (1508), and William Turner's *Libellus de re herbaria novus* (1538), has a much greater range than the earlier *Dictionary.* As Elyot describes in his "Proheme," he had endeavored to make

a general collection by the order of letters of all notable countries, cities, mountains, and rivers, with their true descriptions, bounds, and commodities; the names and natures of sundry beasts, fowls, serpents, and fishes; the declaration of a great number of herbs, trees, fruits, gums, precious stones and metals, which before me were never of any man (that I can hear of) declared and set forth in English; the true definitions of all sicknesses and kinds of maladies, which commonly do happen to men, with the cause whereof they proceed; finally the names of most notable personages, who from the first man Adam until three hundred years after the incarnation of Christ, did anything worthy a special remembrance.

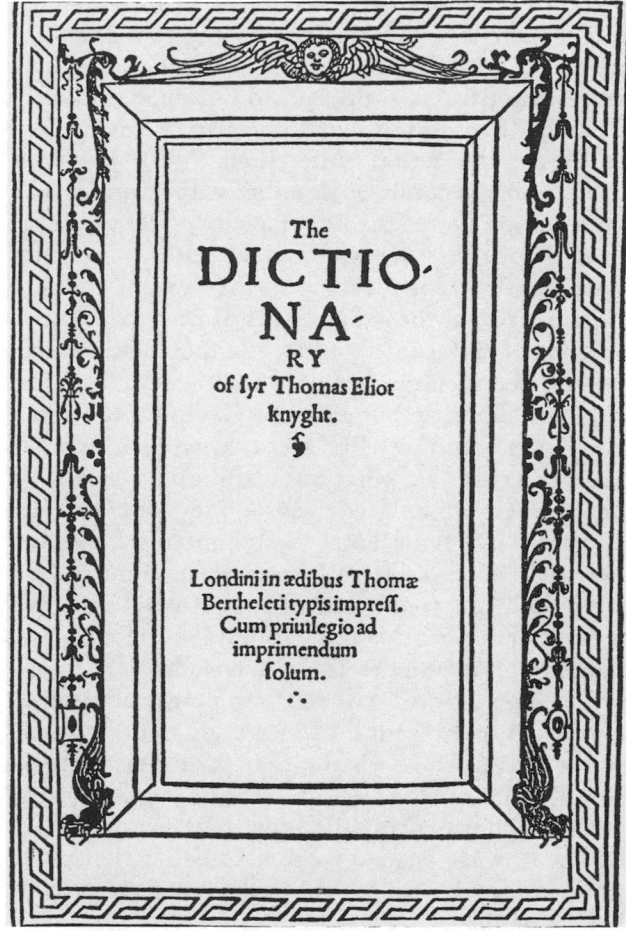

The
DICTIO-
NA-
RY
of fyr Thomas Eliot
knyght.

Londini in ædibus Thomæ
Bertheleti typis impreff.
Cum priuilegio ad
imprimendum
folum.

Title page for Elyot's 1538 work, which he dedicated to Henry VIII

Elyot includes, moreover, information on weights, coins and measures, chronology, proverbs, and the proper terms relating to physic, surgery, and diverse other arts and sciences. His purpose in dedicating the *Bibliotheca Eliotae* to the king can be inferred from his observation that it is "no marvel that great kings have in their councils most witty persons, seeing that the making of great wits is in their puissance." He took as his proof the effect that Henry's encouragement had had on him, with the implied suggestion that he, too, deserved to be considered one of these "witty persons." Clearly, Elyot was still nurturing hopes of being appointed to the King's Council.

When Henry decided to remarry after the death of Queen Jane Seymour, Elyot made a bid for the favor of the new queen by publishing *The Defense of Good Women* (1540). This slim volume is a Platonic dialogue, based upon Boccaccio's *De claris mulieribus* (1364), which revolves around a dispute between Caninius, a misogynist who condemns women, and Candidus, a praiser of women. Candidus's view is proved right by Queen Zenobia, whose example confirms that "women, being well and virtuously brought up, do not only with men participate in reason, but some also in fidelity and constancy be equal unto them." Elyot adapts Boccaccio's account of Zenobia with considerable imagination. Whereas Boccaccio narrates the story from a third-person point of view, setting the events in the past, Elyot places it in the present and has Zenobia reveal the salient facts of her story. As he says in his preface, "to induce that noble princess to declare her own life, I devised a contention between two gentlemen, the one named Caninius, the other Candidus. Caninius like a cur, at women's conditions is always barking, but Candidus, which may be interpreted benign or gentle, judgeth ever well, and reproveth but seldom." Caninius and Candidus are stock figures drawn from Roman comedy (the cynic and the benevolent man), crossed with the moral personifications to be found in the medieval morality plays and the Tudor interludes. The dramatized interaction between these points of view allows Elyot to present his flatteringly implicit praise of the new queen's virtue in a way that is both arresting and novel. Any hopes that he might have entertained of procuring the favor of Anne of Cleves, however, were dashed by the revulsion Henry felt for his new wife, which led to the marriage quickly being annulled.

The Image of Governance (1540) marks Elyot's final bid for patronage. It consists of "the acts and sentences notable" of the Roman emperor Marcus Aurelius Alexander Severus (reigned 222–235), assembled about 1532, soon after Elyot had published *The Governor*. He purported to have gathered the material out of a book written by Alexander's secretary named Eucolpius; but no such source has been traced, and *The Image of Governance* is drawn, in fact, largely from the lives of the emperors by Aelius Lampridius (fourth century A.D.) and political material derived from Herodotus (fifth century B.C.).

Regarding this work, Elyot wrote that he desired "more to make it plain to all readers, than to flourish it with over much eloquence." Consequently, *The Image of Governance* lacks much of the Latinate diction and complex syntactic patterning that he had used to heighten the style of *The Governor*. Instead, he was content to present a simple compendium of events in the life of Alexander Severus that display the emperor's virtuous qualities and practices as a ruler, narrated in a style that is serviceably plain in diction and relatively uncomplicated in sentence structure.

Elyot's purpose is to offer Alexander Severus as "a pattern to knights, an example to judges, a mirror to princes, and a beautiful image to all them that are like to be governors." To do so, he juxtaposes the deeds of Alexander Severus as the ideal against those of Heliogabalus (Roman emperor from 218 to 222) as an archetypal bad prince. In essence, the ideal state that *The Image of Governance* presents is a realization in practice of the blueprint delineated theoretically in *The Governor,* so that the two works may be regarded as complementary.

Elyot dedicated his final political work to the nobles, "as being most ready to be advanced to governance under your prince," claiming that he himself has "more regard to my last reckoning than to any riches or worldly promotion." Nevertheless, his bitter observation that "diverse there be which do not thankfully esteem my labors, dispraising my studies as vain and unprofitable, saying in derision that I have nothing won thereby, but the name only of a maker of books" suggests that he may have been protesting too much.

None of Elyot's hopes for preferment to a major post were to bear fruit. He was called upon to serve in a variety of minor administrative capacities during the late 1530s and early 1540s, being appointed to the commission to visit monasteries in Oxford and Oxfordshire in 1535; the commission of Oyer and Terminer for the Eastern Circuit in 1541; the Commission of Sewers for Cambridgeshire, Huntingdonshire, Lincolnshire, and Northamptonshire in 1540 and 1544; and the commission to take musters for Cambridgeshire in 1546, as well as serving intermittently as sheriff and justice of the peace. He also received a token of the king's favor by being granted on 5 December 1539 some lands in Cambridgeshire that had belonged to the Abbey of Eynsham. But he was never appointed to any of the influential political offices for which he believed his learning qualified him. His true feelings on the matter are expressed in the 1541 edition of *The Castle of Health* when he discusses the emotional effects of lack of promotion: "Oftentimes the repulse from promotion is cause of discomfort: but then consider, whether in the opinion of good men, thou art deemed worthy to have such advancement, or in thine own expectation and fantasy." Evidently, after his abortive career as an ambassador, Elyot was never able to persuade his masters that he was a suitable person to whom political office could be entrusted.

Elyot's final work was *A Preservative against Death,* a devotional treatise "gathered together out of holy scripture" and written during Lent, 1545.

The book is dedicated to Sir Edward North, chancellor of the Court of Augmentations, and consists of a conventional meditation on the attempts of the devil to ensnare men with the temptations of his sisters, the flesh, and the world. Elyot's description of the world places him in the allegorical tradition that would find its fullest expression in Spenser's portrayal of Duessa and Acrasia, the evil enchantresses of *The Faerie Queene* (1596), and Spenser was doubtless influenced by Elyot's lurid image of the world as a lascivious woman:

> She cometh against thee with her paps open, full of serpentine poison, and with her hands decked with rings of gold and rich stones, she proffereth to embrace thee. And with a loud voice and a delectable she saith: 'Lo, I am come for to meet thee, and now have I found thee. I have decked my bed with cloths of Egypt, my bed have I made to smell of myrrh, aloes, and cinnamon. Let us lie together and take our pleasure.'

Elyot's remedy against these enemies is contempt of the world and contemplation of the greater joys of the world to come. Interestingly, in the course of the book he denounces the Protestant doctrine of predestination, which confirms his ultimate adherence to the old religion that his detractors had long suspected.

Elyot died on 26 March 1546, leaving all his lands to his wife, Margaret, and was buried in the parish church at Carlton, Cambridgeshire. In his will he directed that all his books be sold and the proceeds "distributed to poor scholars which be good students" and left various other charitable bequests.

In a final estimation, Elyot cannot be judged a greatly creative or original literary genius, but he is nevertheless an important figure in English literary and intellectual history. In addition to his extraordinary infusion of new words into the English language, his achievement lies in his ability to synthesize humanist learning in order to disseminate and popularize it. By being the first writer to present such material in English, Elyot came to exert a much greater influence on subsequent writers in England than might be expected of someone who was not a deeply original thinker or imaginative writer. For the rest of the century Elyot's books were a common source for most writers, including Spenser and Shakespeare, of basic information concerning moral and political philosophy, medical lore, and semantic matters. In this respect, at least, Elyot made a major contribution to the history of English literature.

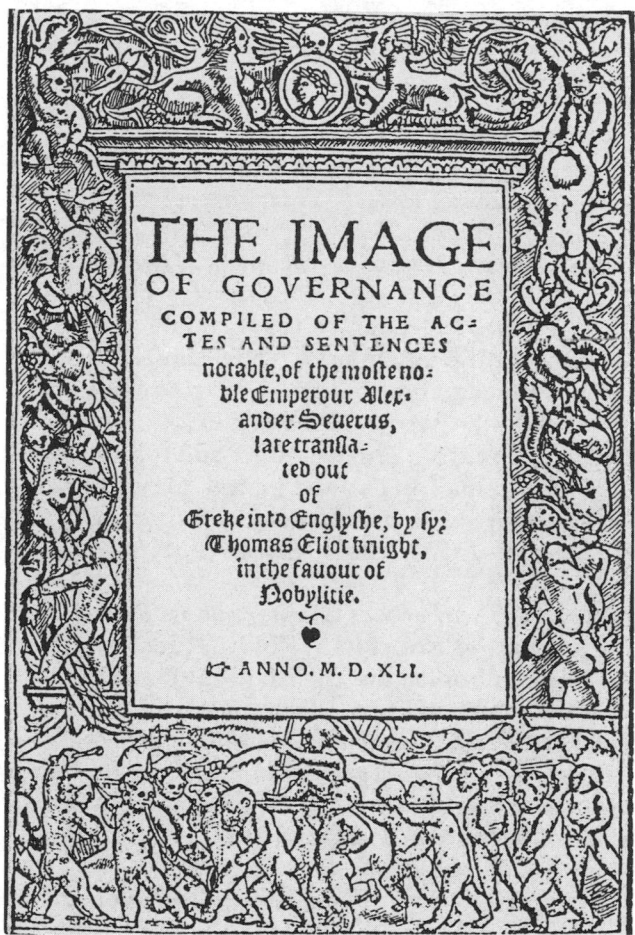

Title page for Elyot's final political work, in which he compares the Roman emperor Alexander Severus, his model of the ideal ruler, with Severus's predecessor, Heliogabulus, Elyot's archetypal bad prince

Letters:

"The Letters of Sir Thomas Elyot," edited by Kenneth Jay Wilson, *Studies in Philology,* 73, no. 5 (December 1976): 1–78.

Bibliographies:

E. J. Freeman, "A Bibliography of Sir Thomas Elyot (1490?–1546)," Ph.D. dissertation, University of London, 1962;

Jerome S. Dees, "Recent Studies in Elyot," *English Literary Renaissance,* 6 (Spring 1976): 336–344.

Biographies:

Stanford E. Lehmberg, *Sir Thomas Elyot, Tudor Humanist* (Austin: University of Texas Press, 1960);

John M. Major, *Sir Thomas Elyot and Renaissance Humanism* (Lincoln: University of Nebraska Press, 1964);

Pearl Hogrefe, *The Life and Times of Sir Thomas Elyot, Englishman* (Ames: Iowa State University Press, 1967).

References:

Constance W. Bouck, "On the Identity of Papyrius Geminus Eleates," *Transactions of the Cambridge Bibliographical Society,* 2, no. 5 (1958): 352–358;

Fritz Caspari, *Humanism and the Social Order in Tudor England* (Chicago: University of Chicago Press, 1954), pp. 76–109;

Henry Wolfgang Donner, "The Emperor and Sir Thomas Elyot," *Review of English Studies,* new series 2 (January 1951): 55–59;

Alistair Fox, "Sir Thomas Elyot and the Humanist Dilemma," in Fox and John A. Guy, *Reassessing the Henrician Age: Humanism, Politics and Reform 1500–1550* (Oxford: Blackwell, 1986), pp. 52–73;

Guy, *The Court of Star Chamber and Its Records to the Reign of Elizabeth I,* Public Records Office Handbooks, no. 21 (London: Her Majesty's Stationers Office, 1985), pp. 11–13, 23;

Richard Foster Jones, *The Triumph of the English Language: A Survey of Opinions Concerning the Vernacular from the Introduction of Printing to the Restoration* (Stanford: Stanford University Press, 1953), pp. 71, 78–82;

Constance Jordan, "Feminism and the Humanists: The Case of Sir Thomas Elyot's *Defence of Good Women,*" *Renaissance Quarterly,* 36 (Summer 1983): 181–201;

Mary Lascelles, "Sir Thomas Elyot and the Legend of Alexander Severus," *Review of English Studies,* new series 2 (October 1951): 305–318;

James Kelsey McConica, *English Humanists and Reformation Politics under Henry VIII and Edward IV* (Oxford: Clarendon Press, 1965);

Donald W. Rude, "On the Date of Sir Thomas Elyot's *Bringinge up of Children,*" *Papers of the Bibliographical Society of America,* 71, no. 1 (1977): 61–65;

Thomas Stapleton, *Tres Thomae,* translated by Philip Edward Hallett (London, 1928);

DeWitt T. Starnes, *Renaissance Dictionaries: English-Latin and Latin-English* (Austin: University of Texas Press, 1954), pp. 45–84;

Starnes, "Shakespeare and Elyot's *Governour,*" *University of Texas Studies in English,* 7 (November 1927): 112–132;

Kenneth Jay Wilson, *Incomplete Fictions: The Formation of English Renaissance Dialogue* (Washington, D.C.: Catholic University of America Press, 1985), pp. 75–107;

Wilson, "*Usque ad aras:* Thomas Elyot's Friendship with Thomas More," in *Actus Conventus Neo-Latini Sanctandreani: Proceedings of the Fifth International Congress of Neo-Latin Studies,* edited by Ian Dalrymple McFarlane (Binghamton, N.Y.: Medieval and Renaissance Texts and Studies, 1986), pp. 531–535;

James Wortham, "Sir Thomas Elyot and the Translation of Prose," *Huntington Library Quarterly,* 11 (May 1948): 219–240.

Desiderius Erasmus

(circa October 1467 – 12 July 1536)

Mary M. Schmelzer
Temple University

SELECTED BOOKS: *Adagiorum collectanea* (Paris: Printed by Johanne Philippo, 1500); revised and enlarged as *Adagiorum chiliades* (Venice: Aldine Press, 1508; revised and enlarged again, Basel: Printed by Johann Froben, 1515); translated by Richard Taverner as *Prouerbes or Adagies with Newe Addicions Gathered out of the Chiliades of Erasmus* (London: Printed by Richard Bances, 1539); edited and translated by Margaret Mann Phillips as *The "Adages" of Erasmus* (Cambridge: Cambridge University Press, 1964);

Moriae encomium (Paris: Printed by Gilles de Gourmont, 1511); translated by Thomas Chaloner as *The Praise of Folie* (London: Printed by Thomas Berthelet, 1569 [1549]); edited and translated by Leonard F. Dean as *The Praise of Folly* (Chicago: Packard, 1946);

De duplici copia rerum ac verborum (Paris: Printed by Jodocus Badius Ascensius, 1512); edited and translated by David H. Rix and Donald B. King as *On Copia of Words and Ideas* (Milwaukee: Marquette University Press, 1963);

Novvm instrumentum omne (Basel: Printed by Johann Froben, 1516); republished as *Novvm testamentvm omne* (Basel: Printed by John Froben, 1519);

Ivlivs. Dialogvs viri cvivspiam ervditissimi festiuus sane ac elegans, quomodo Ivlivs II, attributed to Erasmus (N.p., n.d. [Germany?, 1517?]); translated anonymously as *The Dialoge Betwene Julius the Seconde, Genius, and Saynt Peter* (London: Printed by Richard Coplande for John Byddell, [1534?]); translated by Paul Pascal, edited by Kelley Sowards as *The Julius Exclusus of Erasmus* (Bloomington: Indiana University Press, 1968);

Enchiridion militis christiani, saluberrimis praeceptis refertum, in his *Lvcvbrativncvlae aliqvot* (Antwerp: Printed by Theodor Martens, 1503); republished separately (Basel: Printed by Johann Froben, 1518); translated [by William Tyndale?] as *A Booke Called in Latyn Enchiridion Militis Christiani, and in Englysshe the Manuell of the Christen Knyght* (London: Printed by Wynkyn de Worde for John Byddell, 1533); edited and translated by Raymond Himelick as *The Enchiridion of Erasmus* (Bloomington: Indiana University Press, 1963);

Familiarium colloquiorum formulae (Basel: Printed by Johann Froben, 1518; London: Printed by Wynkyn de Worde, 1519); translated by H. M. Gent as *The Colloquies into English* (London: Fleshen, 1672); edited and translated by Craig Thompson as *The Colloquies of Erasmus* (Chicago: University of Chicago Press, 1965);

Antibarbarorum liber (Basel: Printed by Johann Froben, 1520);

Epistola nvncvpatoria ad Carolvm Caesarem. Exhortatio ad studium Euangelicae lectionis. Paraphrasis in Euangelium Matthaei (Basel: Printed by Johann Froben, 1522);

Tomus primus [–secundus] paraphraseon (Basel: Printed by Johann Froben, 1524);

De recta latini graecique sermones pronuntiatione Des. Erasmi roterodami dialogus. Eivsdem dialogu cui titulus, Ciceronianus sive de optimo genere dicendi (Basel: Printed by Johann Froben, 1529).

Editions: *Omnia opera,* 9 volumes, edited by Rhenanus Beatus (Basel: Printed by Johann Froben, 1539–1555);

Opera omnia, 10 volumes, edited by Jean LeClerc (Leiden: Printed by Petrus Vander Aa, 1703–1706);

Christian Humanism and the Reformation: Selected Writings of Erasmus, edited and translated by John C. Olin (New York: Fordham University Press, 1975);

Opera omnia Desiderii Erasmi Roterodami, recognita et adnotatione critica instructa notisque illustrata, edited by C. M. Bruehl (Amsterdam: North-Holland Publishing Company, 1969–);

The Collected Works of Erasmus, 89 volumes to date, editorial board chair James K. McConica (To-

Desiderius Erasmus in 1517 (portrait by Quentin Metsys; Galleria Nazionale d'Arte Antica, Rome)

ronto: University of Toronto Press, 1974–) – comprises volumes 1–22: *Letters*; volumes 23–29: *Literature and Educational Writings*; volumes 30–36: *Adages*; volumes 37–38: *Apoph thegmata*; volumes 39–40: *Colloquies*; volumes 41–60: *New Testament Scholarship*; volumes 61–62: *Patristics*; volumes 63–65: *Expositions of the Psalms*; volumes 66–70: *Spiritualia and Pastoralia*; volumes 71–84: *Controversies*; volumes 85–86: *Poetry*; volumes 87–89: *Contemporaries of Erasmus: A Biographical Register of the Renaissance and Reformation.*

OTHER: Robert Gaguin, *De origine et gestis Francorum compendium* (Paris, 1495).

In July 1514 Desiderius Erasmus of Rotterdam left England for Basel, Switzerland, and the Froben Press to publish the annotated New Testament and the critical edition of the works of Saint Jerome on which he had been working during his stay at Cambridge. He left behind an imprint on the humanist tradition which would shape the output of every serious writer of the English Renaissance. In *De duplici copia rerum ac verborum* (On Abundance of Things and Words, 1512), a text intended to aid schoolboys in developing rhetorical felicity, he regrouped all discursive practices around a program of wide reading and note taking from the broadest array of classical literature available. Such work was intended to provide a speaker or writer with a storehouse of ideas, words, and phrases which might be deployed effectively as the spectrum of verbal situations he would confront demanded. Such eloquence became the aim and sign of an educated man, and those same qualities, naturalized in the education process, became the hallmark of the richest literary moment in English history. Erasmus has been called the single most important influence on the style and shape of all writing of the period.

As he left England, Erasmus was middle-aged and at the apex of a career that had not come easily. His early years were spent overcoming the humiliation and impoverishment of an illegitimate birth which he was to characterize in so many configurations that the precise facts of his origin are clouded in textual speculation. Erasmus was probably born in October 1467 in Gouda to a priest, Gerald or Roger, and his mistress, Margaret, who openly lived together in the church rectory with their two sons until she left Gouda for Deventer to work as a washerwoman when Erasmus was nine. Although he returned to Gouda a few years later after his mother succumbed to the plague, Erasmus eventually left the town behind forever, using neither his father's name nor attaching his birthplace to his given name as was the custom. Instead he chose to use his maternal grandparents' city as his place of origin and became Erasmus of Rotterdam. He first used the name Desiderius on the title page of the second printing of the *Adagia* in 1508, perhaps to signal the newly won acclaim the book was gaining for him as well as to announce the scholarly work that he desired to accomplish.

At the Cathedral School of Saint Lebwin's overseen by the pious Brethren of the Common Life, Erasmus first learned of Renaissance humanism and began to earn respect for the intellectual acuity which would finally win him an international reputation. This respect manifested itself first in the order's enthusiastic invitations to join them, which he railed against, wanting to instead attend a university. His poverty made this wish impossible. In 1487 he entered the monastery of the Augustinians at Steyn with some reluctance. In pursuit of a humanistic education, he devoured the classics that were available to him while he longed for position and independence in the larger world outside the monastery walls.

Through the likely ministrations of David of Burgundy, bishop of Utrecht, and impelled by a desire to pursue literature and an intellectual life, Erasmus left the monastery in 1492 to become Latin secretary to the bishop of Cambray. By 1495 he was at the Sorbonne in Paris, ostensibly to obtain a degree in theology. With few resources and no financial support he experienced a penury close to destitution. He lived in a communal dormitory with his fellow students, most between the ages of sixteen and twenty, who were interested in little more than Scholastic theology and mortification of the flesh. While ferreting out a living by wooing potential patrons in graceful letters and reluctantly tutoring pupils, he came into contact with the humanist community, which welcomed his graceful Latin style as well as his wit.

There he was encouraged to write. In fact, Erasmus first appears in print in 1495, when the noted humanist Robert Gaguin concluded his long history of France, *De origine et gestis Francorum compendium,* with a complimentary letter from Erasmus. The book achieved wide popularity; when Erasmus met the English classical scholar and theologian John Colet four years later, the latter was already familiar with his name from Gaguin's text. This was not, however, the first piece he had sought to publish. Earlier, in 1489, the constraints of monastic life had impelled him to write *Antibarbarorum liber* (The Book against the Barbarians, 1520). Gaguin advised him against publishing this vitriolic attack on a monasticism that Erasmus saw as ignoring or rejecting the study of literature and the cultivation of learning. Recomposed over intervening decades, it was not published until 1520.

This delayed publication was not a singular incident; in fact, it is difficult to categorize the works of Erasmus chronologically with any accuracy because he never viewed his work as complete or finished and devoted much of his productive energy to expanding and rewriting earlier texts. His works, so often derived from issues Erasmus was personally confronting, remained vital and alive so long as he was. Although Erasmus advocated extensive reading of classical literature, as did most other humanists, his particular concern was with how such knowledge contributed to a person's ability to express himself on issues relating to his own experience. Like Michel Montaigne, he was the subject of his own writing. Unlike Montaigne, however, Erasmus wrote and published entirely in Latin, the common language of educated Europeans of the time who constituted his audience.

While Erasmus met and learned from important men like Gaguin, his life was, nonetheless, constrained by the burdens of his daily existence and his need to obtain the degree in theology for which he had been sent to the Sorbonne, both of which he viewed as obstacles to the pursuit of his real goal: the classically based "New Learning" of the humanists. In 1499 one of his pupils, William Blount, Lord Mountjoy, invited him to England, thus offering Erasmus an escape from these exigencies and the possibility of a more independent, productive life. Here for the first time he was introduced into a circle of intellectually keen but congenial friends who would provide him with a personal and financial security heretofore unknown to him. In all, Erasmus was to make eight trips to England and spend over seven of his most productive years there. He was also to define for himself his own life's vocation and undertake much of his most famous work. At the same time, he was to leave his indelible mark on English education, religion, and letters.

The conditions in England at the time of Erasmus's arrival could not have been more agreeable to him. The New Learning had been alive in the universities and intellectual communities there for the last three decades of the fifteenth century. He was introduced almost immediately to the first-rate minds of Colet, the humanist physician and scholar Thomas Linacre, the rhetorician William Grocyn, and the young Thomas More. He met as well powerful potential patrons such as John Fisher, the future bishop of Rochester; Richard Foxe, bishop of Winchester; and William Warham, archbishop of Canterbury. One of his earliest commissions was from the scholarly Prince Henry, whom he had met while walking with More from Mountjoy's house in Greenwich to the royal estate in the next village. While More had a poem for the prince, Erasmus had nothing. The young prince asked in writing for a poem. Within three days, a poem in praise of England and the Tudors was sent to him. This was Erasmus's first experience of a comfortable patronage that made him seem neither servant nor beggar.

In this atmosphere of easy intellectual freedom, Erasmus felt, perhaps for the first time, at home. Delighted with his new surroundings, he wrote to his friend Fausto Andrelini that he was "learning to act like a courtier, bowing politely, smiling gracefully, and kissing when meeting and departing from acquaintances." He was also being challenged to think more acutely and to define his vocational goals.

Erasmus had come to England as a humanist poet with classical and worldly preoccupations only to find himself among scholars who were enthusiastically considering theology. From discussions with them, he learned a new kind of theology which valued a direct philological attempt to comprehend the Gospels in the light of historical Christianity and textual accuracy over preordained systems and syllogistic subtleties. He was also introduced to a Christian simplicity, one that took seriously the notion that the virtuous person lives as far as possible in imitation of Christ. Under this influence, Erasmus developed the program of religious, moral, and social reform at once genuinely humanist and genuinely Christian to which he would dedicate the remaining thirty-six years of his life. No one was more influential in his coming to terms with this vocation than Colet.

Colet shared with Erasmus a skepticism about dogmatism. Both were interested in developing intellectual skill rather than mastery of form. When Erasmus first attended Colet's lectures on the Epistles of Saint Paul at Oxford, he was struck by the difference from the program of "quadruple interpretation" of the Bible (a hermeneutics which posited four distinct levels of meaning in all divinely inspired texts) so entrenched at the Sorbonne. Colet maintained that Scholastics were doomed to failure when trying to deal with the infinite. He recognized that the real face of God as well as other essentialist ideas of truth were unavailable to postlapsarian man even with the most facile of mental gymnastics. Colet also emphasized the redemptive power of Christ's sacrifice over sacraments and ritual. The experience of Christianity had more significance for him than the schoolmen's theories about it. At the same time, Colet's work was not anti-intellectual, since it centered around a rigorous and accurate understanding of sacred texts.

Erasmus readily accepted Colet's program of biblical study and religious reform because it was thoroughly congenial to the notions of intellectual and spiritual life that had sent him from Steyn to the university. In Colet he found for the first time someone who joined theology to an active religious experience in a program aimed at the soul's salvation. To adapt this program to his own needs, Erasmus knew that he must focus on two things: continued honing of the persuasive rhetorical skills inherent in Colet's program, and the mastery of Greek that he saw as essential for scholarly editing of the New Testament. So at the end of 1500, despite offers of support and growing friendships, especially with More, Erasmus returned to Paris where he was immediately forced to find ways to support his Greek studies.

While learning Greek, running from the plague, and fending off starvation, he managed to publish *Adagiorum collectânae* (Collection of Adages) in June 1500. This compendium of 818 Latin quotations proved enormously popular, and he would continue to expand and republish it in later years. Erasmus did not view this work as *occupatio,* mere pleasure reading, but as a treasured source of collected citations – a foundation for the program of abundant discourse he would later develop in *On Abundance*. In the dedication to Lord Mountjoy, Erasmus states that the *Adages* had been compiled to help its reader increase his rhetorical power with arguments and ideas from the storehouse of ancient wisdom.

The *Adages* helped to spread the classical spirit across Europe. Many Renaissance students discovered ancient culture through the proverbs and quotations drawn from Erasmus's wide reading. At the same time, they provided Erasmus with a testing ground for the exposition of his own political and ethical thought in a text as personal and self-revealing as a journal. In the 1515 edition his own money problems surface in "Felix qui nihil debet" (Happy the Man Who Owns Nothing). He thinks more frequently, however, about larger contemporary issues. "Aut fatuum aut regem nesci" (To Be Born a King or a Fool) takes reigning monarchs to task for their foolish and unchristian actions. "Scarabeus aquilam quaerit" (The Beetle Searches for the Eagle) limns the figure of the tyrant, while "Sparta nactus est, hanc orna" (You Have Obtained Sparta) exhorts the prince to administer his state well. When he adumbrates a theme close to his heart, Erasmus shows little concern for circumspection. In "Dulci bellum inexpertis," he says of warfare:

> All go to war, the decrepit, the priest, the monk, and we mix up Christ with a thing so diabolical! Two armies march against each other carrying the standard of the Cross which in itself might teach them how Christians should conquer. Under that heavenly banner . . . there is a rush to butcher each other and we make Christ the witness and authority for so criminal a thing.

In the *Adages,* Erasmus first performs the extemporaneous display of broad classical learning in a personal style, which he encouraged Colet to develop in his students at Saint Paul's.

Erasmus's deep debt to Colet for his religious, moral, and ethical formation may be seen in how much his *Enchiridion militis christiani* (The Handbook of the Christian Soldier, 1503) reverberates with the notions of Christian simplicity that had been semi-

STVLTICIAE LAVS.

æ uelut umbra quædã,fit ut præmij quoq; illi⁹ aliqñ guſtũ.
aut odoré aliqué ſentiãt. Id tãetſi minutiſlima quædã ſtillu
la eſt ad fonté illũ æternæ felicitatis,tñ longe ſupat uniuer/
ſas corpis uoluptates,etiã ſi oés omniũ mortaliũ delitiæ in
unũ coferant. Vſq̃adeo præſtãt ſpiritaliã corpalib⁹,inuiſi/
bilia uiſibilib⁹.Hoc nimirũ eſt,qd̃ pollicet̃ ꝓpheta, oculus
nõ uidit,nec auris audiuit,nec in cor hois aſcédit, quæ præ
parauit deus diligétibus ſe . Atq̃ hæc eſt Moriæ pars,quæ
nõ aufert̃ cõmutatióe uitæ,ſed pficit̃.Hoc igit̃ qbus ſentire
licuit(cõtingit aũt ꝓpaucis) ij patiunt̃ qddã demétiæ ſimilli
mũ, loquũtur quædã nõ ſatis cohærétia, nec humano mo/
re,ſed dant ſine mēte ſonũ, deinde ſubinde totã oris ſpecié
uertũt,Nũc alacres,nũc deiecti,nũc lachrymãt, nũc rident ,
nũc ſuſpirãt,in ſũma uere toti extra ſe ſunt . Mox ubi ad ſe
ſe redierint,negãt ſe ſcire,ubi fuerint,utrũ in corpe,an extra
corp⁹,uigilãtes,an dormiétes,qd audierint, qd uiderint, qd
dixerint,qd fecerint,nõ meminerũt,niſi tãq̃; p nebulam. ac
ſomniũ,tantũ hoc ſciunt,ſe feliciſſimos fuiſſe, dũ ita deſipe
rēt.Itaq̃; plorãt ſeſe reſipuiſſe,nihilq̃; omniũ malint q̃ hoc
inſaniæ genus ꝓpetuo inſanire. Atq̃; hæc eſt futuræ felicita
tis tenuis quædã deguſtatiuncula. Verũ ego iãdudũ oblita
mei ὑπὲρ τὰ ἐσκαμμένα πηδῶ. Quãq̃; ſiqd petulãtius aut loqua
cius a me dictũ uidebit̃,cogitate & ſtulticiã, & mulierem di
xiſſe.Sed interim tñ memineritis illius Græcanici ꝓuerbij,
πολλάκιϛοι καὶ μωϱὸς ἀνὴϱ κατακαίϱιοϛ ἔιπεμ· Niſi forte putatis hoc
ad mulieres nihil attinere. Video uos epilogũ expectare ,
ſed nimiũ deſipitis, ſi qdē arbitramini me qd dixerim etiã
dũ meminiſſe.Cũ tãtã uerborũ farraginé effuderim. Ve
tus illud,μισῶ μνάμονα ſυμπόταμ.Nouũ hoc,μισῶ μνάμονα ἀκϱο
ατὴν. Quare ualete,plaudite,uiuite,bibite,Moriæ celeberri
mi Myſtæ.

        ΜΟΡΙΑΣ ΕΙΚΩΜΙΩΝ Feliciter abſolutum.

Marginalia by Hans Holbein in his copy of Erasmus's Praise of Folly. *Folly is descending from the pulpit (Öffentliche Kunstammlung, Basel).*

nal to the English scholar's Oxford lectures. In the opening argument of the first edition Erasmus promises to deliver "in a concise fashion some method of living which might help you achieve a character acceptable to Christ." The soldier Erasmus envisions would choose the spiritual against the secular, but not in soulless adherence to dogma. The work encourages its readers not to think "of Christ as an empty word, but that it stands for charity, simplicity, patience, purity, in brief, all that he taught."

His will to devote himself to sacred studies deepened, and in 1504 his letters reflect anger and frustration at the hindrances and delays which beset him. In 1505 he returned to England, apparently at Colet's invitation, entertaining the possibility of an ecclesiastical benefice. By that time he had largely perfected his knowledge of Greek and had begun Latin translations of the New Testament and the church fathers.

During this visit, Erasmus's intellectual companionship and friendship with More deepened as they spent long, happy hours translating Lucian's satires from the Greek. Erasmus at this time refers to More as the sweetest of all his friends. But the pleasures of his English experience were not fully satisfying so long as he was still burdened by the double yoke of his illegitimacy and obligation to the Augustinians at Steyn whom he had left a decade before to pursue a degree in theology. Through the influence of Andrea Ammonio, a cleric in the entourage of the Italian Bishop of Worcester, he was absolved by Pope Julius II from the disadvantages of his illegitimate birth in a letter dated 4 January 1506.

By the spring of 1506 Erasmus had been induced by Bishop John Fisher, chancellor of Cambridge University, to accept an endowed lectureship at Cambridge, where he also applied for a degree in theology. These plans were interrupted, however, when he left for Italy to receive a doctorate, awarded in September 1506 by the authority of the bishop of Torino, a great-nephew of Pope Julius. This was Erasmus's long-awaited first visit to Italy, and his time there was full of contacts and contradictions. Perhaps the most disturbing of the latter was his first sight of the pope, as Julius entered the fallen city of Bologna in triumphal march ahead of a papal army that had sacked it. This vision of Julius may have been what turned Erasmus into a pacifist.

In the fall of 1507, after some traveling in Italy, Erasmus made his way to Venice to the home of the renowned printer Aldus Manutius where the scholar found intellectual companionship and hospi-

tality to rival that of his English friends. He stayed there until late the next year, when he left to visit Padua, Ferrara, and Siena. Through Manutius's Aldine Press, Erasmus published a greatly expanded edition of adages, the *Adagiorum chiliades* (1508), which earned for him some of the international celebrity he desired. This three-thousand-item edition reflects the abundant source material Aldus and other Venetian collectors and bibliophiles made available to him. He read from Plato, Plutarch, Athenaeus, Homer, Pausanius, and Pindar. Most of the new material in this edition had never before appeared in print. Thus, Erasmus greatly expanded the storehouse of ready phrases his serious readers could use to enrich the elegance of their speech and writing. He might have stayed in Italy longer had not his English friends urged his return when Henry VIII ascended the throne in 1509. As he traveled northward, Erasmus sketched out a new work unlike anything he had published previously.

In *Moriae encomium* (1511; translated as *The Praise of Folly,* 1549 – the title could also be punningly translated as "The Praise of More"), the world was first introduced to Erasmus's satiric writing, though the work was not his first satiric venture. His letters make clear that irony and satire were the principal weapons Erasmus used against the injustices he saw in the world generally and in religion especially. *The Praise of Folly* parodies the popular oration of praise that lauded abstractions like Truth, Wisdom, or Philosophy. A personified Folly argues that man "must send for me if he wants to be a father" and that "there are no great actions without my help, no important arts without my collaboration." In the middle of the work Erasmus has Folly consider religious foolishness, a move which drew censure from conservative clerics that would persist for the remainder of the author's life. Of bad preachers Folly says, "This is a style of oratory which is handed down in person from brother to brother like a secret ritual. I'm not one of the initiated, but I'll make a guess at what it's like." The mendicant religious are a "tribe so universally loathed that even a chance meeting is thought to be ill-omened – and yet they are gloriously self-satisfied. In the first place they believe it's the highest form of piety to be so uneducated that they can't even read."

Erasmus is quick to remind his critics that Folly, not he, says that "it is easier to escape from a maze than from the tangles of Realists, Nominalists, Thomists, Albertists, Occamists, and Scotists," but few made that distinction. The meaning of *folly* shifts as the oration progresses: among other things, it is connected with the simplicity of the noble savage and, at the close of the work, to the Christian innocent who is willing to become a fool for Christ by rejecting worldly "wisdom." This ambiguity has engaged critics from the sixteenth century to the twentieth.

The authorship of the pamphlet *Julius Exclusus* (Julius Excluded, circa 1517), a bitingly satiric account of Pope Julius II's exclusion from heaven after his death in 1513, is for sound reasons assumed to be the work of Erasmus, although he denied any connection with it. The pamphlet shows Julius in a most unfavorable light, contrasting the Renaissance papacy with the simple church that Christ and the Apostles intended. It accuses Julius of illegitimacy, drunkenness, bribery, lechery, and simony and finds him guilty of all manner of deadly sin, causing Saint Peter to exclude him from heaven. In light of the favors Julius had procured for Erasmus, such an excoriating condemnation could have been seen as ungrateful even by his most generous supporters and patrons. It is, perhaps, most accurate to characterize this caustic satire as something Erasmus wrote to circulate among his friends but never intended to have published. It was neither polished nor prepared for press and gives an unintended glance at the humanist in a negative-epideictic mode.

In addition to securing the patronage of the powerful, Erasmus also staved off poverty by tutoring young students. A happy result of that occupation was his *Colloquia* (Colloquies, 1518), notebooks intended to aid these pupils in developing graceful conversation and writing. The book began in the late 1490s as a series of simple exercises in Latin conversation; it ended some sixteen editions later in 1533 as a large, heavy book with more than sixty additional dialogues on a broad spectrum of subjects from politics and religion to diet and women's rights. The *Colloquies* were continuously popular, appreciated particularly for their ability to capture the sights and sounds of Erasmus's world. Like the *Adages,* they were intended for use in rhetorically appropriate circumstances, and major literary figures like John Webster, François Rabelais, Robert Burton, Ben Jonson, and perhaps even William Shakespeare borrowed frequently from them.

Although Erasmus lectured in divinity at Cambridge from 1511 until 1514, what secured him a special place in the development of English culture was a work designed to assist educators in their task. At this time, Colet was dean of Saint Paul's School and, as such, was responsible for the intellectual training of young men who were to become the

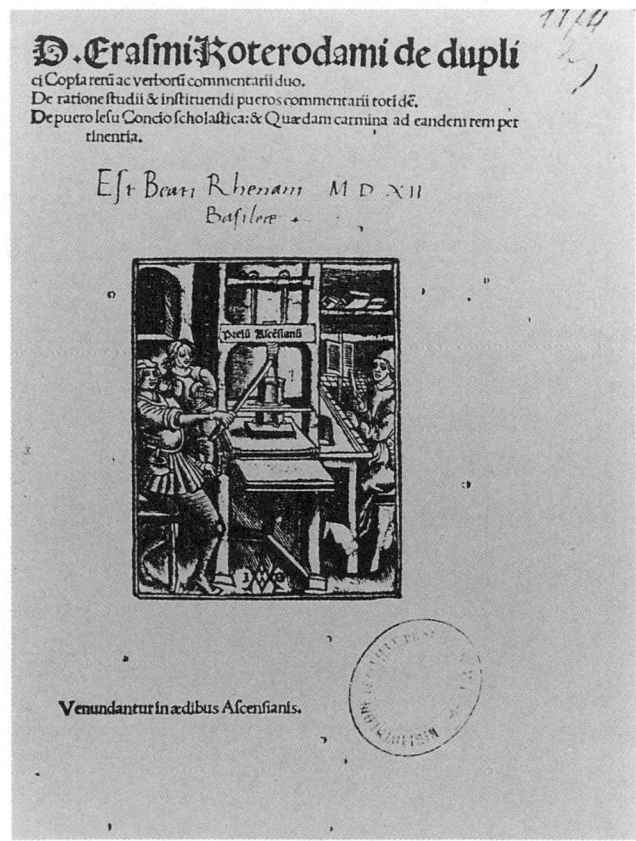

Title page for Erasmus's book on rhetorical embellishments, which became a standard textbook among English educators

nation's statesmen, clergy, and writers. Colet asked Erasmus to assist him in educating these leaders and intellectuals. In response, Erasmus wrote *De duplici copia rerum ac verborum* (On Abundance of Things and Words). First published in Paris in 1512, it aimed to develop verbal richness and eloquence in its readers. It appeared in at least eighty-five editions throughout Europe in the author's lifetime.

Erasmus and Colet believed that intellectual power was determined by one's ability to speak or write fully and convincingly on any subject. Therefore, the single most important goal of education became the acquisition of verbal richness and rhetorical skill through wide reading and the collecting of potentially useful citations. *On Abundance* adumbrates the method of the *Adages* and the *Colloquies* and shows how one might join the classical, the topical, and the personal to produce lively, effective discourse. Students are asked to store up words and ideas from what they read in what should constitute a treasure house: "I want the furnishings of a rich house to exhibit the greatest variety; but I want them altogether in good taste, not with every corner crammed with willow

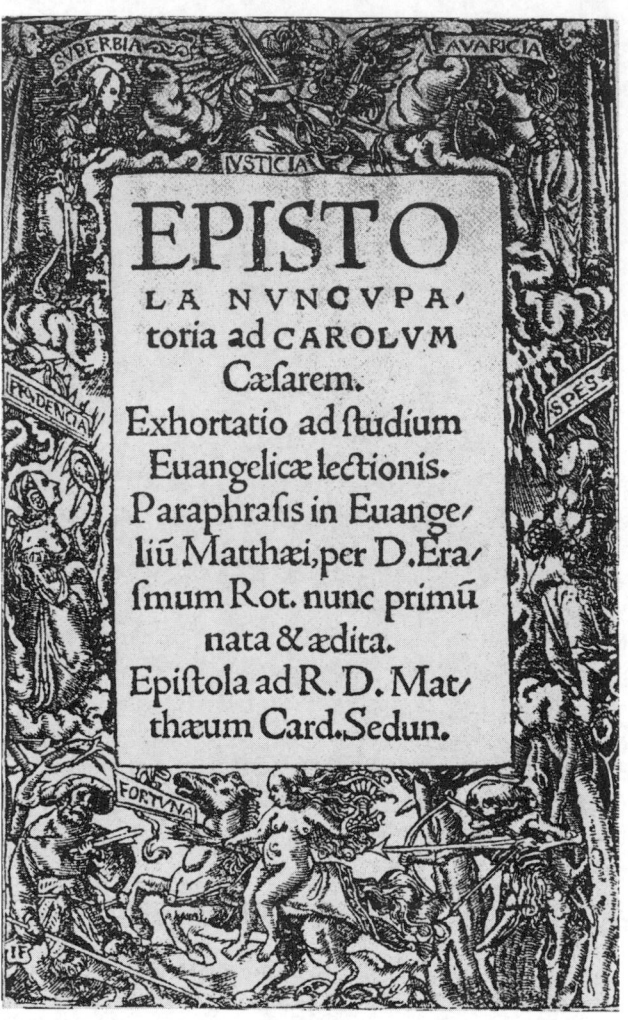

Title page for Erasmus's 1522 paraphrase of the Book of Matthew

and . . . Samian ware. At a splendid banquet I want various kinds of food to be served."

They are further encouraged to rewrite what they have collected in variation exercises which asked them to find new expression for conventional phrases. Book 1 ends in a discursive tour de force as Erasmus performs such a variation exercise on the statement "Your letter has delighted me very much," which undergoes 150 modifications in the course of its elaboration: "In a wonderful way your letter has delighted me . . . your epistle has cheered me exceedingly . . . you should have seen me transported by the extent of my joy when your letter reached me . . . By your letter the wrinkles were straightaway wiped from my brow. He brought me a festal day who brought me your letter. I would have preferred what you wrote to any nectar," and so on.

Modern critics, focusing on this text and seeing it as central to Erasmian thinking, have used it

to reposition him in the English Renaissance. They argue that, in a pedagogy that valued richness, variety, and full speech on any subject, habits of mind were inculcated that produced a corresponding view of literature. Thus the lushness of Sir Philip Sidney's *Arcadia* (written 1580–1581), the excesses of Thomas Nashe's *Unfortunate Traveller* (1594), and the endless contradiction of Burton's *Anatomy of Melancholy* (1621) owe much to Erasmus's widely held discursive theory. In Shakespeare, Beatrice and Benedict's constant repartee in *Much Ado about Nothing* (1599), Iago's facile extemporaneous performance in *Othello* (1604), and the well-known "To be or not to be" speech from *Hamlet* (1601) all reveal the expansive, playful, yet thoughtful sense of language advocated in *On Abundance*.

Erasmus performed his ideas rather than theorized about them. He did not, for example, write about how one might collect sayings from famous people for use in future discourse; he instead collected them and made them available to others in his *Adages*. Moreover, his texts are replete with shifts, tropes, and contradictions that leave him open to multiple readings. For example, what begins in *On Abundance* as a seemingly straightforward discussion of varying by synonym – "The first, then, and simplest method of varying depends upon those words which, although they are different, express exactly the same thought, so that as far as the meaning goes, it makes no difference whether you choose rather to use one or the other" – is immediately complicated when the text notes that "scarcely anywhere will you find two words so close in meaning that they do not differ in some respect" and then "although we grant there to be no difference at all in meaning, yet some words are more becoming than others." Also potentially confusing are the characteristics of "aptness" and "propriety," often portrayed as desirable, but never specifically defined and left to the student's discretion. Furthermore, Erasmus encourages his readers to see every argument from as many points of view as possible, a practice which he lived and for which he was often misunderstood. Nowhere, perhaps, is this more poignantly demonstrable than in his position in the religious quarrels of his final years.

Erasmus left England in 1514 with a working manuscript of his translation of a restored Greek New Testament in hand as well as the notes he had made toward an edition of Saint Jerome (he would return for brief visits in the summer of 1516 and the fall of 1517). He looked forward to overseeing the publication of his works at the press of Johann Froben in Basel. By March 1516, with the New Tes-

Erasmus in the year before his death (woodcut by Hans Holbein)

tament completed, he stood at the pinnacle of his career looking forward to the work which would occupy the next few years, a related project of a series of paraphrases on the books of the New Testament. By the time the book of *Matthew* was published in 1522, Erasmus was the most recognized scholar in Europe and the most important proponent of philological biblical scholarship, and for that reason one of the foremost influences on the Protestant Reformation. His desire to see an accurate text made available to the broadest audience in order to encourage private Christian spirituality mirrored the Reformers' intentions.

Perhaps, as Erasmus contended, the Franciscans of Cologne originated the popular saying that "Erasmus laid the egg that Luther hatched." Both the classical humanist and the reformer shared a revulsion for the excesses of the church, decrying monastic decay and the substitution of superstition and ritual for authentic Christian experience. Erasmus, however, remained faithful to the church while its enemies, Martin Luther in particular, were using his reform writings (the dialogues in the *Colloquia* especially) to support measures more radical than the scholar could countenance. In 1529 the ferocity of the confrontations in Basel between the opposing groups finally forced the ailing Erasmus to a self-imposed exile in Freiburg, Germany, a university town some forty miles to the north. There he continued to write at a remove from a violent world in which his fondest English friend, More, and Bishop Fisher were executed in 1535 when they refused to take an oath impugning the pope's authority. Erasmus returned to Basel to die in 1536, faithful to a church which would declare him a heretic at the Council of Trent in 1559.

A consideration of Erasmus and sixteenth-century English literature cannot be complete without confirming his influence on its religious reformation. While both reformers and conservers invoked him as a source for their ideas, it is really the former who owe him the greatest debt. William Tyndale relied on Erasmus's Greek text and Latin translations of the Bible for English translation. Erasmus's biblical paraphrases, ordered by every church, encouraged the private interpretation of the Bible – a hallmark of the distinctly Protestant humanism of the English Reformation. His own appreciation of a simple and personal imitation of Christ can be cited as a powerful influence on the religious tracts which would proliferate throughout the century.

The influence of Erasmus on the letters of Renaissance England is so pervasive that it is impossible not to see his mark on all of the finest minds of the century. In both aesthetic and polemical endeavors, the richness of Erasmian copiousness shapes most texts, from literary compositions to the abundant religious tracts of the time. The major texts of the late sixteenth and the early seventeenth centuries combine these qualities as Erasmus himself had taught, to produce the most remarkable literary output of any time in English letters.

Letters:

Opus Epistolarum . . . per Autorem Diligenter Recognitum (Basel: Printed by Johann Froben, 1529);

The Epistles of Erasmus from his Earliest Letters to His Fifty-First Year, 3 volumes, edited and translated by Francis M. Nichols (London: Longmans, 1901–1918; New York: Russell & Russell, 1958).

Opus Epistolarum Desiderius Erasmi Roterodami, 12 volumes, edited by Percy Safford Allen, Helen Mary Allen, and Heathcote William Garrod (Oxford: Clarendon Press, 1906–1947; index, 1958).

Bibliographies:

Vander F. Haeghen, *Bibliotheca Erasmiana: Repertoire des Oeuvres d'Erasme,* 3 volumes (Gand: Bibliothèque de l'Université de l'Etat, 1893);

Irmgard Bezzel, *Erasmusdrucke des 16. Jahrhunderts in Bayerischen Bibliotheken* (Stuttgart: Hiersemann, 1979);

E. J. Devereux, *Renaissance English Translations of Erasmus* (Toronto: University of Toronto Press, 1983).

Biographies:

Johan Huizinga, *Erasmus of Rotterdam,* translated by Frederick Hopman (New York: Scribners, 1924; London: Phaidon, 1952);

Roland H. Bainton, *Erasmus of Christendom* (New York: Scribners, 1969);

A. F. C. Koch, *The Year of Erasmus' Birth* (Utrecht: Haentjens, Dekker & Gumbert, 1969);

Gyorgy Faludy, *Erasmus* (New York: Stein & Day, 1970);

James K. McConica, *Erasmus* (Oxford: Clarendon Press, 1991);

Leon-E. Halkin, *Erasmus: A Critical Biography,* translated by John Tonkin (Cambridge, Mass.: Blackwell, 1993).

References:

Terrance Cave, *The Cornucopian Text: Problems of Writing in the French Renaissance* (Baltimore: Johns Hopkins University Press, 1979);

Wallace K. Ferguson, "Renaissance Tendencies in the Religious Thought of Erasmus," *Journal of the History of Ideas,* 15 (October 1954): 499–508;

Elmore Harris Harbison, *The Christian Scholar in the Age of Reformation* (New York: Scribners, 1950) pp. 69–102;

James K. McConica, *English Humanists and Reformation Politics under Henry VIII and Edward VI* (Oxford: Clarendon Press, 1965);

Margaret Mann Phillips, *The Adages of Erasmus: A Study with Translations* (Cambridge: Cambridge University Press, 1964);

Phillips, *Erasmus and the Northern Renaissance* (New York: Macmillan, 1950);

Jesse Kelley Sowards, *Desiderius Erasmus* (New York: Twayne, 1975);

Craig R. Thompson, "Erasmus and Tudor England," in *Actes du Congres Erasme, Rotterdam 27–29 Octobre 1969* (Amsterdam & London: North-Holland Publishing Company, 1971);

Marion Trousdale, *Shakespeare and the Rhetoricians* (London: Scholar Press, 1982).

Geoffrey Fenton

(1539? – 19 October 1608)

Alison Taufer

California State University, Los Angeles

TRANSLATIONS: Matteo Bandello, *Certaine Tragicall Discourses Writtten [sic] oute of Frenche and Latin by Geoffrey Fenton, No Less Profitable than Pleasant, and of Like Necessity to All Degrees That Take Pleasure in Antiquities or Foreign Reports* (London: Printed by Thomas Marshe, 1567);

Antonio de Corro, *An Epistle or Godlie Admonition, of a Learned Minister of the Gospel of Our Sauiour Christ, Sent to the Pastoures of the Flemish Church in Antwerp (Who Name Themselues of the Confession of Ausperge,) Exhorting Them to Concord with the Other Ministers of the Gospell* (London: Printed by Henry Bynneman, 1569);

Jean de Serres, *A Discourse of the Ciuile Warres and Late Troubles in Fraunce, Drawn into Englishe by Geffray Fenton, and Deuided into Three Bookes* (London: Printed by Henry Bynneman for Lucas Harrison & George Bishop, 1570);

Simon Vigor, *Actes of Conference in Religion, Holden at Paris, betweene Two Papist Doctours of Sorbone and Two Godlie Ministers of the Church. Drawen out of French* (London: Printed by Henry Bynneman for William Norton & Humphrey Toye, 1571);

Etienne Pasquier, *Monophylo, Drawne into English by Geffray Fenton: A Philosophicall Discourse, and Diuision of Loue* (London: Printed by Henry Denham for William Seres, 1572);

Jean Talpin, *A Forme of Christian Pollicie Gathered out of French* (London: Printed by Henry Middelton for Rafe Newbery, 1574);

Antonio dé Guevara, *Golden Epistles, Contayning Varietie of Discourse Both Morall, Philosophicall, and Diuine: Gathered as Well out of the Remaynder of Guevaraes Workes, as Other Authors, Latine, French, and Italian* (London: Printed by Henry Middelton for Rafe Newberry, 1575; revised, 1577; revised, 1582);

Francesco Guicciardini, *The Historie of Guicciardin, Conteining the Warres of Italie: Reduced into English* (London: Printed by Thomas Vautroullier for William Norton, 1579).

Editions: Matteo Bandello, *Certain Tragical Discourses of Bandello,* 2 volumes, translated by Fenton, introduction by Robert Langton Douglas, edited by W. E. Henley (London: Nutt, 1898; New York: AMS, 1967);

Bandello, *Tragical Tales: The Complete Novels,* translated by Fenton, introduction by Douglas, edited by Hugh Harris (London: Routledge, 1924; New York: Dutton, 1924);

A Discourse of the Civile Warres and Late Troubles in Fraunce, The English Experience, no. 248 (Amsterdam: Theatrum Orbis Terrarum, 1970; New York: Da Capo, 1970);

A Forme of Christian Pollicie, The English Experience, no. 454 (Amsterdam: Theatrum Orbis Terrarum, 1972; New York: Da Capo, 1972);

A Form of Christian Policy Gathered out of French, introduction by Peter Davison (New York: Johnson Reprint, 1972).

Geoffrey Fenton, Elizabethan translator and statesman, is best known for *Certain Tragical Discourses* (1567), a collection of Matteo Bandello's novellas translated from the French version by François de Belleforest and Pierre Boaistuau, *Histoires tragiques, extraits des oeuvres Italiennes de Bandel* (1559). Like his contemporaries William Painter and George Pettie, Fenton's importance to Elizabethan fiction is derived primarily from his role in introducing the Continental novella to English literature. His work is noteworthy for its elaborate rhetoric and strong didacticism. The stylistic elements of his writing, such as antithesis, alliteration, balanced phrases and clauses, and amplification, predate similar features in the work of John Lyly by more than ten years. His love of moralizing, even when there is no moral to be drawn, appears not only in his translations of fiction but of religious, historical, and political tracts as well. Although some of the works he translated, such as Bandello's *Novelle* (1554), Antonio dé Guevara's *Epístolas familiares* (1539–1542), and Francesco

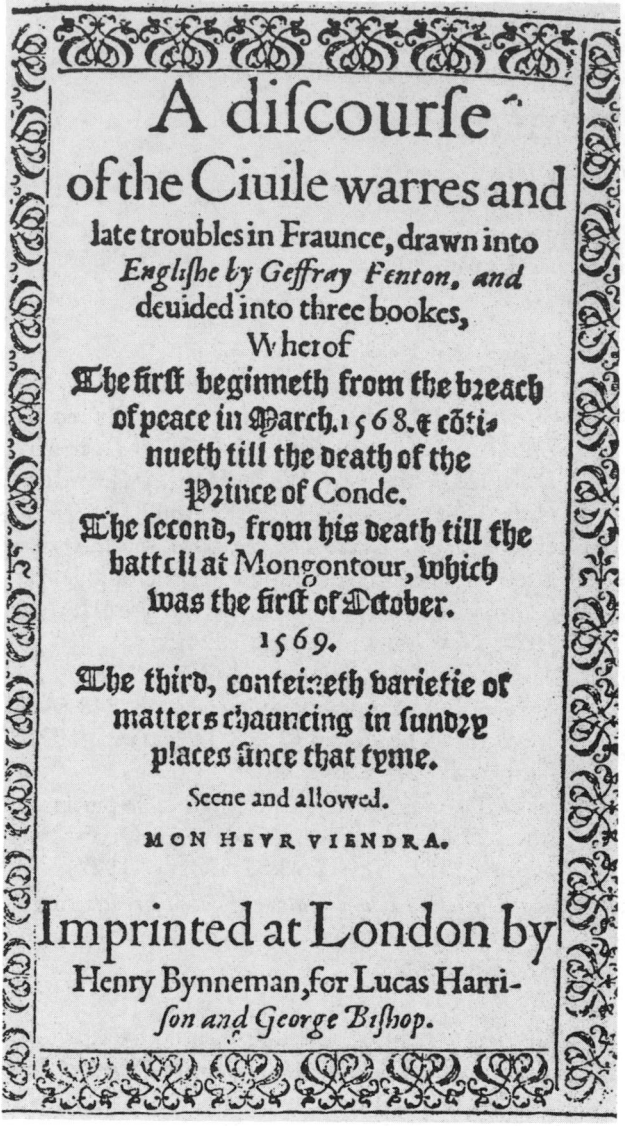

A difcourfe
of the Ciuile warres and
late troubles in Fraunce, drawn into
Englifhe by Geffray Fenton, and
deuided into three bookes,
Wherof
The firſt beginneth from the breach
of peace in March.1568.& côti=
nueth till the death of the
Prince of Conde.
The fecond, from his death till the
battell at Mongontour, which
was the firſt of October.
1569.
The third, confeineth varietie of
matters chauncing in fundry
places ſince that tyme.
Seene and allowed.
MON HEVR VIENDRA.

Imprinted at London by
Henry Bynneman, for Lucas Harri=
fon and George Bifhop.

Title page for Geoffrey Fenton's translation of Jean de Serres's account of France's Third War of Religion

Guicciardini's *Storia d'Italia* (1561–1564), were originally written in Italian or Spanish, his translations all appear to be from French intermediaries.

Of Fenton's early life, little is known. He was born around 1539 in Fenton, Nottinghamshire, to Henry Fenton and Cecily Beaumont Fenton. No evidence exists that he attended either Oxford or Cambridge, the two major universities, but he appears to have received a solid education, including training in French and Latin and possibly in Italian and Spanish. He spent some time in France and was residing in Paris in 1567 when he dedicated *Certain Tragical Discourses* to Lady Mary Sidney.

Fenton's motto, *Mon heur viendra* (My hour will come), which appears on the title page of all but one

of his books, attests to his ambitious nature. The dedications of his translations to Lady Sidney and her husband, Sir Henry Sidney; to Lady Elizabeth Hoby; to William Cecil, Lord Burghley, and his daughter Anne; and to Queen Elizabeth substantiate critics' claims that his devotion to literary pursuits was a means to an end rather than an end in itself. After his influential friends helped him to secure the post of secretary to the lord deputy of Ireland in 1580, Fenton terminated his literary career. He became a spy for Elizabeth in Ireland, reporting on the activities of his superiors and colleagues and, not surprisingly, earning himself a great deal of enmity. In June 1585 he married Alice Weston; they had a son and a daughter. He was made principal secretary of the Irish Council in 1587 and was knighted in 1589. He died on 19 October 1608 and was buried in Saint Patrick's Cathedral, Dublin.

Certain Tragical Discourses is Fenton's first and most important contribution to Elizabethan literature. Consisting of thirteen tales adapted from Belleforest and Boaistuau's French version of Bandello's *Novelle,* Fenton's translations bear little resemblance to the original stories and only a superficial one to his French source. He expands and even adds to the verbose descriptions and constant moralizing of Belleforest and Boaistuau's text, but his rhetorical elaborations do not always detract from the stories. His attention to descriptive detail and his addition of soliloquies often make his characters more psychologically interesting than those of his sources.

Fenton claims to have written *Certain Tragical Discourses* to entertain as well as to instruct "the frail imps" of his day, using "such examples as might best serve to instruct our youth, who, as they may see here the faults of fragility punished with shame, loss of honor, cruel death, and perpetual infamy to their posterity, so have they also, of the contrary, special patterns of virtue, alluring them to imitation of semblable honesty, with diversity of authorities proving the reward of virtue and virtuous living." In providing this service Fenton continually harps on the frailty and wantonness of women, the evils of "the Babylonian or diabolical sect of Rome," and the moral corruption of the Italians.

While English translations of Continental novellas provided Elizabethan and Jacobean dramatists with many of their plots and subplots, Fenton's collection appears to have contributed to only one play: critics have argued that one of William Shakespeare's sources for *Othello* (produced 1604?; published 1622) is Fenton's "Albanoys Captain," the story of an insanely jealous foreign military man

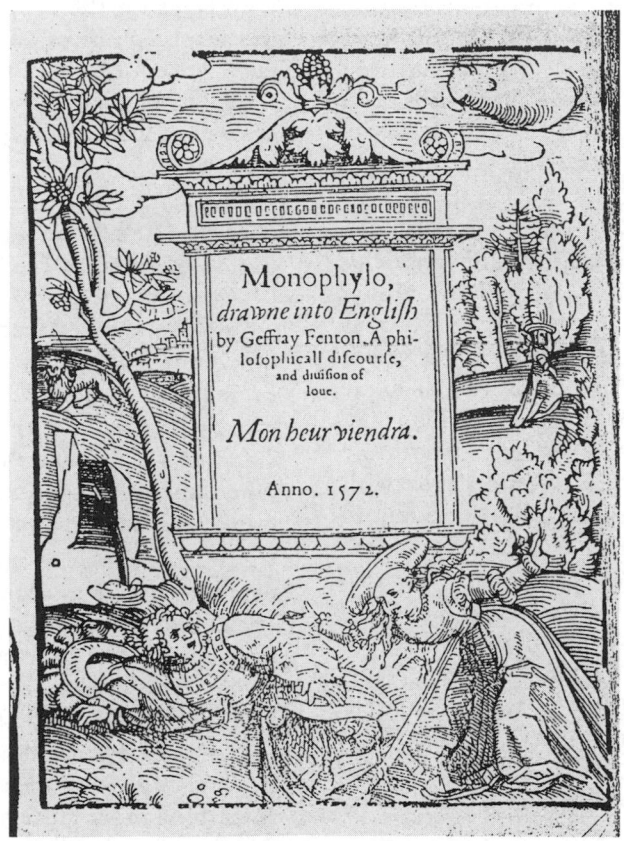

Title page for Fenton's translation of Etienne Pasquier's book on love and marriage, which includes moralistic passages by Fenton

who murders his innocent wife and then commits suicide. Unlike Painter's *Palace of Pleasure* (1566), *Certain Tragical Discourses* does not otherwise appear to have had an influence on the drama of the period.

An Epistle or Godly Admonition . . . Sent to the Pastors of the Flemish Church in Antwerp (1569), Fenton's next translation, is based on a sermon given by the Spanish reformer Antonio de Corro in January 1567. It exhorts a Protestant sect, the "Confession of Auspurge," to reject its belief in transubstantiation and join the rest of the reformed church in its doctrine concerning the Sacrament of the Lord's Supper. The work calls for understanding and an end to slanderous attacks among the various camps within the reformed church, arguing that "we have not been baptized in the names of Martin, Zwinglius, or Calvin, but in the name of the Father, the Son, and the Holy Ghost." Fenton's own prayer for Christian unity appears at the beginning of the text.

A Discourse of the Civil Wars and Late Troubles in France (1570) is an account of France's Third War of Religion. The work is divided into three books: the first begins with the breach of the peace in

March 1568 and ends with the death of Louis I de Bourbon, Prince de Condé; the second covers the period from his death to the battle at Mongontour on 1 October 1569; the third deals with the events of November and December of that year, including the siege of Vezelay and the failed Protestant siege of Bourges on 21 December. In his dedicatory epistle to Sir Henry Sidney, Fenton claims that the events were recorded by a "diligent" eyewitness who "proceeds with great modesty, observing with all such singular integrity as both the good sort may settle and confirm, and the rest suffice and satisfy without cause of offense, unless temperance and truth be offenses to such whose tastes can abide no better dispositions than their own." Despite the professed "truth and indifference of the author," *A Discourse of the Civil Wars and Late Troubles in France* has a definite Protestant slant. In its portrayal of the Princes de Condé and Henry of Navarre as gallant and devout nobles who desire only the right to worship according to their consciences, it ignores the royal ambitions of these Huguenot leaders. The villain of the history is Cardinal Charles de Lorraine, although the work is reticent about the roles that Catherine de Médicis and Charles IX played in the religious antagonism. Fenton's source has been traced to the *Memoires de la trèzieme guerre civile et des derniers troubles de France sous Charles IX* (1570), attributed to the Huguenot Jean de Serres.

Acts of Conference in Religion (1571) records a series of disputes that, according to Fenton, reveal the "rude sophistry of the Papists and mild simplicity of the reformed side." Dedicated to Lady Hoby, widow of the ambassador and translator Thomas Hoby and an accomplished linguist in her own right, *Acts of Conference in Religion* opens as a dialogue but evolves into an exchange of letters on the validity of the Mass versus that of the Sacrament of the Last Supper. The liberties that Fenton took with many of his translations are particularly evident in *Acts of Conference in Religion*. The original French version, *Actes de la dispute et conference tenue à Paris en mois de Juillet et Août 1566, entre deux docteurs de Sorbonne et deux ministres de l'église reformée* (1566), was written by one of the two Catholic disputants, Simon Vigor, archbishop of Narbonne. Fenton turns the archbishop's account into an anti-Catholic tirade, taking every opportunity to vilify the "two Papist doctors of [the] Sorbonne" and extol the two Calvinist ministers.

Also dedicated to Lady Hoby, *Monophylo* (1572) is based on Etienne Pasquier's *Le Monophyle* (1554). In the first book a group of young courtiers retires to a shady grove to discuss loyalty in love and the relationship of love to marriage. They decide to meet again the next day, and the ensuing debate as to whether passionate love is truly ennobling and inspiring or merely destructive constitutes the second book. Although the original *Le Monophyle* bears a resemblance to book 4 of Sir Thomas Hoby's translation of Baldassare Castiglione's *Book of the Courtier* (1561), Fenton's translation indulges his own puritanical prejudices by adding passages on the frailty of women, placing a heavy moralistic emphasis on various practical issues of marriage and on the evils of passion, and downplaying the Neoplatonic elements of Pasquier's text.

Fenton's translation of Jean Talpin's *A Form of Christian Policy* (1574) is a lengthy and detailed prescription for the government and regulation of a Christian commonwealth based on the "true foundations and pillars of commonweals," religion, and civil justice. Scripture is presented as the ultimate authority in affairs of state, and the book draws heavily on the Bible to support its claims. *A Form of Christian Policy* begins with discussions of the duties and qualities of a good magistrate and continues with rules for the proper administration of justice, the responsibilities and conduct of the various estates, the education of the young, the giving of alms, the relationships within the family, and the role of ecclesiastical authority in the Christian commonwealth.

Golden Epistles, Containing Variety of Discourse Both Moral, Philosophical, and Divine (1575) is a continuation of Edward Hellowes's *The Familiar Epistles of Sir Antony of Guevara* (1574). Unlike Hellowes, who closely translated from the original Spanish of Guevara's *Epístolas familiares,* Fenton used the French translation, *Epistres dorées, moralles et familières,* by Jean de Guterry (1556, 1559), as his source. The title's claim that the book contains the work of other authors is false, since all selections in Fenton's translation can be traced back to Guevara.

Epístolas familiares is a series of letters offering personal advice to dignitaries and nobles on a variety of matters. Obviously drawn to the heavily didactic nature of Guevara's work, Fenton often includes additional sermonizing in his translation. He also changes both structure and content by omitting location and date as well as the salutations and closings of the letters, thus turning the epistles into something more closely resembling essays. Furthermore, he deletes all passages relating to Catholicism and to Guevara's personal life; there is nothing in Fenton's *Golden Epistles* that indicates that its original author was a Roman Catholic bishop.

Fenton returned to history in his last and most ambitious book, *The History of Guicciardin* (1579), a loose translation of Guicciardini's *Storia d'Italia.* Next to *Certain Tragical Discourses, The History of Guicciardin* is considered his most significant work. Its influence has been traced to Raphael Holinshed's *Chronicles* (1587) and to Barnabe Barnes's drama *The Devil's Charter* (1607). As in *Certain Tragical Discourses* and *Golden Epistles,* Fenton did not translate from the original but depended on a French intermediary; the wording of Fenton's text is far closer to Jérôme Chomeday's French translation of 1568 than it is to Guicciardini's Italian.

Guicciardini's history records the political fortunes of Italy over the tumultuous years from the death of Lorenzo de Medici in 1492 to the Treaty of Cambrai between Francis I and Charles V in 1529. While Guicciardini's work is considered one of the most dispassionate and objective accounts of the Italian wars, and Chomeday's translation closely follows the tone of the original, Fenton typically adds rhetorical, sentimental, and moral embellishments to his version. He also denigrates other nations, especially Italy, glorifying England and its role in Italian affairs.

Fenton's puritanism, intense distrust of passion, delight in moralizing, and feelings of misogyny and xenophobia have been made unmistakably clear by the time the reader finishes *Certain Tragical Discourses,* and those personality traits dominate every one of his books. Fenton's tendency to make a foreign work his own prompted C. S. Lewis to label him a "semi-original author." As for Fenton's influence on English prose style, his emphasis on rhetoric and character has been credited with beginning a tradition that was further developed in Pettie's *Petite Palace of Pettie His Pleasure* (1576), Lyly's *Euphues* (1578), and Robert Greene's *Planetomachia* (1585) and *Penelope's Web* (1587).

Bibliographies:

James L. Harner, "Geoffrey Fenton," in his *English Renaissance Prose Fiction, 1500–1660: An Annotated Bibliography of Criticism* (Boston: G. K. Hall, 1978), pp. 164–167;

Harner, "Geoffrey Fenton," in his *English Renaissance Prose Fiction, 1500–1660: An Annotated Bibliography of Criticism (1976–1983)* (Boston: G. K. Hall, 1985), pp. 36, 286–290, 673;

Harner, "Geoffrey Fenton," in his *English Renaissance Prose Fiction, 1500–1660: An Annotated Bibliography of Criticism (1984–1990)* (Boston: G. K. Hall, 1992), pp. 48, 51–52, 188–192, 450, 452.

References:

Robert J. Clements and Joseph Gibaldi, *Anatomy of the Novella: The European Tale Collection from Boccaccio and Chaucer to Cervantes* (New York: New York University Press, 1977);

Jeannette Fellheimer, "Barnabe Barnes' Use of Geoffrey Fenton's *Historie of Guicciardin,*" *Modern Language Notes,* 57 (May 1942): 358–359;

Fellheimer, "Geoffrey Fenton's *Histoire of Guicciardin* and Holinshed's *Chronicles* of 1587," *Modern Language Quarterly,* 6 (September 1945): 285–298;

Fellheimer, "Hellowes and Fenton's Translations of Guevara's *Epistolas Familiares,*" *Studies in Philology,* 44 (April 1947): 140–156;

Fellheimer, "Notes on Geoffrey Fenton's Minor Translations," *Philological Quarterly,* 22 (October 1943): 343–346;

Rudolf B. Gottfried, *Geoffrey Fenton's Historie of Guicciardin,* Indiana University Publications, Humanities Series no. 3 (Bloomington: Indiana University Press, 1940);

Stephen A. Gottlieb, "Fenton's Novelle," *Revue de Littérature Comparée,* 40 (January–March 1966): 121–128;

Frank S. Hook, "Introduction," in *The French Bandello: A Selection. The Original Texts of Four of Belleforest's Histoires tragiques Translated by Geoffrey Fenton and William Painter, Anno 1567,* edited by Hook (Columbia: University of Missouri Press, 1948), pp. 9–51;

C. S. Lewis, *English Literature in the Sixteenth Century, Excluding Drama* (Oxford: Clarendon Press, 1954), pp. 309–311, 643;

René Pruvost, *Matteo Bandello and Elizabethan Fiction* (Paris: Champion, 1937);

Paul Salzman, *English Prose Fiction 1558–1700: A Critical History* (Oxford: Clarendon Press, 1985), pp. 7–21;

Paul N. Siegel, "A New Source for *Othello?,*" *PMLA,* 75 (September 1960): 480.

Giles Fletcher the Elder

(November 1546 – 11 March 1611)

Gordon McMullan
University of Newcastle upon Tyne

BOOKS: *Of the Russe Common Wealth. or Maner of Gov-
ernement by the Russe Emperour, with the Manners,
of the People* (London: Printed by T. D[awson]
for Thomas Charde, 1591);

*Licia, or, Poemes of Loue. Whereunto Is Added Richard the
Third,* anonymous (Cambridge: Printed by
John Legat, 1593);

*De literis antiquæ Britanniæ, Regibus praesertim qui
doctrina claruerunt, quique Collegia Cantabrigiae
fundarunt,* edited by Phineas Fletcher (Cambridge: Printed by [Thomas Buck and Roger
Daniel], 1633).

Editions: *Licia and Other Love-Poems and the Rising to
the Crowne of Richard the Third,* in *Miscellanies of
the Fuller Worthies' Library,* volume 3, edited by
Alexander B. Grossart (Blackburn, 1871);

Poems by Giles Fletcher, LLD., edited by Grosart
(Manchester, 1876);

Licia, in *Elizabethan Sonnets,* edited by Sidney Lee,
volume 2 (London: Constable, 1904), pp. 30–
62;

The English Works of Giles Fletcher, the Elder, edited by
Lloyd E. Berry (Madison: University of Wisconsin Press, 1964);

Of the Rus Commonwealth, edited by Albert J. Schmidt
(Ithaca, N.Y.: Cornell University Press, 1966);

Of the Russe Commonwealth, by Giles Fletcher, edited by
Richard Pipes (Cambridge, Mass.: Harvard
University Press, 1966).

OTHER: "The Tartars or Ten Tribes," in *Israel
Redux; or, The Restauration of Israel,* edited by
Samuel Lee (London: Printed by S. Streater
for John Hancock, 1677).

Giles Fletcher the Elder is generally thought of
in connection with the "Spenserian" poets of the
reign of James I, a group of consciously Protestant writers – including Samuel Daniel, Michael
Drayton, William Browne, George Wither, and
Fletcher's sons Phineas and Giles the younger –
who were opposed to many of the king's policies,

especially in matters of foreign affairs, and who attempted to remain faithful to the model of the militant Protestant poet that they found in the work of
Edmund Spenser. The work of Giles Fletcher
the Elder was, however, written during Elizabeth's reign and thus precedes the particular political issues that underpin the writings of his sons and
their associates, and his importance as a writer lies
not only in his influence on the Jacobean and Caroline generations of Protestant poets but also in his
own works, primarily the sonnet sequence *Licia*
(1593) and the geographic treatise *Of the Russe Commonwealth* (1591).

Giles Fletcher, the second son of Richard
Fletcher, was baptized at Watford on 26 November
1546. Giles's father was a friend of the martyrologist John Foxe and one of the first Reformation vicars. He had suffered under the Marian persecution
but became minister at Cranbrook in Kent in the
first year of Elizabeth's reign. Giles's elder brother,
also called Richard, became bishop of London and
was the father of John Fletcher the playwright. Giles
went from Cranbrook to Eton in 1561. He must
have shown poetic promise at an early age, since he
contributed eleven epigrams, twice as many as any
other scholar, to a collection of Latin verses presented to the queen on her visit to Eton in October
1563.

The first phase of Giles Fletcher's mature life
was spent at Cambridge. He went up to King's College as a scholar in August 1565 and was appointed
to a lectureship in 1572, taking his M.A. a year
later. He wrote more Latin poetry while at King's,
the most notable being the eclogue *De literis
antiquæ Britanniæ,* which he revised around 1594
but which was not published until his son Phineas
edited it in 1633. Fletcher was conscious of both
the Protestantism he had inherited from his father
and his status as a Cambridge poet, and it is this
milieu that his sons and their admirer John
Milton were to evoke as part of a Spenserian tradition. Fletcher consistently delineates a

pointed role for Cambridge in the history of English letters: *De literis antiquæ Britanniæ* is an allegorical poem which narrates a Cambridge-centered history of British intellectual endeavor and is an obvious source (via the protagonist, Lycidas, and the narration of the myth of Sabrina) for Milton's *Lycidas* (1638). Four years later Fletcher contributed several poems to a collection of verse in memory of the legal scholar Walter Haddon and his son Clere, who had drowned in the Cam River shortly after his father's death. Two of Fletcher's elegies – particularly "Adonis," on the drowning of the younger man – also influenced Milton. In the same year Fletcher wrote a commendatory poem for the second edition of the *Acts and Monuments* of his father's friend Foxe. It must have been around this time that he met Joan Sheafe; his marriage to her in 1581 obliged him to give up his college fellowship and ushered in the second phase of his life.

Initially, Fletcher and his family settled at his father's home at Cranbrook; but, after his election as member of Parliament for the Cinque Port of Winchelsea in November 1584, they moved permanently to London. Here, Fletcher allied himself with the diplomat Sir Thomas Randolph, and he went with Randolph to Scotland in 1586 to negotiate a league between Elizabeth and James VI. Fletcher's appointment as ambassador to Russia two years later was in all likelihood a result of this patronage, since Randolph had been ambassador there previously.

In December 1585 Fletcher was appointed remembrancer of the City of London, a post he would hold for most of the rest of his life. In May 1587 he was sent on his first major mission as an agent for the queen to negotiate trading rights with Hamburg. After two months' stalemate he made an alternative but advantageous agreement with nearby Stade instead, to the rage of the Hamburg authorities. A year later the queen sent Fletcher as ambassador to Russia with a similar task. By this time English trading privileges in Russia had been eroded almost completely, and relations between the Russia Company and the czar's court were at a low ebb. Fletcher was to attempt to revitalize these links. He was not well received and was even kept for a while under house arrest; eventually, however, by dint of considerable patience, he succeeded in negotiating a favorable agreement. On his return to England in 1590, he presented the first version of his treatise *Of the Russe Commonwealth* to the queen.

Shortly afterward he wrote to the queen's adviser, William Cecil, Baron Burghley, announcing his intention to write a Latin history of Elizabeth's

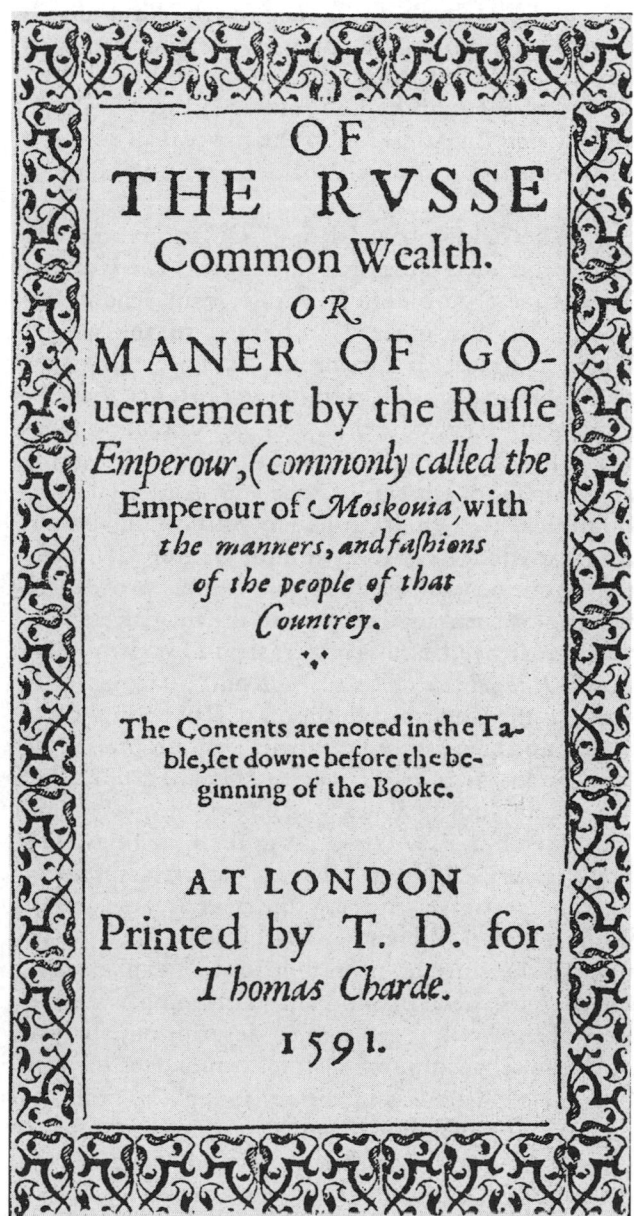

Title page for Fletcher's 1591 geographic treatise, a significant influence on the English conception of Russia in the sixteenth and seventeenth centuries

reign, providing a detailed outline of the projected work, and requesting both patronage and permission to examine the relevant state papers. "Your Lordship knoweth," he wrote, "what is needful to make a story not a tale, besides *res gestae* [actions] to have *consilia rerum gestarum* [the thinking behind the actions]." He carefully adds that he does not need to see "the very *arcana* [secrets] (which are best when they are secretest) but so much as shall be necessary to explain and justify the actions"; but Burghley appears not to have trusted him, more than likely aware of Fletcher's preference for the kind of militant foreign policy he opposed. Fletcher seems to have abandoned the project, despite the detailed nature of the plan he had forwarded to Burghley, and turned his attention to the process of revising *Of the Russe Commonwealth,* which was published in 1591.

The British-based Russia Company immediately requested Burghley to suppress the treatise. This request, considering its tone, is not wholly surprising. In his preface addressed to the queen, Fletcher states his intentions "to note things for mine own experience, of more importance than delight, and rather true than strange" and announces that she may see both these latter qualities in the government of Russia: "A true and strange face of a tyrannical state (most unlike to your own), without true knowledge of God, without written law, without common justice, save that which proceedeth from their speaking law, to wit, the magistrate who hath most need of a law to restrain his own injustice." *Of the Russe Commonwealth* had a strong influence on the English conception of Russia in the sixteenth and seventeenth centuries: Milton praises the book in his own *Brief History of Moscovia* (1682), and others, including Giles's nephew the playwright John Fletcher, made use of it in their writings. The book is divided into twenty-eight chapters in three unequal sections, covering topics as diverse as geographic detail, the emperor's lifestyle, and the liturgy of the church, offering historical explanations for various social phenomena. The comprehensiveness of the book – geographic description, analysis of the state, account of customs – indicates the seriousness of Fletcher's intention; though he claims to be reporting personal observations, he writes a systematic treatise. The central section, devoted to a description of the state, represents the first coherent study of Russian politics ever written. The writing is characterized by a profound contempt for the political life of the country, and the reader gains a strong sense not only of the autocracy of the czar's rule but also of Fletcher's own very clear political preferences. He is appalled that "as touching any law or public order of the realm, it is ever determined of before any public assembly or parliament be summoned," and enraged by the czar's encouragement of corruption in the church "as knowing superstition and false religion best to agree with a tyrannical state." The Russia Company was understandably afraid that the effect of such a blast of contempt from the English ambassador would undo the very trading privileges he had negotiated for them.

In 1593 Fletcher's *Licia; or, Poems of Love* was published anonymously. It is a collection of all of Fletcher's English verse, including a fifty-three-sonnet sequence, several elegies, and a longer poem, "The Rising to the Crown of Richard III." The sonnet sequence is notable both for its clarity and calmness and for its unique dependence upon Anacreontic material for its portrayal of love. Beginning with a limited cast of Venus, Apollo, and Cupid (who is portrayed in nearly half the poems, and characterized as a playful boy rather than the vengeful god of Ovidian tradition), the poems, the bulk of which depended upon Continental models, provide a gradual development from the initial limited grouping of gods into, in the closing sonnet, a full pantheon, each god expressing one of the attributes of Licia's beauty. Sonnet 28 ("In time the strong and stately turrets fall") offers a large political backcloth for the love affair, while sonnet 36 ("Hear how my sighs are echoed of the wind") concentrates on a controlled display of the lover's emotions. Such control diminishes with respect to the physical: sonnets 29 and 48 are both marked by an erotic quality which looks forward to Donne. In sonnet 29 the poet dreams of Licia's "ebon thighs, the wonder of my sight, / Where all my senses with their objects meet," while in 48 he sees a spider run into Licia's house and asks the creature "why of late I saw / Thee loose thy poison, and thy bowels gone?" to find that the spider had come across Licia and mistaken her for the goddess Minerva.

The sonnet sequence is followed by several elegies and "The Rising to the Crown of Richard III," a poetic monologue in the style of the *Mirror for Magistrates.* The poem concentrates on warning of the problems inherent in those with "sparks of ambition" yet is also marked by a wry humor, as when Richard narrates his responsibility for drowning his brother in a butt of malmsey: "My brother George, men say, was slain by me, / A brother's part, to give his brother wine."

The importance of Fletcher's *Licia* has been noted as much for the literary views expressed in the two prefatory epistles as for the poetry itself. *De literis antiquæ Britanniæ* had evoked a Cambridge-centered view of Protestant poetics which traced British intellectual endeavor back to the Druids, to a time before the dominance of the Roman Catholic church, a time of bardic culture when poetry and prophecy were interlinked. This assertion of the native origins of English literature echoes the views of Protestant writers such as John Bale and seeks to create a sense that a militant Protestant tradition predates European and Roman Catholic influences;

thus it provides an appropriate tradition for post-Reformation writers. Fletcher's zeal as a Protestant is clear: in later life he was regularly employed in the interrogation of captured priests, and he passed on to his sons a fiery anti-Catholic religious outlook. Yet he is careful in the dedicatory letter of *Licia* to place distance not only between his own attitudes to the church and those of Brownist Separatists but also between his sense of the Christian propriety of poetic endeavor and the negativity of Puritanism, regretting that "our English *Genevan* purity hath quite debarred us of honest recreation."

His approach to poetics as outlined in the dedicatory letter, addressed to Lady Molineux, consciously echoes that of Sir Philip Sidney, with whose *Defense of Poetry* (circa 1580) he is obviously acquainted. He had contributed to the Cambridge collection of verses in memory of Sidney in 1587, and his reference to Sidney in the *Licia* letter supports his assertion of the Cambridge milieu as a center of learning, gentlemanly accomplishment, and poetic endeavor. He underlines the centrality of his own college by reminding Lady Molineux that Sir John Harington, whose 1591 translation of Ariosto's *Orlando Furioso* (1532) she admired, had studied at King's. The letter coyly alludes to the question of Licia's identity: "It may be she is Learning's image or some heavenly wonder, which the precisest may not mislike: perhaps under that name I have shadowed Discipline. It may be, I mean that kind courtesy which I found at the patroness of these poems; it may be some college; it may be my conceit, and portend nothing." Although we are left none the wiser, we have a sense that what matters about these poems is not their subject matter but their treatment of form and convention, though the mention of "Discipline" appears an oblique but serious reference to the religious underpinnings of Fletcher's writings.

The third phase of Fletcher's life began abruptly in June 1596 with the unexpected death of his brother the bishop, who bequeathed him a large family and substantial debts to the queen. He was reduced to writing two pleas to Elizabeth entitled "Reasons to Move Her Majesty in Some Commiseration towards the Orphans of the Late Bishop of London," yet there was still considerable delay. After Burghley's rejection of the history project and his further denial of Fletcher's appeal for the position of master of requests, it must have been all too clear that no patronage would be forthcoming from that quarter, and Fletcher sought a new patron. He turned to Robert Devereux, Earl of Essex. Fletcher's staunch Protestantism no doubt

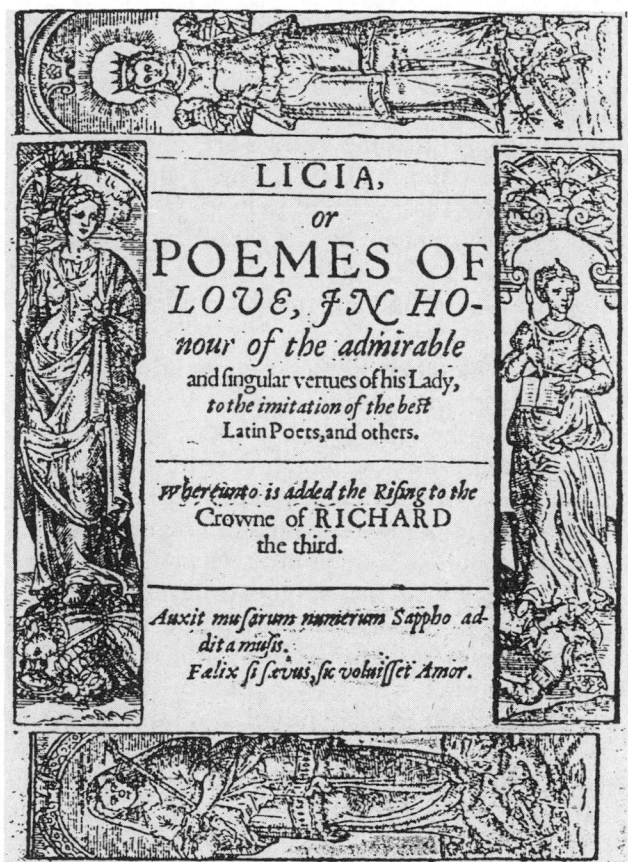

Title page for Fletcher's 1593 sonnet sequence

appealed to Essex, who made use of the former's position as remembrancer on several occasions; in return, the earl appears to have assisted Fletcher to be discharged of his brother's debts.

In May 1597 Fletcher was appointed treasurer of Saint Paul's, and his future seemed secure. He was sent to the Low Countries to negotiate on behalf of the Merchants Adventurers. But domestic matters were becoming troublesome, and Fletcher's health appears to have been on the wane. His financial position improved with the gift of the lease of a profitable parsonage from King's College, but then in 1601 came the Essex rebellion, resulting in Essex's execution and Fletcher's near ruin. He was examined in connection with the abortive coup and was obliged to defend himself against charges of complicity. He was held in private custody for a month and, though he retained his positions of remembrancer and treasurer of Saint Paul's, he seems nonetheless to have remained under the shadow of the affair for the rest of his life. He finally resigned the post of remembrancer under some pressure on 2 July 1605.

It was probably at this late stage that Fletcher wrote a short treatise titled "The Tartars or Ten Tribes," which remained unpublished until 1677. Similar in style to *Of the Russe Commonwealth,* the treatise conjectures that the Tartars are descended from the ten lost tribes of Israel. This appears to have been Fletcher's last piece of writing. In 1610 he was employed once again by the Merchants Adventurers in some trade negotiations, but by February 1611 his health had collapsed completely, and he died on 11 March.

Giles Fletcher the Elder was a minor Elizabethan writer who exerted a quiet but clear influence on subsequent generations of writers up to Milton. He was a vehement Protestant with a strong sense of political justice and a hatred of tyrannical behavior, as is abundantly clear from his writings about Russian politics. His poetry, though by no means brilliant, demonstrates a substantial knowledge of classical precedent and an ability to move beyond the conventions and models with which it begins. The range of his talents is clear, from the antityrannical indignation of passages in *Of the Russe Commonwealth* to the calm detail of several of the *Licia* sonnets, and his combination of learning, religion, and good humor is seen at its best in the prefatory epistles of the *Licia* collection.

Bibliography:

Lloyd E. Berry, "Giles Fletcher, the Elder: A Bibliography," *Transactions of the Cambridge Bibliographical Society,* 3 (1961): 200–215.

References:

Warren B. Austin, "Milton's Lycidas and Two Latin Elegies by Giles Fletcher, the Elder," *Studies in Philology,* 44 (January 1947): 41–55;

Lloyd E. Berry, "Three Poems by Giles Fletcher, the Elder, in 'Poemata Varii Argumenti' (1678)," *Notes & Queries,* 204 (April 1959): 132–134;

Lisle Cecil John, *The Elizabethan Sonnet Sequences* (New York: Columbia University Press, 1938);

Julius Walter Lever, *The Elizabethan Love Sonnet* (London: Methuen, 1956), pp. 144–149;

C. S. Lewis, *English Literature in the Sixteenth Century, excluding Drama* (Oxford: Clarendon Press, 1954), pp. 493–494;

David Norbrook, *Poetry and Politics in the English Renaissance* (London: Routledge & Kegan Paul, 1984);

Anne Lake Prescott, "Licia's Temple: Giles Fletcher the Elder and Number Symbolism," *Renaissance and Reformation,* 2 (1978): 170–181;

Robert R. Raymo, "Three New Latin Poems of Giles Fletcher the Elder," *Modern Language Notes,* 71 (June 1956): 399–401;

Janet Girvan Scott, *Les sonnets élisabéthains* (Paris: Champion, 1929), pp. 103–113.

Papers:

A manuscript copy of *Of the Russe Common Wealth,* with a preface in Fletcher's hand, is located in the library of Queen's College, Cambridge.

George Gascoigne

(1539? – 7 October 1577)

Susan C. Staub

Appalachian State University

BOOKS: *A Hundreth Sundrie Flowres, Bounde vp in One Small Poesie. Gathered Partely (by Translation) and Partly by Inuention* (London: Printed by Henry Bynneman for Richard Smith, 1573); revised and enlarged as *The Posies of George Gascoigne Esquire* (London: Printed by Henry Bynneman for Richard Smith, [1575]);

The Glasse of Gouernement. A Tragicall Comedie (London: Printed by Henry Middleton for Christopher Barker, 1575);

The Princelye Pleasures at the Courte at Kenelwoorth: That Is to Saye, the Copies of All Such Verses . . . and Other Deuices of Pleasure, as Were There . . . Presented . . . Before the Qvene's Maiestie in the Yeare, 1575 (London: Printed by Rychard Jhones, 1576);

The Spoyle of Antwerpe. Faithfully Reported, by a True Englishman, Who Was Present (London: [Printed by John Charlewood for] Richard Jones, [1576?]);

The Steele Glas. A Satyre. Together with the Complainte of Phylomene (London: [Printed by Henry Binneman] for Richard Smith, 1576).

Editions: *The VVhole Woorkes of George Gascoigne, Esquyre: Newlye Compyled into One Volume* (London: Printed by Abell Ieffes, 1587);

The Complete Poems of George Gascoigne, edited by William Carew Hazlitt (London: Printed [by Whittingham and Wilkins] for the Roxburghe Library, 1869–1870);

"Certain Notes of Instruction," in *Elizabethan Critical Essays*, edited by G. Gregory Smith, volume 1 (Oxford: Clarendon Press, 1904), pp. 46–57;

The Complete Works of George Gascoigne, edited by John W. Cunliffe, 2 volumes (Cambridge: The University Press, 1907–1910);

A Hundredth Sundrie Flowres, edited by Bernard M. Ward (London: F. Etchells and H. Macdonald, 1926; Port Washington, N.Y.: Kennikat Press, 1975);

George Gascoigne's A Hundreth Sundrie Flowres, edited by C. T. Prouty (Columbia: University of Missouri Press, 1942);

"A Pleasant Discourse of the Adventures of Master F. J.," in *Elizabethan Prose Fiction,* edited by Merritt E. Lawlis (New York: Odyssey Press, 1967);

A Hundred Sundry Flowers (Menston, U.K.: Scolar Press, 1970);

The Steele Glass and The Complaint of Philomene, edited by William L. Wallace, Elizabethan and Renaissance Studies, no. 24 (Salzburg: Salzburg Studies in English Literature, 1975);

George Gascoigne the Green Knight: Selected Poetry and Prose, edited by Roger Pooley (Manchester: Carcanet New Press, 1982);

"A Pleasant Discourse of the Adventures of Master F. J.," in *An Anthology of Elizabethan Prose Fiction,* edited by Paul Salzman (New York: Oxford University Press, 1987), pp. 1–81.

PLAY PRODUCTIONS: *The Supposes,* London, Gray's Inn, 1566;

Jocasta, London, Gray's Inn, 1566.

OTHER: Jacques de Fouilloux, *The Noble Arte of Venerie or Hunting,* translation attributed to Gascoigne (London: Printed by Henry Bynneman for Christopher Barker, [1575]);

Saint Augustine, *A Delicate Diet, for Daintiemouthde Droonhardes,* translated by Gascoigne (London: [Printed by John Charlewood for] Richard Jones, 1576);

Humphrey Gilbert, *A Discourse of a Discouerie for a New Passage to Cataia,* edited by Gascoigne (London: Printed by Henry Middleton for Richard Jhones, 1576);

Innocent III, *The Droomme of Doomes Day. Wherein the Frailties of Mans Lyfe, Are Portrayed,* translated by Gascoigne (London: [Printed by Thomas East] for Gabriell Cawood, 1576; Printed by John Windet for Gabriell Cawood, 1586);

George Gascoigne (woodcut from The Steel Glass, *1576)*

Anonymous, "The Pleasant Tale of Hemetes the Hermit," Latin translation by Gascoigne, in *A Paradoxe, Prouing by Reason and Example, that Baldnesse Is Much Better than Bushie Haire. Hereunto Is Annexed the Tale of Hemetes the Heremite. Newly Recognised Both in Latine and Englishe, by the Said A. F.,* by Synesius, translated by Abraham Fleming (London: Printed by Henry Denham, 1579).

George Gascoigne, amateur poet and gentleman, was the chief poet of the early Elizabethan period. As a writer supremely interested in proving the English language to be as fit a medium for poetry as other languages, he deserves attention if only as a literary pioneer. Among his other achievements, he is credited with the first prose comedy and Greek-style tragedy in English, the first treatise on English prosody, the first English satire using the Roman form, and, many argue, the first English novel. Gascoigne is impressive, then, for the sheer variety of his literary roles: translator, playwright, editor, sonneteer, satirist, moralist, apologist, novelist, and reporter. Beyond these accomplishments, his works strike a new and sophisticated note in English literature in their experimentation with poetic

voice. An incredibly self-conscious poet, Gascoigne refashioned himself throughout his literary career. From the rakish lover of his early works to the staunch moralist of the later, he is constantly appropriating new identities. Yet he seems unwittingly to have provided the best summary of his career in the autobiographical poem entitled "Gascoigne's Woodmanship," where he characterizes himself as shooting "awry almost at every mark." Constantly seeking preferment, yet invariably alienating his patrons, Gascoigne provides an interesting example of the problems facing the Elizabethan courtier-poet. A fascination with court power colors virtually all his endeavors. His forays into law, military service, courtiership, and literature suggest a man struggling to find a place in a world that offers him none.

The details of Gascoigne's early life are sketchy; even the date of his birth is open to conjecture. Born around 1539 to a prosperous and noble family in Cardington, Bedfordshire, George was the eldest son of Sir John Gascoigne and Margaret Scargill Gascoigne. Sir John was a Catholic and a member of Parliament for Bedford in 1542, 1553, and 1557 and served as justice of the peace. Both parents apparently were litigious and quarrelsome, characteristics that Gascoigne seems to have inherited. There is evidence of Sir John's deathbed disinheritance of George and of Margaret's suing her sister over a gold casting bottle from their father's estate. Other records reveal disputes between mother and son over the ownership of sheep.

According to C. T. Prouty, Gascoigne probably "stole" much of his early education by joining his cousins in their lessons while visiting them in Westmoreland. References in his poetry reveal that he attended Trinity College, Cambridge, but left without taking a degree. In 1555 Gascoigne entered Gray's Inn at the Inns of Court, but his interest in the law quickly waned, and he soon returned to Bedford to assume the life of a country gentleman. Apparently the formative event of the young poet's life occurred when he served as almoner in his sick father's place at the coronation of Queen Elizabeth. This opportunity provided Gascoigne with his first taste of court life that was to entice him for the rest of his days. He describes this fascination in one of his poems written on the theme "Sat cito, si sat bene" (If it be well, let it be quickly done):

In haste, post haste, when first my wandering mind
Beheld the glist'ring court with gazing eye,
Such deep delights I seemed therein to find,
As might beguile a graver guest than I.
The stately pomp of princes and their peers

Did seem to swim in floods of beaten gold.
The wanton world of young delightful years
Was not unlike a heaven for to behold,
Wherein did swarm (for every saint) a dame,
So fair of hue, so fresh of their attire,
As might excel dame Cynthia for fame,
Or conquer Cupid with his own desire.
These and such like were baits that blazed still
Before mine eye to feed my greedy will.

The "stately pomp" and "deep delights" of this "wanton world" would beguile the poet for most of his life and would soon lead to his financial ruin.

From 1558 to 1572 the poet became embroiled in a series of legal difficulties that exhausted him both financially and emotionally. He wrote several poems detailing his life and troubles during this period, most notably "The Green Knight's Farewell to Fancy" and "Gascoigne's Woodmanship." In these conspicuously autobiographical poems Gascoigne chronicles his career as student, lawyer, courtier, and soldier and expresses his disillusionment with each. This habit of developing his works around his own life and experiences, however, later caused great confusion, as readers mistook much that he wrote for historical fact.

What should have marked the end of his financial troubles – his marriage on 23 November 1561 to Elizabeth Bacon Breton, the rich widow of William Breton and mother of the poet Nicholas Breton – only added to his difficulties. Although the records are not completely clear on the legalities, Elizabeth was apparently already married to Edward Boyes at the time she married Gascoigne. In the bitter legal battles that followed to determine which man was her rightful husband, the courts impounded the couple's household belongings and denied Gascoigne access to his wife in "the mean season." The dispute was settled when Elizabeth obtained a legal divorce from Boyes and remarried Gascoigne. But this settlement did not require Boyes to cede control of the Breton children's inheritance, and litigation continued for several more years.

During this time of great legal difficulty Gascoigne decided to "abandon all vain delights" and returned to Gray's Inn in 1565, apparently in an attempt to mend his broken fortunes. The return was marked by one of his most ambitious early efforts, his "Memories," a series of five poems on themes suggested by his fellow students. Gascoigne met the challenge to his virtuosity quite handily, boasting that he devised the five themes, amounting to 158 lines of verse, "riding by the way, writing none of them until he came at the end of his journey, one day in tarrying with his friend, and the third in re-turning to Grey's Inn." These poems, on themes such as "Audaces fortuna juvat" (Fortune favors the brave) and "Satis sufficit" (Enough is enough), have been judged to be some of Gascoigne's finest work.

During this stint at Gray's Inn, Gascoigne also had a hand in writing two plays, *The Supposes* and *Jocasta,* both produced in 1566. *The Supposes,* a play that Jonathan Crewe calls "Gascoigne's major legacy to the English theater and above all to Shakespearean comedy," is the first example of Italian-style comedy in English. With a plot adapted from Lodovico Ariosto's *I Suppositi* (1509), Gascoigne's drama presents a story of disguise, deceit, and mistaken identity. Most important, *The Supposes* anticipated Shakespeare's *Comedy of Errors* (circa 1592) and provided the subplot for *The Taming of the Shrew* (1594).

Also while at Gray's Inn, Gascoigne collaborated with his friend Francis Kinwelmershe on *Jocasta,* a play which has the distinction of being the first Greek-style tragedy played on the English stage. Although the play claims to be translated from Euripides' *Phoenissae,* it was actually borrowed from the Italian Lodovico Dolce's *Giocasta* (1560). Despite its Italian origins, it follows Senecan drama in its five-act division and its use of a chorus and dumb shows.

Although life at Gray's Inn provided an outlet for Gascoigne's literary interests, he quickly grew bored with practicing law, and by 1567 or 1568 he had returned to farming in Cardington. Yet the court still drew him, and he seems to have traveled to London frequently during this period. By May 1570, however, the expense of court life aggravated the continuing financial drain of litigation, and Gascoigne was confined to Bedford jail for failure to pay his debts.

Seeking a way out of his financial distress, he decided to try his luck as a soldier of fortune, joining Sir Humphrey Gilbert's forces in 1572 in support of William of Orange against the Spaniards in the Low Countries. He recounts these experiences in "Dulce Bellum Inexpertis" (War is sweet to those without experience), a poem first published in *The Posies*. Far from the patriotic glorification of war so typical of the martial literature of the time, Gascoigne's depiction is bitter and personal, revealing the cowardice and incompetence of his fellow soldiers. War, he feels, is "the scourge of God," a punishment for the pride that infects all levels of society. Soldiering, he soon discovered, would not reward him with the fame and fortune he so arduously sought.

After returning from the Dutch wars later in the same year, he managed to win election as burgess of Midhurst, a position that would grant him parliamentary immunity from his creditors. But this shift in fortunes proved short-lived when an anonymous letter was sent to the Privy Council accusing him of an assortment of crimes – murder, atheism, and treason being the most damning. Adding insult to injury, the writer of the letter accused Gascoigne of being "a common rhymer and a deviser of slanderous pasquils [lampoons] against diverse persons of great calling." Gascoigne left England soon after these charges were lodged, fearing an investigation into their validity. With nowhere else to turn, he again beat a hasty retreat to Holland, but not before he had arranged for the publication of his collected works.

Having tried his luck as a courtier, lawyer, and soldier, Gascoigne turned his hand to literary endeavors in the early 1570s. Seeking patronage from Arthur Grey, Baron Grey de Wilton, he wrote the autobiographical poem "Gascoigne's Woodmanship," which critic Yvor Winters judges to be one of the two or three finest verses of the century. It wittily compares the poet's poor marksmanship in shooting a deer with his failures in life and becomes an occasion for the poet to reevaluate the whole of his career. The poem opens dramatically, setting the scene and making explicit the analogy between missing the target in hunting and shooting amiss in life:

> My worthy lord, I pray you wonder not
> To see your woodman shoot so oft awry,
> Nor that he stands amazed like a sot,
> And lets the harmless deer (unhurt) go by.
> Or if he strike a doe which is but carrion,
> Laugh not, good lord, but favor such a fault;
> Take well in worth, he would fain hit the barren,
> But though his hart be good, his hap is nought . . .
> Believe me, lord, the case is nothing strange.
> He shoots awry almost at every mark,
> His eyes have been so used for to range,
> That now God knows they be both dim and dark.

The poem then chronicles all the occasions when the poet shot and missed his aim – at law, at court, and at soldiering:

> For proof, he bears the note of folly now,
> Who shot sometime to hit philosophy.
> Next that, he shot to be a man of law,
> And spent sometime with learned Littleton,
> Yet in the end, he proved but a dawe [fool]. . . .
> From thence he shot to catch a courtly grace
> And thought even there to wield the world at will,
> But out alas he much mistook the place,
> And shot awry at every rover still.

Far from being truly self-deprecating, the poem actually affords a chance for self-advertisement. In an ironic reversal at the end of the poem, Gascoigne hints that his recurrent bad luck in worldly endeavors paradoxically highlights his unique worth and virtue. "Woodmanship" achieved its goal and brought the poet a commission to write a masque celebrating the double wedding of Anthony Browne, son and heir to the Viscount Montague, to Mary, daughter of Sir William Dormer, and of Robert Dormer, Mary's brother, to Elizabeth, Montague's daughter by his second wife.

The success of these two forays into poetry persuaded Gascoigne to arrange and publish his works in a single volume. The result was one of the great publishing hoaxes of the Renaissance, the autoanthology *A Hundred Sundry Flowers Bound up in One Small Posy, Gathered Partly (by Translation) and Partly by Invention* (1573). Significantly, the "posy" headed "Meritum petere grave" (To seek reward is serious) appears on the title page in the place normally reserved for the author's name and provides clear motivation for Gascoigne's decision to publish his poems. Presented anonymously as the work of several authors, each distinguished by his own motto or "posy," *The Flowers* gathers together most of Gascoigne's lyric poetry. The volume is as varied as its title suggests: in addition to its sundry verse it includes two plays (*The Supposes* and *Jocasta*), a prose narrative mixed with verse ("The Adventures of Master F. J."), several sonnet sequences and themes, a masque ("Gascoigne's Device of a Masque for the Right Honourable Viscount Montague"), and a lengthy verse narrative ("Dan Bartholomew of Bath").

A masterful authorial dodge, the ruse of sundry authors accomplished several things, the most obvious of which was that it allowed the poet to avoid the stigma of print, since Gascoigne's contemporaries believed that publishing one's work made it common and jeopardized the author's position as a gentleman. But it also allowed Gascoigne an opportunity to capitalize on the popularity of *Tottel's Miscellany* (1557), one of the first anthologies of English poetry. By pretending that the collection represented the work of sundry authors, he could manipulate the form he inherited from Richard Tottel and other miscellanies and explore various poetic voices, perspectives, and genres.

The crucial difference between *A Hundred Sundry Flowers* and the other miscellanies is that the poems in Gascoigne's anthology are not really those of various authors. Although the poet provides enough hints throughout the volume to render this subterfuge fairly transparent, the work has evoked great conjecture regarding its true authorship. In his

1926 edition, for example, Bernard M. Ward, taking Gascoigne at his word, posits that the volume comprises the writing of sundry authors, to which the chief contributor was Edward de Vere, seventeenth Earl of Oxford, a hypothesis which continues to find proponents. Despite their allure, such theories have been largely discredited by Walter Wilson Greg, Fredson Bowers, C. T. Prouty, and others. The scholarly consensus is that Gascoigne is the sole author of *A Hundred Sundry Flowers* and that the collection only pretends to be a miscellany.

To complicate matters further, Gascoigne holds the disparate pieces of his volume together with the commentary of a fictional editor, mysteriously identified by the initials "G. T." Although G. T. claims only to "reduce [the poems] into some good order," he in fact persistently colors the reader's experience of the works. With the creation of this obtrusive editor, Gascoigne departs completely from the miscellany tradition. Although Tottel plays a significant part in the shaping of his finished anthology, he has no visible and continuing presence in it. He regularizes the verse by smoothing out the rhythms and eliminating archaisms, and he adds titles, sometimes inappropriate to the content of the poem. Gascoigne's editor, on the other hand, constantly intrudes to shape the reader's apprehension of the text. Often his voice overwhelms the text on which he is commenting. In "The Adventures of Master F. J.," for instance, he speaks for a full 80 percent of the narrative.

Although it was conventional to present works anonymously or as translations, Gascoigne's tactic of sundry authors achieves something more sophisticated. The claim of multiple authorship combines with the intrusive voice of the putative editor to draw the reader's attention immediately to the rhetorical activity involved in writing. The voice of the author becomes fractured so that the editor appears to be the only reliable center of authority. But the editor, too, turns out to be unreliable, pedantically insisting on setting every poem in its historical context and displaying an annoying literal-mindedness. More than just an intermediary between the reader and the text, then, Gascoigne's editor becomes a coreader whose persona and commentary — however wrongheaded — draw attention to the written word and establish reading as a game.

A Hundred Sundry Flowers proved an ambitious undertaking, a collection that has been called "more brilliant than any before [Sir Philip] Sidney's" and "a worthy antecedent to [Edmund] Spenser's *Shepheardes Calender* (1579)." Keenly aware of the English literary tradition, Gascoigne sought to gain

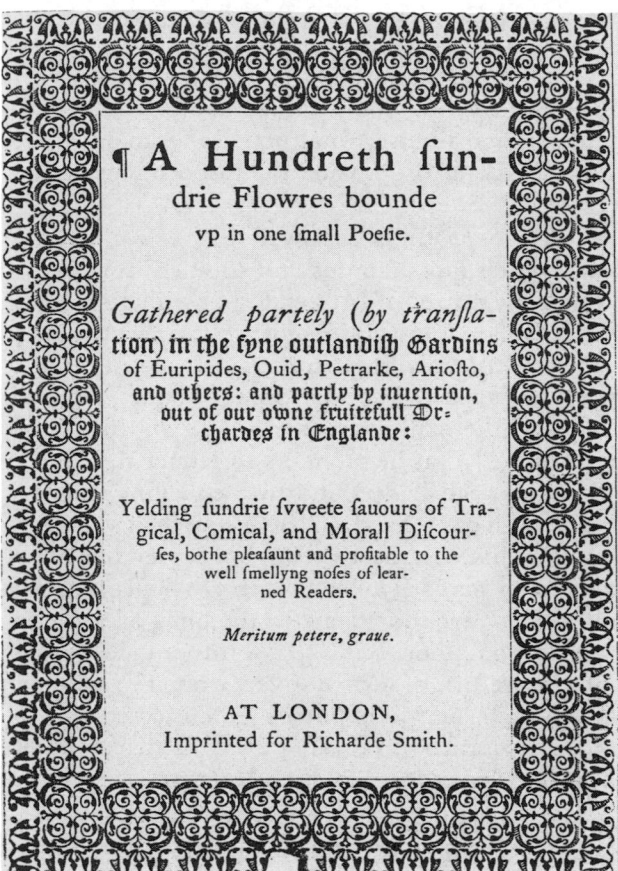

Title page for Gascoigne's first book, published as a collection of works by various authors but in fact written entirely by Gascoigne

"immortal fame" by following "the trace of that worthy and famous knight Sir Geoffrey Chaucer," as G. T.'s dedicatory epistle states. Feeling that poets had neglected Chaucer and the native English tradition, G. T. promises the first volume worthy of such a predecessor: "[none of] our native countrymen . . . have in their verses hitherto (translations excepted) delivered unto us any such notable volume, as have been by Poets of antiquity, left unto the posterity." *A Hundred Sundry Flowers*, however, claims that it will celebrate the English tradition and stand tall alongside the classical.

Fittingly, the volume opens with *The Supposes*, a work whose theme provides a clue to what Gascoigne is attempting. A play full of intrigue and mistaken identities, it forewarns the reader that things are not always as they appear to be. Its prologue or argument — "But understand, this our supposed is nothing but a mistaking or imagination of one thing for another" — might just as easily be applied to *A Hundred Sundry Flowers*. At one point Gascoigne even refers to his poems as "supposes" ("Epistle to the Young Gentlemen"). When he revised the volume in 1575, he retitled it *The Posies,* with its suggestion of "poses," perhaps to make this meaning clearer. Since the court valued subterfuge and intrigue above all else, what better way to advertise his skill at courtly evasion than to produce such a volume?

The Supposes is followed by *Jocasta* and by Gascoigne's most famous and sophisticated work, "The Adventures of Master F. J.," which of all his writings has received the most scholarly attention. Labeled "the first English novel," it has never lost its critical appeal. The story line is simple: it tells of the romantic exploits of a young man, identified only as "F. J.," as he attempts to seduce the beautiful but married Lady Elinor while visiting relatives in the north of England. In true Petrarchan style, F. J. achieves his conquest through a series of poems written to his ladylove. Elinor proves easy prey, and the two are soon depicted tumbling all night on the bedroom floor. But F. J.'s fortunes quickly sour with the return of a rival lover, ironically another writer, in the person of Lady Elinor's secretary. F. J. ends the narrative skulking away in defeat, older though little wiser for all his adventures.

Although the plot is fairly straightforward, it is Gascoigne's presentation that marks his unique contribution to English literature. From its very start the narrative is couched in subterfuge and evasion. It opens with three letters that provide an elaborate explanation of how the work came to be published: the printer claims to have obtained the manuscript through his friend H. W.; H. W. explains that he was given the poems by G. T. on the condition that he promise not to publish them; and finally, G. T., our faithful editor, claims that he received the poems directly from F. J. These letters force the reader to step back from the main narrative and serve as a warning that, as Gascoigne himself explains, "these things are mystical and not to be understood but by the author himself."

Gascoigne's masterstroke is his creation of the editor/narrator G. T. While F. J. chronicles the love affair in his poems, G. T. comments upon F. J.'s activities in prose. The same event is often rendered in two completely different ways. For instance, as F. J. admires Elinor's "heavenly" beauty in Petrarchan imagery, constantly bemoaning his inability to "countervail the least part of [her] goodness," G. T. brings the reader back to earthy reality. Elinor, he posits, is a "cornfed crow," more attractive than the "mounting kite" (Elinor's kinswoman, Frances, who is in love with F. J.) because she is more easily caught. By placing the practical viewpoint alongside

the Petrarchan, Gascoigne forces the reader to see Petrarchan discourse for what it has become: artificial and trite, and ultimately deceitful. The resulting doubling of perspective allows Gascoigne at once to parody the tradition and to burlesque the courtier-poet system of which he himself is a part.

Actually, F. J.'s story is told three more times, in three different ways – as allegory, as autobiography, and as parable – before the narrative draws to a close. G. T. tells only one of these stories, "The Allegory of Suspicion"; different speakers relate the other two. Frances presents a parable about a faithless wife and her patient husband, while Dame Pergo tells of her own misdirected courtship. In these inset stories Gascoigne seems to be honing his craft, artfully exploring the possibilities of perspective, much as the schoolboy discovers the possibilities of language by following the principles of rhetorical *amplificatio.* These apparent digressions amplify and parallel the situation of the larger tale. More important, they refocus our attention on the game of storytelling.

As he closes "The Adventures of Master F. J.," the editor offers the reader a series of shorter poems grouped as "The Devices of Sundry Gentlemen." These devices comprise seventy-four pieces gathered together with various mottoes or "posies." Although the poems by sundry gentlemen do not seem to be in any set order, they do move from light and amatory in tone to more-serious verse. The first set of poems, grouped under the posy "Si Fortunatus infoelix" (If one is fortunate, one is unhappy), is largely playful, portraying kissing contests, letters to friends, flirtations with ladies at court, and various social occasions. Here Gascoigne depicts the same picture of courtly life as in "Master F. J.": a life of dinners and intrigue, games and riddles. And here, too, G. T.'s glosses occasionally overwhelm and even seem more interesting than the poems.

The next sets are largely Petrarchan, treating the many joys and complaints of the various lovers. The love poems, however, are increasingly interspersed with poems emphasizing mutability, failures, the loss of youth, and the fear of dying. Interestingly, Gascoigne presents most of these nonamatory poems openly as his own. Such verses as "Gascoigne's Lullaby" and "Gascoigne's Anatomy" display the plain style that prompted Winters's assessment of Gascoigne as "one of the six or seven greatest lyric poets of the sixteenth century, and perhaps higher." "Gascoigne's Arraignment" and "Gascoigne's Libel of Divorce" also wittily reflect the poet's legal training.

Even in a volume as largely playful as *A Hundred Sundry Flowers,* Gascoigne exhibits some of the serious moralism that so darkly shadows his later work. In "Gascoigne's Good Night," for example, he contemplates the day's activities, looking ahead to death and the Last Judgment (lines 33–38):

And as I rise up lustily, when sluggish sleep is past,
So hope I to rise joyfully, to Judgement at the last.
Thus will I wake, thus will I sleep, thus will I hope to
    rise,
Thus will I neither wail nor weep, but sing in godly
    wise.
My bones shall in this bed remain, my soul in God
    shall trust,
By whom I hope to rise again from death and earthly dust.

Finally, having presented the poems of "various authors," G. T. introduces the last work, "Dan Bartholomew of Bath," with these words: "And now to recomfort you and to end this work, receive the delectable history of sundry adventures passed by Dan Bartholomew of Bath, read it and judge of it." Though not as finely conceived, "Dan Bartholomew" reprises the story of the unhappy love affair told in "The Adventures of Master F. J." and in so doing allows the two works to comment upon one another. This time, however, the tale is told completely in verse and is narrated not by G. T. but by a speaker who provides a more dispassionate rendition of his tale than does G. T. The shifts in form and point of view suggest Gascoigne's interest in playing with various genres and perspectives, the primary concern of *A Hundred Sundry Flowers* as a whole.

But, more practically, Gascoigne recognized the affinities between poetic performance and court conduct. The Elizabethan courtier was expected to possess extraordinary learning and oratorical skill, and be able to argue any side of an issue convincingly. In the "diverse discourses and verses" of *A Hundred Sundry Flowers,* Gascoigne showed that he could write on a variety of subjects from any number of perspectives. By writing and piecing his works together in a single volume, he sought to display his rhetorical virtuosity and thereby assert his fitness for court service. He failed miserably.

The reception of *A Hundred Sundry Flowers* proved disastrous. Gascoigne's hurried retreat to Holland meant that he was away from England while the book was at press, an occurrence that added to the confusion surrounding its publication. Nonetheless, his departure was timely because it allowed him to claim that he had no intention of publishing the volume; judging from the prefatory let-

Gascoigne's signature on the title page of his copy of Petrarch

ters to *The Posies,* however, this ruse did not prevent him from bearing the calumny of his detractors. While he was away, the volume was called in by the Stationers' Company and banned.

Although the lacuna in the Stationers' Register for the period 22 July 1571 to 17 July 1576 prohibits any definitive conclusions, one of the prefatory letters to *The Posies* suggests that "The Adventures of Master F. J." was read as a roman à clef, "written to the scandalizing of some worthy personages." Part of the problem is that Gascoigne's narrative strategies, particularly the subterfuge of initials, taunt his readers into making real-life correspondences. Faced with the controversy surrounding *A Hundred Sundry Flowers,* Gascoigne revised the volume and republished it under his own name as *The Posies* in 1575.

In the prefatory letters to this work, he claims he has thoroughly altered the contents; the reader "shall find it now in this second imprinting so turquened [twisted] and turned, so cleaned from all uncleanly words, and so purged from the humor of inhumanity" that he will hardly recognize it as the same work. Actually, Gascoigne changed the volume very little, omitting a few minor poems and adding a few others. With his overstated claims of a reformed text, Gascoigne probably hoped to placate the censors, anticipating that they would read only the first few pages. But he also seems to have been thumbing his nose at them, dubbing them "curious carpers" and "ignorant readers" in one particularly angry letter.

In the three letters prefacing *The Posies,* Gascoigne attempts to defend his decision to publish, insisting that he did so to advance the cause of English poetry, to provide a public record of his poetic skill, and to offer "a mirror for unbridled youth" so that they might "avoid these perils" which he had experienced. He also discusses how to read his poetry, confronting the age-old problem of how to read imaginative literature. Smiling at the simplicity of those who took "The Adventures of Master F. J." literally, Gascoigne condemns the biographical readings that plague his writings to this day. Anticipating Sidney's *Defence of Poesie* (written in 1579–1580), he contends that even a child viewing a play recognizes it as a play; likewise, his readers should leave their literal-mindedness behind when reading his poetry. Like Sidney, Gascoigne seems to have some notion of poesy as mimesis (the imitation of men's actions). Confusion of fact for fiction, then, reflects the reader's sheer naiveté.

Even a cursory reading of *A Hundred Sundry Flowers,* especially "The Adventures of Master F. J.," indicates that this confusion is exactly what Gascoigne seeks. By including so much intimate detail in his writings and by obscuring the reader's perspective through the voice of a fictitious editor, he deliberately foists a historical reading on his audience. He often alludes to contemporary affairs and scatters references to his own life throughout his work, mingling fiction and reality.

Although the content of the original and revised versions is virtually the same, it is clear from Gascoigne's changes that he had not given up his interest in experimentation. As he reorganized his works around the structural principle of the garden, an idea merely hinted at in the earlier *A Hundred Sundry Flowers,* he created a volume that coheres as a unified book. As an image endlessly rich in cultural and literary associations, the garden provides a loose frame for the encyclopedic range of Gascoigne's poetry. The framework establishes unity by setting the smaller pieces within a larger system. The division of the volume into Flowers (light verse, "more pleasant than profitable"), Herbs

(moral discourses, "more profitable than pleasant"), and Weeds ("neither pleasant nor yet profitable, and therefore meet to be cast away") also allows Gascoigne to defend his poetic practice. Everything in nature has its purpose, he argues in "The Epistle to the Young Gentleman," so that although they might seem worthless, "many weeds are right medicinable, so may you find in this [volume] none so vile or stinking, but that it hath in it some virtue if it be rightly handled." He hopes his collection will provide both pleasure and profit and sees the merit of both.

Gascoigne's belief in the importance of the poetic endeavor becomes clear in the essay "Certain Notes of Instruction Concerning the Making of Verse or Rhyme in English," which is appended to the revised volume. This essay is the first English treatise on prosody and suggests that Gascoigne saw himself as a serious poet. He had earlier hinted his preoccupation with poetic theory in G. T.'s running comments in "The Adventures of Master F. J."; but since that work was so badly misconstrued, he sets forth his ideas more plainly here.

A practical manual concerned basically with the problems involved in writing English poetry, "Certain Notes" presents Gascoigne's precepts on style, diction, and prosody. These range from discussions of the proper use of rhyme and meter to the avoidance of polysyllabic words and inkhorn (antiquated or Latinate) terms. The most important of these concepts is invention, what Gascoigne labels "the first and most necessary point that I ever found meet to be considered in the making of a delectable poem." Although the sixteen notes are written in random order, seemingly as the thoughts occurred to him, Gascoigne actually subsumes all of them under this larger concept. The subject, rhyme, and style must all accord with the invention.

Originally, invention was a term from classical rhetoric, derived from Latin *invenio,* meaning to "come upon" or "find," to discover (that is, *dis + cover*). In the sixteenth century the word *invention* did not have the connotation it does today of something fabricated or created ex nihilo, although it did increasingly come to mean fiction making. In fact, the term was often used precisely because it lacked the negative connotation that plagued the word *fiction.* Usually it signified the mental process of generating concepts from which one produced arguments and literature, and frequently the finished product of that process. Although he is not consistent in his use of the term, most often Gascoigne uses *invention* in the Sidneian sense of a "foreconceit," a preconceived, controlling idea which governs the meaning of the work.

Since his readers had failed to recognize "the invention" governing "The Adventures of Master F. J.," Gascoigne completely revamped the tale. The changes are quite remarkable. Faced with the "busy conjectures" of some readers who "presumed to think that the same was indeed written to the scandalizing of some worthy personages," he thunders, "there is no living creature touched or to be noted thereby." This reworking, which Leicester Bradner calls "one of the most astonishing revisions in literary history," re-creates the tale as "The Pleasant Fable of Ferdinando Jeronimi and Leonora de Valasco, Translated out of the Italian Riding Tales of Bartello."

The "fable" of the new title suggests that Gascoigne will present the narrative as straightforward fiction, and so he does. He abandons his experimentation in favor of a more traditional narrative technique. The letters and initials that might prompt the reader to search for real-life correspondences are replaced with complete names in the new tale. The immediacy and familiarity of the English country-house setting become the "pleasant country of Lombardy . . . not far from the city of Florence." Whereas the Gascoigne of "The Adventures of Master F. J." deliberately wrote in shadows, this Gascoigne seeks total clarity: "And because I do suppose that Leonora is the same name which we call Elinor in English, and that Francischina also does import none other than Frances, I will so entitle them as to our own countrymen may be most perspicuous." Most startlingly, G. T. is obliterated.

The nameless first-person narrator who replaces G. T. claims merely to have translated the tale from an Italian (the fictional Bartello), and he possesses none of the complexities that make G. T. so compelling. Since the new narrator's professed goal is morality, he feels it imperative to show the repercussions of F. J.'s lecherous behavior. Ferdinando spends the "rest of his days in a dissolute kind of life"; Leonora continues her wicked, wanton ways; and long-suffering Francischina dies of a "miserable consumption" brought on by her unrequited love for Ferdinando. The narrator even offers a moral to those who might have missed the point: "Thus we see that where wicked lust does bear the name of love, it does not only infect the light-minded, but it may also become confusion to others which are vowed to constancy."

Although the plots are basically the same, Gascoigne has created two fundamentally different works with two different purposes. Inevitably, the revision is vastly inferior to the original and lacks its sophisticated manipulations of point of view.

The first work shows us the writer writing; the second pummels us with morality. Apparently, the revision came to nothing and was also banned soon after its appearance.

After the furor evoked by *A Hundred Sundry Flowers* and *The Posies,* Gascoigne decided to transform himself from the "idle poet, writing trifles" to "Gascoigne the satirical writer, meditating each Muse that [might] express his reformation." Although this may have been a genuine reformation, the about-face that we witness in most of Gascoigne's remaining works is difficult to reconcile with the cavalier and self-promoting "Green Knight" of his early volumes. The first of these reformed works was *The Glass of Government,* with a dedication dated 26 April 1575.

The Glass of Government represents yet another of Gascoigne's unique contributions to English literature. In it he borrows from the Dutch tradition to create the only English example of the prodigal-son play. As befits the reformed profligate, he presents the story of two fathers of Antwerp, each seeking to educate his two sons, each with a witty and prodigal elder, and a dull but dutiful younger son. Since the play purports to provide "a figure of the rewards and punishments of virtues and vices," the two older sons meet unfortunate ends despite the best efforts of their tutor, Gnomaticus. But the tragedy is offset by the virtue of the younger sons, Gascoigne assures his audience. The moralism of this play is heavy-handed, offering little of the hope of the biblical story, where the father celebrates the return of his wayward son.

In *The Glass of Government* the playfulness of the earlier works disappears; and if the title page is any indication, Gascoigne takes great pains to ensure he will give no offense to the censors. He assures the reader that the work has been "seen and allowed, according to the order appointed in the queen's majesty's injunctions." Reformed plain speech replaces courtly evasion:

> Plain speech to use, if wanton be your will
> You may be gone, wide open stands the port.
> But if you can contented be to hear,
> In true discourse how high the virtuous climb . . .
> Then stay a while . . .[.]

Despite his claims of a newfound morality, Gascoigne clearly had not given up all his worldly ambitions. In 1575 he snatched yet again at the chance to advance his career, this time through his performance in *The Princely Pleasures at Kenilworth,* the most elaborate of the entertainments welcoming Elizabeth on her summer progresses. Two contem-

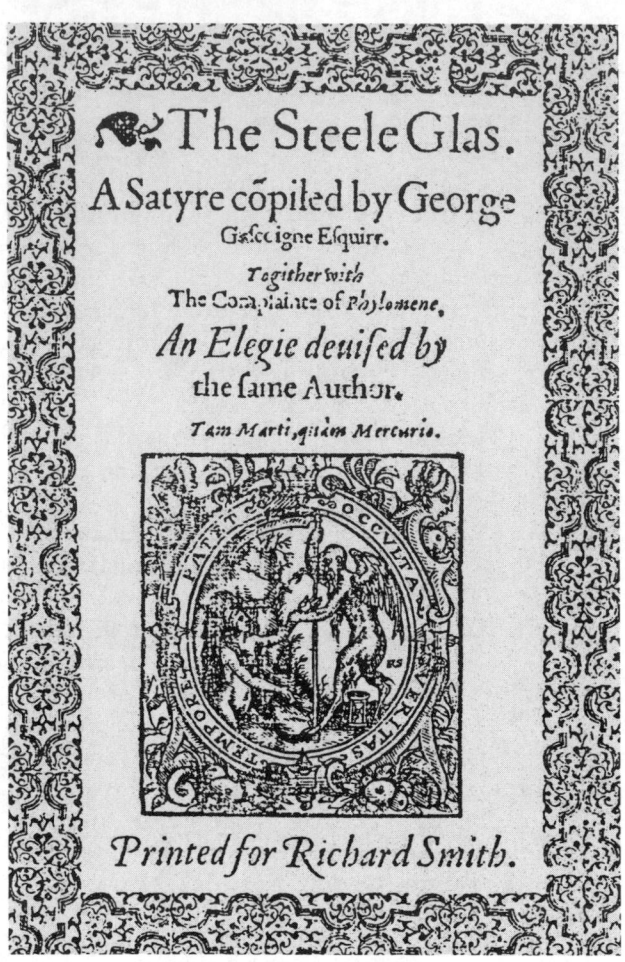

The Steele Glas.

A Satyre cõpiled by George Gascoigne Esquire.

Togither with
The Complaint of Phylomene.

An Elegie deuifed by
the fame Author.

Tam Marti, quàm Mercurio.

Printed for Richard Smith.

Title page for Gascoigne's 1576 satire

porary accounts of this performance survive, one by Gascoigne and one by Robert Laneham. Gascoigne's naturally gives prominence to his own part in the entertainment, but Laneham's account of Gascoigne's bumbled attempts to garner the queen's attention is probably nearer the truth. In this performance we again see him shooting amiss, now with more comic but also with more potentially disastrous results. The first of Gascoigne's misfortunes occurs when his "Masque of Zabeta," written especially for the occasion, was abruptly canceled. According to the poet, "lack of opportunity and seasonable weather" prevented the performance of the play. More likely, it was dropped from the entertainments because Leicester recognized that its impolitic persuasion to marriage would have offended Elizabeth.

Undeterred, Gascoigne next appeared to Elizabeth covered in branches and leaves, representing the Savage Man. Overcome by Elizabeth's beauty, he vows "to submit myself / beseeching you to serve." As luck would have it, in his eagerness to re-

claim Elizabeth's attention and illustrate his complete submission, he tipped his staff and, in so doing, almost hit her horse on the head. The horse startled backward, but Elizabeth managed to keep her seat, exclaiming, "No hurt, no hurt." "Which words I promise you we were all glad to hear and took them to be the best part of the play," Laneham recounts. She also remarked, apparently in annoyance, that "the actor was blind."

One final episode reveals the lengths to which Gascoigne was willing to stoop to gain the queen's favor. This time he assumed the role of Sylvanus, God of the Woods and, as the queen was departing, ran breathlessly alongside her horse reciting lines from his aborted masque. Taking pity on him, Elizabeth offered to slow her pace; but the obsequious poet demurred, protesting that "he would rather be her majesty's footman on earth, than a god on horseback in heaven." As demeaning as all these events must have been to the poet, they brought him the recognition he sought. Later that summer Gascoigne was granted a royal commission.

In August of the same summer, Gascoigne again appeared to Elizabeth when she arrived at Woodstock, the house of Sir Henry Lee. This time he greeted her as the blind hermit Hemetes who is struck with sight in Elizabeth's presence. Hemetes then recites a tale supporting the argument that marriage should be subordinate to the good of the state. As one might expect, Elizabeth was greatly pleased by the performance and asked for a copy. The result was an elaborate manuscript titled *The Tale of Hemetes the Hermit,* embellished with woodcuts of Gascoigne's own devising, which he presented to Elizabeth on New Year's Day 1576.

The tale itself is not of great importance to Gascoigne's literary career because he merely transcribed and translated the work of an anonymous author into Latin, Italian, and French. Nonetheless, the volume is interesting for its carefully constructed portrait of the poet. In a calculated bit of self-promotion, Gascoigne opens the volume with a self-portrait offering the present book to Elizabeth. In what must have been one of the most blatant bids for preferment in the period, the drawing depicts the poet kneeling subserviently before the queen, book in hand, sword and spear at his side. Hovering overhead is a crown of laurel and Gascoigne's favorite motto: "Tam Marti quam Mercurio" (As much to Mars as to Mercury; perhaps because he felt a kinship with the older poet, Sir Walter Ralegh took this motto as his own after Gascoigne's death). He also includes a prefatory poem entitled "A Poet with a Spear" in which he refashions himself as the courtier-poet of "The Adventures of Master F. J." Greeting Elizabeth as a sonneteer does his lady, he offers his service to her "with humble heart, and knees that kiss the ground." Courtiers typically recast the language of love poetry, especially that of Petrarch, into the language of patronage. The imagined relationship between the lover and the lady is literalized in the very real transactions between Elizabeth and her courtiers. Seeking to show his many talents, Gascoigne comes to her both as a soldier and as a poet, "armed with pencil in his ear, with pen to fight, and sword to write a letter." Clearly, the ambition that had dictated Gascoigne's early career had not completely disappeared in the staunch moralist of the later.

The only work of any originality composed during the poet's last years is the verse satire *The Steel Glass,* published in April 1576 along with *The Complaint of Philomene*. Although largely medieval in form (following the format of medieval-estates satire fairly closely), *The Steel Glass* exemplifies several of the concerns of Gascoigne's earlier writing. Continuing his interest in the native English tradition, he draws heavily on William Langland's *Piers Plowman* (written circa 1367–1386) for his themes. But he also seeks to unite the native satiric tradition with the classical tradition of Horace and Juvenal, something no English writer had yet attempted.

The satire opens with "The Epistle Dedicatory," in which Gascoigne laments his misspent youth at court: "I have misgoverned my youth, I confess it: what shall I do then?" He continues, "I am derided, suspected, accused, and condemned: yes more than that, I am rigorously rejected when I proffer amends for my harm." In the work itself he spares no one the harsh glare of his steel glass or mirror, not even himself. The satire is built around the premise that a steel glass truthfully exposes faults and vices while a crystal mirror only flatters and deludes. Holding his trusty mirror up to all levels of English society – kings, knights, soldiers, peasants, and clergy – the poet discovers that all are infected with "peevish pride."

The most revealing aspect of this volume is its opening allegory depicting the birth of satire or Satyra. Here Gascoigne chooses as his persona the female Satyra, daughter of Plain Dealing and Simplicity and sister to Poesy. As the two sisters grow older, "a lusty lad" named Vain Delight begins to woo Poesy. With help from his train of pages (False Semblant, Flearing Flattery, Detraction, and Deceit), he manages to marry her. The two live together happily until one day "a spark of lust did kindle in his breast, / And bade him hark to songs of Satyra." Filled with lust, Vain Delight ravishes Satyra, throws her into the "cage of misery," and brutally cuts her tongue out with the "Razor of Restraint." But Satyra refuses to be silenced and continues to sing her song:

> And yet, even as the mighty gods did deign
> For Philomele, that though her tongue were cut,
> Yet should she sing a pleasant note sometimes:
> So have they deigned, by their divine decrees,
> That with the stumps of my reproved tongue,
> I may sometimes reprovers' deeds reprove
> And sing a verse to make them see themselves.

In mythology, the Athenian princess Philomela was raped and had her tongue cut out by her brother-in-law Tereus but was later changed into a nightingale. Satyra's fate is less poetic, as she must sing with the "stumps" of her tongue. It is hard to resist reading this allegory as representative of Gascoigne's own situation. Like his poetic persona, he, too, was "reproved" by the razor of censorship but had not given up his song. The brutal images seem to betray the powerlessness he must have felt at the negative reception of much of his poetry.

The appeal that the myth of Philomela held for Gascoigne is also clear from the companion piece to *The Steel Glass, The Complaint of Philomene*. In the latter work he recasts the familiar Ovidian story into the native English tradition. Set in the form of a medieval dream vision, the poem opens with the poet listening to the sounds of the various songbirds. Puzzling over the peculiar sound "Nemesis, Nemesis," he falls asleep, leaning on his walking stick. In his dream he is visited by Nemesis, the Greek goddess of retribution, who tells him the story of Philomela and reveals that poetry often originates in pain. The dreamer awakens when his staff slips. Although the tale itself is not original, Gascoigne's contribution to the popular myth is his plain style treatment and his transformation of it to the English countryside. The poem is lively and fast moving but also somewhat bloodthirsty, as Gascoigne revels in the details of violation and revenge.

Late in the summer of 1576, Gascoigne's attempts at recognition finally met with measured success. He was granted an appointment by Elizabeth's adviser William Cecil, Baron Burghley, and sent first to France and then to Antwerp. While in Antwerp, he witnessed the siege and pillage of the city by Spanish troops and four days after returning to England wrote his eyewitness account, *The Spoil of Antwerp, Faithfully Reported, by a True Englishman, Who Was Present*. This work represents one of the earliest

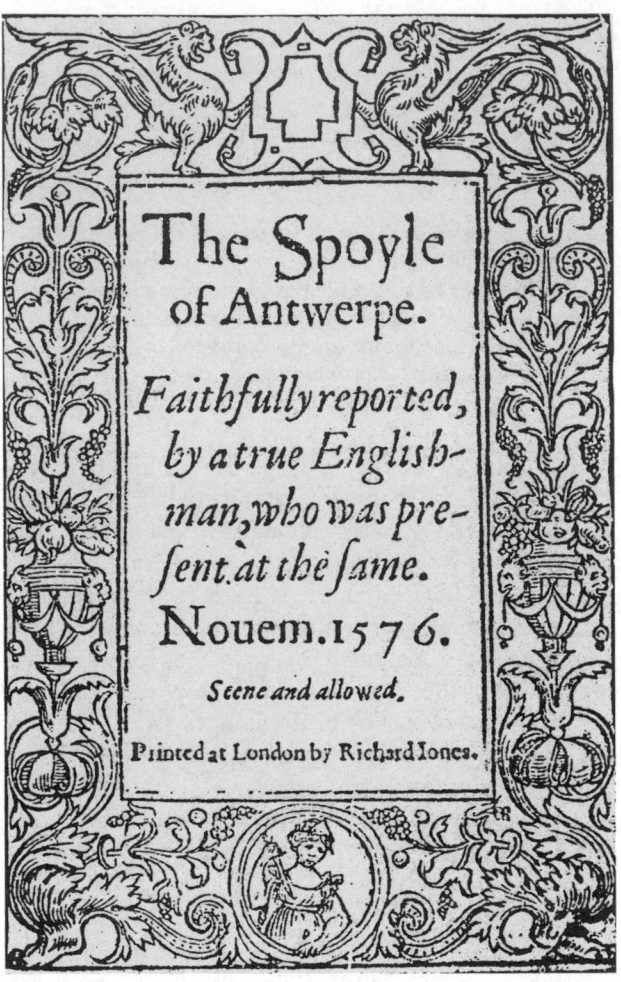

The Spoyle
of Antwerpe.

*Faithfully reported,
by a true English-
man, who was pre-
sent at the same.*

Nouem.1576.

Scene and allowed.

Printed at London by Richard Iones.

*Title page for Gascoigne's account of the siege and pillage of
Antwerp by Spanish troops*

examples of war correspondence in the language
and presents a vivid picture of the horrors of war.

Gascoigne's remaining works are largely derivative, composed almost completely of translations and paraphrases. The first of these, his *Drum of
Doomsday,* a translation of Innocent III's *De contemptu
mundi,* is filled with dire predictions of the end of the
world, further enhanced with vivid woodcuts depicting the tortures of the damned in hell. The volume was written, Gascoigne explains, to show that
he could "abide the correction of learned divines."
Likewise, *A Delicate Diet for Dainty-mouthed Drunkards,*
one of the earliest temperance tracts in the language, is a translation of Saint Augustine's *De ebritate.* Largely Puritan in tone, its reflection on the
proposition "All drunkards are beasts" offers us a
last picture of Gascoigne as disillusioned moralist.

One final work, "The Grief of Joy," shows
Gascoigne still pandering to the queen, this time
with a verse translation of Petrarch's *De remediis*

utriisque fortunae (The Remedies of Both Fortunes).
Here he develops the theme "there is a grief in every
kind of joy" in four songs detailing the vanity of
youth, beauty, strength, and activity. This manuscript
was offered to Elizabeth as a New Year's gift in 1577.

While Gascoigne was busily transforming
himself into the reformed moralist of these final
works, he was also battling ill health. He admits
that he had been sick off and on from at least May
1576. By summer of the same year his career was in
its ascendancy; he had received the recognition he
had sought for so long and had been granted a position as an agent for Burghley. And if the reception
of *The Tale of Hemetes* and *The Grief of Joy* are any indication, his works were well received at court. But
such stability was not to be enjoyed for long. Gascoigne died on 7 October 1577 at the home of his
friend and fellow poet, George Whetstone.

That George Gascoigne was held in high esteem in his own day seems evident from the number
of contemporary references to him. George Puttenham includes him among his "crew of courtly
makers" and praises him for "a good meter and for
a plentiful vein." The gloss to the November eclogue of Spenser's *Shepheardes Calender* calls him a
"witty gentleman" and "the very chief of our late
rhymers." And Robert Tofte, writing in 1615, notes
that he "first broke the ice for our quainter poets."
Although his poetry is sometimes derivative and
often uneven, Thomas Nashe's injunction, written
in 1589, remains valid: "Master Gascoigne is not to
be abridged of his deserved esteem, who first beat
the path to that perfection which our best poets
have aspired to since his departure."

Bibliographies:

Samuel Tannenbaum, *George Gascoigne: A Concise
    Bibliography* (New York: Tannenbaum, 1942);

Robert Carl Johnson, "George Gascoigne," in *Eliza-
    bethan Bibliographic Supplements: Minor Elizabe-
    thans,* volume 9 (London: The Nether Press,
    1968), pp. 21–25;

Jerry Leath Mills, "Recent Studies in Gascoigne,"
    English Literary Renaissance, 3 (Spring 1973):
    322–327;

Evelyn Haynes, "George Gascoigne: A Bibliogra-
    phy of Secondary Sources," *Bulletin of Bibliog-
    raphy,* 49 (September 1992): 209–214.

Biographies:

Felix E. Schelling, *The Life and Writings of George Gas-
    coigne* (Philadelphia: University of Pennsylva-
    nia, 1893; New York: Russell & Russell,
    1967);

C. T. Prouty, *George Gascoigne: Elizabethan Courtier, Soldier and Poet* (New York: Columbia University Press, 1942).

References:

Robert Adams, "Gascoigne's *Master F. J.* as Original Fiction," *PMLA,* 73 (September 1958): 315–326;

Fredson Bowers, "Notes on Gascoigne's *A Hundredth Sundrie Flowres* and *The Posies,*" *Harvard Studies and Notes in Philology and Literature,* 16 (1934): 13–35;

Leicester Bradner, "The First English Novel: A Study of George Gascoigne's 'Adventures of Master F. J.,' " *PMLA,* 45 (June 1930): 543–552;

Bradner, "Point of View in Gascoigne's Fiction," *Studies in Short Fiction,* 3 (Fall 1965): 16–22;

Jonathan Crewe, "Gascoigne's 'Woodmanship': Antioedipal Poetics," in his *Trials of Authorship* (Berkeley: University of California Press, 1990), pp. 118–139;

Roy T. Eriksen, "Typological Form in Gascoigne's 'De Profundis,' " *English Studies,* 66 (August 1985): 300–309;

Frank Fieler, "Gascoigne's Use of the Courtly Love Convention in 'The Adventures Passed by Master F. J.,' " *Studies in Short Fiction,* 1 (Fall 1963): 26–32;

Walter Wilson Greg, "A Hundred Sundry Flowers," *The Library,* 7 (December 1926–1927): 269–282;

Jane Hedley, "Allegoria: Gascoigne's Master Trope," *English Literary Renaissance,* 11 (Spring 1981): 148–164;

Richard Helgerson, *The Elizabethan Prodigals* (Berkeley: University of California Press, 1976);

Daniel Javitch, "The Impure Motives of Elizabethan Poetry," *Genre,* 15 (Spring/Summer 1982): 225–238;

Javitch, *Poetry and Courtliness in Renaissance England* (Princeton: Princeton University Press, 1978);

Ronald Johnson, *George Gascoigne* (New York: Twayne, 1972);

Arthur Kinney, *Humanist Poetics: Thought, Rhetoric, and Fiction in Sixteenth-Century England* (Amherst: University of Massachusetts Press, 1986);

Robert Laneham, "A Letter: Whearin, part of the Entertainment, untoo the Queen'z Maiesty, at Killingworth Castl, in WarwikSheer, in this Soomerz Progress, 1575, Isz signified," in *The Progresses and Public Processions of Queen Elizabeth,* edited by John Nichols, volume 1 (London: Printed by John Nichols & Son, 1823), pp. 426–484;

Richard Lanham, "Narrative Structure in Gascoigne's F. J.," *Studies in Short Fiction,* 4 (Fall 1966): 42–50;

Richard McCoy, "Gascoigne's 'Poemata Castrata': The Wages of Courtly Success," *Criticism,* 27 (Winter 1985): 29–55;

George Puttenham, *The Art of Englishe Poesie,* in *Elizabethan Critical Essays,* edited by G. Gregory Smith, volume 2 (Oxford: Clarendon Press, 1904), pp. 1–193;

George Rowe, "Interpretation, Sixteenth-Century Readers, and George Gascoigne's 'The Adventures of Master F. J.,' " *English Literary History,* 48 (1981): 270–289;

Susan C. Staub, " 'According to My Source': Fictionality in *The Adventures of Master F. J.,*" *Studies in Philology,* 87 (Winter 1990): 111–119;

John Stephens, "George Gascoigne's *Posies* and the Persona in Sixteenth-Century Poetry," *Neophilologus,* 70 (January 1986): 130–141;

Arthur Tennenhouse, "Sir Walter Ralegh and Clientage," in *Patronage in the Renaissance,* edited by Guy Fitch Lytle and Stephen Orgel (Princeton: Princeton University Press, 1981), pp. 235–258;

Germaine Warkentin, "The Meeting of the Muses: Sidney and the Mid-Tudor Poets," in *Sir Philip Sidney and the Interpretation of Renaissance Culture,* edited by Gary Waller and Michael Moore (Totowa, N. J.: Barnes & Noble, 1984), pp. 17–33;

Nancy Williams, "The Eight Parts of a Theme in 'Gascoigne's Memories: III,' " *Studies in Philology,* 83 (Spring 1986): 117–137;

Yvor Winters, "The Sixteenth Century Lyric in England: A Critical and Historical Reinterpretation," *Poetry,* 53, no. 5 (February 1939): 258–272; 53, no. 6 (March 1939): 320–335; 54, no. 1 (April 1939): 35–51.

Papers:
The Tale of Hemetes the Hermit (signed Royal MS. 18 A xlviii) and *The Grief of Joy* (Royal MS. 18 A lxi) are owned by the British Library.

Sir Humphrey Gilbert

(1537 – 9 September 1583)

Mary C. Fuller
Massachusetts Institute of Technology

BOOKS: *A Discovrse of a Discouerie for a New Passage to Cataia,* edited by George Gascoigne (London: Printed by Henry Middleton for Richarde Ihones, 1576);

Voyages and Colonizing Enterprises of Sir Humphrey Gilbert, edited by David B. Quinn (London: Hakluyt Society, 1940).

Editions: "A Discovrse of a Discouerie for a New Passage to Cataia," in Richard Hakluyt, *The Principall Navigations, Voiages and Discoueries of the English Nation, deuided into Three Seuerall Parts* (London: Printed by George Bishop & Ralph Newberie, 1589), pp. 597–615;

A Discovrse of Discouerie for a New Passage to Cataia (Menston, U.K.: Scolar, 1972);

"A Discovrse of a Discouerie for a New Passage to Cataia," in *New American World: A Documentary History of North America to 1612,* volume 3, edited by David B. Quinn (New York: Arno Press & Hector Bye, 1979), pp. 5–23.

OTHER: "The Creation of an Academy in London for Education of Her Majestes Wardes and Others the Youth of Nobility and Gentlemen," in *Queene Elizabethes Achademy,* edited by Frederick James Furnivall (London: Published for the Early English Text Society by N. Trübner & Co., 1869), pp. 1–12;

"A Discourse How Hir Majestie May Annoy the King of Spayne; A Discourse How Hir Majestie May Meete with and Annoy the King of Spayne," in William Gilbert Gosling, *The Life of Sir Humphrey Gilbert: England's First Empire Builder* (London: Constable, 1911), pp. 133–144.

The seventeenth-century historian William Camden described Sir Humphrey Gilbert as *"vir acer et alacer, belli pacisque artibus claris"* (a zealous and eager man, famous in the arts of war and peace).

Sir Humphrey Gilbert; engraving published in 1620

Gilbert was a man of action rather than a man of letters, more important as a military figure than as a writer. The small body of writing he left, most of it unpublished until several centuries after his death, deals with a series of projects, from finding the Northwest Passage to establishing a third university. Many and varied though these projects were, most of them were unsuccessful or not attempted during Gilbert's lifetime. Gilbert is still seen as an important early figure in the history of English colonization and empire, though less so now than earlier in the twentieth century. He held the first letters patent to settle North America and made two attempts to exercise his privileges; in the second, after establishing the first English colony in North America at Saint John's, Newfoundland, he died. After his death the letters passed to his half brother Sir Walter Ralegh, who planted the first English colony in what is now North Carolina.

Gilbert was born in Devon in early 1537 to Otho (or Otes) Gilbert and Katherine Champernowne Gilbert; he was the second of five siblings, the others being John, Adrian, Otho, and Katherine. By his mother's second marriage, to Walter Ralegh the elder, he was half brother to Walter and Carew Ralegh. Gilbert was educated at Eton; at Oxford, where he is said to have studied navigation and the arts of war; and at New Inn. Though as a young man he was intended for the Inns of Court, he was preferred to the service of Elizabeth Tudor through the mediation of his maternal relative Katherine Ashley, governess to the princess. A 1581 letter in which Gilbert writes that he has served Queen Elizabeth for twenty-seven years places the beginning of the connection in 1554 or 1555. He served Elizabeth as a soldier and military commander, a sailor and captain of ships, a member of Parliament, and a discoverer.

Gilbert's interest in voyages of discovery and colonization began as early as 1565, when he petitioned Elizabeth for permission to seek a northwest passage to China. English interest in exploration and overseas trade had been minimal since the voyages of John Cabot under Henry VII but began to grow again in the 1550s. The Merchant Adventurers Company launched searches for a northwest passage in 1553 and 1555, years which also saw the publication of Richard Eden's *Treatise of the New India* (1553) and his translation of Pietro Martire d'Anghiera's *Decades of the New World or West India* (1555). Gilbert could have met Eden during his military service in 1562–1563 in Le Havre-de-Grâce; he may also have met Jean Ribault, then newly returned from attempting to settle a French Huguenot colony in Florida. Ribault's project stimulated several more English-language narratives, including Ribault's *The Whole and True Discovery of Terra Florida* (1563) and Nicholas Le Challeux's *A True and Perfect Description of the Last Voyage* (1566), and at least two plans for Anglo-French collaboration in Florida, neither of which was carried out. Though Gilbert's *A Discourse of a Discovery for a New Passage to Cathay* was not published until 1576, his letter to

his brother Sir John Gilbert, which precedes the text, is dated 1566 and thus forms part of the initial wave of interest and publication of the mid 1560s. Gilbert's 1565 petition for discovery, the first of several to bear his name, was eventually blocked by the Muscovy Company, which saw his proposed search for a northern passage as an infringement of its patent.

Gilbert's military service in Ireland began in 1566, and a proposal to plant an English colony there superseded his transatlantic projects. An attempt by several West Country gentlemen to settle on confiscated lands in Munster in 1568–1569 led to a rebellion, which Gilbert was charged with subduing in Gov. Sir Henry Sidney's absence. Gilbert believed that conquered peoples could be made to obey only by fear, not by love; Thomas Churchyard wrote in the *General Rehearsal of Wars* (1579) that the terror Gilbert inspired made for short wars. Gilbert wrote in a letter of 6 December 1569: "After my first summoning of any castle or fort, if they would not yield it, I would not afterward take it of their gift but win it by force, how so many lives so ever it cost, putting man, woman, and child of them to the sword." Camden's *acer* (zealous) can also be translated as violent, impetuous, or brutal, and Gilbert's camp was decorated with the heads of his enemies. His bravery and effectiveness were admired by his English contemporaries, but later writers criticize his brutality.

Gilbert was knighted by Sidney on 1 January 1570 for his pacification of Munster. Returning to England, he married Ann Ager (or Aucher); they had six sons and a daughter. In 1571 he represented Plymouth in Parliament. In a debate over monopolies he was in the minority as a defender of the Crown's absolute powers. Such a view testified to his strong personal loyalty (he had not yet been paid for his Irish service), as well as, perhaps, to some self-interest. During his life Gilbert held or sought to obtain several patents, ranging from the right to settle and rule "such remote heathen and barbarous lands, countries, and territories not actually possessed of any Christian prince or people" to a monopoly on attempts to transmute iron into gold by alchemical means.

George Gascoigne, in the prefatory material to *A Discourse of a Discovery for a New Passage to Cathay,* records a visit with Gilbert at Limehouse in the mid 1570s during which he asked his host, free from military duties since his unsuccessful campaign in the Low Countries in 1572, how he occupied himself: "he courteously took me up into his study, and there showed me sundry profitable and very com-

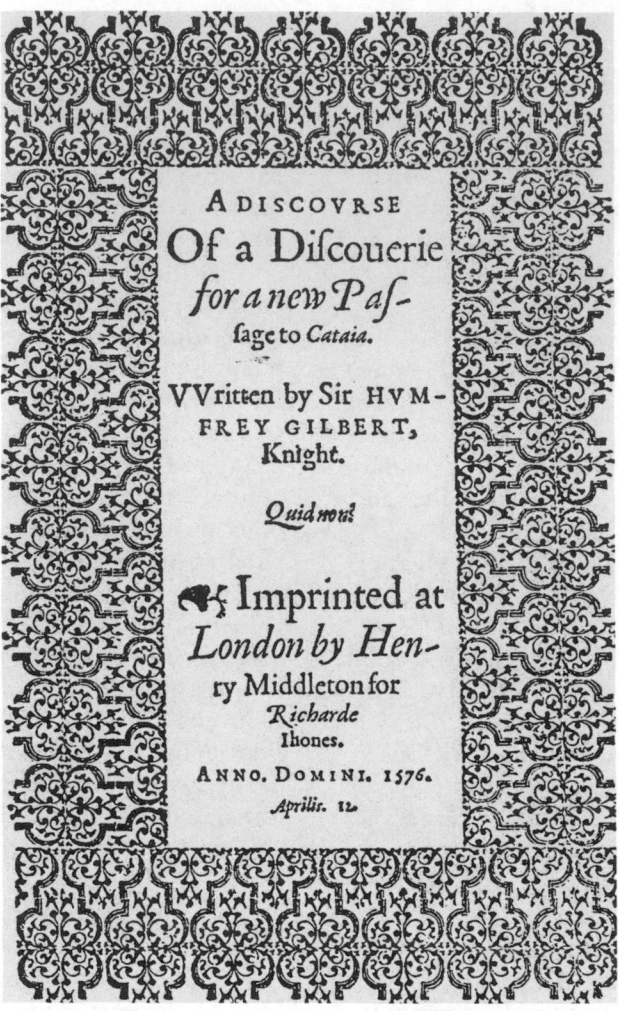

A DISCOVRSE
Of a Difcouerie
for a new Paf-
fage to *Cataia.*

VVritten by Sir HVM-
FREY GILBERT,
Knight.

Quid non?

Imprinted at
London by Hen-
ry Middleton for
Richarde
Ihones.
ANNO. DOMINI. 1576.
Aprilis. 12.

Title page for the book in which Gilbert tried to prove the existence of a northwest passage from Europe to China

mendable exercises, which he had perfected painfully with his own pen: and among the rest this present *Discovery*." Gascoigne borrowed the manuscript and had it printed without Gilbert's consent.

One other "exercise" by Gilbert survived to see print three hundred years later; in "The Creation of an Academy in London for Education of Her Majestes Wardes and Others the Youth of Nobility and Gentlemen" (1869) he proposes to reform the education of the queen's wards by opening a third university that would serve as a practical academy of publicly desirable skills. Though his syllabus begins conventionally, with instruction in Greek and Latin grammar, Hebrew, logic, and rhetoric, the rhetoric curriculum of English orations on historical events, "approving or reproving the matter" by example as well as reason, aims to train students in practical political and military analysis. Gilbert echoes Niccolò Machiavelli in his belief that

constant practice in analyzing "the occasions of . . . victories or overthrows" will produce "wise counsel in doubtful matters of war and state." The science curriculum has a similar practical bent: the mathematics instructors are to focus primarily on applications – artillery, fortification, cosmography, astronomy, navigation, shipbuilding, and mapmaking – with the equivalent of one instructor's yearly salary allocated for the purchase of powder and shot. By such methods "men shall be taught more wit and policy than school learning can deliver . . . for the greatest school clerks are not always the wisest men." In his suggestion that the academy receive a copy of every book printed in England, Gilbert anticipates the endowment of Oxford's Bodleian Library by several decades.

A Discourse of a Discovery, an argument for the existence and accessibility of a northwest passage to China, was the only work by Gilbert published in

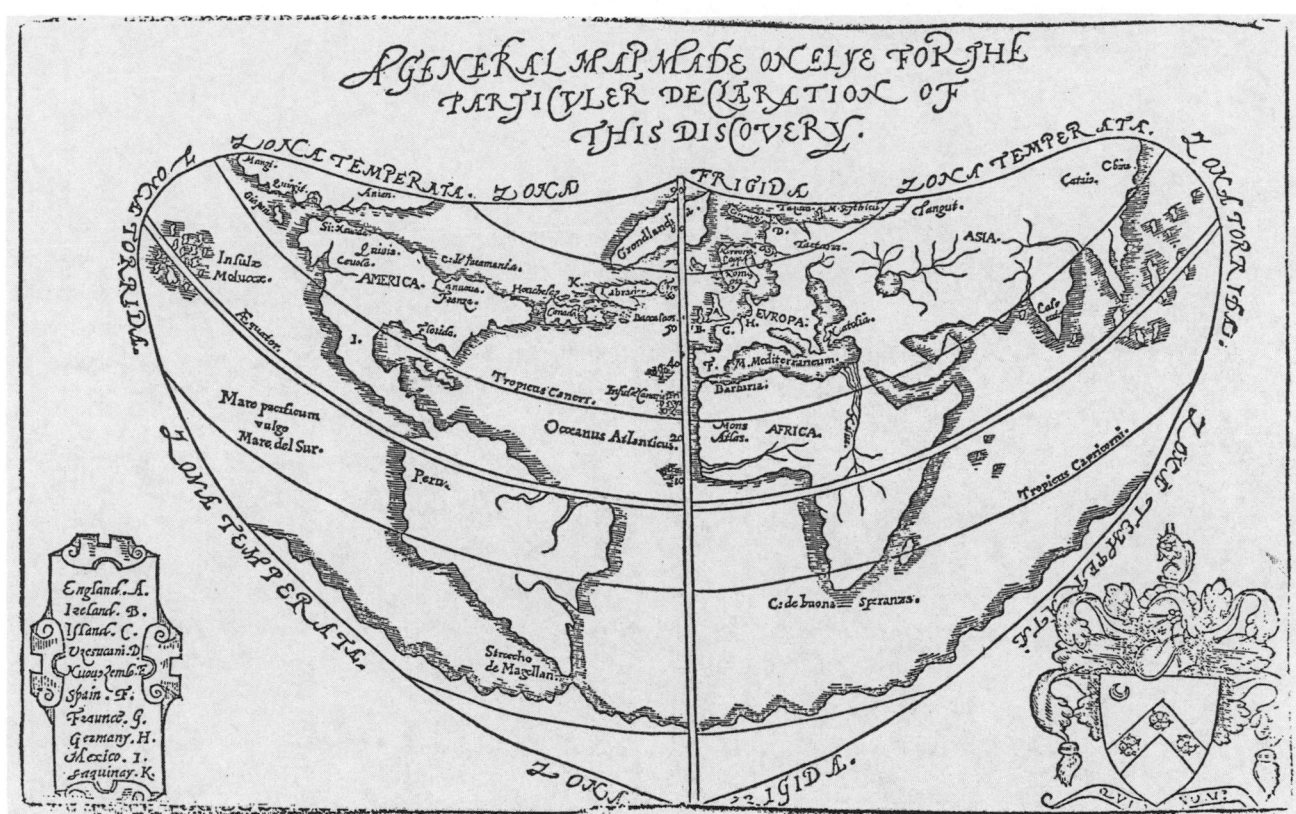

Gilbert's map of the world, from his Discourse of a Discovery

his lifetime. Gilbert's material was at least ten years out of date, and none of it was based on his own observations. The book appeared too late to have any influence on Sir Martin Frobisher's expeditions to the northwest in the mid 1570s, and in any case the information it contained was already well known to Frobisher. *A Discourse of a Discovery* belongs to a preliminary stage of the discovery enterprise, one in which the possibility of such an enterprise was still to be argued in theoretical terms; logic and textual authorities are used in an attempt to assuage uneasy incredulity. Gascoigne's preface gives the circumstances of its conception because "this voyage then seemed strange and had not been commonly spoken of before, as also because it seemed impossible to the common capacities . . . [Sir John] did seem partly to mislike [the author's] resolutions, and to dissuade him from the same: thereupon he wrote this treatise unto his said brother, both to excuse and clear himself from the note of rashness, and also to set down such authorities, reasons, and experiences, as had chiefly encouraged him unto the same. . . ." In his prefatory letter to his brother, Gilbert points out that Cathay (China) is not Utopia but a "country well known to be described and set forth by all modern geographers."

The argument for a northwest passage is divided into ten chapters. Chapter 1 offers a proof by authority, citing such writers as Plato, Aristotle, and Marsilio Ficino. Chapter 2 gives a proof by reason, deducing the existence of a passage from the evidence of currents. Chapter 3 proves by the experience of travelers that at least part of a passage exists. Chapter 4 offers circumstantial proof that a complete passage exists and "hath been sailed throughout." Chapters 5 through 7 work over the implications of "certain Indians . . . driven through the North Seas from India, upon the coasts of Germany, by great tempest," asserting that they could only have come through the Northwest Passage. (Gilbert gives several sources, including Francisco Lopez de Gómara, for this story.) In the concluding three chapters he asserts the convenience of a passage by the northwest and refutes arguments offered before the queen by an unnamed man (possibly Gilbert's onetime associate, Anthony Jenkinson) in favor of "proving a passage by the northeast." Like other early projectors and promoters of American exploration, Gilbert had to make hypothesis stand for proof; he does so by claiming that belief is superior to empirical knowledge: "The diversity between brute beasts and men, or between the wise

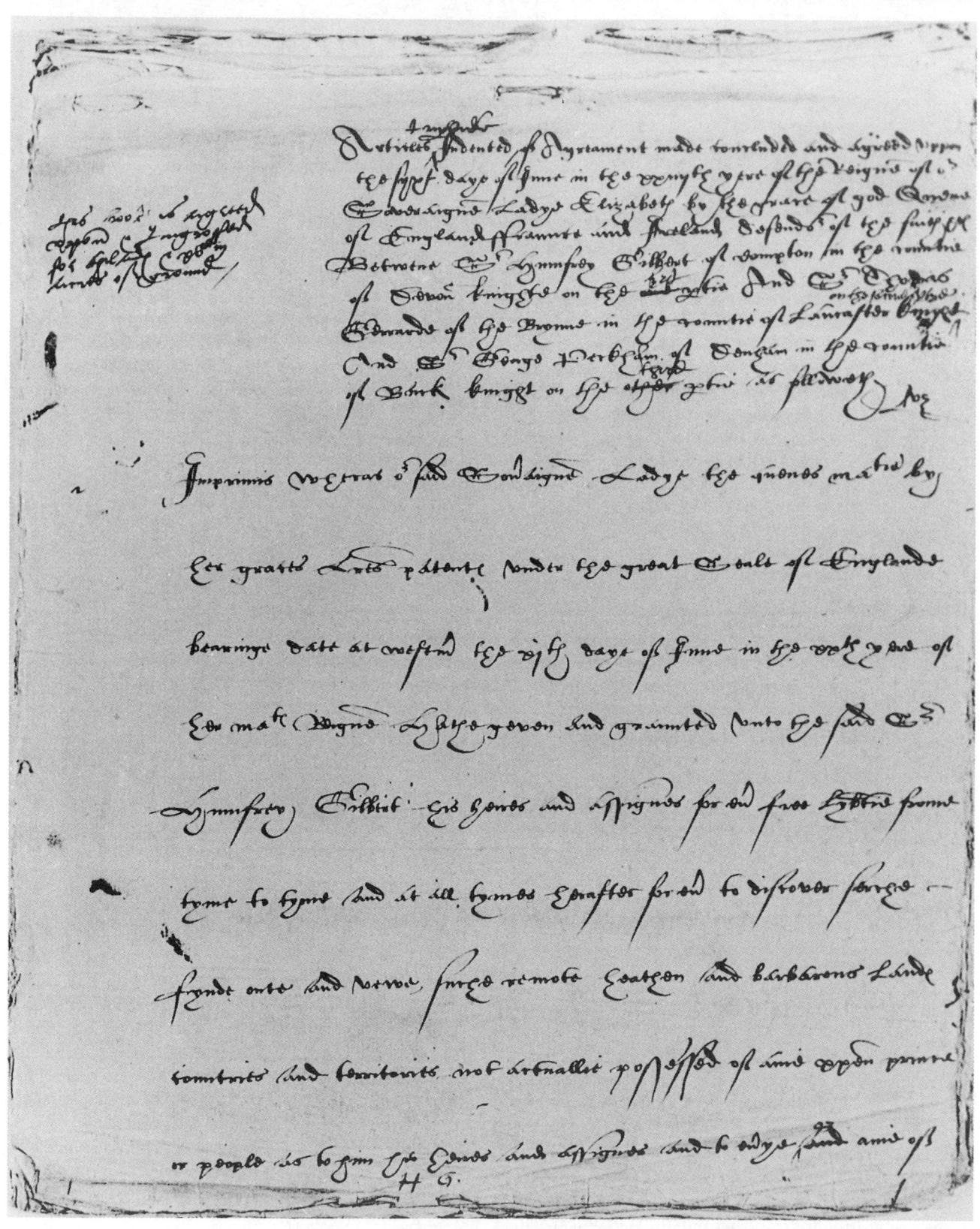

First and last pages of the agreement whereby Gilbert obtained financing for his ill-fated 1583 expedition to Newfoundland. In return for their support he granted 1.5 million acres in America to Sir George Peckham and Sir Thomas Gerrard (Sotheby's auction catalogue, sale 2716, 27 September 1988).

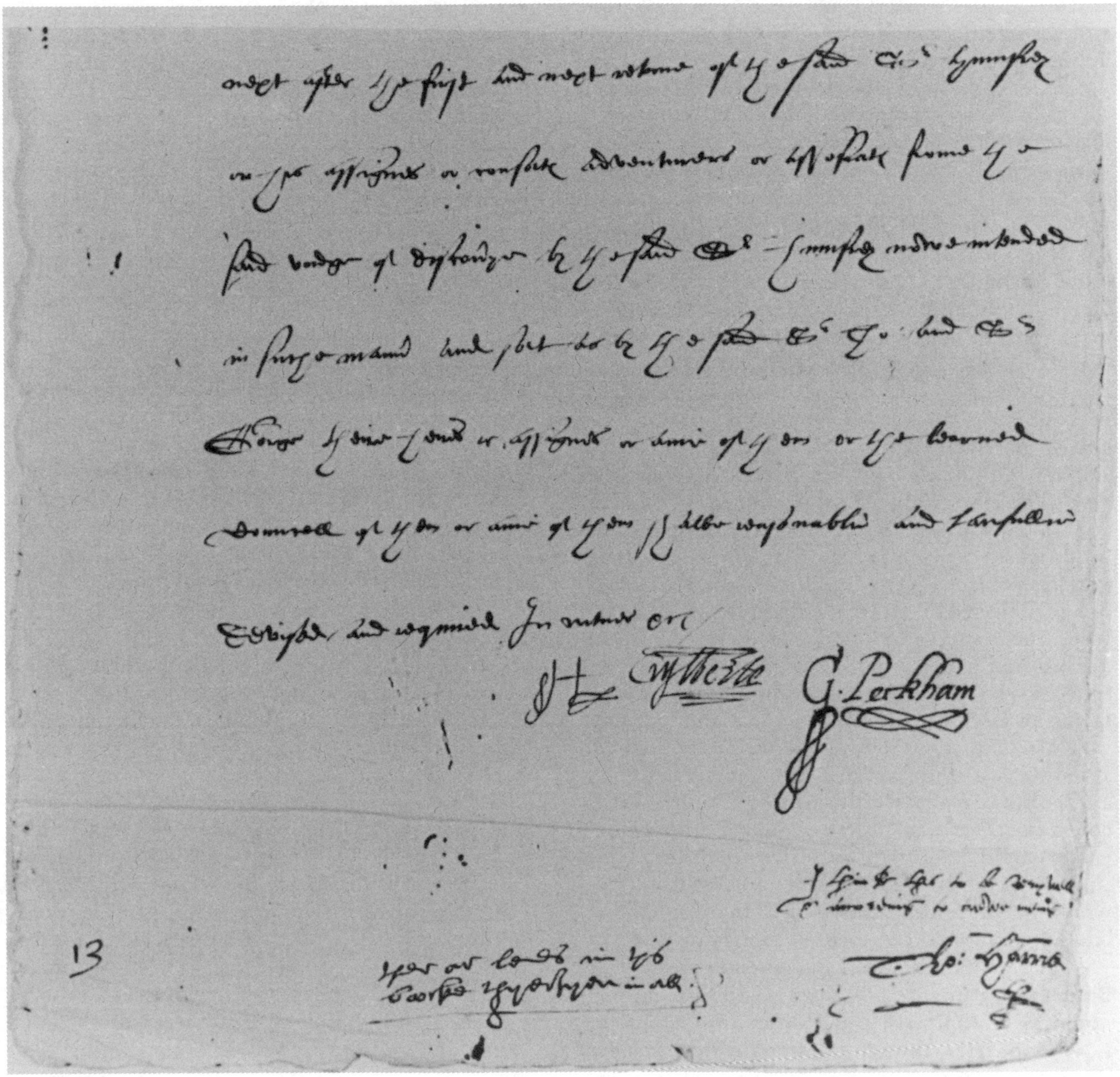
H. Gylberte
G. Peckham
13

and the simple, is that the one judgeth by sense only and gathereth no surety of any thing that he hath not seen, felt, heard, tasted, or smelled: And the other not so only, but also findeth the certainty of things by reason, before they happen to be tried." Gilbert attacks skepticism as brutish or lazy and takes pleasure in the copiousness of his own arguments.

A shorter discourse offers a different perspective on Gilbert's New World projects. It is dated 11 June 1577, the same day he visited John Dee, a mathematician, magician, diarist, and adviser to the Cathay Company. Not only was the text never published, but Gilbert's signature is crossed out as if to conceal it. There were obvious reasons for secrecy: Gilbert proposes that a voyage of discovery serve as "colorable means" for seizing the Spanish fishing fleet off Newfoundland. The expedition would pay for itself, perhaps even draw a profit, since "the N.F. [Newfoundland fish] is a principal and rich and everywhere vendible merchandise," and it would be without danger, since the fishing ships and their crews would be dispersed and off guard. Seizure of the fishing fleet would injure both King Philip's maritime forces and his revenue. Admittedly, England is not actually at war with Spain; Gilbert argues that his plan is, nevertheless, morally justified, since the Catholic Spanish are enemies of God, and politically necessary: since no true friendship could exist between Protestant and Catholic powers, it would be prudent to anticipate Spain's inevitable aggression with a first strike. Prudent, too, would be an official disavowal of the plan. Vague letters patent could be written, indicating that the voyage was for discovery and even expressly forbidding any hostile activities. Gilbert had operated under similarly deniable conditions in the Low Countries, though the Spanish ambassador there had been well advised of his actual activities as well as of his secret report to Elizabeth's government.

No records by Gilbert survive of his two actual voyages. The first is still shrouded in uncertainty as to its intended destination and purpose, neither of which was achieved: his ships took so long to assemble that he was not ready to leave until late September 1578, and when the expedition finally sailed out of Dartmouth, it was dispersed and driven back by wind. By the end of October the fleet had still not left England, and soon afterward it was split into two unequal parts by the disaffection of Henry Knollys, Gilbert's second in command. Both groups of ships departed again in late November; Knollys engaged in a few acts of piracy with no apparent intention of trying a transatlantic voyage, while all that is known of Gilbert's is that they revictualed in Ireland in December and February and returned in April. By the end of April the Privy Council was sufficiently disenchanted with Gilbert to bar him from further voyaging and to require him to put up sureties for the behavior of his crews. His ships were detailed to patrol the coast of Ireland; but he was summoned home, and his crews seized the ships in lieu of wages, which had been stopped for some months. Gilbert suffered a loss he estimated at two thousand pounds, which was uncompensated by the Crown. Churchyard's poem "A Matter Touching the Journey of Sir Humphrey Gilbert, Knight" (1578), written before the expedition's return, praised the nobility and fortitude of Gilbert and his colleagues, though somewhat bathetically: the poem includes a graphic description of seasickness as one of the hazards the heroic voyagers would face.

Gilbert's subsequent actions were driven by his need to take possession of *some* land before the six-year period of his letters patent expired. He began by selling the rights to millions of acres in North America to Dee, George Peckham, Philip Sidney, and others, both to raise money and to encourage potential settlers. Despite his land sales and the subscriptions of supporters, Gilbert's second voyage, in 1583, was inadequately funded and was rushed by the approaching expiration of his patent. Historians see the second voyage as an object lesson in the impracticability of privately funding colonial efforts. Gilbert's ships were so inadequately provisioned that the expedition had to modify its intended southerly direction to revictual in Newfoundland, and piracy by the poorly fed and clothed crews was a continuing problem.

The second voyage was a succession of disasters. The largest of Gilbert's ships, the *Bark Ralegh* (owned by Ralegh), turned back two days out of Plymouth; the *Delight* was lost by poor seamanship off Newfoundland, along with Gilbert's papers and the results of mineral assays taken on the island. Though Gilbert hinted to Edward Hayes, the captain of the *Golden Hind,* that his men had found silver, the expedition's only achievement was its show of strength in Saint John's Harbor, which, along with two hundred leagues in every direction, Gilbert formally claimed for the queen in the presence of fishing fleets from several nations. The provisions extracted from the fishery there went down, for the most part, with the *Delight.* On 9 September, little more than two months out of England, the company agreed to turn back. Gilbert, insisting that he sail on the tiny and overladen *Squirrel,* called out to the *Golden Hind:* "We are as near to heaven by sea as by land." That night the *Squirrel* was lost with all hands.

Gilbert's writing, brief as it is, participates in two developments that would assume increasing importance in English prose thereafter. His proposals for colonization and discovery, along with the texts describing and celebrating his ventures, represent an early and significant stage in an accelerating production of works about the New World that would eventuate in the massive collection of Richard Hakluyt and Samuel Purchas; *A Discourse of a Discovery,* along with Gilbert's proposal for a practical academy in London, forms part of an emergent scientific discourse that would gather momentum in the following century.

Biographies:
Carlos Slafter, *Sir Humfrey Gylberte and His Enterprise of Colonization in America* (Boston: Prince Society, 1903);

William Gilbert Gosling, *The Life of Sir Humphrey Gilbert: England's First Empire Builder* (London: Constable, 1911).

References:
Kenneth R. Andrews, *Trade, Plunder and Settlement: Maritime Enterprise and the Genesis of the British Empire, 1480–1630* (Cambridge: Cambridge University Press, 1984);

William Camden, *The History of the Most Renowned and Victorious Princess Elizabeth, Late Queen of England,* edited by Wallace T. MacCaffery (Chicago: University of Chicago Press, 1970);

Stephen Parmenius, *The New Found Land of Stephen Parmenius,* edited and translated by David B. Quinn and Neil M. Cheshire (Toronto & Buffalo, N.Y.: University of Toronto Press, 1972).

Papers:
Sir Humphrey Gilbert's manuscript for "A Discourse How Her Majesty May Annoy the King of Spain" is in the Public Record Office, London, in State Papers Domestic, Elizabeth (SP 12/118, 12 [i–ii]); the manuscript for "The Creation of an Academy in London" is in the British Museum (Lansdowne MS. 98. folios 2–7v).

Arthur Golding
(1536 – May 1606)

Madeleine Forey
All Souls College, Oxford University

BOOKS: *A Brief Discourse of the Late Murther of Master G. Saunders* (London: Printed by Henry Bynneman, 1573);

A Discourse vpon the Earthquake That Hapned the Sixt of Aprill. 1580 (London: Printed by Henry Binneman, 1580).

Editions: *"Shakespeare's Ovid," being Arthur Golding's Translation of the Metamorphoses,* edited by W. H. D. Rouse (London: De la More Press, 1904);

"The Discourse on the Saunders Murder"; "The Discourse on the Earthquake"; and "Arthur Golding to the Reader," in *An Elizabethan Puritan: Arthur Golding the Translator of Ovid's* Metamorphoses *and also of John Calvin's* Sermons, by Louis Thorn Golding (New York: R. R. Smith, 1937), pp. 164–201;

Ovid's Metamorphoses: The Arthur Golding Translation 1567, edited by John Frederick Nims (New York & London: Macmillan, 1965);

"Arthur Golding's *A Morall Fabletalke:* An Annotated Edition," edited by Nora Rooche Field, Ph.D. dissertation, Columbia University, 1979.

OTHER: "Arthur Golding to the Reader," in *An Aluearie or Triple Dictionarie, in Englishe, Latin, and French,* by John Baret (London: Printed by Henry Denham, 1580).

TRANSLATIONS: Conradus Hubertus, *A Briefe Treatise Concerning the Burnynge of Bucer and Phagius, at Cambrydge* (London: Printed by Thomas Marshe, [1562]);

Leonardo Bruni, *The Historie of Leonard Aretine, Concerning the Warres betwene the Imperialles and the Gothes for the Possession of Italy. Translated out of Latin by A. Goldyng* (London: Printed by Rowland Hall for George Bucke, 1563);

Gnaeus Pompeius Trogus, *Thabridgment of the Histories of Trogus Pompeius, Collected by Justine, and Translated by A. Goldyng* (London: Printed by Thomas Marshe, 1564);

Gaius Julius Caesar, *The Eyght Bookes of Caius Julius Caesar Conteyning His Martiall Exploytes in Gallia, Translated oute of Latin by A. Goldinge* (London: Printed by William Seres, 1565);

Ovid, *The Fyrst Fower Bookes of P. Ouidius Nasos Worke, Intitled Metamorphosis, Translated into Englishe Meter by A. Golding* (London: Printed by William Seres, 1565);

Ovid, *The .XV. Bookes of P. Ouidius Naso Entytuled Metamorphosis, Translated into English Meeter, by A. Golding* (London: Printed by William Seres, 1567);

John Calvin, *A Little Booke . . . Concernynge Offences. Translated out of Latine by A. Goldinge* (London: [Printed by Henry Wykes for] William Seres, 1567);

Neils Hemminsen, *A Postill, or Exposition of the Gospels Vsually Red Vpon the Sundayes and Feast Dayes* (London: Printed by Henry Bynneman for Luke Harrison and George Byshop, 1569);

David Chytraeus, *A Postil or Orderly Disposing of Certeine Epistles Vsually Red in the Church of God. Written in Latin and Translated by A. Golding* (London: Printed by Henry Bynneman for Luke Harrison and George Bishop, 1570);

Calvin, *The Psalmes of Dauid and Others. With J. Caluins Commentaries* (London: Printed by Thomas East and Henry Middleton for Luke Harrison and George Bishop, 1571);

Théodore de Bèze, *A Booke of Christian Questions and Answers. Written in Latin by T. Beza and Translated by A. Golding* (London: Printed by William How for Abraham Veale, 1572);

Heinrich Bullinger, *A Confutation of the Popes Bull against Elizabeth Queene of England* (London: Printed by John Day, 1572);

Benedetto da Mantova, *The Benefite that Christians Receiue by Jesus Christ Crucifyed, Translated out of French by A. G[olding?]* (London: Printed by

Thomas East for Luke Harison and George Bishop, 1573);

Augustine Marlorat, *A Catholike Exposition vpon the Reuelation of Sainct John* (London: Printed by Henry Binneman for Luke Harison and George Bishop, 1574);

Calvin, *Sermons . . . vpon the Booke of Job.* (London: Henry Binneman for Luke Harrison and George Bishop, 1574);

Calvin, *Sermons . . . vpon the Epistle to the Galathians* (London: Henry Bynneman for Luke Harison and George Bishop, 1574);

Anonymous, *A Iustification or Cleering of the Prince of Orendge agaynst the False Sclaunders* (London: Printed by John Day, 1575);

Henry III of France, *The Edict or Proclamation Set Forthe Vpon the Pacifying of the Troubles in Fraunce. The xiiij. Day of May, 1576* (London: Printed by Thomas Vautrollier, [1576]);

Jean de Serres, *The Lyfe of the Most Godly, Valeant and Noble Capteine J. Colignie Shatilion* (London: Printed by Thomas Vautrollier, 1576);

Anonymous, *The Warfare of Christians: Concerning the Conflict against the Fleshe, the World, and the Deuill. Translated out of Latine by A. Golding* (London: Printed by Henry Binneman for John Shepparde, 1576);

Calvin, *The Sermons of M. John Caluin, vpon the Epistle too the Ephesians* (London: Printed by Thomas Dawson for Luke Harison and George Byshop, 1577);

Bèze, *A Tragedie of Abrahams Sacrifice, Written in French and Translated by A. G.* (London: Printed by Thomas Vautroullier, 1577);

Lucius Annaeus Seneca, *The Woorke of the Excellent Philosopher Lucius Annaeus Seneca Concerning Benefyting* (London: [Printed by John Kingston for] John Day, 1578);

Abraham Fleming, *A Godly Prayer, Written by A. Fleming. Translated out of Latine, by A. Golding,* in *Concerning the True Beleefe of a Christian Man, a Dialogue, by S. C.* (London: Printed by Thomas Purfoot, [1582?]);

Francis, Duc d'Anjou, *The Joyful and Royal Entertainment of Prince, Frauncis. Into Antwerpe. Translated out of Frenche by A. Golding According to the Copie Printed by Plantine* (London: Printed by Thomas Dawson for William Ponsonby, 1582);

Calvin, *The Sermons of M. John Caluin vpon Deuteronomie: Gathered as He Preached Them (by D. Raguenier.)* (London: Printed by Henry Middleton for George Bishop, 1583);

Pomponius Mela, *The Worke of P. Mela. The Cosmographer, Concerninge the Situation of the World* (Lon-

don: Printed by John Charlwood for Thomas Hacket, 1585);

Philippe de Mornay, *A Woorke Concerning the Trewnesse of the Christian Religion. Begunne to Be Translated by Sir P. Sidney and Finished by A. Golding* (London: Printed by [John Charlewood and] George Robinson for Thomas Cadman, 1587);

Gaius Julius Solinus, *The Worthie Worke of Julius Solinus Polyhistor. Contayning Many Noble Actions of Humaine Creatures* (London: Printed by John Charlwood for Thomas Hacket, 1587);

Jacques Hurault, *Politicke, Moral, and Martial Discourses* (London: Printed by Adam Islip, 1595);

Jean Froissart, *An Epitome of Frossard: or, A Summarie Collection* (London: Printed by Thomas Purfoot for Percival Golding, 1608);

Anonymous, *A Most Excellent and Profitable Dialogue of the Powerfull Justifying Faith* (London: Printed by Nicholas O[kes] for Samuel Rand, 1610).

Arthur Golding is best known for his translation of Ovid's *Metamorphoses* (1565; 1567), which William Shakespeare used as a source. Yet his significance within sixteenth-century letters extends beyond this work to his translations of many classical and religious texts (particularly the works of John Calvin) into English. Golding's translations were widely read and discussed in literary circles of his day.

Golding was born in 1536, the second son among the seven children born to John Golding by his second wife, Ursula, daughter of William Marston of Horton, Surrey. John Golding was variously resident in London – he was an auditor of the Exchequer and was admitted to the Middle Temple in April 1520 – and in Belchamp Hall in the parish of Belchamp Saint Paul's, Essex, where he was a substantial landholder. Neither the place of Arthur Golding's birth nor the nature of his childhood education has been established, although the removal of the family from Belchamp Hall to Bloomsters Manor near Halstead in 1548, after John Golding's death in the previous year, would have permitted his later schooling at Halstead grammar school. It also brought him into the vicinity of the home of John de Vere, sixteenth Earl of Oxford, who married Arthur's half sister Margery on 5 August 1548 and with whose family he had continued contact.

Golding matriculated at Jesus College, Cambridge, in the Easter term of 1552, being entered as a "fellow commoner." There is no evidence of his receiving a degree nor indication of the length of his residence in Cambridge; his biographer Louis Thorn

*Title page for one of the first translations into English of
John Calvin*

Golding suggests that he left Cambridge during the "purge" of the university in the reign of Mary in which Martin Bucer and Paul Fagius were tried and burned for heresy in 1555. His first known publication was a translation of a Latin pamphlet on this execution; its prefatory address to the reader, denouncing Roman Catholics as Antichrists, marks the virulently anti-Catholic temper of Golding's work, which was maintained throughout his career.

In 1562, following the death of de Vere on 3 August, Golding was appointed by William Cecil as "receiver" (executor) for his nephew Edward de Vere during his minority. Receipts show an involvement on Golding's part in the financial interests of the seventeenth earl and his sister, and in the managing of the de Vere estate. In 1563 he became involved in defending the legitimacy of the earl and his sister,

and hence their right to the estate, against the claims of their half sister Lady Catherine Windsor.

The de Vere connection was also maintained on a literary and educational level. Golding's third publication, Justine's abridgement of the *Histories of Trogus Pompeius* (1564), was dedicated to the earl of Oxford with an exhortation that the example of the classical heroes should "encourage [him] to proceed in learning and virtue." Golding's almost parental concern is again in evidence in the epistle to the earl which prefaces his translation (1571) of Calvin's *Commentaries on the Psalms*, where he urges his nephew's strict adherence to the Protestant faith, adding "the devil hath more shapes than Proteus; first and foremost, the obstinate-hearted Papists, the sworn enemies of God." There is, however, no substantive evidence that Golding acted as tutor to his nephew.

Translations appear to have been Golding's major occupation during the 1560s, which he spent in London at Cecil House while he was acting as receiver for de Vere and at his home in Essex. These translations may broadly be grouped into three categories: religious works; histories; and, in a category of its own, the translation of Ovid's *Metamorphoses*. Among the important religious translations are a large number of works by Calvin, for whom Golding was one of the significant channels in later-sixteenth-century England, and the completion in 1587 of Sir Philip Sidney's translation (following instructions left by Sidney himself) of *The Trueness of the Christian Religion* from the French of Philippe de Mornay (1581). Golding continued to work on Calvin at the same time as his Englished Ovid, four books of which were published in 1565 with a dedication to Robert Dudley, Earl of Leicester, at that time a major patron of Puritan writing. The complete fifteen-book version was published in 1567.

Apart from some verses prefixed to Baret's *Alveary* (1580), only two publications of original work by Golding exist: *A Brief Discourse of the Late Murder of Master G. Saunders* (1573) and *A Discourse upon the Earthquake* (1580). During this period Golding became a member of the Society of Antiquaries, which was established by Matthew Parker, William Camden, Robert Cotton, and others, and in 1573 he was made a member of the Inner Temple (of the Inns of Court) "without payment." He seems, however, to have held no official posts.

It is important to recognize that Golding's various translations and original works form a coherent whole; indeed, his literary practice and theory may be compared with those of Sidney. In his study of Shakespeare's work Charlton Ogburn speculates that much of Golding's translation of Ovid was in fact the work of the young earl of Oxford, on the grounds that the literary work is incongruous with Golding's religious translations and other works. There is, however, a continuity of interests. Both the choice of religious texts, many of them from Calvin and other major Protestant writers, and the prefatory remarks to these translations show both a strong and persistent anti-Catholicism and a concern for the moral improvement and repentance of his Protestant readers that is at times charged with an apocalyptic awareness.

It is appropriate, for example, that, from among the many Protestant commentaries upon Revelation then available, Golding chose Augustine Marlorat's *Catholic Exposition upon the Revelation of Saint John* for translation in 1574, since it combines a conventional Protestant assault upon the papacy with an insistence that the calamities of the Apocalypse occur not by chance but through God's providence in order to provide moral admonition to man. This may be compared with Golding's own *Discourse upon the Earthquake,* another anti-Catholic piece, in which he presents the earthquake as a call to repentance, a forewarning of wrath to come. His reading of the earthquake as moral doctrine – "We have signs and tokens enough at home, if we can use them to our benefit" – prefigures his similar reading of Ovid in the following year. Golding finds the teaching of the earthquake transparent: "forsaking the lusts and the wicked imaginations and devices of our own hearts, let us turn to the Lord our God with hearty repentance and unfeigned amendment of life." His account of the murder of George Saunders in 1573 similarly treats the event as a moral exemplum provided by God: "[God's] purpose is that the execution of His judgments should by the terror of the outward sight of the example drive us to the inward consideration of our selves."

Golding's interest in extracting moral example from stories, whether historical or fictional, may again be seen in his *Moral Fabletalk,* which remained in manuscript until 1979. The work consists of a translation of Arnold Freitag's emblem book *Mythologia Ethica* (1579), comprising 125 Aesopic fables in prose. The intention of the work, which Golding translates into lively and highly idiomatic English, is to provide through stories precepts for the moral benefit of its readers.

Golding's translation of the *Metamorphoses,* the work for which he was most widely known in his own time and is most widely studied today, is presented in similar terms. In the prefatory material he claims the same moral usefulness for Ovid's stories as he found in Aesopic fables, contemporary events, and histories. Just as he treated classical and contemporary history as a narrative from which to derive moral education, so his explanations of Ovid's stories, both in the dedicatory epistle to Leicester and the "Preface to the Reader" added in the 1567 edition, show him to be reading Ovid in the medieval tradition of *Ovide moralisé* (Ovid Moralized, circa 1320). In each tale, he claims, "are pithy, apt and plain / Instructions which import the praise of virtues, and the shame / Of vices." Thus, for example, the tale of Echo's love for Narcissus is tersely expounded in terms similar to those Golding found fitting for George Saunders's wife in 1580: "And Echo in the selfsame tale doth kindly represent / The lewd behavior of a bawd and his due punishment." Although the length and repetition of Golding's moralizing in his prefatory material (over six hundred lines in the epistle alone) may indicate some lack of confidence in his readers' interpretative skills, there is no doubt that he translated Ovid's work with the same attitudes as are expressed in his historical, topical, and religious writings. Indeed, in his epistle to Leicester Golding goes so far as to suggest biblical parallels with Ovid's original text: "Thus partly in the outward phrase, but more in very deed, / He seems according to the sense of Scripture to proceed."

The distinction between Golding's reading of the *Metamorphoses* and the intention of Ovid's sophisticated and capricious original may be paralleled with the marked difference in the style of the English and Latin texts. The Englishing of the text comprises not simply a translation but a shift into English idiom and meter, for although Golding's understanding of the Latin is for the most part highly accurate, he eschews Latinate diction or syntax and ignores subtleties of wordplay and structure which do not easily translate into English. Thus the sophistication of Ovid's text is lost, as are the parodies of other literary genres present in the original.

In place of the Ovidian hexameters Golding chooses rhyming "fourteeners" (heptametric couplets), a popular verse form of the period. His handling of the line and his use of enjambment are at times clumsy and tend toward a comic tone. The expansive meter permits or calls for a large degree of "padding," such as the use of clichéd narrative formulas and multiple synonyms, which is of a piece with the homely, native, and accessible diction which Golding employs. The translation of *torus* (couch) variously as "bedstead" and "costly couch and good soft feather-bed" illustrates both the homeliness of Golding's vocabulary and his expansion of the Latin text.

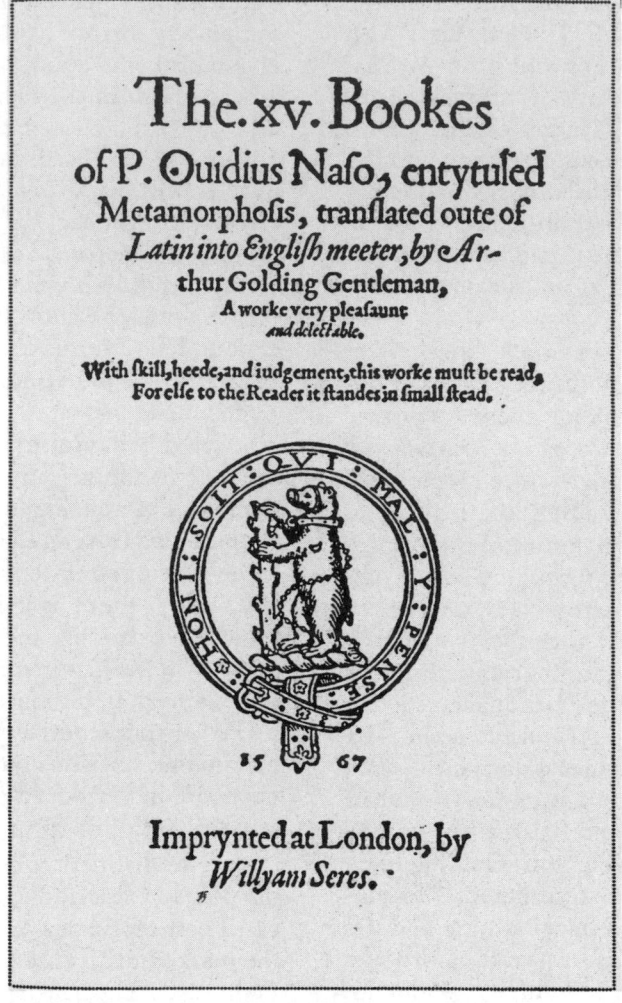

Title page for Golding's most influential work, his translation of Ovid

Golding's diction is predominantly backward-looking; there is a heavy use of intensives ("right," "full," "so") and clichéd rhyme inherited from medieval poetry ("of yore," "so sore," "every wight," "I will recite"). Thus by the time that Shakespeare used the text in the 1590s, it was distinctly old-fashioned. But the translation has a homely vigor and comic vitality and is, paradoxically, most successful when furthest removed from the tone and manner of Ovid. A forthright robustness and generous expansiveness take the place of Latinate sophistication and concision. Ovid's "*parva queror*," for example, is roundly translated as "Tush, these are trifles"; "*nec supplex turba timebat judicis ora sui*" is well developed into "There was no man would crouch or creep to judge with cap in hand." The translation was well received and remained preeminent until the publication of George Sandys's translation in 1626 (enlarged in 1632).

Documentation, mostly concerning finances and property, provides only the outlines of Golding's nonliterary activities in the later part of his life. The date of his marriage to Ursula Roydon is unknown. They had eight children – Henry, George, Thomas, Percival, Jane, Alice, Elizabeth, and Dorothy – and the first mention of their eldest, Henry, appears in 1575. The same year saw a substantial alteration in Golding's financial position, owing to the death of his elder brother Henry, who had inherited his father's estate. Golding was left wealthy, with large but encumbered properties. However, numerous lawsuits over the properties persistently drained his resources over the following twenty years, and Golding was eventually consigned to Fleet Prison for debt. The length of his stay in prison is not clear, but his dedication of his translation (1595) of Jacques Hurault's *Politic, Moral, and Martial Discourses* to William Brooke, Lord

Cobham, acknowledges that he received help from Cobham in his financial troubles. However, there is evidence that again in 1596 Golding had need to borrow money. He died in 1606 intestate and deeply in debt, and he was buried 13 May 1606 in the parish church of Belchamp Saint Paul's.

During his lifetime, as now, Golding was most widely known for his *Metamorphosis,* which achieved considerable popularity, although contemporary mention is also made of his religious translations. The complete fifteen-book *Metamorphosis* ran through seven editions in the sixteenth and early seventeenth centuries (1567, 1575, 1584, 1587, 1593, 1603, 1612), and Golding's achievement received complimentary references from, among others, Thomas Blundeville, George Peele, Thomas Nashe, and Francis Meres. William Webbe, in his *Discourse of English Poetry* (1586), includes among those worthy of praise "Master Arthur Golding, for his labor in Englishing Ovid's *Metamorphoses* for which gentleman, surely our country hath for many respects greatly to give God thanks." Golding's translation again received praise in George Puttenham's *Art of English Poesy* (1589), where Golding is compared to Phaer, the translator of Virgil: Puttenham recommends both men "for a learned and well-corrected verse, specially in translation clear and very faithfully answering their authors' intent."

But it is Shakespeare's use of the *Metamorphosis* in his plays which has been the primary cause of critical attention to Golding's work in the twentieth century. While the extent of Shakespeare's reading of Ovid's Latin text remains a subject for debate, his familiarity with the English translation is clear. Among the most famous of his adaptations from Golding is Prospero's speech from act 5 of *The Tempest* (1611) beginning "Ye elves of hills, brooks, standing lakes, and groves," which strikingly rewrites Medea's speech in book 7 of Golding's version: "Ye airs and winds, ye elves of hills, of brooks, of woods alone, / Of standing lakes, and of the night, approach ye every one." Borrowings from Golding's work may be found from the earliest of Shakespeare's plays and poetry onward and commonly rely on an audience's awareness of the original context for their full effect. This is the case, for example, in act 4 of *The Taming of the Shrew* (1594), where Katherine, commanded by Petruchio to address an old man as a young maiden, aptly adapts Salmacis's words to Hermaphroditus from book 4 of the *Metamorphosis* (appropriate because of the merging of genders in both cases).

Shakespeare's use of the Pyramus and Thisbe story from book 4 of the *Metamorphosis* as a source for *A Midsummer-Night's Dream* (1595) has aroused the most interest among modern critics, however. It has been argued that the language and prosody of Shakespeare's clownish "mechanicals" parodies Golding's diction and verse and that their dramatic presentation of Pyramus and Thisbe in act 5 of Shakespeare's comedy constitutes an amused commentary on a manner of writing which was by the mid 1590s distinctly outmoded. Although Anthony Brian Taylor's detailed study of this episode has somewhat redeemed Golding, the argument that there is some commentary on Golding's text in the scene is strengthened by the fact that Shakespeare's mechanicals, when presenting their play to their aristocratic audience, employ the propitiatory and somewhat ingenuous tone, and at times even the diction, which Golding uses in his own prefatory material. Shakespeare's reading of Golding seems to be more complex than Golding's reading of Ovid.

Despite his popularity in his own day, however, Golding's reputation declined sharply in the seventeenth century and remained negligible until the twentieth. After the edition of 1612 there appears to have been no further printing of Golding's *Metamorphosis* until William Henry Denham Rouse's edition of 1904. The first substantial modern critical attention came in the form of characteristically idiosyncratic praise from Ezra Pound. In his essay "Notes on Elizabethan Classicists," Pound writes, "Golding was no inconsiderable poet . . . His *Metamorphoses* [sic] form possibly the most beautiful book in our language . . . Chaucer and Golding were more likely to find the *mot juste* . . . than were for some centuries their successors."

In its capacity of source material for Shakespeare, Edmund Spenser, and others, Golding's work continues to be recognized, producing each year a handful of short articles on newly discovered borrowings. However, Golding deserves to be recognized on his own merits as well. His association with Sidney, his popularity with Shakespeare, and the critical acclaim which he received in his own day might all suggest that an appreciation of Golding is important not only in establishing the nature of the *Metamorphoses* as it was received by an Elizabethan readership, but also in exploring Elizabethan concepts of the function of literature and its relation to readings of history and biblical texts.

Biography:

Louis Thorn Golding, *An Elizabethan Puritan: Arthur Golding the Translator of Ovid's* Metamorphoses *and also of John Calvin's* Sermons (New York: R. R. Smith, 1937).

References:

Thomas Whitfield Baldwin, Review of *Ovid's Metamorphoses: The Arthur Golding Translation 1567,* edited by John Frederick Nims, *Journal of English and Germanic Philology,* 66 (January 1967): 124–127;

H. Manning Blake, "Golding's Ovid in Elizabethan Times," *Journal of English and Germanic Philology,* 14 (January 1915): 93–95;

Gordon Braden, *The Classics and English Renaissance Poetry: Three Case Studies* (New Haven & London: Yale University Press, 1978);

David G. Hale, "The Source and Date of Golding's 'Fabletalke,'" *Modern Philology,* 69 (May 1972): 326–327;

Caroline Jameson, "Ovid in the Sixteenth Century," in *Ovid,* edited by J. W. Binns (London & Boston: Routledge & Kegan Paul, 1973);

Henry Burrowes Lathrop, *Translations from the Classics into English 1477–1620,* Studies in Language and Literature, no. 35 (Madison: University of Wisconsin Press, 1933);

Myron W. McIntyre, "A Critical Study of Golding's Translation of Ovid's *Metamorphoses,*" Ph.D. dissertation, University of California, Berkeley, 1965;

Kenneth Muir, "Pyramus and Thisbe: A Study in Shakespeare's Method," *Shakespeare Quarterly,* 5 (Spring 1954): 141–153;

Charlton Ogburn, *The Mysterious William Shakespeare* (New York: Dodds, Mead and Company, 1984);

Ezra Pound, *ABC of Reading* (London: Routledge, 1934), p. 42;

Pound, "Notes on Elizabethan Classicists," in *Make It New* (London: Faber, 1934), pp. 95–121;

George Puttenham, *The Art of English Poesy,* edited by Gladys Doidge Willcock and Alice Walker (Cambridge: Cambridge University Press, 1936);

Forrest G. Robinson, "A Note on the Sidney-Golding Translation of Phillipe de Mornay's *De La Verité De La Religion Chrestienne,*" *Harvard Library Bulletin,* 17 (January 1969): 98–102;

K. Sørensen, *Thomas Lodge's Translation of Seneca's "De beneficiis" compared with Arthur Golding's Version: A Textual Analysis with Special Reference to Latinisms* (Copenhagen: Gyldendal, 1960);

Marshall W. S. Swan, "A Study of Golding's *Ovid,*" Ph.D. dissertation, Harvard University, 1942;

Anthony Brian Taylor, "Golding's Ovid, Shakespeare's 'Small Latin,' and the Real Object of Mockery in 'Pyramus and Thisbe,'" *Shakespeare Survey,* 42 (1989): 54–64;

William Webbe, "A Discourse of English Poetry (1586)," in *Elizabethan Critical Essays,* edited by George Gregory Smith, vol. 1 (London: Oxford University Press, 1904), pp. 226–302;

Robert F. Wilson, "Golding's *Metamorphosis* and Shakespeare's Burlesque Method in *A Midsummer Night's Dream,*" *English Language Notes,* 7 (September 1969): 18–25;

James Wortham, "Arthur Golding and the Translation of Prose," *Huntington Library Quarterly,* 12 (August 1949): 339–367.

John Grange

(circa 1556 – ?)

R. W. Maslen
Glasgow University

BOOK: *The Golden Aphroditis: A Pleasant Discourse, Penned by John Grange, Gentleman, Student in the Common Lawe of Englande. Whereunto Be Annexed by the Same Authour as Well Certayne Metres vpon Sundrie Poyntes, as also Diuers Pamphlets in Prose, Which He Entituleth His Garden: Pleasant to the Eare, and Delightful to the Reader, If He Abuse Not the Scente of the Floures* (London: Printed by Henry Bynneman, 1577).

Editions: *The Golden Aphroditis* (New York: Scholars' Facsimiles and Reprints, 1936);

The Golden Aphroditis and Granges Garden, introduction by Hyder E. Rollins (New York: Scholars' Facsimiles and Reprints, 1939).

John Grange was the author of one of the most stylistically flamboyant and idiosyncratic works of Elizabethan prose fiction, *The Golden Aphroditis* (1577). The book is one of a series of experimental fictions produced in England during the 1570s by writers, such as George Gascoigne, George Pettie, and John Lyly, who contributed to and took advantage of the increasing sophistication with which the Elizabethan public engaged in the act of reading. *The Golden Aphroditis* contains important evidence of the influences and preoccupations that helped to shape these experimental fictions.

According to the registry for Queen's College, Oxford, a John Grange of London matriculated in January 1575 at the age of eighteen. If this person is the author of *The Golden Aphroditis,* he, like Pettie, Lyly, and other authors of prose fiction from Oxford, may have been influenced by the complex prose style used by John Rainolds, tutor at Corpus Christi, in his lectures on Aristotle. Nothing else is known of Grange's life except what he says on the title page of his book: that he considered himself a "gentleman" and that at the time of writing he was a "student in the common law of England."

His legal studies repeatedly invade the text of *The Golden Aphroditis.* Grange's opening address to those who suffer from the "doleful dumps" suggests that one of the causes of their melancholy may be imminent participation in a trial: "have ye to deal with the inexorable judges Minos and Rhadamanthus?" Soon afterward, the lovers A. O. and N. O. meet in the course of a legal appeal to the pagan gods, and at the end of the volume the epistles of F. G. are saturated with legal jargon. Grange repeatedly refers to Minerva, who seems to have been the pagan goddess most frequently associated with the Inns of Court at the time he was writing. One of the poems asks, "Alas what one can frame himself his youthful race to spend / All in Minerva's comely court?," and Grange adopts as one of his mottos *Tam Minervae quam Veneri* (dedicated equally to the goddesses of wisdom and of love). The entire work might be seen as a written version of the holiday entertainments put on by the Inns of Court; at one point N. O. stages a Christmas interlude for his fiancée reminiscent of the plays on mythological subjects that were performed by the young lawyers, and Grange's establishment of his own "youthful authority" at the beginning of the book sets him up as a kind of literary lord of misrule.

The principal story told in what Grange calls his "paganical pamphlet" is a deceptively simple one concerning the wooing of A. O., the daughter of Diana and Endymion, by the knight N. O. After a brief period of misunderstanding engineered by I. I., a rival for A. O.'s affections, the lovers reconcile and marry. But this simple narrative is conveyed through an intriguing amalgam of genres. Like Gascoigne's "A Pleasant Discourse of the Adventures of Master F. J." (1573), the story unfolds in a combination of verse and prose narrative interspersed with love letters, coded messages, and parlor games; but Grange introduces his own peculiar variations. The games devised by N. O. invite the participation of the book's readers by leaving out the answers to the problems they pose; and Grange encourages further discussion by hinting that the story he tells is a slightly scurrilous account of actual events, gleaned with investigative zeal from the

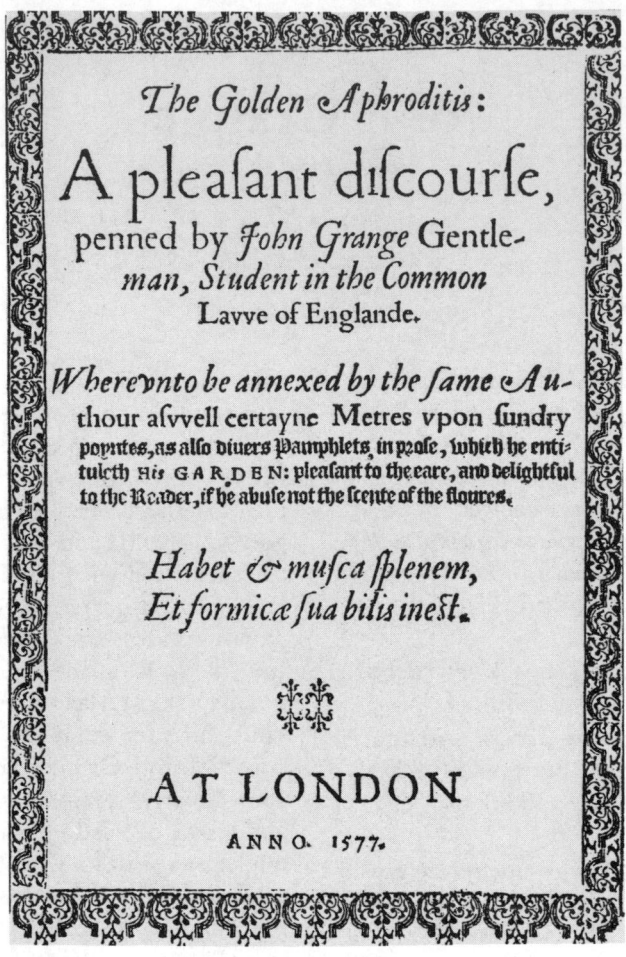

Title page for John Grange's flamboyant and idiosyncratic story
of a love triangle

secret world of Elizabethan high society. The dedicatory epistle insinuates mysteriously that "those which have their clear sight to look steadfastly herein, shall see perchance an ape whipped, which somewhat may delight him. Whereupon certain young gentlemen and those of my professed friends (well viewing this work) requested me earnestly to have entitled it *A Nettle for an Ape,* but yet (being somewhat wedded, as most fools are, to mine own opinion, who would hardly forgo their babble for the Tower of London) I thought it good . . . to set a more cleanly name upon it, that is, *Golden Aphroditis.* For if the other had stood, who most had been bitten herewith peradventure would have sought all the means they could to have turned this whip for mine own tale." Grange reinforces these hints that his work is partly satiric by allusions to the figure of Pasquil, introduced into Tudor literature by Sir Thomas Elyot in his dialogue *Pasquil the Plain* (1533) as the representative of satirical plain speech.

Grange adds to the book's air of mystery by interpolating mythological elements. The narrative opens with an erotic allegory involving the goddess Diana and a stag and closes with a funny account of a drunken wedding attended by all the "Homerical gods." At the end of the narrative he supplies a "Conclusion" that contains critical discussion of his purpose in writing the text and the response he expects from his readers. The book ends with "Grange's Garden," a collection of letters and poems. Few Elizabethan texts give such an impression of disorderly plenty in such a small space.

Of course, this blend of disparate elements is intended as a virtuoso display of erudition and inventiveness, but it also provides a miniature summary of the state of Elizabethan thought about the nature of fiction at a time when writers were intensively questioning its traditional moral function. Grange's work is designed to elude any attempt to categorize it in conventional terms. One sign of its elusive nature is Grange's refusal to adopt unequivocally the role of the penitent prodigal by which his contemporaries tended to justify their less morally uplifting literary productions: he says only that his book provides a "plain mirror of youthful vanities" and that "the shade thereof shall bereave you of your senses." One of the authors of the commendatory verses printed in the book seems to have been so taken aback by this failure to adopt the familiar stance of penitence for literary follies that he claims that the whole work should be read as meaning the opposite of what it seems to say, that Grange has adopted the role of the Vice Ambidexter from Thomas Preston's play *Cambises* (produced 1560–1561; published 1570?), and that he "shows himself still friendliest there, where most of all he loathes."

While Grange is eager to suggest that parts of his book are based on actual events, he is equally eager to plagiarize from authors he admires. The title and many details, including the marriage, are taken from Sir Thomas Chaloner's translation of Desiderius Erasmus's *The Praise of Folly* (1549), and Grange praises Erasmus in his "Conclusion." On the same page he praises John Skelton, whose works had recently been reprinted; and in the poem "I. G. biddeth his friend A. T. good morrow" he makes one of the few Elizabethan attempts to imitate the style of Skelton's satire "Speak, Parrot" (1521). Several of the poems, letters, and games closely resemble those in Gascoigne's "A Pleasant Discourse of the Adventures of Master F. J."; some anecdotes are lifted from James Sanford's translation of Ludovico Guicciardini's *The Garden of Pleasure* (1573), and elsewhere Grange borrows from Arthur Golding, Thomas Howell, and Richard Edwards. The borrowings are so blatant that it is tempting to suppose that an author who knew *The Praise of Folly* so well might have had Erasmus's passage on plagiarism in mind: Folly observes that "the wiser writers are those who put out the work of someone else as their own." The suspicion that Grange's repeated protestations of the hidden meaning of his text are intended to be parodic, guying the pretensions of the learned, would seem to be borne out by the bawdy nature of some of his most "allegorical" passages – especially Diana's account of her encounter with a randy buck. In any case Grange's borrowings are for the most part transformed beyond recognition by the eccentricity and vigor of his prose style.

That style is as energetically eclectic as his blend of genres. Unlike Pettie and Lyly, Grange avoids extensive use of a limited number of rhetorical figures. He makes use, as they do, of alliteration, of multiple comparisons drawn from natural his-

tory, and of classical allusions; but he mixes these formal devices with outbreaks of colloquialism and homely proverbs (one character is said to be "as seemly as a cow in a cage, a dog in a doublet, or a sow in a saddle"). At emotional moments his text breaks into the rhythms of verse: "What better did become her case than moaning weeds to clad her corpse? Who cried and wished ten thousand times that earth it might enclose the same." Above all Grange shows an infectious enthusiasm for the art of eloquence itself; in this respect his text is characteristic of a decade that saw an unprecedented proliferation of handbooks designed to teach the upwardly mobile reader how to gain power through persuasive speech. His characters are always complimenting one another on their rhetorical ingenuity – A. O. tells N. O. that "his tongue was made of massive gold" – or launching into encomiastic hyperboles: N. O. tells A. O. "if springs and seas were turned to ink, if lands were turned to paper, if shrubs and trees were men, if every man took pen in hand, if Apollo and Pallas should give them wisdom, if Mercury ambages, and Arethusa influence, yet would their ink be dried up, their paper spent, their pens stubbed, and (to be short) their wits gravelled: yet would thy features be untouched, the which in number pass the sands in seas, and eke the glittering stars in skies." One wonders whether A. O. appreciated being complimented on the *number* of her features.

Gascoigne's "A Pleasant Discourse of the Adventures of Master F. J." investigated the social and moral implications of stylistic complexity, warning that such complexity could be the instrument of accidental confusion or deliberate deception; but Grange derives only pleasure from the problems inherent in sophisticated discourse. The villain I. I. succeeds only briefly in persuading the lovers to misinterpret one another's words and actions; for the most part rhetorical obscurity is a sign of profundity, and the most precious gift N. O. can get for his lover is a cup of eloquence given him by the Muses. The text overflows with metaphors for verbal abundance: pens, nibs, and paper. By the last page Grange's writing skills have been so violently tested that he says: "My pen is stubbed, my paper spent, my ink wasted, my wits gravelled, and (to be short) time calleth me away." He is aware that his exuberant style will be ridiculed by some ("Think ye that Polyhymnia that rhetorical Muse is commended of all men?"), and he is as conscious as Gascoigne that verbal misunderstandings can have tragic consequences. A poem in "Grange's Garden" narrates in high Senecan style the death of a pair of lovers, victims of just such a deception as I. I. practiced on N. O. and A. O. (the poem adds yet another literary genre to Grange's repertoire, the elegy or tragic lament). But Grange's principal project is to celebrate the heady pleasures of eloquence, and his carnivalesque little book serves as a sparkling if clumsy forerunner of the more spectacular rhetorical achievements of Lyly, Christopher Marlowe, and Thomas Nashe in the next two decades.

In his *Discourse of English Poesie* (1586), William Webbe mentions Grange as one of the foremost living writers, but since then he has been accorded scant attention. *The Golden Aphroditis* deserves further study for the light it throws on the intellectual contexts of early Elizabethan fiction and the relationship of Elizabethan and Tudor literature. It should also take its place in any study of the prose, poetry, and drama associated with the Inns of Court. Above all, it deserves the highest compliment the twentieth-century reader can pay it: to be read.

References:

Marie Axton, *The Queen's Two Bodies* (London: Royal Historical Society, 1977);

Esther Garke, *The Use of Songs in Elizabethan Prose Fiction* (Bern: Francke, 1972);

Richard Helgerson, *The Elizabethan Prodigals* (Berkeley: University of California Press, 1976);

C. S. Lewis, *English Literature in the Sixteenth Century, Excluding Drama* (Oxford: Clarendon Press, 1954);

Percy Waldron Long, "From Troilus to Euphues," in *Anniversary Papers by Colleagues and Pupils of George Lyman Kittredge,* edited by F. N. Robinson (Boston: Ginn, 1913), pp. 367–376;

Charles T. Prouty, "Elizabethan Fiction: Whetstone's 'The Discourse of Rinaldo and Giletta' and Grange's *The Golden Aphroditis*," in *Studies in Honor of A. H. R. Fairchild,* edited by Prouty, University of Missouri Studies 21.1 (Columbia: University of Missouri Press, 1946), pp. 133–150;

William Ringler, "The Immediate Source of Euphuism," *PMLA,* 53 (September 1938): 678–686;

Hyder E. Rollins, "John Grange's *The Golden Aphroditis,*" *Harvard Studies and Notes in Philology and Literature,* 16 (1934): 177–198;

M. P. Tilley, "Borrowings in Grange's *Golden Aphroditis,*" *Modern Language Notes,* 53 (June 1938): 407–412;

William Webbe, *A Discourse of English Poetrie* (London: Printed by John Charlewood for Robert Walley, 1586);

Pamela J. Willetts, *The Henry Lawes Manuscript* (London: Trustees of the British Museum, 1969).

Papers:

The British Library contains several seventeenth-century manuscripts with lyrics attributed to John Grange: the poems "To his thoughts," "Against pride in pedigrees" (both in Additional Ms. 33998, fols. 58, 81), and "On the death of a child" (Ms. Sloane 1446, fol. 37) and three songs in a manuscript of music by Henry Lawes: "Sure thou framed wert by art," "A lover once I did espy," and "Be not proud, cause fair and trim" (Additional Ms. 53723, fols. 56b, 83b, and 137b).

Nicholas Grimald

(circa 1519 – circa 1562)

Seymour Baker House
University of Otago

BOOKS: *Christvs Redivivvs, Comoedia Tragica, sacra et noua* (Cologne: Printed by Johann Gymnicus, 1543);

Archiprophetae, Tragoedia (Cologne: Printed by Martin Gymnicus, 1548);

Oratio ad Pontifices, Londini in aede Paulina, anno domini 1553. 17. Idus Aprilis (London: Printed by Henry Bynneman, 1583).

Editions: *Christus Redivivus,* edited by James Morgan Hart, *PMLA,* 14, no. 3 (1899): 369–448;

Archipropheta: Tragoedia, translated by Charles J. Tibbits (London, 1906);

Christus Redivivus and *Archipropheta,* Latin texts with English translations by Le Roy Merrill, in Merrill, *The Life and Poems of Nicholas Grimald* (New Haven: Yale University Press, 1925; reprinted, Hamden, Conn.: Archon, 1969).

PLAY PRODUCTIONS: *Christus Redivivus,* Brasenose College, Oxford, circa Easter 1541;

Archipropheta, Christ Church College, Oxford, circa Christmas 1548.

OTHER: "Domino Hugoni Latimero Nicolaus Grimoaldus Salutem," "Ad Dominum Guilielmum Turnerum," "Ad Catabaptistam," and "To the reader," in *A Preseruatiue, or Triacle, agaynst the Poyson of Pelagius, Lately Renued, by the Furious Secte of the Annabaptistes,* edited by William Turner (London: Printed by Steven Mierdman for Andrew Hester, 1551);

Thomas Cooper, ed., *Bibliotheca Eliotae Eliotis Librarie: This Dictionarie Now Newly Imprinted, M.D.XLVIII Is Inriched* (London: Printed by Thomas Berthelet, 1552) – includes poems by Grimald;

Marcvs Tullius Ciceroes Thre Bokes of Duties, to Marcus His Sonne, Turned oute of Latine into English, translated by Grimald (London: Printed by Richard Tottel, 1556; enlarged, 1558); edited by Gerald O'Gorman (Washington, D.C.: Folger Shakespeare Library, 1990; London & Toronto: Associated University Presses, 1990);

Songes and Sonnettes Written by the Ryght Honorable Lorde Henry Howard Late Earle of Surrey, and Other, edited by Richard Tottel (London: Printed by Richard Tottel, 1557) – includes poems by Grimald; revised and enlarged as *Tottel's Miscellany 1557–1587,* 2 volumes, edited by Hyder Edward Rollins (Cambridge, Mass.: Harvard University Press, 1928, 1929; revised, 1966);

Virgil, *In P. V. Maronis quatuor libros Georgicorum in oratione soluta paraphrasis elegantissima: Oxonij in aede Christi anno serenissimi regis Edouardi sexti secundo, confecta,* edited by Grimald (London: Printed by George Bishop & Ralph Newbery, 1591).

Classical scholar, playwright, priest, poet – and, to some, Catholic traitor – Nicholas Grimald was one of the second wave of English humanists. His translations of classical works, especially of Cicero's *De officiis* as *Three Books of Duties* (1556), enjoyed immense popularity, and his ability as an orator was renowned. His interest in poetry and the English language led him to revere medieval literature, as the titles of his lost works on Chaucerian subjects attest. This interest sets him apart from the majority of English humanists, who affected to despise the writings of the Middle Ages. Esteemed by his peers as among the best of a generation of Cambridge scholars, Grimald was one of the first to use blank verse in English, and it is for his verse contributions to *Tottel's Miscellany* (1557) that he is chiefly remembered today. He composed English and Latin drama; but of his eight plays, only two Latin works survive. Despite their Protestant viewpoint, these biblical plays, produced at Oxford during the 1540s, are pedagogical rather than polemical, in contrast to much of the vernacular drama of the period. Orthodox in his adherence to the doctrines of the established English church, Grimald participated in contemporary debates by contributing Latin and English verses to William Turner's *Preservative or Treacle* (1551) against Anabaptists and other Protestant sectarians; there he joined company with other notable authors, such as the popular divine Thomas Becon and the future dramatist Thomas Norton (who would become the co-author of one of the first English tragedies, *Gorboduc* [1561]). His few surviving works and the titles of his many lost translations show him to be a moderate classicist who saw the English language as capable of bearing the weight of Latin rhetoric.

Born circa 1519 in the small Huntingdonshire town of Leighton-Bromswold to Giovanni Baptista Grimaldi, a clerk, and Annes Grimaldi, Grimald received his B.A. from Cambridge University in 1540. He continued his studies at Oxford under the patronage of Gilbert Smith, archdeacon of Peterborough, and settled at Brasenose College. While awaiting the arrival of his books he composed his lyrical Latin drama *Christus Redivivus* (1543), dedicated to Smith and performed at the college around Easter 1541. Although Grimald had been tempted to abandon the work, his tutor, John Airy, had urged him on with the play despite its departure from classical dramatic form; Airy praised its lack of frivolity, the prominent comic scenes on the miles gloriosus motif notwithstanding

Grimald wrote *Christus Redivivus,* which blends Virgilian diction with restrained Protestant theology, when Latin biblical drama was at its most popular. His depiction of Christ's triumph over death incorporates many nonscriptural elements and characters, including passages from the *Aeneid,* so that the audience, which included townspeople in addition to students, would "not only pluck the flowers from the language, but would indeed gather the richest fruits from the subject matter." The blending of classical and Christian elements, which had occasioned such an outcry at Oxford a generation earlier that Sir Thomas More had been forced to rise in defense of Greek studies, passed without comment, having yielded to theological debates of more immediacy – although academic quarrels could still rage over correct Greek pronunciation.

Christus Redivivus calls for a large number of players, including a chorus used in the classical manner. Grimald adheres closely to the biblical chronology yet includes little scriptural material in the dialogue – in contrast to traditional vernacular drama, which often presents passages taken verbatim from the Bible. Each act is preceded by a narrative prologue offering a synopsis of the action. The play opens with Jesus' entombment and the visit by

Mary Magdalene to the grave. She laments the cruelty of the Jews and, as night falls, is led away by Nicodemus and Joseph, who attempt to succor her with hope. The second act contains the comic soldiers bragging of their courage, contrasting sharply with the heroic activity of Jesus, who descends into Hell and frees the souls of the damned. In the third act the soldiers are overcome by fear as Jesus rises from the tomb; the disciples return and find the tomb empty. As an example of Grimald's pervasive use of classical diction, the touching scene in which the weeping Mary recognizes the risen Christ contains no scriptural dialogue – indeed, it opens with a quotation from Ovid. Act 4 details the various stratagems by which the Jews, led by a delegation from Hell, try to deny the Resurrection. The fifth and final act closes with Jesus' appearance to the gathered disciples.

Having moved from Brasenose to Merton College as a fellow, Grimald received his M.A. by 1544. Shortly after Henry VIII rededicated Cardinal Thomas Wolsey's Oxford foundation of Cardinal's College as Christ Church in November 1546, Grimald sent his second biblical Latin drama, *Archipropheta* (1548), to its first dean, Dr. Richard Cox; on the basis of this work Grimald was appointed lecturer in rhetoric. Based on the life of John the Baptist, the play was staged around Christmas of the year of its publication. A favorite subject for drama among Protestants and Catholics alike, John the Baptist was the protagonist of many dramatic works, including those of Grimald's friend John Bale (1538) and the Scots humanist George Buchanan (1578) as well as the medieval cycle drama.

Grimald augments his biblical source with Flavius Josephus's account of the beheading of John the Baptist in his *Antiquities of the Jews.* He adopts the same humanist posture as in *Christus Redivivus,* which set out to "delight the learned, but also to profit those of cruder intelligence." But whereas that play had altered the Latin form of comedy to present its tragicomic theme of Christ's death and Resurrection, *Archipropheta* adheres more closely to the classical form of tragedy. While *Archipropheta* lacks the abundant topical references found in Bale's treatment of the Baptist, it urges the resumption of reform under young King Edward VI. Grimald's successful use of the wise fool Gelasimus harks back to Desiderius Erasmus's *Moriae encomium* (1511; translated as *The Praise of Folly,* 1549) and anticipates William Shakespeare's Fool in *King Lear* (1623).

Possibly indebted to Jakob Schöpper's *Ectrachelistes sive Johannes decollatus* (1546) for its comic

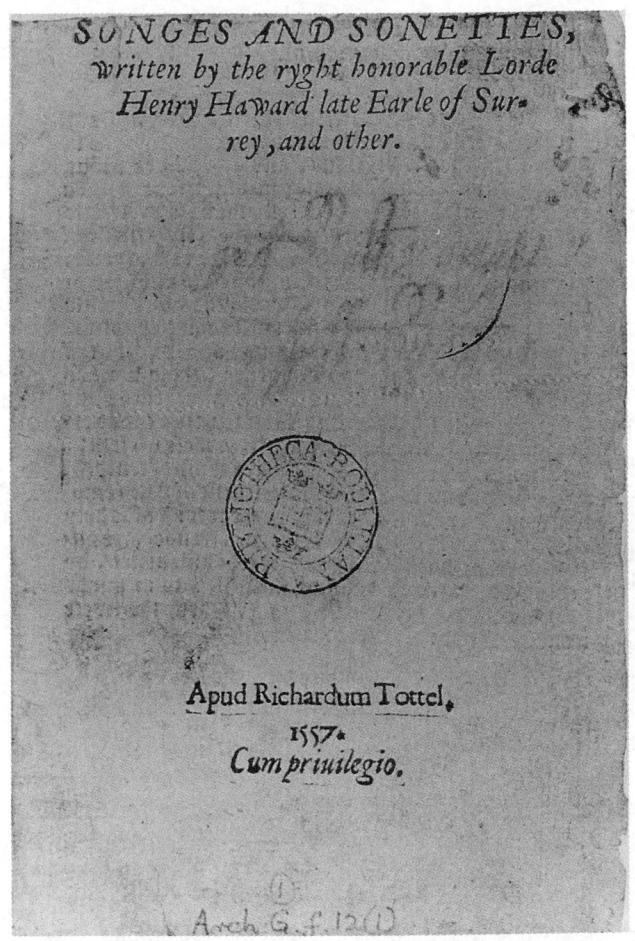

Title page for the first edition of the collection that came to be known as Tottel's Miscellany. *This edition includes at least thirty-eight poems by Nicholas Grimald; later editions dropped most of them.*

fool, certain festive scenes, and most particularly its varied meter, *Archipropheta* is a lyric drama with a wide variety of stage settings, affective soliloquies, and lavish banquet scenes with song and dance. The printed version of the play includes metrical directions for each scene. Act 1 introduces John and his mission to declare an end to all human trappings in light of the promised Savior. In the second act Gelasimus mocks Pharisaic religious practices, the appearance of Herodias introduces the theme of voluptuousness, and John has a favorable interview with Herod. The third act depicts the plans to destroy John concocted by the Pharisees, who are jealous of his growing authority, and by Herodias, who resents his condemnation of her adulterous marriage. Herod, torn by John's call to righteousness and his desire for Herodias, throws John into prison, where he learns of Jesus' ministry. Act 4, the longest, further develops the comic role of Gelasimus, whose unwelcome honesty parallels John's, and contains the elaborate banquet scene in

which Herodias's daughter (here given a Greek name meaning "voluptuous" rather than the traditional Salome) does her dance. Act 5 opens with Jehovah alone onstage, urging constancy under persecution, and concludes with John's farewell to the people and his execution amid general lamentation. The scenes needed no gloss for those who had witnessed the last decade or more of Henry VIII's reign.

In 1552 Grimald became chaplain to London's reforming bishop, Nicholas Ridley, who appointed him to the chantership of Saint Paul's Cathedral that same year. There, in April 1553, he excoriated the assembled clergy for their worldliness in a sermon notable for its classical allusions. His evangelical views, constant throughout Edward VI's reign, wavered during his imprisonment in Oxford's Bocardo in 1555 under Mary. Not the stuff of martyrs, he recanted his Protestant views; but the suggestion – based on slight circumstantial evidence – that he betrayed Ridley, Thomas Cranmer, and

Hugh Latimer finds no support in the writings of his contemporaries.

In June 1557 appeared the first edition of *Songs and Sonnets Written by the Right Honorable Lord Henry Howard, Late Earl of Surrey, And Other,* now known as *Tottel's Miscellany,* which includes at least thirty-eight poems by Grimald in addition to poems by Howard and by Sir Thomas Wyatt. The second edition, which appeared a few weeks later, drops all but ten of Grimald's poems and lists his contributions by his initials rather than by name; and each of the Grimald poems in subsequent editions is a Latin translation, four of them of poems by the Calvinist Theodore Beza. Le Roy Merrill argues that the change was due to the printer's fear that Grimald's name would jeopardize sales because of his "betrayal" of Ridley, Cranmer, and Latimer; but Gladys D. Willcock points out that Grimald's poems, with their somewhat intrusive classicism, cannot compete with those of Howard and Wyatt and were probably excluded for that reason. Hyder Edward Rollins has taken up this suggestion, adding that Grimald's highly personal poems, kept out of print until 1557, were by design unsuitable for publication and were perhaps removed at his own request.

The poems cover a wide range, from eulogies on his mother and university friends to somewhat labored treatments of classical themes. Equally varied are the styles Grimald employs: blank verse, rhyme royal, sonnet, poulter's measure, fourteener, and his favorite measure, the heroic couplet. Many of the poems are translations or paraphrases from Beza or classical sources; but among his original compositions are several poems of a highly personal nature, all of which were suppressed in the second edition. These include the moving funeral song for his mother, in which something of Grimald's early years can be seen, and the equally touching eulogy on William Chambers, a friend at the university:

O Chambers, O thy Grimald's mate most dear:
Why hath fell fate ta'en thee, and left him here?
But whereto these complaints in vain make we?
Such words in winds to waste, what moveth me?
Thou holdest the haven of health, with blissful Jove;
Through many waves, and seas, yet must I rove.
Not worthy I, so soon with thee to go:
Me still my fates retain, bewrapt in woe.
Live, our companion once, now live for aye:
Heaven's joys enjoy, while we die day by day.

Other poems omitted from the second and subsequent editions are original well-wishing verses to Edward Seymour's daughters and to other former ladies of the court; epitaphs to Sir James Wilford, Lady Margaret Lee, and Lord Mautravers; and translations of several early love poems by Beza.

Few modern commentators discuss Grimald outside the context of *Tottel's Miscellany,* although some attention has been focused on his Latin drama and, more recently, his translation of Cicero's *Three Books of Duties,* which has been published in a modern critical edition (1990). Using textual as well as biographical material, H. J. Byrom argues for Grimald's editorship of *Tottel's Miscellany* against the traditional ascription of that role to Tottel himself. George Shannon analyzes Grimald's use of the heroic couplet and concludes that he was a pioneer of the neoclassical movement, while Merrill and Hoyt Hudson identify his reliance on Beza and various classical sources for much of his poetry. Rollins sees Grimald as inferior to Surrey but nonetheless a valuable addition to the ranks of mid-Tudor poets and traces the enormous influence *Tottel's Miscellany* had throughout Elizabethan England. Unfortunately, attention to his two Latin plays has been sparse following an initial flurry of activity earlier in the twentieth century. Frederick S. Boas places *Christus Redivivus* in its university context and discusses Grimald's remarkable ability to adapt his style to the dramatic occasion. George C. Taylor and Patricia Abel have isolated the medieval Hegge and Digby Resurrection Plays as possible sources for *Christus Redivivus,* and Howard Norland discusses *Archipropheta* as a fusion of native English religious drama (the saint's play) with the language and form of classical tragedy, concluding that it may have served as a model for the later popularization of academic drama.

Grimald's reputation has not fared well, despite the popularity of *Tottel's Miscellany* and his translation of Cicero. His later years are shrouded in obscurity, as is the date of his death. Most agree that he died in 1562, in which year an epitaph by his friend Barnabe Googe appeared. Renewed attention to Tudor humanism may restore some luster to his reputation as dramatist, poet, and translator of classical texts during the early years of England's literary Renaissance.

Bibliographies:

John Bale, *Index Britanniae Scriptorum,* edited by Reginald Poole and Mary Bateson (Oxford: Clarendon Press, 1902), pp. 301–304;

Le Roy Merrill, *The Life and Poems of Nicholas Grimald* (New Haven: Yale University Press, 1925; reprinted, Hamden, Conn.: Archon, 1969), pp. 15–34;

Bale, *Scriptorum Illustrium Majoris Britanniae Catalogus,* 2 volumes (Farnborough: Gregg International, 1971), I: 701–702.

Biography:

Le Roy Merrill, *The Life and Poems of Nicholas Grimald* (New Haven: Yale University Press, 1925; reprinted, Hamden, Conn.: Archon, 1969).

References:

Patricia Abel, "Grimald's *Christus Redivivus* and the Digby Resurrection Play," *Modern Language Notes,* 70 (May 1955): 328–330;

Frederick S. Boas, "Biblical Plays at Oxford," in his *University Drama in the Tudor Age* (Oxford: Clarendon Press, 1914), pp. 26–42;

H. J. Byrom, "The Case for Nicholas Grimald as Editor of *Tottel's Miscellany,*" *Modern Language Review,* 27 (April 1932): 125–143;

Hoyt Hudson, "Grimald's Translations from Beza," *Modern Language Notes,* 39 (November 1924): 388–394;

John King, *English Reformation Literature: The Tudor Origins of the Protestant Tradition* (Princeton: Princeton University Press, 1982), pp. 242–244, 297–299;

Le Roy Merrill, "Nicholas Grimald, the Judas of the Reformation," *PMLA,* 37 (June 1922): 216–227;

Howard Norland, "Grimald's *Archipropheta:* A Saint's Tragedy," *Journal of Medieval and Renaissance Studies,* 14 (Spring 1984): 63–76;

George Shannon, "Nicholas Grimald's Heroic Couplet and the Latin Elegiac Distich," *PMLA,* 45 (June 1930): 532–542;

Shannon, "Nicholas Grimald's List of the Muses," *Modern Language Quarterly,* 8 (March 1947): 43–46;

George C. Taylor, "The *Christus Redivivus* of Nicholas Grimald and the Hegge Resurrection Plays," *PMLA,* 41 (December 1926): 840–859;

Thorlac Turville-Petre, "Nicholas Grimald and *Alexander A,*" *English Literary Renaissance,* 6 (Spring 1976): 180–186;

Gladys D. Willcock, "A Hitherto Uncollated Version of Surrey's Translation of the Fourth Book of the *Aeneid,*" *Modern Language Review,* 17 (April 1922): 131–149.

Elizabeth Grymeston

(before 1563 – before 1604)

Betty S. Travitsky
New York Public Library

BOOK: *Miscelanea, Meditations, Memoratives* (London: Printed by Melchisidec Bradwood for Felix Norton, 1604; revised and enlarged edition, London: Printed by George Elde for William Aspley, 1606?); republished as *Miscellanea, Prayers, Meditations, Memoratives* (London: Printed by Melchisidec Bradwood for William Aspley, 1608?).

Elizabeth Grymeston is easily the most polished and possibly the most learned of the seventeenth-century writers of the "mother's advice book," a tract of advice ostensibly directed by a mother to her child, providing (invariably pious) guidance for that child's instruction. The mother's advice book, a genre which seems to be a novelty of the early-modern period, was often composed by a dying mother, apparently impelled to write as an extension of her motherhood, the most authoritative function open to her in early-modern English society. Indisputably the Grymeston tract, probably written without any intention of publication, succeeds in combining pious thoughts, questions, and paraphrases, most of them of a decidedly Roman Catholic cast, into a wonderful whole compounded of direct, simple language and arresting, concrete images. The *Miscelanea* (1604) so persuasively conveys Grymeston's intentions and thoughts that Charlotte Kohler, in her study of women writers of the Elizabethan era, compares it to Robert Burton's *Anatomy of Melancholy* (1621) "on a smaller scale" and calls it "the first autobiography of an Elizabethan woman's mind." The printing history of this posthumous work, reprinted three times in the early seventeenth century, provides testimony to the popularity of Grymeston's sentiments, if not of her specific beliefs.

Most circumstances of the life of Elizabeth Grymeston, daughter of Martin Bernye and Margaret Flynte of Gunton, Norfolk, and wife of Christopher Grymeston of Smeeton, Yorkshire, are shrouded in mystery. It has been established that she was born before 1563, and lines in Simon Grahame's prefatory poem to the first edition of her *Miscelanea* indicate that she had died before the work appeared. Although college regulations forbade the marriage of fellows, Grymeston's husband was associated from 1578 with Caius College, Cambridge, as fellow and bursar, even after their marriage (by 1584) and the births of several children. It is unclear whether Christopher's separation from the college in 1592 was a result of the discovery of the marriage. Alternately, there may have been difficulties connected with Grymeston's religious leanings, for records indicate that both the Bernye and Grymeston families had Catholic connections, and an Elizabeth Grymeston of Yorkshire was fined in 1593 as a recusant; moreover, such leanings fit many of the sentiments of the *Miscelanea*. Whatever the cause, in 1592 Christopher entered Gray's Inn of the Inns of Court. Grymeston alludes to "eight several sinister assaults" on her husband's life, although she does not explain their nature or cause. These attacks may have been related to religious matters; however, they may have resulted from quarrels over family legacies. After her marriage a serious feud erupted between Grymeston and her mother, and the cruel behavior of the latter seems to have resulted in Grymeston's chronic invalidism. By the time Grymeston composed her *Miscelanea*, only one of the nine children born to her still survived, her husband's life had been threatened, and her own health was endangered by dissension.

Because of these troubles, Grymeston writes in the introductory letter addressed to her son, Bernye, that she felt authorized to pen her *Miscelanea*. Since her health was so poor and her husband, Bernye's father, had been repeatedly attacked and his whereabouts were unknown, she felt impelled to leave a book of advice to her son as a "portable veni [*sic*] mecum" in place of his parents. "There is nothing so strong as the force of love," she writes; "there is no love so forcible as the love of an affectionate mother to her natural child: there

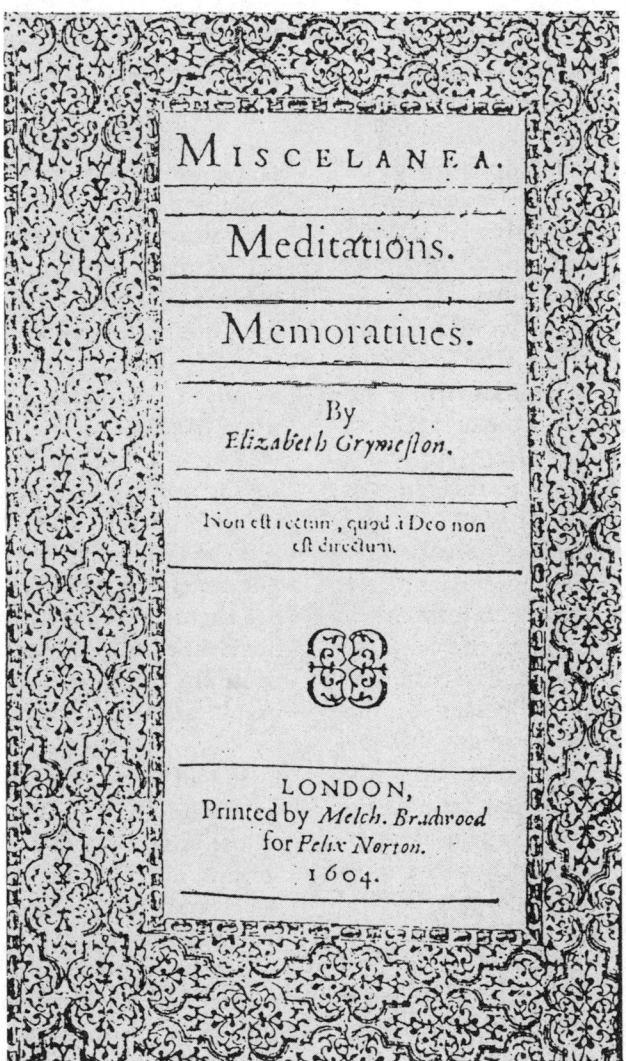

Title page for the advice book Elizabeth Grymeston addressed to her son

is no mother can either more affectionately show her nature, or more naturally manifest her affection, than in advising her children out of her own experience, to eschew evil, and encline them to do that which is good." This is a strongly expressed justification echoed by many women who wrote such books of advice, revealing their uneasiness with public utterance, a questionable act that needed to be explained or excused.

It is not surprising, in light of the particular educational advances of the English Renaissance, that some mothers such as Grymeston wrote books of advice to their children. For in England, due to the relatively late onset of humanism and the advent of religious reform, both Christian humanists and Protestant reformers had developed an interest in women's education in the sixteenth century. The

new theories stressed the need for women to conduct their homes religiously and, most especially, to raise and educate their children in religion. These theories had resulted in the development of a "new mother," who was a learned and pious woman, responsible both for raising her children and developing her own potential as a private person.

The inevitability, centrality, and hazards of motherhood were facts of life for the early-modern Englishwoman, at a time when the only alternative career option to marriage, the convent, had been closed to them, when there were no reliable methods of birth control, and when childbirth was extremely dangerous. What was new in early-modern England was an appreciation of the importance of the mother's influence on the child and the subsequent increase in the education of women for the sake of fulfilling this responsibility. However, the theorists of both the humanist and Protestant camps agreed on the importance of female subordination, including an abstinence from public speech that extended to print, so it is understandable that the writers of mother's advice tracts, women who were essentially conforming to social expectations, were uneasy at transgressing the prohibition on writing and expressed this uneasiness in print, penning apologies and explanations for their temerity.

Indeed, some advice books by women remain in manuscript, while most of those that did reach print appeared only after the deaths of their authors. An example of the latter, Elizabeth Joceline's *Mother's Legacy to Her Unborn Child* (1624), provides an exquisitely poignant testimony to the sense of duty the writer felt for her child as well as to the dangers of childbirth in the early-modern period. Sent abroad by Joceline's grieving husband, to whom she had penned a touching prefatory letter, the work reached multiple editions in the century, in translation as well as in the original English. *The Mother's Blessing* (1616), a tract addressed by the widowed Dorothy Leigh to her three sons – its composition, she perhaps craftily suggests, the only means by which she could fulfill their father's injunction to educate them – also appeared after Leigh's death and also reached many editions. The highly interesting *Countess of Lincoln's Nursery* (1622), by Elizabeth Clinton, Dowager Countess of Lincoln, perhaps wrung fewer heartstrings with its highly emotional appeal to women that they breastfeed their children in order to raise them to virtue, and it was not reprinted.

As a group the advice books by mothers are particularly interesting when compared with contemporary advice books by fathers. Several such books are known in the period, those by William Cecil, Lord Burghley; Francis Osborne; Sir Walter Ralegh; and Richard Vaughan, Earl of Carbery, being perhaps the best known. Generally fathers writing in the genre make no apology for doing so; in fact they self-righteously preen themselves on taking such pains. Their children, they sometimes note, may not be ready for this good advice, but they express the hope that they will grow into it; certainly they will realize how well-meaning and kind their fathers are, even when their advice may not seem palatable.

The paternal advice books also adopt a much more secular viewpoint than their maternal counterparts. Indeed, this is a central difference since the woman writers often justify their writing on religious grounds. Given these grounds, the mothers could hardly provide nonreligious advice to their children, and in fact they show no desire to do so: their works are permeated with deep religious concern.

Such examples suggest that the genre in which Grymeston chose to write was loaded with a set of socially derived constraints based on the sex of the author, with two contrasting traditions: the strong, self-assured, and worldly masculine voice; and the weaker, hesitant, and religious feminine speaker. This contrast has led critic Elaine Beilin to suggest that Grymeston's introductory portrayal of herself as physically weak and dying is a clever rhetorical ploy. According to Beilin, the alleged physical weakness of the speaker disguises what is, in fact, "a strong mind, one that cleverly resolves the woman writer's chronic dilemma, how to possess 'masculine' knowledge and use 'masculine' language without sacrificing feminine virtue." Yet, while granting the rhetorical benefits of Grymeston's report of her physical condition, there is no reason for the reader to doubt the biographical veracity of her autobiographical introduction.

Another important distinction between the male and female writers of this genre is that the latter come from humbler ranks than the fathers whose advice books have survived, and less hard information about the women's lives is available; this is certainly true of Grymeston. Yet, despite the relative scarcity of corroborating biographical data, mother's advice books (inadvertently) provide the reader with a window into the minds of the women who composed them. The sentiments of Grymeston's *Miscelanea,* for example, are heavily Catholic. The first edition of the work is divided into fourteen chapters, largely concerned with religious topics. Citations of Catholic notables and martyrs, and quotations and paraphrases from the works of the church fathers are rife, as in the final chapter, comprising a collection of moral maxims and headed "Memoratives." Even more essential, Grymeston makes extensive use, particularly in chapter 11, the "Morning Meditation," of the poetry of her kinsman the Catholic poet Robert Southwell, who was martyred in 1595. And she also draws heavily on the *Odes in Imitation of the Seven Penitential Psalms,* by the Catholic poet Richard Rowlands (or Verstegan), in chapter 13 (19 in the subsequent, enlarged editions), which consists of Grymeston's versions of the seven odes. Grymeston has also been shown to be indebted to Robert Allott's *England's Parnassus* (1600) for many lines of poetry, and she may be indebted to Sir Hugh Plat's *Flores Patrum* (1594) for much of her prose.

Though the *Miscelanea* demonstrates Grymeston's great familiarity with a range of learned sources, particularly the poetry of Robert Southwell, it does not display her as a poet, as she is designated in the *Dictionary of National Biography*, since she did not originate any of the poetry she includes but instead altered existing verses to suit her meaning when she deemed this appropriate. Grymeston goes so far as to state clearly that she could not see the point in saying weakly what other writers had said better: "the spider's web is neither the better because woven out of his own breast, nor the bee's honey the worse for that gathered out of many flowers: neither could I ever brook to set down that haltingly in my broken style, which I found better expressed by a graver author." Paradoxically, in doing this she created for her son an amalgam that was, in her own words, "the true portraiture of thy mother's mind."

References:

Elaine Beilin, *Redeeming Eve: Women Writers of the English Renaissance* (Princeton: Princeton University Press, 1987), pp. 266–271;

Elizabeth Clinton, *Countess of Lincoln, Countess of Lincoln's Nursery* (Oxford: John Lichfield and James Short, 1622);

B. Y. Fletcher and Christine Sizemore, "Elizabeth Grymeston's *Miscelanea. Meditations. Memoratives:* Introduction and Selected Text," *University of Pennsylvania Library Chronicle,* 45, nos. 1–2 (1981): 53–83;

Dorothy Gardiner, *English Girlhood at School* (London: Oxford University Press, 1929);

Virgil B. Heltzel, "Richard Earl of Carbery's Advice to His Son," *Huntington Library Bulletin,* no. 11 (April 1937): 59–105;

Ruth Hughey, "Cultural Interests of Women in England, from 1524–1640, Indicated in the Writings of the Women," Ph.D. dissertation, Cornell University, 1932, pp. 66–77;

Hughey and Philip Hereford, "Elizabeth Grymeston and Her *Miscelanea,*" *Library,* fourth series 15 (June 1934): 61–91;

Elizabeth Joceline, *The Mother's Legacy to Her Unborn Child* (London: John Haviland, 1624);

Charlotte Kohler, "Elizabethan Woman of Letters: The Extent of Her Literary Activities," Ph.D. dissertation, University of Virginia, 1936;

Dorothy Leigh, *The Mother's Blessing* (London: For John Budge, 1616);

Mary R. Mahl and Helene Koon, "Elizabeth Grymeston, d. 1603," in *The Female Spectator: English Women Writers before 1800,* edited by Mahl and Koon (Bloomington: Indiana University Press, 1977), pp. 52–61;

Christine Sizemore, "Early Seventeenth-Century Advice Books: The Female Viewpoint," *South Atlantic Bulletin,* 41 (January 1976): 41–48;

Betty Travitsky, "The New Mother of the English Renaissance (1489–1659): A Descriptive Catalogue," *Bulletin of Research in the Humanities,* 82 (Spring 1979): 63–89;

Travitsky, "The New Mother of the English Renaissance: Her Writings on Motherhood," in *The Lost Tradition: Mothers and Daughters in Literature,* edited by C. N. Davidson and E. M. Broner (New York: Ungar, 1979), pp. 33–43;

Travitsky, ed., *Paradise of Women: Writings by Englishwomen of the Renaissance* (Westport, Conn.: Greenwood, 1981), pp. 51–55;

Foster Watson, *Vives and the Renaissance Education of Women* (London: Edward Arnold, 1912);

Rachel Weigall, "An Elizabethan Gentlewoman," *Quarterly Review,* 215 (1911): 119–138;

Louis B. Wright, ed., *Advice to a Son: Precepts of Lord Burleigh, Sir Walter Raleigh, and Francis Osborn* (Ithaca, N.Y.: Cornell University Press, 1962).

Everard Guilpin

(circa 1572 – after 1608?)

D. Allen Carroll
University of Tennessee, Knoxville

BOOKS: *Skialetheia. Or, A Shadowe of Truth, in Certaine Epigrams and Satyres,* anonymous (London: Printed by James Roberts for Nicholas Ling, 1598);

The Whipper of the Satyre His Pennance in a White Sheete: Or, The Beadles Confutation, anonymous (London: Printed [by William White] for Thomas Pavier, 1601).

Editions: *Skialetheia. Or, A Shadowe of Truth, in Certaine Epigrams and Satyres,* edited by John Payne Collier (London, 1870);

Skialetheia of Edward Guilpin. (1598), edited by Alexander B. Grosart (Blackburn, U.K: Printed for the subscribers by C. E. Simms, 1878);

Skialetheia, 1598, edited by George Bagshawe Harrison (London: Published for the Shakespeare Association by H. Milford, Oxford University Press, 1931);

"The Whipper of the Satyre His Pennance," in *The Whipper Pamphlets, 1601,* 2 volumes, edited by Arnold Davenport (Liverpool, U.K.: University Press of Liverpool, 1951), II: 35–49;

Skialetheia. Or, A Shadowe of Truth, in Certaine Epigrams and Satyres, edited by D. Allen Carroll (Chapel Hill: University of North Carolina Press, 1974).

Everard (sometimes Edward) Guilpin (sometimes Gilpin) is remembered primarily as the writer of *Skialetheia; Or, A Shadow of Truth, in Certain Epigrams and Satires* (1598), a collection of seventy epigrams and seven formal verse satires modeled after Martial and Juvenal, the major classical influences, respectively, on Elizabethan epigram and satire. In accounts of formal verse satire in England, Guilpin ranks just behind John Donne, Joseph Hall, and John Marston; in studies of the influence of Martial he is grouped with John Harington, John Davies (to whose epigrams his are related, perhaps indebted), and Ben Jonson. Although published anonymously, *Skialetheia* can readily be attributed to Guilpin because excerpts in the anthology *England's Parnassus*

(1600) carry his initials. He had connections with Donne and Marston, both of whose satires are quite like those in *Skialetheia.* Donne dedicated a verse letter "To Mr. E. G.," and Marston, whose uncle seems to have been Guilpin's stepfather, dedicated "To his very friend, Master E. G." a poem that attacks the satirist Hall. *Skialetheia* sounds that peculiarly negative, melancholic, and malicious note that is associated with the late 1590s, with all of these verse satirists, with Jonson's *Humour* plays, and with William Shakespeare's *Hamlet* (1603). While some of the material in the book may have been written early in the 1590s, certain allusions make it impossible for it to have been finished until a few weeks before publication.

Guilpin's family apparently resided for a while in Highgate, just north of London, and later in Bungay, Suffolk, where they had relatives. He matriculated at Emmanuel College, Cambridge, in 1588; in 1591, presumably without a degree, he went to Gray's Inn of the Inns of Court.

Guilpin seems to have participated at the turn of the century in what Arnold Davenport has labeled the Hall-Marston-Guilpin-Jonson-[John] Weever-[Nicholas] Breton quarrels." His contribution was a defense of satire in an unsigned pamphlet, *The Whipper of the Satire His Penance* (1601), which reacted to a pamphlet by "W. I." (Weever?) attacking him as the "Epigrammatist" and Marston as the "Satirist." After the turn of the century he seems to have settled in Boyscott, Suffolk, where he married in 1607.

Guilpin is identified with that extraordinary set of young men who came from the universities in the 1590s to the Inns of Court to study law and to find preferment at court. They were well educated, of fairly good families, ambitious, quick-witted, frustrated, active almost the point of desperation, and became quickly and thoroughly skilled in the ways of city and court. *Skialetheia* is a product of the limited world of the Inns, with its special values and sensibilities. For these young men writing was a form of self-advertisement, though Guilpin, so far as is known, never received a position in the government.

Skialetheia was one of several books that were considered socially disruptive, called in, and burned by the archbishop of Canterbury, John Whitgift, in June 1599. The epigrams, approximately a third of which are based on Martial, treat subjects traditional with epigrammatists such as loose women, absurd fashions, dishonest lawyers and merchants, fops, eccentrics, and poetasters, and do so under conventional type-names such as Lais, Clodius, Matho, Licus, and Naevia. Some are especially topical, such as number 68 with its list of London sights and sounds; number 8, "To Deloney"; and number 24, "Of Fuscus" (who is probably Thomas Nashe). All give the impression not of Martial's Rome but of Elizabeth's London. Epigram 40 is typical:

Naevia is one while of the Inns of Court,
Toiling in *Brooke, Fitzherbert,* and in *Dyer* :
Another while th'Exchange he doth resort,
Moiling as fast, a seller, and a buyer:
    Will not he thrive (think ye) who can devise,
    Thus to unite the law and merchandise?
    Doubtless he will, or cozen out of doubt;
    What matter's that? His law will bear him out.

The Satiric Prelude (*Satyre Preludium*), on poets and poetry, attacks contemporary tastes and particular works by defending epigram and satire as literary forms. Satire 1, on hypocrisy, lashes out at the times in general, listing various guises of hypocrisy. Satire 2 describes cosmetics and details the horror of their effects. Satire 3, on inconstancy, attacks one overly fashionable former friend in particular and others in passing. Satire 4, on jealousy, portrays the jealous husband's antics and exposes his own guilt. Satire 5, on vanity, presents in the form of a city walk the variety of vanities to be met in the streets of London. Satire 6, on opinion, the most philosophical of the satires, attacks the sway this inferior function has over reason in Guilpin's time.

The most obvious feature of the book is its tone – the angry, crude, sputtering voice of the satirist, who was thought to be related to the half-man, half-goat satyr. In Guilpin the satirist is by turns a beadle with whip and cord, a Puritan lecturer, a fencer with rapier in his fist, a foul-mouthed jester, and a physician who "heals with lashing." The satirist points out as many depravities as possible, categorizes them, and castigates them. Usually, though not always, some irony is generated because the satirist himself is susceptible to the very sins he sees in others. Satire 1, for example, ends:

SKIALETHEIA.
OR,
A shadowe of Truth, in certaine Epigrams and Satyres.

At London,
Printed by I. R. for Nicholas Ling, and are to bee solde at the little West doore of Poules. 1598.

Title page for Everard Guilpin's book of epigrams and verse satires

Methinks already I applaud my self,
For nettle-stinging thus this fairy elf:
And though my conscience says I merit not
Such dear reward, dissembling yet (God wot)
I hunt for praise, and do the same expect:
Scoffs make me know myself, I must not err,
Better a wretch than a dissembler.

Partly in reaction to the ease and sweetness of Elizabethan lyricism, Guilpin, like Hall, Donne, and Marston, deliberately renders the style of this satirist especially harsh. Epigram 70 shows this sense of a difference in style:

I know they are passing filthy, scurvey lines,
I know they are rude, harsh, unsavory rimes;
Fit to wrap plaisters, and odd unguents in . . . .

The lines are also, as part of the method, more or less obscure and hard to read, with abrupt shifts in syntax, exclamations, ambiguous expressions, frequent allusions and puns, suppressed transitions, questions, and so on. But a reader with some patience can get on; the lines do scan and make sense.

They are, moreover, frequently what Elizabethans would call obscene, using bawdy words to describe bawdy situations, and turn often to excretory bodily functions. "How your tongue rioted in bawdry, I am ashamed to rehearse," W. I. complains against "the Epigrammatist." Perhaps it was this salacity more than anything else that caused the archbishop to burn the book.

The book is, finally, filled with references to real places and people of the day. There are scores of London place-names and other details of the times, so that *Skialetheia* is often quoted by editors of other, more significant works of the 1590s for purposes of elucidation. The book makes explicit reference to Geoffrey Chaucer, John Gower, Edmund Spenser, Sir Philip Sidney, Michael Drayton, Samuel Daniel, Gervase Markham, and Thomas Deloney; it seems to allude to Nashe, Davies, Christopher Marlowe, Thomas Lodge, and Gabriel Harvey; and it probably alludes to many others whom contemporaries could recognize, or thought they could, which was no doubt part of its appeal. Modern readers need a better sense of the kinds of codes used in such allusions so that they can understand more of what goes on in this book; Satire 3, for example, is almost certainly an extended attack on Francis Davison. Guilpin's preoccupation with his craft and fellow craftsmen has made the book a valuable resource for literary scholars interested in the late sixteenth century.

References:

Christopher P. Baker, "Francis Davison and Guilpin's 'Satire III,' " *Etudes Anglaises,* 31 (July–December 1978): 360–362;

R. E. Bennett, "John Donne and Everard Gilpin," *Review of English Studies,* 15 (January 1939): 66–72;

R. E. Brettle, "Everard Guilpin and John Marston (1576–1634)," *Review of English Studies,* new series 16 (1965): 396–399;

Arnold Davenport, "The Quarrel of the Satirists," *Modern Language Review,* 37 (April 1942): 123–130;

Philip J. Finkelpearl, "Donne and Everard Gilpin," *Review of English Studies,* new series 14 (1963): 164–167;

M. Thomas Hester, " 'All the players': Guilpin and 'Prester *Iohn*' Donne," *South Atlantic Review,* 49 (January 1984): 3–17;

Alvin Kernan, *The Cankered Muse* (New Haven: Yale University Press, 1959);

Francis Meres, "Wit's Treasury (1598)," in *Elizabethan Critical Essays,* 2 volumes, edited by G. Gregory Smith (Oxford: Clarendon Press, 1904), II: 308–324;

John Peter, *Complaint and Satire in Early English Literature* (Oxford: Oxford University Press, 1956).

Edward Hake

(flourished 1566 – 1604)

Luke Wilson
Ohio State University

BOOKS: *A Touchestone for This Time Present, Expresly Declaring Such Ruines, Enormities, and Abuses as Trouble the Churche of God and Our Christian Common Wealth at This Daye. Wherevnto Is Annexed a Perfect Rule to Be Obserued of All Parents and Scholemaisters, in the Trayning vp of Their Schollers and Children in Learning* (London: Printed by [William Williamson for] Thomas Hacket, 1574);

A Commemoration of the Most Prosperous and Peaceable Raigne of Our Gratious and Deere Soueraign Lady Elizabeth by the Grace of God of England, Fraunce and Irelande, Queen, &c. Now Newly Set Foorth This .xvii. Day of Nouember, Beyng the First Day of the .xviii. Yeare of Her Maiesties Sayd Raigne (London: Printed by William How for Richard Johnes, 1575); enlarged as *A Joyfull Continuance of the Commemoration of the Reigne of Elizabeth. Now Newly Enlarged With an Exhortation Applied to This Present Time* (London: Printed for Richard Jhones, 1578);

Newes out of Powles Churchyarde Now Newly Renued and Amplifued according to the Accidents of the Present Time, 1579, and Otherwise Entituled, Syr Nummus. Written in English Satyrs (London: Printed by Iohn Charlewood & Richard Ihones, 1579);

An Oration Conteyning an Expostulation aswell with the Queenes Highnesse Faithfull Subjects for Their Want of Due Consideration of Gods Blessings Enijoyed by Means of Her Maiestie: As Also with the Vnnaturall English for Their Disloyaltie and Vnkindnesse towards the Same Their Soueraygne. At the First Pronounced vpon the Queens Maiesties Birthday (London: Printed [by Thomas Orwin] for Edward Aggas, 1587);

Of Golds Kingdome, and This Vnhelping Age. Described in Sundry Poems Intermixedly Placed after Certaine Other Poems of More Speciall Respect: And before the Same Is an Oration or Speech Intended to Haue Bene Deliuered by the Author Hereof vnto the Kings Maiesty (London: Printed by Iohn Windet, 1604);

Epieikeia: A Dialogue on Equity in Three Parts, edited by D. E. C. Yale, Yale Law Library Publications, no. 13 (New Haven: Yale University Press, 1953).

Editions: "A Commemoration of the Most Prosperous and Peaceable Raigne of Our Gratious and Deere Soveraigne Lady Elizabeth," edited by Thomas Park, in *The Harleian Miscellany,* volume 9, edited by William Oldys (London: Printed for R. Dutton, 1809), pp. 123–139;

"An Oration Conteyning an Expostulation," in John Nichols, *The Progresses and Public Processions of Queen Elizabeth,* volume 2 (London: Printed by John Nichols, 1823), pp. 460–480;

Newes out of Powles Churchyarde. Written in English Satyrs. Accurately Reprinted fro the Excessively Rare Edition of 1579 in the Possession of Sir Charles Isham, Bart., edited by Charles Edmonds (London: Sotheran, Baer, 1872);

A Touchstone for This Time Presently Declaring Such Ruines, Enormities, and Abuses as Trouble the Churche of God, The English Experience, no. 663 (Amsterdam: Theatrum Orbis Terrarum, 1974; Norwood, N. J.: Johnson, 1974).

OTHER: Desiderius Erasmus, *One Dialogue, or Colloquye of Erasmus (Entituled Diuersoria) Translated oute of Latten into Englyshe: And Imprinted, to the Ende That the Judgement of the Learned Maye Be Hadde before the Translator Procede in thereste,* translated by Hake (London: Printed and sold by William Griffyth, 1566); republished in *The Earliest English Translations of Erasmus' Colloquia, 1536–1566: Two Dyaloges, A Mery Dialogue, Ye Pylgremage of Pure Deuotyon, Diuersoria,* edited by Henry de Vocht (Louvain: Librarie Universitaire, Uystpruyst, 1928); republished as *One Dialogue or Colloquye: London 1566,* The English Experience, no. 244 (Amsterdam: Theatrum Orbis Terrarum, 1970; New York: Da Capo, 1970);

Thomas à Kempis[?], *The Imitation or Following of Christ, and the Contemning of Worldly Vanities: At*

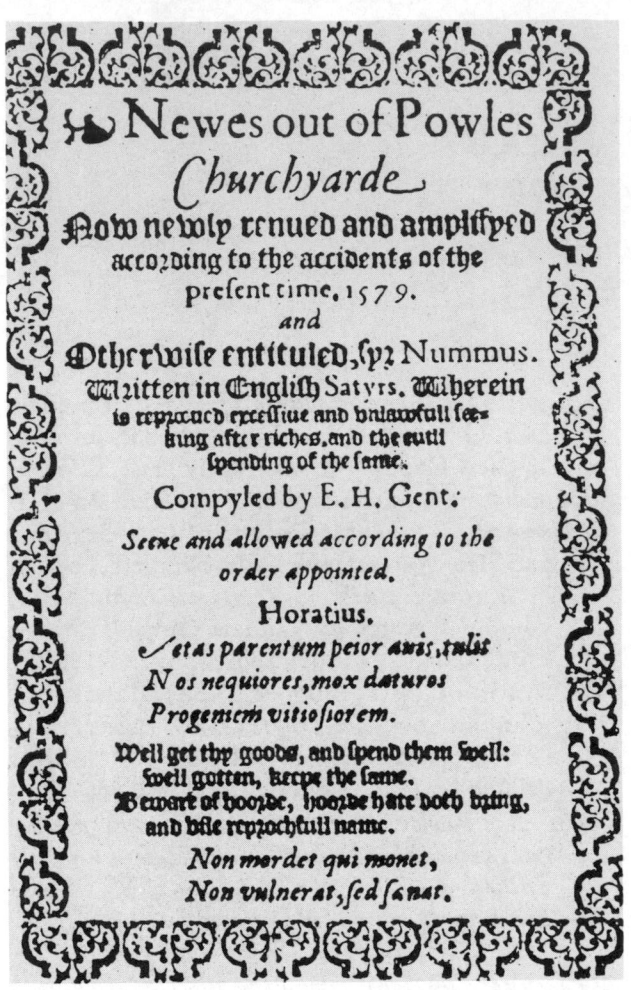

Title page for the first extant edition of Edward Hake's series of
eight verse satires

Hake produced a wide variety of other works: at least one other volume of poems, encomiastic verses on Queen Elizabeth, prose condemnations of contemporary social abuses, and translations of a work by Desiderius Erasmus and one attributed to Thomas à Kempis. A practicing lawyer who had studied law at Barnard's and Gray's Inns, Hake is also of interest to legal historians as the author of a legal treatise, *Epieikeia* (1953), that is a unique source of information about late-sixteenth-century conceptions of Chancery and common-law equity.

Almost nothing is known of Hake's parentage. A 1581 entry in the *Calendar of the Patent Rolls* records that in that year Isabel Hake, widow, and her son Edward Hake leased property in the lordship of Clewer, adjacent to New Windsor, Berkshire. Thus, Hake's family may have resided near New Windsor, and it is possible that Hake was born there; he did spend much of his life there, holding various posts in city government. He was educated by the schoolmaster John Hopkins, who was well known for his translation with Thomas Sternhold of the Psalms. Hake's last published work appeared in 1604, but he was still alive in 1608, when his signature appears in court pleadings.

Record of Hake's literary career begins with the appearance in 1566 of his translation – the first into English – *One Dialogue or Colloquy of Erasmus (Entitled Diversoria)*. A satirical comparison of French and German inns, *Diversoria* is the eighth of the ten colloquies by Erasmus that were published as *Familiarium colloquiorum formulae* in 1523. Also in 1566 William Griffith, who had already published the *Diversoria*, entered in the Stationers' Register *A Most Delectable Conference between the Wedded Life and the Single*, "by master Henry Hake." Edward Hake was probably meant, but the work is lost and nothing else is known about it. Hake's *Merry Meeting of Maids in London*, also lost, was entered in the Stationers' Register in 1567; it is mentioned in a poem by John Long prefixed to the 1579 edition of *News out of Paul's Churchyard*. A response to Hake's work, *A Letter Sent by Maidens of London* (1567), suggests that Hake's book was a rather ungenerous attack on the moral conduct of London's female servant class.

In 1567 also appeared the first edition, now lost, of *News out of Paul's Churchyard*, as well as *The Imitation or Following of Christ*, Hake's translation of *De imitatione Christi* (1426), usually attributed to Thomas à Kempis. Hake's translation was republished in 1568 with the addition of "Another Pretty Treatise Entitled The Perpetual Rejoice of the Godly, Even in This Life." Both editions bear the same dedication to Thomas Howard, Duke of Nor-

the First Written by Thomas Kempise a Dutchman, Amended and Polished by Sebastianus Castalio, an Italian, and Englished by E. H., translated by Hake (London: Printed by Henry Denham, 1567); enlarged as *The Imitation or Following of Christ, and the Contemning of Worldly Vanities: Whereunto as Springing out of the Same Roote We Haue Adioyned Another Pretie Treatise, Entituled, The Perpetuall Reioyce of the Godly, Even in This Lyfe* (London: Printed by Henry Denham, 1568);

The Whole Booke of Psalms, Collected into Englysh Metre, translated by Thomas Sternhold, W. Whitington, and John Hopkins, edited by Hake, music by William Damon (London: Printed by John Daye, 1579).

Edward Hake, satirist, poet, lawyer, and Puritan, is best known as the author of *News out of Paul's Churchyard*, a series of eight energetic satires first published in 1567 in an edition that is now lost. But

folk, who was executed in 1572 at the urging of Robert Dudley, Earl of Leicester, for communicating with Mary, Queen of Scots.

During this early period of remarkable productivity, which in the preface to the 1579 edition of *News out of Paul's Churchyard* he refers to as his "childish years," Hake studied law in the Inns of Chancery – presumably at Barnard's Inn, from which he dates the epistle to his *Commemoration of . . . Elizabeth* (1575). In *News out of Paul's Churchyard* he speaks of having spent his first three years at the Inns of Chancery "about a dozen years" before; he may thus have been associated with Barnard's for as long as eleven years.

Hake's work attracted mockery in print from George Turberville, who in his translation of Dominicus Mancinus's *A Plain Path to Perfect Virtue* (1568) puns on his name:

> I neither write the News of Paul's
> > Of late set out to sale,
> Nor Meeting of the London Maids,
> > For now that fish is stale.

Evidently Hake's work was well enough known at least to earn contempt. Perhaps the "fish" (Hake) was stale both because the popularity of *News out of Paul's Churchyard* had already peaked and because *A Letter Sent by Maidens of London* had demolished the moralistic pretensions of his *Merry Meeting of Maids in London*.

Hake's *A Touchstone for This Time Present* (1574), dedicated to "Edward Godfrey, Merchant," is a cranky prose polemic directed against social maladies vaguely associated by the Puritan mind with the evils of popery. It assails the misgovernment of the church, the miseducation of girls, and the evils of face painting and intemperate dancing. Appended to the work is an abridged verse rendering of Erasmus's *De pueris statim ac liberaliter instituendis declamatio* (1529); written in heptameters, it is a dialogue between Philopas and Chrisippus. In the dedication to John Harlowe, whom Hake calls a fellow pupil under Hopkins, Hake says that, having recently become an attorney, he had resolved by intensive study of the law to save himself from the disrepute associated with that rank, but, being "tied unto solitariness in the country" on account of his marriage, decided to exercise his mind by undertaking the translation instead. This is the earliest indication that Hake was married; a suit filed jointly in 1603 shows that his wife at that time was named Joan. It was in 1574, too, that Hake garnered the only praise he is known to have received in print from a contemporary: Richard Robinson, in his *Reward of Wickedness* (1574), commends Hake, John Studley, and William Fulwood for their "stately style."

Hake's *A Commemoration of . . . Elizabeth* was published in 1575 and enlarged in 1578 as *A Joyful Continuance of the Commemoration . . . of Elizabeth*. Dedicated to Edward Eliott, the queen's surveyor in Essex, the work consists of heptameter quatrains addressed to Elizabeth, with some additional pentameter quatrains addressed to her counselors and a prose meditation thanking God for the nation's prosperity. By the time the enlarged edition appeared Hake was involved in the local government of New Windsor. According to the *Annals of Windsor* he was appointed deputy steward in 1576, though when he commenced his duties is unclear. He was serving as recorder in September 1576 and in June 1578 as bailiff.

A revised edition of *News out of Paul's Churchyard* appeared in 1579, dedicated to Leicester, whom Hake had praised in *A Commemoration of . . . Elizabeth*. The foremost literary patron of Elizabeth's early reign and the recipient of dedication from writers including Turberville, Arthur Golding, Edmund Spenser, and John Stow, Leicester since 1567 had become for tactical reasons a supporter of Puritan causes. *News out of Paul's Churchyard* begins with an address to the reader, verses by Long and Richard Matthews, and some pentameter lines by "The Author to the Carping and Scornful Sycophant" in which Hake disclaims any intent to slander and lashes out at the papists for their hostile reception of the first edition.

News out of Paul's Churchyard shows Hake as a satirist in the tradition of William Langland, Robert Crowley, and George Gascoigne. Its eight dialogues, in lively and alliterative heptameter couplets, attack contemporary versions of those figures that had, since the fourteenth-century *Piers Plowman*, attributed to Langland, formed the butt of domestic satire in the medieval mode. Hake's central premise, that the profit motive is at the root of most social ills, is a familiar one; and it may be fairly said, as Hallet Smith does, that he "never moves very far from the economic and social phenomena of the time, bringing to bear upon them a Christian, Protestant, common-man indignation."

The satires are organized as dialogues between Bertulph and Paul, who meet in the aisle at Saint Paul's Cathedral and fall into a discussion, overheard by the poet, of corrupted justices and greedy pettifoggers; stingy, clotheshorse quack physicians; conspicuous consumers headed for penury and crime; bawds; brokers; and usurers. In satire 6 Hake deplores the desecration of Saint Paul's by licentious talk and by papists plotting insurrection in the south aisle. Hypocritical Catholics elicit his most vehement and alliterative versifying, often with unintentionally comic effect: "O . . . *Janus* Jacks and double-faced dogs, O

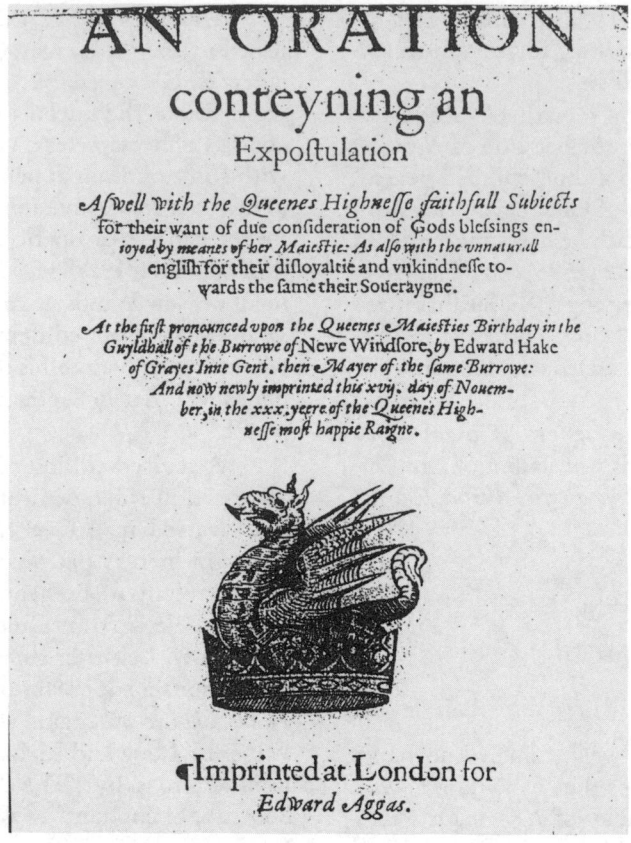

AN ORATION conteyning an Expostulation

Aſwell with the Queenes Highneſſe ꝼaithfull Subiects for their want of due conſideration of Gods bleſsings enioyed by meanes of her Maieſtie: As alſo with the vnnaturall engliſh for their diſloyaltie and vnkindneſſe towards the ſame their Soueraygne.

At the firſt pronounced vpon the Queenes Maieſties Birthday in the Guyldhall of the Burrowe of Newe Windſore, by Edward Hake of Grayes Inne Gent. then Mayer of the ſame Burrowe: And now newly imprinted this xvij. day of Nouember, in the xxx. yeere of the Queenes Highneſſe moſt happie Raigne.

¶Imprinted at London for Edward Aggas.

Title page for the printed version of the speech in which Hake reproached the English for their ingratitude to Queen Elizabeth I's government and denounced what he perceived as Catholic threats to national security

wily winking wizard wolves, O grunting, groaning hogs." Hake's enthusiastic description of the merchant-gourmand's feast in satire 4 illustrates the proximity, for the Puritan temperament, of pleasure and disgust:

> Both capon, swan, and heronsew good, fast bittern, lark and quail:
> Right plover, snipe, and woodcock fine, with curlew, wipe and rail:
> Stonetivets, teal, and peckteals good, with bustard fat and plum,
> Fat pheasant, pout, and plover base, for them that after come.
> Stint, stockard, stampine, tanterveal, and widgeon of the best:
> Puyt, partridge, blackbird and fat shoveller with the rest.
> . . . .
>
> He must foresee that he ne lack cold bakemeats in the end:
> With custards, tarts, and florentines, the banquet to amend.
> And (to be short and knit it up) he must not wanting see

> Strange kinds of fish at second course to come in their degree,
> As porpoise, seal, and salmon good with sturgeon of the best,
> And turbot, lobster, and the like to furnish out the feast.
> All this they'll have, and else much more, 'sides marchpane and green cheese,
> Stewed wardens, prunes, and sweet conserves with spiced wine like lees,
> Greenginger, sucket, sugar plate, and marmaladie fine:
> Blanched almonds, pears, and ginger. . . .

Hake's incessant harangues work best when, as here, though somewhat mechanical, they disclose a pleasure in words that outruns any strict moral intention.

Also in 1579 appeared *The Whole Book of Psalms, Collected into English Metre,* with a preface by Hake and set to music by his friend William Damon. The text is that of Sternhold's translation of Psalms, on which Hake's old schoolmaster Hopkins had collaborated; but some of the translations are by a J. Hake, who might be Hake's wife, Joan.

By 1586 Hake was mayor of New Windsor. The *Annals of Windsor* records his performance of various duties, among them offering acts to pave the town's streets and build a new market house, and relates that "at the pitiful complaint of divers of the commonality of this town for the redress of the smallness of the market bushel, Edward Hake, gentleman, then mayor, travelled to Greenwich and thence to Westminster divers journeys till he found the Clerk of the Market, carrying with him the brazen gallon, and obtained the amending of the bushel." On the queen's arrival in New Windsor on 10 August 1586 he welcomed her with a short speech; on 7 September, her birthday, he delivered in the town's Guildhall *An Oration Containing an Expostulation* (1587). Dedicated to Lady Anne, Countess of Warwick – the wife of Ambrose Dudley, elder brother of the earl of Leicester – *An Oration Containing an Expostulation* reproaches the English for their ingratitude toward Elizabeth's government and, apparently with reference to the Babington conspiracy uncovered a month before, denounces Catholic threats to national security. The title page describes Hake as a member of Gray's Inn, and while there is no record of his admission, he probably belonged; Barnard's was a feeder school for Gray's, and in proceeding there Hake would have followed a timeworn path. The *Pension Book of Gray's Inn* records that he contributed to "the building of the gate" in 1593.

In 1588 Hake was elected member of Parliament for New Windsor. The Commons journal for this period is lost, and there is no way to know what part he may have taken during the debates. Parliament was dissolved on 29 March 1589, and Hake was not reelected.

In the nineteenth century Thomas Warton apparently saw a work by Hake, published in 1588, titled *The Touchstone of Wits;* he quotes Hake's praise in that work of William Baldwin's *A Mirror for Magistrates* (1559). But no contemporary reference to such a work by Hake has been found, and no copy of it is known to exist.

Hake's sole legal work, *Epieikeia: A Dialogue on Equity in Three Parts,* remained unpublished until 1953, but Hake presented it in manuscript both to James I in 1603 and to the prominent lawyer Sir Julius Caesar in 1597. A letter from Hake to Caesar in 1603 indicates that Lord Chancellor Thomas Egerton had read *Epieikeia* and commended its author, as had Chief Justice Edmund Anderson, Justice Thomas Walmesley, and Edward Bruce, Lord Kinloss, Master of the Rolls. (Hake had been acquainted with Egerton at least as early as 1600, when he signed an entry in the *Calendar of the Patent Rolls* indicating that he knew the parties in a legal

transaction, including Egerton, the antiquarian and legal historian William Lambarde, and Richard Temple, who had been mayor of New Windsor in 1581.) Modeled on Christopher Saint German's *Dialogues between a Doctor of Divinity and a Student* (1530), *Epieikeia* is a dialogue among three characters called Hake, Lovelace, and Eliott. Lovelace may refer to Richard Lovelace, whom Hake praises in a poem in *Of Gold's Kingdom* (1604), and Eliott may have been suggested by Edward Eliott, to whom Hake had dedicated *A Commemoration of . . . Elizabeth.*

Epieikeia preceded the emergence of jurisdictional friction between the Chancery and the common-law courts, but it is nevertheless of great interest as a source of information about equity and the Chancery in the 1590s. It also shows Hake ruminating on the relation between his legal career and his poetic vocation, as he had in *A Commemoration of . . . Elizabeth* and was to do again in *Of Gold's Kingdom.* To illustrate the operation of equity, for example, *Epieikeia* includes a poem directed to judges that contrasts theft motivated by need and that motivated by covetousness. Hake's attempts to synthesize legal thought and poetic practice compare usefully to Abraham Fraunce's much more ambitious undertaking in *The Lawyer's Logic* (1588).

Of Gold's Kingdom, dedicated to Edward Vaughn, is a remarkably diverse collection of poems ostensibly organized around the theme that had dominated *News out of Paul's Churchyard,* namely, the pernicious influence of money over human behavior. The poems in fact vary widely in subject, length, and verse form and cover a wide range of genres: verse fable, counsel for the king, satire, encomium, and lyric. The best of them are short, modest poems in the plain style of Turberville, Gascoigne, and Barnabe Googe. "A carefull debtor," for example, combines epigrammatic terseness with a vague and charming melancholy reminiscent of the lyrics of Sir Thomas Wyatt:

> I live in debt, yet love not to do so,
> I pay no debt, but not because I would not:
> ' Tis debt's disease that breedeth all my woe,
> It kills my heart (alas) because I could not.
> But hence I go to seek some change of soil
> Whereby to pay my debt with body's toil.

In the same mode is "Though wit be the woer, Yet gold is the speeder." "Of one near dead through thought" shows an attempt to negotiate plain and ornate styles; Hake begins to develop a conceit involving the paradox of thought as its own murderer but abandons it in the second stanza, reverting to his usual simplicity.

> Thought is a secret that doth kill
> And with the dead itself doth die,
> As with his ruin *Sampson* fell
> Himself and with him all perdie,
> And is not my poor case much nigh,
> Near dead through thought both Thought and I?
>
> I thought no Thought could have prevaild
> Against my cheereful mind,
> But cross with cross hath so assailed,
> That now not so I find:
>   For Thought is come and joy is gone,
>   The body pines and death draws on.

Over the course of his career Hake made signal contributions in a wide range of endeavors. His earliest known work, the translation of Erasmus's *Diversoria,* earns him a place in the history of the English reception of humanist thought. The satires in *News out of Paul's Churchyard,* through which he first came to wide public notice, were among the earliest of the period; they exhibit admirable vigor, even if their moralistic griping is at times too dreary for modern taste. Hake's skill as a lyric poet in *Of Gold's Kingdom* has not received the attention it deserves; and while his legal skills can hardly be compared with those of the great jurists of the age, his *Epieikeia* supplies an unparalleled account of late-sixteenth-century thinking on equity, a concept central to Renaissance jurisprudence, at the same time as it offers a striking glimpse into the conceptual and institutional interconnections between the literary and legal enterprises.

References:

John Payne Collier, *A Bibliographical and Critical Account of the Rarest Books in the English Language,* 3 volumes (New York: Francis, 1866), II: 103–113, 267–272; III: 330–335;

Mark Eccles, "Brief Lives: Tudor and Stuart Authors," *Studies in Philology,* 79 (Fall 1982): 58–59;

R. J. Fehrenbach, "*A Letter sent by the Maydens of London* (1567)," *English Literary Renaissance,* 14 (Autumn 1984): 285–304;

Reginald J. Fletcher, ed., *The Pension Book of Gray's Inn,* volume 1 (London: Chiswick, 1901), p. 99;

James E. Ruoff, *Crowell's Handbook of Elizabethan and Stuart Literature* (New York: Crowell, 1975), p. 370;

Hallet Smith, *Elizabethan Poetry: A Study in Conventions, Meaning, and Expressions* (Cambridge, Mass.: Harvard University Press, 1952), pp. 215–216;

Robert Richard Tighe, ed., *Annals of Windsor, Being a History of the Castle and Town, with Some Account of Eton and Places Adjacent,* volume 2 (London: Longman, Brown, Green, Longmans & Roberts, 1858), pp. 643, 648, 650, 653–655, 660;

Thomas Warton, *History of English Poetry from the Twelfth to the Close of the Sixteenth Century,* volume 4, edited by W. Carew Hazlitt (London: Reeves & Turner, 1871; reprinted, Hildesheim, Germany: Olms, 1968), pp. 203, 249, 305.

Papers:

Two manuscript copies of Edward Hake's *Epieikeia* are in the British Museum (Additional MS. No. 35,326, fol. 2; Lansdowne MS. No. 161, fol. 103). The British Museum also possesses a transcript of Hake's *Commemoration of . . . Elizabeth* (Additional MS. No. 30,370, fol. 34), an extract from his preface to the *Book of Psalms* (Additional MS. 6,193, fol. 64), and a series of letters from Hake (Lansdowne MS. No. 161, fols. 19, 42, 101, 233, 247; Additional MS. No. 12,503, fol. 47).

Richard Hakluyt

(1552? – 23 November 1616)

Mary C. Fuller
Massachusetts Institute of Technology

WORKS: *Divers Voyages Touching the Discoueie of America, and the Ilands Adiacent vnto the Same, Made First of All by Our Englishmen, and Afterward by the Frenchmen and Britons: And Certaine Notes of Aduertisements for Obseruations, Necessarie for Such as Shall Heereafter Make the Like Attempt, with Two Mappes Annexed Heereunto for the Plainer Vnderstanding of the Whole Matter,* edited by Hakluyt (London: Printed by Thomas Dawson for Thomas Woodcocke, 1582);

René de Laudonnière, *A Notable Historie Containing Foure Voyages Made by Certayne French Captaynes vnto Florida,* translated by Hakluyt (London: Printed by Thomas Dawson, 1587);

Pietro Martire d'Anghiera, *De orbe novo Petri Martyris Anglerii Mediolanensis,* edited by Hakluyt (Paris: Guilliam Awray, 1587);

The Principall Navigations, Voiages and Discoueries of the English Nation, Made by Sea and Ouer Land, to the Most Remote and Farthest Distant Quarters of the Earth at Any Time within the Compasse of These 1500. Yeeres: Deuided into Three Seuerall Parts, according to the Positions of the Regions whereunto They Were Directed . . . Whereunto Is Added the Last Most Renowned English Nauigation, round about the Whole Globe of the Earth, edited by Hakluyt (London: Printed by George Bishop & Ralph Newberie, 1589); revised and enlarged as *The Principal Navigations, Voiages, Traffiqves and Discoueries of the English Nation, Made by Sea or Ouer-Land, to the Remote and Farthest Distant Quarters of the Earth, at Any Time within the Compasse of These 1500. Yeeres: Deuided into Three Seuerall Volumes, according to the Positions of the Regions, whereunto They Were Directed,* 3 volumes (London: Printed by George Bishop, Ralph Newberie & Robert Barker, 1598-1600);

Antonio Galvano, *The Discoveries of the World from Their First Originall vnto the Yeere of Our Lord 1555,* edited and translated by Hakluyt (London: Printed by George Bishop, 1601);

Ferdinando de Soto, *Virginia Richly Valued, by the Description of the Maine Land of Florida, Her Next Neighbour,* translated by Hakluyt (London: Printed by Felix Kyngston for Matthew Lownes, 1609); republished as *The Worthye and Famous History, of the Travailes, Discovery, and Conquest of That Great Continent Terra Florida* (London: Printed for Matthew Lownes, 1611); edited by William B. Rye as *The Discovery and Conquest of Terra Florida* (London: Printed for the Hakluyt Society, 1851);

A Discourse on Western Planting, Written in the Year 1584, edited by Charles Deane, introduction by Leonard Woods (Cambridge, Mass.: Press of J. Wilson & Son, 1877).

Editions: *Divers Voyages Touching the Discovery of America and the Islands Adjacent,* edited by John Winter Jones (London: Printed for the Hakluyt Society, 1850);

The Principal Navigations, Voyages, Traffiques, and Discoveries of the English Nation, 16 volumes, edited by Edmund Goldschmid (Edinburgh: Goldschmid, 1885-1890);

The Principal Navigations, Voyages, Traffiques & Discoveries of the English Nation, Made by Sea or Overland to the Remote and Farthest Distant Corners of the Earth at Any Time within the Compass of These 1600 Yeeres, 12 volumes (Glasgow: Maclehose, 1903-1905);

The Original Writings and Correspondences of the Two Richard Hakluyts, edited by E. G. R. Taylor (London: Printed for the Hakluyt Society, 1935);

The Principall Navigations, Voiages and Discoveries of the English Nation, made by Sea and Ouer Land, to the Most Remote and Farthest Distant Quarters of the Earth at Any Time within the Compasse of These 1500. Yeeres: Deuided into Three Seuerall Parts, according to the Positions of the Regions whereunto They Were Directed . . . Whereunto Is Added the Last Most Renowned English Nauigation, round about the Whole Globe of the Earth, introduction

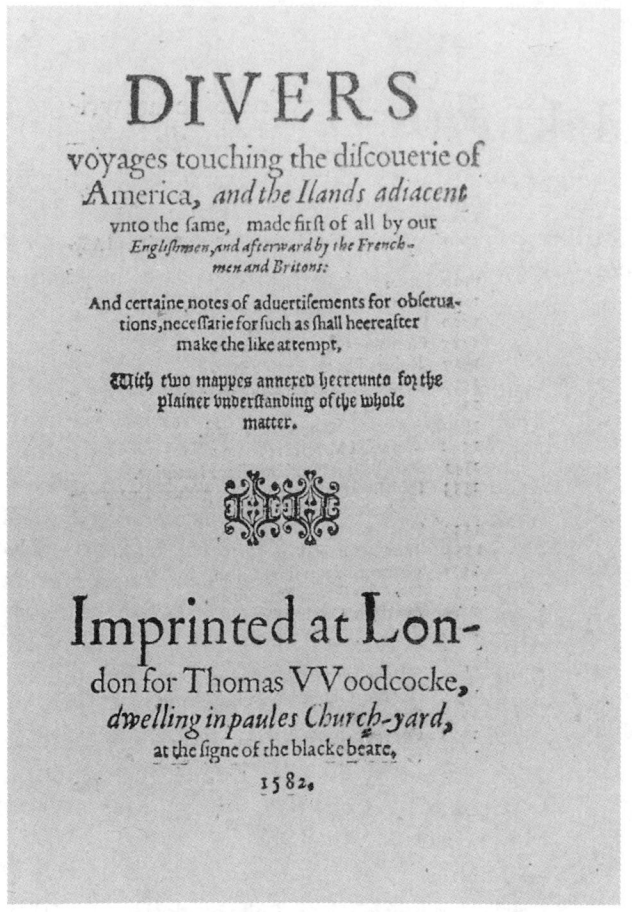

DIVERS

voyages touching the difcouerie of
America, *and the Ilands adiacent*
vnto the fame, made firft of all by our
*Englifhmen, and afterward by the French-
men and Britons:*

And certaine notes of aduertifements for obferua-
tions, neceffarie for fuch as fhall heereafter
make the like attempt,

With two mappes annexed heereunto for the
plainer vnderftanding of the whole
matter.

Imprinted at Lon-
don for Thomas VVoodcocke,
dwelling in paules Church-yard,
at the figne of the blacke beare,
1582.

*Title page for Richard Hakluyt's collection of documents
concerning European voyages to America*

by David Beers Quinn and Raleigh Ashlin
Skelton (London: Hakluyt Society, 1965);
"A particuler discourse concerninge the greate
  necessitie and manifolde comodyties that are
  like to growe to this Realme of Englande by
  the Westerne discoveries lately attempted,
  Written in the yere 1584," in *English Plans for
  North America: The Roanoke Voyages; New En-
  gland Ventures,* volume 2 of *New American
  World: A Documentary History of North America to
  1612,* edited by David B. Quinn (New York:
  Arno Press & Hector Bye, 1979), pp. 70–123.

Richard Hakluyt was the preeminent collector
and editor of documents relating to the first decades
of England's trade and exploration outside of Europe, chiefly in his massive, three-volume *Principal
Navigations, Voyages, Traffics and Discoveries of the English Nation* (1598–1600) – a work the historian
James A. Froude labeled "the prose epic of the modern English nation." Hakluyt was not the first Englishman to publish collections of such narratives –

Richard Eden in the 1550s and Richard Willis in
1577 had preceded him – nor the most comprehensive: after his death Samuel Purchas would take
over his unpublished papers and acquire more of
his own until *Hakluytus Posthumus: or, Purchas His Pilgrims* (1625) filled four folio volumes. Nonetheless,
Hakluyt has become a general name for the activity
of publishing and promulgating such accounts. His
books are valued by historians as unmatched
sources of relatively untouched primary documents
on English mercantile and colonial expansions and
as a landmark in the development of a new kind of
prose that David Beers Quinn describes as "practical, objective, clear, exciting."

Born around 1552, Hakluyt was the second of
five children of Margery and Richard Hakluyt of
London. He later traced his enthusiasm for the voyages and the new economic and physical geography
they generated to the influence of an older cousin,
also named Richard Hakluyt. The elder Hakluyt became guardian of his cousins at their father's death,
when the younger Hakluyt was five years old. A
student at the Middle Temple at that time and subsequently a lawyer, the elder Hakluyt was deeply
involved with the international networks of merchants, cosmographers, and travelers who were beginning to generate materials for a new geography;
he was active in acquiring, generating, and passing
on information as well as devising new ways to
make it accessible and practical. In the late 1560s,
for instance, he commissioned the Flemish cosmographer Abraham Ortelius to construct a world map
on rollers that could easily be consulted in ordinary
rooms. The map was to contain a northwest passage
to the orient along the lines of the one Humphrey
Gilbert was currently "proving," using the same tes-
timonies Gilbert cited. This Hakluyt, like his younger cousin later, was in close contact with practical
projects of overseas exploration, and the needs of
these projects helped determine both the shape of
the information assembled by the two Hakluyts and
the timing of its dissemination. The elder Hakluyt
wrote up a set of notes for Gilbert's first, abortive
voyage in 1578, and his hand is seen in his cousin's
compilations as a source of letters and narratives by
others as well as of his own advice to a series of
travelers. Like his cousin later, this Hakluyt was
praised by contemporaries for his efforts as a
scholar and editor.

In the dedication to *Principal Navigations* the
younger Hakluyt recalls his interest in geography
and travel as beginning with a visit to his cousin's
chambers in the Middle Temple when he was a
queen's scholar at the Westminster School:

"I found lying open upon the board certain books of cosmography, with a universal map; he seeing me somewhat curious in the view thereof began to instruct my ignorance by showing me the division of the earth into three parts after the old account, and then according to the latter, and better distribution into more . . . with declaration also of their special commodities and particular wants which by the benefit of traffic and the intercourse of merchants are plentifully supplied. From the map he brought me to the Bible, and turning to the 107th Psalm, directed me to the 23rd and 24th verses, where I read, that they which go down to the sea in ships and occupy by the great waters, they see the works of the Lord and his wonders in the deep, etc."

Doubly fired by the words of the Bible and his cousin's exposition, Hakluyt writes, he resolved to pursue the study of geography. Having completed his requirements at Christ College, Oxford, where he took his B.A. in 1574 and his M.A. in 1577, he began to read all the voyage narratives he could find in Greek, Latin, Italian, Spanish, Portuguese, French, or English. (His linguistic proficiency would be exemplified in several translations.) Sometime after 1574 he purchased a copy of Giovanni Battista Ramusio's *Delle navigationi et viaggi* (1550–1556), a collection he would imitate in its preference for firsthand narratives and in its organization by region, which contrasted with the more haphazard arrangements of earlier collections. He lectured at Oxford and describes himself as the first to make educational use of both the old and new maps as his cousin had displayed them to him. After further studies in theology, he was ordained in 1580.

By 1580 Hakluyt was knowledgeable enough to prepare a memorandum for Francis Walsingham, the secretary of state, on the prospect of taking the Strait of Magellan after Henry of Portugal's death. His first collection of documents on America, *Divers Voyages* (1582), was published with a dedication to Sir Philip Sidney. The implied thesis of Hakluyt's collection can be gathered from the title page: *Divers Voyages Touching the Discovery of America and the Islands Adjacent unto the Same, Made First of All by Our Englishmen and Afterward by the Frenchmen and Britons: And Certain Notes of Advertisements for Observations, Necessary for Such as Shall Hereafter Make the Like Attempt, with Two Maps Annexed Hereunto for the Plainer Understanding of the Whole Matter.* Though his initials follow the dedication, Hakluyt's name does not appear on the title page or in the book's front matter.

Divers Voyages is divided into three parts. Part 1, aimed at asserting the priority of England's claim, consists mainly of Henrician documents: John Cabot's letters patent from Henry VII (1491) in Latin and English; notes on Sebastian Cabot's voyage, ex-

cerpted from the Great Chronicle of London and from Ramusio's *Delle navigationi et viaggi*; Robert Thorne's representations to Henry VIII on the desirability of a northern passage to the Indies (1527); and a map of the world, showing North and South America, procured by Thorne. The second part reprints accounts of voyages by Giovanni da Verrazano and the Zeno brothers from Ramusio's work and part of Jean Ribaut's *The Whole and True Discovery of Terra Florida* (1563), along with a second map. This map, prepared by Michael Lok and dedicated to Sidney, gives a fragmentary representation of North and South America, imagining them as giving way quite quickly to the China Sea. The third part is made up of practical suggestions for Englishmen who would succeed the Cabots in making the kinds of voyages described in part 2. It includes notes prepared by Hakluyt's cousin for Arthur Pet and Charles Jackman's northeast passage voyage of 1580: geographical features to look for (islands, straits, harbors) and how to take advantage of them; what to take along for trade and show; what to trade for; and what to notice about the inhabitants. A shorter set of notes by the elder Hakluyt "to one that prepared for a discovery, and went not" and a list of American commodities garnered from printed sources complete the section.

Divers Voyages was probably intended as support for the Gilbert expedition of 1583, for which Hakluyt made a trip to Bristol soliciting funds that year. If this was the intention, it was successful to the extent that the dedicatee, Sidney, purchased rights to three million acres in America under Gilbert's patent in July 1582; Sidney also appears on a list of the adventurers associated with Gilbert's voyage. Few copies of the first edition of *Divers Voyages* have survived, and it is now a rare item of Americana.

The Gilbert expedition was a failure: Gilbert's own ship was lost with all hands, and Hakluyt's Oxford friend, the Hungarian scholar Stephen Parmenius, also drowned on the voyage after writing a descriptive letter to Hakluyt from Newfoundland. Hakluyt was in Paris as chaplain to the English ambassador Sir Edward Stafford. As the expiration of Gilbert's patent approached in 1584, Hakluyt wrote to Walsingham urging that the enterprise not be abandoned; as an inducement he describes seeing in one man's house in Paris "the value of five thousand pounds worth of furs" from Canada and offers to go on the voyage himself.

Instead, he was to spend the years 1583 to 1588 moving between Paris and London. In Paris he had access to French travelers and Portuguese

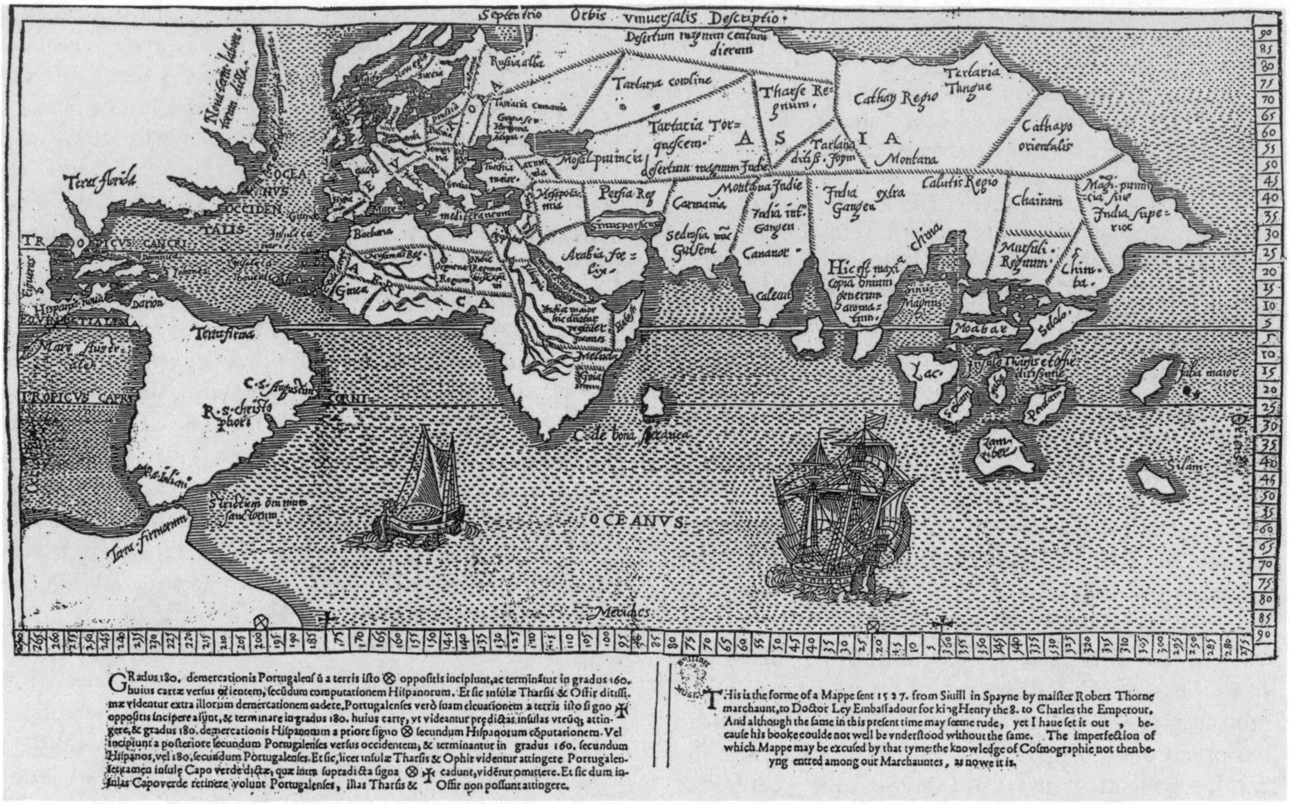

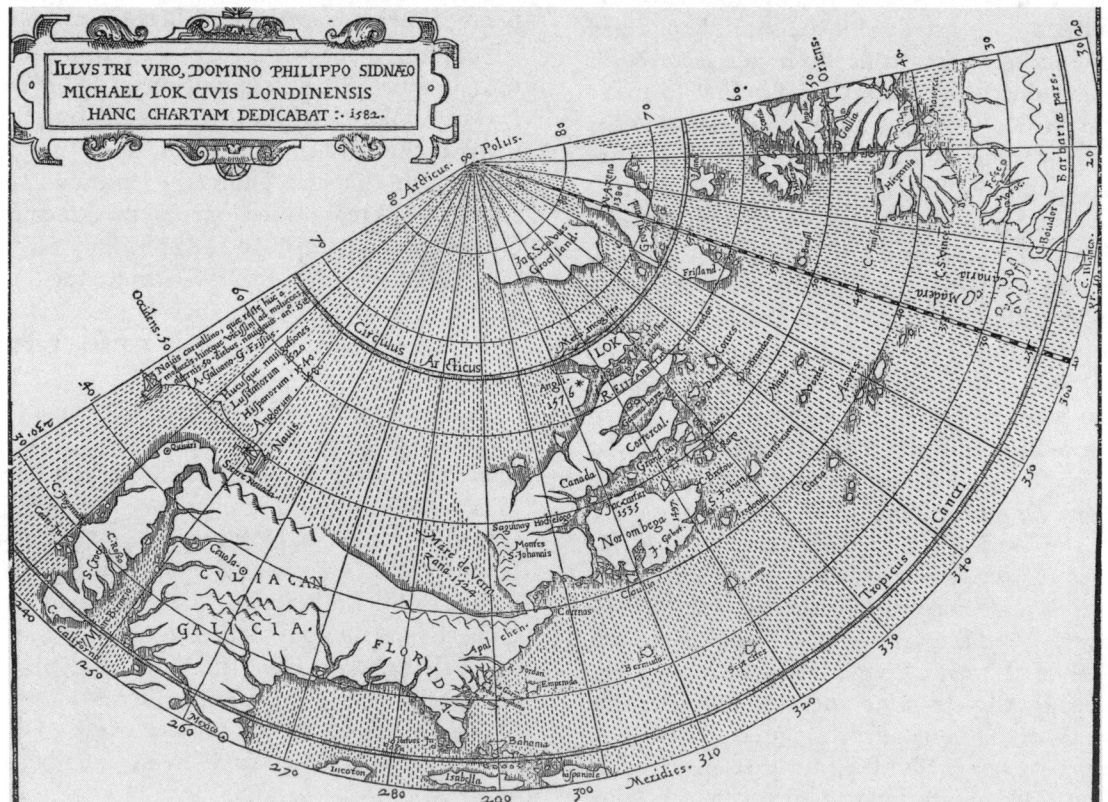

Maps by Robert Thorne and Michael Lok, from Hakluyt's Divers Voyages Touching the Discovery of America

exiles who had actually been to America as well as manuscript accounts of their voyages; there he also heard the English accused of laziness for their failure to pursue enterprises of discovery. Impressed with the competitive lectureship in mathematics established at Paris by Peter Ramus, he wrote to Walsingham urging the establishment of a similar lectureship at Oxford and one in navigation at London; the pursuit of such knowledge was no merely academic concern, he said, but vital for "the service of wars . . . and for our new discoveries and longer voyages by sea."

New letters patent for American discovery were granted to Sir Walter Ralegh on 25 March 1584, and during the next few years Hakluyt was involved with Ralegh's plans for Virginia. At Ralegh's request he composed a confidential memorandum for the queen, titled "A Particular Discourse Concerning the Great Necessity and Manifold Commodities That Are Likely to Grow to This Realm of England by the Western Discoveries Lately Attempted"; the work was edited and published in 1877 as *A Discourse on Western Planting,* the title by which it is usually known. Hakluyt completed the memorandum in September 1584, consulting the favorable reports of the first Virginia voyage by Philip Amadas and Arthur Barlowe, and presented it to the queen in October along with a manuscript analysis of Aristotle's *Politics.* The queen was pleased; her grant of the reversion of a prebend at Bristol Cathedral to Hakluyt is dated the day of this audience.

A Discourse on Western Planting is Hakluyt's longest original work and contains the fullest articulation of his rationale for exploring and colonizing North America. Although the work should have been influential, the manuscript was neither published in the author's collections nor disseminated, as far as is known, outside a restricted circle; a letter survives in which Hakluyt offers a copy to an unknown correspondent.

Hakluyt was also active during his Paris years in translating and publishing voyage narratives. He procured for publication a narrative of Antonio de Espejo's voyage (1586); he edited Pietro Martire d'Anghiera's *De orbe Novo* (1587) with a dedication to Ralegh; finally, he and Martin Basanier procured from André Thevet, the royal French cosmographer, the manuscript for René de Laudonnière's *Histoire notable,* an account of French voyages to Florida, and published it first in French without permission in 1585 and in English translation, with a dedication to Ralegh, in 1587. The dedications would suggest that these publications were proba-

bly part of the campaign for Ralegh's Virginia; the first colony had gone over in 1585, to be removed by Sir Francis Drake in 1586, and the second departed in 1587. Ralegh's client Thomas Harriot, a mathematician, accompanied the first colony as scientific observer, and his *Brief and True Report of the Newfound Land in Virginia* (1588) became the first printed English report of what would later become America.

Hakluyt's second collection, *The Principal Navigations, Voyages, and Discoveries of the English Nation, Made by Sea and Over Land, to the Most Remote and Farthest Distant Quarters of the Earth at Any Time within the Compass of These 1500 Years,* appeared in 1589 with the editor's name on the title page: "By Richard Hakluyt, Master of Arts, and Student sometimes of Christ Church in Oxford." *Principal Navigations* was a different kind of book from its predecessor of 1582. Instead of a quarto, Hakluyt's second collection was a stout folio volume published by the queen's printer. There was more material to include: accounts of Gilbert's voyage to Newfoundland in 1583, of Sir Thomas Cavendish's circumnavigation in 1586, and of the Ralegh-sponsored voyages to Virginia in the 1580s, along with Harriot's "Brief and True Report of the Newfound Land in Virginia." *Principal Navigations* also includes a vast amount of earlier material, such as accounts of Martin Frobisher's voyages in the late 1570s; Gilbert's "Discourse of Discovery," first published in 1576; and accounts of English incursions into Africa and Russia dating back to Marian times. This inclusiveness seems to reflect a new aim of authoritative completeness, of obtaining and printing everything within the compass of English activities.

"Everything" turned out to be a vastly heterogeneous collection. The section on the north and northeast begins with the apocryphal voyage of King Arthur to Iceland in 517, taken from Geoffrey of Monmouth, and concludes with an up-to-date account of Jerome Horsey's overland voyage to Moscow in 1584 – probably from the archives of the Muscovy Company, if not from Horsey himself. The accompanying documents range from the diplomatic (letters between Elizabeth and the Russian and Persian governments concerning privileges and safe conduct for merchants) to the practical ("The Necessary Instruments and Appurtenances Belonging to the Killing of the Whale") and the sociological ("Of the Religion of the Persians"). Hakluyt's documents were bound together by a coherent set of intentions: to further English knowledge of the world outside Europe; to promote English mastery of that world; and, by setting the voyages of the

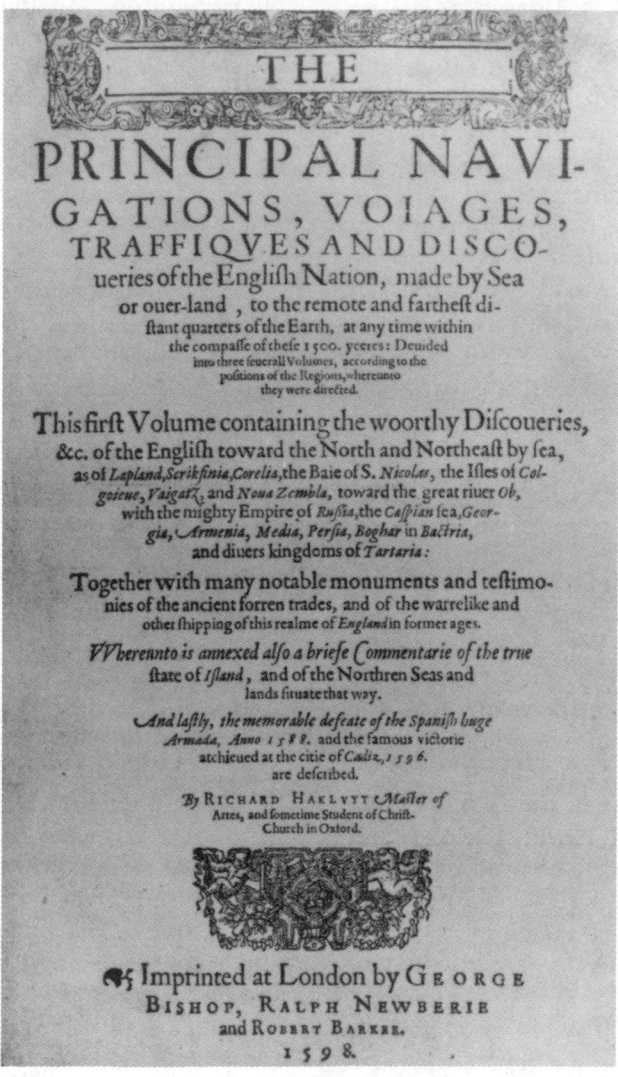

THE

PRINCIPAL NAVI-
GATIONS, VOIAGES,
TRAFFIQVES AND DISCO-
ueries of the English Nation, made by Sea
or ouer-land , to the remote and farthest distant quarters of the Earth, at any time within
the compasse of these 1500. yeeres: Deuided
into three seuerall Volumes, according to the
positions of the Regions, whereunto
they were directed.

This first Volume containing the woorthy Discoueries,
&c. of the English toward the North and Northeast by sea,
as of Lapland, Scrikfinia, Corelia, the Baie of S. Nicolas, the Isles of Col-
goieue, Vaigatz, and Noua Zembla, toward the great riuer Ob,
with the mighty Empire of Russia, the Caspian sea, Georgia, Armenia, Media, Persia, Boghar in Bactria,
and diuers kingdoms of Tartaria:

Together with many notable monuments and testimo-
nies of the ancient forren trades, and of the warrelike and
other shipping of this realme of England in former ages.

VVhereunto is annexed also a briefe Commentarie of the true
state of Island , and of the Northren Seas and
lands situate that way.

And lastly, the memorable defeate of the Spanish huge
Armada, Anno 1588. and the famous victorie
atchieued at the citie of Cadiz, 1596.
are described.

By RICHARD HAKLVYT Master of
Artes, and sometime Student of Christ-
Church in Oxford.

Imprinted at London by GEORGE
BISHOP, RALPH NEWBERIE
and ROBERT BARKER.
1598.

Title page for the first issue of volume one of the second edition of Hakluyt's collection of documents concerning English explorations. After Robert Devereux, second Earl of Essex, fell from royal favor, the title page was reprinted to omit the reference to his victory at Cadiz, and the account of his expedition was excised from some copies.

1570s and 1580s in the context of much earlier documents, to provide a foundation for that mastery in historical precedent. Additional documents – charters, letters patent, and privileges – assert a formal, legal dimension to English claims. Hakluyt's preface asserts that posterity will admire England's opening of a sea route to Russia at least as much as the achievements of Vasco da Gama and Christopher Columbus.

By this time Hakluyt was, beyond doubt, a name in circles that shared his interests. His "singular and deep insight in all histories of discovery" is praised in the prefatory matter to Robert Parke's translation of Juan González de Mendoza's history of China (1588); and Philip Jones, in the dedication to his translation of Albertus Meierus's *Certain Brief*

and Special Instructions (1589), praises Hakluyt's "special carefulness for the good of our nation," as the "rare and excellent work which now he plyeth" (*Principal Navigations*) will give testimony. Hakluyt was also involved in translating, suggesting, and procuring materials for Theodor de Bry's *America* (1590), a collection of documents in four languages that brought Harriot's account of Virginia, along with John White's illustrations, to the attention of an international audience.

Hakluyt became rector of Wetheringsett, Suffolk, in 1590. He married Douglas Cavendish in 1590; she bore his only child, Edmond, in 1593 and died four years later. The enlarged second edition of *Principal Navigations* began to appear in 1598; the first volume, of voyages to the north and northeast, was withdrawn in September 1599, following the return from Ireland of Robert Devereux, second Earl of Essex. Republished along with volume two later in the year, it had acquired a new title page and map but no longer included an account of the Cadiz expedition that had cast Essex in a favorable light. As in the 1589 edition, documents are divided up by region and arranged chronologically; voyages to the south and southeast are now divided into those inside the Strait of Gibraltar and those outside it; and the third volume now refers to "America" rather than "the West, Southwest, and Northwest regions." In the interests of comprehensive coverage, the volume of American voyages prints accounts by nationals of countries other than England when no comparable English document is available. While the 1589 *Principal Navigations* contained 77 American documents, the third volume of the second edition boasts 198. This edition also includes the "new map with the augmentation of the Indies" referred to in William Shakespeare's *Twelfth Night* (1623).

Hakluyt dedicated volume one to Lord High Admiral Charles Howard, and volumes two and three to Sir Robert Cecil. These dedicatory epistles, along with the preface to volume one, are virtually Hakluyt's only original contributions to the work as he follows the procedure he had announced in the preface to the first edition: "Whatever testimony I have found in any author of authority appertaining to my argument, . . . I have recorded the same word for word, with his particular name and page of book where it is extant. . . . And to the ends that those which were the painful and personal travelers might reap that good opinion and just commendation which they have deserved, and further, that every man might answer for himself, justify his reports, and stand accountable for his own doings, I have referred every voyage to his author which both in person hath performed, and in writing hath left the same."

Through his dedications Hakluyt attempted to secure powerful support for the needs of discovery, such as Crown funding of colonies and of lectures on navigation, for Walsingham's death had left England's overseas enterprise without a strong supporter at court. He gives a historical account of English trade dating back to Cornelius Tacitus, reflecting the expanded medieval documentation amassed for the second edition, and vigorously advocates renewal of the Virginia enterprise as a means of occupying the "increasing youth of the realm" in years of peace and of giving room for the "variable humors of all sorts of people." One of the gems of Hakluyt's last collection is a Latin treatise on China

by Duarte Sande, first published in Macao in 1590. Part of the spoils from the interception of the *Madre de Dios* in 1592, it was found "enclosed in a case of sweet cedar wood, and lapped up almost an hundred fold in fine calicut-cloth, as though it had been some incomparable jewel." Hakluyt presents Japan and China to Cecil's attention not as sources of exotic goods and wealth but as potential markets for English woolen cloth, the "natural commodity of this our realm."

Though Hakluyt has no firsthand report to give, the prefatory material emphasizes the magnitude of his own efforts in memorable language: "what restless nights, what painful days, what heat, what cold have I endured, how many long and chargeable journeys I have traveled; how many famous libraries I have searched into; what variety of ancient and modern writers I have perused . . . what expenses I have not spared; and yet what fair opportunity of private gain, preferment, and ease I have neglected albeit thyself can hardly imagine, yet I by daily experience do find and feel, and some of my friends can sufficiently testify."

Hakluyt's labors had not been entirely unremunerated; he had charged the governor of Zeeland twenty pounds for a professional opinion on the Northwest Passage in 1594, for example. *Principal Navigations,* however, brought him significant patronage. Cecil and Howard petitioned the queen to grant Hakluyt the reversion of a prebend at Westminster, and though she initially refused, Hakluyt's second dedication to Cecil in 1600 reflects his gratitude for the petition's success, as well as for a chaplaincy at the Savoy acquired through Cecil's efforts.

Hakluyt's activities did not cease with the appearance of *Principal Navigations.* He wrote up notes for the East India Company shortly after it was chartered; he was also a publicist for and shareholder in the South Virginia Company since its inception. He married Frances Smithe in 1604. His last publication was a translation of Ferdinand de Soto's *Virginia Richly Valued* (1609), with a dedication to the Council of Virginia. In 1612 he became rector of Gedney, Lincolnshire. He died in London on 23 November 1616.

Unlike his successor, Purchas, Hakluyt was less a historian than a compiler of an archive. His collections had a powerful impact on his time, both practical and imaginative. Sir Thomas Smith attributed to the improved knowledge gained by study of *Principal Navigations* a twenty-thousand-pound increase in the East India Company's profits; the multitudinous place-names of John Milton's *Paradise Lost* (1667) also reflect a reading of Hakluyt's works. As *Principal Navigations* was succeeded by more up-to-date information Hakluyt's reputation waned; but he found a second audience in the imperial England of the nineteenth century, which looked back to Elizabethan times as a moment of national origins and identified Hakluyt, along with Shakespeare, as the heralds of a distinctively English greatness. Hakluyt's work of collection and publication was renewed in 1846 by the founding of the Hakluyt Society, whose projects reflected the conviction that England had a historic right to find markets abroad and that this right could be buttressed by publishing reliable early accounts of European trade and overseas expansion. This use of such information was well understood and intended by Hakluyt; the dedication to the 1600 volume of American voyages assigns to *Principal Navigations* an aggressively nationalist purpose: "I have used the uttermost of my best endeavor, to get, and having gotten, to translate out of Spanish, and here in this present volume to publish such secrets of theirs as may any way avail us or annoy them, if they drive and urge us by their sullen insolencies, to continue our courses of hostility against them." The society's activities, however, have outlasted their origins, and Hakluyt's name continues to preside over well-prepared modern editions of otherwise hard-to-find documents.

Bibliography:

David Beers Quinn, *The Hakluyt Handbook,* 2 volumes (London: Hakluyt Society, 1974).

Biography:

George B. Parks, *Richard Hakluyt and the English Voyages* (New York: American Geographical Society, 1928).

References:

James A. Froude, "England's Forgotten Worthies," in his *Short Studies on Great Subjects,* 3 volumes (London: Longmans, Green, 1867), I: 294–333;

Juan González de Mendoza, *The Historie of the Great and Mightie Kingdome of China,* translated by Robert Parke (London: Printed by John Wolfe for Edward White, 1588);

Christopher Hill, *Intellectual Origins of the English Revolution* (Oxford: Clarendon Press, 1965);

Edward Lynam, ed., *Richard Hakluyt and His Successors* (London: Hakluyt Society, 1946);

Albertus Meierus, *Certaine Briefe, and Speciall Instructions for Gentelmen, Merchants, &c. Employed in Seruices Abroad,* translated by Philip Jones (London: Printed by John Woolfe, 1589);

David Beers Quinn, *Richard Hakluyt, Editor* (Amsterdam: Theatrum Orbis Terrarum, 1967);

E. G. R. Taylor, *Tudor Geography 1485–1583* (London: Methuen, 1934).

Papers:

The manuscript for Richard Hakluyt's "Particular Discourse" is in the New York Public Library Division of Manuscripts, Astor, Lenox, and Tilden Foundations.

Sir John Harington

(1560 – November 1612)

D. H. Craig
University of Newcastle

BOOKS: *A New Discourse of a Stale Subject, Called the Metamorphosis of Ajax,* as "Misacmos" (hater of filthiness) (London: Printed by Richard Field, 1596);

Epigrams Both Pleasant and Serious, Never Before Printed (London: Printed [by George Purslowe] for John Budge, 1615);

The Most Elegant and Witty Epigrams of Sir J. Harington, Digested into Foure Bookes: Three Whereof Never Before Published (London: Printed by G[eorge] P[urslowe] for John Budge, 1618).

Editions: *A Briefe View of the State of the Church of England, as It Stood in Q. Elizabeths and King James His Reigns, to the Yeare 1608,* edited by John Chetwind (London: Printed for Joseph Kirton, 1653);

Nugae Antiquae: Being a Miscellaneous Collection of Original Papers in Prose and Verse, edited by Henry Harington, includes J. Harington's "A Treatise on Play," and "A Discourse Showing That Elias Must Personally Come before the Day of Judgment" (London: Printed for W. Frederick, at Bath, 1769); enlarged edition, 2 volumes (London: Printed for W. Frederick, at Bath, 1775); revised and enlarged edition, 2 volumes (London: Printed for J. Dodsley, 1779); revised edition, edited by Thomas Park, 2 volumes (London: Vernor & Hood, 1804);

A Short View of the State of Ireland, edited by William Dunn Macray (Oxford: James Parker, 1879);

A Tract on the Succession to the Crown (A.D. 1602), edited by Clemens R. Markham (London: Printed by J. B. Nichols & Sons for the Roxburghe Club, 1880);

The Letters and Epigrams of Sir John Harington, Together with "The Prayse of Private Life," edited by Norman Egbert McClure (Philadelphia: University of Pennsylvania Press, 1930);

A New Discourse of a Stale Subject, Called the Metamorphosis of Ajax, edited by Elizabeth Story Donno (London: Routledge, 1962);

Sir John Harington; portrait by Hieronimo Custodis; (Collection of Nina, Lady Deramore)

Orlando Furioso. Translated into English Heroical Verse by Sir John Harington (1591), edited by Robert McNulty (Oxford: Clarendon Press, 1972);

A Supplie or Addicion to the Catalogue of Bishops, to the Yeare 1608, edited by R. H. Miller (Potomac, Md.: Turanzas, 1979);

The Sixth Book of Virgil's "Aeneid," translated by Harington, edited by Simon Cauchi (Oxford: Clarendon Press, 1991);

The Elizabethan Courtier Poets: The Poems and Their Contexts, edited by Steven W. May (Columbia: University of Missouri Press, 1991) — includes seven of Harington's Psalms translations.

OTHER: I. C., *Alcilia: Philoparthens Louing Follie,* enlarged edition, includes epigrams by Harington (London: Printed [by Thomas Snodham & Thomas Creede] for Richard Hawkins, 1613).

TRANSLATIONS: Ludovico Ariosto, *Orlando Furioso in English Heroical Verse* (London: Printed by Richard Field, 1591; London: Printed by Richard Field for John Norton & Simon Waterson, 1607); revised edition, includes epigrams by Harington (London: Printed by George Miller for John Parker, 1634 [1633]);
Joannes de Mediolano, *The Englishman's Docter. Or, The Schoole of Salerne,* anonymous translation attributed to Harington (London: Printed [by William Jaggard] for John Helme & John Busby, Jr., 1607).

Sir John Harington was a courtier, a well-connected landowner and builder, and an opinionated member of the Church of England. His writing was an occasional activity, and it always had close links with his other pursuits. He wrote a treatise describing an improvement to the lavatory, for instance, which is both a contribution to the sanitation of the great house and a satire on the pride and hypocrisy of certain of his contemporaries. He wrote tracts on Ireland, on who should succeed Elizabeth on the throne, and on the marriage of the clergy. Even his 1591 translation of the Italian romance epic *Orlando Furioso* was done at the queen's behest, and he draws from his Italian original all kinds of morals for English manners and English government in his printed commentary on the poem. His epigrams, his major contributions in original verse, concentrate on the follies of his immediate family and his wider circle of acquaintances. Yet far from limiting the interest of his work, this engagement with his own times is perhaps what makes Harington most worth reading for later generations, for he was exceptionally frank and interested in everyday detail in an age which habitually censored or simply did not see aspects of its world that are of interest to our century. This bias went with a quality in him his cousin called "that damnable uncovered honesty." Moreover, a certain individual outlook is developed through the various parts of Harington's oeuvre: that of a humorous, mildly skeptical, but always optimistic moralist.

Harington's father, also John, had served Sir Thomas Seymour, high admiral of the fleet under Edward VI, and was imprisoned with Seymour in the Tower when the latter was accused of treason. His fortunes improved, however, and he went on to become a confidential undertreasurer to Henry VIII. In addition the elder Harington's first wife was an illegitimate daughter of the king, bringing properties into the family from the Crown. The younger John was born in 1561 to Harington and his second wife, the former Isabella Markham, who had been a maid of honor in Elizabeth's household when she was princess. The son thus inherited connections at court – Elizabeth was his godmother – and, after his father's death in 1582, estates such as the one in Somerset where he completed the building of Kelston Manor. He was sent to Eton and then to King's College, Cambridge, in 1576. He took the Master of Arts degree in 1581, and in November of that year entered Lincoln's Inn in London, where he studied law for a short time before his father's death. Harington thus came into possession of his estate and in 1583 married Mary Rogers, daughter of another Somerset landowner. They had eleven children in all, two of whom died at birth.

In 1591 Harington published his translation of the forty-six cantos, or books, of Ludovico Ariosto's *Orlando Furioso* (1516). He says in *A New Discourse of A Stale Subject, Called the Metamorphosis of Ajax* (1596) that this translation was done as a penance set him by the queen. The story, first told by Thomas Park in his 1804 edition of *Nugae Antiquae,* is that Harington's crime was circulating a bawdy rendition of canto 28 among the queen's maids of honor; she therefore set him the task of translating the rest. The final product is an exceptionally elaborate book. There are marginal notes; for each canto both an engraving illustrating the action and a commentary under various heads at the end; apologies for the poet, the poem, and the translation; a life of Ariosto; a summary of the allegory; and an index. Some of this – the illustrations, for instance, and much of the "Brief Apology for Poetry" at the beginning – is largely taken over from Italian editions of the poem. But a great deal of the apparatus is specifically designed for Harington's English readers. While aware that intruding English references in the text or changing the story would be "wronging mine author," Harington fills the spaces around his translation with reminders and observations which make him a remarkably immediate presence in the book. The translation itself is readable, sustaining narrative momentum with a brisk, sometimes spritely, use of the ottava-rima stanza (eight lines of iambic pentameter, rhyming *ababab<i>cc</i>*). An account of the fight between Ferraw (Ariosto's "Ferraù") and Renaldo over Angelica in book 1 may serve as an example:

Between them two a combat fierce began
With strokes that might have pierced the hardest
    rocks.
While they thus fight on foot and man to man
And give and take so hard and heavy knocks,
Away the damsell posteth all she can;
Their pain and travail she requites with mocks.
So hard she rode while they were at their fight
That she was clean escaped out of sight.

Harington is also capable of following his original in developing cumulative effects of suspense and irony through a canto. Generally his *Orlando Furioso* is a compression of Ariosto's, frequently scanting details of description, though he also amplifies on occasion, including original verses of devotional meditation (book 7, stanzas 35–37) and a greatly expanded tour of Jerusalem for Astolfo and his brothers (book 15, stanzas 73–77).

In Harington's attitude toward his source, an enthusiastic response to what he sees as the poem's wisdom about human behavior, and to the pathos in its episodes of unlucky love or betrayed innocence, is allied with a defensive reaction to the poem's more fantastic adventures. The commentary aims to temper skepticism about the supernatural, while at the same time defending the poem against attacks from the literal-minded, who associate all imaginative writing with moral laxity and false doctrine. Fending off these assaults from different quarters, Harington is more pragmatic than systematic. Protection by magic or the existence of the Amazons may be taken seriously; other departures from the familiar or the probable may be explained as allegory; still others are regarded as mere fables. In general the poem presents for Harington examples which whether "true" or "feigned" have a moral intent (as he notes in the "Moral" to book 22) and can in fact teach good lessons (as he argues in his "Brief Apology for Poetry").

Orlando Furioso in English Heroical Verse thus represents an exceptionally complex act of translation. By a variety of means it reframes and in some ways domesticates the sophisticated ironies and the provocative mixture of romance and epic in Ariosto's poem. At the time it won its translator some fame as a poet and a learned man; he continued to read passages to his acquaintances for the rest of his life, to King James, to Prince Henry, to lords and ladies in Ireland as well as in England. He published a new edition, with many revisions, in 1607. Francis Bacon and Robert Burton quoted Ariosto from Harington's version, and John Milton noted in his copy that he had read it twice.

Title page for Harington's 1591 translation of Ariosto, a "penance" set him by Queen Elizabeth

In the 1590s Harington also completed, but did not publish, his *Discourse Showing That Elias Must Personally Come before the Day of Judgment,* defending a literal interpretation of passages in the Bible concerning the return of the prophet Elijah. The exact date of its composition is unknown, but he refers to accusations that he has maintained a "popish" position on the subject in *The Metamorphosis of Ajax.* The latter was Harington's second effort at advancement through publication, a pamphlet which brought him another kind of fame altogether. A jakes is a privy, and the metamorphosis presented involves flushing with water stored in a cistern and a stopper to keep out smells from below. There is evidence that the first readers of this tract found it shocking. Thomas Nashe, a contemporary writer of satirical pamphlets, wrote to a correspondent that Harington was "bid[ding] a turd in all gentle readers' teeth"; reactions generally suggested that Harington's witty elaboration of the metaphor failed to compensate for the breach of decorum involved in writing about the privy at all. There was in his tract an authentic

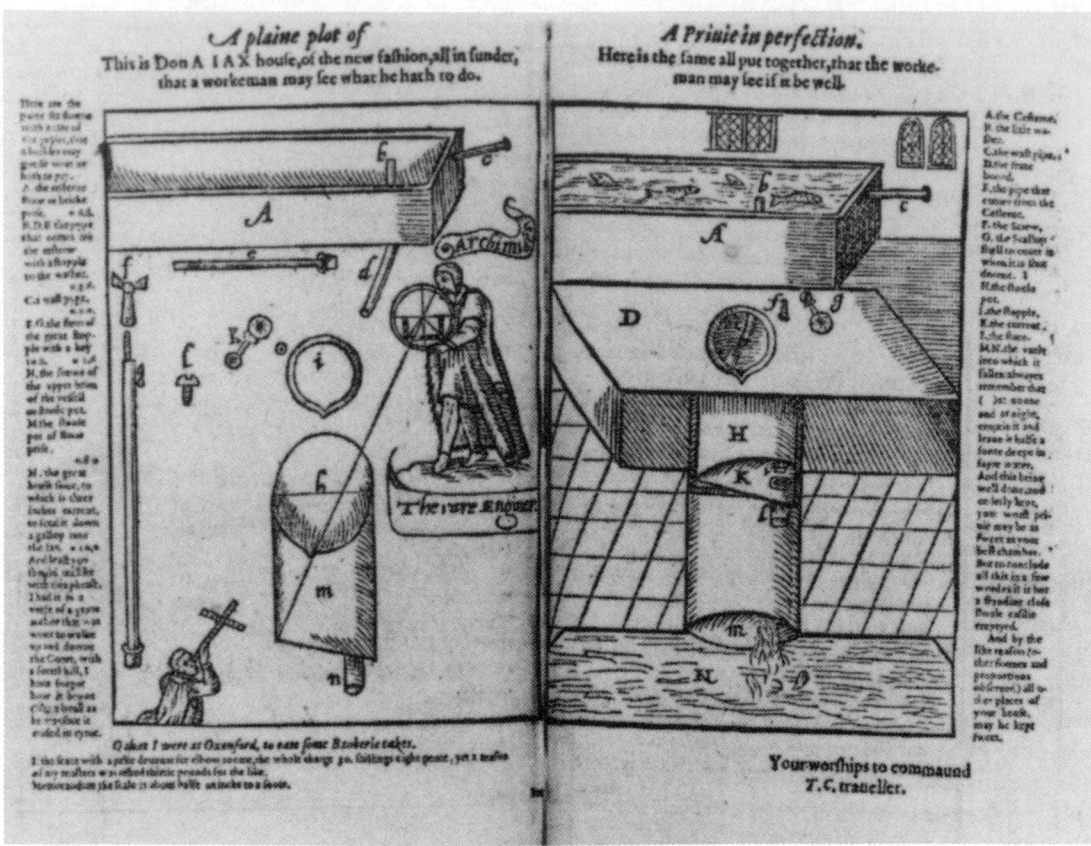

Diagrams of Harington's water closet, from The Metamorphosis of Ajax

technical improvement, presented in a few lines (and in some diagrams, in the practical section contributed by Thomas Combe, Harington's manservant), and many pages on the connections between the purifying of "privy vaults" and the reforming of "privy faults." Yet what persisted in his readers was a distaste for the whole enterprise, and "Monsieur Ajax" became a name not for wit but for what Nashe in his *Have with You to Saffron Walden* (1596) called "excremental conceits." As Harington himself anticipated in the book, his readers were puzzled that, though by no means base by birth, he had been so "fantastical" as to take "so strange a subject."

The queen was uneasy with an alleged slur on the earl of Leicester in the pamphlet, and with its risqué humor. She banished Harington from court. Yet a year or so later one of Harington's correspondents reported that though Elizabeth had expressed displeasure for form's sake, she liked "the marrow" of Harington's book. In this she was in sympathy with what Harington says himself about his intentions in the pamphlet. The scurrilous subject matter was there to attract attention to his serious message, he says, like putting pills in an apple, or wormwood

in raisins. Further, while the privy was beneath notice, it would not be improved: *The Metamorphosis of Ajax* was to make it visible, surprising readers into a shift of perception, just as within the book Harington describes a reader's surprise at being told of all the passages in Scripture there are on the topic, passages which are never mentioned by preachers or commentators. At another, perhaps the most important level, readers were to be repelled initially by all the talk of urine and ordure but then reminded that vice (however painted and perfumed) was a far more serious offense against moral sensibilities. Harington's story of the angel who found that a finely dressed harlot stank far worse than the cartload of night soil on the other side of the street puts the point in a nutshell.

Such madcap reasoning and oblique moralizing are in a long tradition of humanist prose. *The Metamorphosis of Ajax* is a mock-encomium, a treatise in praise of an unworthy subject, like Desiderius Erasmus's *Moriae encomium* (Praise of Folly, 1509); it is also a scabrous fantasy like those of the fifteenth-century French writer François Rabelais. Nearer still in time and place as models are the satirical pamphlets of Nashe. The exuberant and allusive prose in Harington's tract draws on other kinds of discourse as well. At times it is presented as a collection of pleadings, with jurors (twelve of the most distinguished of Harington's relations and friends) named and sworn and judgment passed. At others Harington makes use of the rhetorical figure of *prolepsis,* anticipating objections to his work within its pages. Some of the objections are by characters created for the moment, like the occasional Bible reader whose worldliness is obvious despite his declaration that he reads the Old Testament "at least half an hour by the clock." The third part of *The Metamorphosis of Ajax,* the "Apology," was issued shortly after the first part and begins with an account of certain diners at a tavern shown reading the first part and objecting strongly.

School friends, relations, patrons, and (more obscurely) enemies make appearances in Harington's pages in gossipy references, some still explicable, many not. Allusions abound to classical writers and to the Scriptures, with scarcer references to contemporary writers like Sir Philip Sidney and Edmund Spenser. The topicality of the tract makes it frustrating to read for those outside the circle of courtiers and gentry for whom it was written; but the more general message, about readjusting values from fastidiousness and superficial propriety to genuine humility, still has an impact, and the bonhomie of the writing, the witty nimbleness of the prose, is still impressive.

Harington's epigrams, of which more than four hundred survive, were also produced in the 1590s and, like *The Metamorphosis of Ajax,* mix satire with jest. Only one of them was published in his lifetime but many were widely circulated. Harington's own manuscript collections show his careful arrangement of the epigrams into books, with an address to the reader at the beginning and significant juxtapositions of related items. Harington was among the first in an Elizabethan revival of the epigram, traditionally a brief, witty, and sardonic poetic statement, and he is capable of great succinctness in the form: "Treason doth never prosper, what's the reason? / For if it prosper, none dare call it treason."

His great model was the Roman poet Martial, who with harsh wit depicted a cynical, urban milieu in epigrams depicting the follies and crimes of those around him. "Against Lying Lynus" shows Harington attacking an enemy with a characteristic play on words:

I wonder *Lynus,* what thy tongue doth ail,
That though I flatter thee, thou still dost rail?

Thou think'st, I lie, perhaps thou think'st most true:
Yet to so gentle lies, pardon is due.
A lie, well told, to some tastes is restority;
Besides, we poets lie by good authority.
    But were all lying poetry, I know it,
    Lynus would quickly prove a passing poet.

"Lynus" is one of many Latin pseudonyms which reappear in the collection, apparently concealing a real person. In some cases it is possible to deduce the identity of such individuals: for example, "Paulus" is Sir Walter Ralegh and "Peleus" Sir Matthew Arundel.

Harington borrowed also from an English tradition of jesting, already represented in the epigram by Thomas More and John Heywood. In this tradition epigrams are more expansive, more anecdotal (Ben Jonson, who himself included a variety of short poems under the title *Epigrams,* told William Drummond that Harington's epigrams were mere "narrations"). Many of the more extended epigrams are about Harington's wife, Mall, and his mother-in-law, Lady Rogers. Yet as well as recording family life and sniping at adversaries, Harington aims in his epigram collection to imitate those of "Dr. Dale," who "wisely could mix serious things with jests." It is, as he tells fellow epigrammatist Thomas Bastard, "an act of virtue and of piety, / To warn us of our sins in any sort, / In prose, in verse, in earnest, or in sport."

Two particular kinds of sinners attract Harington's attention in the epigrams: the self-consciously "pure" or "precise," Puritans by temperament or doctrine; and the complacent libertines, the "atheists." With the first, the epigrammatist's tactic is to remind them of their fleshly frailty. The condition of an unmarried "pregnant pure sister" is enough to overthrow her pretensions to be above any mortal weaknesses. Harington contrives to suggest that the venality and unscrupulousness of self-confessed hedonist characters like Lesbia and Paulus are not willed freedom but something determined and relentless, leading remorselessly to damnation. Paulus pours scorn on the idea that spirits are ever to be seen on earth, which is true in the sense that, wherever he goes, he "a fiend worse than himself, shall never see."

Harington was frequently in attendance on Queen Elizabeth in these years, though his family connections with her produced no great preferment. He shows his familiarity with the court in his "A Treatise on Play" (1769), written in 1597, which describes a scheme to reduce gambling for high stakes by allowing players to use large-denomination coins as chips to be exchanged later for comparatively small sums. The treatise shows that there is tedium and discomfort in waiting in the presence rooms of princes, and that vanity is often rampant there, but it aims at regulating excesses rather than at drastic reform. In the matter of gambling Harington is not, in his own phrase, so "severe and Stoical" as to banish it altogether but would allow a safe form which is "gentlemanly for show, little for loss, and pleasant for company and recreation."

In 1599 Harington served with Robert Devereux, second Earl of Essex, on his expedition to Ireland to put down a major rebellion. There Essex infuriated Elizabeth by negotiating a treaty without approval and by knighting many of his followers in the field, including Harington. The latter tried to atone for his involvement in the affair by presenting Elizabeth with his highly critical journal of the campaign.

With the new century and an approaching change of monarch, Harington's interests became markedly more serious. In the closing years of Elizabeth's reign he courted James, whose succession he supported in his "Tract on the Succession" (written in 1602). It is notable for its moderation in church matters. Harington argues that the motives of extremists among both Reformers and Roman Catholics were more mixed than they would admit. Soon after James's accession, Harington, as one of the new king's learned subjects, was summoned to an interview. But the new reign brought him little advancement; indeed, he was imprisoned for debt in 1603 and again in 1604, as a result of incautiously standing surety for his uncle Thomas Markham, who had by then fallen on hard times. He tried to persuade Thomas Sutton, a wealthy moneylender, to buy various properties to save his uncle's fortunes (and his own) and in the end succeeded with one large manor, Castle Camps; in 1607 he intrigued unsuccessfully to have Sutton bequeath his estate to the duke of York, the future Charles I.

Among Harington's readings while he was in prison for debt in 1604 was Saint Augustine. The frequent references to Virgil therein seem to have inspired Harington to return to a translation he had begun earlier of book 6 of the *Aeneid,* which describes Aeneas's voyage to the Shades and to Elysium. For the translation he adopted once again the ottava-rima stanza familiar from his Ariosto. Frequently, it must be admitted, his end-stopped lines struggle somewhat unavailingly to render the density and subtle structures of the original; nevertheless, a naturalistic passage of dialogue or a well-phrased set-piece description occasionally catches the eye. The pleasures of the virtuous in Elysium, for instance, are rendered with great gusto:

> Look what delight they had on earth to frame
> Their chariots and their stately steeds to war,
> Their noble minds retaineth still the same,
> For pleasure not for use where now they are.
> Some make great feasts, some play at pleasant game,
> All in sweet peace all void of hateful jar.
> Their woods are laurel sweet, a pleasant stream
> Like our Euridanus runs through the realm.

In his marginal notes to the poem, and in the longer commentaries at the end, Harington once again gives precious evidence of attitudes toward moral and religious issues and gives some detailed readings of poetry. This time the context is specifically theological, and consideration of the proper bounds for belief in the supernatural is focused through the particular case of Virgil's account of Aeneas's adventures, which, both as a pagan document and as a fictional one, raises questions of interpretation for Harington. Virgil's paganism can be properly dealt with in Harington's view by the guiding notion that, though denied the Christian revelation, the Roman poet saw much of truth through "the light of nature"; what is remarkable, and reassuring, is how close Virgil came even as a pagan to "the mysteries of our faith" in dealing with the afterlife. The problem of fiction is analogous to the problem of a pagan theology: readers must avoid foundering on the rock of superstitious credulity, believing everything they read in a pagan author or in a poem, while at the same time steering clear of the "gulf" of unbounded skepticism or atheism, believing nothing in such writings. Harington's own conviction is that if proper rules for reading poetry are observed, "a good mind almost may be edified, and an ill mind, if not rectified, yet terrified," by passages like those in the book of Virgil he chose to translate.

Shortly after his pronouncements on theology in the commentary on Virgil, Harington actually proposed himself as archbishop and lord chancellor of Ireland. He was aware that contemporaries might find the idea risible; but in *A Short View of the State of Ireland* (1879), written in 1605, he presents his qualifications by expounding remarkably liberal and conciliatory proposals for a religious and legal settlement in that country. His proposals met with no success. In 1607 he drafted an essay in favor of celibacy for the clergy, in reply to a pamphlet by Joseph Hall. He was also collecting material on the bishops of the English church, and in 1608 he sent Prince Henry a supplement to Francis Godwin's *Catalogue of the Bishops of England* (1601). Here his

Sir John Harington and Lady Harington (from Norman Egbert McClure, The Letters and Epigrams of Sir John Harington, *1930)*

harshest criticism is reserved for those who exploited the weakness of the various sees after the Reformation and plundered their wealth. He had also sent the Virgil translation and commentary to Prince Henry.

The last of Harington's works to be published in his lifetime was a verse translation of a medical treatise, which he called *The Englishman's Doctor* (1607). It returns once again to some of the topics of *The Metamorphosis of Ajax.* Sometime around 1612 he completed a metrical paraphrase of the Psalms, sent in manuscript to King James with a letter calling attention to his verses' happy combination of correct doctrine and "smooth verse." The Psalms are the last of his writings to remain in manuscript. Only a handful has been edited. In the best of them he rediscovered some of the freshness and colloquial directness of his Ariosto translation. Their metrical virtuosity — rhyme schemes are especially varied — shows that he continued to the end to experiment in verse forms. Letters from this time shows he was anxious to promote the translations and to have them published. He had been reported "sick of a dead palsy" in May 1612, and he died in November of that year.

Harington declared in a note to book 32 of his *Orlando Furioso* that he found prose "a fair green way" and verse "a miry lane," and the temperament revealed in his writings might best be called prosaic. He was base-minded enough to deal with subjects his contemporaries thought unworthy of notice, and he was always especially suspicious of pretension and hypocrisy. As critic P. J. Croft points out, Harington characteristically reacted to some of the more high-flown passages in Sidney's *Arcadia* (written 1580–1581) by rewriting them to make descriptions more naturalistic and a sexual reference here and there more explicit. In poetry he remains, as Ben Jonson in his own time evidently regarded him, an amateur, though a gifted and industrious one. As a prose writer, on the other hand, he is genuinely original. Taken together, his diverse writings — in private letters, in the pronouncements of a self-appointed public counselor, in margins both literal and metaphorical — constitute a remarkable set of annotations on the life around him. It serves as a constant challenge to convenient simplifications about the Elizabethans and Jacobeans and their writing, and for that reason alone the attitudes expressed there, and the spontaneity and independence of Harington's writing, deserve to be more fully absorbed than they are in our picture of the period and its literature.

References:

Peter Beal, *Index of English Literary Manuscripts,* volume 1 (London: Mansell, 1980), pp. 121–157;

Simon Cauchi, "The 'Setting Foorth' of Harington's Ariosto," *Studies in Bibliography,* 36 (1983): 137–168;

D. H. Craig, *Sir John Harington* (Boston: Twayne, 1985);

P. J. Croft, "Sir John Harington's Manuscript of Sir Philip Sidney's *Arcadia,*" in Croft and Stephen Parks, *Literary Autographs: Papers Read at a Clark Library Seminar 26 April 1980* (Los Angeles: Clark Library, 1983), pp. 39–75;

Robert C. Evans, "Sir John Harington and Thomas Sutton: New Letters from Charterhouse," *John Donne Journal,* 7, no. 2 (1988): 213–237; 8, nos. 1, 2 (1989): 195;

Marcus Selden Goldman, "Sidney and Harington as Opponents of Superstition," *Journal of English and Germanic Philology,* 54 (October 1955): 526–548;

Ian Grimble, *The Harington Family* (London: Cape, 1957);

Ruth Hughey, *John Harington of Stepney, Tudor Gentleman: His Life and Works* (Columbus: Ohio State University Press, 1971);

Daniel Javitch, *Proclaiming a Classic: The Canonization of "Orlando Furioso"* (Princeton: Princeton University Press, 1991);

Ben Jonson, *Ben Jonson,* edited by Charles H. Herford and Percy and Evelyn Simpson, volume 1 (Oxford: Clarendon Press, 1925), p. 33;

Kathleen M. Lea, "Harington's *Folly,*" in *Elizabethan and Jacobean Studies Presented to Frank Percy Wilson* (Oxford: Clarendon Press, 1959), pp. 42–58;

Judith Lee, "The English Ariosto: The Elizabethan Poet and the Marvelous," *Studies in Philology,* 80 (Summer 1983): 277–299;

John Leland, "A Joyful Noise: *The Metamorphosis of Ajax* as Spiritual Tract," *South Atlantic Review,* 47 (May 1982): 53–62;

M. H. M. MacKinnon, "Sir John Harington and Bishop Hall," *Philological Quarterly,* 37 (January 1958): 80–86;

R. H. Miller, "Unpublished Poems by Sir John Harington," *English Literary Renaissance,* 14 (Spring 1984): 148–158;

Thomas Nashe, *The Works,* 5 volumes, edited by Ronald B. McKerrow (London: Bullen, 1904–1910);

T. G. A. Nelson, "Death, Dung, the Devil, and Worldly Delights: A Metaphysical Conceit in Harington, Donne, and Herbert," *Studies in Philology,* 76 (July 1979): 272–287;

Nelson, "Sir John Harington and the Renaissance Debate over Allegory," *Studies in Philology,* 82 (Summer 1985): 359–379;

Nelson, "Sir John Harington as a Critic of Sir Philip Sidney," *Studies in Philology,* 67 (January 1970): 41–56;

Walter Raleigh, "Sir John Harington," in his *Some Authors: A Collection of Literary Essays 1896–1916* (Oxford: Clarendon Press, 1923), pp. 136–155;

Townsend Rich, *Harington and Ariosto: A Study in Elizabethan Verse Translation* (New Haven: Yale University Press, 1940);

N. R. Shipley, "The History of a Manor: Castle Campes, 1580–1629," *Bulletin of the Institute of Historical Research,* 48 (November 1975): 162–181.

Papers:

Sir John Harington was responsible for a great many manuscripts still extant, both of his own works and of others' which he had copied for his personal use. The most important examples of these are in the British Library in London, the Bodleian Library at Oxford, and the Folger Library in Washington, D.C.

Thomas Harman

(flourished 1566 – 1573)

Elizabeth Hanson
Queen's University

BOOKS: *A Caueat for Commen Cursetors Vulgarely Called Vagabones. Newly Agmented* (London: Printed by William Gryffith, 1567); revised as *A Caueat or Warening [etc.]* (London: Printed by Henry Middleton, 1573).

Editions: *The Fraternitye of Vacabondes, by John Awdeley . . . from the Edition of 1575 in the Bodleian Library. A Caueat or Warening for Commen Cursetors Vulgarely Called Vagabones, by Thomas Harman Esquiere, from the 3rd Edition of 1567 . . . A Sermon in Praise of Thieves and Thievery, by Parson Haben or Hyberdyne, from the Landsdowne Ms. 98, and Cotton Vesp. A. 25. Those Parts of the Groundworke of Conny-catching (ed. 1592) that Differ from Harman's Caueat*, edited by Edward Viles and Frederick James Furnivall (London: Published by N. Trübner for the Early English Text Society, 1869), pp. 17–91; republished as *Rogues and Vagabonds of Shakespeare's Youth* (London: Published by N. Trübner for the New Shakespeare Society, 1880);

The Elizabethan Underworld, edited by Arthur Valentine Judges (London: George Routledge & Sons, 1930) – includes Harman's "Caveat," pp. 61–118;

Coney-Catchers and Bawdy Baskets, edited by Gamini Salgado (Harmondsworth, U.K.: Penguin, 1972) – includes Harman's "Caveat," pp. 79–153.

Thomas Harman's *Caueat for Common Cursitors* (first published in 1566, though the earliest extant edition is from the 1567 second printing) is a classic Elizabethan crime or "coney-catching" pamphlet which purports to describe the stratagems, language, and cultural practices of the vagrants (or "cursitors," as Harman calls them) wandering the sixteenth-century English countryside as a result of such social upheavals as the enclosure of lands for sheep grazing, which resulted in the expulsion of many rural tenants by landowners. To some extent

Title page for Harman's 1567 "coney-catching" pamphlet

already a redaction of material from earlier pamphlets, the *Caveat* was copied or borrowed from in subsequent pamphlets and plays purporting to expose "underworld" life and in dictionaries of cant until the end of the eighteenth century. Until recently it was also assumed to be an accurate record of Elizabethan criminal culture. One of the earliest examples of crime writing in English, Harman's little book initiates the construction of the lower classes as an object of ethnographic study which finds its full expression in works such as Henry Mayhew's *London Labour and the London Poor* (1851–1862).

The principal sources of biographical information on Harman are the *Caveat* itself and the historical records of Kent. In the former, Harman styles himself "a poor gentleman," while the latter suggest that he was a reasonably wealthy member of the lesser gentry. His grandfather Henry Harman had been clerk of the crown during the reign of Henry VII and had acquired in about 1480 the estates of Ellam and Maystreet in the parish of Crayford (on the Thames about fifteen miles from London), which were passed to his son, William, and from William to Thomas in 1547. From his father Harman also inherited the manor of Maxton, which he apparently sold. *Hasted's History of Kent* (1886), a vast nineteenth-century compilation of county records, shows several real estate transactions involving Harman and his family. As befitted a person of his station, he appears to have served as a justice of the peace, for he remarks at one point in the *Caveat* that he was "in commission of the peace" when a particular incident occurred; moreover, he writes his book in order that "Justices and shrieves may in their circuits be more vigilant to punish these malefactors." He was evidently not acting in the capacity of justice when he wrote the *Caveat,* however, for his name appears nowhere in the Elizabethan Assize records for Kent from this period. Nevertheless, subsequent appropriators of Harman's material, beginning with the anonymous author of *The Groundwork of Conny-catching* (1592), insist on his status as justice, and one "S. R.," in *Martin Markall, Beadle of Bridewell* (1610), specifies that Harman was "Justice of the Peace in Queen Mary's day."

The *Caveat* seems to be the only work Harman ever published, but it was enough for William Lambard in his *Perambulation of Kent* (1576) to list the former among "the Kentish writers." The picture of Harman that emerges from the *Caveat* is of an energetic man, interested in the welfare of his community and intrigued by vagrant culture but often self-promoting (he was obviously delighted by the opportunity to become a published author) and occasionally brutal. He sets out to restore a social order in which gentlemen "set up houses and keep hospitality in the country to the comfort of their neighbors, relief of the poor, and amendment of the commonwealth," and his text promotes neighborliness and charity; but these commitments do not preclude Harman from torturing a beggar to force him to reveal that his disability is false.

The *Caveat* presents itself as an anatomy of vagrant life developed from Harman's firsthand experience as a crafty interrogator of vagabonds who has had occasion to "talk and confer daily with many of these wily wanderers of both sorts, as well men and women, as boys and girls by whom I have gathered and understand their deep dissimulation and detestable dealing." After an introduction describing Harman's investigative methods, there are entries for each of the various types of vagrants, such as a "dummerer" (beggar who feigns muteness), "walking mort" (unmarried female vagrant), "counterfeit crank" (false epileptic), and so on. Typically each entry will describe the characteristics of the vagrant type and then proceed to a firsthand or secondhand narrative of an encounter with such a person. Although on the order of traditional jests, these little stories usually involve a fair bit of local, even personal, detail. Thus, for example, the account of the counterfeit crank, which involves a lengthy tale of a tangle among Harman, the printer of the *Caveat* (William Griffith), and one such "crank," begins: "Upon Allhallow Day in the morning last, *Anno Domini* 1566, [before] my book was half printed, I mean the first impression, there came early in the morning a counterfeit crank under my lodging at the Whitefriars, within the cloister in a little yard or court, whereabouts lay two or three great ladies, being without the liberties of London, whereby he hoped for the greater gain."

The book concludes with a list of names of male vagrants who "walk about Essex, Middlesex, Sussex, Surrey, and Kent," a dictionary of the canting tongue (underworld jargon), and a sample dialogue between "an upright man" and a "rogue" with interlineated translation, which commences as follows:

UPRIGHT-MAN. *Bene lightmans to thy quarroms! In what libken hast thou libbed in this darkmans, whether in a libbege or in the strummel?*

Good-morrow to thy body! In what house hast thou lain in all night, whether in a bed or in the straw?

ROGUE. *I couched a hogshead in a skipper this darkmans.*

I laid me down to sleep in a barn this night.

The picture Harman paints is of a highly organized culture with well-defined social roles, distinctive sexual practices, and its own language.

The basic format of Harman's book, an anatomy of vagrant types coupled with a lexicon of their language, derives ultimately from the German *Liber Vagatorum* of 1475 (republished by Martin Luther in 1528), although the more immediate source is John Awdeley's *Fraternity of Vagabonds* (1561), which details the orders of "ruffling vagabonds" (but does not provide a lexicon) and upon which Harman claims to be expanding. What distinguishes Harman's work from these predecessors is his extensive narration of how he acquired his knowledge, and the text's wealth of detail (dates, place-names, and proper names of vagrants) — features which produce an effect of documentary accuracy and empirical observation. What had been lore becomes in Harman's treatment fact and personal experience.

The *Caveat* went through four editions in Harman's lifetime, the later ones expanding the unfolding episode of the counterfeit crank and taking up matters of language that seem to have arisen out of correspondence with readers of previous editions. The text seems to have been taken seriously insofar as Harman is cited as an authority on the vagrancy problem in the 1587 version of William Harrison's "Description of England." It was also, however, recognized as a valuable literary commodity. Much of his material was republished in the anonymous *Groundwork of Conny-Catching,* a text which appears to be capitalizing on the vogue started by Robert Greene's coney-catching pamphlets of the same year. The title page of *Groundwork* promises "the manner of peddler's French and the means to understand the same . . . done by a Justice of the Peace of great authority who had the examining of divers of them."

Harman's material appears again in Thomas Dekker's anonymously published *Bellman of London* (1608) and more extensively in the same author's *Lantern and Candlelight; or, The Bell-man's Second Night's Walk* (1608). The former tells of the same types of vagrant that Harman describes. The latter begins with a disquisition on canting and furnishes a dictionary borrowed from Harman, then proceeds through the obviously fictional and not very fully realized figure of the Bellman to describe new types of scoundrels and their stratagems. Gone in these pamphlets is the reasonably realistic account Harman provides of how he made his discoveries and the personalized touches in his accounts of vagrant stratagems. What remains is the classification of rogues by type and the focus on the canting tongue. These pamphlets, then, continue to represent classification and decoding as strategies for dealing with shifters and vagabonds at the same time that they treat the whole enterprise as a kind of literary game. This effect is even more pronounced in the anonymous *Martin Markall, Beadle of Bridewell,* which accuses the Bellman of having merely plagiarized his dictionary from Harman and then proceeds to update Harman's dictionary with new cant words.

The feature of the *Caveat* that seems to have had the most persistence is its fascination with the

Page from A Caveat for Common Cursitors *with a woodcut depicting a member of the Elizabethan underworld, Nicolas Blunt, as an upright man and as a "counterfeit crank" (a beggar pretending to be afflicted with a serious disease)*

canting tongue. Harman's is the first written record of cant, and in the pamphlets which borrow from it the canting lexicon is given pride of place, becoming the focus of the quarrel over authenticity between the Bellman of London and the Beadle of Bridewell — a quarrel in which Harman is credited as the true author and first compiler of the lexicon. These pamphlets were part of a canting vogue in the early decades of the seventeenth century. Plays such as Thomas Middleton and Dekker's *Roaring Girl* (1608), John Fletcher's *Beggar's Bush* (1615), and Richard Brome's *Jovial Crew* (1641) present canting beggars, as does Ben Jonson's masque, *The Gypsies Metamorphosed* (1621).

Versions of Harman's material, particularly the lexicon of cant, continued to appear throughout the seventeenth and into the eighteenth centuries in texts such as the anonymous *English Villainies* (1638) and Richard Head's *English Rogue* (1680), *A Dictionary of the Canting Crew* (1710), *A New Canting Dictio-*

nary (1725), and *The Scoundrel's Dictionary* (1751). At the end of the eighteenth century Francis Grose published *A Classical Dictionary of the Vulgar Tongue* (1785), which (in its pretentious title as well as in its content and presentation) marks a shift in the purpose of the canting lexicon from entertainment to edification and clearly uses Harman as a source. Harman's inscription within serious scholarly endeavor is even more pronounced in John Camden Hotten's *Slang Dictionary* (1873), which reprints Harman's lexicon in its introduction and credits Harman as the first scholar of English slang.

Hotten's recognition of Harman as his forebear is part of a nineteenth- and early-twentieth-century reconstruction of Harman as a bona fide social observer and critic. For Frank Aydelotte, the *Caveat* has "the interest that belongs to honest and real descriptions of a little-known phase of sixteenth-century life." This same approach obtains in A. V. Judges's marvelous compendium of crime pamphlets, *The Elizabethan Underworld* (1930). Each of these works selects the putative foundation of Harman's text in firsthand observation as its distinguishing characteristic, as opposed to the later coney-catching pamphlets, which are categorized as works of purely literary interest, merely plagiarisms of Harman leavened with an inventiveness born of the hack writer's scramble to earn a living.

Recently, however, social historians have called into question the accuracy of Harman's depiction of Elizabethan vagrancy, particularly his account of a highly organized vagrant society with developed criminal specializations. A. L. Beier writes that "vagrant crime was protean rather than specialized," the vagrants themselves simply the rural poor who had been cast off of their land, desperately struggling to stay alive. He lumps Harman's work in with other rogue pamphlets as being primarily of "literary" rather than historical in interest. Never-theless, Beier admits, some of Harman's particular anecdotes can be corroborated by contemporary court records.

Although Harman's pamphlet has lost some of its historical credibility, it has piqued the interests of present-day literary critics because of the way it repeatedly implicates itself in the very social instability that it strives to eradicate. Thus, critic Stephen Greenblatt cites the *Caveat* as an instance of Renaissance authority generating and containing its own subversion because of the way in which Harman's pride at his own craftiness identifies him with the vagrants. In another recent study of Harman's work, Barry Taylor analyzes the *Caveat* as a text that reveals a connection between the very act of writing and social disorder. His argument usefully turns attention from Harman's ostensible subject matter (the Elizabethan criminal classes) to Harman's activity as a writer. But it might be worthwhile to situate this activity with greater historical specificity, to consider what the *Caveat* tells us about the position of the parish gentry in the mid sixteenth century. The interest of Harman's little book has yet to be exhausted.

References:

Frank Aydelotte, *Elizabethan Rogues and Vagabonds* (Oxford: Clarendon Press, 1913);

A. L. Beier, *Masterless Men: The Vagrancy Problem in Early Modern England* (London & New York: Methuen, 1985);

Frank Wadleigh Chandler, *The Literature of Roguery,* 2 volumes (New York: Burt Franklin, 1907);

Stephen Greenblatt, "Invisible Bullets," in *Shakespearean Negotiations* (Berkeley: University of California Press, 1988), pp. 21–65;

Barry Taylor, *Vagrant Writing: Social and Semiotic Disorders in the English Renaissance* (London & New York: Harvester Wheatsheaf, 1991), pp. 1–24.

Thomas Harriot

(1560 – 2 July 1621)

William H. Sherman
University of Maryland at College Park

BOOKS: *A Briefe and True Report of the New Found Land of Virginia* (London: Robert Robinson, 1588); enlarged as *The True Pictures . . . of the People in Virginia,* 2 volumes (Frankfurt am Main: Printed by Johann Wechel for Theodor de Bry, 1590);

Artis analyticae praxis, ad aequationes algebraicas nova, expedita, & generali methodo, resolvendas (London: R. Barker, 1631).

Editions: *A Briefe and True Report of the New Found Land of Virginia,* abridged by Richard Hakluyt, in *The Principall Navigations, Voiages and Discoueries of the English Nation* (London: Printed by George Bishop and Ralph Newberie, 1589), pp. 748–764;

A Briefe and True Report of the New Found Land of Virginia, edited by W. Harry Rylands (Manchester: Printed by A. Brothers for the Holbein Society, 1888);

A Briefe and True Report of the New Found Land of Virginia, edited by Henry Stevens (London: Privately printed, 1900);

A Briefe and True Report of the New Found Land of Virginia, The English Experience, no. 384 (Amsterdam: Theatrum Orbis Terrarum / New York: Da Capo, 1971);

A Briefe and True Report of the New Found Land of Virginia (New York: Dover, 1972).

Thomas Harriot

Thomas Harriot (also spelled "Hariot"; "Heriot"; "Harriots"; and so on) was among the most distinguished of the Elizabethan polymaths. According to his epitaph, he "cultivated all the sciences / And excelled in all." Indeed, his friend the poet George Chapman called him "master of all essential and true knowledge." He was a valued intellectual servant of several noblemen, an expert mathematician and astronomer, and a pioneering ethnographer and linguist. In spite of the paucity of his published work, Harriot was an extremely influential scholar and remains an exceptional representative of his age.

As Anthony à Wood put it, Harriot "tumbled out of his mother's womb into the lap of the Oxonian Muses [in] 1560." Although many Harriots have been identified, it is impossible to trace Thomas's lineage or to assign him a birthplace more precise than Oxfordshire. Nothing is known of his early years, and the first official notice of him came on 20 December 1577, when he was entered in the Matriculation Records of Saint Mary's Hall, Oxford. Despite the general constraints on scientific learning in sixteenth-century Oxford, Harriot's college years were productive. It was in Oxford that he first forged his links with many important friends – among them Richard Hakluyt, Thomas Allen, Chapman, and George Peele.

After leaving Oxford Harriot moved to London, where he offered private instruction in mathematics. He may well have been taken into the household of a young gentleman with maritime aspirations: Sir Humphrey Gilbert, who in 1583 established the first British colony in North America, is perhaps the most likely candidate. By the spring of 1584 Harriot was certainly in the service of Sir Walter Ralegh, assisting the latter in his preparations for New World exploration. Harriot conducted classes in navigation for Ralegh's seamen at Durham House, and from these lectures he wrote his "Arcticon," of which only rough notes survive. A year later Sir Richard Grenville led Ralegh's expedition to Virginia; when his ship left Plymouth on 9 April 1585, Harriot was on board.

Harriot accompanied Grenville's voyage as the official geographer, chronicler, and interpreter – having made some headway, while still in England, into the intricacies of the Algonquian language. He had devised his own phonetic alphabet to transcribe the speech of the Indians, a system far in advance of the linguistic science of his day. Both for the sake of accuracy and for the aid of prospective colonists and traders, he compiled an extensive glossary of commodities and place-names.

But Harriot's greatest service to the Roanoke enterprise, and the one for which he is chiefly remembered, was *A Brief and True Report of the New Found Land of Virginia* (1588), which he penned upon his return to England. In contrast to his official chronicle of the voyage (which has not survived and may never have been completed), *A Brief and True Report* is neither a neutral nor an exhaustive account. It was written rather as a defense of the voyages of Ralegh, who probably commissioned it, at a time when the colonizing venture was in jeopardy, and it was patently designed both to attract new financial support for further colonization and to convince potential colonists of the abundance and relative safety of the New World. As the title page advertises, the work was "directed to the adventurers, favorers, and well-willers of the action, for the inhabiting and planting there."

Harriot's text, significantly, takes the form of a "report" rather than the more conventional narrative or chronological annal. He begins by answering the "many envious, malicious, and slanderous" rumors which have circulated since the venture, but he quickly moves to the survey of "commodities," which constitutes the bulk of the text. This lists first the "merchantable commodities" (silk, flax, wine, oil, sugar, furs, skins, minerals, gems, and dyes) and then the commodities necessary for the "victual and sustenance" of the colonizers (grains, vegetables, roots, fruits, berries, animals, fish, and trees). He concludes with what is for modern readers the most original and interesting section, on the "nature and manners" of the "natural inhabitants."

It is not surprising, in light of the fact that he was the only one of the party who could begin to converse in the language of the natives, that he is markedly more sensitive toward the Indians than his compatriots. He expresses a sort of backhanded respect for many of their practices, granting that, "considering the want of such means as we have, they seem very ingenious." And while he understood his mission to entail both the colonization and Christianization of the natives, he was unable to hide his indignation at their treatment by some of the Englishmen: "some of our company towards the end of the year showed themselves too fierce in slaying some of the people, in some towns, upon causes that on our part might easily enough have been borne withall."

Harriot's rhetorical strategy in *A Brief and True Report* is a tribute to his argumentative skill. After explicitly and repeatedly drawing attention to his credit as an eyewitness, he effaces his voice by offering an inventory of observations, materials, and customs. This manages both to create an illusion of the land's speaking for itself and to leave an impression upon the reader of a sensitive anthropologist at work.

Despite the modest and local concerns guiding its creation, *A Brief and True Report* enjoyed considerable success in its own day and is now considered the first, and possibly the most important, major text of English colonialism. Its first edition, printed in 1588 by Robert Robinson, was a cheap pamphlet. But in 1589 Hakluyt took it up in an abridged form for inclusion in the first edition of *The Principal Navigations*. Hakluyt also persuaded the Frankfurt-based engraver Theodor de Bry to publish Harriot's text along with some of the drawings by John White, the artist who accompanied Harriot on the Grenville expedition. In 1590 de Bry issued this grand edition, in four different languages, as the first part of his great "America" series. In the twentieth century the work has been acknowledged as the first original book about the earliest English colony in Amer-

An illustration from the 1590 edition of A Brief and True Report of the New Found Land of Virginia, *an engraving based on a drawing by John White, who was a member of the expedition*

ica and therefore one of the fundamental books on which the English built their empire. Its central place in Stephen Greenblatt's essay "Invisible Bullets" has recently brought it to the attention of historical-minded literary critics. Greenblatt vividly maps the complex power relations at work in the imposition of an English, Christian order on the American Indians.

As Greenblatt asserts, Harriot's presentation of this order was sufficiently ambiguous to call his own religious orthodoxy into question. Throughout his life he struggled with slanderous allegations of heresy and atheism, the most famous being the testimony of Richard Baines in the 1593 case against Christopher Marlowe: Marlowe, he claimed, had said that "Moses was but a juggler, and that one Heriots being Sir W Raleigh's man can do more than he." Another came by way of a cynical epitaph in 1621: when Harriot died of nasal cancer, one of his contemporaries seized upon his challenge to the doctrine of creation ex nihilo and remarked, "a *nihilum* killed him at last: for in the top of his nose came a little red speck (exceeding small), which grew bigger and bigger, and at last killed him."

Such persecutions, particularly the more official and threatening ones which came in the wake of the Gunpowder Plot in 1605, were responsible for the overwhelmingly private nature of Harriot's intellectual efforts. *A Brief and True Report* proved to be the first and last text published during his life. For the remainder of his career he channeled his efforts into the service of Ralegh and Henry Percy, the "Wizard Earl" (so called because of his scientific experiments) and into a massive collection of looseleaf notes. While established with a generous pension at Percy's Syon House, Harriot made major advances in optics, algebra, and astronomy and built up an impressive circle of young mathematicians. He left to one of these, Nathaniel Torporley, the unpleasant task of sifting through the ten thousand folio pages of undigested notes, measurements, diagrams, and calculations and deciding what was fit for publication. Aside from the appearance in 1631 of a short textbook on algebra (published as *Artis analyticae praxis,* under the direction of Walter Warner rather than Torporley), these papers remain in manuscript. One of his inheritors, the mathematician John Pell, noted that if Harriot had "published all he knew in algebra, he would have left little of the chief mysteries of that art unhandled." Preliminary work on Harriot's notes suggests that he was indeed a scientist of the highest stature and that he carried out within private walls a virtual, albeit quiet, scientific revolution.

While many of his contemporaries would have found this hard to believe, some Renaissance writers considered him the very embodiment of wisdom. George Chapman, who had consulted Harriot in preparing his translation of Homer's *Iliad,* found him one "whose depth of soul measures the height, / And all dimensions of all works of weight." For one contemporary, then, Harriot's "clear eyes" were not the eyes of an atheist but "the spheres where reason moves."

Biography:

John W. Shirley, *Thomas Harriot: A Biography* (Oxford: Clarendon Press, 1983).

References:

Gordon R. Batho, *The Household Papers of Henry Percy, Ninth Earl of Northumberland (1564–1632)* (London: Camden Society, 1962);

George Chapman, *Achilles' Shield* (London: John Windet, 1598);

Wayne Franklin, *Discoverers, Explorers, Settlers: The Diligent Writers of Early America* (Chicago & London: University of Chicago Press, 1979), pp. 104–113;

Stephen Greenblatt, "Invisible Bullets," in *Shakespearean Negotiations: The Circulation of Social Energy in Renaissance England* (Berkeley: University of California Press, 1988), pp. 21–65;

John Parker, *Books to Build an Empire: A Bibliographical History of English Overseas Interests to 1620* (Amsterdam: N. Israel, 1965);

David B. Quinn, *The Roanoke Voyages, 1584–1590* (London: Hakluyt Society, 1955);

Muriel Rukeyser, *The Traces of Thomas Harriot* (London: Gollancz, 1972);

John W. Shirley, ed., *A Source Book for the Study of Thomas Harriot* (New York: Arno, 1981);

Shirley, ed., *Thomas Harriot: Renaissance Scientist* (Oxford: Clarendon Press, 1974);

Henry Stevens, *Thomas Hariot, the Mathematician, the Philosopher, and the Scholar* (London, 1900; New York: Lenox Hill, 1972);

Eva Germaine Rimington Taylor, *Late Tudor and Early Stuart Geography, 1583–1650* (London: Methuen, 1934);

David W. Waters, *The Art of Navigation in England in Elizabethan and Early Stuart Times* (New Haven: Yale University Press, 1958);

Anthony à Wood, *Athenae Oxonienses,* volume 2 (London: F. C. & J. Rivington, 1815), p. 299.

Papers:

Nineteen volumes of Thomas Harriot's papers can be found among the British Library's Additional Manuscripts and the manuscripts at Petworth House, Sussex. Various letters and documents also survive at Alnwick Castle, Northumberland, the Guildhall Library, London, Hatfield House, Hertfordshire, and the Public Record Office in London.

William Harrison

(18 April 1535 – 9 November 1593)

G. J. R. Parry
Victoria University of Wellington

BOOKS: *A Historicall Description of the Island of Britaine, with a Briefe Rehearsall of the Nature and Qualities of the People of England, and Such Commodities as Are to Be Found in the Same,* in *The Chronicles of England, Scotlande, and Irelande,* volume 1, edited by Raphael Holinshed (London: Printed by Henry Bynneman for John Harrison, 1577); revised and enlarged as *The Description of Britain,* in *The First and Second Volumes of Chronicles. Newlie Augmented and Continued by J. Hooker Alias Vowell Gent. and Others,* volume 1, edited by John Hooker, John Stow, and others (London: Printed by Henry Denham, 1587).

Editions: *Harrison's Description of England in Shakspere's Youth, Being the Second and Third Books of His Description of Britaine and England,* edited by Frederick J. Furnivall (London: Printed by N. Trübner for the New Shakespeare Society, 1877–1881); enlarged edition, edited by Furnivall and Charlotte C. Stopes (London: Chatto & Windus, 1908;

The Description of England, by William Harrison, edited by Georges Edelen (Ithaca, N.Y.: Cornell University Press for the Folger Shakespeare Library, 1968).

TRANSLATIONS: Hector Boece, *The Description of Scotland, Written at the First by Hector Boetius in Latine, and Afterward Translated into the Scottish Speech by John Bellenden . . . and Now Finallie into English by R. H.,* translated by Harrison, in *The Chronicles of England, Scotlande, and Irelande,* volume 2, edited by Holinshed (London: Printed [by Henry Bynneman] for John Harrison, 1577).

William Harrison's *Historical Description of the Island of Britain* (1577) provides the fullest contemporary account of social institutions and behavior in Elizabethan England. Recent research has put the *Historical Description* into its proper context by emphasizing the substantial differences between the 1577 edition and the fuller 1587 edition, the source of so much vivid detail, and by discovering some of Harrison's many unpublished historical and chronological works. These previously unknown writings extend the range of Harrison's learning, already impressively wide in the *Historical Description;* establish him as a major figure in Elizabethan historical scholarship; and also demonstrate a more profoundly Protestant social vision than a cursory mining of the *Historical Description* would suggest.

By his own account Harrison was born in the "house next to the Holy Lamb toward Cheapside," in Cordwainer Street, London, at "*hora* 11, *minut* 4, *Secunde* 56," on Sunday, 18 April 1535. He less precisely described his parents, Anne and John Harrison, as "honorable citizens." John was probably not John Harrison the Elder, one of the printers of Holinshed's *Chronicles* criticized by William for their hasty negligence, but probably instead a Merchant Adventurer of that name, since in the *Historical Description* Harrison modestly suppresses the name of a wealthy ship-owning merchant.

Despite the scholarly attention since paid to it, Harrison described his *Historical Description* in its dedication as merely the "crumbs" from his "Great English Chronology." The "Chronology" absorbed his attention from the mid 1560s until his death, while the sixty-five chapters of the 1577 *Historical Description,* surveying the geography, history, and society of England were scrambled together in a few summer weeks in 1576. The second edition of 1587 benefited more from the "Chronology." While the "Chronology" is more outspoken, for example in its criticism of noble misbehavior and the English icon Constantine the Great, both works exhibit a consistently Protestant worldview reflecting Harrison's education in Renaissance values and his traumatic experience of the Reformation.

In the 1540s Harrison attended Saint Paul's School, where he learned from John Colet's curriculum and Desiderius Erasmus's textbooks to despise both scholastic barbarisms and the pursuit of private self-interest at the expense of the commonweal. These prejudices were reinforced a few years later while he was an "unprofitable grammarian" at Westminster School under the Protestant humanist Alexander Nowell. Harrison's early training in grammarian pedantry also explains his later fruitful obsession with detail in the *Historical Description* and the "Chronology," the latter well described by Holinshed in his preface to the *Chronicles* as "a large discourse of most things worthy remembrance, done since the world began," compiled with "exquisite diligence." Harrison's consistently "commonwealth" interpretation of that material emphasizes the continuities between humanism and the reformed religion, which he had encountered at Oxford.

In 1554 Harrison entered Christ Church, Oxford, taking his B.A. in 1557. He became a probationary fellow of Merton in July 1557 and received Catholic ordination in April 1558. Harrison resigned the fellowship, however, sometime before July 1558 to become household chaplain to William Brooke, Lord Cobham. The move reflects less his stated distaste for the shallow learning and corrupt fellowship elections of the college than the first stage of his psychological conversion from Catholicism to a fundamentally Protestant, Pauline faith. After all, Christ Church, like Merton, had fervently embraced Queen Mary's reestablishment of the Catholic church in England in 1555. Cobham presented Harrison to the rectory of Radwinter, Essex, on 16 February 1559, and he went on to take his M.A. from Oxford in June 1560.

In autobiographical marginalia written around 1565, Harrison recalls his personal crisis, claiming to have been cured of popish "insanity" by the secret preaching of the Oxford martyrs, Thomas Cranmer, Hugh Latimer, and Nicholas Ridley. Harrison fitted this unverifiable experience into a prophesied historical scheme that justified his faith and increasingly directed his writing. The preaching of the Martyrs led him to perceive an unceasing conflict filling all of history: between the True Church, descending through the spiritual generations of the elect since Adam, and the Church of Cain, descending from the first apostate and shaped by Satan through paganism into a parody of the true religion. Contemporary popery perpetuated this pagan debasement under anti-Christian forms. Harrison's realization encapsulated a common Protestant scheme, adumbrated notably in the text of John Bale's *Scriptorum illustrium majoris Britanniae . . . catalogus* (1557–1559), in a copy of which Harrison penned his "autobiography." Therefore, in claiming his own place in the continuing True Church, personified in the Oxford martyrs, and bewailing his popish ordination as "a shaved worshipper of Baal," Harrison adopted a resonantly prophetic worldview, the detailed historical implications of which he worked out in his writings.

Also in the 1560s Harrison married Marion Isebrand, a refugee from Andern in the Calais Pale, lost by the English in 1558. The couple had four children. Their daughter Anne went on to marry George Downham, a leading Cambridge Ramist and the bishop of Derry, Ireland, during the reign of James I. Their son Edmund proceeded B.D. from Cambridge in 1603 and held livings in his brother-in-law's diocese, where his books, added to those of his father and Downham, became the core of the diocesan library. Harrison's son William predeceased him, and an unnamed daughter is mentioned in his will.

Harrison's conversion gave the study of time new importance. Chronology with geography formed "the eyes of history," while time gave fulfillment to the divine will; but in minutely studying chronology Protestan's not only organized the past but also could arrange it and their personal experiences according to a prophetically comprehensible pattern. Thus Harrison's 1565 autobiography claims that he had written in English "Chronological computations from the beginning of the world to his own times" and "Reflections on the same." He had also completed a life of Saint Paul, a central figure in Protestant soteriology. However, these works remained unarticulated components of developing historical vision, because he was then writing "an uncommon compendium of history in imitation of Aelian, Gellius, Macrobius, Petrarch, and Politian," clearly a work of humanist historical biography, illustrating desirable types of moral conduct. Not until Harrison abandoned that work some time after 1565 did he begin his great "Chronology," articulating a Pauline conception of religion and history in which the precise chronological and historical demonstration of God's care for his elect aimed to reorient individual perceptions, creating "lively stones" who would through their godly behavior build up Christ's church. Harrison probably acquired this Pauline outlook while completing the requirements for his B.D., taken in 1571 at Cambridge, where evangelical Protestantism was dominant in the later 1560s. The earliest work on the

"Chronology" can perhaps be dated to this further radicalization of his thought, for in that work Harrison depicted historical events as ominously significant for contemporary actions and assumed that chronology revealed God's plan in its periods, patterns, and parallels.

Until recently, only one version of the "Chronology" was extant, a vast manuscript dating from around 1570 to 1580, now located at Trinity College, Dublin. The title page, written around 1580, includes a descriptive list of other manuscript works now lost and reveals Harrison's immersion in the strange world of chronological complexities, utterly alien to the genially prolix Harrison of scholarly tradition. The list begins with the *Description,* followed by a detailed proof of Harrison's chronological calculations, then "Certain Tables" setting out "the several successions of sundry monarchies and empires"; of these the British succession appeared in the 1587 *Historical Description,* and a fragmentary copy of the whole survives in the recently discovered final manuscript of the "Chronology," discussed below. Next comes "An observation of certain great and notable eclipses," an increasingly fashionable attempt to tie astronomical patterns to historical data. Then follow three books entirely devoted to proving that, through errors in the Easter cycle devised by Dionysius Exiguus, the Latin church placed the Incarnation one year too late. Another book followed Gerardus Mercator in calculating the Creation at the first moment of Leo in 3966 B.C., rejecting "sinister imaginations" about the world's horoscope. Yet another synchronized the Hebrew Sabbath cycle with the Julian year, later accomplished by Joseph Justus Scaliger with more public success. Last are "An Historical Calendar" of English and foreign rulers, related to scriptural prophecy, and "Certain Rules and Brief Tables" for understanding the "Chronology." The Trinity manuscript also mentions Harrison's discriminating "annotations" on the prophecies of Merlin, and a far more significant, almost completed treatise on "the Antiquities of this land"; the context suggests a work resembling Laurence Nowell's projected "Topographical Dictionary," a study of historic remains carried on by Harrison's colleague William Lambarde but discontinued when Lombarde saw the manuscript of Camden's *Britannia.*

Harrison may have followed that wise example, but all the works listed would seem to have contributed to Harrison's ongoing argument that the God of history required Englishmen to abandon their sinful ways and conform to the models of godly behavior in the True Church, which alone had escaped God's historical wrath. This theme is obscured, however, for the reader of the Trinity chronology, for apart from being manifestly a work in progress, the "Chronology" is not a continuous, coherent argument, but an interpretation of an immense number of discrete historical events set in series, beginning with the Creation in 3966 B.C. and ending at the year A.D. 1412 in the extant manuscript, though Harrison originally took the work up to A.D. 1579.

Harrison wrote entries for the "Chronology" according to several of seventeen different dating systems, resulting in many early blank spaces and later chaotic congestion, justifying the work's ironic subtitle: "Chronological Chaos." Harrison's myriad revisions riddle the manuscript, verifying his complaint that "so diverse is the observation of true years that a man shall hardly guess how to lean unto the likeliest." Such minute care justifies Holinshed's subsequent praise of Harrison's "most exquisite diligence" but also shows the historian's profound religious purpose in tracking God through history, for he considered his three complementary tasks to be "the exact correction of the time, confirmation of doctrine, and disclosing of necessary antiquity," and he sought "the certainty of the history . . . to the uttermost of my power next unto the preaching of the word which is my chief vocation."

Harrison wrote the "Chronology" at Radwinter and in his adjacent Essex parish of Wimbish, but its wealth of learning indicates the size of his library and his important scholarly connections in Cambridge and London. Although only 165 titles with his ownership marks survive (at Derry, Trinity, and the Ipswich Town Library), the Trinity manuscript refers to upwards of five hundred authors, few of whom could have been consulted in any known epitomes. The "Chronology" also names sixty-five manuscripts once in Harrison's possession, though none of these is extant. Two other manuscripts from his library, the medieval chronological collections and a Wycliffite Saint Matthew's Gospel survive in the collections of the Bodleian and British Libraries.

Harrison also exploited scholarly friendships to obtain access to the libraries of Gabriel Harvey, Alexander Nowell, Saint Paul's Cathedral, several Cambridge and Oxford colleges, and many others. More relevantly, he acquired information from Reginald Wolfe, the inspiration behind a projected "Universal Cosmography" only partially realized in Holinshed's *Chronicles,* and by 1575 he had seen important manuscripts, including an early version of his friend John Stow's *Survey of London* (1598), in the "storehouse of antiquities" belonging to the latter.

Harrison in turn shared information with Holinshed, which explains why, although the chronology was not known to Holinshed until after Wolfe's death in December 1573, Holinshed commissioned Harrison in June or July 1576 to write the *Historical Description.* References in the "Chronology" to "the history of Raphael Holinshed if it may happen to come abroad" and which "ere long I hope shall be brought forth," together with Harrison's dedication of the 1577 *Historical Description,* confirm that until 1576 he worked independently of Holinshed, initially refusing his commission because "the dealing therein might prove an hindrance" to the "Chronology." Doubtless he was daunted by Holinshed's ambitious plans for a vast chorographic study of Britain, with descriptions and maps of twenty-six English cities, including an early version of Stow's *Survey of London;* but he relented because, in the expansive mood gripping the Holinshed group before printing began, someone made rash promises of publishing the "Chronology" in the *Chronicles.*

In spite of the exaggerated hopes of its publishers, the first edition of the *Historical Description* is a relatively short, hurried compromise, a book which, due to the printers' haste was, "no sooner penned than printed" in the late summer of 1576. Harrison overcame serious obstacles in concocting from printed, oral, and personal information three engrossing books on the history and physical and social geography of Britain. The Holinshed group mislaid materials already collected, and other antiquaries who had given Harrison assurances of help failed to follow through, so that with "the leaf under the press" the historian "was left destitute" and forced to rely for chorographic information on John Leland's "motheaten, mouldy, and rotten" historical manuscripts borrowed from Stow. Nor could Harrison use the "Chronology" but only glance at his researches for it in chapters on the nations that had formerly inhabited Britain, its ancient names, the evidence for giants, its former languages, kingdoms, and religions, which better fit his chosen title of "Historical Description."

Holinshed cites the "Chronology" sixty-one times in his *Chronicles,* sometimes as a radical contrast to predominant historical interpretations. While writing the *Historical Description* in 1576, Harrison abandoned the "Chronology," because his time in London exposed his highly susceptible conscience to the city's narrowly scripturalist Protes-

tants, who reinforced the arguments of his Radwinter curate, Richard Rogers, that "it is much unfitting for him that professeth divinity, to apply his time unto . . . contemplation of civil histories."

Back in Radwinter, however, the usefulness of history as a "store of examples" for preaching undermined Harrison's godly self-denial, and he resumed work on his manuscript by the autumn of 1578, abandoning it only around 1583 for an even larger version in three volumes, organized around the "Four Monarchies" of the Book of Daniel. This final version of the "Chronology" disappeared from Derry Diocesan Library in the 1890s, though the last volume, "Containing the period of time from the coming of the Normans unto the year of expectation which is of grace 1588 expired wherin the age of the world runneth all by fire," but in fact continuing until Harrison's death in 1593, was rediscovered in 1992.

Study of this vast manuscript continues, but its form clearly benefits from some printer's advice to Harrison. It is a fair copy made by an amanuensis, with careful additions in Harrison's hand and changes in layout making it easier to print than the chaotic Trinity manuscript. The section dealing with sixteenth-century history reveals Harrison's increasing obsession with Satan's plots against Elizabethan England, whether openly through Catholic missions and Spanish military might or more covertly by the maneuverings of powerful courtiers against the wealth of the church, masked by the agitation of Presbyterian radicals.

Panicked by the way in which these plots fitted into what Harrison saw as a recurrent pattern of history, wherein the destruction of learned preaching brought about the ruin of commonwealths, he abandoned his earlier tolerance of principled dissent and chose to defend unflinchingly the concept of an established church, justified by its pastoral effectiveness. This outlook was implicit in the way Harrison was revising the *Historical Description* by around 1580, integrating it with the "Chronology" and its associated books into one huge historical enterprise, so that the "Chronology" supplied the many vital historical parallels to the 1587 *Historical Description.* Harrison presented these parallels as a warning to his countrymen to avoid a repetition of God's judgments by reforming their church and society in accordance with the True Church's examples. Thus the more carefully organized and dramatically expanded *Historical Description,* which appeared in the 1587 edition of Holinshed's *Chronicles* and is often quoted on the evils of enclosure, excessive consumption, or church corruption, more fully reflects the Protestant worldview of the "Chronology."

Yet like Stow, who failed to publish his enormous "History of This Island," Harrison discovered that Holinshed's volume, to which they had both contributed, had swamped the market for large histories. He continued to work on his "Chronology," however, until he died on 9 November 1593 at Saint George's Chapel, Windsor, to which Elizabeth had appointed him a prebendary in April 1586. Despite their previous friendship Stow blamed Harrison for his failure, wrongly accusing him in his 1598 *Survey of London,* and more vehemently in the 1603 edition, of plagiarizing the entire *Historical Description* from Leland's manuscripts. As an editor of the 1587 edition of the *Chronicles,* Stow avenged himself for this alleged wrong by altering Holinshed's praise for Harrison's "exquisite Chronology" into a dismissal of "some that will seem the precisest calculators."

Surprisingly, the *Historical Description* chapter discussing the ancient religions of Britain aroused most controversy, prompting the Jesuit Robert Parsons in his *Three Conversions of England* (1603) to bracket Harrison with John Bale and John Foxe as "lying heretics" out to diminish England's religious indebtedness to Rome. The contemporary historian John Speed was more concerned with Harrison's reliance on Annius of Viterbo's forged "Berosus" for the earliest evidence of true religion in Britain, forcing Speed in his *History of Great Britain* (1611) to reconstruct slightly firmer foundations for Protestant church history. James Ussher acquired and read the Trinity "Chronology," but Harrison made no discernible impact upon Ussher's massive chronological learning.

Harrison's writings mingled Renaissance and Reformation scholarly impulses. The prudent self-censorship he exercised in the *Historical Description* could not disguise his despair at England's failure to emulate the ideals he drew from humanist and Reformed traditions of social criticism. Yet even the darker, prophetic vision of the "Chronology" preserves flashes of the ironic wit who turned away Gabriel Harvey's question why he did not proceed to the D.D., perhaps prompted by concerns about Presbyterian scruples, with the droll excuse that he only lacked will, skill, and [to] bear it out." Elizabethan literature benefitted in the *Historical Description* from greater perseverance in his competing historical studies. Harrison's modern literary reputation is being rapidly reassessed in the light of his rediscovered manuscript works. Furnivall's edition of the *Historical Description* imparted to Harrison some of the editor's genial but slightly dotty character, a reputation which the *Historical Description* still retains among uncritical writers of the "merry England" type of social history. Georges Edelen's modern edition partially reestablishes Harrison in his proper historical context, enabling Arthur B. Ferguson, for example, to see the *Historical Description* as an important piece of Protestant humanist social analysis. More recently, the rediscovery of substantial parts of his "Chronology" reveals Harrison as seriously engaged with not only the scholarly but also the political and religious controversies of his day and establishes him as an important Elizabethan literary figure.

References:

Georges Edelen, "William Harrison (1535–1593)," *Studies in the Renaissance,* 9 (1962): 256–272;

Arthur B. Ferguson, *Clio Unbound: Perception of the Social and Cultural Past in Renaissance England* (Durham, N.C.: Duke University Press, 1979), pp. 91–96;

Glyn J. R. Parry, "John Stow's Unpublished 'Historie of this Iland': Amity and Emnity amongst Sixteenth-Century Scholars," *English Historical Review,* 102 (July 1987): 633–647;

Parry, *A Protestant Vision: William Harrison and the Reformation of Elizabethan England* (Cambridge: Cambridge University Press, 1987);

Parry, "Trinity College Dublin MS 165: The Study of Time in the Sixteenth Century," *Historical Research: The Bulletin of the Institute of Historical Research,* 62 (February 1989): 15–33;

Parry, "William Harrison and Holinshed's Chronicles," *The Historical Journal,* 27 (December 1984): 789–810.

Papers:

William Harrison's manuscript for "The great English Chronology, entitled by the author his Chronological Chaos, or supputation of time" is in James Ussher's collection at Trinity College, Dublin (MS 165). The last volume of Harrison's final three-volume manuscript of the "Chronology," entitled "The fourth and last part of the great English Chronology, written by W[illia]m H[arrison], containing the period of time from the coming of the Normans unto the year of expectation which is of grace 1588 expired wherin the age of the world runneth all by fire," is held by the British Library (Additional MS 70984).

John Heywood
(1497? – 1580?)

Edmund M. Hayes
Worcester Polytechnic Institute

BOOKS: *A Mery Play betwene Johan Johan the Husbande, Tyb His Wyfe & Syr Jhän the Preest*, anonymous (London: Printed by William Rastell, 1533);

A Mery Play betwene the Pardoner and the Frere / the Curate and Neybour Pratte (London: Printed by William Rastell, 1533);

A Play of Loue, a Newe and a Mery Enterlude Concernyng Pleasure and Payne in Loue (London: Printed by William Rastell, 1533);

The Play of the Wether: A New and a Very Mery Enterlude of All Maner Wethers (London: Printed by William Rastell, 1533);

The Playe Called the Foure PP: A Newe and a Very Mery Enterlude of A Palmer. A Pardoner. A Potycary. A Pedler (London: Printed by William Myddylton, 1544?);

A Dialogue Conteinyng the Nomber in Effect of All the Prouerbes in the Englishe Tongue, Compacte in a Matter Concernyng Two Maner of Mariages (London: Printed by Thomas Berthelet, 1546; enlarged, 1550);

An Hundred Epigrammes (London: Printed in the house of Thomas Berthelet, 1550);

A Balade Specifyienge Partly the Maner, Partly the Matter, in the Mariage betwene Our Soueraigne Lord, and Our Soueraigne Lady (London: Printed for William Ryddell, 1554);

Two Hundred Epigrammes Vpon Two Hundred Prouerbes, With a Thyrde Hundred Newely Added (London: Printed by Thomas Berthelet, 1555);

The Spider and the Flie: A Parable (London: Printed by Thomas Powell, 1556);

A Breefe Balet Touchyng the Traytorous Takynge of Scarborow Castell (London: Printed by Thomas Powell, 1557);

A Fourth Hundred of Epygrams, Newly Inuented (London: Printed in the house late Thomas Berthelettes, 1560);

A Ballad against Slander and Detraction (London: Printed by John Allde, 1562);

Woodcut depicting a man often identified as John Heywood (from his The Spider and the Fly, *1556)*

John Heywoodes Woorkes: A Dialogue Conteyning the Number of the Effectuall Prouerbes in the Englishe Tounge, Compact in a Matter Concernyng Two Maner of Maryages. With One Hundred of Epigrammes, and Three Hundred of Epigrammes vpon Three Hundred Prouerbes, and a Fifth Hundred of Epigrams. Whereunto Are Now Newly Added a Syxt Hundred of Epigrams (London:

Printed by Thomas Powell, 1562; republished, with epilogue by Thomas Newton, London: Printed by Thomas Marsh, 1587);

A Dialogue on Wit and Folly, by John Heywood, Now First Printed from the Original Manuscript in the British Museum. To Which Is Prefixed, an Account of That Author, and His Dramatic Works, edited by Frederick William Fairholt (London: Printed for the Percy Society by T. Richards, 1846).

Editions: *The Proverbs and Epigrams of John Heywood (A.D. 1562): Reprinted from the Original (1562) Edition, and Collated with the 2d (1566) Edition; with an Appendix of Variations* (Manchester: Printed for the Spenser Society by C. Simms, 1867);

The Proverbs of John Heywood: Being the "Proverbes" of That Author Printed 1546, edited by Julian Sharman (London: Bell, 1874);

The Spider and the Flie: By John Heywood. Reprinted from the Edition of 1556 (Manchester: Printed for the Spenser Society by C. E. Simms, 1894);

The Dramatic Writings of John Heywood, Comprising: The Pardoner and the Friar — The Four P.P. — John the Husband, Tyb His Wife, and Sir John the Priest — Play of the Weather — Play of Love — Dialogue Concerning Witty and Witless — Note-book and Word-List, edited by John S. Farmer (London: Privately printed for the subscribers by the Early English Drama Society, 1905);

The Proverbs, Epigrams, and Miscellanies of John Heywood, Comprising A Dialogue of the Effectual Proverbs in the English Tongue Concerning Marriages — First Hundred Epigrams — Three Hundred Epigrams on Three Hundred Proverbs — The Fifth Hundred Epigrams — A Sixth Hundred Epigrams — Miscellanies — Ballads — Note-book and Word-list, edited by Farmer (London: Privately printed for the subscribers by the Early English Drama Society, 1906); republished as *Proverbs, Epigrams, and Miscellanies* (New York: Barnes & Noble, 1966);

A Dialogue of the Effectual Proverbs in the English Tongue Concerning Marriage, edited by Farmer (London: Gibbings, 1906);

The Spider and the Fly, Together with an Attributed Interlude Entitled Gentleness and Nobility, edited by Farmer (London: Privately printed for the subscribers by the Early English Drama Society, 1908); republished as *The Spider and the Fly and Gentleness and Nobility* (New York: Barnes & Noble, 1966);

John Heywood's "Works" and Miscellaneous Short Poems, edited by Burton A. Milligan (Urbana: University of Illinois Press, 1956);

A Dialogue of Proverbs, edited by Rudolph E. Habenicht (Berkeley: University of California Press, 1963).

OTHER: John Redford and others, *The Moral Play of Wit and Science, and Early Poetical Miscellanies: From an Unpublished Manuscript,* edited by James Orchard Halliwell, contributions by Heywood (London: Shakespeare Society, 1848).

John Heywood lived in an era of political, religious, and social unrest. As a poet, musician, and dramatist he served four monarchs — Henry VIII, Edward VI, Mary I (Mary Tudor), and Elizabeth I. Heywood was an innovator and experimenter in language who tried to explore new poetic possibilities in English. Often his efforts were crude; but when he succeeded, he produced striking results. Heywood was not interested in poetry for its own sake; he wrote to serve God and his monarch and to expose human folly. Heywood's reputation as a dramatist rests on six works: *Johan Johan* (1533), *A Play of Love* (1533), *The Play of the Weather* (1533), *The Pardoner and the Friar* (1533), *The Four PP* (1544?), and *Witty and Witless,* published as *A Dialogue on Wit and Folly* (1846). Probably all of these works were performed before 1530. *Johan Johan,* the most "dramatic" of them, is a translation of a French farce, a genre that was popular with Cardinal Thomas Wolsey and the court of Henry VIII. The rest are not plays in the modern sense but dramatized dialogues or debates.

Heywood was born in London, probably in 1497, for he gives his age as seventy-eight in a letter written in 1575. An examination of public records suggests that he was one of four sons of a lawyer, William Heywood. His biographer, Robert Bolwell, quotes Anthony à Wood as suggesting that Heywood briefly attended Broadgates (now Pembroke) College, Oxford, but left there because the "crabbedness of logic did not suit his airy genie." Two of Heywood's epigrams indicate a knowledge of Oxford, but they are hardly conclusive evidence that he attended the university. He may have been a choirboy for the Chapel Royal and might have been sent to Oxford when his voice changed. It is not known for certain where Heywood received his early training in music, but it is reasonable to assume that he studied under masters at the university.

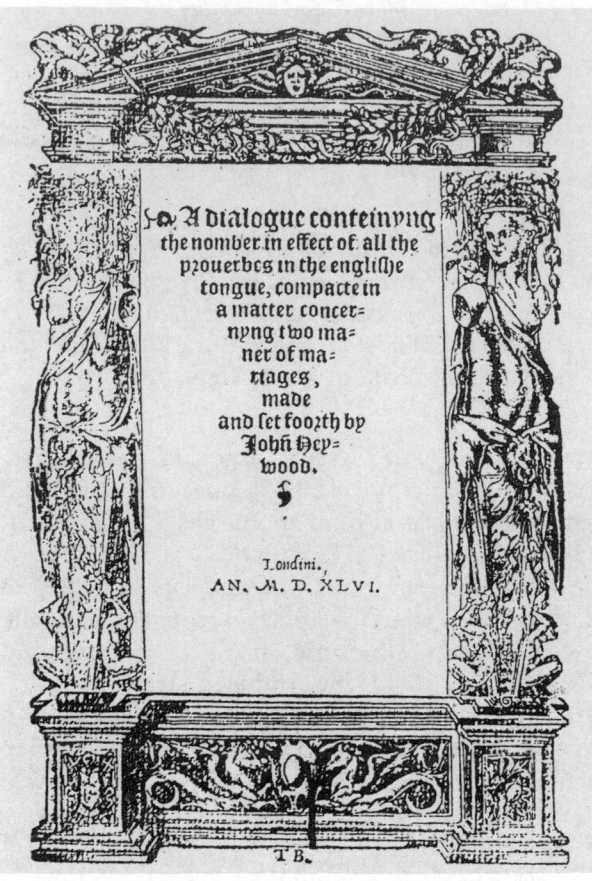

Title page for Heywood's narrative poem that examines the question of whether one should marry for love or for money

He had a successful career at court as singer, musician, and playwright from 1519 to 1528. Pensioned in 1528, he may have spent the years between 1528 and 1548 associated with the choir at Saint Paul's Cathedral and the Chapel Royal. He was also a measurer of linen clothes for the City of London and a member of the prestigious Mercers' Company, and he had ties with prominent members of the Inns of Court. He drew generous payments and gifts from those he served, so that he became a gentleman of some means.

Sometime between 1523 and 1529 Heywood married Eliza Rastell, daughter of the printer and playwright John Rastell. They had five children; their daughter Elizabeth became the mother of the poet John Donne, and their sons Ellis and Jasper became prominent Jesuit priests. Jasper was also the translator of Seneca's *Troas* (1559), *Thyestes* (1560), and *Hercules Furens* (1561).

John Rastell had married Sir Thomas More's sister; thus, it was probably through Heywood's connections with the Rastells that he met More and became a member of his circle. Heywood's poems

reflect the influence of More's love of wordplay, wit, and the intellectual probing of complex questions, and More's example as a religious thinker had a potent influence on Heywood's religious convictions. Heywood lived through Henry's divorce problem, the break with the Catholic church, the death of Cardinal Wolsey, the rise of Thomas Cranmer as archbishop of Canterbury, the dissolution of the monasteries, and the Pilgrimage of Grace in protest of the dissolution in 1536. He took part in 1544 in the attempt to overthrow Cranmer and was arrested, accused of treason, and imprisoned. He publicly recanted on 6 July and was pardoned, and his properties were restored to him. An anecdote in Sir John Harington's *Metamorphosis of Ajax* (1596) tells how Heywood's reputation helped him avoid execution: "What think you by Heywood that escaped hanging with his mirth? The king being graciously and (as I think) truly persuaded that a man that wrote so pleasant and harmless verses could not have any harmful conceit against his proceedings; and so, by the honest motion of a gentleman of his Chamber, saved him from the jerk of the six-stringed whip. This Heywood for his proverbs and epigrams is not yet put down by any of our country."

Heywood favored Queen Mary I and was favored by her. He wrote in praise of her beauty as early as 1534, when she was eighteen. His years at court under the Catholic Mary may have been his happiest. Appointed steward of the queen's chamber in 1555, Heywood resigned that post in 1558 and received from the queen a lease of Bolmer Manor for forty years. During Elizabeth's reign he continued at court as an entertainer. Elizabeth's settlement of the religious question in the Act of Uniformity in 1564, however, posed a problem for Catholics in England because Rome prohibited them from participating in the new worship. On 20 July 1564 Heywood and his son Ellis fled England. Heywood lived in Malines, France, until 1575 and at the Jesuit College in Antwerp, where Ellis was a preacher, until a mob expelled the residents in 1578. He is believed to have died at Louvain, Belgium, around 1580. Heywood gives a description of himself in his "Fifth Hundred of Epigrams" in *John Heywood's Works* (1562):

Art thou Heywood with the mad merry wit?
Yea forsooth, master, that same is even hit.
Art thou Heywood that applies mirth more than thrift?
Yea, sir, I take merry mirth a golden gift.
Art thou Heywood that has made many mad plays?
Yea, many plays, few good works in all my days.
Art thou Heywood that has made men merry long?

Yea, and will, if I be made merry among.
Art thou Heywood that would be made merry now?
Yea, sir: help me to it now I beseech you.

A Dialogue Containing the Number in Effect of All the Proverbs in the English Tongue, Compact in a Matter Concerning Two Manner of Marriages (1546) was the most popular of Heywood's nondramatic works and went through several printings during his lifetime. Actually, the book does not contain "all the proverbs in English"; it is a narrative poem built on as many proverbs as Heywood could appropriately use for his purposes. As he says in his preface, "In this tale, first talked with a friend, I show / As many of them as we could fitly find." (The *we* possibly refers to Thomas Whithorne, Heywood's servant.) Creating a narrative out of as many proverbs as one can "fitly find" strikes the modern reader as artificial – a tour de force, not something one would want to sit down and read. Julian Sharman, who edited the *Dialogue* in 1874 as *The Proverbs of John Heywood,* did so in part because it represented the "first assemblage of colloquial sayings" and "will meet with approbation from other gleaners in the same field of antiquarianism."

Proverbs were popular well before Heywood: the first book in England from William Caxton's press was Anthony Wydeville, Earl Rivers's translation of *The Dictes or Sayings of the Philosophers* in 1477; Desiderius Erasmus's *Adagiorum Collectanea,* a collection of classical proverbs, appeared in 1500; and Nicholas Udall's printed *Apophthegmes,* a collection of wise sayings from classical authors and some English proverbs, appeared in 1542. In his preface to the *Dialogue* Heywood tells his readers "That almost in all things good lessons they [proverbs] teach." He adds, however, that "this write I not to teach, but to touch. For why, / Men know this as well or better than I." Heywood is not going to preach but to awaken the reader's feelings and thoughts regarding love and marriage. The poem is comic yet puts forth a mirror of human selfishness without moralizing. The characters in all of Heywood's poems lack the capacity to understand properly their own shortcomings and blindness; as a result, the reader is left with the task of answering the questions the poems raise. Joel B. Altman's description of Heywood's plays is applicable to the nondramatic works because they, too, "functioned as media of intellectual exploration for minds that were accustomed to examine the many sides of a given theme, to entertain opposing ideals, and by so exercising the understanding, to move toward some fuller apprehension of truth that could be discerned only through the total action of the drama."

In the *Dialogue* Heywood creates a narrator – an older, married man "experienced" in the ways of the world – who is visited by a youth seeking advice as to whether or not he should marry. The young man is no romantic: he wants to marry wisely. The narrator is a comic figure, not a sage or a moralist. During the course of his narrative he weaves in proverbs to deprecate his own so-called wisdom. He is not the author's voice but a character who is more witness than adviser. Through the first five chapters the two carry on a contest of proverbial wisdom. The narrator launches into a string of "Haste makes waste" sayings, while the youth answers him with such adages as "Take time when time comes, lest time steal away" and act now before "other men catch birds." The youth then describes the two women he is thinking of marrying: one is young and beautiful but poor; the other is old and ugly but rich.

In chapter 6 the narrator decides to tell his companion a story, "since this tale contains the counsel I can give." He once lived next to two couples: one couple was young and poor and had married for love; the other couple consisted of a young man married to an old widow whom he had wed for her money. Both couples had come to him to complain about their plights and to seek his advice. The young couple was unhappy because of their poverty. The narrator advised them to visit their relatives to seek assistance. They did so and returned to relate their experiences. The young woman visited her aunt and was treated rudely and denied assistance. While her uncle slept and snored like a hog, her aunt and a vicious companion and gossip, Alice, whose great lust was to "tell tales out of school" and who understood "dissimulation," mocked the young woman. The aunt made it clear that because the young couple married without her approval, she would not help her niece or her husband, even though the girl admitted that she was wrong and sought pity and forgiveness. The aunt told Alice, "I took her for a rose, but she breeds a burr." Disheartened, the girl returned home empty-handed.

The young man visited his uncle's house and was similarly rejected. Starting out on his journey he met his uncle's servant, who turned out to be a Good Samaritan and befriended him. When the uncle rebuffed the young man for willfully marrying, the servant counseled him to visit another relative. The young man made the visit but was unsuccessful because the relative was greedy, lived poorly on purpose, and hoarded his wealth. Leaving the relative's house, the servant and the young man spent a night in a tavern, the servant paid the bill, and the young man, like his wife, returned home to endure poverty. On his return journey he reflected: "Many kinsfolk and few friends. . . ." The three sets of relatives, the sympathetic servant, and the gossip are part of Heywood's attempt to achieve "balance," to spread the debate in as many quarters as necessary to make his case.

The youth interprets the narrator's tale as showing that "Haste does make waste": he who would marry for love is headed for disaster. He decides that he will marry the rich old widow and is impatient to be on his way. The narrator promises a second story after dinner; the youth wants to hear it immediately, but the narrator prevails. After dinner he presents the story of the young husband and the rich old widow.

In the first story the narrator was not directly involved in the experiences of the young man and his bride but reported those experiences as told to him. But in this story he is a participant and observer who was in a position to see the gradual breakup of the couple's marriage. The husband was unfaithful and a prodigal; the old wife was dominating and a shrew. The narrator did not want to become involved in their quarrels, for "To meddle little for me it is best. / For little meddling [there] comes great rest." Nevertheless, he could not escape involvement: the husband and wife took turns visiting him for advice, and in two scenes they quarreled or debated with one another in his presence. In his arbor he overheard the husband persuade his wife to render to him her last bag of money; the husband squandered the money, and he and his wife separated, became beggars, and ultimately died. The narrator concludes with a comment on the two couples: "Thus failed all four of all things less and more, / Which they all, or any of all, married for."

After hearing the tales the youth is initially discouraged; but he finds a "spark of hope" in the realization that although these four suffered, others have "lived and loved full well." The narrator says that of those who have suffered and those who have lived and loved well, "I have seen the one, and heard of the other." He explains that he has put these cases before the youth for the latter's benefit; he will say no more. It is up to the youth (and the reader) to interpret the stories of this playful narrator. The youth decides that he will not marry at all. His final assessment of love and marriage may be the closest approach to a "message" in the poem: at first, he says, "I was wedded unto my will"; now he will be "wedded to my wit." This remark appears to be good Renaissance thinking: wit or reason should prevail over willfulness. He will not wed "only for

love, or only for good." He realizes that though the chief reason for wedding should be love, "yet must more things join." The reader is left to decide what must be added to love. Kindness? Forgiveness? Selflessness? Humility? The poem is open-ended; proverbial wisdom can support or deny virtually any position.

While the verse is halting at times, and the strings of proverbs can glaze the eyes of the reader, there are many finely wrought humorous passages and others that delineate character and scene with surprising depth and sensitivity. The final exchange of proverbs between the young husband and his old wife in chapter 9 of part 2, while the narrator "did closely my ear incline," is deftly rendered; and the gentle irony of the closing line of the chapter, coming just after the young man has received his wife's last bag of money – "They rose, and went to dinner lovingly" – is Heywood at his best.

Heywood's *An Hundred Epigrams* was published in 1550, *Two Hundred Epigrams upon Two Hundred Proverbs, with a Third Hundred Newly Added* in 1555, and *A Fourth Hundred of Epigrams* in 1560. His collected works of 1562 includes "A Fifth Hundred" and "A Sixth Hundred of Epigrams." Although Heywood was not the first to write epigrams, he may have been the first to write them in English. His friend and mentor More's *Epigrammata* had been published as early as 1518, and, through quotation, translation, and imitation, the influence of More's Latin epigrams was present in England throughout the period. The form was also popular on the Continent, and literary convention demanded that a man of learning should produce them.

An epigram, in general, is a short poem that ends in a witty or ingenious turn of thought. The length may vary from two lines to twenty or more; most English epigrams run to about six lines. An epigram may be sententious, moral, punning, humorous, or satiric, and the scope of subject matter is unlimited. Finally, sixteenth-century epigrams were always written to be heard rather than read silently.

Heywood's epigrams are playful, are filled with good humor, and reflect his enthusiasm for the vitality and complexity of language. In prefaces to "A Fifth Hundred" and "A Sixth Hundred of Epigrams" Heywood emphasizes the "mirth" and "good cheer" of his inventions. He played on words for their various senses much as did More and Erasmus and thus placed himself in the intellectual camp of contemporaries who enjoyed and encouraged verbal wit.

In *An Hundred Epigrams* the tenth is an animal fable, "The Fox and the Maid." In thirty-eight lines

Heywood tells how the fox in Finsbury field, "nodding, and blessing, staring on Paul's steeple," duped a maid out of her hens. The moral is spoken by the gulled maiden:

> Woe worth (quoth she) all crafty inventions,
> And all inventors, that by false intentions,
> Invent with intent to blind or blear blunt eyes,
> In case as this fox to me does devise.

In his "Third Hundred" epigrams Heywood questions conventional wisdom: "Haste makes waste: which perceived by Sloth, / Sloth will make no haste, he swears by his truth." In "Of Wits" he writes, "So many heads, so many wits, nay, nay. / We see many heads, and no wits some day." In many of the epigrams he cites a proverb, then goes on to an alternate rendering or what he calls "otherwise," as in "No Lack in Love":

> In love is no lack, true I dare be borrow.
> In love is never lack of joy or sorrow.
>   Otherwise
> In love is no lack, no in no wooing day.
> But after wedding day, let's hear what you say.

In "A Fifth Hundred" and "A Sixth Hundred of Epigrams" Heywood returns to conventional subjects. In "Short Checks between a Man and His Wife" the epigram almost becomes a dialogue:

> I am careful to see you careless, Jill.
> I am woeful to see you witless, Will.
> I am anguished to see you an ape, Jill.
> I am angry to see you an ass, Will.

The longest and most complex of Heywood's nondramatic writings, *The Spider and the Fly* (1556), is a "parable" on the times in which he lived. There is no way of positively identifying the spider, the fly, or most of the other figures; it is known that the maid who kills the spider at the end of the piece represents Queen Mary, because Heywood says so in the conclusion. He also says that the poem had lain untouched for nineteen years. Thus, it must have been begun in the 1530s.

The poem, written in rhyme royal, is divided into ninety-eight chapters. It includes a full-length portrait of the narrator, a scholarly-looking man who might be Heywood, and many woodcuts showing the narrator listening to the debate between the spider and the fly in a spiderweb stretched across a windowpane. The preface warns the reader in typical Heywood fashion not to look for others in the piece to blame for one's own faults; the reader should look for himself or herself in order to mark and mend his or her own life.

Contemporary opinions of *The Spider and the Fly* are difficult to find; unlike his proverbs and epigrams, this poem did not achieve popularity. William Harrison, in his "A Historical Description of the Island of Britain," prefixed to Raphael Holinshed's *Chronicles of England, Scotland, and Ireland* (1577), wrote that Heywood "has made a book of *The Spider and the Fly,* wherein he deals so profoundly and beyond all measure of skill that neither he himself that made it, neither any one that reads it, can reach unto the meaning thereof."

The poem begins in a mock-heroic vein. A fly lands on a spider's web and laments his fate while deriding the fickleness of fortune. His landing jars awake the spider, who has been sleeping with his wife and two children. He assures his family that he will kill the interloper; the fly, however, begs for a fair trial, and the spider agrees to try him according to reason, law, custom, and conscience. The fly asks for bail, but the spider denies it and charges him with burglary and trespassing. In the process of this debate the spider becomes "lordly," while the fly acts and speaks like a commoner and takes on the name of "Buzz." Where did the fly learn about the law and debating? Why, at Westminster Hall, where spiders are not allowed. The debate turns to the question of whether the fly is a "tenant" of the window or, as he claims, that windows are the freehold of every fly by common law. The fly pleads his case in a long speech in which he argues for the rule of justice and mercy, only to discover that the spider has fallen asleep. Later the fly asks that other flies be called to act as judges; the spider rejects the request, which leads to a debate on the relative merits of the Lords versus the Commons. The spider favors "authority" and hierarchy in government, while the fly denies the efficacy of a "clerk's sayings," for simple experience shows that the ideal commonwealth can be ruled just as well by a senate as by a king. The spider interjects a disclaimer in which he makes clear he does not mean to debase the state by comparing royalty and commoners to spiders and flies; that would be "most rude of us."

The spider and the fly agree that they need an arbitrator to decide the case. The fly chooses a blunt but honest butterfly, the spider a small but brainy ant. After instructions from the spider and the fly, the two arbiters separate to hear from other spiders and flies. They cannot decide who is right and say, "Let's at last leave it as we found it." This interlude makes clear reference to the enclosure crisis of the time.

Woodcut from The Spider and the Fly *depicting the maid, who represents Queen Mary I, putting the spider to death*

A new turn occurs as spiders begin "clustering and cluttering" and the flies "murmuring." When talk fails, there are preparations for war. Armies gather, and their various arms are described. The flies capture the ant and are going to hang him on the "Tree of Reformation" (this detail has been linked to the hanging of Robert Ket, the leader of the Rebellion of 1549, who was hanged on the "Oak of Reformation"), but they allow him to speak. He frightens the flies with his description of the horrors of war. He is so effective that they send him to speak to the spiders, where he makes another chilling antiwar talk; but the spiders decide to fight on anyway, and a fierce battle ensues in which hundreds of spiders and thousands of flies are killed. Representatives of both sides link their cause to God's will regarding who should rule, making the political war a religious one as well.

With the failure of the war to resolve whether the flies have freeholder's rights to windows, the opponents return to a debate. It is clear that both spiders and flies are looking desperately for peace. The ant is once again called upon to arbitrate. After more debating, the spider agrees to give the flies a limited number of holes at the bottom of the windows. The flies agree, even though the terms are not good ones, and the war ends. The chastened and wiser ant summarizes his adventures for his fellow ants and tells them: "Yet must we live in order

here, perdie!" He also warns his fellow ants to stay out of politics.

The last twenty chapters of the poem contain religious allegory. The spider returns to his prisoner to decide the latter's fate. Since law and reason have not proved helpful, he promises to abide by conscience and custom in making his decision. The spider and fly change places for a moment, and, ironically, the fly takes on the pride and vanity of his oppressor. When they return to their original identities the spider rules out conscience and determines to execute the fly according to custom. As he is about to destroy the fly, the maid (Queen Mary) intercedes, frees the fly, and condemns the spider to death. The maid asserts that custom has corrupted the spider's conscience. Spiders are guilty of abuse of power: they would take over with more and more webs until their power is absolute. She will not grant the spider mercy – no more than he would have granted it to the fly. Before his death the spider is allowed to meet with his councillors and his son. To the latter he makes a long speech that is part advice, part a public confession of his wrongs. He asks forgiveness of God and the maid, then prepares for death. After killing the spider, the maid calls together twelve flies and twelve spiders and explains that the flies have offended her master and mistress by buzzing around their meat, while the spiders have offended by taking over the windows. The maid admonishes them "to keep order" so that by obeying her, "We may live in love all, each in his degree." She cleans the window, and the narrator, satisfied with what he has seen, departs for dinner.

In the conclusion Heywood salutes "Lady, Queen Mary, and maid":

Whose sword like a broom that sweeps out filth clean
Not a sword that fills the house by bloody mean,
This merciful maiden took in hand to sweep,
Her window, this realm, not to kill, but to keep
All in quiet....

He adds that all should display their love and "banners of obedience" to the queen and to Lord Philip.

The Spider and the Fly is not a great work of art: the rhyme royal is often tedious, and the number of debates is excessive. Part of the problem with decoding the allegory is due to Heywood's putting the poem aside for nearly twenty years; when he resumed writing it he probably had different persons and events in mind than he had had when he started it. Another problem with the poem is its mixed content. The first seventy-eight chapters deal with secular issues, while the final twenty focus on religious concerns. In the early chapters the spiders represent the nobility and the flies the commoners; later the spiders represent the Protestants and the flies the Catholics. There is a piousness to the last books that is missing from the first two-thirds of the poem.

John Redford's *The Moral Play of Wit and Science* (1848) contains a miscellany of songs and poems by Heywood. Among the more important of Heywood's occasional poems are two tributes to Queen Mary. "A Description of a Most Noble Lady" was, according to the last stanza, written when Princess Mary was eighteen. It stresses her beauty, virtue, and intelligence. Though young, she has maturity and wisdom:

> Among her youthful years,
>   She triumphs over age,
> And yet she still appears
>   Both witty, grave, and sage.

In his lengthy "Ballad Specifying the Most Excellent Meeting and Like Marriage between Our Sovereign Lord and Our Sovereign Lady" Heywood creates an allegory in which Philip, the Eagle, flies to England, where he finds a beautiful rose that is both red and white and falls in love with a beautiful lion, representing Mary. In lines that seem to anticipate the closing act of William Shakespeare's *A Midsummer Night's Dream* (1600), Heywood tries to justify the metaphor:

> But mark, this lion, so by name,
> Is properly a lamb to assign,
> No lion wild, a lion tame,
> No rampant lion masculine,
> But lamblike lion feminine.
> Whose mild meek property allures
> This bird to light, and him assures.

Perhaps Thomas Newton, who supplied an epilogue for the 1587 edition of *John Heywood's Works*, captured the essence of Heywood when he wrote:

> Now, as we may a lion soon discern even by his paw,
> So by this work we quickly may a judgment certain draw,
> What kind of man this author was, and what a pleasant vein
> Of fancy's forge and modest mirth lay lodged in his brain.

Heywood was not a major poet, but one cannot read the works of John Lyly or Shakespeare and not see that Heywood's wordplay and epigrammatic style and the way he compelled a reader to look at all sides of a question had an impact on those authors. Heywood was one of a group of poets who discovered the rich possibilities of the English language and were not afraid to experiment with it. In politics, religion, and morality he articulated the thinking of his age, and his poetry lives today because of its historical significance.

Bibliography:
Philip C. Kolin, "Recent Studies in John Heywood," *English Literary Renaissance,* 13 (Winter 1983): 113–123.

Biography:
Robert Bolwell, *The Life and Works of John Heywood* (New York: Columbia University Press, 1921).

References:
Joel B. Altman, *The Tudor Play of the Mind: Rhetorical Inquiry and the Development of Elizabethan Drama* (Berkeley: University of California Press, 1978);

Rupert De La Bere, *John Heywood, Entertainer* (London: Allen & Unwin, 1937);

Jakob Haber, *John Heywood's "The Spider and the Fly"* (Berlin: Emil Felber, 1900);

David R. Hauser, "The Date of John Heywood's *The Spider and the Fly,*" *Modern Language Notes,* 70 (January 1955): 15–18;

Pearl Hogrefe, *The Thomas More Circle: A Program of Ideas and Their Impact on Secular Drama* (Urbana: University of Illinois Press, 1959);

Hoyt Hopewell Hudson, *The Epigram in the English Renaissance* (Princeton: Princeton University Press, 1947);

Robert Carl Johnson, *John Heywood* (New York: Twayne, 1970);

John Walker McCain, "Oratory, Rhetoric and Logic in the Writings of John Heywood," *Quarterly Journal of Speech,* 26 (February 1940): 44–47;

Burton A. Milligan, "Humor and Satire in Heywood's Epigrams," in *Studies in Honor of T. W. Baldwin,* edited by Don Cameron Allen (Urbana: University of Illinois Press, 1958), pp. 16–33;

A. W. Reed, *Early Tudor Drama* (London: Methuen, 1926);

Robert Withington, "Paronomasia in John Heywood's Plays," *Smith College Studies in Modern Languages,* 21 (1939–1940): 221–239.

Papers:
The British Museum has manuscripts for John Heywood's songs and ballads.

Maurice Kyffin

(circa 1560? – 2 January 1598)

William H. Sherman
University of Maryland at College Park

BOOK: *The Blessednes of Brytaine, or a Celebration of the Queenes Holyday* (London: Printed by John Windet, 1587; revised and enlarged edition, London: [Printed by John Windet for] John Wolfe, 1588).

TRANSLATIONS: Terence, *Andria the First Comoedie of Terence, in English* (London: Printed by T[homas] E[ast] for Thomas Woodcocke, 1588);
John Jewel, *Deffynniad Ffydd Eglwys Loegr* (London: Printed by Richard Field, 1595).
Edition: *Deffynniad Ffydd Eglwys Loegr, A Gyfieithwyd i'r Gymraeg, o Ladin yr Esgob Jewel, yn y Flwyddyn 1595, gan Maurice Kyffin,* edited by William Prichard Williams (Bangor, U.K.: Jarvis & Foster, 1908).

Maurice Kyffin is not a household name – not even among Elizabethan literary historians. He was, however, one of Renaissance England's exemplary scholar-soldiers. He was not only an accomplished poet and translator, capable of producing fluent verse and prose in English, Latin, and Welsh, but he became a high-ranking military official, serving as a soldier and paymaster in Elizabeth's major foreign campaigns.

Kyffin's origins and early career are obscure. William Prichard Williams, in his 1908 edition of Kyffin's *Deffynniad Ffydd Eglwys Loegr* (1595), states that Kyffin was an increasingly common surname at that time and that the author has been confused with at least three other Maurice Kyffins. His exact birthdate remains unknown, but it was most likely in the early 1560s. His father, Thomas, though illegitimate, was of noble extraction, as was his mother, Catrin Iengaf. Both sides of the family had coats of arms, and the arms that Maurice later adopted combined elements from each. He grew up in North Shropshire, Wales, near the town of Oswestry, which, although now an English-speaking region, was in Kyffin's day home to a thriving Welsh community. His education was probably informal and grounded in traditional Welsh literature: his village teacher was the poet William Llyn, to whom some of Kyffin's surviving poems are dedicated. The eldest of four children, Kyffin seems to have died unmarried.

Kyffin was in London by 1578, in the service of the great scholar (and Welshman) John Dee. He departed from Dee's household on 25 October 1580 but remained a friend: in his diary Dee recorded visits from Kyffin in 1582 and 1594, and in his will Kyffin bequeathed ten pounds to Dee and his wife "as a memorial of my love towards them." Sometime before 1582 Kyffin joined the household of Thomas Sackville, Lord Buckhurst, where he tutored his sons William, Henry, and Thomas. In his Latin tuition he evidently – like many other contemporary teachers – took Terence as a model, and the Sackvilles encouraged him to publish a translation of Terence's comedy *Andria*. Kyffin's dedicatory epistle to the young Sackvilles was signed, "At London. December 3 1587," and the text was published in 1588. In the prefatory letter he explains that he first produced a verse translation but rejected it in favor of prose. From the commendatory verses included in the volume – one of which is by the eminent historian and schoolmaster William Camden – it is clear that Kyffin was already well established in London.

Another sign of his considerable status, and of his desire for more-official employment, is the eulogy he published in 1587 for the anniversary of Queen Elizabeth's Accession Day. *The Blessedness of Britain* was a celebration of the queen's "entrance into the thirtieth year of her reign" and an exhortation to loyalty, provoked by the previous year's plot organized by Roman Catholic Anthony Babington to murder Elizabeth. In his dedication to Robert Devereux, Earl of Essex, Kyffin claims that his father had served Devereux's father and grandfather.

Although he lamented his "leaden skill" in this "golden cause," Kyffin's versification in *The Blessed-*

ness of Britain is competent and occasionally ingenious, displaying a knowledge of the conventions of both classical and Elizabethan panegyric. He begins by calling upon the Muses to help him "Unfold her fame (with words forth sounding fit), / Whom kings adore, and Lords . . .":

> A monarch maiden queen adorned rare
> With regal heavenly dowers of diverse kind:
> In whom, who list dame Nature's works compare
> With those rich thews and virtues of her mind,
>   Shall much admire, at such a mirror sheen,
>   At such a prince, at such a peerless queen.

As if anticipating the "Ditchley" portrait of 1592, in which Elizabeth brings peace to the realm and calm to the skies, Kyffin employs a meteorologic simile to celebrate the restoration of security:

> As shining sun reclears the darkened sky
> And forth recalls each thing from shivering shrouds,
> So hath our second sun, both far and nigh,
> By brightening beams outcleared erroneous clouds. . . .

Kyffin goes on to praise Elizabeth for improving the coinage; for founding a mighty navy; for begetting truth, virtue, and faith instead of children; and for inspiring Welsh bards with her illustrious Welsh lineage.

While many of his devices are commonplace, Kyffin denounced in his preface the fashionable practice of giving to Elizabeth "pestering names of fained gods, goddesses, nymphs, Persians, Grecians, Romans, etc.," calling it a "beaten highway" and "a thing of some sometimes used, too too much and to little effect." The defeat of the Spanish Armada in August 1588 gave Kyffin grounds for publishing a continuation of the poem, which he again dedicated to Essex.

A manuscript ode signed by Kyffin survives in which he dresses up a simple supplication with a flattering portrait of his potential patron:

> Most worthy counsellor of a mighty queen,
>   Vouchsafe to read this humble poor request.
> O let your Honor's justice here be seen,
>   Righting the wrong of him that is distressed.
>   . . . Some grateful service, one day, may deserve it;
>   Which I have vowed to your honored name;
> I shall for evermore in mind reserve it;
>   And labor to acquit me of the same.
>   Wisdom's dear choice extract of noble race!
>   Weigh, and redress your suppliant's grievous case.

This ode has generally been taken to refer to Robert Cecil. It is more likely, however, that the "extract of noble race" was Essex and that the poem passed

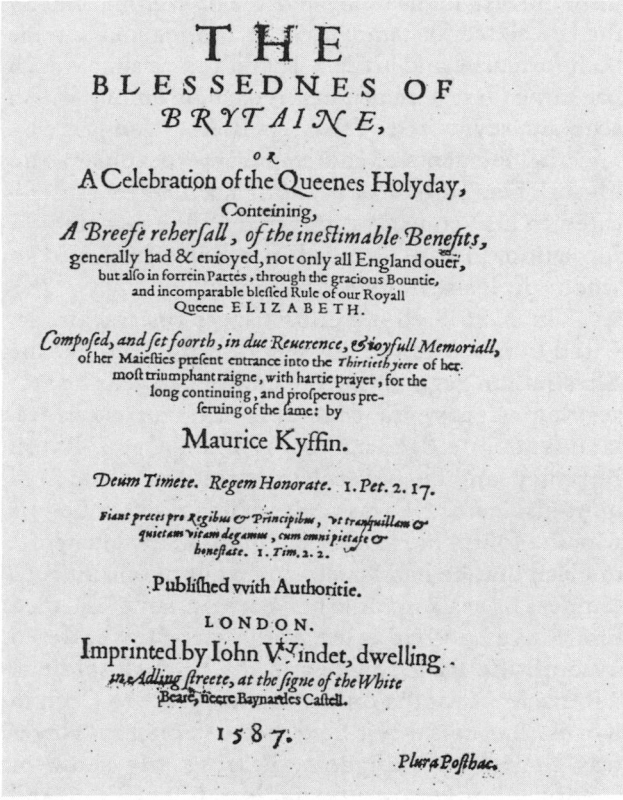

Title page for Kyffin's poem celebrating the beginning of the thirtieth year of Queen Elizabeth's reign

into the Cecil archive with many of the other Essex papers.

With these dedications and verses Kyffin was probably fishing for military employment, and through the agency of Sir Thomas Wilkes he soon got it. By the end of 1588 he had been appointed surveyor of the muster rolls in the Low Countries. In England's next major military action, in Normandy in 1591, he not only served as vice-treasurer but took command of some of the forces.

After Normandy, Kyffin's military career suffered two major interruptions. First, he was wrongfully accused of misappropriating funds and was jailed for a time. Once again he turned to verse, in this instance to vent his despair, penning a moving quatrain describing his view through the bars of his cell. The second interruption was of a more positive nature, as Kyffin spent much of 1594 preparing a Welsh translation of Bishop John Jewel's *Apologia pro Ecclesia Anglicana* (1562). This volume, the *Deffynniad Ffydd Eglwys Loegr,* must be set alongside William Salesbury's Welsh translation of the Bible as one of the most interesting contributions to the propagation of the Reformation in Wales. It is remarkable not only for its piety and political commitment but also for its innovative use of Welsh idiom. By the late sixteenth century Welsh writing had become both formulaic and archaic. Kyffin's translation, which has earned him a tremendous reputation among Welsh scholars, revitalized Welsh as a literary language by injecting elements of contemporary vocabulary and idiom. The *Deffynniad Ffydd Eglwys Loegr* was dedicated to his "cousin" and friend William Meredith, for whom Kyffin secured a military post and to whom (in his will) he left his library.

In 1596 Kyffin's efforts were once again devoted to more-active intervention on behalf of the Elizabethan regime. By the end of the year he was serving as surveyor general of the musters in Ireland and intelligencer for William Cecil, Baron Burghley, and his son Robert – posts he would hold until his death. He was understandably horrified by what he found in Ireland. Upon his arrival he wrote to Cecil that he had "lately come out of one hideous tempest at sea into another here on land." His letters convey a vivid sense of the atrocities suffered by both the Irish people and the English soldiers. After a few months on the job he wrote to Cecil in words that could not have been stronger: "Never was there poor kingdom, bearing any show or shadow of government, so miserably afflicted and distressed as this is." He attributed many of the causes of this situation to the queen's officers and held his fellow paymaster Sir Ralph Lane particularly responsible. Much of Kyffin's time was spent fighting not the Irish rebels but Lane and his corrupt henchmen – who, for their part, considered Kyffin to be "but a wandering commissary."

The historian Charles Greig Cruickshank asserts of this period that any muster master who tried to protect the interests of the Crown or the common soldier instead of lining the pockets of the captains "found himself fighting a losing battle." After putting up a valiant fight, for which he was praised by the English government's representatives

in Ireland, Kyffin finally lost the battle on 2 January 1598, when he died of an unknown ailment. He was buried in Christ Church, Dublin, though no trace of his grave remains. His last acts were rehearsed with considerable pathos by his faithful servant Hugh Tuder in a letter to Lord Burghley on 26 March 1598. Tuder's service continued after the death of his master: on his deathbed Kyffin charged him (under an oath of secrecy to be broken only under threat of torture) with the mission of conveying his papers back to Burghley. Tuder never made it. He was imprisoned and threatened with the rack; and though he was soon released and promoted, he was dead by the end of the year.

Kyffin's motto, *Haud frustra spero* (I do not hope in vain), was cruelly mocked by his fate. Nonetheless, his career remains an instructive example of the place of literary production in Elizabethan politics and patronage and a valuable reminder of the crucial part played by Welshmen and Welshwomen in the English Renaissance.

References:

Charles Greig Cruickshank, *Elizabeth's Army*, enlarged edition (Oxford: Clarendon Press, 1966), pp. 68, 69, 141;

Dictionary of Welsh Biography down to 1940 (London: Cymmrodorion Society, 1959);

James Orchard Halliwell, ed., *The Private Diary of Dr. John Dee* (London: Camden Society, 1842).

Papers:

Many of Maurice Kyffin's letters survive in the State Paper Department, Her Majesty's Public Record Office, London (especially for the period 1596–1598), and there are a few in the Cecil Papers at Hatfield House, Hertfordshire. Miscellaneous autograph poems are found scattered throughout the manuscript collections of the British Library.

Hugh Latimer

(1492? – 16 October 1555)

D. S. Dunnan

Saint James School

BOOKS: *Concio quam habuit Reuerendiss. in Christo pater Hugo Latimer, epus Worcestrie in Coueto spiritualiu* (London: Printed by James Nicolas for John Gough, 1537);

The Sermon That the Reuerende Father in Christ, Hugh Latimer, Byshop of Worcester, Made to the Clergie, in the Conuocation, before the Parlyament Began, the 9. Day of June, the .28. Yere of the Reigne of Our Souerayne Lorde Kyng Henry the VIII. Nowe Translated out of Latyne into Englyshe, to the Intent, That Thing Is Well Said to a Fewe, May Be Understande of Many, and Do Good to Al That Desyre to Be Better (London: Printed by Thomas Berthelet, 1537);

A Notable Sermon of ye Reuerende Father Maister Hughe Latemer, Whiche He Preached in ye Shrouds at Paules Churche in London, on the .xviii. Daye of January, 1548 (London: Printed by Ihon Daye & William Seres, 1548);

The Fyrste Sermon of Mayster Hughe Latimer, Whiche He Preached before the Kynges Maiestie wythin His Graces Palayce at Westmynster M. D. XLIX. the viii. of Marche (London: Printed by Ihon Daye & William Seres, 1549);

The Seconde Sermon of Master Hughe Latemer, Whych He Preached before the Kynges Maiestie, in Hys Graces Palayce at Westminster ye .xv. Day of Marche (London: Printed by Ihon Daye & William Seres, 1549);

A Moste Faithfull Sermon Preached before the Kynges Most Excellete Maiestye, and Hys Most Honorable Councel, in His Court at Westminster (London: Printed by Iohn Daye, 1550);

A Sermon of Master Latimer, Preached at Stamford the .ix. Day of October. Anno. M. ccccc. and Fyftie (London: Printed by Iohn Daye, 1550);

27 Sermons Preached by the Ryght Reuerende Father in God and Constant Matir of Jesus Christe, Maister Hugh Latimer, as Well Such as in Tymes Past Haue Bene Printed, as Certayne Other Commyng to Our

Hugh Latimer; portrait by an unknown artist (National Portrait Gallery, London)

Handes of Late, Whych Were Yet Neuer Set Forth in Print (London: Printed by Iohn Daye, 1562);

Frutefull Sermons Preached by the Right Reuerend Father, and Constant Martyr of Iesus Christ, M. Hugh Latymer, Newly Imprinted: With Others, Not Heretofore Set Forth in Print, to the Edifying of All Which Will Dispose Them Selues to the Readyng of the Same (London: Printed by Iohn Daye, 1571).

Editions: *The Works of Hugh Latimer, Sometime Bishop of Worcester, Martyr, 1555,* 2 volumes, edited by George Elwes Corrie (Cambridge: Cambridge University Press, 1844, 1845);

The Sermons and Life of the Right Reverend Father in God, and Constant Martyr in Christ, Hugh Latimer, Some Time Bishop of Worcester, 2 volumes, edited by John Watkins (London: Aylott, 1858);

Sermons by Hugh Latimer, Sometime Bishop of Worcester, edited by Henry Charles Beeching (London: Dent / New York: Dutton, 1906);

Selected Sermons of Hugh Latimer, edited by Allan G. Chester (Charlottesville: University of Virginia Press, 1968).

OTHER: John Foxe, ed., *Actes and Monuments of These Latter and Perilous Dayes, Touching Matters of the Church,* contributions by Latimer (London: Printed by John Day, 1563).

Hugh Latimer is not as accessible or as attractive to the modern reader as other sixteenth-century literary figures because he was a preacher, and preachers no longer command the interest they did in his day. Furthermore, he was a preacher in a particular religious cause – Protestantism – that no longer elicits the strong favorable or unfavorable reactions it did when Latimer preached it. His theology is not original, but his genius and enduring legacy is that he is the one who made the Reformers' arguments understandable to the people. In doing so he used contemporary images and diction drawn from secular life and a lively colloquial style designed to link court with country and magistrate with yeoman. As perhaps the greatest popularizer of the most significant intellectual, moral, and social movement of his time, Latimer remains an essential vehicle for understanding sixteenth-century England's religion, society, and language. No anthology of sixteenth-century English literature would be complete without Latimer's "Sermon of the Plow," his "Sermon before Convocation," and at least one of his "Sermons before King Edward."

Latimer was probably born around 1492. His father, also named Hugh, appears to have farmed a small holding near Thurcaston in Leicestershire. As was the custom at that time, Latimer went to Cambridge when he was still a boy to pursue a career in the church. In the first sermon he preached before King Edward VI at court during Lent of 1549 he recalls his father with evident pride: "My father was a yeoman and had no lands of his own, only he had a farm of three or four pound by year at the uttermost, and hereupon he tilled so much as kept half-a-dozen men. He had walk for a hundred sheep, and my mother milked thirty kine. He was able, and did find the king a harness, with himself and his horse, while he came to the place that he should receive the king's wages. I can remember that I buckled his harness when he went unto Blackheath field. He kept me to school, or else I had not been able to have preached before the king's majesty now. He married my sisters with five pound or twenty nobles apiece, so that he brought them up in godliness and fear of God. He kept hospitality for his poor neighbors, and some alms he gave to the poor. And all this he did of the said farm, where he that now hath it payeth sixteen pound by year, or more, and is not able to do any thing for his prince, for himself, nor for his children, or give a cup of drink to the poor."

Converted to the Protestant cause by his friend and mentor Thomas Bilney in 1524 when they were at Cambridge, Latimer was soon notorious at the university as an outspoken Protestant of the "early evangelical" or "Bilneyan" type. Like Bilney, he pursued an argument for reform that reflects a mixture of humanist, early Lutheran, and Lollard influences. In his early preaching the Lollard influence is dominant: he attacked the penitential system of the medieval church as "unscriptural" and contrary to the "law of God." He was particularly opposed to the cult of images and the making of pilgrimages; he advocated the translation of Scripture into English and the promotion of "true" or "scriptural" preaching.

In his *Jewel of Joy* (1550?), Thomas Becon provides a firsthand recollection of Latimer's preaching in Cambridge at this time:

> I was present when, with manifest authorities of God's word and arguments invincible, besides the allegations of doctors, [Latimer] proved in his sermons, that the Holy Scriptures ought to be read in the English tongue of all Christian people, whether they were priests or layman, as they be called; which thing divers drowsy duncers, with certain false flying flattering friars, could not abide, but openly in their unsavory sermons resisted his godly purpose. . . .
>
> Neither was I absent when he inveighed against temple-works, good intents, blind zeal, superstitious devotion, etc., as the painting of tabernacles, gilding of images, setting up of candles, running on pilgrimage, and such other idle inventions of men, whereby the glory of God was obscured, and the works of mercy the less regarded.

John Foxe summarizes two of Latimer's "Sermons of the Card" from this period in his *Actes and Monuments* (1563). These sermons appear to be drawn from a series in which Latimer likened a Christian's salvation to the contemporary card game triumph, an ancestor of whist: "Now I trust you wot what your card meaneth: let us see how that we can play with the same. Whensoever it shall happen you to go and make your oblation unto God, ask of yourselves this question, Who art Thou? The answer, as you know, is I am a Christian man. Then you must again ask unto yourself, What Christ requireth of a Christian man? By and by cast down your trump, your heart, and look first of one card, then of another. The first card telleth thee, thou shalt not kill, thou shalt not be angry, thou shalt not be out of patience. This done, thou shalt look if there be any more cards to take up; and if thou look well, thou shalt see another card of the same suit, wherein thou shalt know that thou art bound to reconcile thy neighbor. Then cast thy trump upon them both, and gather them all three together, and do according to the virtue of thy cards; and surely thou shalt not lose." In the second sermon Latimer makes a distinction between works of piety, which are "voluntary," and works of mercy and charity, which are "necessary." This distinction, which he inherited from Bilney, is a feature of his early preaching. By insisting that the traditional works of devotion commended by the medieval church are "voluntary" and that the moral laws of Scripture are "necessary," Latimer was able to attack the devotional apparatus of the church without absolutely rejecting it. Still, he clearly argues against the penitential and devotional practices of the medieval church and in favor of the scriptural good works of charity and mercy: "Again, if you list to gild and paint Christ in your churches and honor him in vestments, see that before your eyes the poor people die not for lack of meat, drink, and clothing. Then do you deck the very true temple of God, and honor him in rich vestures that will never be worn, and so forth use yourselves according unto the commandments: and then, finally, set up your candles, and they will report what a glorious light remaineth in your hearts; for it is not fitting to see a dead man light candles."

Foxe also preserves an anonymous letter written to Henry VIII in December 1530 "for restoring again the free liberty of reading the Holy Scriptures"; he attributes this letter to Latimer. The letter distinguishes between the false leaders of the church, who are marked by their worldly power and wealth, and the true preachers of God's Word, who are marked by their suffering and persecution. Likening the contemporary leaders of the church to the scribes and Pharisees who opposed Jesus, the letter argues that they oppose translating the Bible into English because the plain meaning of the Bible clearly shows that their teachings are contrary to the Law of God: "Therefore, good king, seeing that the right David, that is to say, our Savior Christ, hath sent his servants, that is to say, his true preachers, and his own word also, to comfort our weak and sick souls, let not these worldly men make your grace believe that they will cause insurrections and heresies, and such mischiefs as they imagine of their own mad brains, lest that he be avenged upon you and your realm, as was David upon the Amonites, and as he hath ever been avenged upon them which have obstinately withstood and gainsaid his word."

Like many of the Cambridge Evangelicals, most notably his friend Thomas Cranmer, Latimer found favor with Henry VIII because of his support for the king's divorce from Catherine of Aragon. In March 1530 he was invited to preach at Windsor, and he was appointed to the living of West Kington in Wiltshire in January 1531. He was a Lenten preacher at court in 1534, and he was appointed bishop of Worcester in August 1535.

In a remarkably radical sermon delivered to Convocation in June 1536, preaching on the text "the children of this world to be much more prudent and politic than the children of light in their generation" (Luke 16:8), Latimer makes a distinction between the corrupt "children of this world" who are powerful within the church and the "children of light" who are persecuted: "The children of this world be like crafty hunters; they be misnamed children of light, forasmuch as they so hate light, and so study to do the works of darkness. If they were the children of light, they would not love darkness. It is no marvel that they go about to keep others in darkness, seeing they be in darkness, darker than is the darkness of hell." Latimer appeals to his fellow bishops to prove themselves "children of light" by acting against the "children of this world" within the church.

Latimer was a violent and committed iconoclast who joined with enthusiasm in the king's 1538 campaign against the shrines. In a notorious letter to Thomas Cromwell, the king's chief minister, Latimer wrote with evident anticipation about his assigned role as preacher at the approaching execution of the conservative Catholic Friar Forest, one of the Observant Friars of Greenwich who had refused to accept the royal supremacy, on 22 May 1538: "And, Sir, if it be your pleasure, as it is, that I shall play the fool after my customary manner when Forest shall suffer, I would wish that my stage stood near unto Forest: for I would endeavor myself so to content the people that therewith I might also convert Forest, God so helping, or rather altogether working: wherefore I would that he should hear what I shall say."

Henry reasserted Catholic dogma in the Six Articles of 1539, and Latimer resigned his see in July of that year. After spending a year under house arrest he was forbidden to preach and was exiled to the country. He seems to have spent most of the rest of Henry's reign as a guest in Protestant households in Warwickshire and Lincolnshire. In 1546 he returned to London, where he was questioned by the Privy Council regarding his friendship with the outspoken Protestant Dr. Edward Crome and then was imprisoned in the Tower. After the accession of Edward VI in February 1547 Latimer was released and was designated by Protector of the Realm Edward Seymour, Duke of Somerset, as the official apologist for the protector's more radical program of Protestant reforms. In this role he preached a series of eight sermons at Paul's Cross in January 1548, including his famous "Sermon of the Plow."

According to Latimer, the preacher is like a plowman: "And well may the preacher and the plowman be likened together: first, for their labor of all seasons of the year; for there is no time of the year in which the plowman hath not some special work to do: as in my country in Leicestershire, the plowman hath a time to set forth and to assay his plough, and other times for other necessary works to be done. And they also may be likened together for the diversity of works and variety of offices that they have to do. For as the plowman first setteth forth his plow, and then tilleth his land, and breaketh it in furrows, and sometime ridgeth it up again; and at another time harroweth it and clotteth it, and sometime dungeth it and hedgeth it and weedeth it, purgeth and maketh it clean: so the prelate, the preacher, hath many diverse offices to do." Against this ideal of the simple, hardworking plowman-preacher stands Latimer's old enemy, the "unpreaching prelate" or "lording loiterer": "But this much I dare say, that since lording and loitering hath come up, preaching hath come down, contrary to the apostles' times: for they preached and lorded not, and now they lord and preach not. For they that be lords will ill go to plow: it is no meet office for them; it is not seeming for their estate. Thus came up lording loiterers: thus crept in unpreaching prelates; and so have they long continued." Latimer's distinction between "voluntary" and "necessary" works has hardened into a distinction between works that "honor God" and works that serve the devil: "Where the devil is resident, that he may prevail, up with all superstition and idolatry, censing, painting of images, candles, palms, ashes, holy water, and new service of men's inventing; as though man could invent a better way to honor

God with than God himself hath appointed. Down with Christ's cross, up with purgatory pickpurse, up with him, the popish purgatory, I mean. Away with clothing the naked, the poor and impotent; up with decking of images, and gay garnishing of stocks and stones: up with man's traditions and his laws, down with God's traditions and his most holy word."

One respect in which Latimer's ideas appear to have developed in a Lutheran direction is in his new use of the doctrine of salvation by faith alone. Both Latimer and Martin Luther describe salvation as a three-stage progression from preaching to conversion to good works; but whereas Luther stressed the conversion that is elicited by preaching and bears fruit in good works, Latimer stresses the preaching and the good works: the preacher "hath first a busy work to bring his parishioners to a right faith, as Paul calleth it, and not a swerving faith; but to a faith that embraceth Christ, and trusteth to his merits; a lively faith, a justifying faith; a faith that maketh a man righteous, without respect of works. . . . He hath then busy work, I say, to bring his flock to a right faith, and then to confirm them in the same faith: now casting them down with the law and with threatenings of God for sin; now ridging them up again with the gospel and with the promises of God's favor: now weeding them, by telling them their faults and making them forsake sin; now clotting them, by breaking their stony hearts and by making them supplehearted, and making them to have hearts of flesh, that is, soft hearts, and apt for doctrine to enter in: now teaching to know God rightly, and to know their duty to God and their neighbors: now exhorting them, when they know their duty, that they do it, and be diligent in it; so that they have a continual work to do."

Another area in which Latimer's preaching seems to have become more Lutheran is his now-open opposition to the Catholic teaching that the Eucharist is offered by the priest as a sacrifice to God for sin. Like Luther, Latimer argues that this doctrine turns the Eucharist into a work whereby people try to win salvation with their own sacrifices when they should trust in the one perfect sacrifice of Christ on the Cross: "And this way the devil used to evacuate the death of Christ, that we might have affiance [trust] in other things, as in the sacrifice of the priest; whereas Christ would have us to trust in his only sacrifice." In neither case, however, can one conclude with certainty that Latimer's doctrine had changed; it is more likely that he had avoided asserting these Lutheran aspects of his doctrine while the anti-Lutheran Henry was king. Neither aspect is central

Latimer preaching before King Edward VI; woodcut from John Foxe's Actes and Monuments *(1563)*

to his fundamental argument, which remained consistent: he rejects images, pilgrimages, and all the "false" works of the medieval church, and he promotes the free preaching of the law of God.

Latimer preached at court during Lent of 1548, 1549, and 1550; seven of his 1548 sermons survive, as does the last sermon of 1550. At court he was an outspoken supporter of Somerset's efforts at social and moral reform and an acknowledged leader of the new "commonwealth school" of Edwardian preachers. These preachers believed that Protestant preaching should lead to a more Christian society in which magistrates would honor their duty to govern justly, the rich would fulfill their responsibility to care for the poor, and education would be promoted for the sake of better government and better preaching. Latimer reprimands his noble audience for their lack of charity and their greed, condemns the contemporary administration of the law as unjust, and opposes the enclosing of the common lands formerly available to humbler farmers to secure pasture for the sheep of great landowners. Like the prophets of the Old Testament, Latimer pleads for social justice: "The poorest plowman is in Christ equal with the greatest prince that is. Let them, therefore, have sufficient to maintain them and to find them their necessaries. A plow-land must have sheep; yea, they must have

sheep to dung their ground for bearing of corn; for if they have no sheep to help to fat the ground, they shall have but bare corn and thin. They must have swine for their food, to make their veneries or bacon of: their bacon is their venison, for they shall now have *hangum tuum* [your hanging], if they get any other venison; so that bacon is their necessary meat to feed on, which they may not lack. They must have other cattle: as horses to draw their plow and for carriage of things to the markets, and kine for their milk and cheese, which they must live upon and pay their rents. These cattle must have pasture, which pasture if they lack, the rest must needs fail them: and pasture they cannot have, if the land be taken in, and enclosed from them. . . . Therefore, for God's love, restore their sufficient unto them, and search no more what is the cause of rebellion."

After the fall of his patron, Somerset, in 1550 Latimer again retired to the countryside, staying with the Protestant Frances Grey, Duchess of Suffolk at Grimsthorpe, Lincolnshire. Most of his surviving sermons come from this period; they are in many ways the most attractive of his sermons, as they show him preaching to a simple audience in a pastoral role. There are still strong echoes of his earlier opposition to the teachings and practices of the medieval church, but his purpose is more practi-

The burning of Latimer and Bishop Nicholas Ridley at Oxford, 16 October 1555; woodcut from
Foxe's Actes and Monuments

cal and more positive: to bring the new Protestant doctrines into the lives of common men and women so that they can be inspired to do those works that are "necessary" and to leave behind "false" works of "idolatry and superstition." His emphasis is always on the essential role of the preacher in effecting conversion and on the moral good works that true preaching should produce.

His sympathy for the poor notwithstanding, Latimer's conception of society remained hierarchical: his Lincolnshire sermons stress the commoner's Christian obligation to obey the magistrate. In his sermon at Stamford in 1550, for example, he declares: "The office of a magistrate is grounded upon God's word and is plainly described of Saint Paul, writing unto the Romans, where he showeth that all souls, that is to say, all men ought to obey magistrates, for they are ordained of God: and to resist them is to resist against God." What remains radical about Latimer's social ideas, however, is his assertion that the king is accountable to the Law of God. This means that the faithful preacher is ultimately more powerful, because it falls to the preacher to remind the king of his duty: "There is no king, emperor, magistrate, and ruler, of what state soever they be, but are bound to obey this God, and to give credence unto his holy word, in directing their steps ordinately according unto the

same word. Yea, truly, they are not only bound to obey God's book, but also the minister of the same, 'for the word's sake,' so far as he speaketh 'sitting in Moses's chair'; that is, if his doctrine be taken out of Moses's law. For in this world God hath two swords; the one is a temporal sword, the other a spiritual. The temporal sword resteth in the hands of kings, magistrates, and rulers under him; whereunto all subjects, as well the clergy as the laity, be subject, and punishable for any offense contrary to the same book. The spiritual sword is in the hands of the ministers and preachers; whereunto all kings, magistrates, and rulers, ought to be obedient; that is, to hear and follow, so long as the ministers sit in Christ's chair that is speaking out of Christ's book."

After the accession of the Catholic Mary Tudor in January 1553 Latimer again found himself in danger. His adoption of the Reformed Eucharistic doctrine of the spiritual presence in 1548 and his subsequent preaching against the Catholic doctrine of transubstantiation marked him as a heretic. Refusing to flee the country, Latimer was arrested in September 1553 and imprisoned with Cranmer and Bishop Nicholas Ridley in the Tower. In March 1554 the three were moved to Oxford, where they were forced to take part in a formal disputation on the Eucharist from 14 to 20 April. Latimer was tried for heresy from 30 September to 1 October 1555 and was executed with Ridley in Oxford on 16 October. In his correspondence with Ridley before the disputation and in his comments at the disputation, at his trial, and at his execution Latimer appears almost eager for martyrdom. His vision of the church as the mixed company of the worldly and powerful children of the devil and the innocent and persecuted "children of light" proved his greatest comfort, for he chose to die as a child of light in a time of darkness. Writing from prison in May 1555, he concludes his letter to "all the unfeigned lovers of God's truth": "Die once we must; how and where, we know not. Happy are they whom God giveth to pay nature's debt (I mean to die) for his sake. Here is not our home; let us therefore accordingly consider things, having always before our eyes that heavenly Jerusalem, and the way thereto in persecution. And let us consider all the dear friends of God, how they have gone after the example of our Savior Jesus Christ, whose footsteps let us also follow, even to the gallows (if God's will be so), not doubting, but as he rose again the third day, even so shall we do at the time appointed of God. . . . Comfort yourselves with these words, and pray for me, for the Lord's sake, and God be merciful unto us all! So be it." Latimer's last defiant statement to Ridley at their burning in Oxford is recorded by Foxe in *Actes and Monuments:* "Be of good comfort, Master Ridley, and play the man. We shall this day light such a candle, by God's grace, in England, as I trust shall never be put out."

Latimer's reputation as a theologian, preacher, and hero has suffered from the decline of classical Protestantism as a social and religious force and from the development of a more secular society. Thus, in modern studies of the sixteenth century, Latimer does not loom as large as he once did. Still, he was the most famous (or infamous) preacher of his day and the most effective proponent of early English Protestant doctrine.

Biographies:
Robert Demaus, *Hugh Latimer: A Biography* (London: Religious Tract Society, 1869; revised, 1881);
Harold S. Darby, *Hugh Latimer: A Biography* (London: Epworth Press, 1953);

Allan G. Chester, *Hugh Latimer, Apostle to the English* (Philadelphia: University of Pennsylvania Press, 1954).

References:
Margaret Aston, *England's Iconoclasts* (Oxford: Clarendon, 1988);
J. W. Blench, *Preaching in England in the Late Fifteenth and Sixteenth Centuries* (Oxford: Blackwell, 1964);
Peter Newman Brooks, *Thomas Cranmer's Doctrine of the Eucharist* (London: Macmillan, 1965);
Allan G. Chester, "The 'New Learning': A Semantic Note," *Studies in the Renaissance,* 2 (1955): 139-147;
John F. Davis, *Heresy and Reformation in the South-East of England, 1520–1559* (London: Royal Historical Society, 1983);
D. Stuart Dunnan, *The Preaching of Hugh Latimer: A Reappraisal* (Oxford: Oxford University Press, forthcoming 1994);
Charles M. Gray, *Hugh Latimer and the Sixteenth Century: An Essay in Interpretation* (Cambridge, Mass.: Harvard University Press, 1950);
Elizabeth T. Hastings, "A Sixteenth Century Manuscript Translation of Latimer's First Sermon before Edward," *PMLA,* 60 (December 1945): 959-1002;
Anne Hudson, *The Premature Reformation* (Oxford: Clarendon, 1988);
Robert L. Kelly, "Hugh Latimer as Piers Plowman," *Studies in English Literature,* 17 (Winter 1977): 13-26;
James B. Lane, "Two Masters, God and Monarch: The Political Philosophy of Hugh Latimer," *Journal of Church and State,* 15 (Winter 1973): 33-47;
Marcus C. Loane, *Masters of the English Reformation* (London: Hodder & Stoughton, 1954);
Nicholas Ridley, *The Works of Nicholas Ridley,* edited by Henry Christmas (Cambridge: Cambridge University Press, 1843);
Hastings Robinson, ed., *Original Letters Relative to the English Reformation,* 2 volumes (Cambridge: Cambridge University Press, 1846-1847);
John K. Yost, "Hugh Latimer's Reform Program, 1529-1536," *Anglican Theological Review,* 53 (April 1971): 103-114.

John Leland
(1503? – 18 April 1552)

James P. Carley
York University, Toronto

BOOKS: *Naeniae in mortem Thomae Viati Equitis incomparabilis* (London: [Printed by Reyner Wolfe] Ad signum aenei serpentis, 1542);

Genethliacon Illustrissimi Eäduerdi principis Cambriae: Libellus ante aliquot annos inchoatus, nunc vero absolutus, & editus (London: Printed by Reyner Wolfe, 1543);

Assertio inclytissimi Arturij Regis Britanniae (London: Printed by Reyner Wolfe at the shop of John Herford, 1544); translated by Richard Robinson as *A Learned and True Assertion of the Original Life, Actes, and Death of the Most Noble Prince Arthure, King of Great Britaine* (London: Printed by Iohn Wolfe, 1582);

Fatum Boniae Morinorum (London: Printed by Richard Wolfe, 1544);

Bononia Gallo Mastix: In laudem felicissimi victoris Henrici octaui (London: Printed by John Mayler, 1545);

κυκνειον ασμα: *Cygnea cantio* (London: Printed by Reyner Wolfe, 1545);

Naeniae in mortem Splendidissimi Equitis Henrici Duddelegi (London: Printed by John Mayler, 1545);

Εγκωμιον τηδ ειρηνηδ: *Laudatio Pacis* (London: Printed by Reyner Wolfe, 1546);

The Laboryouse Journey & Serche of John Leylande, for Englandes Antiquitees Geuen of Hym as a Newe Yeares Gyfte to Kynge Henry the VIII. in the XXXVII. Yeare of His Reygne, with Declaratyons Enlarged: by Johan Bale (London: Printed by Steven Mierdman for John Bale, to be sold by Richard Foster, 1549);

Principvm, ac Illustrium aliquot & eruditorum in Anglia virorum, Encomia Trophaea, Genethliaca, et Epithalamia. A Joanne Lelando Antiquario conscripta, nunc primum in lucem edita. Quibus etiam adiuncta sunt, Illustrissimorum aliquot herôum, hodiè viuentium, aliorumq; hinc inde Anglorum, Encomia quaedam, edited by Thomas Newton (London: Printed by Thomas Orwin, 1589);

Eighteenth-century engraving by C. Grignion of a bust of John Leland at All Souls College, Oxford University. No such bust exists there today.

Commentarii de scriptoribus Britannicis, auctore Joanne Lelando Londinate, 2 volumes, edited by Anthony Hall (Oxford: Sheldonian Theatre, 1709); edited and translated by Caroline Brett as *De Viris Illustribus: Commentaries on British Writers,* Oxford Medieval Texts (Oxford: Oxford University Press, forthcoming);

The Itinerary of John Leland the Antiquary, 9 volumes, edited by Thomas Hearne (Oxford: Printed at the Theatre for the publisher, 1710–1712);

Joannis Lelandi Antiquarii De rebus Britannicis collectanea, 6 volumes, edited by Hearne (Oxford: Sheldonian Theatre, 1715).

Editions: *The Itinerary of John Leland in or about the Years 1535–1543,* edited by Lucy Toulmin Smith, 5 volumes (London: Bell, 1906–1910);

"*Assertio Inclytissimi Arturii Regis Britanniae,* with the Translation First Published by Richard Robinson in 1582," edited by William Edward Mead, in *The Famous Historie of Chinon of England,* edited by Christopher Middleton, Early English Texts Society, original series 165 (London: Oxford University Press, 1925);

The Laboryouse Journey & Serche of John Leylande, for Englandes Antiquitees Geuen of Hym as a Newe Yeares Gyfte to Kynge Henry the VIII. in the XXXVII. Yeare of His Reygne, with Declaratyons Enlarged: by Johan Bale (Norwood, N. J. & Amsterdam: Johnson & Theatrum Orbis Terrarum, 1975).

OTHER: "Verses on the Coronation of Anne Boleyn," by Leland and Nicholas Udall, in *The Progresses and Public Processions of Queen Elizabeth,* volume 1, edited by John Nichols (London: Printed by John Nichols, 1788).

Although John Leland was never officially made "King's Antiquary," as some have claimed, he is nevertheless the founder of modern antiquarian studies in England and was acknowledged as such by his sixteenth-century successors John Bale, William Camden, and William Lambarde. His surviving papers provide the single most important source of information about the contents of the dissolved English monasteries and stand as a prototype for the various county histories that subsequently appeared. Moreover, Leland's view of the term *antiquarius,* with which he proudly distinguished himself, was much more general than modern usage would suggest. He saw himself as a humanist scholar in the widest sense: a judicious editor of texts, a careful historian of the Arthurian legend, and a connoisseur of *bonae litterae,* whose excellence he celebrated in his own well-turned verses in purest classical meters.

Most information about Leland's early life comes from his poetry. He was born in London; the precise year of his birth is not certain. By his own account he was slightly older than his friend Wil-

liam Paget, and it would seem, therefore, that he was born around 1503. There is reference in the poetry to an older brother – also named John Leland – who became a physician, and to a patron, Thomas Myles, who adopted him at an early age and sent him to Saint Paul's School. It was at Saint Paul's – founded by John Colet in the early sixteenth century along humanist lines – that Leland became interested in the study of the classics; it was also there that he formed the circle of acquaintances – including Paget, Anthony Denny, Thomas Wriothesley, and Edward North – with whom he would be linked for the rest of his life.

From Saint Paul's School, Leland proceeded to Christ's College, Cambridge, receiving his B.A. in 1522 and becoming tutor to Thomas, son of Thomas Howard, second Duke of Norfolk. He seems to have been a member of the circle of young men associated with the Thomas More household.

After the duke's death in 1524 Leland went to Oxford, where he remained, possibly associated with All Souls' College, until 1526. In subsequent writings he would disparage his time among the noisy sophists at Oxford. Before the end of 1528 Leland was made a king's scholar and traveled to Paris, where he worshiped, he says, at the feet of the great humanists of the generation: Guillaume Budé, Jacques Lefèvre d'Etaples, Paolo Emilio, Jean Ruel, John Lascaris, Nicolas Bérault, and François Du Bois. There, according to his account, he perfected the poetic arts: "Parhisii at Musas mihi persuasere colendas, / Hinc variis cecini carmina mista modis" (But it was Paris that taught me to honor the Muses, / And henceforth I sang songs composed in varying meters). Of profounder importance in the long run, his mentors encouraged his interest in ancient manuscripts and taught him the principles of humanist textual criticism. Du Bois in particular seems to have fostered the young scholar's studies.

While in Paris, Leland sought the support of Henry VIII by writing encomiastic verse to those who might advocate his case at court. By late 1529 he was back in England in receipt of a royal chaplaincy and more than one living. External evidence would suggest a substantial income for the next decade and a half; his verses, however, were regularly addressed to potential patrons, and there were equally regular pleas for funds.

By the late 1520s Henry VIII was actively culling evidence from ancient documents housed at the universities and the monasteries to justify a divorce from Catherine of Aragon; this endeavor would culminate in the *Censurae academiorum* of 1531. Although there is no evidence that Leland was part of

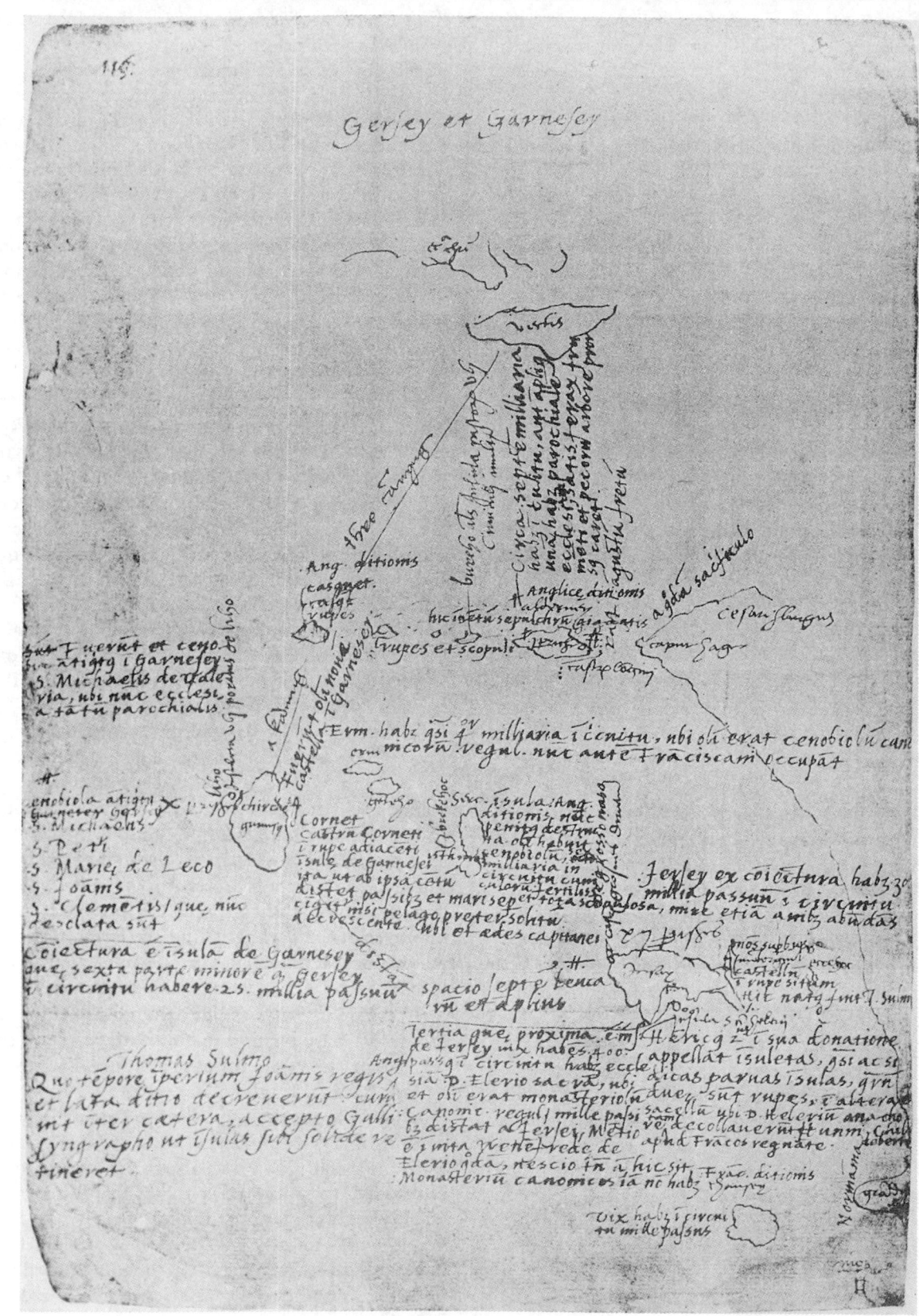

Page from the manuscript for Leland's De rebus Britannicis collectanea *with a map of the Channel Islands by an unknown cartographer, annotated by Leland (Bodleian Library, Oxford, MS. Gen. Top. c. 3 fo. 116)*

this search, it suggested to him the need to determine what was contained in the English libraries; by 1533 he had received a royal commission to examine the monastic and college libraries. The lists he compiled provide the most significant – sometimes the only – information about the contents of English monastic libraries. Leland's lists were in no sense comprehensive, however, and they formed only the preliminary steps toward a complete history of English writers. As it became clear that the monasteries were going to fall, Leland hit on the idea of establishing a royal collection and transferred a variety of treasures to palace libraries at Greenwich, Hampton Court, and Westminster. The salvation of many manuscripts from the destruction that occurred at the time of the dissolution of the monasteries is directly attributable to Leland's efforts.

At some point Leland's interests broadened from manuscripts and writers to a whole range of historical and topographical concerns. In the late 1530s he initiated a series of annual journeys that took him throughout the kingdom, so that "there is almost neither cape nor bay, haven, creek or pier, river or confluence of rivers, breeches, washes, lakes, meres, fenny waters, mountains, valleys, moors, heaths, forests, woods, cities, burgs, castles, principal manor places, monasteries and colleges, but I have seen them, and noted in so doing a whole world of things very memorable." The notebooks he compiled form the main portion of the volumes Thomas Hearne published in the eighteenth century under the titles *The Itinerary of John Leland the Antiquary* (1710–1712) and *Joannis Lelandi De rebus Britannicis collectanea* (1715).

His preliminary explorations completed, Leland outlined his publishing projects in 1545–1546: a dictionary of British writers in four books, to be called *De Viris Illustribus;* a map of Britain accompanied by descriptive material, with the title "Liber de Topographia Britanniae Primae"; a history of Britain in fifty books – with six books concerning the adjacent islands – to be called "De Antiquitate Britannica" or "Civilis Historia"; a study of British noble families in three books, to be titled "De Nobilitate Britannica"; and a book of descriptions of Britain by classical and medieval writers, to be titled "Antiquitates Britanniae." The dictionary was nearing completion in 1547 but was not published until 1709, when it appeared under the title *Commentarii de scriptoribus Britannicis*. The materials in *The Itinerary of John Leland the Antiquary* and *De rebus britannicis collectanea* form the cornerstones for his second, third, and fourth projects. The outline of

the fifth can be found in an unpublished notebook in the British Library.

Shortly after he presented the plan for his projects to Henry VIII, Leland "fell beside his wits," as his friend John Bale put it. He was lodged in the home of the printer Reyner Wolfe, incurably insane. Various theories of the cause of his madness were propounded: his friends alleged grief over the death of Henry VIII or resentment over spiteful treatment by enemies; others suggested recognition of his inability to produce the grandiose works he had promised for so long or divine retribution for heresy or vainglory. Later generations saw Leland's madness as a symbol of the fate of the antiquary, a warning against overapplication to abstruse studies. In an unpublished diagnosis, Dr. Henry Rollin of the Royal College of Psychiatrists has suggested that Leland suffered from manic-depressive illness aggravated by the trauma of Henry's death, as well as from a "magpie complex," an obsession with collecting from which insanity provided the only escape.

Whatever controversialists might have felt about Leland's religious allegiances – he was criticized by extreme Reformers and Catholics alike – it was generally realized that his papers were extremely precious: they provided direct and detailed witness to a way of life that had entirely disappeared with the dissolution and destruction of the monasteries. When Leland died on 18 April 1552 his manuscripts were entrusted to Sir John Cheke, former tutor to Edward VI; but when Cheke fled England during Mary's reign, they appear to have been dispersed. Bale had access to the papers when he was living in the London house of Mary Fitzroy, Duchess of Richmond, and John Stow made copies that Camden later used. At some point five volumes of what would become *De rebus britannicis collectanea* came into the possession of Humphrey Purefoy, whose son gave them to William Burton, the historian of Leicestershire, in 1612. The papers that would be printed as *The Itinerary of John Leland the Antiquary* passed to Leland's old school friend Paget, then to William Cecil, Lord Burghley, and next to Burton, who gave the *De rebus Britannicis collectanea* and seven of the eight volumes of what would become *The Itinerary of John Leland the Antiquary* to the Bodleian Library at Oxford in 1632; the eighth he had lent to a friend and could not recover. It was subsequently given by Charles King.

De rebus Britannicis collectanea and *The Itinerary of John Leland the Antiquary* consist of rough notes packed with detailed information about the Tudor landscape and its medieval remains. They display

Leland's intense intellectual curiosity, love of landscape, and desire for topographical accuracy. The clue to the past, Leland seems to suggest, lies in an analysis of surviving monuments of all sorts, local legends as well as architecture. Leland's book lists provide vital information about the makeup of monastic libraries and are key witnesses to the existence of subsequently destroyed medieval texts. The almost completed *Commentarii de scriptoribus Britannicis* – "the supreme mark of my labor.... Wherefore I, knowing by infinite variety of books and assiduous reading of them who hath been learned, and who hath written from time to time in this realm, have digested into four books the names of them with their lives and monuments of learning" – is the first attempt to provide a comprehensive historical guide to British writers and contains much information available nowhere else. It was envisaged in patriotic terms and stands as a response to Johann von Tritheim's *Catalogus illustrium virorum Germaniae* (1496). Although some of its conclusions seem suspect by modern standards, the *Commentarii de scriptoribus Britannicis* may be seen as the model for later biographical histories, culminating in the *Dictionary of National Biography* (1882–). In other words, it has played a significant role in the formation of the canon of medieval English writers. And the Old Royal Library, now housed in the British Museum, is itself a tangible monument to Leland.

Stow's *A Survey of London* (1598) grew out of Leland's enterprise, as did William Harrison's "An Historical Description of the Island of Britain," published in the first volume of Raphael Holinshed's *Chronicles of England, Scotlande, and Irelande* (1577); both Stow and Harrison were accused of plagiarism by certain of their contemporaries. Some seventeenth-century antiquaries postulated that Holinshed had access to Leland's papers through Wolfe and that these papers were used in compiling his chronicles. Leland's enterprise, moreover, stands as a model for the great work undertaken by Camden. Even if modern scholars reject the charges of plagiarism made by Ralph Brooke in *A Discovery of Certain Errors Published in Print in the Much Commended Britannia* (1596), it is clear that Camden's *Britannia* (1586) represents the book that Leland would have written if his mind had held.

The influence of Leland's poetry is less clear, partly because Leland never wrote in English, his generation being the last in which Latin was a truly living poetic medium. Even if one accepts J. W. Binns's judgment that "Leland stands to the Lat-

in poetry of sixteenth-century England as [Sir Thomas] Wyatt and [Henry Howard, Earl of] Surrey do to the English," one must realize that the Latin poetry so excitedly celebrated by the humanists ultimately represented a road not taken. Nevertheless, Leland's long river poem, the *Cygnea cantio* (1545) – a pioneer in the "topo-chrono-graphical" mode defined by George Wither in the seventeenth century – can be seen as a direct influence on Camden's "De connubio Tamae et Isis," on Edmund Spenser's *Prothalamion* and *Epithalamion Thamesis,* and on Michael Drayton's *Poly-Olbion* (1612).

As much as he is quoted, Leland's life, his intellectual milieu, his place in the religious controversies of Tudor England (concerning which his unpublished "Antiphilarchia" provides a substantial amount of information), and the degree of his reliability as a witness to medieval documents and Tudor topography have rarely been examined. A full-scale, modern biography remains a modern desideratum in sixteenth-century studies.

Biographies:

William Huddesford, "The Life of John Leland," in *The Lives of Those Eminent Antiquaries, John Leland, Thomas Hearne, and Anthony à Wood,* volume 1, edited by Huddesford (Oxford: Clarendon Press, 1772);

Edward Burton, *The Life of John Leland (the First English Antiquary) with Extensive Notes and a Bibliography of His Works, Including Those in MS: Printed from a Hitherto Unpublished Work* (London: Cooper, 1896).

References:

J. W. Binns, *Intellectual Culture in Elizabethan and Jacobean England: The Latin Writings of the Age* (Leeds: Cairns, 1990), pp. 18–26;

Leicester Bradner, "Some Unpublished Poems by John Leland," *PMLA,* 71 (September 1956): 827–836;

Caroline Brett, "John Leland and the Anglo-Norman Historian," *Anglo-Norman Studies,* 11 (1989): 59–76;

Brett, "John Leland, Wales, and Early British History," *Welsh Historical Review,* 15 (1990): 169–182;

Ronald E. Buckalew, "Leland's Transcript of Aelfric's *Glossary," Anglo-Saxon England,* 7 (1978): 149–164;

James P. Carley, "John Leland and the Contents of English Pre-Dissolution Libraries: Glastonbury Abbey," *Scriptorium,* 40, no. 1 (1986): 107–120;

Carley, "John Leland and the Contents of the English Pre-Dissolution Libraries: Lincolnshire," *Transactions of the Cambridge Bibliographical Society,* 9 (1989): 330–357;

Carley, "John Leland and the Contents of English Pre-Dissolution Libraries: The Cambridge Friars," *Transactions of the Cambridge Bibliographical Society,* 9 (1986): 90–100;

Carley, "John Leland and the Foundations of the Royal Library: The Westminster Inventory of 1542," *Bulletin of the Society for Renaissance Studies,* 7 (1989): 13–22;

Carley, "John Leland at Somerset Libraries," *Somerset Archaeology and Natural History,* 129 (1985): 141–154;

Carley, "John Leland in Paris: The Evidence of His Poetry," *Studies in Philology,* 83 (Winter 1986): 1–50;

Carley, "John Leland's 'Cygnea Cantio': A Neglected Tudor River Poem," *Humanistica Lovaniensia,* 32 (1983): 225–241;

Carley, "The Manuscript Remains of John Leland: 'The King's Antiquary,'" *Text,* 2 (1985): 111–120;

Carley, "Polydore Vergil and John Leland on King Arthur: The Battle of the Books," *Arthurian Interpretations,* 15 (1984): 86–100;

Hoyt H. Hudson, "John Leland's List of Early English Humanists," *Huntington Library Quarterly,* 2 (April 1939): 301–304;

James Hutton, "Leland's 'Laudatio Pacis,'" *Studies in Philology,* 58 (October 1961): 616–626;

T. D. Kendrick, *British Antiquity* (London: Methuen, 1950), pp. 45–64;

F. J. Levy, *Tudor Historical Thought* (San Marino, Cal.: Huntington Library, 1967), pp. 126–132;

Joseph M. Levine, *Humanism and History: Origins of Modern English Historiography* (Ithaca, N.Y.: Cornell University Press, 1987), pp. 79–82;

T. C. Skeat, "Two 'Lost' Works by John Leland," *English Historical Review,* 65 (October 1950): 505–508.

Papers:

The manuscript for John Leland's unpublished "Antiphilarchia" is in the Cambridge University Library (MS. Ee.V.14); the manuscript for his unpublished "Antiquitates Britanniae" is in the British Library (MS. Cotton Julius C.VI, fols. 1–89). The Bodleian Library, Oxford, contains the manuscripts for *De rebus Britannicis collectanea* (MS. Gen. Top. c. 1–3), *Commentarii de scriptoribus Britannicis* (MS. Gen. Top. c. 4), and *The Itinerary of John Leland the Antiquary* (MS. Gen. Top. e. 8–15). For stray leaves and early copies, see Peter Beal, *Index of English Literary Manuscripts,* vol. 2 (London: Mansell, 1980), pp. 299–310.

Thomas Moffet

(1553 – June 1604)

Victor Houliston
University of the Witwatersrand

BOOKS: *De venis mesaraicis obstructis ipsarumque ita affectarum curatione theses sive pronunciata LX a Thoma Moufeto Londinate Anglo publicae velitationi proposita* (Basel: L. Oftenius, 1578);

De anodinis medicamentis eorumque causis et usibus physica et medica consideratio in theses aliquot digesta (Basel: Brylinger, 1578);

De ivre et praestantia chymicorum medicamentorvm dialogus apologeticus (Frankfurt am Main: Heirs of Andreus Wechel, 1584); reprinted in *Theatrum chemicum,* edited by Laurence Zetzner (Strasbourg: Heirs of E. Zetzner, 1659–1661), I: 70–108;

Nosomantica Hippocratea, sive Hippocratis prognostica cuncta, ex omnibus ipsius scriptis methodice digesta (Frankfurt am Main: Heirs of Andreus Wechel, Claude Marnius & Johann Aubrius, 1588);

The Silkewormes and Their Flies: Liuely Described in Verse, by T. M. a Countrie Farmer, and an Apprentice in Physicke. For the Great Benefit and Enriching of England (London: Printed by Valentine Simmes for Nicholas Ling, 1599);

Insectorum sive minimorum animalium theatrum: olim ab Eduardo Wottono, Conrado Gesnero, Thomaque Pennio inchoatum: tandem T. Moufeti opera concinnatum, auctum, perfectum, edited by Theodore de Mayerne (London: Thomas Cotes, 1634); translated by John Rowland as *The Theater of Insects; or, Lesser Living Creatures, as Bees, Flies, Caterpillars, Spiders, Worms, etc., a Most Elaborate Work,* volume 3 of Edward Topsell, *The History of Four-footed Beasts and Serpents and Insects,* edited by Rowland (London: Printed by E. Cotes for G. Sawbridge, 1658);

Healths Improvement; or, Rules Comprizing and Discovering the Nature, Method, and Manner of Preparing All Sorts of Food Used in This Nation, edited by Christopher Bennet (London: Printed by T. Newcomb for S. Thomson, 1655).

Editions: *Nobilis; or, A View of the Life and Death of a Sidney, and Lessus Lugubris,* edited and trans-

An unpublished title page for Thomas Moffet's Latin essays on insects, with a portrait of Moffet at the bottom. This title page was printed in about 1590, but the manuscript was then put aside, and the work remained unpublished until 1634.

lated by Virgil B. Heltzel and Hoyt H. Hudson (San Marino, Cal.: Huntington Library, 1940);

The Silkewormes and Their Flies, edited by Victor Houliston (Binghamton, N.Y.: Medieval and Renaissance Texts and Studies, 1989).

Thomas Moffet was a distinguished physician, natural historian, and man of letters attached to the literary circle of Mary Herbert, Countess of Pembroke, at Wilton House. As a scientific author, chiefly in Latin, he was influential in the early development of pharmacology and entomology; his lively arguments and style exemplify the manner of pre-Baconian scientific rhetoric. He successfully championed Paracelsian chemical medicine in the College of Physicians of London, secured an international reputation by collecting and embellishing the entomological studies of his friend Thomas Penny, and in recording his dietary recommendations wrote a highly entertaining commentary on Elizabethan dining habits and attitudes. His connection with the well-known courtier and poet Sir Philip Sidney led to patronage and eventually a pension from Sidney's brother-in-law, Henry Herbert, second Earl of Pembroke, and the composition of one of the earliest biographies of the poet. *The Silkworms and Their Flies* (1599), written in an ambitious attempt to interest Queen Elizabeth in establishing an English silkworm industry, can lay claim to the title of the first Virgilian georgic in English.

Moffet was born in 1553, the second son of a well-to-do London haberdasher, Thomas Moffet (originally of Whitby, Yorkshire), and Alice Ashley Moffet of Kent. His surname, spelled "Moffet" in the genealogy and other English manuscripts, is also rendered as "Moffett," "Moufet," or "Muffet." He is said to have attended the Merchant Taylors' School and, like his brothers, was educated at Cambridge, where he graduated, along with fellow student Edmund Spenser, in 1572. He migrated twice between Trinity and Caius Colleges, took his M.A. from Trinity in 1576, and developed an interest in medicine through contacts with Dr. John Caius, Thomas Lorkin (Regius Professor of Physic), and Penny (physician to the earl of Essex), who became a lifelong friend.

Penny introduced Moffet to Theodore Zwinger, professor of medicine in Basel, which from the time of Queen Mary's reign (1553–1558) had become a popular destination for English Protestants wishing to study abroad. He journeyed to Basel in early 1578 and, under the influence of Zwinger and Felix Platter, became an enthusiastic proponent of Paracelsian medicine, publicly debating several of his own theses, including *De venis mesaraicis* and his doctoral thesis, *De anodinis medicamentis,* which supported the French Paracelsian, Jean Fernel. An implied attack on the leading anti-Paracelsian, Thomas Erastus, caused the latter thesis to be seized in press by the medical faculty in December 1578. Both the original thesis and the enforced revision survive.

After receiving the degree of M.D., Moffet toured Germany and Italy and practiced successfully in Frankfurt. During his travels he met and won the admiration of medical celebrities, including Thaddeus Hajek and Petrus Monavius at the court of Rudolf II in Prague and Joachim Camerarius, Jr., in Nuremberg. In Strasbourg he was welcomed by Johannes Sturm, the founder of the gymnasium, the model for German secondary classical education, and introduced there to fellow Englishman Robert Sidney, brother of Sir Philip Sidney.

Soon after his return to England, Moffet married Jane Wheeler at Saint Mary Colechurch, London, on 23 December 1580. For the next few years, he vigorously promoted Paracelsian medicine despite considerable opposition from the College of Physicians, to which he was admitted as a candidate only in 1585. In his apologetic dialogue *De jure et praestantia chymicorum medicamentorum* (1584) he characterizes the conservative medical establishment as somnolent, obstructive, and provincial. The dialogue portrays the conversion of Philerastus ("lover of Erastus") to the opinion of Philalethes ("love of truth"), who argues for the rationality, openness to experiment, and Protestant integrity of the new movement. By dedicating this work to the Danish royal physician Petrus Severinus, Moffet sought to align himself with a broadly humanist approach to chemical medicine.

During this period he was both maintaining his international scientific connections and cultivating influential patrons. He accompanied Lord Willoughby on a diplomatic mission to Denmark in 1582, when he conferred with the astronomer Tycho Brahe. Willoughby encouraged him to publish his medical recommendations for the benefit of aristocratic patrons, a project which Moffet, then residing in Ipswich, tackled in Ramist fashion in his *Nosomantica Hippocratea* (1588), written in 1585, which purported to "methodize" Hippocrates. In it he scourged the Galenists in the College of Physicians as idle bons vivants; but by 1590 he was entertaining them as colleagues to a "sumptuous feast" at his London residence. Once admitted to the college, he had passed quickly through its ranks. In 1589 he was entrusted with drafting a significant part of the ambitious but abortive London "Pharmacopeia," an attempt by the college to standardize pharmaceutical practice throughout England. It was not published until 1618.

Professional and social advancement left Moffet free for more-gentlemanly pursuits. Penny, whom he had often accompanied into the field in search of entomological specimens, died in 1588, leaving Moffet to salvage his papers from destruction by his brother and publish his findings. This involved amalgamating Penny's notes with earlier descriptions by Conrad Gesner and Edward Wotton. In his *Insectorum sive minimorum animalium theatrum* (1634) Moffet worked up the material into elegant Latin essays with a strongly humanist flavor, as in his encomium on the fly, in imitation of Lucian. As sketches, paintings, and contributions poured in from correspondents as far afield as John White in Virginia and Camerarius in Nuremberg, he continued to embellish the manuscript for the rest of his life, in due course altering the dedication from Elizabeth to James. Although Penny's observations were faithfully transcribed, Moffet was an elaborator rather than an original entomologist, and the *Insectorum theatrum* displays little modern scientific method. The manuscript was passed on to Theodore de Mayerne, the royal physician, who published it in 1634. This work had a wide circulation throughout Europe in the seventeenth century, was frequently consulted by Sir Thomas Browne, and was translated into English by John Rowland in 1658.

Moffet's association with Sir Philip Sidney may have begun at the time of the latter's marriage to Frances Walsingham in 1538, because he claims to have been consulted about her infertility. He had met Sidney's brother, Robert, in Strasbourg and knew Timothy Bright, who was connected both with Sidney and Sir Francis Walsingham, Frances's father, in Ipswich.

After a period of traveling between London and Wiltshire as physician to both Robert Devereux, second Earl of Essex, who married Sidney's widow in 1590, and Henry Herbert, second Earl of Pembroke, husband of Sidney's sister Mary, he settled at Wilton House in 1593 as Pembroke's pensioner. He later moved to Bulbridge Farm nearby. Feeling that a decent interval had elapsed since Philip Sidney's death, he composed *Nobilis,* an exemplary life of the poet in Latin prose. The work was a New Year's gift (probably 1594) for the thirteen-year-old William Herbert and included some Latin elegies, *Lessus Lugubris,* possibly written some years earlier. The biography is modeled on Plutarch's *Lives* and emphasizes Sidney's remarkable aptitude for learning. Not published until 1940, it has provided Sidney's modern biographers with insights into his childhood and evidence of lost works such as his translation of *La sepmaine* (1578) by the French poet Guillaume de Salluste, Seigneur du Bartas.

At Wilton, Moffet enjoyed considerable favor. He accompanied Pembroke, who was president of the Welsh Marches, to Ludlow, witnessed his will in 1596, and was returned as member of Parliament for Wilton in 1597. In his next undertaking, the dietary treatise *Health's Improvement* (1655), he wrote in familiar terms of Sir John Harington, another member of the countess of Pembroke's literary circle, and Harington's satiric pamphlet *Metamorphosis of Ajax* (1596). Apart from dealing systematically with the qualities of animals, fish, birds, fruit, and grain, he broaches several classical themes such as simplicity of diet, vegetarianism, and the timing of meals, so that the work approximates to the "table-talk" genres of Athenaeus and Plutarch. The treatment of individual foods is enlivened by personal reminiscence, bons mots, rhymes, and anecdotes culled from histories, cosmographies, and encyclopedic compilations:

> Drusus the tribune, purposing to accuse Quintus Cæpio of giving him poison, drank goat's blood a good while before, whereby he waxed so pale and colorless that many indeed suspected him to have been poisoned by Cæpio: whereby it is manifest that blood hath been a very ancient nourishment and not lately devised by our country pudding-wrights or curious sauce-makers, as Jason Pratensis and other foolish dietists have imagined. Nay (which is more), not only the blood of beasts hath been given for meat, but also the blood of men and striplings hath been drunk for a restorative; yea, in Rome (the seat and nurse of all inhumanity) physicians did prescribe their patients the blood of wrestlers, causing them to suck it warm, breathing, and spinning out of their veins, drawing into their corrupt bodies a sound man's life, and sucking that in with both lips, which a dog is not suffered to lick with his tongue.

Air, too, is regarded as a kind of food, whose purification could help to prevent the plague. Moffet's technical discussion is eclectic, based chiefly on the qualities hot, dry, cold, and moist, with minimal reference to Paracelsus, but the argument is for the most part informal, often witty, paradoxical or ironic, appealing to common sense. Anti-Catholic satire is directed at Lenten restrictions, contrasted with a glad Protestant reliance on Providence: "Puffins, whom I may call the feathered fishes, are accounted even by the holy fatherhood of cardinals to be no flesh but rather fish; whose Catholic censure I will not here oppugn, though I have just reason for it, because I will not increase the Pope's coffers, which no doubt would be filled if every puffin-eater bought a pardon upon true and certain knowledge that a puffin were flesh — albeit perhaps if his Holiness would say that a shoulder of mutton were fish, they either would not or could not think it flesh." Although *Health's Improvement* was not published in

Moffet's lifetime, the absence of any reference to John Gerard's *Herbal* (1597) suggests that it was substantially complete by 1597.

A projected visit to Wilton House by Queen Elizabeth in 1599 (which did not occur) prompted Moffet to write an imitation of the Italian humanist poet Marco Girolamo Vida's *Bombyx* (1517) in commendation of the silkworm. *The Silkworms and Their Flies* was dedicated to the countess of Pembroke and appeared in a handsome quarto printed by Valentine Simmes in 1599. The poem consists of eighteen hundred lines in ottava rima, divided into two books. Book 1 praises the antiquity of silk and the virtues of silkworms, while book 2 is given over to more-practical instructions, culminating in an appeal to husbandmen to plant mulberry trees, shepherdesses to feed a miniature flock, and the "Queen of Queens" (Elizabeth) to nurse the little creatures in her bosom. The speaker lures the silkworms to their death in the cocoons by offering them a vision of their transformation, in which conventional hyperbole is rescued by accurate description and irony of situation:

> Wings whiter than the snow of Taurus high,
> Feet fairer than Adonis ever had,
> Heads, bodies, breasts and necks of ivory,
> With perfect favor, and like beauty, clad:
> Which to commend with some variety,
> And shadow as it were with color sad,
>   Two little dusky feathers shall arise
>   From forehead white, to grace your ebon eyes.

The Virgilian high style, combined with mockheroic techniques borrowed from Lucian and the paradoxical encomium, has led some modern critics into speculating, mistakenly, that the Pyramus and Thisbe interlude in William Shakespeare's *A Midsummer Night's Dream* (1595) might be a parody of a hypothetical early manuscript version of Moffet's account of the origin of the black mulberry. In fact *Silkworms* has more affinities with Harington's *Metamorphosis of Ajax* and Thomas Nashe's *Lenten Stuff: In Praise of the Red Herring* (1500). Contemporaries recognized it as both a jeu d'esprit and a serious piece of versified natural history which anticipated James I's mulberry-tree campaign.

After the death of his wife in 1600, Moffet married a Wiltshire widow, Catherine Brown, who lived until 1626. Patience, his only daughter by his first wife, is popularly supposed to have inspired the nursery rhyme "Little Miss Muffet" because of her father's interest in spiders. The publication of Ulisse Aldrovandi's *De animalibus insectis* in 1602 prompted Moffet to tinker further with his *In-*

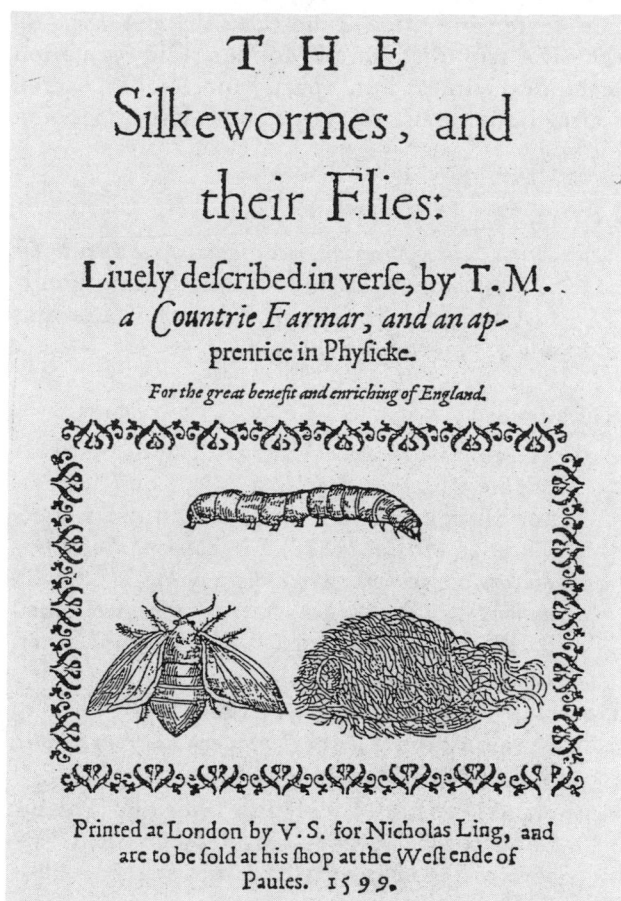

Title page for Moffet's 1599 poem, the first Virgilian georgic in English

sectorum theatrum, including the preparation of an engraved title page by John Rogers, but Moffet fell ill and died in June 1604 before it could come to press.

The characteristic quality of Moffet's work, in both Latin and English, is a blend of scientific argument, facetious classical allusion, and Protestant didacticism. The theme of the importance of little things recurs frequently, from the modesty topoi of his early pamphlets to the microscopic imagination of his silkworm georgic. His literary career follows a broadening of interest: from academic and polemical Paracelsian tracts to compendious projects aimed at public education in health and natural history. Moffet enjoyed a considerable reputation in medical and scientific circles at least until the middle of the eighteenth century, when *Health's Improvement* was reprinted (1746) and the *Insectorum theatrum* praised by Albertus ab Haller (1751). The work of greatest literary interest, *The Silkworms and Their Flies,* was presented as a holiday from more-serious occupations but also claimed to be written "for the great benefit and enriching of England." Sir Sidney

Lee's extensive entry in the *Dictionary of National Biography* is an indication of Moffet's solid reputation in modern times; but, apart from Shakespearean source-hunters, literary critics have largely ignored his work.

Letters:

Epistolarum philosophicarum, medicinalium, ac chymicarum . . . volumen, edited by Laurence Scholz (Frankfurt am Main: Heirs of A. Wechel, C. Marnius and J. Aubrius, 1598).

References:

Robert-Henri Blaser, "Un rare témoignage de fidélité envers Paracelse à Bâle: Les Theses de anodinis medicamentis du médicin anglais Thomas Moffet (1578)," in *Current Problems in History of Medicine: Proceedings of the XIXth International Congress for the History of Medicine,* edited by Blaser and Heinriek Buess (Basel: Karger, 1966), pp. 502–512;

Douglas Bush, "The Tedious Brief Scene of Pyramus and Thisbe," *Modern Language Notes,* 46 (March 1931): 144–147;

Katherine Duncan-Jones, "Pyramus and Thisbe: Shakespeare's Debt to Moffet Cancelled," *Review of English Studies,* 32 (August 1981): 296–301;

Victor Houliston, "Sleepers Awake: Thomas Moffet's Challenge to the College of Physicians of London, 1584," *Medical History,* 33 (April 1989): 235–246;

Kenneth Muir, "Pyramus and Thisbe: A Study in Shakespeare's Method," *Shakespeare Quarterly,* 5 (Spring 1954): 141–153;

Charles E. Raven, *English Naturalists from Neckam to Ray* (Cambridge: Cambridge University Press, 1947), pp. 172–191;

Kitty W. Scoular, *Natural Magic: Studies in the Presentation of Nature in English Poetry from Spenser to Marvell* (Oxford: Clarendon Press, 1965), pp. 38–48;

George Urdang, "How Chemicals Entered the Official Pharmacopeias," *Archives Internationales d'Histoire des Sciences,* 7 (Spring 1954): 303–314;

Manfred E. Welti, "Englisch-baslerische Beziehungen zur Zeit der Renaissance in der Medizin, den Naturwissenschaften und der Naturphilosophie," *Gesnerus,* 20 (1963): 105–130.

Papers:

Manuscripts of Thomas Moffet's works are held by the British Library (*Insectorum theatrum*) and the Huntington Library, San Marino, California (*Nobilis*). His correspondence with Theodore Zwinger is in the Basel University Library.

Sir Thomas More

(6 or 7 February 1477 or 1478 – 6 July 1535)

Elizabeth McCutcheon
University of Hawaii

BOOKS: *A Mery Gest How a Sergeaunt Woldel Erne to Be a Frere,* anonymous (London: Printed by Julyan Notary, 1516?);

Libellus vere aureus nec minus salutaris quam festiuus de optimo reip. statu, deque noua Insula Vtopia (Louvain: Printed by Thierry Martin, 1516); second edition, *Habes candide lector opusculum illud vere aureum Thomae Mori non minus vtile quam elegans de optimo reipublicae statu, deque noua Insula Vtopia* (Paris: Printed by Gilles de Gourmont, 1517); third edition, *De Optimo Reip. Statv Deque noua insula Vtopia libellus uere aureus, nec minus salutaris quam festiuus* (Basel: Printed by John Froben, 1518; fourth edition, 1518); translated by Ralph Robynson as *A Fruteful and Pleasaunt Worke of the Beste State of a Publyque Weale, and of the Newe Yle Called Utopia* (London: Printed by Abraham Vele, 1551; revised edition, London: Printed by Richard Tottell for Abraham Vele, 1556);

Epigrammata clarissimi disertissimique viri Thomae Mori Britanni, pleraqve e graecis versa, by More, William Lily, and Desiderius Erasmus, edited by Beatus Rhenanus [in *De Optimo Reip. Statv Deque noua insula Vtopia libellus uere aureus, nec minus salutaris quam festiuus,* above] (Basel: Printed by John Froben, 1518); revised edition, *Epigrammata clarissimi disertissimique viri Thomae Mori Britanni ad emendatum exemplar ipsius autoris excusa* (Basel: Printed by John Froben, 1520);

Thomae Mori Epistola ad Germanum Brixium: Qui quum Morvs in libellum eius quo contumeliosis mendacijs incesserat Angliam: Lusisset aliquot epigrammata (London: Printed by Richard Pynson, 1520);

Eruditissimi viri Ferdinandi Barauelli opus elegans, doctum, festiuum, pium, quo pulcherrime retegit, ac refellit insanas Lutheri calumnias: Quibus inuictissimum Angliae, Galliaeque regem Henricum eius nominis octauum (London: Printed by Richard Pynson, 1523); enlarged as *Eruditissimi Viri Guilielmi Rossei opus elegans, doctum, festiuum,*

Sir Thomas More; oil painting, dated 1527, by an unknown artist after Hans Holbein the Younger (National Portrait Gallery, London)

pium, quo pulcherrime retegit, ac refellit insanas Lutheri calumnias: Quibus inuictissimum Angliae, Galliaeque regem Henricum eius nominis octauum (London: Printed by Richard Pynson, 1523);

A Dyaloge of Syr Thomas More Knyghte: One of the Counsayll of Our Souerayne Lorde the Kyng & Chauncellour of Hys Duchy of Lancaster. Wherin Be Treatyd Dyuers Maters, as of the Veneration & Worshyp of Ymagys & Relyques, Prayng to Sayntys, & Goyng on Pylgrymage. Wyth Many Othere Thyngys Touchyng the Pestylent Sect of Luther and Tyndale, by the Tone Bygone in Saxony, and by the Tother Laboryd to Be Brought in to Englond (London: Printed by John

Rastell, 1529; revised edition, London: Printed by William Rastell, 1531);

The Supplycacyon of Soulys (London: Printed by William Rastell, 1529);

The Confutacyon of Tyndales Answere (London: Printed by William Rastell, 1532);

A Letter of Syr Tho. More Knyght Impugnynge the Erronyouse Wrytyng of John Fryth agaynst the Blessed Sacrament of the Aultare (London: Printed by William Rastell, 1533);

The Second Parte of the Confutacion of Tyndals Answere in Whyche Is Also Confuted the Chyrche That Tyndale Deuyseth. And the Chyrche also That Frere Barns Deuyseth (London: Printed by William Rastell, 1533);

The Apologye of Syr Thomas More Knyght (London: Printed by William Rastell, 1533);

The Debellacyon of Salem and Bizance (London: Printed by William Rastell, 1533);

The Answere to the Fyrst Parte of the Poysened Booke, Whych a Namelesse Heretyke Hath Named the Souper of the Lorde (London: Printed by William Rastell, 1534 [i.e., 1533]);

A Dialoge of Comfort against Tribulacion, Made by Syr Thomas More Knyght, and Set Foorth by the Name of an Hungarien, Not before This Time Imprinted (London: Printed by Richard Tottell, 1553); revised by John Fowler (Antwerp: Printed by John Fowler, 1573);

The Boke of the Fayre Gentylwoman, That No Man Shulde Put His Truste, or Confydence in: That Is to Say, Lady Fortune (London: Printed by Robert Wyer, 1556? [traditionally dated 1540]).

Editions and Collections: *The Workes of Sir Thomas More Knyght, Sometyme Lorde Chauncellour of England, Wrytten by Him in the Englysh Tonge,* edited by William Rastell (London: Printed for John Cawood, John Waly & Richarde Tottell, 1557);

Lvcubrationes, ab innumeris mendis repurgatae. Vtopiae Libri II. Progymnasmata. Epigrammata. Ex Lvciano conuersa quaedam. Declamatio Lucianicae respondens. Epistolae. Quibus additae sunt duae aliorum epistolae de uita, moribus & morte Mori, adiuncto rerum notabilium indice (Basel: Printed by F. Episcopius, 1563);

Omnia, quae hucusque ad manus nostras peruenerunt, Latina Opera (Louvain: Printed by John Bogard, 1565);

Epistola, in qua non minus facete quam pie, respondet Literis Ioannis Pomerani (Louvain: Printed by John Fowler, 1568);

Dissertatio Epistolica, De aliquot sui temporis Theologastrorum ineptijs; Deque correctione translationis vulgatae N. Testamenti: Ad Martinum Dorpium Theologum Lovaniensem (Leiden: Printed by Elzevier, 1625);

Epistola Thomae Mori ad academiam Oxoniensem. Cui adjecta sunt quaedam poemata in mortem clarissimi viri Roberti Cottoni & Thomae Alleni, edited, with contributions, by Richard James (Oxford: Printed by John Lichfield for Thomas Huggins, 1633);

Epigrammata Thomae Mori Angli, Viri eruditionis pariter ac virtutis nomine clarissimi, Angliaeque; olim Cancellarii (London: Printed by John Haviland for Humphrey Mosley, 1638);

The Historie of the Pitifull Life, and Unfortunate Death of Edward the Fifth, and the Then Duke of Yorke His Brother: With the Troublesome and Tyrannical Government of Usurping Richard the Third, and His Miserable End (London: Printed by Thomas Payne for William Sheares, sold by Michael Young, 1641);

Utopia, translated by Gilbert Burnet (London: Printed by Richard Chiswell, 1684);

Opera Omnia (Frankfurt am Main: Printed by Christian Gensch, 1689);

The Yale Edition of the Selected Works of St. Thomas More, 5 volumes (New Haven & London: Yale University Press, 1961–1980) – comprises *Selected Letters,* edited by Elizabeth F. Rogers (1961); *Utopia,* edited by Edward Surtz, S. J. (1964); *"The History of King Richard III" and Selections from the English and Latin Poems,* edited by Richard S. Sylvester (1976); *A Dialogue of Comfort against Tribulation,* edited by Frank Manley (1977); *The Tower Works: Devotional Writings,* edited by Garry E. Haupt (1980);

The Yale Edition of the Complete Works of St. Thomas More, 14 volumes to date, executive editors Sylvester and Clarence H. Miller (New Haven & London: Yale University Press, 1963–) – comprises volume 1: the English poems, the *Life of Pico,* and *The Last Things,* with Latin sources for material More translated in the *Life,* edited by Anthony Edwards and Katherine Gardiner Rodgers (forthcoming); volume 2: *The History of King Richard III,* edited by Sylvester (1963); volume 3, part 1: *Translations of Lucian,* edited by Craig R. Thompson (1974); volume 3, part 2: *Latin Poems,* edited by Miller, Leicester Bradner, Charles A. Lynch, and R. P. Oliver (1984); volume 4: *Utopia,* edited by Surtz, S. J., and J. H. Hexter (1965); volume 5, parts 1 and 2: *Responsio ad Lutherum,* edited by John M. Headley (1969); volume 6, parts 1 and 2: *A*

Dialogue Concerning Heresies, edited by Thomas M. C. Lawler, Germain P. Marc'hadour, and Richard C. Marius (1981); volume 7: *Letter to Bugenhagen, Supplication of Souls, Letter against Frith,* edited by Manley, Marc'hadour, Marius, and Miller (1990); volume 8, parts 1, 2, and 3: *The Confutation of Tyndale's Answer,* edited by Louis A. Schuster, Marius, James P. Lusardi, and Richard J. Schoeck (1973); volume 9: *The Apology,* edited by J. B. Trapp (1979); volume 10: *The Debellation of Salem and Bizance,* edited by John Guy, Ralph Keen, Miller, and Ruth McGugan (1987); volume 11: *The Answer to a Poisoned Book,* edited by Stephen Merriam Foley and Miller (1985); volume 12: *A Dialogue of Comfort against Tribulation,* edited by Louis L. Martz and Manley (1976); volume 13: *Treatise on the Passion, Treatise on the Blessed Body, Instructions and Prayers,* edited by Haupt (1976); volume 14, parts 1 and 2: *De Tristitia Christi,* edited by Miller (1976); volume 15: *In Defense of Humanism: Letter to Martin Dorp, Letter to the University of Oxford, Letter to Edward Lee, Letter to a Monk, with a New Text and Translation of "Historia Richardi Tertii,"* edited by Daniel Kinney (1986);

Thomas More's Prayer Book, edited by Martz and Sylvester (New Haven & London: Yale University Press, 1969);

Utopia, edited by George M. Logan and Robert M. Adams (Cambridge: Cambridge University Press, 1989);

"Utopia": A Revised Translation, Backgrounds, Criticism, edited by Adams (New York: Norton, 1992).

OTHER: Lucian, *Luciani compluria opuscula longe festiuissima,* translated into Latin by More and Desiderius Erasmus, with a declamatio by More answering Lucian's *Tyrannicida* (Paris: Printed by Badius Ascensius, 1506); republished as *Luciani Erasmo interprete dialogi et alia emuncta* (Paris: Printed by Badius Ascensius, 1514);

Gianfrancesco Pico, *Here Is Conteyned the Lyfe of Iohan Picus Erle of Myrandula . . . with Dyuere Epistles & Other Warkis of the Seyd Johan Picus,* translated by More (London: Printed by John Rastell, 1510?);

Lucian, *Necromantia: A Dialog of the Poete Lucyan,* translated into Latin by More ([Southwark]: Printed [by Peter Treveris?] for John Rastell, 1530?);

"Kyng Edward the Fifth. (King Richard the Third)," edited by Richard Grafton, in *The Chronicle of Jhon Hardyng in Metre, from the First Begynnyng of Englande, unto ye Reigne of Edwarde ye Fourth,* edited by Grafton (London: Printed by Richard Grafton, 1543);

Edward Hall, *The Vnion of the Two Noble and Illustrate Famelies of Lancastre & Yorke,* includes More's lives of Edward V and Richard III (London: Printed by Richard Grafton, 1548);

Psalmi, sev Precationes D. Ioan. Fisheri, includes prayers by More (Lyons: Printed by Sebastian Gryphius, 1572);

"A Brief Treatise to Receiue the Blessed Bodie of Our Lord Sacramentally, & Virtually Both" and "Certaine Deuout Praiers and Ghostly Meditations," in *A Brief Fourme of Confession,* translated by John Fowler (Antwerp: Printed by John Fowler, 1576);

G. Flinton, ed. and trans., *A Manval of Prayers Newly Gathered Out of Many and Diuers Famous Authours aswell Auncient as of the Tyme Present,* includes prayers by More (Rouen: Father Parsons' Press, 1583).

Sir Thomas More is — in the phrase associated with him since the early sixteenth century — a man for all seasons. World renowned as the author of *Utopia* (1516), he wrote humanist, polemical, and spiritual works in Latin and English and thereby contributed to the development of the vernacular. A lawyer, politician, humanist, and statesman — for two and a half years lord chancellor — he was executed on grounds of high treason; he died a martyr, and he was canonized by the Roman Catholic church in 1935. More's character and personality continue to attract, inspire, challenge, and perplex. His life and death, his beliefs, and his writings are the subjects of countless interpretations.

More was the first son and second child of John More, a successful London lawyer, and Agnes Graunger More, whose father, Sir Thomas Graunger, was also a lawyer. He was born on 6 or 7 February 1477 or 1478; contradictions in John More's entry for his son's birth give support for any of these dates. More began his formal education at Saint Anthony's School in London, where he would have studied Latin grammar, rhetoric, and logic. Around 1490 his father placed him as a page in the household of John Morton, who was then the lord chancellor of England and archbishop of Canterbury and subsequently became a cardinal. The two years More spent in Morton's household gave him an opportunity to observe firsthand the political life of England. As William Roper, More's son-in-law and biographer, tells it, Morton said of More that "This child here waiting at the table, whosoever shall live to see it, will prove a marvelous man." Roper also tells how More would step in and improvise a part of his own when actors put on plays and pageants during the Christmas season.

More attended Oxford University for about two years, probably from 1492 to 1494. Brought back to London by his father to study law, he attended the New Inn for about two years, transferring to Lincoln's Inn on 12 February 1496. He began to practice law around 1501. At the same time, he tested his vocation for a spiritual life: from about 1500 to 1504 he lived within the precincts of the London Charterhouse, participating in the Carthusian monks' life of austere devotion. More remained deeply attracted to the ascetic life and wore a hair shirt until the day before he was put to death. But he could not sublimate the desires of the body; Desiderius Erasmus observed in a letter to Ulrich von Hutten in 1519 that More "chose to be a god-fearing husband rather than an immoral priest." More also seems to have been more attracted to an active life in this world than some early biographers acknowledged. In late 1504 or early 1505 he married Jane Colt, the oldest daughter of John Colt of Netherhall, Essex. They had four children: Margaret, born in 1505; Elizabeth, born in 1506; Cecily, born in 1507; and John, born in 1509. Their education, which More oversaw, became a model throughout Europe of the "new" classical and humanistic learning, especially for women, and by the 1520s Margaret More Roper was a woman of letters; her translation of Erasmus's commentary on the Lord's Prayer, *Precatio Dominica* (1523), was published anonymously as *A Devout Treatise upon the "Pater Noster"* (1526?). Jane Colt More died in 1511; soon afterward More married Alice Middleton, a wealthy widow who proved to be a good manager of the large household.

By 1499 More had become part of a circle of humanists that included John Colet, Thomas Linacre, and William Grocyn. The humanists shared scholarly, educational, and literary ideals based on the study of classical languages and culture: they emphasized the learning of grammar, rhetoric, history, poetry, and moral philosophy (ethics), opposing the late Scholastic emphasis on dialectic, and they were concerned with reform and with moral and social problems. Little is known about the lectures More delivered on Saint Augustine's *City of God* around 1501 at the Church of Saint Lawrence in London, where Grocyn was rector. But Thom-

as Stapleton, another early biographer, repeats Erasmus's information that they were well attended; Stapleton adds that More treated the work "from the standpoint of history and philosophy" rather than from a "theological point of view," signaling More's humanist orientation.

Two early works indicate the range and complexity of More's humanism. Around 1505 More translated Gianfrancesco Pico's biography of his uncle, Count Giovanni Pico della Mirandola, from Latin into English, adding translations of several short works by Pico della Mirandola: three letters, an interpretation of Psalm 16, three prose pieces in verse paraphrase, and a hymn; the collection was published in 1510. Pico della Mirandola was a well-known Italian humanist and philosopher whose life became increasingly devout in the years preceding his early death, and the biography is, in a sense, a saint's life: "All praise of people, and all earthly glory, he reputed utterly for nothing," More's translation reads; "Liberality only in him passed measure." Because Pico della Mirandola, like More, was attracted to a religious vocation yet remained a layman, several biographers have argued that More saw him as a model for his own life. Unlike More, however, Pico della Mirandola never married and did not attach himself to a court. More sent the work as a New Year's gift to Joyeuce Leigh (Lee), a cloistered nun in the convent of the Poor Clares, for "the happy continuance and gracious increase of virtue" in her soul.

More's translations of four of Lucian's works from Greek into Latin appeared in 1506 as *Opuscula,* his first work to be published except for a few epigrams. On the face of it, Pico della Mirandola and Lucian seem worlds apart: Lucian was a cynic, atheist, and mocker of sacred things. More was sensitive to the issue and defended what he called the first fruits of his Greek studies in his dedicatory letter to the royal secretary, Thomas Ruthall: emphasizing how well Lucian "fulfilled the Horatian maxim and combined delight with instruction," he insists that he "everywhere reprehends and censures, with very honest and at the same time very entertaining wit, our human frailties." A Lucianic impulse is an important element in much of More's humanist writing, which values irony, drama, and seriocomic wit and tests and exercises its readers. It can be related to More himself, given his ability to play so many parts so well and his inimitable combination of engagement and detachment.

Opuscula was a joint effort with Erasmus, by 1515 northern Europe's leading classical and patristic scholar and humanist. More had met him in

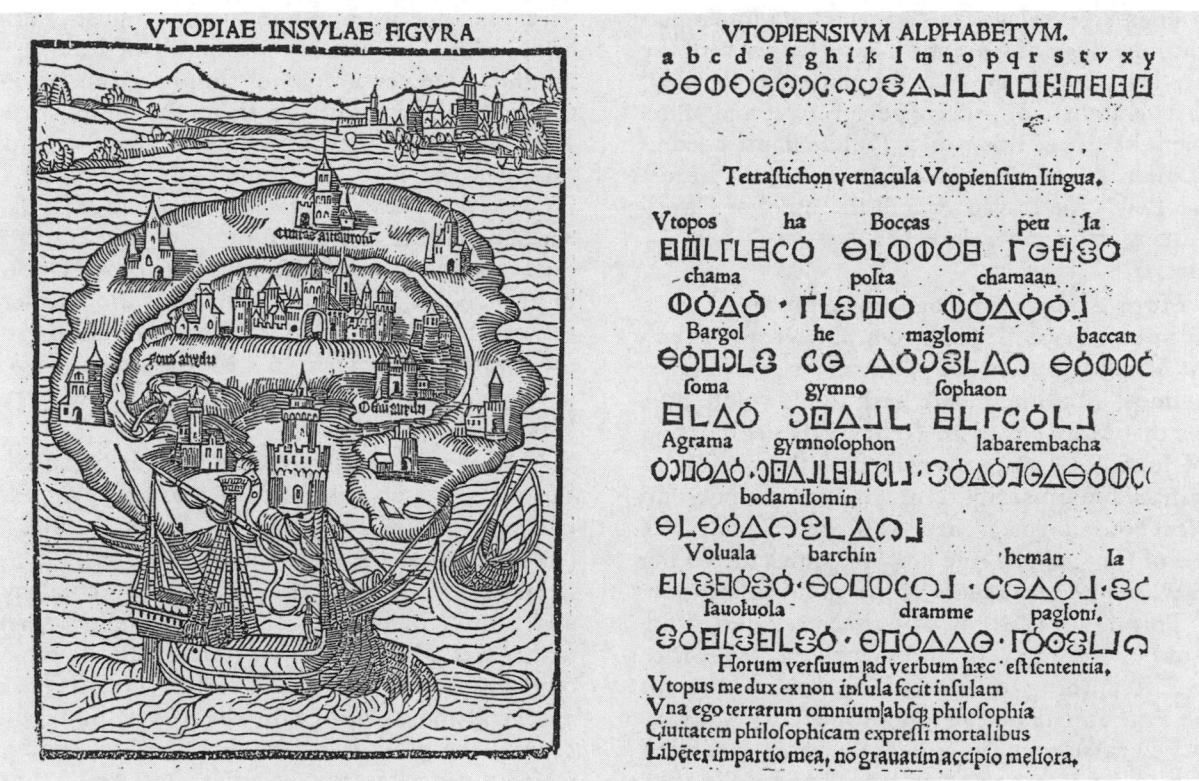

Map of the Island of Utopia, the Utopian alphabet, and a poem in Latin and Utopian from the first edition of More's Utopia

1499, and they became good friends and collaborators. Erasmus's best-known work, the *Moriae encomium* (1511; translated as *The Praise of Folly,* 1549), is a praise not only of folly but also of More (*Moriae* is a play on words) and was written at More's house in 1509. More's four translations in *Opuscula* are of *Cynicus,* a short dialogue in which a Cynic debates the nature of human happiness; *Menippus* (or *Necromantia*), in which Menippus sets out to discover what kind of life is best; *Philopseudes,* a dialogue that satirizes credulity; and *Tyrannicida,* a highly rhetorical declamation in which a speaker claims the reward for killing a tyrant, although he actually killed the tyrant's son and the grief-stricken tyrant killed himself. In a friendly competition More and Erasmus wrote rejoinders to *Tyrannicida;* speaking as the opponent of the claimant, they refuted his position and demonstrated their mastery of rhetorical modes that were a central part of the humanists' program.

More was a poet as well as a rhetorician – in his *Ciceronianus* (1528) Erasmus claims that More was a poet even when he wrote prose. Latin epigrams by More appear at the beginning and end of John Holt's grammar book, *Lac Puerorum,* which was written before 1500 but is known only in editions from about 1505 on. More wrote several poems in English as well; they are collected in *The Works of Sir*

Thomas More (1557). One is a "merry jest" in tail rhyme about an officer of the law who dresses up as a friar to arrest a debtor but is beaten up. It was probably written as part of a celebration, perhaps of a livery company – More and his father were members of the Mercers' Company. More's other verses are generally in rhyme royal; they include the "Pageant Verses," in which More draws upon the ages-of-man motif and Petrarch's *Trionfi* to interpret nine "pageants" about the cycle of life on a "fine painted cloth" in his father's house. He also wrote an elegy for the wife of Henry VII, Elizabeth of York, who died in 1503. Because the speaker is Elizabeth herself, a traditional lament becomes a poignant farewell:

> Adieu, lord Henry, my loving son, adieu.
> Our lord increase your honor and estate.
> Adieu, my daughter Mary, bright of hue.
> God make you virtuous, wise, and fortunate.
> Adieu, sweet heart, my little daughter Kate.
> Thou shalt, sweet babe, such is thy destiny,
> Thy mother never know, for lo now here I lie.

There are also his verse paraphrases in the biography of Pico della Mirandola and stanzas on Fortune in More's *Book of the Fair Gentlewoman, Lady Fortune* (1556?). Though uneven and experimental, these early poems reveal various aspects of More's personality: his love of a practical joke, his sense of the ironic, his fascination with the parts people play, and his awareness of shifting perspectives and of the transient nature of this world. (While imprisoned in the Tower, More wrote two rhyme-royal stanzas: one as Lewis the lost lover and the other as Davey the dicer, who now has the leisure "to make rhymes.")

More achieved recognition, however, as a Latin poet, not an English one. He wrote his epigrams around 1497 to 1520, but according to Erasmus almost all of them date back to his youth. Five poems that More wrote for Henry VIII's coronation on 24 June 1509 were presented to the king in an illuminated manuscript. Humanist encomium and political consciousness meet as More celebrates the return of the Golden Age and welcomes the young king, whom he represents as the savior of his people: "This day is the limit of our slavery, the beginning of our freedom, the end of sadness, the source of joy." According to Roper, More had spoken out in the Parliament of 1504 against Henry VII's attempts to raise money by new taxation, incurring the king's displeasure and endangering his life. The trenchant criticism of the fiscal and legal abuses and stratagems of the last years of Henry VII's reign that More makes in the first of these poems reflects actual historical circumstances: Henry VIII had his father's chief councillors, Edmund Dudley and Richard Empson, arrested and later executed.

On 3 September 1510 More became undersheriff of London. Besides his official duties as judge in the Sheriff's Court, he was busy as a private lawyer and held various commissions, sometimes representing the merchants of London. While undersheriff, he twice served as a royal ambassador for Henry VIII, meeting Peter Giles and Jerome Busleyden, humanist friends of Erasmus, in Flanders during the so-called Utopian Embassy from 12 May to around 25 October 1515. By 1517 he was a member of the King's Council, although he did not receive his first stipend as a royal councillor until 21 June 1518. He resigned as undersheriff on 23 July 1518.

More continued his literary studies, notwithstanding his many professional, public, and family responsibilities. His major humanist works – *The History of Richard III, Utopia, Epigrams,* and defenses of humanism – were written or published between 1513 and 1520. According to More's nephew William Rastell, More was at work on *The History of Richard III* around 1513; editors today argue that he wrote it between 1514 and 1518. More wrote two

versions, one in Latin and one in English, but left both unfinished; neither was published during his lifetime. One version is not simply a translation of the other. The Latin version, first published in 1565, is more compact and stops with the coronation of Richard III. (Volume 15 [1986] of the *Yale Edition of the Complete Works of St. Thomas More* [1963-   ] contains a critical edition of a better text, discovered in a manuscript at the Bibliothèque Nationale in Paris.) The English version adds the murder of Edward IV's two sons in the Tower of London and the equivocal remarks by Morton that, in part, prompted the revolt of Henry Stafford, second Duke of Buckingham.

Both versions begin with the death in 1483 of Edward IV, who tries to avert the very dangers of factional division that will undo his plans. The protector, Richard, outmanipulates everyone else until he has removed all of his potential or actual rivals and gained the throne. But, as the English version makes clear, he ironically prepares the way for his own downfall. As Alistair Fox observes, "If there is a central moral design in the *History,* it revolves around the motive of 'the biter bit,' according to which those who prey on others become victims of their own devices."

Both the Latin and the English versions offer dramatic, ironic, and psychologically acute studies of the exercise of power and factional politics in recent English history. The world as More represents it is a dark and troubled one, where "matters be king's games, as it were stage plays, and for the more part played upon scaffolds." Subtly reworking classical historical models and many other literary works, along with oral sources, More creates a powerful portrait of Richard III and other men and women of the period that deeply influenced William Shakespeare's *The Tragedy of King Richard the Third* (1597). Historians have questioned the way More represents Richard: "He was close and secret, a deep dissimuler [dissembler], lowly of countenance, arrogant of heart, outwardly coumpinable [sociable] where he inwardly hated, not letting [omitting] to kiss whom he thought to kill." But many of More's critics have called *The History of Richard III* one of his greatest works, singling out its development of character and motivation and its dramatic and dynamic representation of history.

Utopia, which has given its name to and become the model for a literary form, is More's best-known and most influential work. There is no consensus about its meaning: where one reader finds a jeu d'esprit, another sees a blueprint for actual social reform and another a catalyst for thought about urgent and fundamental sociopolitical issues. It has a dialogic relationship with many other texts and writers, including Plato's *Republic* and *Laws*, Aristotle, Lucian's satires and *True History*, Cicero, Seneca, Pliny, the Bible, and the church fathers, as well as More's contemporaries – notably Erasmus. It also has a dialogic relationship with itself since it both creates and questions its vision of a better world.

Like the *History*, the *Utopia* is concerned with social and political life and with the nature of human beings and their relationships. But here More initiates a multi-faceted and open-ended inquiry about the "respublica," an elastic term that includes what Tudor England thought of as the commonwealth. The long title, which the Yale edition translates as *The Best State of a Commonwealth and the New Island of Utopia*, calls attention to *Utopia*'s complex structure and the mix of modes that helps to explain part of its elusiveness. At once a political and philosophical discourse and a deeply imagined seriocomic work of fiction, *Utopia* juxtaposes a critique of actual societies with a description of a hitherto-unknown island in the New World – a better, the best, or the only true commonwealth – and invites readers to "see" societies with new eyes. Erasmus wrote Guillaume Cop, a physician, in 1517: "If you have not yet read [*Utopia*], be sure to ask for it when you want to be amused, or more truly, if you wish to see the very wellsprings of all troubles in the commonwealth."

The first edition of *Utopia*, published in Latin in 1516, is a small but dense work. The title page is followed by a map of Utopia; the Utopian alphabet; a short poem in Utopian and Latin that makes high claims for the island; another short poem, by the poet laureate Anemolius, ("the windy one"), which suggests that Utopia (the word means a place that is not) is Eutopia (the happy land); poems and letters of commendation solicited from fellow humanists; and a letter from More to Giles, a humanist who was the chief secretary of the city of Antwerp and had a hand in the publication of the work. This material, with additions and other changes made in the editions of 1517 and 1518, is now called the *parerga* (subordinate or secondary matter); it reinforces Utopia's putative reality, frames books 1 and 2, and makes the reader's experience even more complex.

More's 1516 letter to Giles is more than a *parergon*, however: the first edition rightly sets it off as the "Prefatio" (Preface), and it is an essential prelude to the two books that follow. According to Erasmus, More wrote the second book first; J. H. Hexter argues that More wrote almost all of book 2

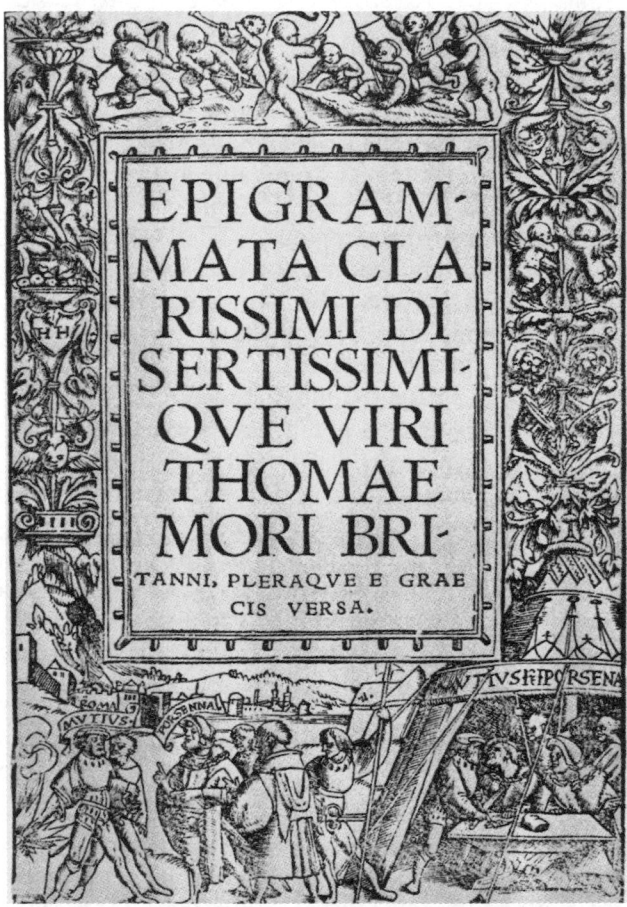

Section title page for More's collection of epigrams, published in the third edition of Utopia *(1518)*

and the early part of book 1 between May and October 1515 in Flanders, inserting the long dialogue of counsel in book 1 after he returned to England. Other critics have suggested a longer period of composition.

The prefatory letter to "my dear Peter" lets More introduce his interlocutors, who should not be confused with the author, and develop an elaborate fiction that insists on its factuality. Writing as mere reporter, he sends a written version of an "historia" or narrative by the elusive Raphael Hythlodaeus – a narrative he is not sure he ought to publish – to a fellow auditor, representing himself as an extremely busy lawyer, a family man, and a literalist, an essential part of his reportorial guise. The letter also enacts rhetorical strategies that point to an aesthetics of honest deception; signaling its duplicities and ambiguities, the text startles the reader and encourages an ongoing dialogue with an unstable text.

Book 1 continues the play of fact and fiction, placing Morus (More as he represents himself in

Utopia) in Antwerp in the summer of 1515. Through Giles he meets Hythlodaeus, philosopher and world traveler, who was with Amerigo Vespucci on his last three voyages and stayed behind in the New World, where he visited many countries and observed their customs and institutions. As Hythlodaeus starts to speak about the "manners and customs of the Utopians," Giles breaks in, introducing an issue that many critics argue applies to a crisis More faced in 1516: Why does Hythlodaeus not serve some king? Hythlodaeus rejects this role, a common one for the civic humanist; he prefers his freedom and insists that no one would listen to him anyway. Nor can he compromise with the truth, which has no place at court. By contrast Morus advocates accommodation and an indirect or oblique approach, rejecting Hythlodaeus's "academic philosophy" for "another philosophy, more practical for statesmen, which knows its stage, adapts itself to the play in hand, and performs its role neatly and appropriately." The scenes Hythlodaeus describes at Cardinal Morton's, at the court of the king of France, and at the court of a nameless king build a picture of England and western Europe at a critical moment of disequilibrium. The poor and helpless are being systematically exploited by a powerful and wealthy elite, which causes the problems it ostensibly wishes to solve, while kings and councillors manipulate the legal, fiscal, and economic systems and foreign policy for their own ends. In a particularly telling moment Hythlodaeus graphically represents the effects of enclosures in England: the sheep, "usually so tame and so cheaply fed," have become "so greedy and wild that they devour human beings themselves and devastate and depopulate fields, houses, and towns." He admits that some of these abuses could be reformed, but he is convinced that the only real solution is that of Utopia, where all things are held in common.

Most of book 2 is Hythlodaeus's description, praise, and defense of Utopia, a place that could not exist – its measurements are self-contradictory. It is both like and unlike its antipodes, England; marginalia draw out these comparisons and contrasts, which may surface in the text, too – as when the Anemolian ambassadors parade down the main street of Amaurotum, Utopia's capital, hoping to impress by their cloth of gold and gold chains, which are very flimsy compared to those that slaves wear there. A child, perplexed by this odd spectacle, points to one of the ambassadors and nudges his mother, who says, "Hush, son, I think it is one of the ambassador's fools [morionibus]" – the text self-reflexively playing on More's and Morus's name and office.

Preserving "natural" differences (including age, sex, intelligence, and aptitude) while adhering to a hierarchy of goods that places the soul above the body, the Utopians, as Hythlodaeus describes them, have achieved a well-ordered – indeed regimented – society in which everyone is entitled to food, water, clothing, housing, education, work (which is also an obligation), leisure, and medical care. The Utopians, who control what they consider false desires, despise gold, although, ironically, they have it in huge quantities. They value everything in accordance with its use; and they have eliminated the waste, luxury, and conspicuous consumption of western Europe. They subscribe to a philosophy of pleasure but prize only virtuous pleasures. Though not Christian, they embrace a version of the Golden Rule and believe in the immortality of the soul. Hythlodaeus, a Stoic as well as a Platonist, is disturbed by their philosophy of pleasure; it smacks of Epicureanism. Many readers are perplexed by the slavery, colonization, and warfare practiced by the Utopians; they also ask about civil and other sorts of freedom.

Hythlodaeus winds up his description with a powerful peroration. Only Utopia can "claim the name of a commonwealth" because only there, "where nothing is private, they seriously concern themselves with public affairs." In other countries he finds only injustice and "a kind of conspiracy of the rich." Combining an economic with a psychological and ethical analysis, he identifies the ultimate cause of these defects: pride, a "serpent from hell" that wraps itself around the hearts of human beings and "measures prosperity not by her own advantages but by others' disadvantages." Morus, on the other hand, finds "not a few" customs and laws of the Utopians "absurd," including their way of waging war, their ceremonies and religion, and especially "their common life and subsistence – without any exchange of money": this "alone utterly overthrows all the nobility, magnificence, splendor, and majesty which are, in the estimation of the common people, the true glories and ornaments of the commonwealth." Critics continue to debate whether this remark is sincere or ironic. But Morus shifts his point of view again, observing that "there are very many features in the Utopian commonwealth which it is easier for me to wish for in our countries than to have any hope of seeing realized." Polysemous and open-ended, *Utopia* encourages its readers to add their voices to a dialogue about community and the common good – issues that the text clarifies but never resolves.

More's collected epigrams were first published with Erasmus's epigrams in the third edition of *Uto-*

pia in March 1518; they did not appear separately until 1520. The epigrams did much to establish More's literary reputation and his fame as a humanist; perhaps only his translations of Lucian and *Utopia* were more important in this respect. Frequently reprinted in anthologies, they were used as models in Renaissance classrooms. The first eighteen epigrams are called "progymnasmata" (literally, a series of warm-up exercises). In each case More and an older humanist, William Lily, translate the same Greek text into Latin, offering examples of imitation, emulation, and rhetorical *copia* (fullness).

Sixteen of the progymnasmata are from the Greek Anthology, and many of the epigrams that follow are translations from the Planudean Anthology – More's most important single source. In many instances More was the first to translate a particular epigram from Greek into Latin. His collection differs from fifteenth-century collections in several ways: it eschews their licentiousness and their religiosity, and its choice of subjects is far broader and its mindset far livelier – "the world of merchants, lawyers, and courtiers" has replaced the scholar's or cleric's study is the way Leicester Bradner and Charles A. Lynch, two of the editors of volume three, part 2 (1984), of *The Yale Edition of the Complete Works of St. Thomas More* explain it. It is difficult to summarize the contents – More tells jokes, laughs at astrologers, mocks the false pride of a king by adopting the point of view of a peasant, writes about meeting a woman he was attracted to many years ago, protests the cruelty of the hunt, speculates about the best form of government, attacks Germanus Brixius (a French writer who attacked him in turn), and writes an epitaph in which he wishes that his deceased first wife, his present wife, and he "could have lived all three together." One of his most powerful epigrams is "On the Vanity of This Life": "Damnati ac morituri in terrae claudimur omnes" (We are all shut up in the prison of this world under sentence of death). In his longest and perhaps best-known epigram he tells Candidus how to choose a wife: he should be concerned with her virtuous and pleasant disposition rather than her beauty or her dowry. Many of More's original epigrams are on political subjects. He "always had a special hatred of absolute rule and a corresponding love for equality," according to Erasmus, and there are several attacks on tyrants, such as: "A tyrant rules his subjects as slaves; a king thinks of his as his own children." The good king is a watchdog, "who by barking keeps the wolves from the sheep. What is the bad king? He is the wolf." The epigrams are like *Utopia* in other ways as well as in their political outlook: they are dramatic, dialogic, paradoxical, inviting of reflection, and deeply ironic.

Four essays in epistle form that More wrote in defense of humanism and a fifth one defending his own Latin poetry span this period and complement his other humanist works. He wrote the "Letter to Dorp" in 1515, which makes it almost contemporary with the *Utopia,* the "Letter to Oxford" in 1518, the "Letter to Lee" and "Letter to a Monk" in 1519, and the "Letter to Brixius" in 1520. Each one was precipitated by a particular occasion or situation. Maarten van Dorp, a theologian and humanist at Louvain, had objected to Erasmus's *Praise of Folly* and his plan to publish a new translation of the New Testament; a preacher at Oxford had attacked the study of Greek; Edward Lee, a churchman, was circulating a manuscript volume attacking Erasmus's translation of the New Testament; a London Carthusian, now known to be John Batmanson, had written a general attack on Erasmus; and Brixius had recently published his *Antimorus* (1520), attacking the style and substance of More's epigrams. In answering these charges, More is sometimes exploratory and dialogic, sometimes apologetic, and sometimes polemic, taking on various critical roles to explore what humanism meant, to come to the defense of Erasmus and his writings, and to defend his own Latin poems. The first four humanist defenses, in particular, show More working out what Daniel Kinney, the editor of volume fifteen of *The Yale Edition of the Complete Works of St. Thomas More* (1986), calls "a truly progressive prescription for the continual renewal and refinement of the 'living gospel of faith,' " while the fifth one creates an ars poetica.

More's already-demanding life became even more demanding after his entry into the king's service in 1517 as a Latin secretary, diplomat, and orator; he also performed a variety of judicial duties and was liaison between Henry and Thomas Wolsey, the lord chancellor. In 1521 he was knighted and became under treasurer; in 1523 he was the Speaker of the House of Commons; in 1524 he became high steward of Oxford University; in 1525 he became high steward of Cambridge University and chancellor of the Duchy of Lancaster.

The three works More wrote in the early and mid 1520s are all proleptic. "The Last Things," which Rastell dated around 1522 when he published it in his edition of More's works (1557), is an unfinished meditative treatise that foreshadows the devotional writings of More's last years. More reflects on Ecclesiasticus 7:40, "Remember the last things, and thou shalt never sin." Structuring his work around the four last things – death, judgment,

⊂A dyaloge of syr Thomas More knyghte: one of the
counsayll of oure souerayne lorde the kyng
τ chauncellour of hys duchy of Lancaster. Wherin be treatyd dyuers
maters/as of the veneration
τ worshyp of ymagys τ
relyques/prayng to
saynts/τ goyng
ō pylgrymage.
Wyth many othere
thyngys touchyng the
pestylent sect of Luther and
Tyndale / by the tone bygone in
Saxony / and by the tother
laboryd to be brought in
to Englond.∵

*Title page for the first of More's English-language polemics
against heresy*

hell, and heaven (which he calls "death," "doom," "pain," and "joy") — More set out to develop a medicine for the soul. But he completed less than one-quarter of this scheme; treating death and the seven deadly sins to show how sick the soul is, he has just begun to discuss the sixth sin, sloth, when the work breaks off. The work is diffuse, and readers have found it tedious and grim. Yet it has gallows humor: More enlivens his analysis of covetousness with a story about the thief who "cut a purse at the bar," though he would be hanged the next day, because "it did his heart good, to be lord of that purse, one night yet." It is a densely imagined work, full of metaphoric comparisons: this world is likened both to a stage play and to a prison in which "old and young, man and woman, rich and poor, prince and page" are condemned and put to death, "thrown in an hole, and either worms eat him under ground or crows above." It also includes More's preoccupation with how everyone confuses the false pleasures of this life with the true pleasures of the soul.

With the *Responsio ad Lutherum* (1523), written in Latin for a learned international audience and published under a Spanish pseudonym, Ferdinand Baravellus, More turned from the humanist issues

of previous polemics to the theological controversies that would dominate his writing until 1534. He wrote it initially to defend Henry VIII's book "asserting" the seven sacraments against Martin Luther's *De Captivitate Babylonica Ecclesiae* (1520). He himself had some role (at least as an editor) in Henry's *Assertio Septem Sacramentorum* (1521), which prompted Luther's vitriolic attack on the king in 1522. More defends both the sacramental system of the Catholic church and the understanding of authority and tradition behind it. More refutes Luther's rejoinder to the king point by point, citing extensive passages from both the king's and Luther's texts. This method, to which he returns in later polemics, results in the argument becoming tedious, at times self-defeating. Neither side really talks to the other; much of the time More treats Luther as a clown, buffoon, "abuser," "cashiered friarlet," "Hussite," or "Satanist from hell." And his language, like Luther's to the king, can be painfully violent, even scatological, as when he claims "the posterior right to proclaim the beshitted tongue of this practitioner of posterioristics most fit to lick with his anterior the very posterior of a pissing she-mule until he shall have learned more correctly to infer posterior conclusions from prior premises."

The issues are fundamental here and in More's later polemical works. Against Luther's insistence on "sola scriptura" (only the Scripture), More argues for a tradition that is both written and unwritten; he defends the authority of the church, animated by the Holy Spirit, to distinguish truly inspired tradition from a tradition invented by human beings. He attacks the idea of the church as an invisible and spiritual group defined by inner faith, insisting that the church is "the common multitude of those who profess the name and faith of Christ," whether they be good or bad, and that its structure is specific, visible, and divinely instituted. Only after writing the first version did More realize the centrality of this issue, and he added a long chapter on the identity of the church. He also changed his pseudonym and persona, writing as an Englishman, William Ross, instead of as a Spaniard.

Between December 1525 and February 1526 More wrote a second Latin polemic, his *Epistola in Qua Respondet Literis Pomerani* (1568). "Pomeranus" was Johann Bugenhagen, pastor of Wittenberg and author of *Epistola ad Anglos* (Letter to the English, 1525). More's letter attacks him, Luther, and Lutheran doctrine — especially the idea of justification by faith alone — and defends traditional Catholic beliefs.

By 1526 More was becoming increasingly involved in attempts to suppress and prevent heresy in England. In his *Apology* (1533) he defines heresy as that "whereby a Christian man becometh a false traitor to God" and says that it "is in all laws spiritual and temporal both, accompted as great a crime as is the treason committed against any worldly man." For More, the Protestant Reformers were malicious and seditious heretics who threatened the order of church and state, and in the epitaph he composed for himself he characterizes himself "as a source of trouble to thieves, murderers, and heretics."

The second phase of More's written attack on heresy began on 7 March 1528 when the bishop of London, Cuthbert Tunstall, authorized him to read heretical books and commissioned him to refute them in English. *A Dialogue of Sir Thomas More* (1529), now called *A Dialogue Concerning Heresies,* is the first and the best of his English controversial writings: C. S. Lewis has called it a "great Platonic dialogue: perhaps the best specimen of that form ever produced in English." Here More puts his understanding of drama and dialogue to good use; there are four long conversations, with a two-week interval supposedly occurring between the second and the third. He imagines an extended dialogue between the author, who is a busy court official and concerned father figure, and the messenger, a university-trained young man who has been sent to him by an unnamed friend; the published work purports to be More's report of the dialogue to the friend. The messenger, a good Christian, has some sympathy with Lutheran ideas and is confused and puzzled. Gradually he comes to understand the Catholic church's position and to see Luther and William Tyndale as heretics. The pace, as so often in More's writing, is leisurely, sometimes digressive or recursive. Here is the messenger's flow of thought, for instance, at the beginning of a chapter: " 'Truly sir,' quod he, 'me thinketh it is well said that ye have said. And in good faith, to say the truth, I see not what I should answer it withall. And yet, when I look back again upon Holy Scripture and consider that it is God's own words, which I wot well ye will grant, I find it hard in mine heart to believe all the men in the whole world, if they would say any thing, whereof I should see that the Holy Scripture saith the contrary, since it is reason that I believe God alone far better than them all.'" But the recursive nature of the text mimes a psychological and educational process: the messenger must not simply know something, he must integrate it into his whole being so that he truly remembers it. More likewise models a larger educative process for others trying to refute Protestant ideas and for

those who, like the young man, are interested in or are of two minds about them.

The conversation is familiar and friendly; it includes merry tales and jokes, sometimes at the expense of women. More explains at length the fundamental beliefs of the Catholic church, refuting Lutheran ideas about justification by faith. He stands by what he calls the common consent of the church, which, inspired by the Holy Spirit, cannot be mistaken; he defends the practices that the Reformers were attacking – including images, pilgrimages, relics, and praying to saints – and the whole sacramental life of the church. He also treats more immediate issues, including Tyndale's translation of the New Testament; the judgment of the court in Thomas Bilney's heresy case; the case of Richard Hunne, which had aroused strong anticlerical feeling; Luther's books; and the treatment of heretics.

On 25 October 1529 More was appointed lord chancellor following the downfall of Wolsey, whose foreign policy and attempts to obtain the king's divorce from Catherine of Aragon through the papacy had both failed. As the king's chief magistrate More was heavily involved in judicial work and the implementation of legal reforms in the courts of Chancery and Star Chamber. He also pursued a determined campaign against heresy and tried to defend the church from anticlericalism and from attacks by religious reformers. His position was a difficult one, however, because the king's "great matter," his divorce, which More privately opposed, became increasingly entangled with issues affecting both the church and secular authority.

His six other polemical pieces in English, all directed at specific instances of subversive writing, are increasingly defensive and violent. Like his Latin polemics, they usually proceed point by point against the work being refuted, often at great length, with More's legal mind much in evidence. In *The Supplication of Souls* (1529) More answers the lawyer Simon Fish's *Supplication for the Beggars* (1529), an anticlerical pamphlet that More elsewhere calls "a piteous beggarly book, wherein [Fish] would have all the souls in purgatory beg all for nought." In his rejoinder More challenges Fish's claim that the clergy is responsible for the sad plight of the beggars and other poor in England and defends the idea of purgatory, which Fish, like other Reformers, denied. He ends with the plea of the souls themselves, who beg the reader to disregard the "jesting and railing of those uncharitable heretics, mortal enemies unto us and to themselves both," to "consider you our pains, and pity them in your hearts, and help us with your prayers, pilgrim-

Page from the copy of The Book of Hours *that More had with him in the Tower of London, with the first two lines of his "Godly Meditation"
written in the top and bottom margins (Beinecke Rare Book and Manuscript Library, Yale University)*

ages, and other almsdeeds," especially "the holy mass, whereof no man living so well can tell the fruit as we that here feel it."

In 1531 Henry claimed the title of supreme head of the Church in England, and by 1532 More and others supporting Catherine of Aragon found themselves isolated and outmaneuvered by a radical group led by Thomas Cromwell. On 15 May 1532 the clergy made their submission to the king. The next day More surrendered the great seal to the king, resigning as lord chancellor and withdrawing from public life. But he became even more active in his verbal warfare against heresy, remaining a figure of high visibility.

In 1532 appeared the first part of his *Confutation of Tyndale's Answer,* the only polemical work he wrote while lord chancellor; the second part was published the following year. Over one thousand pages long in the Yale edition of the complete works (volume eight, 1973), the *Confutation* is More's long-est polemic; even so, the two parts cover only one-quarter of Tyndale's *Answer to Sir Thomas More's Dialogue* (1531). In his preface to the first part of the *Confutation* More surveys the contemporary situation and itemizes the many heretical books that "like the children of vipers would now gnaw out their mother's belly." Thereafter he discusses Tyndale's preface, his translation of the New Testament, and the question of whether the church preceded the Gospel or the Gospel the church. In the second part he continues his attack on the Reformers' ideas of the church, Tyndale's interpretation of Scripture, and the idea of a feeling faith; a fragmentary ninth book, also on the church, was first published in *The Works of Sir Thomas More* in 1557.

The *Letter against Frith* was completed on 7 December 1532 and printed that month but not released for publication until December 1533. It is More's shortest polemical piece, with many asides about this "young man," John Frith: "I will not for courtesy say he is stark mad, but surely I will say that for his own soul, the young man playeth a very young wanton pageant." Written as a letter to an unnamed person, it refutes Frith's first treatise on the Eucharist, which More saw in manuscript – it was later printed anonymously as *A Christian Sentence and True Judgment of the Sacrament of Christ's Body and Blood Declared, Both by the Authority of the Holy Scriptures and the Ancient Doctors* (1548?) – and exposes Frith, then being courted in royal circles, as a grievous heretic. Against Frith's denial of the real presence More argues that "in the blessed sacrament the whole substance of the bread and the wine is transmuted and changed into the very body and blood of Christ."

The Apology and *The Debellation of Salem and Bizance,* written and published in 1533, answer anticlerical works by an anonymous author now identified as the lawyer Christopher Saint German. The exchange began with Saint German's *Treatise Concerning the Division between the Spirituality and Temporality* (1532?), which attacks the treatment of heretics in ecclesiastical courts. Objecting to the use of secret evidence that jeopardized the innocent, Saint German makes proposals for legal reform that would limit the authority of the clergy. In his *Apology* More upholds church court procedures, defends the clergy and canon law, and impugns the motives of his opponent, whom he ironically calls the Pacifier, saying that the latter, "under his fair figure of *some say . . .* bring[s] in all the mischief that any man can say." He also defends himself and his polemical writing against various faults the "brethren" complained about: they found his writing "over long, and therefore too tedious to read." More continues his defense of heresy laws in *The Debellation of Salem and Bizance,* an answer to Saint German's answer to *The Apology.* The most legalistic of his polemical works, *The Debellation of Salem and Bizance* was rendered largely moot by the reform of heresy law in 1534.

In his last polemical work, *The Answer to a Poisoned Book,* printed in 1533 but dated 1534, More returns to questions about the nature of the Eucharist that he had treated in his *Letter against Frith,* which he released for sale with *The Answer.* Published anonymously, the "poisoned" book, *The Supper of the Lord,* seems to have been printed in Antwerp in 1533 and smuggled into England the same year; it denies the real presence of Christ's body and blood in the Eucharist. In his rejoinder to the author (who was probably George Joye) More develops a fuller defense of the real presence. His exposition of the sixth chapter of the Gospel of Saint John and his interpretation of traditional Christian doctrine are particularly important and anticipate his approach in works written just before and during his imprisonment.

On 23 March 1534 Parliament passed the Act of Succession, declaring Henry's marriage to Catherine null and his marriage to Anne Boleyn lawful. On 12 April, More received a summons to sign an oath endorsing this and all other acts and statutes passed by Parliament since 1529, including the Act of Supremacy – declaring Henry supreme head of the Church of England – and the Act of Treasons, both passed in 1534. More refused to swear the oath and on 17 April was sent to the Tower of London. The letters he sent to his daughter Margaret tell of his interrogations and the attempts that were made to intimidate and trap him. Because More kept silent, not explaining his refusal to sign the oath except by referring to his conscience, the government had no legal grounds for proceeding against him. But on 1 July 1535 he was convicted of treason on false evidence. Before the sentence of death was passed More spoke out against the judgment, declaring that the Act of Supremacy was "directly repugnant to the laws of God and His Holy Church" and that he was not bound "to conform my conscience to the council of one realm against the general council of Christendom." Five days later, on 6 July 1535, More was led to the scaffold on Tower Hill, where he was beheaded, dying as "the King's good servant," yet God's first.

At the end of *The Answer* More had announced his plans to answer a second book by Frith against "the blessed sacrament." His next work, "A Treatise upon the Passion," probably written in the early months of 1534 and published in *The Works of Sir Thomas More,* is in large part on the Eucharist. But he subsumes his attack on heretical ideas to concerns that are historical, instructional, and devotional. He explains that he wants "to show and set forth the truth before the eyes of the reader, that he may rather of the truth read, increase in faith, and conceive devotion." "A Treatise upon the Passion," though technically pre-Tower, can thus be considered the first of the Tower works, which are focused on Christ's passion and More's wish to live his life in conformity with Christ's.

"A Treatise upon the Passion" promises the good Christian reader "a treatise historical, containing the bitter passion of our savior Christ" from the first "contriving" of his death through his burial. The introduction deals with the fall of the angels, the creation and fall of "mankind," and the determination by the Trinity to restore humanity through Christ. More gets no further than the Last Supper, and the text breaks off with a "lecture" on how "we ought to use our self in the receiving" of the Sacrament. The homiletic chapters are expositions of the text of Jean Charlier de Gerson's *Monotessaron* (1480?), a Gospel harmony (combination of corresponding phrases and passages from the four Gospels); they end with short prayers. Thus More moves from cause to response, from cosmic circumference to redemptive action and the sacrament of the altar that was instituted at the Last Supper, linking biblical reading with doctrine and devotion.

The brief "A Treatise to Receive the Blessed Body of Our Lord," written some time in 1534, presumably as a corollary to "A Treatise upon the Passion," begins where the latter breaks off. More writes about how "to receive the blessed body of our lord, sacramentally and virtually both." The focus is on receiving the Eucharist "virtually" or "worthily," by which More means receiving the "virtue" or grace to become "lively members incorporate in Christ's holy mystical body." Addressing the inward disposition and outward manifestations of such grace, he encourages his readers to imitate such diverse examples as Elizabeth, Martha, Mary, and the good publican Zaccheus, who received Christ "with a sure earnest virtuous mind" and "proved it by his virtuous works."

Five instructions, meditations, and prayers are a particularly personal reflection of More's agonizing spiritual struggles while he was imprisoned in the Tower. In the first, written with a piece of coal, More says that he would "Bear no malice nor evil will to no man living"; in the second he reflects on the difference between a temporal and an eternal death and emphasizes the need "to stand stiff" and have "a strong and steadfast faith." In the "Imploratio," a long meditation composed of selections from the Psalms, he seeks divine help against temptation; and in a prayer sequence written early in July 1535 he prepares for his imminent death. Best known and loved is the "Godly Meditation" that More wrote in the top and bottom margins of his copy of the *Book of Hours,* adding his voice to the voice of the church to pray, "Give me thy grace good Lord / To set the world at nought."

A Dialogue of Comfort against Tribulation (1553) is the only Tower work to be published before 1557. Written in English, like the treatises and three of the prayers (with which it has many affinities), it is the longest and the most multifaceted of More's spiritual writings; some readers have considered it his greatest single work. The form, a dramatized dialogue, let More achieve hard-won detachment from the suffering and pain facing him and those he loved. It also let him write for any reader, for friends and family, and for and to himself, as he drew upon classical consolation and Christian belief in a dual search for comfort in the midst of tribulation and for strength to endure to the end for what he believed.

Set in Hungary after the Turks' first invasion in 1526 but before a second invasion in 1529, *A Dialogue of Comfort* is historically precise and metaphorically allusive. The speakers are the old Antony, who feels his age, and his young nephew, Vincent, who comes to him for "some comfortable counsel against tribulation." Readers have recognized aspects of More in both speakers, and Vincent also resembles Margaret, who appears in a dialogue with her father in a letter that More, Margaret, or both wrote in August 1534. Vincent is a solicitous and attentive listener, but he also asks leading questions, and his objections become increasingly tough as he voices fears that take three books to overcome. The conversation moves easily – Louis L. Martz characterizes it as an "art of improvisation" – but there is an underlying structure, despite the garrulity and digressions. Here is Antony as he moves into a discussion of suicide, a fear that he "forgot" or perhaps repressed: "Surely, cousin, but yet there are many more than I can either remember or find, howbeit one yet cometh now to my mind, of which I before nothing thought, and which is yet in my opinion of all the other fears the most horrible – that is to wit, cousin, where the devil tempteth a man to kill and destroy himself."

The dialogue is grounded in a faith that transforms suffering into an act of love. In the first book Antony argues that tribulation is actually a gift that can be seen as a cure, a preservative, or a test and exercise of one's patience and love. True comfort is not transient pleasure or prosperity but "the consolation of good hope that men take in their heart of some good growing toward them" – namely, of God's favor. In contrast to the sobriety of the first book, the second is full of tales that bind the two men and speak to their common humanity. But it also explores various impediments to the willing acceptance of tribulation, including the faint heart, the too-scrupulous conscience, the temptation to suicide, and worldly prosperity.

In the third book, which is also the most inward-looking, More treats the most painful tribulation of all: persecution for the faith. Antony and Vincent first ponder the loss of "outward things" – riches, fame, and authority. Harder still are im-

Page from the transcription of More's Dialogue of Comfort against Tribulation *that is the basis for all modern editions of the work (Bodleian Library, Oxford University, MS. Corpus Christi College D. 37)*

prisonment and death. Antony encourages Vincent to cleave to God and pray for grace, explaining that God is faithful and will not allow him "to be tempted above that you may bear, but giveth also with the temptation a way out." And he calls for a radical perspective from which the whole world can be seen as a prison from which no one escapes except by death. The last part of the dialogue is a meditation on the last things and the passion and death of Christ: "In our fear let us remember Christ's painful agony, that himself would for our comfort suffer before his passion, to the intent that no fear should make us despair; and ever call for his help, such as himself list to send us; and then need we never to doubt, but that either he shall keep us from the painful death or shall not fail so to strength[en] us in it, that he shall joyously bring us to heaven by it, and then doth he much more for us than if he kept us from it."

More's last major Tower work, *De Tristitia Christi* (The Sadness of Christ), was written sometime before 12 June 1535, when his books and writing materials were taken away. The text breaks off just as Jesus is being taken into custody. *De Tristitia Christi* used to be considered a continuation of "A Treatise upon the Passion," but it is now recognized as an independent work. As in the English treatise, More comments on the biblical narrative from Gerson's *Monotessaron*. Here, however, he concentrates on one scene, Christ's agony in the garden of Gethsemane, and he is more meditative: Garry E. Haupt, an editor of the Yale edition of More's complete works, speaks of his "dramatic and psychological penetration of the biblical texts." Prayer, the humanity of Christ, martyrdom (and two kinds of martyrs, brave and fearful), the apostles' failure to keep watch with Christ, Judas's betrayal, and the escape of a young disciple are some of the topics that engage him. More is often expository and reflective, sometimes satiric, polemical, or ironic. But he writes most intensely about the mental anguish of Christ, whose bloody sweat he sees as a consolation for those who are fearful at the thought of torture and might succumb to despair. He imagines Christ comforting the fearful martyr: "O faint of heart, take courage and do not despair. You are afraid, you are sad, you are stricken with weariness and dread of the torment with which you have been cruelly threatened. Trust me. I conquered the world and yet I suffered immeasurably more from fear, I was sadder, more afflicted with weariness, more horrified at the prospect of such cruel suffering drawing eagerly nearer and nearer. Let the brave man have his high-spirited martyrs, let him rejoice in imitating a thousand of them. But you, my timorous and feeble little sheep, be content to have me alone as your shepherd, follow my leadership; if you do not trust yourself, place your trust in me. See, I am walking ahead of you along this fearful road. . . . Take heart, and use the sign of my cross to drive away this dread." He carried a red cross of wood on his way to Tower Hill, where he was beheaded on 6 July – dying, as he is reported to have said, as the king's good servant yet God's first.

More played many parts: he was a successful lawyer and judge; a civil servant, political figure, and statesman; a humanist, critic, and brilliant intellectual; a jester and a man of consummate wit; a storyteller and poet; a loving father, good friend, and genial host; an educator; a fierce polemicist, single-minded in his pursuit of heresy; an ascetic; a man of conscience; and a man of faith who died for his beliefs. For this reason, it is hard to see his writings whole. He wrote in two languages and helped to shape both the international culture of early-sixteenth-century humanism and the culture of early Tudor England. His output was enormous, even though he left many works, including some of his most important ones, unfinished. By far the largest amount of his writing is polemical, and his counterattacks on the Protestant Reformers are extremely important historically and culturally. Yet his literary reputation has depended far more on his humanist pieces and on the letters and devotional works he wrote as a prisoner in the Tower of London, while *Utopia,* at once his most enigmatic and most powerful work, has a worldwide reputation and a life of its own. And only when the St. Thomas More Project at Yale University is completed with the publication of volume one will his extant verse and almost all of his prose be readily available in critical editions. Without his complete works critics have been handicapped in trying to assess More's development, his ideas, his achievements as thinker and writer, and the relations between so many and such diverse works.

More rapidly attained fame as a Latinist in sixteenth-century Europe, and he has long held an important place in English literature. His name heads the list of sixteenth-century English writers in Ben Jonson's *Timber; or Discoveries Made upon Men and Matter* (1641), and Samuel Johnson drew heavily on More's English verse, along with material from *The History of Richard III* and a Tower letter, to illustrate the history of the English language in his dictionary (1755). Johnson speaks of More's works as "models of pure and elegant style," and comparable claims – focused on the prose – have been made and questioned in the twentieth century. On the one hand, R. W. Chambers argued that More was the first writer with a vernacular prose style equal "to all the needs of Sixteenth-Century England." On the other hand, Lewis objected to the "stodgy and dough-like" quality of More's prose, concluding that he "never really rose from a legal to a literary conception of clarity and completeness."

This debate has not been so much resolved as abandoned, as critics have become increasingly interested in More's rhetoric and have rethought the politics of his writing as well as its biographical and historical contexts. More is seen today as a writer who was engaged in virtually all of the most fundamental and controversial issues of his day – issues to which he brought his energy, his extraordinary irony (one reason for the complexity and elusiveness of his writing), his subtle mind, his inexhaustible inventiveness, his mix of the comic and the serious, his genius for conversation and dialogue, and his ability to transform literary genres. More the writer is at his best when he turns to the letter and the dialogue, and most readers would agree that *Utopia, A Dialogue Concerning Heresies,* and *A Dialogue of Comfort against Tribulation* are his greatest works. So often writing at a time of crisis, whether for society or for himself, More explored the human condition and asked about its reformation from multiple perspectives: sociological, political, legal, historical, philosophical, ethical, psychological, doctrinal, and spiritual. Though the positions taken and answers given vary widely from work to work, he addressed problems of the community and the common good from the beginning of his career to the end of his life. Here, as in so many other ways, Thomas More remains a man for all seasons.

Letters:

Opus Epistolarum Des. Erasmi Roterodami, 12 volumes, edited by P. S. Allen, H. M. Allen, and H. W. Garrod (Oxford: Clarendon Press, 1906–1958);

The Correspondence of Sir Thomas More, edited by Elizabeth Frances Rogers (Princeton: Princeton University Press, 1947);

Sir Thomas More: Neue Briefe, edited by Hubertus Schulte Herbrüggen (Münster: Aschendorff, 1966);

Herbrüggen, "Three Additions to More's Correspondence," *Moreana,* 20, no. 79/80 (1983): 35–41;

Herbrüggen, "Seven New Letters from Thomas More," *Moreana,* 27 (September 1990): 49–66.

Bibliographies:

Frank and Majie Padberg Sullivan, *Moreana 1478–1945: A Preliminary Check List of Material by and about Saint Thomas More* (Kansas City, Mo.: Rockhurst College, 1946);

R. W. Gibson and J. M. Patrick, *St. Thomas More: A Preliminary Bibliography of His Works and of Moreana to the Year 1750* (New Haven & London: Yale University Press, 1961);

Frank and Majie Padberg Sullivan, *Moreana: Materials for the Study of Saint Thomas More,* 4 volumes (Los Angeles: Loyola University, 1964–1968);

Majie Padberg Sullivan, *Index to Moreana: Materials for the Study of Saint Thomas More* (Los Angeles: Loyola University, 1971);

Sullivan, *Moreana: Materials for the Study of Saint Thomas More: Supplement and Chronology to 1800* (Los Angeles: Loyola Marymount University, 1977); *Supplement II* (Los Angeles: Loyola Marymount University, 1985);

Judith Paterson Jones, "Recent Studies in More (1945–1976)," *English Literary Renaissance,* 9 (Autumn 1979): 442–458;

Constance Smith, *An Updating of R. W. Gibson's "St. Thomas More: A Preliminary Bibliography"* (Saint Louis: Center for Reformation Research, 1981);

Albert J. Geritz, "Recent Studies in More (1977–1990)," *English Literary Renaissance,* 22 (Winter 1992): 112–140.

Biographies:

Thomas Stapleton, *Tres Thomae* (Douai: Printed by J. Bogard, 1588); translated by Philip E. Hallett as *The Life and Illustrious Martyrdom of Sir Thomas More,* edited by E. E. Reynolds (New York: Fordham University Press, 1966);

William Roper, *The Mirror of Virtue in Worldly Greatness; or, The Life of Sir Thomas More* (Paris [Saint Omer: Printed by the English College Press], 1626); republished as *The Lyfe of Sir Thomas Moore, Knighte,* edited by Elsie Vaughan Hitchcock (London: Oxford University Press for the Early English Text Society, 1935); republished as "The Life of Sir Thomas More by William Roper," in *Two Early Tudor Lives: The Life and Death of Cardinal Wolsey, by George Cavendish; The Life of Sir Thomas More, by William Roper,* edited by Richard S. Sylvester and Davis P. Harding (New Haven & London: Yale University Press, 1962);

Cressacre More, *The Life and Death of Sir Thomas Moore* (Douai: Printed by B. Bellere, 1631?);

T. E. Bridgett, *Life and Writings of Sir Thomas More* (London: Burns & Oates, 1891);

Nicholas Harpsfield, *The Life and Death of Sr Thomas Moore, Knight, Sometymes Lord High Chancellor of England,* edited by Hitchcock (London: Oxford University Press for the Early English Text Society, 1932);

R. W. Chambers, *Thomas More* (London: Cape, 1935);

Ro. Ba., *The Lyfe of Syr Thomas More, Sometymes Lord Chancellor of England,* edited by Hitchcock and Hallett (London: Oxford University Press for the Early English Text Society, 1950);

Germain P. Marc'hadour, *L'Univers de Thomas More: Chronologie critique de More, Erasme, et leur époque (1477-1536)* (Paris: Librairie Philosophique, J. Vrin, 1963);

E. E. Reynolds, *The Field Is Won: The Life and Death of Saint Thomas More* (London: Burns & Oates, 1968);

J. A. Guy, *The Public Career of Sir Thomas More* (Brighton, U.K.: Harvester, 1980);

Richard Marius, *Thomas More* (New York: Knopf, 1984).

References:

Robert P. Adams, *The Better Part of Valor: More, Erasmus, Colet, and Vives, on Humanism, War, and Peace, 1496-1535* (Seattle: University of Washington Press, 1962);

Peter R. Allen, "*Utopia* and European Humanism: The Function of the Prefatory Letters and Verses," *Studies in the Renaissance,* 10 (1963): 91-107;

Judith H. Anderson, "More's *Richard III:* History and Biography," in her *Biographical Truth: The Representation of Historical Persons in Tudor-Stuart Writing* (New Haven & London: Yale University Press, 1984), pp. 75-109;

Shlomo Avineri, "War and Slavery in More's *Utopia,*" *International Review of Social History,* 7 (1962): 260-290;

Dominic Baker-Smith, *More's "Utopia"* (London & New York: HarperCollins*Academic,* 1991);

Baker-Smith, *Thomas More and Plato's Voyage* (Cardiff, U.K.: University College, 1978);

Harry Berger, Jr., "The Renaissance Imagination: Second World and Green World," *Centennial Review,* 9, no. 1 (1965): 36-77;

David M. Bevington, "The Dialogue in *Utopia:* Two Sides to the Question," *Studies in Philology,* 58 (July 1961): 496-509;

Ladislaus J. Bolchazy, Gregory Gichan, and Frederick Theobald, eds., *A Concordance to the "Utopia"*

of St. Thomas More and a Frequency Word List (Hildesheim & New York: Olms, 1978);

R. Bracht Branham, "Utopian Laughter: Lucian and Thomas More," *Moreana,* no. 86 (1985): 23-43;

R. W. Chambers, "The Continuity of English Prose from Alfred to More and His School," in Nicholas Harpsfield, *The Life and Death of Sr Thomas Moore, Knight, Sometymes Lord High Chancellor of England,* edited by Elsie Vaughan Hitchcock (London: Oxford University Press for the Early English Text Society, 1932), pp. xlv-clxxiv;

J. C. Davis, "The Re-Emergence of Utopia: Sir Thomas More," in his *Utopia and the Ideal Society: A Study of English Utopian Writing 1516-1700* (Cambridge: Cambridge University Press, 1981), pp. 41-61;

Leonard F. Dean, "Literary Problems in More's *Richard III,*" *PMLA,* 58 (March 1943): 22-41;

J. Duncan M. Derrett, "The Trial of Sir Thomas More," *English Historical Review,* 79 (July 1964): 449-477;

P. Albert Duhamel, "Medievalism of More's *Utopia,*" *Studies in Philology,* 52 (April 1955): 99-126;

Douglas Duncan, "More," in his *Ben Jonson and the Lucianic Tradition* (Cambridge: Cambridge University Press, 1979), pp. 52-76, 239-240;

G. R. Elton, "The Real Thomas More?," in *Reformation Principle and Practice: Essays in Honour of Arthur Geoffrey Dickens,* edited by Peter Newman Brooks (London: Scolar, 1980), pp. 21-31;

Alistair Fox, "Thomas More and Tudor Historiography: *The History of King Richard III,*" in his *Politics and Literature in the Reigns of Henry VII and Henry VIII* (Oxford: Blackwell, 1989), pp. 108-127;

Fox, *Thomas More: History and Providence* (New Haven & London: Yale University Press, 1982);

Fox, *"Utopia": An Elusive Vision* (New York: Twayne, 1993);

Brian Gogan, *The Common Corps of Christendom: Ecclesiological Themes in the Writings of Sir Thomas More* (Leiden: Brill, 1982);

Walter M. Gordon, "The Monastic Achievement and More's Utopian Dream," *Medievalia et Humanistica,* new series 9 (1979): 199-214;

Gordon, "The Platonic Dramaturgy of Thomas More's *Dialogues,*" *Journal of Medieval and Renaissance Studies,* 8 (Fall 1978): 193-215;

Damian Grace, "Thomas More's *Epigrammata:* Political Theory in a Poetic Idiom," *Parergon,* new series 3 (1985): 115–129;

Patrick Grant, "Thomas More's *Richard III:* Moral Narration and Humanist Method," *Renaissance and Reformation / Renaissance et Réforme,* new series 7 (August 1983): 157–172;

Stephen Greenblatt, "At the Table of the Great: More's Self-Fashioning and Self-Cancellation" and "The Word of God in the Age of Mechanical Reproduction," in his *Renaissance Self-Fashioning: From More to Shakespeare* (Chicago & London: University of Chicago Press, 1980), pp. 11–114;

Richard Helgerson, "Inventing Noplace, or the Power of Negative Thinking," *Genre,* 15 (Spring-Summer 1982): 101–121;

J. H. Hexter, *More's "Utopia": The Biography of an Idea* (New York: Harper & Row, 1965);

Frederic Jameson, "Of Islands and Trenches: Naturalization and the Production of Utopian Discourse," *Diacritics,* 7 (Summer 1977): 2–21;

Robbin S. Johnson, *More's "Utopia": Ideal and Illusion* (New Haven & London: Yale University Press, 1969);

Judith P. Jones, *Thomas More* (Boston: Twayne, 1979);

Karl Kautsky, *Thomas More and His "Utopia,"* translated by H. J. Stenning (New York: Russell & Russell, 1959);

Anthony Kenny, *Thomas More* (Oxford & New York: Oxford University Press, 1983);

Arthur F. Kinney, "*Encomium Sapientiae:* Thomas More and *Utopia,*" in his *Humanist Poetics: Thought, Rhetoric, and Fiction in Sixteenth-Century England* (Amherst: University of Massachusetts Press, 1986), pp. 57–88;

Kinney, *Rhetoric and Poetic in Thomas More's "Utopia"* (Malibu, Cal.: Undena, 1979);

Daniel Kinney, "Kings' Tragicomedies: Generic Misrule in More's *History of Richard III,*" *Moreana,* no. 86 (July 1985): 128–150;

Kinney, "More's *Letter to Dorp:* Remapping the Trivium," *Renaissance Quarterly,* 34 (Summer 1981): 179–210;

C. S. Lewis, *English Literature in the Sixteenth Century, Excluding Drama* (Oxford: Clarendon Press, 1954), pp. 113, 165–181;

George Logan, *The Meaning of More's "Utopia"* (Princeton: Princeton University Press, 1983);

Frank E. Manuel and Fritzie P. Manuel, "The Passion of Thomas More," in their *Utopian Thought in the Western World* (Cambridge,

Mass.: Belknap Press of Harvard University Press, 1979), pp. 117–149;

Louis Marin, "Toward a Semiotic of Utopia: Political and Fictional Discourse in Thomas More's *Utopia,*" in *Structure, Consciousness, and History,* edited by Richard Harvey Brown and Stanford M. Lyman (Cambridge: Cambridge University Press, 1978), pp. 261–282;

Marin, *Utopics: Spatial Play,* translated by Robert A. Vollrath (Atlantic Highlands, N. J. & London: Humanities Press & Macmillan, 1984);

Richard C. Marius, "Thomas More and the Early Church Fathers," *Traditio,* 24 (1968): 379–407;

Louis L. Martz, *Thomas More: The Search for the Inner Man* (New Haven & London: Yale University Press, 1990);

James McConica, "The Patrimony of Thomas More," in *History and Imagination: Essays in Honor of H. R. Trevor-Roper,* edited by Hugh Lloyd-Jones, Valerie Pearl, and Blair Worden (London: Duckworth, 1981), pp. 56–71;

Elizabeth McCutcheon, "Denying the Contrary: More's Use of Litotes in the *Utopia,*" *Moreana,* no. 31–32 (1971): 107–121;

McCutcheon, *My Dear Peter: The "Ars Poetica" and Hermeneutics for More's "Utopia"* (Angers, France: Moreanum, 1983);

Michael J. Moore, ed., *Quincentennial Essays on St. Thomas More: Selected Papers from the Thomas More College Conference* (Boone, N.C.: Albion, 1978);

Stanley Morison and Nicolas Barker, *The Likeness of Thomas More: An Iconographical Survey of Three Centuries* (London: Burns & Oates / New York: Fordham University Press, 1963);

Gary Saul Morson, *The Boundaries of Genre: Dostoevsky's "Diary of a Writer" and the Traditions of Literary Utopia* (Austin: University of Texas Press, 1981);

Clare M. Murphy, Henri Gibaud, and Mario A. Di Cesare, eds., *Miscellanea Moreana: Essays for Germain Marc'hadour* (Binghamton, N.Y.: Medieval and Renaissance Texts and Studies, 1989);

Alan F. Nagel, "Lies and the Limitable Inane: Contradiction in More's *Utopia,*" *Renaissance Quarterly,* 26 (Summer 1973): 173–180;

Rainer Pineas, *Thomas More and Tudor Polemics* (Bloomington & London: Indiana University Press, 1968);

A. F. Pollard, "The Making of Sir Thomas More's *Richard III,*" in *Historical Essays in Honour of James Tait,* edited by J. G. Edwards, V. H. Galbraith, and E. F. Jacob (Manchester, U.K.: Printed for the Subscribers, 1933), pp. 223–238;

Martin N. Raitiere, "More's *Utopia* and *The City of God*," *Studies in the Renaissance*, 20 (1973): 144–168;

Wayne A. Rebhorn, "Thomas More's Enclosed Garden: *Utopia* and Renaissance Humanism," *English Literary Renaissance*, 6 (Spring 1976): 140–155;

Timothy J. Reiss, "From the Middle Ages to the (W)Hole of *Utopia*," in his *Discourse of Modernism* (Ithaca, N.Y. & London: Cornell University Press, 1982), pp. 108–139;

Peter Ruppert, *Reader in a Strange Land: The Activity of Reading Literary Utopias* (Athens & London: University of Georgia Press, 1986);

Richard J. Schoeck, " 'A Nursery of Correct and Useful Institutions': On Reading More's *Utopia* as Dialogue," *Moreana*, no. 22 (1969): 19–32;

Quentin Skinner, *The Foundations of Modern Political Thought*, 2 volumes (Cambridge: Cambridge University Press, 1978);

Skinner, "Sir Thomas More's *Utopia* and the Language of Renaissance Humanism," in *The Languages of Political Theory in Early-Modern Europe*, edited by Anthony Pagden (Cambridge: Cambridge University Press, 1987), pp. 123–157;

Edward Surtz, S. J., *The Praise of Pleasure: Philosophy, Education, and Communism in More's "Utopia"* (Cambridge, Mass.: Harvard University Press, 1957);

Surtz, *The Praise of Wisdom: A Commentary on the Religious and Moral Problems and Backgrounds of St. Thomas More's "Utopia"* (Chicago: Loyola University Press, 1957);

Richard S. Sylvester, " 'Si Hythlodaeo Credimus': Vision and Revision in Thomas More's *Utopia*," *Soundings*, 51 (1968): 272–289;

Sylvester, ed., *St. Thomas More: Action and Contemplation* (New Haven & London: Yale University Press, 1972);

Sylvester and Germain P. Marc'hadour, eds., *Essential Articles for the Study of Thomas More* (Hamden, Conn.: Archon, 1977);

J. B. Trapp and Hubertus Schulte Herbrüggen, comps., *"The King's Good Servant": Sir Thomas More 1477/8–1535* (London: National Portrait Gallery, 1978);

Andrew W. Weiner, "Raphael's Eutopia and More's *Utopia*: Christian Humanism and the Limits of Reason," *Huntington Library Quarterly*, 39 (November 1975): 1–27;

Thomas White, "Aristotle and *Utopia*," *Renaissance Quarterly*, 29 (Winter 1976): 635–675;

White, "Pride and the Public Good: Thomas More's Use of Plato in *Utopia*," *Journal of the History of Philosophy*, 20 (October 1982): 329–354;

K. J. Wilson, "The Transformation of Dialogue," in his *Incomplete Fictions: The Formation of English Renaissance Dialogue* (Washington, D.C.: Catholic University of America Press, 1985), pp. 137–175;

Warren W. Wooden and John N. Wall, Jr., "Thomas More and the Painter's Eye: Visual Perspective and Artistic Purpose in More's *Utopia*," *Journal of Medieval and Renaissance Studies*, 15 (Fall 1985): 231–263.

Papers:

Because of Thomas More's execution and the political situation in the 1530s and later, many of his papers were hidden, lost, or destroyed. The most important extant manuscript in More's hand is the Valencia Manuscript, which contains the *De Tristitia Christi*, with extensive autograph revisions and a catena of scriptural passages, in the Chapel of the Relics, Royal College of Corpus Christi, Valencia, Spain. A Latin Book of Hours and a liturgical psalter that More used while he was a prisoner in the Tower of London contain many marginalia; bound together as "Thomas More's Prayer Book," they are at Yale University.

Richard Morison

(1514? – 20 March 1556)

Janice Liedl
Laurentian University

BOOKS: *A Lamentation in Whiche Is Shewed What Ruyne Cometh of Seditious Rebellyon,* anonymous (London: Printed by Thomas Berthelet, 1536);

A Remedy for Sedition, anonymous (London: Printed by Thomas Berthelet, 1536);

Apomaxis calumniarum, convitiorumque, quibus íoannes cocleus, . . . Henrici Octaui, famam impetere, . . . stuauit (London: Printed by Thomas Berthelet, 1537);

A Comfortable Consolation Wherin the People May Se, Howe Far Greatter Cause, They Haue to Be Glad for the Ioyful Byrth of Prince Edwarde, than Sory for the Dethe of Quene Jane (London: Printed by Thomas Berthelet, 1537);

An Inuectiue ayenste the Great and Detestable Vice, Treason (London: Printed by Thomas Berthelet, 1539);

An Exhortation to Styrre All Englyshemen to the Defence of Theyr Countreye (London: Printed by Thomas Berthelet, 1539);

A Defence of Priestes Mariages . . . Agaynst T. Martin, edited by Matthew Parker (London: Printed by John Kingston for Richard Jugge, 1567).

Editions: *A Remedy for Sedition,* edited by E. M. Cox (London: Golden Hours, 1933);

An Exhortation to Styre All Englyshemen to the Defense of Theyr Countreye (New York: Da Capo Press, 1972);

An Inuectiue ayenste the Great and Detestable Vice, Treason (New York: Da Capo Press, 1972);

A Remedy for Sedition and *A Lamentation in Which Is Shown What Ruin Cometh of Seditious Rebellion,* in *Humanist Scholarship and Public Order: Two Tracts against the Pilgrimage of Grace by Sir Richard Morison,* edited by David Sandler Berkowitz (Washington, D.C.: Folger Books, 1984).

TRANSLATIONS: Johannes Sturm, *The Epistle That Johan Sturmius, a Man of Great Learning and Judgment, Sent to the Cardynalles and Prelates* (London: Printed by Thomas Berthelet, 1538);

Sextus Julius Frontinus, *The Strategies, Sleights, and Policies of War* (London: Printed by Thomas Berthelet, 1539);

Juan Luis Vives, *An Introduction to Wysedome* (London: Printed by Thomas Berthelet, 1540).

Richard Morison's pamphlets played an integral role in the defense of the Henrician Reformation. His writings defended the king and his councillors against the conservative uprisings of 1536 and 1539 as well as responding to criticism levied against the Reformation at home and abroad. Morison emphasized obedience and loyalty in his popular pamphlets, themes which were further developed in his Latin compositions and manuscript proposals. A fervent supporter of Lutheran Protestantism, Morison strongly supported the official Reformation under the last two Tudor kings, and his writings carried the principles of reform into the areas of law, education, and government. In reward for his services at court, in Parliament, and as a propagandist, Morison was knighted in the reign of Edward VI, yet he ended his days as an exile in Protestant Strasbourg.

Richard Morison was born around 1514 to Thomas Morison of Hertfordshire and a daughter of Thomas Merry of the same county. Little is known about him before his arrival at Oxford, where he was educated at Archbishop Thomas Wolsey's Cardinal College. He received his B.A. in 1528 and entered Wolsey's service, but his prospects for advancement were dashed by Wolsey's fall from favor and death in 1529. Probably in the company of some of his fellow Oxford scholars, Morison traveled to Paris in the household of Wolsey's bastard son, Thomas Winter. With this new source of patronage Morison later moved to Padua to study civil law at the university there. After his father's fall Winter's own finances grew tight, and Morison found himself virtually penniless. Only the

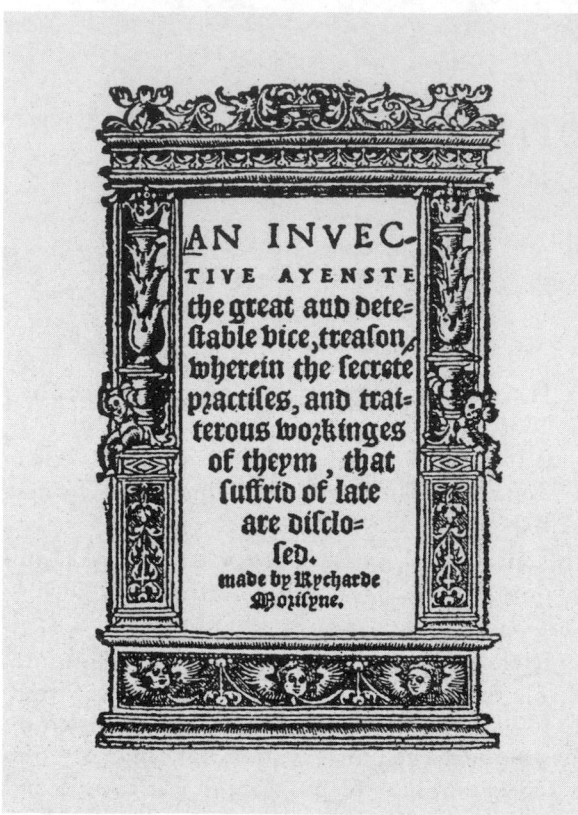

Title page for Morison's 1539 work, in which he attacks Reginald Pole, who was believed to be forming a Continental army to restore Roman Catholicism in England by force

largesse of Reginald Pole kept him from destitution, he wrote to his friend Thomas Starkey in 1535. Portraying himself as an able Italianist and humanist author, Morison sought new patronage to support his studies. In 1536 his pleas for relief from England finally had some effect. The king's chief minister, Thomas Cromwell, patron to Morison's good friend Starkey, first gave Morison some support apparently to remain abroad and offer intelligence of foreign affairs for the minister. However, Cromwell soon invited him to join his household, and in May 1536 Morison left Padua for England.

Within a few months Morison found himself playing a critical role in the defense of the Henrician Reformation. In autumn 1536 the "Pilgrimage of Grace," a militant and conservative uprising in the north of England, stunned the nation. The pilgrims demanded the restoration of Catholic worship in the realm and the replacement of Cromwell and other lowborn ministers with nobles and gentlemen. King Henry VIII was outraged and summoned a royal army to march north and subdue the rebels. In addition to this force of arms, Cromwell saw to it that the rebels' demands were answered

with loyal rhetoric and directed Morison to produce anonymous pamphlets denouncing the rebellion. The two works that resulted, *A Lamentation in Which Is Shown What Ruin Cometh of Seditious Rebellion* (1536) and *A Remedy for Sedition* (1536), emphasize the need for obedience and attack the presumption of subjects who dare to correct the king and his ministers. They established their author's reputation as a reliable and effective government propagandist. Morison boasted in a letter to his friend Henry Phillips that he wrote the *Lamentation* while still in his boots, in an afternoon and a night. This first pamphlet speaks in the voice of an educated and loyal Englishman railing against the rebellious lower classes and charging, "Look the histories, you shall evermore . . . find that never great realm or commonwealth hath been destroyed without sedition at home. Dissension, dissension hath been the ruin, the venom, the poison of all great estates."

Morison's second tract of the year came hard on the heels of the first. Whereas *A Lamentation* was a hasty response to the first rebellion in Lincolnshire, *A Remedy for Sedition* is a more polished answer to the second stage of the rebellion in Yorkshire, filled with biblical and classical references to the rewards of obedience and the punishment for rebellion, some of them derived from Morison's readings of Niccolò Machiavelli. In this pamphlet Morison expands upon his earlier reproaches against the disordered commons, whose upstart objections to King Henry's religious reforms and lowborn council he rejects summarily. But *A Remedy for Sedition* also blames the English nobles who ally themselves with the pilgrims, for by their example, Morison argues, the nobles lead their servants astray: "If the nobles be evil taught in points concerning religion, as if they be popish (to put one example for many), how can their servants choose but be so too?" The root of old troubles, as far as he is concerned, lies in the old religion and its mindless adherents who rebel against their king. Morison concludes *A Remedy* with a stirring exhortation to expand and increase the reformation of the English church and nation as one: "We must agree in religion, we must serve but one master; one body will have but one head. It is not possible [for] men to agree long that dissent in religion."

The following year saw two further publications to Morison's credit. The first was his Latin tract begun the previous year, *Apomaxis calumniarum* (1537), which had been delayed by the Pilgrimage of Grace. The *Apomaxis* responds to the German humanist Johannes Cochlaeus's *Defensio Clarissimorum Virorum* (1535), which had attacked Henry VIII for his break with Rome, his divorce of Catherine of Aragon, and the executions of Sir Thomas More and John Fisher, bishop of Rochester. Morison cites the arguments of English authorities such as Archbishop Thomas Cranmer, Bishop Stephen Gardiner, and Bishop Cuthbert Tunstall in counter to Cochlaeus's interpretation. Those whom the German portrayed as martyrs Morison redefines as stubbornly misguided men. The *Apomaxis* is filled with examples drawn from classical history and literature to support further the authority of Henry's Reformation, and it serves as elegantly humanistic propaganda for a more learned audience.

The second treatise that Morison produced in 1537 was occasioned upon the death of Queen Jane Seymour after giving birth to Henry's long-sought male heir, Prince Edward. *A Comfortable Consolation* proposes two chief arguments to counter English unhappiness at the death of their queen. First, Morison explains, Queen Jane, by reason of her virtuous life, must surely have gone to heaven. Second, and for him far more important, she left England with a prince to succeed Henry, which demonstrates God's favor toward England and her godly reformation. Therefore, there is nothing for any true Englishman or Englishwoman to mourn. On the contrary, Morison hints darkly that any complaint or disobedience on the part of Henry's subjects could negate the queen's sacrifice: "If it shall please God to send our prince [Edward] life, to wear the crown after his father, as undoubtedly he will, if he shall not find us unworthy [of] such felicity."

During this time Morison wrote many pieces which never made it to print, among them an address proposing to codify English common law along the model of Roman civil law and a treatise on the seven sacraments. His continued interest in Continental matters probably sparked an English translation of the German humanist educator Johannes Sturm's *Epistle* (1538), which incidentally praised the Henrician Reformation while it condemned the slow process of papal reform proceeding on the Continent.

In 1539 fears of invasion and rebellion stirred again as a plot on the part of Pole's noble family was discovered. Morison, basking in the favor of his powerful patron, Cromwell, was installed as a gentleman of the king's bedchamber but remained ready to defend his country with pen and paper. The Exeter conspiracy had brought down two important English families, the Courtenays and the Poles, and it was feared that the newly made cardinal Pole would assemble an invasion army on the

Hans Holbein the Younger's portrait of Prince Edward, with a Latin inscription by Morison which begins, "Little one, imitate your father and be the heir of his virtue, the world contains nothing greater." (Mellon Collection, National Gallery of Art, Washington, D.C.)

Continent to restore Catholicism to England. Once again, Morison proved his worth as a propagandist in two compositions. The first, *An Invective against the Great and Detestable Vice, Treason* (1539), openly attacks the perfidy of Pole, a man who had abandoned both God and country in Morison's eyes. Using biblical and classical examples, Morison shows Pole's defection to be ungrateful and unnatural. Such a rebellion was also clearly destined to failure, as God would ever allow "his chosen king, a prince that chiefly above all things, has sought and seeks to set forth his glory, to restore his holy word, to put down hypocrisy, to banish idolatry, and finally to bring this once to pass, that all his people, may be as they are called, that is, true Christians." Morison's second printed pamphlet of 1539, *An Exhortation to Stir all Englishmen to the Defense of Their Country,* was completed shortly before he sat in the House of Commons that helped to condemn the Exeter conspiracy. Once again Pole's perfidy is rehearsed: "The Pole, then a pearl of his country, now a foul pock to it . . . hath this always in his mouth, Roma mihi patria est, Rome is my native country." But the primary aim of *An Exhortation* was to stir up the militant impulse of the English when an imminent invasion by Catholic troops was expected.

Morison's preoccupation with military questions also led him to translate a military manual by the classical author Sextus Julius Frontinus, *The Stratagems, Sleights, and Policies of War* (1539). In the introduction to his translation Morison explicitly connects this volume to *An Exhortation,* writing, "I have besides this my translation in another trifle of mine, exhorted all my country men, peace laid aside, to prepare for war." With service now in court, in Cromwell's propaganda machine, and in Parliament, Morison continued to accumulate favor and reward, receiving grants of houses, lands, and profitable offices in 1540 and 1541. Cromwell's execution for treason in 1540 ended Morison's service as a pamphleteer. In fact Morison was not published again in his lifetime, though he continued to exploit his offices at court, receiving in 1545 the lordship of Cassiobury, Hertfordshire, which became his country residence. He contracted a marriage to Bridget Hussay in September 1546, shortly before embarking on an embassy to the king of Denmark and the Hanseatic towns, where he remained until the accession of Edward VI. Morison was now addressed with the title of king's councillor, continued to serve in Parliament, and was knighted in the summer of 1550. Later that fall he was appointed ambassador to the imperial court, where his enthusiastic support of Lutheranism alienated Emperor Charles V. His career as an ambassador to the imperial court ended with an indiscreet reference in an official letter to Guildford Dudley, the husband of Lady Jane Grey, as king, and he was recalled to England on 5 August 1553, early in the reign of Mary.

In 1554 Sir Richard began a voluntary exile in Strasbourg, where he was accounted an important member of the English Protestant community. During this period he could have written the last work attributed to him, *A Defense of Priests' Marriages* (1567), an answer to Thomas Martin's *Tract Declaring and Plainly Proving That the Pretended Marriage of Priests Is No Marriage* (1554). *A Defense of Priests' Marriages* condemns the new direction the church was taking under Mary and Philip. Referring to the new English bishops, the tract claims, "They profess to know God in word, passing all others: but by their doings they plainly deny him. Yea, they persecute him in his members: they persecute the faith and doctrine that he has left behind him." The subject matter and historical examples cited in this ex-

tremely detailed refutation of the value of clerical celibacy are certainly reminiscent of Morison's earlier writings. But while the defiantly Lutheran tone of the tract accords well with accounts of Morison's increasing devotion to his religion in exile, *A Defense* lacks the humanist flare that marked his Henrician works. Sir Richard Morison died in Strasbourg on 20 March 1556, leaving a young son, Charles, three daughters, Jane, Elizabeth, and Mary, and several illegitimate children. His enviable estate was administered by his widow, who returned to England and married Henry Manners, second Earl of Rutland, and after Rutland's death married Francis Russell, second Earl of Bedford.

Morison's literary career went largely unacknowledged until his anonymous tracts were properly attributed by C. R. Baskerville in 1936. Warren G. Zeeveld made Morison's propagandizing one of the central concerns of *The Foundations of Tudor Policy* (1948), and since then Morison's work has been recognized as an integral part of Cromwell's campaign for order and obedience. Most recently, David Sandler Berkowitz has produced an outstanding critical edition of Morison's books against the Pilgrimage of Grace, complete with introductory chapters on his early career and his sources.

Letters:

Letters and Papers, Foreign and Domestic, of the Reign of Henry VIII, edited by J. S. Brewer, and others, 21 volumes (London: Her Majesty's Stationer's Office, 1864–1932), 9: nos. 101–103; 10: nos. 320–321, 417–419, 660–661; 11: 1481–1482; 13.1: nos. 1296–1297.

References:

C. R. Baskerville, "Sir Richard Morison as the Author of Two Anonymous Tracts on Sedition," *Library,* 17 (June 1936): 83–87;

Cissie Rafferty Bonini, "Richard Morison, Humanist and Reformer under Henry VIII," Ph.D. dissertation, Stanford University, 1974;

Sharon Kay Christie, "Richard Morison: An Analysis of His Life and Work," Ph.D. dissertation, West Virginia University, 1978;

Helen Miller, "Richard Morison," in *The House of Commons, 1509–1558,* 3 volumes, edited by S. T. Bindoff (London: History of Parliament Trust, 1982);

William G. Zeeveld, *The Foundations of Tudor Policy* (Cambridge, Mass.: Harvard University Press, 1948).

William Painter

(1540? – February 1594)

Renée Pigeon
California State University, San Bernardino

BOOKS: *The Palace of Pleasure* (London: Printed by Henry Denham for Richard Tottell and William Jones, 1566; revised and enlarged edition, London: Printed by Thomas Marshe, 1575);

The Second Tome of the Palace of Pleasure (London: Printed by Henry Bynneman for Nicholas England, 1567);

A Moorning Ditti vpon the Deceas of Henry Earl of Arundel (London: John Allde, 1580);

Luctus consolatorius. svper morte nuper D. cancellarij Angliæ, Nouembr. 1591 (London: Thomas Orwin, 1591).

Editions: *The Palace of Pleasure,* edited by Joseph Haselwood, 3 volumes (London: R. Triphook, 1813); edited by Joseph Jacobs, 3 volumes (London: David Nutt, 1890); edited by Hamish Miles, 4 volumes (London: Cresset Press, 1929);

An Elizabethan Story-Book: Famous Tales from "The Palace of Pleasure," edited by Peter Haworth (London: Longmans, Green, 1928).

OTHER: William Fulke, *Antiprognosticon That Is to Saye, an Inuectiue Agaynst the Astrologians,* translated by Painter (London: Printed by Henry Sutton, 1560);

Anonymous, *Delectable Demaundes, and Pleasaunt Questions, with Their Seuerall Aunswers, in Matters of Loue, Naturall Causes, with Morall and Politique Deuises,* translated by Painter (London: Printed by John Cawood for Nicholas England, 1566);

Cælius Secundus Curio, *Pasquine in a Traunce: A Christian and Learned Dialogue (Contayning Wonderfull Newes out of Heauen, Purgatorie, and Hell),* translation attributed to Painter (London: Printed by William How for Abraham Veale, 1575).

William Painter's place in English literary history is derived from the collection of tales he trans-lated into English from diverse sources — most notably Matteo Bandello, Margaret of Navarre, and Giovanni Boccaccio — which he brought together as *The Palace of Pleasure* (1566). This collection of "pleasant histories and excellent novels" achieved immediate popularity and has been credited with inspiring Roger Ascham's attack in *The Schoolmaster* (1570) against "bawdy" translations of Italian works. *The Palace of Pleasure* is notable both because it inaugurated the fashion for translating Continental novellas, inspiring imitators such as Geoffrey Fenton and George Pettie in the years following its first publication, and because it was an important source for William Shakespeare, John Webster, and other dramatists of the period. Tales found in *The Palace of Pleasure* which later appeared in dramatic form on the Elizabethan and Jacobean stage include "The Duchess of Malfi," "Romeo and Julietta," and "Giletta of Narbonne," the latter being the source of Shakespeare's *All's Well That Ends Well* (1598).

Little is known of Painter's early life. His family may have had its origin in Kent, where Painter in later years acquired two estates, but even the year of his birth is uncertain. Joseph Jacobs's 1890 edition of *The Palace of Pleasure* gives 1525, repeated by certain other authorities; but since Painter was matriculated at St. John's College, Cambridge, as a sizar in November 1554, circa 1540 seems more likely. No record exists of his having taken a degree at Cambridge; by 1560 he was headmaster of the Sevenoaks School, and on 9 February 1561 he was appointed clerk of the ordnance of the Tower of London. His superior was Ambrose Dudley, Earl of Warwick, master of the ordnance, to whom Painter dedicated the first volume of *The Palace of Pleasure,* thanking him for "benefits and commendation undeserved." The title page of the first edition of *The Palace of Pleasure* displays the Dudley emblem of the bear and the ragged staff.

In fact, the "benefits" Painter acquired in his office seem to have gone well beyond the eight pence per diem the position offered: he was accused

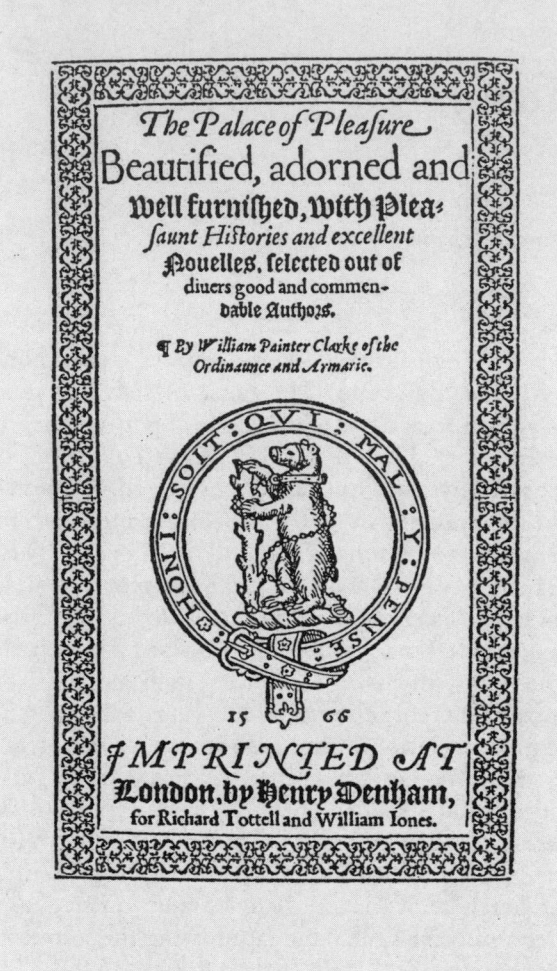

Title page for Painter's 1566 translation of Italian novellas, sources for plays by William Shakespeare and John Webster

der of the Sultan Solyman," a narrative detailing the sultan's murder of his eldest son, Mustapha, which Painter later included in the second edition of *The Palace of Pleasure.* He also translated William Fulke's *Antiprognosticon* (1560), a treatise attacking astrologers. In 1562 the printer William Jones entered "The City of Civility, translated into English by William Painter," in the Stationers' Register, probably the original title of *The Palace of Pleasure.* Four years later the first volume of sixty tales appeared; the "Second Tome," with thirty-four tales, followed in 1567. In 1575 a second edition of volume one appeared, featuring six new translations of tales from Navarre's *Heptameron* (1559), and an undated second edition of volume two was published (possibly in 1582) with the addition of "The Murder of Sultan Solyman." It is clear from the preface to the first volume that Painter planned the second to follow rapidly on its heels, since he notes that he has translated more tales from Boccaccio's *Decameron* (1353) than the eight which appear in the first volume, saving them "until I adjoin to this another tome . . . which with all my heart I wish and desire." Painter also apparently intended to publish a third volume, noting in an "advertisement to the reader" which concludes the second that "because suddenly (contrary to expectation) this volume is risen to greater heap of leaves, I do omit for this present time sundry novels of merry device"; however, no further new installments appeared.

In keeping with conventional Elizabethan attitudes regarding the purpose of literature, Painter announces his didactic intent in his preface to the first volume of *The Palace of Pleasure,* promoting his work as suitable for a variety of readers: "the lady, gentlewoman or other of the feminine kind," as well as the gentleman, the merchant, and the yeoman. In short he promises, "for all states and degrees, in these novels be set forth singular documents and examples, right commodious and profitable to them that will vouchsafe to read them." Having promised to instruct, Painter does not neglect the other desideratum of Elizabethan literature, delight: his readers will find the tales in *The Palace of Pleasure* "pleasant so well abroad as at home, to avoid the grief of winter's night and length of summer's day . . . delectable they be (no doubt) for all sorts of men, for the sad, the angry, the choleric, the pleasant, the whole, and the sick, and for all other with whatsoever passion rising either by nature or use they be affected."

Classical authors are well represented in the 101 tales that form the complete *The Palace of Pleasure;* nearly one-third of the tales are translations of the works of Livy, Herodotus, Plutarch, and other

during the 1580s of substantially increasing his personal wealth by embezzlement. According to the allegations against him, he transferred powder from Windsor to the Tower of London, then charged it to the accounts as newly purchased. His accuser states that "he deceived Her Majesty and made her pay for that which was her own." The validity of these charges is not incontrovertible, but both he and his son Anthony did admit to certain "irregularities" in the discharge of their duties. Despite the accusations against him, Painter retained his office until his death in 1594, which probably occurred not long after 14 February, when he dictated his will. After his father's death, Anthony Painter wrote to Sir Robert Cecil asking to be appointed surveyor of the ordnance, "having been brought up in that office," but his application was unsuccessful.

Painter's earliest known work is a translation of a Latin account of "The horrible and cruel mur-

writers of antiquity. Among his classical sources, Painter drew most frequently on Aulus Gellius (circa A.D. 130–180), whose *Noctes Atticae* is the source of twelve tales; but this number is misleading, since these are not, for the most part, novellas but brief anecdotes, "pretty jests," and fables from Aesop, such as the story of Androcles and the lion. For example, as the twenty-third novel in the first volume of *The Palace of Pleasure,* Painter translates from Gellius advice to mothers to breast-feed their own children rather than employ wet nurses. From Livy, Painter derived eight tales, including "Coriolanus" and "The Rape of Lucrece," the source of Shakespeare's poem.

Noting that in the first volume of *The Palace of Pleasure* Painter repeats three stories found in popular Elizabethan jestbooks (the eighteenth, twenty-first, and twenty-sixth tales, translated from Gellius), Douglas Bush suggests that in the first volume Painter was modeling his work in part on that very successful genre; by the second volume, however, he had a firmer sense of what his audience desired and included far fewer tales — only five out of thirty-four — from classical sources, while the second volume includes eighteen tales translated from Bandello and six from Boccaccio. It is also possible, however, that Painter's selection of tales in each volume was more random than Bush suggests and was based on the translations he had completed and had ready at hand, rather than a conscious response to the first volume's reception.

The greatest number of tales in the complete collection from a single author — twenty-six — are translations of the *Novelle* (1554–1573) of Bandello, frequently derived from the French translations by Boaistuau and François de Belleforest, which Painter preferred to the original Italian, describing Bandello's own language as "barren soil." The most familiar tale from Bandello in *The Palace of Pleasure* — and one of the longest — is "The Duchess of Malfi." Painter relied upon Belleforest's translation of Bandello and adopts his harshly moralistic stance with regard to the duchess, in contrast to Bandello's original account, which was both more succinct and less judgmental. At the conclusion of a series of seven stories from Bandello in the first volume of *The Palace of Pleasure,* Painter includes a note to the reader which demonstrates his awareness of the sensationalism in these works: "after these tragical and dolorous histories of Bandello, I have thought good for thy recreation to refresh thy mind with some pleasant devices and disports lest thy spirits and senses should be appalled and astonished with the sundry kinds of cruelties" that occur in Bandello's fiction.

After Bandello, Navarre's *Heptameron* and Boccaccio's *Decameron* provided Painter with the next greatest number of tales, sixteen from each source. Of the sixteen translations from the *Heptameron,* ten appeared in the first edition of volume one of *The Palace of Pleasure,* and the remaining six appeared for the first time in the second edition (1575). The remaining tales are from other contemporaries — among them Cinthio (Giambattista Giraldi), Fiorentino, Gianfrancesco Straparola, and Antonio de Guevara.

While Painter's versions of Navarre's tales are generally quite faithful translations, he omits all but a few rather inexplicable fragments of the framing discussions by the storytellers and audience which occur in the original text, and in doing so subtly alters the impact of the stories. The *Heptameron*'s thirty-second story, for example, tells of an adulterous woman punished by confinement to the chamber in which she committed her transgression in the company of the skeleton of her lover (who was slain by her husband) and forced to drink from a cup made from her lover's skull, until a visitor persuades the husband that, as the couple is childless and she is contrite, he should forgive her and secure heirs to his fortune. Painter quite accurately translates this macabre tale (the fifty-second tale in volume one, "A Strange Punishment for Adultery"); but in the original text the woman's punishment is debated by the courtly audience, while in *The Palace of Pleasure* its validity goes unquestioned. Similarly, Painter translates the thirty-sixth novel of the *Heptameron* as "The President of Grenoble," in which an unfaithful wife is poisoned by the husband who has successfully concealed her adultery from public notice, thus maintaining both his private and public honor. In this instance Painter does include a few sentences of the *Heptameron*'s ensuing debate among teller and audience over the ethics of the husband's action, but in the original the debate is as long as the tale itself.

In translating sixteen tales from Boccaccio's *Decameron,* Painter also eliminates the frame story and the varied tellers of the tales. His principle of selection is apparent from his remark in the introduction to *The Palace of Pleasure* that among Boccaccio's one hundred tales "there be some (in my judgment) that be worthy to be condemned to perpetual prison, but of them such have I redeemed . . . as may be best liked and better suffered." Clearly, Painter wanted to omit the more ribald and bawdy tales from the *Decameron.* Of the sixteen he includes, five are from the *Decameron*'s second day, when stories are told of those who achieved unexpected happy endings after a series of adventures; his other selections include four tales each from days one and ten, and one each from days three and eight. Yvonne Rodax terms Painter's translation of Boccaccio "conscientious but humorless," noting that he "sometimes reproduces a whole tale almost exactly but misses the point." His translation of the *Decameron*'s "Gilietta of Narbonne" is the first appearance in English of the story which Shakespeare recast as *All's Well That Ends Well.* As he did with the *Heptameron,* Painter achieves a tone that, while consistent with the balance of *The Palace of Pleasure,* is not representative of the original. Addressing Painter's subtly revisionist approach to his sources in *The Palace of Pleasure,* Howard Cole asserts that the "relatively accurate version of the *All's Well* story was bound to be misleading."

The two volumes of *The Palace of Pleasure* differ quite significantly in the way in which Painter links the stories. In the first, he occasionally comments briefly on the tale to be told: for example, he introduces the twenty-seventh novel, "The Love of Antiochus with Fair Stratonica," by noting that "although the wise philosopher Plutarch elegantly and briefly describeth this history in the life of Demetrius, yet because Bandello aptly and more at large doth discourse the same, I thought good to apply my pen to his style." As noted previously, he includes an "advertisement to the reader" to justify (rather clumsily) a shift in tone after his final selection from Bandello in volume one. In the second volume, however, Painter introduces every tale, with some of his introductions as long as the tales that they precede and he frequently concludes with an introduction to the next tale, or draws comparisons suggesting thematic links among a series of tales. His introductions include both moralizing commentary and literary asides. He introduces his thirty-second tale, for example (from the *Decameron,* day eight, novel seven), by first justifying a shift in mood: "divert we now a little from these sundry haps to solace ourselves with a merry device." In his lengthy introduction to this tale of a scholar who exacts revenge on a widow who tricked him into standing all night in the snow, Painter summarizes the action, notes that "one Girolamo Ruscelli, a learned Italian making pretty notes for the better elucidation of the Italian *Decameron* of Boccaccio, judgeth Boccaccio himself to be this scholar" and adds the warning that "if women wist what dealings are with men of great reading, they would among one hundred other, not deal with one of the meanest of those that be bookish." Perhaps Painter sensed a

need in some way to replace the framing stories he encountered in Navarre and Boccaccio, but in any event the overall effect is of a writer far surer of himself and of his purpose, taking the opportunity to create a personal narrative voice to link his diverse selections.

In general, *The Palace of Pleasure,* while effectively introducing the Continental novella to an English audience, is a very different sort of work in many respects from the original texts which Painter often faithfully translates: while he retains sensational incident and is capable of vivid storytelling, through his process of selection and omission he achieves a moral tone more serious and weighty, and at times more sententious, than that of the original authors, especially in the thirty-five selections that comprise the second volume, where Painter points to a specific moral for his reader in each instance.

A few other minor works are attributed to Painter, including *A Mourning Ditty* (1580), and *Luctus consolatorius* (1591), elegies on the deaths of two prominent Elizabethans, Henry Fitzalan, Earl of Arundel and Sir Christopher Hatton. He is also credited with the translation from the French of the anonymous *Delectable Demands and Pleasant Questions* (1566), a series of questions and answers about love and moral and natural philosophy. He may have been the "W. P." who translated Caelius Secundus Curio's *Pasquine in a Trance* (1575), "turned but lately out of the Italian into this tongue" in which a dialogue between Pasquine and his friend Marforius enumerates abuses of the clergy, and is followed by "Questions of Pasquine to be disputed in the council now holden in Trent."

The importance of *The Palace of Pleasure* as a source for dramatists has long been acknowledged: C. S. Lewis's reference to that work as "dung or compost for the popular drama" is characteristic. But, as Robert J. Clements and Joseph Gibaldi point out, the novella tradition introduced into England by *The Palace of Pleasure* not only provided plots for Elizabethan dramatists but also influenced the direction their works took, "moving English drama away from the classical direction it might well have taken, as the example of *Gorbuduc* (first performed in 1561) clearly indicates." Rodax credits Painter with imparting to his work "an indefinably English stamp" through the process of selection, his choice of graphic tales, and the addition to them of local color and detail.

Painter's prose style, unlike that of, for example, John Lyly, was neither distinctive nor influential; Lewis called it "tolerably plain," though "workmanlike" might be a more impartial characterization. His significance in the development of prose fiction lies not in innovative style or narrative technique, but in his popularizing of the Continental novella. Despite the attacks of opponents such as Roger Ascham to his "bawdy" works, Painter offered to Elizabethans an array of tales which, while they imparted didactic lessons, also emphasized plot and character, encouraging the emerging synthesis of Renaissance genres that fostered the development of prose fiction. The steady increase in attention paid to Renaissance prose fiction in recent years should secure his continuing prominence in English literary history.

Bibliography:

James L. Harner, "William Painter," in his *English Renaissance Prose Fiction, 1500–1660: An Annotated Bibliography of Criticism* (Boston: G. K. Hall, 1978), pp. 360–370; and supplements for 1976–1983 (1985), pp. 131–135, and 1984–1990 (1992) pp. 101–104.

References:

Max Bluestone, *From Story to Stage: The Dramatic Adaptation of Prose Fiction in the Period of Shakespeare and His Contemporaries* (The Hague: Mouton, 1974);

Douglas Bush, "The Classical Tales in Painter's *Palace of Pleasure*," *Journal of English & Germanic Philology*, 23 (July 1924): 331–341;

Robert J. Clements and Joseph Gibaldi, *Anatomy of the Novella: The European Tale Collection from Boccaccio and Chaucer to Cervantes* (New York: New York University Press, 1977);

Howard Cole, *The All's Well Story from Boccaccio to Shakespeare* (Urbana: University of Illinois Press, 1981) pp. 72–89;

C. S. Lewis, *English Literature in the Sixteenth Century, Excluding Drama* (Oxford: Clarendon Press, 1954) pp. 309, 310;

René Pruvost, *Matteo Bandello and Elizabethan Fiction* (Paris: H. Champion, 1937);

Yvonne Rodax, *The Real and the Ideal in the Novella of Italy, France and England* (Chapel Hill: University of North Carolina Press, 1968), pp. 94–99;

Paul Salzman, *English Prose Fiction 1558–1700: A Critical History* (Oxford: Clarendon Press, 1985), pp. 7–21.

Catherine Parr

(1513? – 5 September 1548)

Jeanne Costello
Fullerton College

BOOKS: *Prayers or Meditacions, Wherin the Mynde Is Styrred Paciently to Suffre all Afflictions Here* (London: Printed by Thomas Berthelet, 1545); also published as *Prayers Stirryng the Mynd Vnto Heauenlye Medytacions Collected oute of Holy Workes* (London: Printed by Thomas Berthelet, 1545);

The Lamentacion of a Sinner, Made by ye Most Vertuous Ladie, Quene Caterine, Bewayling the Ignoraunce of Her Blind Life (London: Printed by Edward Whitchurche, 1547).

Editions: *The Lamentation, or Complaint of a Sinner, Made by the Most Virtuous . . . Ladie, Queene Catherine; Bewailing the Ignorance of Her Blind Life, Led in Superstition,* in *The Harleian Miscellany,* volume 5 (London: Robert Dutton, 1810), pp. 293–313;

Writings of Edward the Sixth, William Hugh, Queen Catherine Parr, Anne Askew, Lady Jane Grey, Hamilton, and Balnaves (Philadelphia: Presbyterian Board of Publication, 1842);

Prayers or Medytacions, facsimile edition (Amsterdam & Norwood, N. J.: Theatrum Orbis Terrarum & Walter J. Johnson, 1976).

OTHER: "Considerant ma vie mis rable," in *Hatfield House Manuscripts,* volume 1 (London: Historical Manuscripts Commission, 1883), p. 53.

Catherine Parr; portrait attributed to William Scrots (National Portrait Gallery, London)

Queen Catherine Parr played a vital role in promulgating Protestantism and humanist learning in Tudor England both by producing and patronizing religious works in the vernacular. Her first work, *Prayers or Meditations* (1545), was a volume of meditational pieces collected from other texts. It is important for its status as one of the first popular publications of courtly devotional literature in the English Protestant tradition. Her *Lamentation of a Sinner* (1547) was among the earliest Protestant spiritual autobiographies in England. Her influence as a patron enabled such Protestant humanists as Roger Ascham, John Foxe, and Thomas Wilson (to name a few) to acquire appointments as tutors in noble households. The support they received from her court circle of intellectual women provided the impetus for such works as Ascham's *Schoolmaster* (1570) and Wilson's *Art of Rhetoric* (1553) and *Rule of Reason* (1551) as well as a wide array of other sermons, tracts, and translations by religious Reformists. Queen Catherine was directly responsible for patronizing the English translation of the first volume of Desiderius Erasmus's Latin *Paraphrases of the New Testament* (1548).

Catherine Parr was born around 1513, either at Kendal Castle, Westmoreland, her father's ancestral estate, or in Blackfriar's, London, into an influential and wealthy family. Her father, Sir Thomas Parr, who served as master of the wards and comptroller of the household to Henry VIII, was son to Elizabeth Fitzhugh, a close friend of Henry's well-known grandmother, Margaret Beaufort. He married Maud Greene, a principal lady-in-waiting to Queen Catherine of Aragon, in 1508.

Catherine received nearly as excellent an education as was possible for a woman of her day. Her mother was in charge of the royal nursery and school in a court where the new humanist learning flourished. Thus young Catherine was educated in the company of Princess Mary and Sir Thomas More's children, among other aristocratic offspring, by their tutor, the illustrious Spanish scholar Juan Luis Vives. Catherine studied English, French, Latin, and some Greek and even at a young age was praised for her wisdom by Lord Dacre, grandfather to one of her prospective suitors. After being told by a fortune-teller that she was destined to sit in the highest seat of imperial majesty, the young girl reportedly refused her tasks with the comment, "My hands are ordained to touch crowns and scepters, and not spindles and needles."

Two marriages to wealthy nobles preceded Catherine's royal liaison. Because her father had died in 1517, she was betrothed early and at age fourteen married Edward, Lord Borough of Gainsborough in Lancashire, a man nearly four times her age. In 1527 she joined him on his northern estate, where she developed a friendship with Anne Askew, who was later to be executed during Henry's reign on charges of heresy. This relationship may well have sown the seeds of Parr's Reformist interest in religious matters. Her tenure as a lady-in-waiting to Queen Catherine of Aragon following the death in 1529 of Lord Borough certainly reinforced the intellectual bent demonstrated early in her life. At court she acquired a reputation for scholarliness and virtue, qualities strongly encouraged among the queen's intelligent and well-educated circle of women.

Catherine left the court when Anne Boleyn married King Henry, and in 1533 she married her second husband, John Neville, Lord Latimer, of the powerful northern Catholic family. Their marriage lasted nearly ten years, the most eventful of which was 1536. In October of that year Lord Latimer participated in an uprising known as the Pilgrimage of Grace, taking charge of a group of northern rebels outraged at Lord Privy Seal Thomas Cromwell's handling of church property following the dissolution of the monasteries. While Latimer eventually took a leading role in negotiating a resolution of the conflict between the rebels and the king's forces,

careful diplomatic maneuvering on his wife's part, through her influential sister and brother, was required to save the Latimers from the fate of many other participants in the uprising – imprisonment and death. Catherine was widowed again in December 1542 but shortly thereafter fell in love for the first time, with Thomas Seymour, brother of Catherine Howard, Henry's third wife. This relationship was not to be, though, for Queen Catherine Howard was convicted of infidelity to the king, and thus treason, and was executed on 13 February 1543. Parr next became the object of the king's attentions, and they were married by Stephen Gardiner, bishop of Winchester, on 12 July 1543.

It may be that Parr's greatest success as queen was her uniting of the royal children; under her care they all lived together for the first time, and she convinced Henry to acknowledge both Mary and Elizabeth as legitimate, bringing them once more into the line of succession. She certainly contributed to the excellent educations of Edward and Elizabeth, hiring the best humanist scholars to instruct them. She encouraged all three royal children to produce religious works. With the queen's encouragement, Princess Mary contributed a translation of the Saint John's Gospel portion of the Erasmian paraphrases Parr had sponsored. Princess Elizabeth acknowledges Parr's influence on her translation of Margaret of Navarre's *Mirror of the Sinful Soul* in an introductory letter which accompanied the gift on New Year's Day 1545. In correspondence with the queen Prince Edward expresses his appreciation for her encouragement in his scholarly endeavors.

While she was close to the sources of new learning whenever she was at court, Parr did not begin her career as a writer until late in life. *Prayers or Meditations* was probably composed during the summer of 1544, while Henry led his army in France. Catherine served as regent during his absence from 7 July to 10 October, and several of the prayers speak of battle and express her desire for victory and subsequent reconciliation. This little volume was extremely popular, going through ten editions during the sixteenth century alone. Its publication in an inexpensive octavo format fulfilled the humanist goal of making religious literature more widely available to a popular readership.

While the prayers are collected from a variety of sources, with perhaps some original compositions, the "meditation" section is a recasting of book 3, chapters 15–50 of Thomas à Kempis's *Imitation of Christ*, closely based upon a 1530 translation by Richard Whitford. Unrelated to liturgical observances, the prayers seem to be intended for private

PRAYERS OR
Medytacions, wherein the
mynd is stirred, paciently to
suffre all afflictions here, to
set at nought the vayne pro=
speritee of this worlde, and
alwaie to longe for the euer=
lastynge felicitee : Collected
out of holy woorkes by
the most vertuous
and graciouse
Princesse
Kathe=
rine
quene of Englande,
Fraunce, and
Irelande.
Anno dñi
1545.

Title page for Parr's first book, an early example of a religious work in the vernacular

devotion, most focusing traditionally upon the self-denial required for spiritual discipline and connection to God.

Much of the scholarship devoted to Parr's work attempts to determine the degree to which it represents a truly Protestant or merely Henrician-Catholic frame of mind. While earlier critics tend to insist that Parr's thinking was circumscribed by Erasmian notions and Henrician doctrinal attitudes, more-recent critics have called attention to the various influences that make the work more individually Protestant in conception. The consensus is that *Prayers* expresses no distinct religious alignment, although Parr's next book would clearly demonstrate her new association with Reformist Protestantism.

The famous anecdote of Parr's near brush with the fate of earlier queens given to us in Foxe's *Acts and Monuments* also suggests that Parr's religious views may have manifested a more radical perspective than her husband's. Gardiner feared the queen was pressing Henry to greater reforms of the church than were desirable. He witnessed a conversation between her and Henry in which she took issue with her husband in a religious matter. Gardiner later questioned the queen's loyalty and convinced Henry to allow him to search the chambers of her closest ladies for incriminating evidence of noncompliance with the Six Articles and to take the queen into custody. As Foxe tells the story, Henry went along with Gardiner only to trap him and allowed the accusations to find their way to Catherine, who immediately fell sick. When she spoke with her husband, she cleverly assured him that she was a weak woman only seeking to be educated by her husband in such matters as she could not pretend to understand. Henry was satisfied with her acknowledgement of his authority; and when Lord Chancellor Thomas Wriothesley arrived to take her and her ladies into custody, he was surprised by an indignant king who dismissed him as a "Beast, fool, and knave."

This is elusive evidence at best of the queen's convictions, but the preface by William Cecil, later Baron Burghley, to Parr's *Lamentation of a Sinner* certainly casts the work in a political light by presenting it as a call for reform. Parr's presentation of her conversion also marks it as distinctly Reformist in perspective, particularly when reinforced by the critique of "corrupted" clergy which falls in the last part of the book. In addition, the fact that the *Lamentation* was not published until after Henry's death, though it was written while he was still alive, suggests that Parr was aware of its departure from the king's rather orthodox doctrinal views. It must be said, though, that she also includes overzealous reformers in her criticism, calling them "contentious disputers."

The *Lamentation* is loosely arranged in three parts. It begins with a report of the author's conversion in which she confesses her sinful ways and recounts her struggle to achieve faith by understanding the meaning of Christ's passion. The middle section elaborates this meaning, moving from devotional to doctrinal discussion. She applies the ideas from this section to the wider social arena in the third part, where she takes to task those who would hinder reform and exhorts all to remain true to their callings and to reform their lives. Within this general structure, individual reflections upon topics and biblical verses are organized serially.

Parr's relationship with John Parkhurst, the Reformist chaplain she chose soon after she became queen, may have contributed to her conversion, but she attributes her own change of heart and mind simply to her reading of the Scriptures in translation. This experience becomes the basis for her belief that the Bible should be available in the vernacular to all English people. In this view Parr trod on delicate ground with the king, who in 1536 had allowed William Tyndale, author of the controversial English translation of the Bible (1525–1531), to be executed as a heretic. Though this idea and others, like her criticism of theological squabbling, reveal significant Erasmian influence upon the *Lamentation,* Parr also differs from Erasmus, most importantly in her view that goodness can be achieved only through justifying faith. The views and writing styles of Tyndale, Hugh Latimer, and Thomas Cranmer also influenced Parr. Parr's personalized synthesis of important Reformist ideas proved consistently popular throughout the century, and the *Lamentation* stands as a rare Tudor confessional work in a period when women wrote primarily translations.

While her writing remains a seminal part of the body of early Protestant devotional work, Catherine Parr's patronage of other writers was equally important. Throughout her tenure as queen from 1543 to 1547, Parr exerted her influence at court by supporting the careers of many important humanists. She saw to it that Cranmer and Latimer remained influential in spite of the conservatism of Henry's final years, and she advanced scholars such as Ascham, John Cheke, and William Grindall. Parr's most important legacy as a patron, though, was the English translation of Erasmus's *Paraphrases of the New Testament,* which she commissioned. While she was directly responsible only for the first volume (Anne Seymour, Duchess of Somerset, taking over the project of the second volume), the continuation of the Parr coat of arms on the second title page attests to her influence on the project as a whole. Parr engaged Nicolas Udall (best known as the playwright of the earliest known English comedy, *Ralph Roister Doister* [circa 1552]), Thomas Kay, and Princess Mary (later replaced by Francis Malet) as translators for the Gospels. In a dedicatory letter prefacing the Gospel of Saint Luke, Udall tells the queen that "by procuring the whole paraphrase of Erasmus to be diligently translated into English, [you] have minced it and made it ever English man's meat, though his stomach be never so weak and tender." The presence of the translation in every church, by Edward VI's royal decree, attests to the extent of its potential influence.

Parr's role in this project and the young king's affection for his devoted stepmother no doubt saved her from the disapproval of Edward Seymour, the earl of Hertford and lord protector, over her fourth and final marriage. Within a month of Henry's death on 28 January 1547, Thomas Seymour, made baron of Sudeley and lord high admiral when his brother was appointed protector, began to court her. They married sometime before 17 May 1548, receiving the reluctant approval of the young king and the lord protector only after the private wedding. Shortly after the couple settled at the palace which Catherine had inherited at Chelsea, Princess Elizabeth, then sixteen, came to live with them. Always concerned with the royal children's education, Catherine procured first Grindall and then Ascham as tutors for the princess. On 30 August, after a difficult pregnancy and labor, she gave birth to her first and only child, a daughter, at Sudeley Castle. Complications followed, and she grew delirious, accusing friends and family of having neglected her. She drew up her will on 5 September, and on 7 September she died. She was buried in Sudeley chapel, the first member of English royalty to be given a Protestant funeral, in a ceremony presided over by Miles Coverdale, the prominent minister who had been responsible for the first English translation (1535) of the whole Bible.

While she is lauded by Foxe as a Reformist, the predominant strain in all of Catherine Parr's work, both as queen, patroness, and author, is a desire to see the kingdom of England unified in its belief, free of the political and religious squabbles that characterized the court during her last ten years. She felt that the act of reading the Scriptures could

She felt that the act of reading the Scriptures could accomplish this goal; and like Erasmus, to whom her work is so clearly indebted, she believed that all believers should have access to the Word of God. The works she wrote, immensely popular in her time, are currently receiving renewed recognition, and the writers and scholars she encouraged produced some of the best examples of English humanist thought.

References:

Roland H. Bainton, *Women of the Reformation in France and England* (Minneapolis: Augsburg Publishing House, 1973), pp. 161–179;

Desiderius Erasmus, *The First Tome of the Paraphrases of the New Testament* (Delmar, N.Y.: Scholars Facsimiles & Reprints, 1975);

John Foxe, *Acts and Monuments,* volume 5 (London: Seeley, Burnside & Seeley, 1843–1849), pp. 553–561;

William P. Haugaard, "Katherine Parr: The Religious Convictions of a Renaissance Queen," *Renaissance Quarterly,* 22 (Winter 1969): 346–359;

Charles Fenno Hoffman, "Catherine Parr as a Woman of Letters," *Huntington Library Quarterly,* 23 (August 1960): 349–367;

Martin Hume, *The Wives of Henry the Eighth and the Parts They Played in History* (New York: Brentano's, 1926);

John N. King, "Patronage and Piety: The Influence of Catherine Parr," in *Silent but for the Word: Tudor Women as Patrons, Translators, and Writers of Religious Works,* edited by Margaret Patterson Hannay (Kent, Ohio: Kent State University Press, 1985), pp. 43–60;

Anthony Martienssen, *Queen Katherine Parr* (New York: McGraw-Hill, 1973);

James Kelsey McConica, *English Humanists and Reformation Politics under Henry VIII and Edward VI* (London: Oxford University Press, 1965);

Janel Mueller, "A Tudor Queen Finds Voice: Katherine Parr's *Lamentation of a Sinner,*" in *The Historical Renaissance: New Essays on Tudor and Stuart Literature and Culture,* edited by Heather Dubrow and Richard Strier (Chicago: University of Chicago Press, 1988), pp. 15–47;

Agnes Strickland, *Lives of the Queens of England,* volume 5 (Philadelphia: Blanchard & Lea, 1844), pp. 5–99.

Papers:

Most of the extant letters of Catherine Parr are either in the British Museum manuscript collection or among the holdings of the Public Record Office, London. Corpus Christi College, Cambridge, possesses several letters which she wrote in support of the university and individual scholars, while the remainder are scattered among a few private collections catalogued by the Historical Manuscripts Commission.

George Pettie

(circa 1548 – July 1589)

Juliet Fleming
University of Southern California

BOOK: *A Petite Pallace of Pettie His Pleasure; Contayning Many Pretie Histories* (London: Printed by Richard Watkins, 1576).

Editions: *The Court of Good Counsell. Wherein Is Set Downe the True Rules, How a Man Should Choose a Good Wife from a Bad, and a Woman a Good Husband from a Bad* (London: Printed by Ralph Blower, Sold by William Barley, 1607);

A Petite Pallace of Pettie His Pleasure, edited by Herbert Hartman (London & New York: Oxford University Press, 1938).

TRANSLATION: Stephano Guazzo, *The Civile Conuersation of M. Steeuen Guazzo Written First in Italian, and Nowe Translated out of French by George Pettie, Deuided into Foure Bookes* (London: Printed for Richard Watkins, 1581); enlarged as *The Civile Conversation of M. Stephen Guazzo . . . the fourth now translated out of Italian into English by Bartholomew Young* (London: Printed by Thomas East, 1586); edited by Edward Sullivan as *The Civile Conuersation of M. Steeven Guazzo: The First Three Books Translated by George Pettie, Anno 1581, and the Fourth by Barth. Young, Anno 1586,* 2 volumes (London: Constable, 1925; New York: Knopf, 1925).

According to his great-nephew Anthony à Wood, whose biographical sketch of George Pettie in *Athenae Oxonienses* (1691–1692) contains most of what is known about his life, Pettie was, in his time, "excellent for his passionate penning of amorous stories, equal for poetical invention with his dear friend William Gager, and as much commended for his neat stile as any of his time." By 1692, however, Pettie's work had worn so badly that Wood claimed to keep his copy of *A Petite Palace of Pettie His Pleasure* (1576) out of family sentiment: " 'Tis so far now from being excellent or fine, that it is more fit to be

Title page for George Pettie's book of twelve stories in which questions of love and marriage are debated

read by a schoolboy or rustical amoratto, than by a gentleman of mode or language." Centuries of critical neglect of *A Petite Palace* were disrupted by Friedrich Landmann's pronouncement in 1880 that the book anticipated, "to the minutest detail, all the specific elements of euphuism," and by Morris P. Tilley's elaboration in a 1926 study of John Lyly's

269

debt to Pettie. Since then criticism of Pettie's work has been concerned with this issue of influence and with his 1581 translation of Stephano Guazzo's *La Civil Conversatione* (1574). The importance of Pettie as an author who wrote specifically for women has been remarked on only recently.

Few details of Pettie's life are known. Born circa 1548, the fourth son of John and Mary Charnell Pettie, George Pettie was the child of a "gentle and ancient" Oxfordshire family, according to Wood. In 1564 Pettie became a scholar at Christ Church College, Oxford. After leaving Oxford in 1570 he served as a soldier in France and the Lowlands. He died in Plymouth in July 1589, "a captain and a man of note," according to Wood.

Pettie diversified his military career with writing and claimed that his first published work, *A Petite Palace,* made him as famous "as he which fired the Temple of Diana." Pettie's book – the title of which invokes William Painter's *Palace of Pleasure* (1566-1567) – had gone through six editions by 1613. It comprises twelve tales based on classical sources but "so transformed that they would often be unrecognizable but for the names. . . . Character and incidents, dialogue, soliloquies, letters are invented for romantic purposes," according to Douglas Bush. Each tale debates questions of love and marriage and ends with a tendentious summary of its action that seems designed to provoke Pettie's female readers into joining the discussion:

> Now I would wish you blazing stars which stand upon your chastity, to take light at this lot, to take heed by this harm, you see the husband slain, the ruffian fled, the lover poisoned, the wife dead, the friends comfortless, the children parentless. And can the preservation of one simple woman's chastity countervail all these confusions? Had not the loss of her chastity been less than of her life? . . . But it is naturally incident to women to enter into extremities.

A Petite Palace is prefaced by three letters that fictitiously describe how it came to press against the will of its author. In the first, "To the Gentle Gentlewoman Readers," one "R. B." recounts his role in the "faithless enterprise," claiming that he named the work after Painter's *Palace of Pleasure.* Having heard Pettie give the stories "in a manner *ex tempore*" on many "private occasions" and having learned that he had then written them down, R. B. apparently begged the manuscript from his friend, promising to keep it for private use. But fervent admiration for the opposite sex drove R. B. to "transgress the bounds of faithful friendship" and publish the stories for the "common profit and pleasure" of

readers "whom by my will I would have only gentlewomen."

This address to women, of which Pettie could have found an instance in Giovanni Boccaccio's *Decameron* (1349-1351), enjoyed a minor vogue during the English Renaissance. It informs, for example, the "prodigal" writings (those done while the writers were waiting for preferment at court) of Lyly, Barnabe Riche, Robert Greene, Thomas Lodge, Nicholas Breton, and Sir Philip Sidney. Pettie, whose text regularly and overtly addresses its female readers, is one of the earliest and most fully articulate proponents of literature for women in early modern England. *A Petite Palace* is, however, a storehouse of misogynist tropes and stereotypes put into dizzying play by an always unreliable narrator, and it ends with the story of Alexius, who saves his soul by abjuring the company of women forever. Pettie seems to provoke his female readers more than he charms them.

In the second prefatory letter – supposed to have accompanied the manuscript when Pettie confided it to his treacherous friend – Pettie asks R. B. to keep the manuscript secret because "divers discourses touch nearly divers of my near friends." The third letter is from the printer, who claims to know neither Pettie nor R. B. but to have been given the manuscript by a third party. Alarmed by the "too wanton" nature of the work, the printer then "gelded" it of "such matters as may seem offensive." Authorial disavowal of an intention to publish was not uncommon in the late sixteenth century; such a stance represents an attempt to circumvent the class derogation attached to print. But Pettie's second work, *The Civil Conversation,* maintains the fiction that his first was published without his permission. Here Pettie calls *A Petite Palace* "a trifling work (which by reason of the lightness of it, or at the least of the keeper of it, flew abroad before I knew of it)" and claims that he intends his translation to counterbalance the frivolity of his former work. He thus represents himself as following a "prodigal" career: one in the course of which the young university-trained humanist was forced to waste his talents writing fiction while he waited for preferment at Elizabeth I's court.

Entered in the Stationers' Register in November 1579 and first published by Richard Watkins in 1581, Pettie's *Civil Conversation* is dedicated to Lady Marjorie Norris, whom Elizabeth I nicknamed the "black crow" because of her dark complexion. Based on the 1579 French version by Gabriel Chappuys, Pettie's translation made available in English what was, after Baldassare Castiglione's *Il Libro*

THE CIVILE CON-
uerſation of M. Steeuen Guazzo
written firſt in Italian, and nowe tranſlated out of
French by George Pettie, *deuided into foure bookes.*

In the firſt is conteined in generall, the fruites that
may bee reaped by conuerſation, and teaching howe to knowe
good companie from yll.

In the ſecond, the manner of conuerſation, meete for
all perſons, which ſhall come in any companie, out of their owne
houſes, and then of the perticular points which ought to
bee obſerued in companie betwéene young men and olde,
Gentlemen and Yeomen, Princes and priuate perſons,
learned and vnlearned, Citizens and Stran-
gers, Religious and Secular, men & women.

In the third is perticularly ſet foorth the orders to bee obſerued in conuerſation within dores, betwéene the huſband
and the wife, the father and the ſonne, brother and bro-
ther, the Maiſter and the ſeruant.

In the fourth, the report of a banquet.

¶ *Jmprinted at London by*
Richard Watkins.
1581.

*Title page for Pettie's translation of a well-known Italian
conversation book*

del Cortegiano (1528; translated by Thomas Hoby as *The Courtyer,* 1561), "probably the best known Italian book in England," according to John Leon Lievsay. Pettie translated only the first three books of Guazzo's work, omitting the fourth (supplied in subsequent editions with a translation by Bartholomew Young) on the grounds that it had "much trifling matter in it," a claim that is more descriptive of Pettie's new seriousness than of Guazzo's text. In spite of a tendency toward local expansion and decoration – exemplified by a recurrent use of doublets, some occasional pro-Protestant modifications of religious debate, and the incongruous addition of a two-page eulogy of the excommunicated Queen Elizabeth – Pettie's translation has been sufficiently respected to remain the standard English version of Guazzo's work.

Written as a dialogue, the work defines civil conversation as "an honest, commendable, and virtuous kind of living in the world." Two interlocutors discuss the evils of solitude, the selection of company, the cultivation of the intellect, the role of religion in a state, and the conduct of a variety of social and political relations. Book 3 – selected portions of which were reprinted with minor changes as *The Court of Good Counsel* (1607) – discusses "domestical" conversation: relations between men and women, parents and children, and masters and servants. Guazzo, who opposes wife beating, has been given credit as an early feminist, but *Civil Conversation* is still conducted from the perspective (and in the interest) of a wealthy male citizen who is advised to keep "conversation" with women to a bare minimum.

In his preface to the translation Pettie advances a defense of English, undertaking to write in it "as copiously for variety, as compendiously for brevity, as choicely for words, as pithily for sentences, as pleasantly for figures, and every way as eloquently, as any writer." It has been suggested that in *A Petite Palace* Pettie develops the style that is named after Lyly's *Euphues* (1579) and has historically been credited to Lyly. Euphuism is a prose style in which antithetical ideas are expressed and weighed in balanced clauses, pointed by alliteration and assonance, as seen in this passage from *A Petite Palace:* "And so much the less I like this lot, by how much the less I looked for it, and so much the more sour it is, by how much the more sudden it is." Its tropes include proverbs, exempla, sententiae, rhetorical questions, and similes drawn from myth and an exotic and largely invented natural history.

The search for the origin of euphuism has halted before a realization that the style represents the accretion of a variety of prose mannerisms with widely scattered antecedents. Janel Meuller, following Jacobus Schwart, has convincingly argued, however, that while Pettie's writing mobilizes all the formal features of euphuism, he does not use surface symmetries to construct the opaque and enigmatic effect associated with Lyly's style. Perhaps, then, Pettie's future critical reputation rests on the pointed address of *A Petite Palace* to women as the readers of English literature.

References:

Douglas Bush, "The Petite Pallace of Pleasure," *Journal of English & Germanic Philology*, 27 (1928): 162–169;

Juliet Fleming, "George Pettie, Barnaby Rich, and Delights for Women 'Only,'" in *Sexuality and Gender in Early Modern Europe*, edited by James Grantham Turner (Cambridge: Cambridge University Press, 1993);

Richard Helgerson, *The Elizabethan Prodigals* (Berkeley: University of California Press, 1976);

Friedrich Landmann, "Shakespeare and Euphuism," *New Shakespeare Society Transactions*, part 2 (1880–1885): 241–276;

John Leon Lievsay, *Stephano Guazzo and the English Renaissance, 1575–1675* (Chapel Hill: University of North Carolina Press, 1961);

Caroline Lucas, "George Pettie and the Premature Closure of the Text," in her *Writing for Women: The Example of Woman as Reader in Elizabethan Romance* (Philadelphia: Open University Press, 1989), pp. 52–73;

Janel Meuller, "Manner and Modality: Euphuizing in Pettie and Lyly," in her *Native Tongue and the Word: Developments in English Prose Style, 1380–1580* (Chicago: University of Chicago Press, 1984), pp. 372–383;

Jacobus Schwart, "Lyly and Pettie," *English Studies*, 23 (1941): 9–19;

Morris P. Tilley, *Elizabethan Proverb Lore in Lyly's "Euphues" and in Pettie's "Petite Pallace," with Parallels from Shakespeare*, University of Michigan Publications in Language and Literature, no. 2 (New York: Macmillan, 1926);

Anthony à Wood, *Athenae Oxonienses*, volume 1, edited by Philip Bliss (London: F. C. & J. Rivington, 1813), cols. 552–555.

Papers:

George Pettie's will is at Somerset House, London.

Richard Rainolde

(circa 1530 – December 1606)

Michael McClintock
University of Toronto

BOOKS: *A Booke Called the Foundacion of Rhetorike, Because All Other Partes of Rhetorike Are Grounded Thereupon, Every Parte Sette Forthe in an Oracion upon Questions, Verie Profitable to bee Knownen and Redde* . . . (London: Printed by John Kingston, 1563);

A Chronicle of All the Noble Emperours of the Romaines, from Iulius Caesar, Orderly to . . . *Emperour Maximilian, that Now Gouerneth, with the Great Warres' of Iulius Caesar* . . . (London: Printed by Thomas Marshe, 1571).

Editions: *The Foundacion of Rhetorike,* edited, with an introduction, by Francis R. Johnson (New York: Scholars' Facsimiles & Reprints, 1945);

The Foundacion of Rhetorike (Amsterdam: Theatrum Orbis Terrarum / New York: Da Capo Press, 1969);

The Foundation of Rhetoric, 1563 (Menston, U.K.: Scolar Press, 1972).

Richard Rainolde's literary career was concentrated in roughly one decade, the 1560s, during which he produced three substantial works on rhetoric, history, and political theory. While his rhetorical treatise, *The Foundation of Rhetoric* (1563), has received the most attention, his literary output as a whole is of interest for the ways in which it reflects both his life and the dominant concerns of the decade in which it was created: his writings display a humanist's concern with active applications of learning, a nationalist's concern with political order and stability, and a Protestant's concern with the dangers of Catholicism. No matter what the subject, Rainolde saw his work as vitally important, convinced that it could play a practical role in promoting the well-being of the commonwealth. All three of his treatises emphasize the need for political order and stress "the duty of a subject, the worthy state of nobility, the pre-eminent dignity and majesty of a prince, the office of counsellors (worthy [of] chief veneration)," according to *The Foundation of Rhetoric.* The ambitious dedications of these works to Elizabeth's most powerful courtiers can be seen as attempts by Rainolde to gain an office in which he could apply his learning for the commonwealth's benefit.

Rainolde was born in Essex, most likely in the early years of the 1530s; the precise location and date of his birth are unknown. He entered Saint John's College, Cambridge, in 1546 as a sizar, but a year later he was a scholar on the Lady Margaret Foundation. At some point in 1548 he transferred to the newly founded (1546) Trinity College, from which he received his B.A. in 1550; he was a fellow of Trinity in 1551, and his M.A. was conferred in 1553. The Protestant-humanist education Rainolde received at Cambridge might explain the lack of any accounts of him during the reign of Mary I (1553–1558) as well as his subsequent zeal for political stability and the Protestant faith during the first decade of Elizabeth I's rule.

Rainolde's most important work is *The Foundation of Rhetoric,* the first English example of a so-called formulary rhetoric, which instructs by formula and example. The work is based on the fourth-century *Progymnasmata* of Aphthonius and in particular on Reinhard Lorich's often-reprinted 1542 Latin edition of Aphthonius's Greek text. Lorich's work was one of the most popular school textbooks during the Renaissance. Rainolde's book is not simply a translation of Lorich's but rather a loose adaptation that alters much of Lorich's material and incorporates many of Rainolde's own passages.

Progymnasmata, or preliminary exercises, were a common feature of Tudor grammar-school education, and Aphthonius was prescribed in the statutes of several sixteenth-century schools. The *progymnasmata*'s place in the curriculum was between the study of grammar and the study of rhetoric. These exercises allowed students to apply the knowledge that they had gained from their study of the poets; at the same time, the *progymnasmata* laid the foundation for students' study of full-fledged orations.

Each exercise is in effect a miniature oration, in which a given theme is developed and organized according to the pattern provided. The aim of Rainolde's exercises was not concision but rather development of the copious, expansive style favored by humanist educators.

While the first *progymnasmata* – written by Theon (circa A.D. 100) and Hermogenes (circa A.D. 200) – merely provide the rules for each exercise, both Lorich and Rainolde follow Aphthonius by adding samples of fully developed themes. The fourteen topics of the *progymnasmata* gradually increased in difficulty, building on the skills learned in the preceding ones. The first orations developed the ability to expand a narrative, while later ones concentrated on argumentative skills and evaluation. Students were asked to impersonate historical and fictional figures in their compositions and to create pictorially vivid descriptions of events. The final exercises moved into the realm of deliberative rhetoric, examining questions and hypothetical laws from opposing perspectives. By the time the students had worked their way through the *progymnasmata,* they had built up a repertoire of narrative devices that they could call on in their own compositions. While such formulaic learning might seem to restrict creativity unduly, "the justification for such exercises is that they provided a framework within which a student could develop his own individuality," according to Brian Vickers's *In Defence of Rhetoric* (1988). Nearly all sixteenth-century authors learned their basic composition skills from the *progymnasmata.*

Rainolde's contributions to *The Foundation of Rhetoric* are notable for their insistent political concern. For Rainolde, the true virtue of rhetoric lies in its political effectiveness. He imagines orators as eloquent statesmen with the ability to "draw unto them the hearts of a multitude, to pluck down and extirpate affections and perturbations of the people, to move pity and compassion, to speak before princes and rulers, and to persuade them in good causes and enterprises, to animate and incense them to godly affairs and business, to alter the counsel of kings, by their wisdom and eloquence, to a better state." He applies this theory in his treatise by drawing out the political implication of whatever theme he is developing. For example, in his first exercise, the Fable, Rainolde glosses the fable of the shepherds and the wolves with the expected moral: beware of feigned friendship. He then, however, goes on to expand the fable into a political allegory in which the wolves stand for foreign and domestic threats to the commonwealth and the shepherds represent

Title page for Rainolde's best-known work, the first English rhetorical treatise to instruct its readers by formula and example

the monarch and the royal counselors who keep these threats in check:

> So of like sort it always chanceth, tyrants and bloody men do seek always a means and practice policies to destroy all such as are godly affected. . . . For by cruelty their wolfish natures are known; their glory, strength, kingdom, and renown cometh of blood, of murders, and beastly dealings. . . . The state of everyone universally would come to perdition, if the invasion of foreign princes, by the wisdom and policy of counsellors, were not repelled. The horrible acts of wicked men would burst out, and a confusion ensue in all states, if the wisdom of politic governors, if good laws, if the power and sword of the magistrate, could not take place. The peers and nobles, with the chief governor, standeth as shepherds over the people.

Similar political applications appear in other exercises as Rainolde seizes nearly every opportunity to stress the importance of social order.

The choice of *The Foundation of Rhetoric* for a title indicates not only the educational status of the *progymnasmata* as preparation for rhetoric but also connects the work to the tradition of English rhetorics inaugurated by Thomas Wilson's *Art of Rhetoric* (1553). Rainolde shares with Wilson the belief that the English language is capable of producing eloquent expression and sees Wilson's work as a necessary vernacular precursor to *The Foundation of Rhetoric*: "Though in [a] few years past, a learned work of rhetoric [was] compiled and made in the English tongue, of one who floweth in all excellency of art, who in judgement is profound, in wisdom and eloquence most famous," but "as yet the very ground of rhetoric is not heretofore entreated of, as concerning these exercises." Rainolde may have hoped that the popularity of Wilson's work would ensure a large readership for his own. In 1563 *The Art of Rhetoric* was reprinted for the fourth time by John Kingston, who in that same year also published *The Foundation of Rhetoric*. But, for whatever reasons, Rainolde's rhetoric did not match the popularity of Wilson's.

Rainolde's treatise, however, did not go unnoticed. In 1568 William Fulwood published *The Enemy of Idleness: Teaching the Manner and Style How to Indite, Compose, and Write All Sorts of Epistles and Letters,* a formulary work similar to *The Foundation of Rhetoric* that sets out epistolary patterns and examples. In a discussion of style Fulwood suggests that "whoso will more circumspectly and narrowly entreat of such matters let them read the Rhetoric of Master Doctor [Thomas] Wilson, or of Master Richard Rainolde." In 1579 John Jones enlisted a different aspect of Rainolde's rhetoric to bolster the argument of his *Art and Science of Preserving Body and Soul in Health, Wisdom, and Catholic Religion.* In chapter 12 Jones attacks a communal religious sect, the Family of Love, deploring its disregard of authority and social hierarchy. Many of the points he makes in favor of social divisions and a strong monarchy recall Rainolde's arguments, and Rainolde is invoked approvingly at one point when Jones recommends that "we mark but the use of our own [bodies'] parts, the pattern of all laws, regiment, and unity, as Mr. Rainolde well noteth in his *Foundation of Rhetoric.*" So although Rainolde's book was not reprinted, both its rhetoric and its politics had some impact on his contemporaries.

Rainolde's concern with political order and stability marks his other two works as well. *A Chronicle of All the Noble Emperors of the Romans* was entered in the Stationers' Register between June 1566 and July 1567 and was published in 1571. The work, which may derive in part from Pedro Mexia's *Historia Imerial y Cesárea* (History of the Emperors and Caesars, 1545), presents moralized histories, arranged chronologically, of the reigns of all the Roman emperors from Julius Caesar to the Holy Roman emperor Ferdinand I, the predecessor of the then-reigning emperor, Maximilian II. Rainolde's moral approach to history makes the past the record of God's justice, showing the triumphs of good over evil: "In this history . . . I do set forth the great providence of God in preserving commonwealths, in raising and exalting to government godly princes, in throwing down tyrants, rebels, and all maintainers of rebellion, how God by his mighty hand overthroweth the persecutors of his church, and all devilish practices: the devil hath his limits and bonds appointed which he shall not pass." Although the *Chronicle* is a history of the Roman emperors, Rainolde repeatedly draws parallels between Roman and English history, using the English chronicles for examples of virtuous and tyrannical rulers and at other times using the past as an exhortation to cherish Elizabeth I's rule and to abhor rebellion.

At some point during the 1560s Rainolde produced a Latin manuscript, "De statu Nobilium Virorum et Principum" (The Condition of Noblemen and Rulers). This work, which is probably in Rainolde's hand, allowed him to focus all his attention on the political concerns that appear as subthemes in his other two works. His treatise celebrates monarchy in general, and Elizabeth I's reign in particular, and counterbalances this with attacks on the pope and Roman Catholicism. Rainolde also devotes a chapter to the topical questions of Elizabeth I's marriage and her successor. The dedication of the work to Thomas Howard, fourth Duke of Norfolk, may put the date of its composition around 1566, at which time Norfolk was working in conjunction with Parliament to persuade Elizabeth to resolve the succession issue.

As the dedication to Norfolk shows, Rainolde was always ambitious when seeking a patron for his writings. All his works are dedicated to some of the most powerful people in England short of Queen Elizabeth: *The Foundation of Rhetoric* is dedicated to Robert Dudley (later first earl of Leicester), Elizabeth's favorite; while the *Chronicle* is dedicated to William Cecil, Lord Burghley, Elizabeth I's secretary of state and chief administrator. Norfolk was the first peer of the realm, one of Elizabeth I's privy councillors, and the head of the large and powerful Howard family. However, there is no evidence to suggest that Rainolde knew any of these men. In fact, he turns unfamiliarity into a virtue in his dedication to Dudley: "Whoso is adorned with nobility and virtue, of necessity nobility and virtue will move and allure them to favor and support virtue in any other; yea, as Tully the most famous orator doth say, even to love those whom we never saw, but by good fame and bruit beautified to us." Despite these efforts Rainolde's dedications failed to assist him in any way.

With his literary ambitions frustrated, Rainolde eventually settled for a career in the church. In the decade that he produced his writings he also studied toward a degree in medicine. In 1567 he received permission to go through the final steps needed for the degree and anticipated its completion, signing himself "Doctor in Physic" in the *Chronicle*. But instead of completing the degree, he went to Russia for a short time with testimonial letters from Cambridge University. After his return he became rector of Stapleford-Abbots, Essex, in 1568, and a year later he became rector of Lambourne, Essex, as well. In 1571, the year the *Chronicle* was published, the College of Physicians found Rainolde unlearned. He confessed that he had been practicing medicine for two years, and the college ordered his imprisonment until he paid a twenty-pound fine. Between 1578 and 1584 he was also the vicar of West Thurrock, Essex. In 1579 John Aylmer, bishop of London, summoned him to answer an unspecified charge. Instead of complying, however, Rainolde and the constable of Stapleford-Abbots assaulted the process server and were committed to the Marshalsea prison. He petitioned the Privy Council for a pardon later that year. After this the only surviving records of Rainolde's activities involve his performance of routine ecclesiastical duties in Lambourne. He died in December 1606.

While Rainolde remains one of the more minor figures of the English Renaissance, his *Foundation of Rhetoric* continues to attract occasional attention. Interest in sixteenth-century theories of composition has led some critics to consider the connection between *progymnasmata* such as *The Foundation of Rhetoric* and various types of literature. His other two works remain virtually untreated: the re-lationship between English and Roman history in the *Chronicle* has been briefly considered, while the manuscript treatise still awaits critical examination.

References:

Donald Lemen Clark, "The Rise and Fall of Progymnasmata in Sixteenth and Seventeenth Century Grammar Schools," *Speech Monographs,* 19, no. 4 (1952): 259–263;

William G. Crane, *Wit and Rhetoric in the Renaissance: The Formal Basis of Elizabethan Prose Style* (New York: Columbia University Press, 1937);

Paul Dean, "Contemporary English History in Elizabethan Roman Histories," *Notes and Queries,* new series 33 (1986): 312–316;

Wilbur S. Howell, *Logic and Rhetoric in England, 1500–1700* (Princeton: Princeton University Press, 1956);

Arthur F. Kinney, *Humanist Poetics: Thought, Rhetoric, and Fiction in Sixteenth-Century England* (Amherst: University of Massachusetts Press, 1986);

Kinney, "Rhetoric and Fiction in Elizabethan England," in *Renaissance Eloquence: Studies in the Theory and Practice of Renaissance Rhetoric,* edited by James J. Murphy (Berkeley: University of California Press, 1983), pp. 386–388;

Wallace MacCaffrey, *The Shaping of the Elizabethan Regime* (Princeton: Princeton University Press, 1968);

Eleanor Rosenberg, *Leicester: Patron of Letters* (New York: Columbia University Press, 1955);

Marion Trousdale, *Shakespeare and the Rhetoricians* (Chapel Hill: University of North Carolina Press, 1982);

Brian Vickers, *In Defence of Rhetoric* (Oxford: Clarendon Press, 1988).

Papers:
Richard Rainolde's manuscript "De statu Nobilium Virorum et Principum" (Harleian MS. 973) is in the British Library, London.

John Rastell

(1475? – 20 April 1536)

Peter C. Herman
Georgia State University

BOOKS: *A New Interlude and a Mery of the Nature of the .iiii. Elements,* anonymous (N.p., n.d. [London: Printed by Rastell, 1520?]);

Expositiones terminorum legum anglorum, attributed to Rastell (N.p., n.d. [London: Printed by Rastell, circa 1523]); translated by Rastell as *The Exposicions of the Termes of the Lawes of England, with Diuers Rules. Whereunto Are Added the Olde Tenures* (London: Printed by Richard Tottel, 1563);

A New Comodye in Englysh in Maner of an Enterlude Wherein is Dyscrybyd as Well the Bewte & Good Propertes of Women as Theyr Vycys (London: Printed by Rastell, [circa 1525]);

Of Gentylnes & Nobylyte a Dialoge, anonymous (London: Printed by Rastell, [circa 1525]);

The Pastyme of People (N.p., n.d. [London: Printed by Rastell, 1530?]);

A New Boke of Purgatory Whiche Is a Dyaloge Betwene Comyngo & Gyngemyn (London: Printed by Rastell, 1530).

Editions: *The Pastime of People,* edited by Thomas F. Dibdin (London: Printed for F. C. and J. Rivington, 1811);

Three Rastell Plays: Four Elements, Calisto and Melebea, Gentleness and Nobility, edited by Richard Axton (Cambridge: D. S. Brewer; Totawa, N. J.: Rowman & Littlefield, 1979);

The Pastyme of People and a New Boke of Purgatory, edited by Albert J. Geritz (New York: Garland, 1985).

John Rastell belongs to the circle of humanists which flourished during the first decades of Henry VIII's reign. Because he was the brother-in-law of Sir Thomas More, the father of William Rastell (the first editor of More's collected English works), the father-in-law of Thomas Heywood, and the great-grandfather of John Donne, his family connections alone earn him a place in Renaissance studies. But his importance also stems from his authorship of several interesting prose works, dramatic interludes, and legal texts, as well as his significant contributions to the development of printing, especially the printing of music. Furthermore, Rastell participated in religious controversies, acted as a government lawyer, helped design political spectacles, made an early attempt to colonize the New World, and designed the first permanent theater in England. His energy and incredibly wide range of achievements give his life a paradigmatically Renaissance quality, and his two prose works, *The Pastime of People* (1530?) and *A New Book of Purgatory* (1530), display an almost avant-garde willingness to question convention.

John Rastell was born into a politically prominent family in Coventry, probably in 1475. His early years are obscure, although he may have studied at Oxford. Afterward, he spent several years in London reading law as a member of the Middle Temple, where he probably met More, who was then studying law at Lincoln's Inn. After completing his studies, Rastell returned home to take up a legal practice established by his father and grandfather. He married Elizabeth More, Thomas More's sister, fathered three children (William, John, and Joan), took part in local politics, and generally prospered.

In 1510, for reasons that remain unclear but probably involved the decline in Coventry's economy, his increasing ambitions, and his increasing involvement with More and his circle, Rastell moved himself and his family to London. He found a patron in Sir Edward Belknap, Privy Councillor to both Henry VII and Henry VIII. Belknap employed him as an overseer for various building projects, which might seem like an odd way to use a lawyer, but Rastell was nothing if not versatile. In 1515

One of the devices Rastell used in his books

Belknap secured for him the lands, tenants, and wealth of Richard Hunne, a London tailor imprisoned for refusing to pay a mortuary tax to the clergy upon the death of his son, and who was later found hanging in his cell. The authorities, including More, alleged suicide; many others alleged murder. The affair caused widespread controversy, and Rastell had to fight constant legal battles to keep his wealth.

The year 1510 also marks Rastell's entry into the fledgling publishing industry. Again his motivation remains cloudy, especially since a small market did not yet promise much return. Perhaps he recognized the possibilities of rising profits and wanted to establish himself before others did. Or, fired by the idealist humanist notion that education would solve everyone's problems, he might have regarded printing useful books as a means of profiting the masses as well. Whatever spurred him on, between 1510 and 1529 Rastell published a stream of legal, religious, and literary works, including More's opening salvo against Lutheranism, *A Dialogue . . . of the Veneration & Worship of Images* (1529).

In addition to printing, Rastell busied himself with many other schemes. In 1517 he sailed for the New World, planning to establish there the first English colony. However, the crew mutinied and left him stranded in Ireland, where, never at a loss for developing projects, he composed his interlude, *The Nature of the Four Elements* (1520). In 1520 Rastell transferred his energies to the design of public pageants. His patron, Belknap, employed him to construct and paint the roofs of the banquet hall for the Field of the Cloth of Gold, the setting of the extravagantly chivalric meeting between King Henry VIII and King Francis I of France in June 1520. The result of Rastell's commission is described in the state papers as "curiously garnished under with knots and batons gilt and other devices." His work must have been well received because in 1522 he was asked to design a pageant for the visit of the Holy Roman Emperor Charles V. His most significant contribution to the development of English drama, however, may be his building of the first permanent stage in Tudor England sometime between 1524 and 1529. Though an important precedent, the stage was probably a simple covered platform. Costumes were Rastell's greatest expense, and, always the entrepreneur, he rented them out for other performances, the price being determined by the season.

Rastell's third major interest, which he pursued alongside printing and dramatic writing, was his political career. Precisely when he entered government service remains unknown, but in August 1523 he was in France, digging trenches for Henry VIII's wars under the leadership of Charles Brandon, Duke of Suffolk. By the mid 1520s his career took a more administrative turn. Under Thomas Cardinal Wolsey's chancellorship the government employed Rastell to check whether bills were worthy of royal consideration, and he served as a member of a commission to determine the status of foreigners in the London business world. In 1529 he was elected to the Reformation Parliament which effected the break with Rome; and between 1529 and 1530 he spent six months in France, probably trying to drum up support for Henry's divorce.

Although Rastell's amazingly varied career may appear to have no unifying theme, in fact the common denominator for his many activities is the humanist emphasis on applying learning to practical uses. He clearly used his printing press as an instrument of self-aggrandizement but also to publish works that he thought would benefit the commonwealth. And although he did not rise to the same heights as his more illustrious brother-in-law, he evidently took very seriously More's advice to Hythlodaeus in the *Utopia* (1516) and tried to serve the state as best he could. If he could make a profit while helping others, so much the better.

Somehow, in the midst of all his projects, Rastell managed to carve out time for a fourth venture that neatly, if problematically, combined humanism, civic service, and commerce: the writing of a popular history, *The Pastime of People,* which he brought out around 1530. *The Pastime of People* recounts the history of England from its mythological origins through the Roman and Anglo-Saxon periods and concludes with the death of Richard III. Rastell recounts the history of the rest of Europe (especially France, the empire, and the papacy), although he primarily focuses on England. As an added attraction, he included some fairly crude woodcuts of English monarchs. Interestingly, the layout indicates Rastell's willingness to experiment with typographical arrangement. Instead of separating the various national histories into discrete sections, Rastell arranges them in parallel columns on each page so that the reader can tell at a glance the state of Europe in any given year. Thus chronology is the basis of the book's organization rather than geographic or political criteria.

Rastell's treatment of his sources in *The Pastime of People* strongly indicates his humanist sensibility. Throughout the work he summarizes large portions of Robert Fabyan's *Chronicle* (1516), and he also relies on standard Roman and medieval texts: those of Julius Caesar, Bede, Brut, and Geoffrey of Monmouth as well as Ralph Higden's *Polychronicon.* He does not, however, merely repeat his sources without attribution or accept them blindly, for he acquired from his humanist friends a healthy dose of skepticism and an awareness of anachronism. For example, Rastell has little patience with the legendary accounts of England's being inhabited before the coming of Brutus by a race of giants engendered by the Devil. Rastell points out that no other writers corroborate them and, more important, they make no sense at all: "And I marvel in my mind that men having any good natural reason will to such a thing give credence, for no man can tell who is the author of this story, nor of whom it should come, nor of any writer of name in this land that ever wrote thereof, nor also we read in no histories of any other country of any such king ... And also it standeth neither with good faith or reason that the Devil should by such manner engender with women, which if the Devil had such power, then why should he not now have like power at this day, whereof nowadays we see no such generation, and also if the Devil had such power I see not why those children so gendered should be giants ... But yet other writers of histories there be which claim that this land was first called Albion by reason of the white cliffs and rocks at Dover." Rastell frequently gives several different accounts of the same event, prefacing each opinion with "some say that" or "diverse men think that."

Although Rastell may have shared the humanist sense that one can never recover the past in its entirety, that, as William Shakespeare writes in Sonnet 12, something always gets lost "in the wastes of time," *The Pastime of People* implies that he may not have agreed entirely with the humanist concept of history's function of instilling virtue and promoting goodness. Nor may he have subscribed entirely to the court-sponsored appropriation of history as a political tool for shoring up the slender claims of the Tudors to the throne. Unlike most other Tudor histories, such as Edward Hall's *Union of the Two Noble ... Families of Lancaster and York* (1548) and Polydore Vergil's *Anglicae Historiae* (1534), Rastell's does not begin by trum-

Title page for Rastell's popular history of England, from its mythical origins through the death of Richard III

peting history's purpose as an agent of fame or touting the moral benefits of reading about the past. Instead he launches into his narrative without any theoretical prelude. God is noticeably absent in the text. Rastell makes no attempt to moralize his story, to show that good kings are rewarded and bad kings punished. Instead he presents his reader with an unending procession of violence, betrayals, and usurpations that are punished, if at all, by more violence, betrayals, and usurpations.

Nor does Rastell endorse a providentialist theory of history that casts the destruction of monarchs as an offense against God and the state. Take as an example the deposition of King Richard II. According to the Tudor myth propagated by Henry VII's court historians – Vergil, Hall, and Raphael Holinshed – this act brought down God's judgment upon England in the form of the Wars of the Roses and ultimately the "bottled spider," King Richard III. Rastell, however, merely relates that

while King Richard II was in Ireland, the exiled Henry Bolingbroke landed at Ravenspur and "with that much people resorted unto him." Unlike others writing history during the early Tudor period, he makes no mention of divine retribution for usurping the Crown from an anointed monarch or blaming this crime for the Wars of the Roses. Henry IV's reign may have been filled with bloody rebellions, but no more so than those of most of the other kings , including Richard III.

Moreover, Rastell implicity calls the glorification of Henry VII into question by casting the marriage between the white rose of York and the red rose of Lancaster as a tawdry political bribe: "Also in the second year of King Richard divers and many gentlemen went over the sea unto the Earl of Richmond, then being in France, and covenanted with him that if he would marry Elizabeth, the eldest daughter to King Edward IV, that then they would aim him to be the king of England." Note that Rastell says nothing about concluding the Wars of the Roses, let alone Henry VII's bringing to a close God's punishment upon England for Henry Bolingbroke's usurpation and murder of Richard II.

In sum, even though Rastell wholeheartedly served Henry VII and worked hard at promoting the king's interests, his *Pastime of People* participates in neither the humanist moralization of history nor in the promotion of the Tudor mythology. He does not overtly deny the version of history being encouraged by the Tudor monarchs, but neither does he overtly endorse it. Given the politicization of history writing during the reigns of both Henry VII and Henry VIII, Rastell's refusal to join openly in the chorus is highly unusual and suggests a more original sensibility than most critics have allowed him.

The independence of mind that Rastell shows in *The Pastime of People* also crops up in his next prose work, *A New Book of Purgatory*, which marks his entry into the dangerous world of religious polemics, an involvement that would ultimately lead to his disgrace and death. In 1529 the Reformer Simon Fish published a satire on purgatory called *The Supplication for the Beggars*, and More responded a few months later with a polemic of his own, *The Supplication of Souls*. Why Rastell chose to enter the debate with his own defense of purgatory, no one knows. His relations with More were strained at this point, so he might have intended the book to help strengthen their friendship. Or he might have seen this one as more opportunity to make himself invaluable to the government. Or he may have just liked controversy.

Whatever the motivation, *A New Book of Purgatory* is in many ways a singular text. It consists of three dialogues between a Turk named Gyngemen and a German, Comyngo, who may or may not represent the "new variance in Christendom." The first dialogue "showeth and treateth of the marvelous existence of God," the second "treateth of the immortality of man's soul," and the third "treateth of Purgatory." Rastell's text, however, is no dry compendium of theological argumentation; instead *A New Book of Purgatory* partakes of the same seriocomic ethos that permeates More's *Utopia,* evincing the same sense of playfulness, of tolerance for multiple perspectives, and of irony.

Perhaps echoing the beginning of *Utopia,* Rastell presents himself as a man of affairs whose business brings him to a "great city" where representatives from all the nations of Christendom and Islam gather: "And because of interchanging of merchandises, the said merchants do daily meet together in divers places within the same city, and when they have talked together of things concerning their own business, yet for a recreation among themselves, they be desirous each of other to know news and strange things of other countries." The author witnesses their debate, which he reports, "so well pleased me that immediately after that I took pen and ink and titled it in writing and reported every argument and reason as nigh as my wit and remembrance would serve me." Despite the debate's polemical aim, however, Rastell turns this encounter into an argument for religious toleration between competing religions. First Gyngemen suggests, and Comyngo agrees, to conduct their debate relying solely upon reason and without recourse to any outside texts, including the "Alcoran" and the Bible. In addition to suggesting Rastell's faith in the universality of reason, this ground rule establishes an acceptance of cultural difference without insisting upon Christianity's superiority to Islam:

Gyngemen. For thou mayest well know it will be but a thing in vain to allege such texts or authorities to me, for that I and all other Turks of our laws and sect will utterly deny many of the principles and many of the texts and authorities of thy Christian belief and faith.

Comyngo. Because thou sayest so I shall not trouble thee with alleging of any such texts and authorities of our faith or law. And therefore I pray thee likewise use the same manner unto me.

Furthermore, Rastell even allows the Islamic Gyngemen to understand divine matters better than the German Comyngo. In a fascinating reversal of expectations. Gyngemen not only gets all the good lines in this dialogue, he also gets all the true ones. In this way Rastell's antiheretical dialogue tests the limits of humanist "thought experiments," for in the process of supporting one aspect of Catholic dogma, he implicitly destabilizes his religion's claim to be the sole fountain of truth.

A New Book of Purgatory, doubtless much to Rastell's dismay, received little notice until the Cambridge Reformer John Frith refuted it, along with the views of More and Bishop John Fisher, in *A Disputation of Purgatory* (1533). Rastell then responded to Frith's attack (More and Fisher ignored it) with a further book on Purgatory that has been lost, and he may have spoken personally with his antagonist. Frith, by now imprisoned in the Tower, answered with *Another Book against Rastell Named the Subsidy or Bulwark to His First Book made by John Frith, Prisoner in the Tower* (1533). However, as John Foxe reports in his *Acts and Monuments* (1563), this quarrel differed from the usually interminable feuds of contemporary pamphlet writers, in that Frith actually succeeded in convincing his opponent of the error of his ways: Rastell converted to Protestantism.

At first Rastell's newfound religion was advantageous since it followed the government's bent. He found a patron in Thomas Cromwell, who regularly commissioned him to do administrative work; and by 1534 Rastell reached the height of his success, when Cromwell appointed him and one Roland Lee, bishop of Lichfield and Coventry, to crush a rebellion in Wales. The same year, however, he suffered a financial crisis, lost his house in Monken Hadley, and embroiled himself in a series of lawsuits. Perhaps thinking that a return to printing would help his balance sheet, Rastell proposed a variety of schemes, including a book on how religious laws affected the courts and a book of prayers in English, but neither project went beyond the planning stage. Rastell's final schemes show that he had become a radical Reformer, and in 1535 he attempted to convert the monks of London's Charterhouse, much to their amusement.

Rastell's Protestantism, unfortunately, also led to his downfall. One year after Henry executed More for refusing to grant the king's supremacy in religious affairs, the government threw Rastell into the Tower for refusing to pay tithes and for arguing that the clergy should live on free offerings, not tithes — a position more radical than the government's and a deeply ironic one, given the source of Rastell's much-contested wealth. Rastell was tried by Archbishop Thomas Cranmer, who tired very quickly of the prisoner's obstinancy. Rastell had no more success with Cranmer than he had with Frith, although with different consequences. He died of natural causes in 1536, defeated and imprisoned.

Rastell clearly belongs to the second rank of English writers; indeed, his once-antagonist and later-spiritual-ally John Frith once commented rather acidly that "the beams of his brains be nothing so radiant" as More's. But even if he lacked More's brilliance and even if his works never quite live up to their promise, Rastell's life is emblematic of the intellectual ferment stirred up by humanism in England, and his writings show how humanism could encourage its adherents to question conventions, to expand their literary and intellectual horizons.

Significant work has been done on Rastell's dramatic output, yet critics have almost entirely ignored his prose works. This neglect is partly due to a general marginalization in Renaissance studies of pre-Elizabethan Renaissance literature, but there are also causes related specifically to the nature of Rastell's work. Rastell's amazingly varied career and interests recently led the influential scholar Richard Marius to dismiss him as "bizarre and unstable." Also Rastell studies have suffered from a paucity of reliable editions. No modern edition existed of *A New Book of Purgatory* until 1985, and before that date the only edition of *The Pastime of People,* from the nineteenth century, is of limited use because the editor replaced the original typographical schema with a conventional arrangement. Both of these works are now available in a reliable edition, however, making possible a reevaluation of Rastell's

contributions to English humanism, Reformation polemics, and English historiography.

Bibliography:
Albert J. Geritz, "Recent Studies in John Rastell," *English Literary Renaissance,* 8 (Autumn 1978); 341–350.

References:

William A. Clebsch, *England's Earliest Protestants* (New Haven: Yale University Press, 1964);

Arthur Geoffrey Dickens, *The English Reformation* (London: Batsford, 1964);

Albert J. Geritz and Amos Lee Lane, *John Rastell* (Boston: G. K. Hall, 1983);

Fred Jacob Levy, *Tudor Historical Thought* (San Marino, Cal.: Huntington Library, 1967);

Richard Marius, *Thomas More* (New York: Knopf, 1984), p. 7;

James McConica, *English Humanists and Reformation Politics under Henry VIII and Edward VI* (Oxford: Clarendon Press, 1965);

Samuel Eliot Morison, *The European Discovery of America,* 2 volumes (New York: Oxford University Press, 1971–1974);

Arthur William Reed, *Early Tudor Drama: Medwall, the Rastells, Heywood, and the More Circle* (London: Methuen, 1926) pp. 1–28;

Louis A. Schuster, "Thomas More's Polemical Career, 1523–1533," in *The Complete Works of St. Thomas More,* volume 8, part 3 (New Haven: Yale University Press, 1973), pp. 1135–1268.

Barnabe Riche
(1542 – 10 November 1617)

Donald Beecher
Carleton University

BOOKS: *A Right Exelent and Pleasaunt Dialogue, betwene Mercury and an English Souldier* (N.p., n.d. [London: Printed by John Day, 1574]);

Allarme to England, Foreshewing What Perilles Are Procured, Where the People Liue Without Regarde of Martiall Lawe (London: Printed by Christopher Barker, 1578);

The Straunge and Wonderfull Aduentures of Don Simonides (London: [Printed by John Kingston for] Robert Walley, 1581);

Riche His Farewell to Militarie Profession (London: [Printed by John Kingston for] Robert Walley, 1581; enlarged edition, London: Printed by G[eorge] E[ld] for Thomas Adams, 1606);

The True Report of a Late Practise Enterprised by a Papist, with a Yong Maiden in Wales (London: [Printed by John Kingston for] Robert Walley, 1582);

The Second Tome of the Trauailes and Aduentures of Don Simonides, Enterlaced with Historie (London: [Printed by John Kingston for] Robert Walley, 1584);

A Path-way to Military Practise (London: Printed by John Charlewood for Robert Walley, 1587);

The Aduentures of Brusanus Prince of Hungaria (London: [Printed by Thomas Orwin for] Thomas Adames, 1592);

Greenes Newes Both from Heauen and Hell, attributed to Riche (London: [Printed by Alice Charlewood for] Thomas Adams, 1593);

A Martial Conference, Pleasantly Discoursed betwene Two Souldiers, the One Captaine Skil, Trained Vp in the French and Low Country Seruices, the Other Captaine Pill, Only Practised in Finsburie Fields (London: Printed by John Oxenbridge, 1598);

A Souldiers Wishe to Britons Welfare (London: [Printed by Thomas Creede] for Jeffrey Chorlton, 1604); republished as *The Fruites of Long Experience* (London: Printed by Thomas Creede for Jeffrey Chorlton, 1604);

Faultes Faults, and Nothing Else but Faultes (London: [Printed by Valentine Simms] for Jeffrey Chorleton, 1606);

Roome for a Gentleman, or the Second Part of Faultes Collected for the True Meridian of Dublin (London: Printed by J[ohn] W[indet] for Jeffrey Chorlton, 1609);

A Short Survey of Ireland. Truely Discovering Who Hath Armed that People with Disobedience (London: Printed by N[icholas] O[kes] for Bartholomew Sutton & William Barenger, 1609);

A New Description of Ireland: Wherein Is Described the Disposition of the Irish (London: [Printed by William Jaggard] for Thomas Adams, 1610); republished as *A New Irish Prognostication, or Popish Callender* (London: Printed for Francis Constable, 1624);

A True and a Kinde Excuse Written in Defence of That Booke, Intituled a Newe Description of Irelande (London: [Printed by Thomas Dawson] for Thomas Adams, 1612);

A Catholicke Conference betweene Syr Tady Mac. Mareall and Patricke Plaine (London: [Printed by Thomas Dawson] for Thomas Adams, 1612);

The Excellency of Good Women (London: Printed by Thomas Dawson, 1613);

Opinion Diefied. Discovering the Ingins, Traps, and Traynes, That Are Set to Catch Opinion (London: [Printed by Thomas Dawson] for Thomas Adams, 1613);

The Honestie of This Age (London: [Printed by Thomas Dawson] for T[homas] A[dams], 1614);

My Ladies Looking Glasse. Wherein May Be Discerned a Wise Man from a Foole (London: [Printed by John Legat] for Thomas Adams, 1616);

The Irish Hubbub or, The English Hue and Crie (London: [Printed by George Purslowe] for John Marriot, 1617).

Editions: *Greenes Newes Both from Heaven and Hell, by B. R., 1593, and Greenes Funeralls by R. B., 1594,* edited by Ronald B. McKerrow (Stratford-upon-Avon: Shakespeare Head, [1922]);

Title page for Riche's 1581 book, a collection of eight stories written in the style of the Italian novella

Rich's Farewell to Military Profession, edited by Thomas Mabry Cranfill (Austin: University of Texas Press, 1959);

Faultes Faults and Nothing Else but Faultes, edited by Melvin H. Wolf (Gainesville, Fla.: Scholars' Facsimiles & Reprints, 1965);

Farewell to Military Profession, edited by Donald Beecher (Ottawa: Dovehouse Editions / Binghamton, N.Y.: Medieval and Renaissance Texts and Studies, 1992).

For many years Barnabe Riche was remembered largely due to William Shakespeare's choice of the second story of *Riche His Farewell to Military Profession* (1581) as a source for *Twelfth Night* (1601). Much of the critical interest in Riche has been because of literary borrowing or lending, especially in the use of his work as source material by contemporary dramatists. But recently Riche's achievements in the novella, in satire, and in romance are being increasingly acknowledged. He was not given to the

kinds of stylistic play and ambiguity that resulted in "problem" texts or that demanded the kinds of close readings favored by New Critics. But as critical interests expand to include questions concerning genre, narrative, gender, myth, conventions of romance, and the social uses and reception of fiction, Riche's texts are beginning to receive more attention. Meanwhile his importance as a military writer has never been in doubt among specialists. The historian Henry J. Webb went so far as to claim that Riche's "contributions to military literature [were] historically speaking every bit as important as Shakespeare's to drama." Riche's references to his age in various introductions to his books indicate that he was born in 1542, presumably in Essex, perhaps in Maldon, or possibly to a Thomas Riche residing in Colchester. Further comments in his prefatory writing suggest that his formal education was modest. There is no record of university attendance.

By profession Riche was a soldier. For over forty years he campaigned in both Holland and Ireland, rising early in his career to the rank of captain. He first saw action in 1562 at Le Havre, where a typhus epidemic slew thirty-eight hundred of the garrison of five thousand. In 1565 he joined a privateering venture that failed and left him seriously in debt. That matter haunted Riche for many years, leading to his arrest in 1570 and a brief period spent in prison. A short time after his release he was posted to Ireland. Between 1570 and 1582 he was constantly on the move between the Dutch and the Irish fronts. Thomas Churchyard drew upon Riche's notes for his account of the 1572 battle of Zutphen in *A True Discourse Historical of the Succeeding Governors in the Netherlands and the Civil Wars There* (1602). Riche must have been an eyewitness of the battle if not an actual participant.

In *A Right Excellent and Pleasant Dialogue between Mercury and an English Soldier* (1574), in *Alarm to England* (1578), and in *A Pathway to Military Practice* (1587), Riche touches upon issues critical to military life: adequate pay for soldiers; the use of capital punishment for unsoldierly conduct in time of war; the need for disciplined and professional soldiers and officers; the corrupt use of impressment and the low quality of soldier such means obtained; the complacent attitudes of civilians toward the strategic role of the military; and the privations of the common soldier. His *Dialogue* is noteworthy for its literary framing device based on the medieval dream motif in which Mercury leads the dreamer to the castle of Mars, while *A Pathway* is a remarkable document for its detailed descriptions of the echelons, duties, battle strategies, and formations of the English army. Riche's sustained sense of the importance of the military as protection against invasion and the danger of leaving England's defense in the hands of a hastily conscripted rabble was clairvoyant in light of the events that followed.

During idle moments in Ireland in the late 1570s, Riche turned to writing fictional narratives. The first of these, *The Strange and Wonderful Adventures of Don Simonides* (1581), combines the romance form with that of the Italian collections of novellas and is his best piece of longer fiction. The lovelorn protagonist seeks adventure in order to cure his melancholy passion. During his travels he becomes a hermit bent on leading a contemplative life, but in due course he finds himself in Venice, where he becomes a voyeur-confessor to a lady who recounts to him her amorous adventures. The Don's pilgrimage creates the framing structure for a series of tales, while at the same time his own character is altered and educated by his experiences.

In a sequel to this work, *The Second Tome of the Travels and Adventures of Don Simonides* (1584), the euphuistic and satiric elements become more prominent, while the narrative structures and the governing conventions become less coherent. The hero travels to Athens to meet the title character of John Lyly's *Euphues, the Anatomy of Wit* (1579) and then passes through London to visit Euphues' friend Philautus before returning to his native Seville. Memorable among the many stories that mark the journey is that of Priscilla, met by Don Simonides in a desert near Naples, weeping over the bodies of two Italian princes dead for love of her and for her inability to choose between them. The London episode turns into a satire on English manners, while the homecoming tells of total disillusionment when the hero discovers that his beloved has married an ugly old man for his money. This eclectic work is of interest for its narrative variety, for its handling of romance conventions, and for the satiric treatment of the then-fashionable affectations of melancholy love.

Riche His Farewell to Military Profession (1581) was written before the renewal of hostilities provoked by the Catholic insurrectionist James Fitzmaurice's return to Ireland in July 1579, an action in which Riche had a part. The work's title signifies a change in his literary interests and not a renunciation of his profession. It is a collection of eight love stories which he claims to have written to delight and edify a specifically female readership. The posturing of the soldier as courtier-raconteur creates a personalized audience within a more general reader-

ship: the ladies are invited to read as women sitting in judgment of what a man might offer to win their favors, even as he pretends to lecture them on fashions and morals. Despite its unassuming style and manner, the *Farewell* is arguably the finest set of Elizabethan stories written in imitation of the Italian novella, a genre that enjoyed twenty-five years of popularity following the publication of William Painter's *Palace of Pleasure* in 1566. Three of the eight stories are reworkings of Lodowick Bryskett's translation of the *Hecatommithi* (1565), by Cynthius, but the remaining five are new creations, pieced together from many sources ranging from the Italians Matteo Bandello and Giovanni Francesco Straparola to the English anthologies of Painter and George Pettie. The *Farewell* makes use of a wide range of narrative conventions, from traditions as disparate as the romance, the fabliau, and the fairy tale. In addition, Riche's collection escapes the stylistic excesses and moralizing that for many modern readers blemish Elizabethan fiction generally.

Riche returned to the long, episodic romance form in *The Adventures of Brusanus* (1592), but with rather less control over the unity of the work than he exercised in *Don Simonides*. Brusanus is a prodigal-type hero resembling prototypes in the works of Lyly. By degrees, however, he is metamorphosed into a model of perfection in a tale of ideal friendship drawn from the story of Pyrocles and Musidorus in Sir Philip Sidney's *Arcadia* (written 1581; published 1590). Yet another contrast emerges in the final section, where a willful lady is tamed in anticipation of marriage to the hero. Three standard motifs emerge in sequence: the cautionary humanist tale in which woman is the temptress; the story of retreat into ideal masculine friendship; and the comic romance in which the woman is granted sufficient wit and charm to make her fit for union with the protagonist. These are, in fact, three motifs that dominate Elizabethan fiction, and they are present here either because Riche's attention drifted uncritically from model to model or because he attempted a cumulative literary essay in the form of romance comedy.

Although *Brusanus* was published in 1592, it was written in 1584 or 1585, and shortly after its completion Riche was called to another military command. He had enjoyed a three-year interlude in London after escaping in the spring of 1582 a period of terrible pestilence and famine in Ireland. His new assignment was to end abruptly, however, for on 18 November 1585, while Riche was away in Dublin, the hundred men under his command in the north of Ireland were lured out of their fortifica-

MY
LADIES LOO-
KING GLASSE.

WHEREIN MAY BE
DISCERNED A WISE MAN
FROM A FOOLE, A GOOD WO-
MAN FROM A BAD: AND THE
true resemblance of vice, masked
vnder the vizard of vertue.

By *Barnabe Rich* Gentleman, seruant to the Kings
most excellent Maiestie.

Malui me diuitem esse quam vocari.

LONDON,
Printed for *Thomas Adams.*
1616.

Title page for one of Riche's satiric works

cil took his allegations against these prelates seriously and temporarily restrained their powers.

Riche's first commercial pamphlet on Ireland, *A Looking Glass for Ireland,* appeared in 1599, though no copies of this work have survived. He spent a few years in London after the turn of the century, presumably as a trainer of new recruits at Finsbury Fields or at Mile End, Stepney, near his home. Riche also received honorable mention for his part in the quelling of the Essex rebellion in 1601. *A Short Survey of Ireland* appeared in 1609, followed by *A New Description of Ireland* in 1610, his *Defense of . . . "A New Description"* in 1612, and finally *The Irish Hubbub* in 1617. The question of Ireland had become a literary industry for Riche, one which presumably augmented his income and which has left to specialists in Anglo-Irish relations a legacy of documentation and opinion.

In addition to his work on the pamphlets Riche also turned away from the novella and the romance during this period in order to write social satire, a move which must be attributed largely to the changing literary fashions of the age. If the past ethos for Riche had been created essentially by Painter, Lyly, and Sidney, the new ethos originated in the works of Joseph Hall, John Marston, and Ben Jonson. Yet Riche's satires are not the work of an angry young intellectual, as satire so often is, for when *Faults, Faults, and Nothing Else but Faults* appeared in 1606, he was sixty-four. This work features conventional themes: greed; political corruption and favoritism; excessive courtly fashions; false melancholiacs; and decadent travelers. In *Faults* Riche includes some twenty character sketches — worthy precursors to the Theophrastan characters presented in the collections of Hall, Thomas Overbury, and John Earle. *Faults* lacks structural design and is characterized by frequent digression, though it is unified by its satiric tone, a kind of sneering outrage, and satisfied self-righteousness.

Riche produced several other satirical works, such as *Room for a Gentleman* (1609), *The Excellency of Good Women* (1613), *Opinion Defied* (1613), *The Honesty of This Age* (1614), and *My Lady's Looking Glass* (1616). These works continue his unflattering observations on the social foibles and enormities of the age, many of which had become commonplace in the theater: social climbing and the extravagance of women, the bankrupting of husbands, immodesty and sexual license, the mobility of women, the rage for fashions, and the use of cosmetics. By implication, Riche espoused yeoman values of modesty, industry, and honesty, but his ambivalent

tions and massacred almost to the last man. Somehow Riche made the transition from Ireland back to London in time for his wedding on 12 January 1586. He was forty-four, and his bride was Katherine Easton, a lady with influential family ties, although that fact does not seem to have brought the Riches much material benefit.

In March 1587 Riche published his *Pathway to Military Practice* and astutely dedicated it to the queen, which may have brought the small pension she offered him that September. Once back in Ireland, he sent a series of booklets, letters, and reports to various officials as well as to the queen that deal with the treacheries of the Irish and the corruption of English officials in Dublin. Riche was particularly critical of the Anglican leaders who showed tolerance to Irish recusants. Not surprisingly he made numerous enemies, including Adam Loftus, lord chancellor of Ireland and archbishop of Dublin, and Thomas Jones, bishop of Meathe. In 1592 he was beaten by Loftus's men and barely managed to escape to England. The high tide of Riche's career as an informer occurred when the Privy Coun-

opinions on the conduct of women places his satire on both sides of the so-called controversy over women. He draws upon a store of commonplace material, much of it no doubt from his notebooks. He was not above borrowing from himself to the point of self-plagiarism, and that habit is particularly in evidence in his later writings. Yet his satirical works are of value for the historian, reflecting as they do the values and customs of the age.

Even during his declining years in Dublin, Riche kept up a steady correspondence with London officials concerning the corruption of the principal administrators in Ireland. A confidential report went to Chief Minister Robert Cecil in 1610, another to Chancellor of the Exchequer Sir Julius Caesar in 1612, and *The Anatomy of Ireland* (1615) was addressed directly to King James. In dedicating so many of his books to members of the royal family, Riche seemed particularly zealous in his search for royal favor. Such favor was not easily obtained in the best of circumstances, but he may have had an additional handicap in the form of an indiscretion committed in the conclusion of the *Farewell,* where he had made the king of Scotland a victim of demonic possession. James had protested the passage officially in 1595, and there is reason to think that Riche himself made the revisions in the edition of 1606 that removed the slight. James probably held a long grudge, but in the end he relented, for in July 1616 a warrant went out from Westminster "to pay Barnaby Riche, the oldest captain of the kingdom, £100 as a free gift." Riche had only eighteen months to enjoy this royal windfall, however, as he died on 10 November 1617.

In writing novellas, romances, quixotic adventures, character sketches, pamphlets, and social satires as well as several military books, Riche reveals a remarkable range of interests and talents. He was uneven as a writer and was never an accomplished stylist, but he is, at his best, an engaging and rewarding storyteller. Certainly he was prolific as a writer, claiming in his last book (published when he was seventy-four or seventy-five years old) that he had authored twenty-six. He may have been stretching the count by including shorter pamphlets and works reissued under different titles, but he does have a clear claim to some twenty-two books and longer pamphlets ranging from 40 to 212 pages in their original printed formats. Moreover, that the

Farewell to Military Profession went through four editions in his lifetime and served as a full or partial source for at least nine plays attests to a certain favor he found with contemporary readers. Imitation was a working principle of the age, and the practice included language, character types, plot situations, and structural ideas. Working in this way, Riche was receptive to a variety of literary fashions; and in imitating the novella he may have brought the genre to its apogee in England. He is a remarkable example of the dogged patriot who devoted his life as soldier and informer to two monarchs, and, as a writer, he did his part in attempting to improve the conduct of the age.

Biography:

Thomas Mabry Cranfill and Dorothy Hart Bruce, *Barnaby Riche: A Short Biography* (Austin: University of Texas Press, 1953).

References:

Max Bluestone, *From Story to Stage: The Dramatic Adaptation of Prose Fiction in the Period of Shakespeare and His Contemporaries,* Studies in English Literature, no. 70 (The Hague: Mouton, 1974);

Thomas Mabry Cranfill, "Barnaby Rich's 'Sappho' and *The Weakest Goeth to the Wall,*" *University of Texas Studies in English* (1945–1946): 142–171;

Walter Davis, *Idea and Act in Elizabethan Fiction* (Princeton: Princeton University Press, 1969);

Paul A. Jorgensen, "Barnaby Rich: Soldierly Suitor and Honest Critic of Women," *Shakespeare Quarterly,* 7 (Spring 1956): 183–188;

John Leon Lievsay, "A Word about Barnaby Rich," *Journal of English & Germanic Philology,* 55 (July 1956): 381–392;

Leo G. Salingar, "The Design of *Twelfth Night,*" *Shakespeare Quarterly,* 9 (Spring 1958): 117–139;

DeWitt Talmage Starnes, "Barnabe Riche's 'Sappho Duke of Mantona': A Study in Elizabethan Story-Making," *Studies in Philology,* 30 (July 1933): 455–472,

Henry J. Webb, "Barnabe Riche – Sixteenth Century Military Critic," *Journal of English & Germanic Philology,* 42 (April 1943): 240–242;

Louis B. Wright, *Middle-class Culture in Elizabethan England* (Ithaca, N.Y.: Cornell University Press, 1958).

Reginald Scot

(circa 1538 – 9 October 1599)

Jeffrey Powers-Beck
East Tennessee State University

BOOKS: *A Perfite Platforme of a Hoppe Garden* (London: Printed by Henrie Denham, 1574; revised and enlarged, 1576); reprinted in *The Country-man's Recreation* (London: Printed by Bernard Allsop & Thomas Fawcet for Michael Young, 1640);

The Discouerie of Witchcraft, Wherein the Lewde Dealing of Witches Is Notablie Detected, the Knauerie of Coniurors, [etc.] (London: Printed by William Brome, 1584) – includes "A Discourse vpon Diuels and Spirits . . . "; republished as *Scot's Discovery of VVitchcraft: Proving the Common Opinions of Witches Contracting with Divels, Spirits, or Familiars; and Their Power to Kill . . . to Be but Imaginary, Erronious Conceptions and Novelties . . . Whereunto Is Added, a Treatise upon the Nature, and Substance of Spirits and Divels, &c. . . .* (London: Printed by R. C., sold by Giles Calvert, 1651); republished as *The Discovery of Witchcraft: Proving that the Compacts and Contracts of Witches with Devils and All Infernal Spirits of Familiars Are but Erroneous Novelties and Imaginary Conceptions . . .* (London: Printed for Andrew Clark, 1665).

Editions: *The Discoverie of Witchcraft,* edited by Brinsley Nicholson (London: E. Stock, 1886; Totowa, N.J.: Rowman & Littlefield, 1973);

The Discoverie of Witchcraft, introduction by Montague Summers (London: Rodker, 1930; New York: Dover, 1972);

The Discoverie of Witchcraft, introduction by Hugh Ross Williamson (Arundel, U.K.: Centaur, 1964; Carbondale: Southern Illinois University Press, 1964);

The Discoverie of Witchcraft, The English Experience, no. 299 (New York: Da Capo Press, 1971);

A Perfite Platforme of a Hoppe Garden, The English Experience, no. 620 (New York: Da Capo Press, 1973).

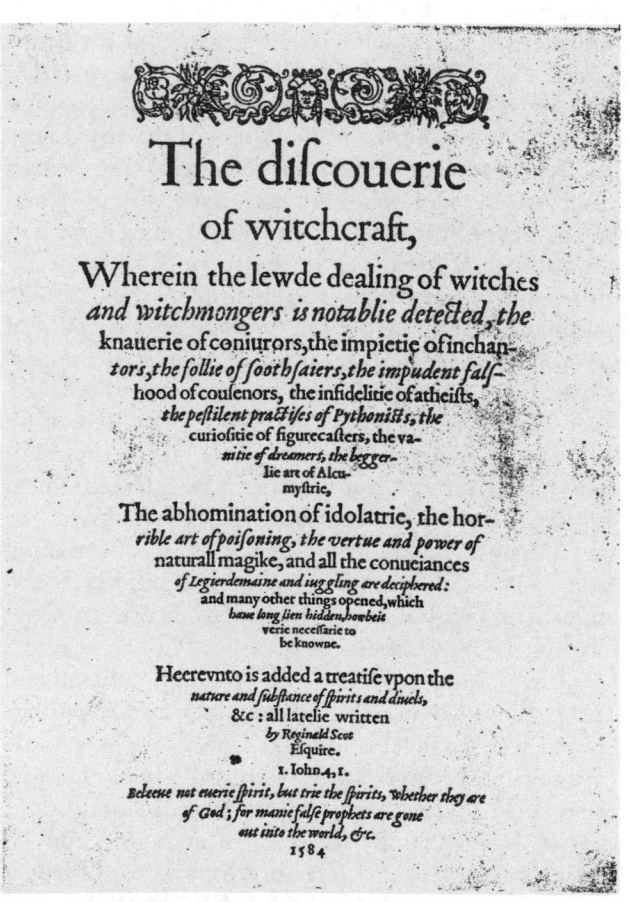

Title page for Reginald Scot's treatise on witchcraft, notable for its skeptical and humane approach to the subject

In encyclopedia entries Reginald Scot is typically credited with a set of obscure "firsts." He wrote the first tract on hop farming in English, introducing Flemish methods of hop cultivation to Kent. He also wrote the first discourse on witchcraft and conjuring tricks in English, exposing the illusions of supernatural phenomena and the cruelties of Elizabethan witch trials in a vast, skeptical, and humane treatise. The obscurity of these distinctions somewhat belies Scot's character as a pragmatic man of business and a keen critic of Elizabethan laws and religion. His *Discovery of Witchcraft* (1584) had an impressively broad influence on English society, attracting the attention of theologians, judges, doctors, playwrights, and even King James VI of Scotland (later James I of England) and initiating a critique of supernatural events that would flourish in the seventeenth and eighteenth centuries.

The son of Richard Scot and Mary Whetenall, Reginald (or Reynold) Scot was born circa 1538 in Smeeth, Kent. Belonging to a prosperous gentry family, he matriculated at age seventeen at Hart College, Oxford, but he returned to Smeeth sometime later without a degree. He married his first wife, Jane Cobbe, in 1568, and she gave birth to their daughter, Elizabeth. After Jane's death, probably in the 1580s, he married a widow, Alice Collyar, who brought a stepdaughter, Marie, to his family. Scot's first biographer, Anthony à Wood, wrote at the end of the seventeenth century that the young man "gave himself up solely to solid reading, to the perusing of obscure authors that had by the generality of scholars been neglected, and at times of leisure to husbandry and gardening." Although Scot investigated these subjects exhaustively for his two books, he was hardly the retiring pedant of Wood's sketch. Scot's biographers have characterized him as an active man of business with diverse interests.

As a member of the gentry with the title "armiger" or "esquire," Scot devoted much of his life to the governance and cultivation of his native Kent. He inherited part of his aunt Lady Winifred Rainsford's estate in 1575 and appears (from a sentence in his will) to have succeeded to other lands upon his second marriage. In the next century Thomas Ady wrote that Scot was "a student of the laws and learned of the Roman Laws," leading biographers to speculate that he may have practiced law for a time as a justice of the peace. Cases cited in *The Discovery* testify to his professional knowledge of the law and to his intimate acquaintance with witchcraft trials in Kent.

Throughout his life Scot's finances apparently suffered vicissitudes. In a prefatory letter to *The Discovery* he speaks of having his hand in his cousin Sir Thomas Scot's purse and his foot under his cousin's table. With this statement in mind, biographers have conjectured that Reginald acted as his cousin's land agent or estate manager, or that Thomas subsidized the writing of *The Discovery of Witchcraft*. Reginald certainly worked closely with his cousin on the project of draining Romney Marsh, serving four years as a surveyor of land. He earned brief mention by Raphael Holinshed for acting in 1583 as

Thomas's agent in negotiations with Secretary Francis Walsingham for the reconstruction of Dover Harbor. He also collected subsidies for the lathe of Shepway in 1586–1587, stood as a member of Parliament for New Romney in the infamous year of 1588, and apparently served as captain of a troop of foot soldiers in order to help repel the Spanish Armada that summer. With the Romney Marsh and Dover projects completed, Sir Thomas died in 1594, and Reginald reputedly wrote his cousin's epitaph. Having written his own will and provided for his wife and daughters, Reginald died on 9 October 1599 in Smeeth. If he did write the sixty-four-line epitaph for his cousin, he might well have wished for the same recognition of his services to Kent:

> Let Romney Marsh and Dover say,
>   Ask Norborn Camp at leisure,
> If he were wont to make delay
>   To do his country pleasure.

In both of his works Scot sought to "do his country pleasure," and he did so in *A Perfect Platform of a Hop Garden* (1574) by the practical means of agriculture. The fifty-six-page manual gives full and careful instructions on the cultivation of hops. The Dutch had recently entered into a profitable trade in hops and hopped ales, and Scot, who knew of the hop gardens in Poppering, Flanders, discerned that his neighbors in Kent could join in this trade. In his prefatory letters and epilogue he urges his readers to take up hop farming with diligence and industry. And Scot persuades them with characteristic humor in his epilogue comparing those sluggards who drink Dutch beers and refuse to raise English hops to "alehouse knights": "for that many of these ale knights having good drink at home of their own, can be content to drink worse abroad at an Alehouse."

The body of *A Perfect Platform* instructs farmers on every step of hop growing. These steps include how to choose and prepare the ground for a hop garden; how to plant and set hops; how to cut poles, shape hills, and fertilize hops; how to harvest, dry, and store hops; and especially how to use an oast or hop oven. Fifteen woodcut diagrams accompany the text, illustrating the directions. The success of *A Perfect Platform* is demonstrated by the three editions in Scot's lifetime, another in the seventeenth century, and Kent's rising fame as England's leader in hop production. Scot's contribution to English agriculture is still recognized. In his history of hop cultivation and use, Abraham Hale Burgess asserts that "the cultural operations which Scot describes are excellent for the type of hop growing of the period;

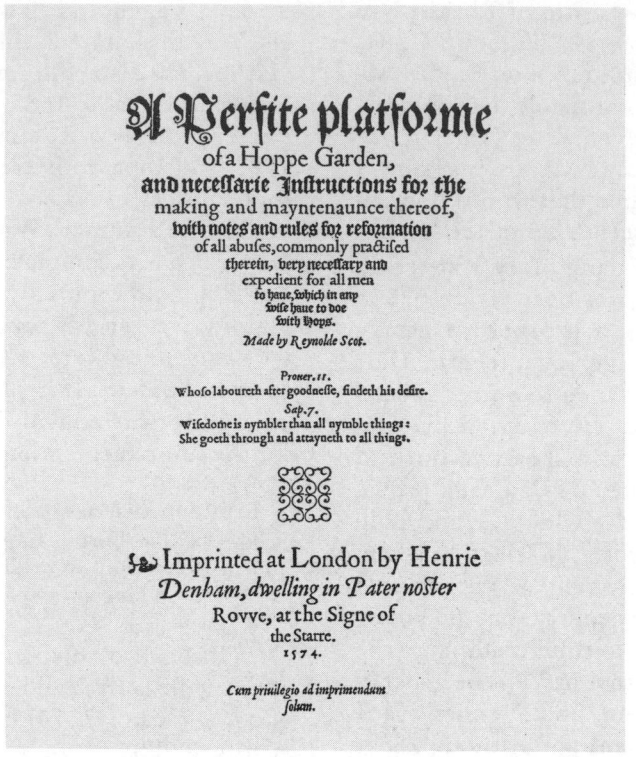

A Perfite platforme

of a Hoppe Garden,
and necessarie Instructions for the
making and mayntenaunce thereof,
with notes and rules for reformation
of all abuses, commonly practised
therein, very necessary and
expedient for all men
to have, which in any
wise have to doe
with Hops.

Made by Reynolde Scot.

Prover. 11.
Whoso laboureth after goodnesse, findeth his desire.

Sap. 7.
Wisedome is nymbler than all nymble things:
She goeth through and attayneth to all things.

Imprinted at London by Henrie
Denham, dwelling in Pater noster
Rovve, at the Signe of
the Starre.
1574.

Cum privilegio ad imprimendum
solum.

*Title page for Scot's 1574 book, which introduced Flemish
methods of hop cultivation to England*

they still apply, in a general way, today, and the English hop-growing industry was fortunate to have in its early stages such a reliable textbook."

Although *A Perfect Platform* is foremost an agricultural text, the prefatory letters and epilogue are of some literary interest. While Scot is never pretentious, he takes some pains to show that he is a cultivated gardener. His letter "To the Reader" begins with a cento of Solomon's proverbs on hard work and sloth (for example, "A simple man that worketh is in better case than a gorgeous man that wanteth"), and he mingles his praise of the "mystery" (or craft) of hop growing with a pleasant defense of his own style. He writes in well-balanced phrases, justifying his "homely style" with respect to his earthy subject and his humble audience: "and to say the truth, to use eloquent school phrases in a homely rustical matter, were to bring the country people to a new form of hearing, wherein they should be longer in learning to understand the curiosity of the style than the knowledge of the art. . . ." Scot then concludes his long sentence cleverly: "and therefore it sufficeth if in a rude cask I exhibit wholesome fruit, and write plainly to plain men of the country, and yet, *Saepe etiam est holitor valde oportuna locutus* [Even a green grocer can sometimes speak aptly]." Thus he appeals to his gentry readers as a "plain man of the country" himself, who trusts direct speech more than inkhorn terms, but who can still wink at the scholars with a Latin proverb.

Yet Scot's greatest contribution to Kent and to English law, religion, and literature came in *The Discovery of Witchcraft.* "Discovery" is used in the sense of the modern "exposé," and this 560-page work is a vast encyclopedia of occult lore with a constant skeptical refrain: "Witchcraft is in truth a cosening art. . . . The manner thereof is so secret, mystical, and strange, that to this day there hath never been any credible witness thereof." For his part, Scot thought that all witches were either the hapless sufferers of delusions, conniving impostors, or the innocent victims of village superstition and animosity.

Concurrent with this thesis is Scot's plea that English judges view witch mongers with suspicion and alleged witches with compassion. In all four of his prefatory letters and in much of *The Discovery* he stresses the need to treat accused witches with mercy: "For (God knoweth) many of these poor wretches had more need to be relieved than chastised; and more meet were a preacher to admonish them, than a jailer to keep them; and a physician more necessary to help them, than an executioner or tormentor to hang or burn them." Given the superstitions that led to the executions of tens of thousands of supposed witches in Europe from 1500 to 1800, Scot's humane plea was as bold as it was necessary.

In book 2 of *The Discovery,* Scot builds a convincing case that prosecution of witches is unjust because (1) the alleged witches are being tried for committing impossibilities, as if they had plucked the moon from the sky; (2) these women frequently suffer from melancholy delusions; (3) they are sometimes compelled to testify against themselves by humiliation and torture; (4) they are often condemned by the testimony of enemies and gossips; and (5) they are often convicted on the basis of a coincidence, such as the mysterious death of a cow. Similarly, while Scot was ages removed from modern feminism, he still recognized the injustice in the fervid persecution of women as witches and the simultaneous leniency toward male conjurors: "We for our parts would have killed five poor women, before we would suspect one rich butcher."

Throughout *The Discovery* Scot refers to recent witch cases, sometimes recounting them in detail. These include the trial of Margaret Simons at Rochester in 1581; the ventriloquism episode of Mildred Norrington, "the holy maid of Kent," in 1574; the deception of Thomas Eps's family by Mother Baker in Romney, Kent; the execution of witches at the Saint Osyth trials in Essex in 1582; and the poignant story of Ade Davie of Selling, Kent, who suffered from melancholy fears that she was a witch.

In book 13 of *The Discovery,* Scot also relies on his own experiences, as he ascribes much apparent magic to the sleight-of-hand tricks of skilled conjurors. He gives multiple examples of illusions with cards, money, balls, and animals, illustrating his explanations with woodcuts of trick knives and the decollation of John the Baptist at Bartholomew Fair in 1583. Much of this information Scot obtained in person from a French-born conjuror named John Cautares, who is "in conversation an honest man" but who "hath the best hand and conveyance (I think) of any man that liveth this day."

While Scot's subject is indeed serious and his treatment of it humane, he uses humor and earthy simplicity to satirize the ideas of such major European treatises on witchcraft as Jean Bodin's *De la Demonomanie* (1580) and Heinrich Krämer and Jacob Sprenger's *Malleus Maleficarum* (circa 1486). He cites the Belgian physician Johann Wier and scores of other writers in his arguments, but his most memorable passages combine wry humor and rustic phrases, as when he ridicules the notion that witches travel vast distances on broomstick: "For their furthest fetches that I can comprehend are but

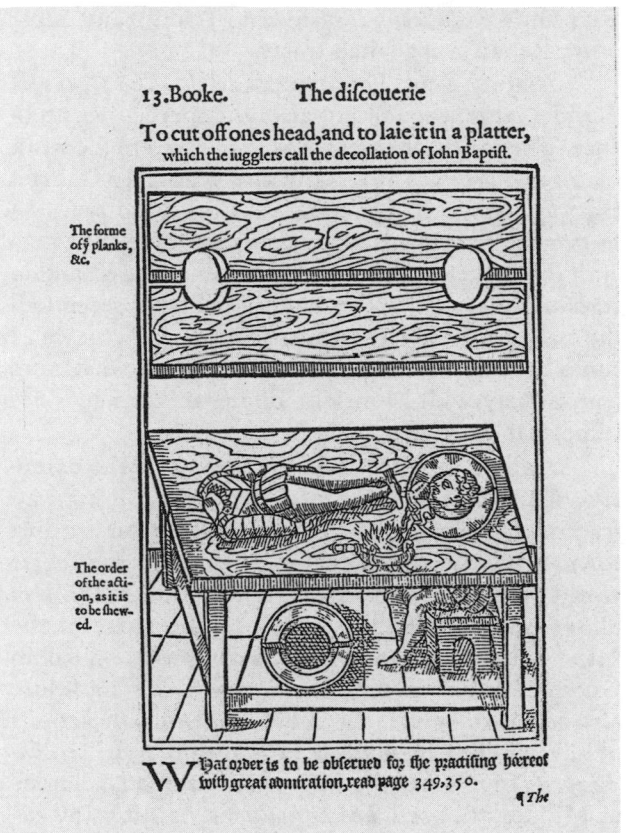

Woodcut from The Discovery of Witchcraft, *exposing the secret of a popular illusion, the decollation of John the Baptist*

to fetch a pot of milk . . . from their neighbor's house, half a mile distant from them." Elsewhere, in making a droll philosophical query, he mocks Bodin's story of a witch who transformed a sailor into an ass: "But was this man an ass all this while? Or was this ass a man?" Scot, who had a taste for Geoffrey Chaucer's *The Canterbury Tales* (circa 1388), also satirized with Chaucerian bawdry the legend of Saint Martin expelling a spirit out of a man's fundament: "O stinking lie!"

Certainly, these irruptions into drollery mark Scot's character as a nonacademic writer, and in the next century the learned Joseph Glanvill disdained his penchant for humor: "For the author doth little but tell odd tales and silly legends, which he confutes and laughs at, and pretends this to be a confutation of the being of witches and apparitions." Glanvill is right that Scot often prefers jest to scholarly argument, and that some of his scriptural arguments (for example, that the Witch of Endor was a ventriloquist) are unconvincing and tainted with anti-Catholic prejudice. Yet four centuries later *The Discovery* is more readable and compelling than

Glanvill's *Saducismus Triumphatus* (1689) and most other Renaissance witch tracts.

Among Scot's contemporaries, *The Discovery* found a large, though not always appreciative, audience. The satirist Thomas Nashe referred to the work in *Strange News* (1592), and the scholarly Gabriel Harvey rendered Scot some very qualified praise in *Pierce's Supererogation* (1593): "Scot's discovery of witchcraft dismasketh sundry egregious impostures, and in certain principal chapters and special passages hitteth the nail on the head with a witness: howsoever, I could have wished he had either dealt somewhat more courteously with Monsieur Bodin, or confuted him somewhat more effectually."

Almost in spite of Scot's opinions, the extensive witch lore of *The Discovery* also made it an attractive literary source. In creating Bottom's transformation, the character of Puck, and the faerie world of *A Midsummer-Night's Dream* (1596), William Shakespeare probably turned to the story of the "ass-headed man" and to Scot's comments on Robin Goodfellow and diminutive fairies. Scot's spirit lore also seems to be present in Shakespeare's depictions of the witches in *Macbeth* (1606) and Ariel in *The Tempest* (1609). Another important dramatist, Thomas Middleton, used *The Discovery* in naming and describing the familiar spirits in his play *The Witch* (circa 1614).

More infamous, in his *Demonology* (1597) King James VI condemns Scot's view of witchcraft as "damnable" and imputes to him "the old error of the Sadducees, in denying of spirits." While Scot rejected the name of Sadducee in his "Discourse upon Devils and Spirits," his position was too close to materialism for the comfort of his contemporaries. According to Scot's biographer Brinsley Nicholson, a German writer in the seventeenth century named Gisbert Voetius reported that *The Discovery* was burned by order of King James. While the many surviving copies of the first edition (more than two dozen in British and American libraries) seem to discount this legend of book burning, fear of censorship may have prevented a second edition during the author's lifetime and during James's reign as king of Great Britain. *The Discovery* may have been "the principal threat" to the king's attempt to enhance his English reputation with Scottish witch lore: Scot's book was reasonably scholarly and influential enough to be potentially dangerous to James; compared to the compendious learning and long bibliography of *The Discovery*, King James's slim book was inconsequential.

Scot's reputation grew steadily in the seventeenth century with the printing of two more English editions and a Dutch translation of *The Discovery*. The argument over the existence of spirits and supernatural events was waged fiercely between, on one side, skeptics like Thomas Hobbes, Samuel Harsnet, Ady, and John Webster and, on the other, spiritualists like William Perkins, Meric Casaubon, Glanvill, and Henry More. *The Discovery* helped to define the standard skeptical position toward witchcraft in the English debate. As the seventeenth century progressed, Scot's position experienced increasing sway with judges and doctors, and the Jacobean witchcraft statutes were finally repealed in 1736. Exemplifying those changes, Joseph Addison's essay on Moll White in a 1711 issue of the *Spectator* is a sympathetic portrait of an accused witch that owed a great deal to Scot's critique: "There is scarce a village in England that has not a Moll White in it. When an old woman begins to dote, and grow chargeable to a parish, she is generally turned into a witch and fills the whole country with extravagant fancies. . . . This frequently cuts off charity from the greatest objects of compassion." With Addison, Scot's arguments had found approval in the coffeehouse and the mainstream press, and in spite of lingering superstitions the spectacle of Moll White in the dock was vanishing from English life.

While Scot will be remembered by literary critics primarily in footnotes on Shakespeare and Middleton, he offers a wealth of material to social historians interested in the development of European skepticism and in the practice and legal prosecution of witchcraft. His accounts of witch trials are of special interest to scholars studying the treatment of women in Renaissance courtrooms. Readers of Ben Jonson's *Bartholomew Fair* (1614) and of "coney-catching" literature (Elizabethan exposés of confidence tricksters) may also be intrigued to see some popular carnival tricks of the time exposed by an inquisitive country squire. Thus *The Discovery of Witchcraft* continues to be a useful source for folklorists and historians as well as a potentially serendipitous experience for students of literature.

Bibliography:

Robert Hunter West, *Reginald Scot and Renaissance Writings on Witchcraft* (Boston: Twayne, 1984).

References:

Joseph Addison, "No. 117," in *Selections from "The Tatler" and "The Spectator,"* edited by Angus Ross (Harmondsworth, U.K.: Penguin, 1982), pp. 536–538;

Charles Boyce, *Shakespeare A to Z* (New York: Facts on File, 1990);

Geoffrey Bullough, *Narrative and Dramatic Sources of Shakespeare,* volume 1 (London: Routledge & Kegan Paul, 1964), pp. 371–373;

Abraham Hale Burgess, *Hops: Botany, Cultivation, and Utilization* (New York: Interscience Publishers, 1964);

Joseph Glanvill, *Saducismus Triumphatus,* facsimile edition (Gainesville, Fla.: Scholars' Facsimiles, 1966);

Trevor Hall, "The Discoverie of Witchcraft," in *Old Conjuring Books* (London: Duckworth, 1972), pp. 47–62;

Gabriel Harvey, *Pierce's Supererogation,* facsimile edition (Menston, U.K.: Scolar, 1970);

Standish Henning, "The Fairies of 'A Midsummer Night's Dream,'" *Shakespeare Quarterly,* 20 (Autumn 1969): 484–486;

Raphael Holinshed, *Holinshed's Chronicles of England, Scotland, and Ireland,* volume 4, edited by Henry Ellis and others (London: Rivington, 1807–1808), pp. 853–868;

James VI of Scotland, *Daemonologie,* edited by George Bagshawe Harrison (London: John Lane, 1924);

Christina Larner, *Witchcraft and Religion: The Politics of Popular Belief,* edited by Alan Macfarlane (Oxford: Blackwell, 1984);

Thomas Nashe, "Strange News, of the Intercepting of Certain Letters," in *The Works of Thomas Nashe,* volume 1, edited by Ronald B. McKerrow (Oxford: Blackwell, 1966), pp. 247–335;

Brinsley Nicholson, Introduction to Scot's *The Discoverie of Witchcraft* (London: E. Stock, 1886), pp. x–xlvii;

Gareth Roberts, "A Re-examination of the Sources of the Magical Material in Middleton's 'The Witch,'" *Notes and Queries,* new series 23 (May-June 1976): 216–219;

James Renat Scott, "Reginald Scott," in *Memorials of the Family of Scott, of Scot's-hall, in the County of Kent* (London: J. R. Scott, 1876), pp. 188–190;

Keith Thomas, *Religion and the Decline of Magic* (New York: Scribners, 1971);

Anthony à Wood, "Reynolde Scot," in *Athenae Oxoniensis,* Sources of Science no. 55, volume 1 (New York: Johnson Reprint, 1967), pp. 679–680.

Luke Shepherd

(flourished 1547 – 1554)

Seymour Baker House
University of Otago

BOOKS: *John Bon and Mast Person,* anonymous (London: Printed by John Day and William Seres, [1548?]);

Antipus. To Heare of Such Thinges Ye Be Not Wont, anonymous (N.p., n.d. [London: Printed by John Day, 1548?]);

The Comparison betwene the Antipus and the Antigraphe or Answere Thereunto, with. An Apologie of the Same Antipus, anonymous (N.p., n.d. [London: Printed by John Day, 1548?]);

Doctour Doubble Ale, anonymous (N.p., n.d. [London: Printed by Anthony Scoloker?, 1548]);

A Godlye and Holesome Preseruatyue against Desperation, anonymous (London: [Printed by John Herford for] James Burrell, [1548?]);

Pathose, or an Inward Passion of the Pope for the Losse of Hys Daughter the Masse, anonymous (London: Printed by John Day and William Seres, [1548?]);

Phylogamus, anonymous (N.p., n.d. [London: Printed by William Hill, 1548?]);

A Pore Helpe, The Buklar and Defence of Mother Holy Kyrke, anonymous (N.p., n.d. [London: Robert? Wyer, 1548?]);

The Vpcheringe of the Messe, anonymous (London: Printed by John Day and William Seres, [1548?]).

Editions: W. Carew Hazlitt, ed., *Remains of the Early Popular Poetry of England* (London: John Russell Smith, 1866) – includes "John Bon and Mast Parson," IV: 1–16; "Doctor Double Ale," III: 297–321; and "A Poor Help," III: 349–367;

"John Bon and Mast Parson," in *Tudor Tracts 1532–1588,* edited by Albert Frederick Pollard (Westminster: Constable, 1903), pp. 159–169.

Rising out of obscurity around 1547 and sinking back just as rapidly, Luke Shepherd's works spring from quite disparate motives and display a variety of styles. They range from a single-sheet folio poem (a precursor of the broadside ballad) to pious meditations on death. His verse is often com-

pared with that of John Skelton for its skewed meter and macaronic Latin parodies. Shepherd's decidedly anti-Catholic works display a certain virtuosity in combining personal invective against conservative priests and their theological positions with various fictional and recognizably Protestant literary devices. His satiric verse lies at the core of the Tudor ballad tradition – works written with an eye on literary form while adhering to an explicitly partisan political or theological agenda. With the exception of *A Godly and Wholesome Preservative against Desperation* (1548?), they are voices in a chorus of protest during the Reformation using native English literary styles for political ends and thus are as representative of Tudor poetry as are the poems of Sir Thomas Wyatt and the sonnets of Henry Howard, Earl of Surrey.

Luke Shepherd was born in Colchester, a major Essex town northeast of London with a history of dissent. Nothing is known of his parentage nor his early years save that at some time he probably received medical training, for he is described as a Protestant physician by the only contemporary to leave an extended account of him. At some point he moved to London, where he set up his medical practice on Coleman Street, a known Lollard area. He appears to have spent some time in the Fleet prison on account of his writings, although it is unclear whether this was under Henry VIII, Edward VI, or Mary.

In December 1547, within a year of his accession, King Edward VI issued a proclamation prohibiting discussion of the Eucharist. Despite this ban the number of works from London presses in 1548 was more than twice its 1547 level, a rise due almost entirely to the torrent of Protestant tracts dealing specifically with the Mass, including those attributed to Luke Shepherd. Both he and his printer John Day were called before London's mayor, Sir John Gresham, in early 1548 for publishing Shepherd's *John Bon and Mast Parson,* which, in defiance of the royal proclamation, presents a Protestant denial of the real presence of Christ in the Eucharist. It chanced that Shepherd's friend, the courtier Edward Underhill, was dining with the lord mayor and presented him with a copy of the offending literature with the comment that "there is many of them in the court." After examining the work firsthand, Gresham pronounced it "both pithy and merry" and took no further action against either printer or author.

In the space of two years Shepherd wrote up to nine works which, owing to the dangerous circumstances, display varying degrees of anonymity – his real name appears on none, nor are there dates assigned in the texts or colophons. They formed part of a body of theological flytings between radical Protestants and their conservative opponents which circulated around London and penetrated the countryside from the latter part of Henry VIII's reign into Mary's and beyond. Some conceits found in Shepherd's works, such as the "Mistress Missa" persona, became Protestant satiric conventions while others, notably the plainspoken uplander of *John Bon and Mast Parson,* were already traditional; their appearance in Shepherd underscores the popular nature of his verse.

John Bon and Mast Parson is cast as a dialogue on the eve of Corpus Christi, which feast serves as a background for the ensuing discussion of the Eucharist. The ploughman John Bon's seemingly naive questions to the parson concerning the presence of Christ in the sacrament of the altar deliver the Protestant polemic against transubstantiation, while his speech (which renders Corpus Christi as "copsi cursty") provides a comic element heightened by the learned priest's inability to overcome this bucolic questioner. John's mocking tone, his simple questions, and the repeated references to heresy and treason (and by implication the punishments for these crimes) hint at the dangers of doctrinal disputes. Having urged the parson to leave off saying Mass and instead to adopt the communion of the Protestants, the ploughman orders his team homeward.

As a salvo in the doctrinal disputes of late 1547 over the nature of Christ's presence in the Eucharist, *John Bon and Mast Parson* stands firmly in the Protestant camp which denied transubstantiation as a medieval accretion. As poetry it employs the native English conceit of the theological ploughman – the spiritual ancestor of England's Protestants associated with anticlerical sentiments since the fifteenth century in works such as the pseudo-Chaucerian *Jack Upland, The Plowman's Tale,* and *The Prayer and Complaint of the Plowman unto Christ* (all written

Title page for the work in which Luke Shepherd argues against transubstantiation despite a royal proclamation prohibiting discussion of the Eucharist

circa the fifteenth century and printed circa 1531–1536) – who would become a mainstay of later English Protestant literature.

Despite his near imprisonment because of *John Bon and Mast Parson,* Shepherd wrote at least seven more controversial works, all anonymous and printed without date but traceable to around 1548, before the appearance of the first official Edwardian formulary, *The Book of Common Prayer* (1549). Two works from this group are against transubstantiation: *Pathos; or, An Inward Passion of the Pope for the Loss of His Daughter the Mass* and *The Upcheering of the Mass.* Both were openly printed by John Day and were part of a flood of works issued around 1548 against the Mass and the Corpus Christi procession in defiance of the royal injunction.

Pathos is a lively and varied lament by the Pope for the loss of his daughter, the Mass, through whom he used to control princes and kings. Shepherd uses many techniques common in Tudor polemic such as a list of authorities and heavily nuanced references to historical and contemporary figures. The poem also contains much medical lore which supports the physician Shepherd's authorship; indeed, the entire poem is couched in terms of a bedside lament for a sick patient. The identification of the author with London's medical community is made explicit by the apparent precision of the revelation by the Pope that in London "Physicians that there be / I have a score and three / That still doth worship me." The poem also includes satiric Latin verses which, when translated, reveal truths about the Pope concealed from the people only by their ignorance of the language. This popular Protestant device reinforces the Catholic conspiracy motif used by John Bale quite successfully in his drama and by other writers agitating for an English service. In the closing description of a funeral procession carrying the Mass down to Hell, Shepherd mocks the Latin liturgy and Catholic funeral practices.

The Upcheering of the Mass is quite similar to *Pathos,* including its attack on Bishop Stephen Gardiner, the ranking conservative figure in England (then in the Tower of London) and his conservative allies. The Mass is depicted as a "Winchester gosling," that is, a street prostitute from the stews located in Gardiner's diocesan headquarters of Southwark. The unnamed speaker narrates a history of the recent troubles over the Mass and ironically laments its demise by pointing out the various idolatrous and unauthorized uses for the Sacrament:

> Some say she is good for biles
> And good for humbled heels
> And good for cow or ox
> That chafed be with yokes
> And good for hens and cocks
> To keep them from the fox
> They say she is good for the pox
> And such as have sore docks.

Shepherd also rejoices over Gardiner's imprisonment:

> I dare say at this hour
> Though he be in the Tower
> Yet doth he still honor
> The mass that sweet a flower.

He closes with a mock Latin satire of the service for the dead in memory of both the Mass and Gardiner himself.

The attack on conservative London clergymen is more clearly seen in the satiric *Doctor Double Ale* (1548?), where Shepherd lampoons Henry George, curate of the conservative parish of Saint Sepulcher. The simple narrator contrasts George's

drunken irresponsibility with the unlearned scriptural wisdom of a cobbler's boy whose artisan background suggests connections with native English Protestantism and may in fact refer to the anonymous *Disputation between a Shoemaker and a Popish Parson* (1548), a popular Protestant tract.

Shepherd's comments on the course of the Reformation in London and his detailed criticisms of George suggest personal acquaintance, although here George clearly personifies the clerical abuses of those unwilling or unable to adapt to the demands of the new learning. And again Shepherd closes in Skeltonic mock Latin which parodies the inebriated ecclesiastical learning of his subject and, by implication, champions the simple English of the unlearned narrator and the Protestant views he represents.

A Poor Help, the Buckler and Defense of Mother Holy Church (1548?) is an ironic complaint against Protestant "Gospellers" in an ostensible attempt to succor the Catholic church, and it lampoons both Catholic praxis and specific practitioners, notably George and the Catholic poet Miles Hoggarde. Previously thought to be by Skelton, the poem charts once again the progress of the Reformation; but the main targets are clearly the doctrine of transubstantiation and a certain priest, whose imprisonment the narrator ironically laments. Various clues identify the unnamed cleric as Bishop Gardiner of Winchester, who was imprisoned from September 1547 to January 1548 over his defense of transubstantiation and finally, in July of that year, sent to the Tower, where he faced a much more serious situation — execution for either treason or heresy. The narrator mentions this imprisonment and delights in distinguishing the two different forms of execution which may await him — drawing to Tyburn on a wooden hurdle to be hanged for treason or burned at Smithfield as a heretic: "Your hap may be to wag / Upon a wooden nag / Or else a fair fire / May hap to be your hire." He points out that the prisoner's kinsman Germain Gardiner has already suffered a similar fate: "Though Germain his man / Were hanged, what then?" Shepherd's precise attack on known conservatives reveals the personal dimension of the polemical atmosphere in which he wrote and serves as a good example of the theological flyting which typifies this flurry of controversial tracts from the early part of Edward's reign.

Shepherd's single-sheet folio *Antipus, to Hear of Such Things Ye Be Not Wont* (1548?) continues his attack on conservative Londoners, this time against William Leighton, a prebend and canon of Saint Paul's who defended transubstantiation in his public sermons. In poulter's measure Shepherd highlights the absurdity of traditional teaching on the real presence, in which a priest changes bread into the body of Christ, by comparing it to other false inversions: "As verily as Adam created first his God, / So verily he tasted not the fruit that was forbod," and leads to the conclusion that "As verily as bread doth make and bake the baker, / So verily these thieves the priests can make their maker." In one rhyme-royal stanza beneath these eleven couplets, Shepherd makes explicit the object of his attack: "If Leighton will needs his maker make, / That these are true he can not forsake."

The *Antipus* was answered in kind by an unknown writer, possibly Sir John Mason, which provoked Shepherd to republish his original folio along with both the offending answer entitled *Antigraphium* and his own rejoinder entitled "Apologia Antipi." Together these form *The Comparison between the Antipus and the Antigraph or Answer Thereto with an Apology or Defense of the Same Antipus* (1548?). Quite possibly a collaboration, *The Comparison* sets out to refute the *Antigraphium* and to continue the ad hominem attacks by naming not only Leighton and Mason but also Dr. Richard Smith and other presumably conservative Londoners.

The "Apologia Antipi" is divided into three parts, each addressing a different aspect of the controversy. The first part criticizes the writer of *Antigraphium* not only for adopting Shepherd's format, but also for defending transubstantiation in the first place. The second part treats the defense of Leighton, and the third castigates Leighton's presumed allies by name. The comparison serves as a detailed example of the techniques of repetition and rebuttal common during the Reformation, as well as the personal component of Tudor public debate.

The obscure *Philogamus* (Longing for Marriage, 1548?) addresses the issue of clerical marriage, prohibited until 1549. In it Shepherd again satirizes the poet who opposed him in the *Antigraphium*:

> He wrote I tell you plain
> An Antigraph full main
> None such on this side Spain
> Antipus to suppress.

Mason is armed with supreme poetic gifts. Complete with papal insignia ("He may wear upon his bonnet / A double P well set"), the poet's name is concealed in easily penetrated riddles; for example, "He is skilled so wonderously / In the science of Masonry," and later, "But this I will you tell / Thee Mason doth excell."

In praising the poet's verse, Shepherd digresses into Latin liturgical parodies, and when praising the poet himself, he ironically relates how this new champion of the Muses has rendered obsolete all other poetry. But his attack on Mason is also an attack on mandatory clerical celibacy, repeating the popular Protestant charge that its advocates merely wish to preserve lechery and fornication rather than to permit the institution of marriage. Shepherd also denounces one "Smith" (probably Thomas Smith, a flyter with some experience), author of a lost book called "The Testimony and Latter Will of Heresy," and criticizes several other conservatives. He closes with an obscure broken Latin sequence which, when pieced together, denounces unwed priests as unchaste hypocrites more intent on satisfying their lusts and keeping their power over the laity than exercising any spiritual guidance. In passing, Shepherd makes reference to other verse polemicists who have addressed this theme, including Pantolabus (John Huntington), author of "The Genealogy of Heresy."

In addition to his polemical poems Shepherd is credited with writing *A Godly and Wholesome Preservative against Desperation,* the anonymous devotional tract based on 1 Peter, chapter 5, in which Paul calls upon the Christian to resist his adversaries and rely on faith. Shepherd's pious treatise reiterates the Pauline image of the armor of God but again challenges conservative teaching on the Mass. In a passage notable for its restraint, Shepherd again espouses a Protestant view of the Eucharist, "which we are commanded to receive in remembrance of his benefits," yet he also supports the conservative doctrine of the intercession of saints. Intended to give comfort during sickness or death by confirming the remission of sins through faith, the work received a second edition in 1551.

Assessments of Shepherd have varied through the years. His contemporary John Bale mentions Shepherd's translations of the Psalms (which do not survive) and saw his works written against the papists as comparable to those of Skelton in their poetry, while Thomas Warton, writing in the 1770s, states that Shepherd was nothing more than "a petty pamphleteer in the cause of Calvinism." His satire was so clever at times that some readers were confused as to whose side he was on. The early-eighteenth-century antiquarian John Strype thought *A Poor Help* was lampooning Protestants, and even today there is no consensus on Shepherd's literary style, despite tentative agreement on which works should be attributed to him.

More recently, John King, in an examination of English Reformation literature, emphasizes elements in Shepherd's works linking them to a native English literary tradition and sees the *Antipus/Antigraphium/* "Apologia Antipi" as a satiric triptych composed entirely by Shepherd. Other scholars, such as Cathleen Wheat and Susan Brigden, focus on the biographical references in Shepherd's works and place them firmly in their historical context. As poetry these pieces pale beside the studied calm of later Tudor verse. But as windows onto the dangerous and uncertain years surrounding Edward VI's accession – years which saw the renewal of intense confessional strife in England – Shepherd's poetry discloses the closely knit and rapidly changing face of mid-Tudor England.

Bibliographies:

John Bale, *Scriptorum Illustrium Majoris Britanniae Catalogus,* volume 2 (Basel: John Oporinus, 1557–1559; facsimile edition, Farnborough: Gregg International, 1971), p. 109;

Bale, *Index Britanniae Scriptorum,* edited by Reginald Poole and Mary Bateson (Oxford: Clarendon Press, 1902; Cambridge: Cambridge University Press, 1990), p. 283.

References:

Susan Brigden, *London and the Reformation* (Oxford: Clarendon Press, 1989), pp. 438, 440;

Sir Samuel Egerton Brydges, *Censura Literaria,* 10 volumes (London: Longman, Hurst, 1805–1809), V: 277–280; VII: 337;

Friedrich Germann, *Luke Shepherd, ein Satirendichter der englischen Reformationzeit* (Augsburg: Theodore Lampart, 1911);

John King, *English Reformation Literature: The Tudor Origins of the Protestant Tradition* (Princeton: Princeton University Press, 1982), pp. 95, 116–118, 157, 252–270, 287;

M. Channing Lenthicum, "*A Pore Helpe* and Its Printers," *Library,* fourth series 9 (September 1929): 169–183;

John Nichols, ed., *Narratives of the Days of the Reformation,* Camden Society, old series 77 (Westminster: Nichols & Sons, 1859), pp. 171–172, 325–326;

Thomas Warton, *History of English Poetry,* volume 3, edited by René Wellek (New York & London: Johnson Reprint Corporation, 1968), p. 316;

Cathleen Wheat, "Luke Shepherd's *Antipi Amicus,*" *Philological Quarterly,* 30 (January 1951): 58–68;

Wheat, "*A Pore Helpe, Ralph Roister Doister,* and *Three Laws,*" *Philological Quarterly,* 28 (April 1949): 312–319.

John Skelton

(2? May 1463 – 21 June 1529)

Arthur F. Kinney
University of Massachusetts, Amherst

BOOKS: *Here Begynneth a Lytell Treatyse Named the Bowge of Courte* (Westminster: Printed by Wynkyn de Worde, circa 1499);

A Ballade of the Scottisshe Kynge, anonymous (London: Printed by Richard Faques, 1513);

The Tunning of Elinor Rumming (London: Printed by Wynkyn de Worde?, circa 1521); republished as *Elynour Rummin, the Famous Ale-Wife of England* (London: Printed by Bernard Alsop for Samuel Rand, 1624);

A Ryght Delectable Tratyse vpon a Goodly Garlande or Chapelet of Laurell (London: Printed by Richard Faukes, 1523);

Skelton Laureate Agaynste a Comely Coystrowne (London: Printed by John Rastell, circa 1527);

Here Folowythe Diuers Balettys and Dyties Solacyous (London: Printed by John Rastell, circa 1528);

Honorificatissimo, Amplissimo, . . . A Replycacion Agaynst Certayne Yong Scolers (London: Printed by Richard Pynson, circa 1528);

Magnyfycence, a Goodly Interlude and a Mery (Southwark: Printed by Peter Treveris for John Rastell, circa 1530);

Here After Foloweth a Lytell Boke Called Collyn Clout (London: Printed by Thomas Godfrey, circa 1531);

Here After Foloweth the Boke of Phyllyp Sparowe (London: Printed by Robert Copland for Richard Kele, circa 1545);

Here After Foloweth a Lytell Boke, Whiche Hath to Name, Why Come Ye Nat to Courte (London: Printed by Robert Copland for Richard Kele, circa 1545);

Pithy Pleasaunt and Profitable Workes of Maister Skelton, Nowe Collected and Newly Published (London: Printed by Thomas Marsh, 1568).

Editions: *The Tunning of Elinor Rumming* (London: Printed by Isaac Dalton for W. Bonham, 1718);

The Tunning of Elinor Rumming in *The Harleian Miscellany,* volume 1 (London: Printed for Thomas Osborne, 1744), pp. 402–410;

Woodcut of John Skelton in the first edition of Speke Parrot

The Tunning of Elinor Rumming in *The Harleian Miscellany,* volume 1 (London: Printed for John White, John Murray & John Harding 1808), pp. 415–422;

Select Works of the British Poets, from Chaucer to Jonson, with Biographical Sketches, edited by Robert Southey (London: Longman, Rees, 1831), pp. 61–75;

The Poetical Works of John Skelton, 2 volumes, edited by Alexander Dyce (London: Thomas Rodd, 1843); revised edition, 3 volumes (Boston: Little, Brown, 1856);

The Poetical Works of Skelton and Donne, with a Memoir of Each, 2 volumes (Boston: Houghton Mifflin, circa 1855);

"A Ballade of the Scottysshe Kynge," in *Athenaeum*, 2790 (16 April 1881): 325;

"A Ballade of the Scottysshe Kynge," edited by John Ashton (London: Elliot Stock, 1882);

"A Ballade of the Scottysshe Kynge," in *A Century of Ballads*, edited by Ashton (London: E. Stock, 1887), pp. xiii–xvii;

Magnyfycence, A Moral Play, edited by Robert Lee Ramsay, Early English Text Society, no. 48 (1908);

Magnificence, a Goodly Interlude and a Merry, edited by John S. Farmer, Tudor Facsimile Texts, no. 43 (1910);

"A Laureate Poem by Skelton," edited by C. C. Stopes, *Athenaeum*, 4514 (2 May 1914): 625;

Poems by John Skelton, edited by Richard Hughes (London: William Heinemann, 1924);

The Garland of Laurell, in *English Verse Between Chaucer and Surrey*, edited by Eleanor Prescott Hammond (Durham, N.C.: Duke University Press, 1927), pp. 342–367;

"Skelton's Speculum Principis," edited by Frederick M. Salter, *Speculum*, 9 (January 1934): 25–37;

Skelton: Poems by John Skelton, edited by Roland Gant (London: Grey Walls Press, 1949);

John Skelton: A Selection from His Poems, edited by Vivian de Sola Pinto (New York: Grove, 1950);

"A Ballad of the Scottish King," in *The Common Muse*, edited by de Sola Pinto and Allan Edwin Rodway (London: Chatto & Windus, 1957), pp. 32–33;

The Complete Poems of John Skelton Laureate, edited by Philip Henderson (London: Dent; New York: Dutton, 1959);

"A Ballad of the Scottish King," edited by Ashton (Detroit: Singing Tree Press, 1969);

John Skelton: Poems, edited by Robert S. Kinsman, Clarendon Medieval and Tudor Series (Oxford: Clarendon Press, 1969);

Pithy, Pleasant, and Profitable Works of Master Skelton, Poet Laureate, Now Collected and Newly Published (Menston, U.K.: Scolar Press, 1970);

John Skelton: Selected Poems, edited by Gerald Hammond (Manchester: Carcanet New Press, 1980);

Magnificence, edited by Paula Neuss, The Revels Plays (Manchester: Manchester University Press / Baltimore: Johns Hopkins University Press, 1980);

John Skelton: The Complete English Poems, edited by John Scattergood, Penguin English Poets (Harmondsworth, U.K. & New York: Penguin, 1983);

The Book of the Laurel, edited by F. W. Brownlow (Newark: University of Delaware Press / London, U.K. & Mississauga, Ontario: Associated University Presses, 1990);

"The Latin Writings of John Skelton," edited by David R. Carlson, in *Studies in Philology*, 88 (Fall 1991): 1–125.

TRANSLATIONS: Titus Calpurnius Siculus, *Bibliotheca Historia of Diodorus Siculus* [photographic facsimile of 1488 manuscript] (New York: Modern Language Association, 1925);

Siculus, *Bibliotheca Historia of Diodorus Siculus*, edited by Frederick M. Salter and H. L. R. Edwards, Early English Text Society, volumes 233, 239 (London: Oxford University Press 1956, 1957).

No one can deny the power, endurance, and memorable lines of the work of John Skelton; he is indisputably the first major Tudor poet, writing during the reigns of Edward IV, Richard III, and (for most of his career) Henry VII and Henry VIII. His poems are by turn lyric, passionate, vitriolic, learned, allusive, bewildering, scriptural, satiric, grotesque, and even obscene; his one extant play, *Magnificence* (circa 1530), makes dramatic allegory sternly didactic and pointedly political. Yet while Skelton's importance is clear enough, just how he is to be read and evaluated has always been contested. His poems might be royalist in tone, or they might be highly critical of government; he could write for the court and his patrons, the Howard family, yet still need political sanctuary; he could write a moving lament for a young novitiate's loss of a pet sparrow at the same time that he was castigating his own parish curate, the archbishop of York, and the lord chancellor. While his poems seem to have circulated widely, few of them were published in his lifetime. Nor have readers in later times fared much better in penetrating his meaning and appreciating his style. After the Reformation, George Puttenham found this very Catholic poet a "rude railing rhymer," and Ben Jonson used him as a character, but in an antimasque; by the time of Alexander Pope he was "beastly Skelton," offensive for his attack on a village alewife in *The Tunning of Elinor Rumming* (circa 1521), a poem which nevertheless remained in print throughout the eighteenth and nineteenth centuries, often as the single representation of his art.

In recent scholarship, there remains much disagreement. John M. Berdan, without much quarrel, called Skelton in 1920 "the greatest English poet to have been born in the fifteenth century"; he is seen as an erudite and clever poet of considerable breadth by F. W. Brownlow; an early-Tudor humanist steeped in classical learning by William Nelson; a poet primarily concerned with the literary aspect of his poems, as in his play with the medieval strategies of satire, by A. R. Heiserman; a chiefly rhetorical poet who invokes a reader response through his personal engagements and disengagements with his subjects for Stanley Eugene Fish; and essentially a priest who used poetic and dramatic works to instruct the laity by basing them in scriptural lessons and liturgical services of the Roman Catholic church for Arthur F. Kinney. Perhaps the best way to recover and understand Skelton's work is to consider all of these perspectives.

One fundamental difficulty in understanding Skelton is that very little is known of his life, and the absence of facts has been filled in over the centuries with legend and myth as well as, on occasion, questionable evidence – there were about one hundred John Skeltons born in the fourteenth and fifteenth centuries – or conflicting evidence – he seems to have written *The Garland of Laurel* both near the middle and the end of his life, and the result is a layered poem with some obscure passages. There are few extant documents that can be associated with him with certainty, so that the biography of the poet whom William Wordsworth once described as "a demon in point of genius" rests on such demonizing Protestant works as the anonymous *Merry Tales of Skelton* (1567), which make him into a legendary subject for jest and even scurrility, and on the genius Skelton inscribes for himself in his work. Both sources can be unreliable if not treacherous unless the reader is careful, so that any reconstruction of his life is more or less conjectural.

There are, for instance, no records of his birth or baptism, although allusions in his work point to a birthplace in the north of England, perhaps Yorkshire. As F. W. Brownlow points out, *The Garland of Laurel* (1523) alludes to Skelton's horoscope and birth on 2 May 1463. Nothing is recorded of his early schooling, but his display of learning suggests a strong early education, and his extensive knowledge and love of music suggest he may have been trained at a monastic choir school. In one poem he speaks affectionately of Cambridge as his *alma parens* from whom he took his sonship – "Namque tibi quandam carus alumnus eram" – and adds a marginal note that Cambridge first nourished Skelton laureate with "the pap of her knowledge." William Caxton, in his preface to his translation of Virgil's *Eneydos* (1489), calls Skelton "the late created poet

laureate in the University of Oxford," and in 1493 Skelton was given the only laureateship ever awarded at Cambridge. The Oxford laureation may have come in 1488, because some important event that year inspired Skelton to begin a personal calendar to which he later alludes. It is also fairly certain that at about this time he took up duties at court in the service of King Henry VII, where, he notes in a short poem, he was given his own "habit," a robe in the Tudor colors of green and white with Calliope embroidered on it in gold. Skelton was one of only a few poets and a few native English scholars chosen by the king. Finally, Brownlow notes that in late 1488 Thomas Howard was released from the Tower of London by the king and that Skelton's patronage by the Howard family was likely reaffirmed; his livelihood secure, his career as a poet thus had a new and lasting rebirth.

Indeed the best scholarly guess, now approaching consensus, is that from his time at Cambridge Skelton served as the poet and servant of the Howard family, the most powerful Catholic family in northern England. Quite likely he began, as a traditional humanist scholar might, as a tutor to the Howard children, for Caxton's tribute speaks of Skelton as a translator of classical texts; he "late translated the epistles of Tully [Cicero] / and the book of Diodorus Siculus, and diverse other works out of Latin into English, not in rude and old language, but in polished and ornate terms craftily." The Howards are more directly implicated in other early works. *The Bouge of Court* (circa 1499) is set at Powers Quay, a place in Harwich then belonging to John Howard, Duke of Norfolk, at the date of the poem's dream vision, encoded in the first stanza as 19 August 1482.

Howard was also "bannerer" at the funeral of Edward IV and as such may have prompted Skelton's moving lament for the king. In this elegy of eight twelve-line stanzas the king recalls his own life, listing his accomplishments (the Tower and city wall of London, the fortification of Dover, the royal palaces of Nottingham, Windsor, and Eltham) only to realize that worldly things are motivated by vanity and bound by time: "Where is now my conquest and victory? / Where is my riches and my royal array?" Instead he must, like anyone else, eventually yield to Death: "Humbly beseeching thee, God, of thy grace! / O ye courteous commons, your hearts unbrace," and sleep forever in dust: "Et, ecce, nunc in pulvere dormio!" is the poem's moral, mourning refrain.

In 1485 John Howard was killed at Bosworth Field, fighting on behalf of Richard III; his son and heir, Thomas Howard, Earl of Surrey, was

Woodcut depicting "Poeta Skelton," the persona of The Garland of
Laurel *(from the first edition)*

wounded, captured, attainted for treason, stripped
of his property, and put in the Tower of London.
When Henry VII released Howard in late 1488,
Skelton may have composed *The Garland of Laurel,*
reaffirming his love of the Howards and his duty to
them. In 1489 Howard was charged by the king to
put down the northern rebellion that had killed
Henry Percy, Earl of Northumberland, and Skelton
followed his patron's lead by writing an elegy for
Northumberland. This longer elegy blames the
earl's death on "fickle" Fortune's frown and on
"Fortune's double dice," commending Northumberland to the Virgin Mary.

The most important poem of this earliest period is *The Bouge of Court,* with "bouge" meaning
"rewards" or "provisions." It appears to be a traditional dream vision in rhyme royal with allegory,
personification, and a formulary incipit. But Skelton
moves his dream vision from the typical garden or
hillside to a public house in the Suffolk seaport of
Harwich and changes the season from spring to autumn, "when the sun [is] *in Virgo*" and Luna is

prominent and "full of mutability." He names his
protagonist Drede (dread) and puts him on ship-
board with seven tempters but no one of virtue:
Favell (flattery), palsied Suspicion, Harvey Hafter
(a rogue), ashen-faced Disdain, Riot, Dissimulation
(with a two-sided cloak), and Deceit. Each in turn
welcomes Drede, befriends him, and then apparently, alone or conspiratorially, betrays
him. Drede's meetings accelerate and accumulate
as his anxiety grows into an incurable fear; his final
decision to commit suicide by jumping overboard
causes the dreamer to awaken and write Drede's
story as an admonitory poem.

Clearly Skelton's ship, roughly contemporary
with Sebastian Brant's *Narrenschiff* (1494), is a ship
of fools, but it is also a ship of young courtiers
whose temptations are, like those at court, the temptations of political favor. If the poem is a study in
the growth not of dream but of nightmare, then one
moral is a warning against the evils of political life,
bred by greed and jealousy and promoted by dissimulation and betrayal. That Drede can initially be
tempted is revealed when he follows merchants on
board the ship; it is in this context that Desire, telling him that Fortune guides and rules the ship, at
first presents no threat. But the danger is there from
the start for Drede, because in following a Dame
Fortune that does not really appear, he is seduced
by self-interest. Fortune proves illusory; truth resides not in dreams but in life and not in favors but
in belief in the true Church. Thus the language of
unholy parody – where the tempters frequently
swear in blasphemous delusion themselves – leads
the reader of Skelton's poem to recall Saint
Bernard's spiritual ages of man and his sense of
man's fallen state, a state in which one is undirected
and in which the surrender of the self to secularism
divides man from Holy Mother Church. On board
a ship no longer guided by Christ but instead by an
antitype of the Holy Virgin (during the sign of the
Virgin), where favor and success are measured by
power and by material gain, Drede realizes that life
is no longer a pilgrimage but an increasing exile
from Eden.

The Garland of Laurel, which Skelton wrote in
1495 at Surrey's Sheriff Hutton Castle, treats a
more secular subject. (The castle, which once belonged to Richard III, was the royal outpost to secure peace in the rebellious northern part of England.) The poem purports to recount Skelton's life
at midpoint – he was in his early thirties – in a
dream vision which recounts his works and in
which Dame Occupation, with the support of Dame
Pallas (wisdom), helps to secure Skelton's place in

the Palace of Fame. The story is complicated and comprehensive; while it treats the value of art as creative and even redemptive, it also makes amusing comments about those who try to take Fortune by storm, about those whose work is not fully understood (like Skelton), and those who, like members of the Howard household and their friends, are charming students and companions.

The narrative of *The Garland* is located precisely in time and place. Brownlow, in his edition of the poem, has decoded the astrological description to locate the precise time at which it is set: between 7:00 and 7:30 on the morning of 8 May 1495. The place is more explicit: the marshy woods of the Forest of Galtres outside Sheriff Hutton Castle, where the Howards reside. Together the heavens and landscape reflect "Poeta Skelton" – the poem's persona – and his twin desires: the longing for immortality and the desire for earthly fame as a poet. At first he is melancholy and depressed, in a dull half-sleep of exhaustion and a sense of failure, before his dazzling dream takes him to the pavilion of Dame Pallas and the palace of the Queen of Fame. What could be serious and dull, however, is enlivened by characterization. Poeta Skelton is the hapless artist who has stopped creating art, and the Queen of Fame is petulant and complaining, for although Poeta Skelton is enrolled in her books, he has lost his right to be there because he is no longer producing poetry. Fame suggests he write in favor of women, since they are his audience. Pallas understands the wider learning in Poeta Skelton's work and appreciates a writer's difficulties. If he writes poems of praise in lovely English, he is accused of lies and flattery; if he tells the truth, he is called stupid and his plainspokenness threatened with punishment. On one hand, he must write to earn his place in the roll of fame; on the other, he risks calling down complaints on himself.

Pallas and Fame decide to resolve this predicament by holding a Court of Fame at which the poet will speak on his own behalf. When Eolus, the god of wind, blows his trumpet, a motley crowd of the rude and stupid comes running, passionately longing for fame. Fame tells Pallas that success alone will not win entry to her palace but that hard work and virtue are needed for success and admittance; she confesses to maintaining high standards and a keen sense of responsibility. Actually, she has neither. Those in the rabble that arrives are not the sort of people with whom the poet wishes to associate, and he disengages himself from them. Pallas, old and plain in appearance, is the real keeper of standards; Fame, in comparison, is incompetent and

even destructive. Her court, by extension, is unjust, and so are her complaints about Skelton. Someone else must judge his case.

The poem proceeds, like *The Bouge of Court,* by associational or psychological development – a dream logic. Eolus's trumpet draws not only the usual untalented seekers of reputation but the entire college of true poets, both living and dead. They too have taken an interest in Skelton's case and appear not in motley but in splendid dress, many of them carrying their own works. They gladly drink the wine Bacchus offers them. But the reader learns that their magnificent and musical language, inspired by Apollo, began at first in pain, grief, and failure; their laurels are the sign of Apollo's hopeless love for Daphne, who in mythology turned into a laurel tree to escape the god's amorous pursuit. Pain, not fame, causes poets to write. Poetry is also the process of healing – another application of Apollo as the god of medicine – and poets must win their own return to health. The poets thus form their own court to render an independent judgment. They send Poeta Skelton three English predecessors – John Gower, Geoffrey Chaucer, and John Lydgate – to assure him that there is a place for him in their college and that they intend to present him to Fame's court. They also fetch Lady Occupation, Fame's registrar, who is the poet's old best friend, having supported him for long hours at his desk. But she is also admonitory and shows him a dreadful vision of the life of mere ambition.

Occupation's vision depicts the world as a walled field, with gates for past and present nations, the gate of Anglia culminating in a royal leopard and strange verses of warning; it has been seen as a world governed by time and history, of growth and death, and a vision of the English court especially as dangerous. Poeta Skelton claims to be "no thing proud/Of that adventure," suggesting he has strayed from the vocation of a poet to activities at court and that Lady Occupation is urging him to return. At one point, in what may be a later-interpolated passage, "one there was there – I wondered of his hap – / For a gun stone, I say, had all to-jagged his cap, / Ragged and dagged [bemired] and cunningly cut; / The blast of the brimstone blew away his brain." Although this strange man is not identified and at least one scholar has thought it a self-portrait of Skelton endangered by court, it may instead be a portrait of Thomas Cardinal Wolsey, whose ambition to Skelton seemed greatest and most dangerous.

After this, an enveloping mist clouds the vision, and Occupation returns the poet-dreamer to a formal, enclosed garden where Apollo plays his harp and the Muses are led in a dance by Flora, the goddess of spring. Only a bad fiddler named Envious Rancor mars this paradise; the character has been decoded as Roger Statham, a courtier Skelton disliked. Between the dangers of court and the personal dangers of envy, Occupation leads the poet to a winding stair which goes to a chamber where Skelton discovers the countess of Surrey, her three daughters, and seven attendant ladies, all weaving a garland of laurel for him. Like Pallas, the countess is an older woman who becomes the poet's sponsor, and the poet addresses the ladies with some of his most charming, and perhaps most personal, poetry. Occupation returns Poeta Skelton to Fame's palace, where she reads aloud Skelton's bibliography. The queen can only ratify his case; when Occupation arrives at *The Garland* itself, the audience of poets bursts into applause. This noisy response awakens the poet-dreamer, and he gives himself a new-year greeting, marking 1488 as the beginning of his rededication to poetry.

Despite the seriousness of the theme, the poem is also witty – in the case of Eolus (who may also suggest the Last Judgment), Poeta Skelton wearing his garland for a hat, and even the brainsplattered syphilitic intruder. The cluster of poems surrounding the countess is itself a garland analogous to the one Skelton is awarded in the poem, and while they align the larger work to the Howards, they make of Skelton's employment at Sheriff Hutton a pleasurable experience at some distance from the bouge of court with its competitive politics and daily harangues. Despite the eccentricity of some of the lines, the changing of moods, and the visionary shifts in subject, *The Garland* remains one of the age's greatest poetic tributes.

Sometime in the 1490s Skelton left Sheriff Hutton for court in London, perhaps to accompany the Howards, or as an extension of his service to Henry VII, which may have begun in 1492 when he accompanied the king to France. Perhaps he was called to court by Lady Margaret Buford, Countess of Richmond, to tutor her grandson Prince Henry (later Henry VIII) for his place as archbishop of Canterbury and head of the church. In any event Skelton seems to have been acting as the court poet when in 1494 he celebrated Prince Henry's creation as duke of York with some Latin verses, "Carmen ad principem, quando insignitus erat ducis Ebor. titulo." In addition he was apparently involved in creating court entertainments, although one later play, *Magnificence,* written in 1516, is all that survives. His role as court poet is supported by the single autograph copy of "The Rose Both White and Red," possibly a coronation poem for Henry VIII, found between the leaves of an account book of the royal revels; several of his other poems were set to music by William Cornish, the music master of the children of Westminister Abbey and later Master of the Children of the Chapel Royal. The only manuscript of Skelton's translation of Diodorus Siculus was written for Robert Pen – like Cornish, a Gentleman of the Chapel Royal – so that Skelton's activities at court may also have connected him to the King's Chapel.

Among the lost works attributed to Skelton in *The Garland of Laurel* is his translation of a moral allegory, *La Pélerinage de la vie humaine* (The Pilgrimage of Human Life, 1330–1331) by Guillaume de Deguileville, done for Lady Margaret. He also wrote for her a "devout prayer," and a record of December 1497 notes a payment of sixty-six shillings and eight pence (a large sum) given by her "to my lady the king's mother's poet." Whether her influence, the influence of the Chapel Royal, or some other factors were in play, in 1498 Skelton decided to take orders in the Roman Catholic Church, and in March, April, and June he was swiftly ordained as subdeacon, deacon, and priest by the bishop of London. A series of religious poems at this time – "Vexilla Regis," "Upon a Dead Man's Head," and "Woefully Arrayed" – may have been inspired by these events, and Henry VII probably attended Skelton's first celebration of Holy Mass when on 16 November 1498 he gave the new priest a gift of twenty shillings, about three times his usual Sunday offering.

Skelton nevertheless continued teaching the prince. His *Speculum principis,* signed "At Eltham, 28 August 1501," is a "little mirror" written in rhyming Latin prose to teach "the princes in their minority." (Later, when the prince became king, Skelton revised the work and presented it to him formally.) But his job ended suddenly in 1502 – quite likely because in April of that year Prince Arthur, the first son of Henry VII, died, and young Prince Henry was sent off with a new instructor to prepare for a life of politics rather than religion. A record from 29 April 1502 shows that the "Duke of York's schoolmaster" was paid forty shillings by the king, likely to discharge him from his duties.

At that time the king's mother may have become Skelton's patroness, for the next record, dated 10 April 1504, shows him to be the parson of the parish church of Saint Mary the Virgin in Diss, a prosperous wool town and trading center in East Anglia on the road from Bury Saint Edmonds to Norwich, and a living in the gift of Lady Margaret. Diss, in the powerful diocese of Norwich, was also well located near sites of political and ecclesiastical power: Skelton's church was four miles from Hoxne Abbey, where the bishop of Norwich was often in residence, and eight miles from Redgrave, where in 1506 Thomas Wolsey was appointed parson of the parish church. Also, Diss was about twenty miles from Framlingham Castle, the chief residence of his patrons, the Howard family, and one of the most impressive and fortified castles in Tudor England.

At East Anglia he wrote, among other works, "Epitaphs of Two Knaves of Diss," "Ware the Hawk," and "Philip Sparrow," perfecting a verse form composed of short, cascading lines of dimeter and trimeter phrasings, which has been named "Skeltonic" verse. The form, however, was not new with Skelton but was a variation on the musical form of plainsong (Gregorian chant) which is strophic, not metrical, and varies the accents and the number of accented syllables at will for better expression, thus emphasizing a feeling for spoken language. Various interpretations of plainsong rhythms exist – mensuralist, rhythmicist, and nonmensuralist – but from the viewpoint of a student of Skeltonics, plainsong is always nonmetrical and allows for a free placing of accent. Usually the lines are dimeters or trimeters controlled by the substance and meaning of lines as much as their mood, allowing a mixture of long and short lines such as can be found in a later Skelton poem such as "Colin Clout." Furthermore, extensions of plainsong which were first connected to the "Alleluia," known as sequences, in time became detached and used as independently shaped melodies that could also vary, as Skelton varies poetic form in *The Garland of Laurel*. Finally, plainsong became in time the basis of troping, those long, digressive poems that often occur at the "conductus" of the Mass. This kind of troping lies behind Jane's Mass of Birds, where it follows its liturgical model in seeming both formed and formless, accretive and endless, digressive and an extended analogy of the basic meaning of the larger poem (or service) to which it is attached through performance. A more secular troping is found in a later Skeltonic poem, *The Tunning of Elinor Rumming*, which extends the title in a way that is only apparently formless.

In "Epitaphs of Two Knaves of Diss" the juxtaposition of mock epitaphs for John Clark, soul priest (a curate who prays for the souls of others), and Adam Uddersall, bailiff, draws on the satiric strains of late-medieval goliardic poetry, but it also pairs the two quarrelsome troublemakers as if they were figures for John and James, the equally quar-

relsome disciples in the Gospels of Mark and Luke. Clark may have earned his role as knave because in his will, dated 2 February 1506, he gives money to the local guild foundation in Skelton's parish but pointedly excludes Skelton's own benefice. The form Skelton uses for the mock-epitaphs is that of the trental of pilgrim's prayers at Lent; for Skelton this becomes thirty Masses, said one after another over thirty days and all revealing how Clark, like Peter at the Last Supper, betrays Holy Service: he is portrayed as mocking the Eucharist by his desire to acquire a red amice, the liturgical color for the Passion as well as for those who celebrate the Black Mass; he eats intestines of sheep, goats, and oxen rather than the blessed elements of Host and wine; he reverses the prayer "Orate, fratres" in the Canon; he kneels before a football as if it were the Host; he chants "Bibite multum" instead of the proper "bibite ex eo" at the elevation of the chalice; and he kisses the Devil's *culum* (ass) rather than sacred elements. In short, John Clark's heresies, according to this epitaph, show him to be a soul priest whose own soul is misdirected.

Just as Clark is attacked for betraying his vocation, so Uddersall is blamed for misusing his authority as a bailiff. Like Clark, he subverts the talents and the office given him by God, and so reveals his disobedience to Him. He is compared to a foe of Israel: Agag, King of Amalek, defeated by Saul (1 Samuel 15:5–9). Both poems are figural, seeing their specific subject matter as typological behavior open to interpretation and judgment on a spiritual spectrum.

"Ware the Hawk" is a more complicated and powerful poem. The title is a proverbial cry used to encourage a hawk to obtain its prey; the poem tells the story (presumably autobiographical) of the rector of Diss's finding a neighboring curate hawking in his church during his absence, a practice that Pope Innocent III had specifically forbidden in an injunction of the Fourth Lateran Council (1215). Although hawking was a common offense and the hawking parson a commonplace of poetic satire – already having been employed by Chaucer and Gower – Skelton portrays this instance as a desecration of the church since this "lewd curate, / A parson beneficed," has allowed the hawk to pollute the altar and eventually to defecate on it. Not only is the altar stained, but the blood of the hawk's prey falling on the Host and chalice mocks the blood of Christ whose suffering is the very heart of Holy Mass celebrated there.

What follows this initial narration is the body of the poem, a sermon which interprets the situation as exegesis does a biblical text. In form, this sermon is

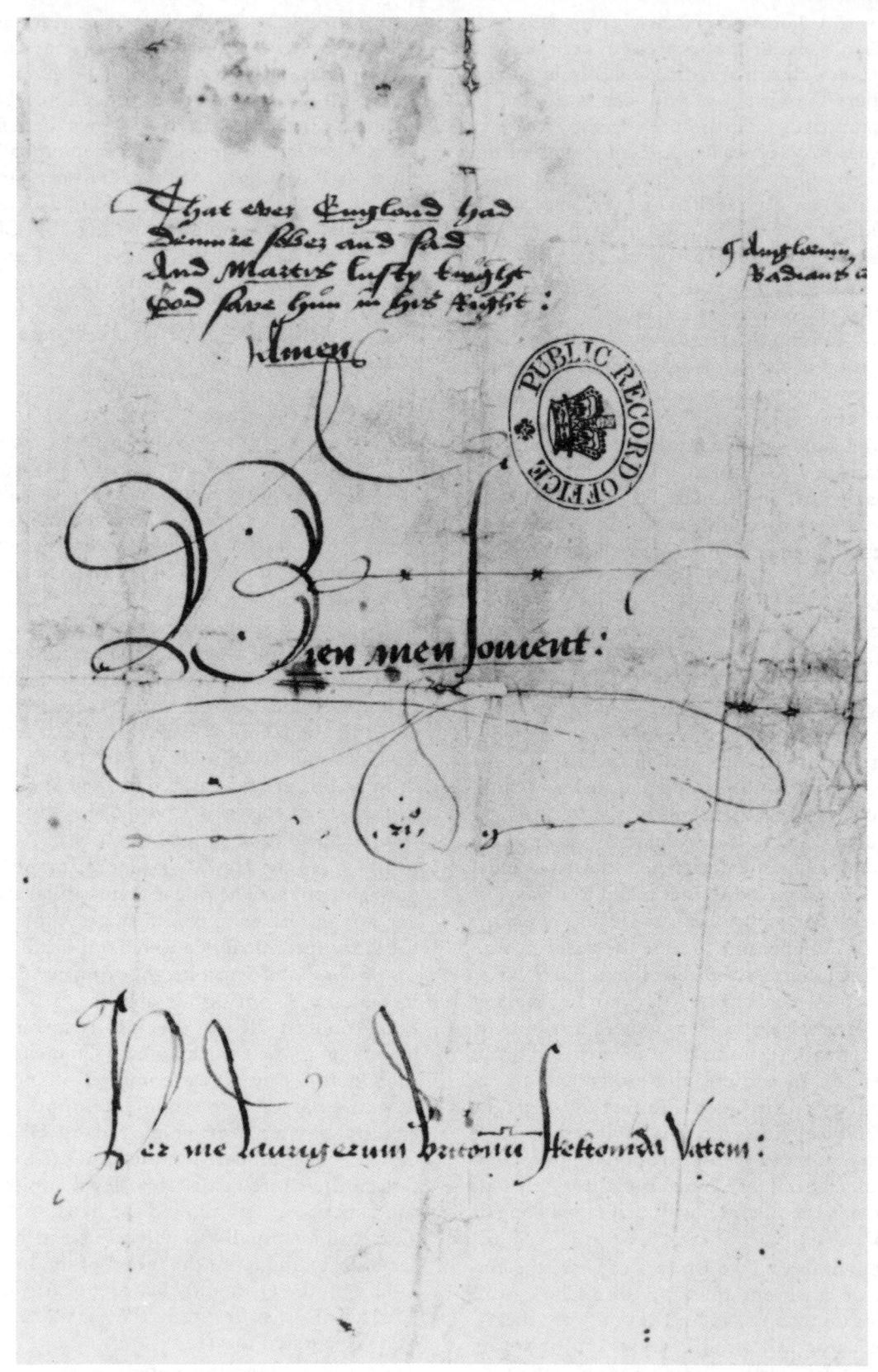

Last page of Skelton's manuscript for his poem on the accession of Henry VIII, 22 April 1509 (Public Record Office, London)

a penitential one, divided into eight parts labeled "Observate," "Considerate," "Deliberate," "Vigilate," "Deplorate," "Divinate," "Reformate," and "Pensitate" and followed by a new "table" of laws to replace the Ten Commandments. This table can hardly be for the erring curate, for he has been called irredeemable; rather, as the imperative mode of the subtitles suggests, it is meant for the poet's congregation and for his readers. Furthermore, by setting this incident on 29 August, the feast day of the Decollation of Saint John the Baptist, Skelton stresses the idea of sacrifice by death; by alluding to the desecration of the Temple in 2 Kings 16 and 2 Chronicles 28, Skelton shows that the curate is prefigured by Ahaz, who "defiled . . . all the furniture of the temple." Even in the section called "Reformate," Skelton provides a long catalogue of Roman emperors who persecuted Christians and more recent pagans, such as the Turks, who in 1453 desecrated the Church of Saint Sophia in Constantinople, the mother church of the Eastern papacy where Saint John's head was taken as a relic. As God provided a Hezekiah to overcome the savage destruction of Ahaz, so he has caused Skelton to see (and to overcome through his poem) the destruction wrought by the curate. The dark denunciations suggest that the matter of the poem is God's prophecy, not an idle boast by Skelton who, after all, was surprised to find the curate hawking in his church. That was the doing of God, just as the appointment of Skelton to punish the curate is God's decision. In confronting the curate with his crime, the exasperated Skelton is reduced to calling him "Doctor Dawcock" and "Domine Dawcock."

Since the nineteenth century, "Philip Sparrow" has been Skelton's best-loved poem. Its occasion is the death of a pet sparrow trained and beloved by Jane Scrope, a young novitiate then living with her mother, the recently widowed Lady Eleanor Windham, at the Benedictine Priory of Saint Mary at Carrow just outside Norwich. Part 1 of the poem is based on a single liturgical service, the vespers of the Office of the Dead, and opens with a brief antiphon after which the service is named: "Placebo Domino in regione vivorum" (I shall please the Lord in the land of the living). It concludes with an augmented version of the same antiphon, to which there is the reply "Hei mihi, Domine, qui incolatus meus prolongatus est" (Woe is me, O Lord, that my sojourn is prolonged).

But, unlike the service, Jane's "Placebo" begins and remains antiphonal:

Pla ce bo,
    Who is there, who?

Di le xi,
    Dame Margery,
Fa, re, my, my.
    Wherefore and why, why?
For the soul of Philip Sparrow,
That was late slain at Carrow,
Among the Nuns Black.
For that sweet soul's sake,
And for all sparrows' souls
Set in our bede rolls [mourners' prayer rolls]
Pater noster qui
With an *Ave Mari,*
And with the corner of a Creed,
The more shall be your meed [reward].

These opening lines indicate the thrust of the entire "Placebo" of the poem: clearly what Jane has done — the first half of the poem is in her voice and in her thought — is to turn a liturgical service which she is attending into an antiphon, and she responds with the plainsong of her own stream of consciousness, which is in turn directed by the service. Because her entire thought pattern is a projection of her own suffering over the recent loss of her sparrow, the antiphonal exchange following the opening of the Office of the Dead is rendered keenly autobiographical. She is sorrowful herself at her prolonged sojourn, separated as she is from Philip; she asks how, left in the land of the living without her sparrow, she can possibly be expected to please the Lord. The dialectic proposed by the text in her primer becomes the basic dilemma that her private meditation must work out even as the more public service is impersonally sung around her. That Jane is prompted to such thoughts is parodic in a special sense meant to underscore how seriously, and how personally, she applies the text of the Divine Office: while others say or sing it, she lives it.

Other versicles from Psalms are sung, and then the service invokes the Magnificat, at which point Jane awards Philip with his own more fitting Requiem Mass of Birds. While this may seem intrusive, even digressive, it comes at a point in the service roughly analogous to where the sequence of the proper of any mass might be "troped" (extended by a fitting digression), and in accommodating her Requiem to Philip, Jane acts as intercessor just as Mary, in the Magnificat, is made intercessor between God and man; notably, Saint Philip is the historic saint of intercession. The more dolorous matter of the requiem transforms the young novitiate for the moment into the Mater Dolorosa, the sorrowing mother at the cross of a misunderstood Christ. Those who might laugh at Jane for her excessive grief over a pet do not measure truly the need and function of intercession: it is, after all, the sparrow for whom Christ says God has special providence.

Part 2 of "Philip Sparrow" follows exactly a service complementary to the "Placebo": the Commendation of All Souls, found in the same primers and Books of Hours. This service is also named for a formulary which suggests intercession: "Tibi, Domine, commendamus animam famuli tui N. et animas famulorum famularumque tuarum" (To thee, O Lord, we commend the soul of thy servant N. and the souls of thy servants both men and women), this latter formula providing the last liturgical reference in the poem. The eight main sections in part 2, each introduced by a versicle from Psalms, have appeared to many critics as erotic stanzas cataloguing Jane's physical charms, astonishingly out of place in this poem. But the point is that they are based on praises of the Virgin drawn from popular carols and rounds, the Canticle of Canticles, and Saint Valentine's Day poems to the Virgin. Skelton follows part 1, based loosely on the Seven Sorrows of the Virgin, with his own more celebratory Seven Joys of the Virgin; he returns (as Jane does with the Magnificat) to the relationship between mother and child marked by pleasure and happiness.

The two parts of the poem thus function as one by realizing the double interpretation of Christ's death as derived from Saint Origen: the first resurrection, by which the soul rises from the death of the body (as Philip rises from his death by the cat Gib) and the second resurrection – Philip's, the cat's, and the reader's – by which the body finds occasion to be freed from all corruption, to renew spiritual dedication, and to take joy in newfound spiritual health.

Such a poem grows directly out of the experience of life in the convent, where Skelton likely met Jane Scrope and her mother. But the allusions of such figural poetry, which find their meaning only in light of received liturgy and Scripture, apparently confused Skelton's first readers as they have most readers until recently. Skelton remarks in *The Garland of Laurel:* "What ail them to deprave / Philip Sparrow's grave? / His *Dirige,* her Commendation / Can be no derogation, / But mirth and consolation / Made by protestation, / No man to miscontent / With Philip's entrement." To prevent misreading, Skelton wrote a brief part 3, the "Addition," in which he replies directly to his critics. In writing this, he follows part 1 (the intercession of Jane for Philip) and part 2 (the intercession of Jane to God) by interceding on Jane's behalf to the poem's readers. This final act of intercession becomes, as the others have become, an act of commendation; and all three become acts of pleasing ("Placebo").

After 1511 Skelton's name no longer appears in records at Diss; on 5 July 1511 he was in London dining with the prior of Westminster Abbey. By 1512 the poet appears to have given Henry VIII three manuscripts: a revised copy of his *Speculum Principis;* a poem titled "Complaint," decrying "Skelton Laureate, onetime royal tutor" as being "quiet in soliloquy with himself " and "wholly given over to oblivion, or like one dead from the heart"; and an annotated copy of the old *Chronique de Rains* about Richard the Lion-Hearted, inscribed with a new dedication to Henry. The *Speculum Principis* ends with an allusive jab at one of Henry's advisers, possibly Wolsey, who had left the parish of Redgrave and by 1512 was royal almoner and privy councillor to the king: "Grow strong, prince, easily a prince of all princes. Understand that a king must rule and not be ruled. Listen to Samuel, read Daniel, banish Ishmael. Banish! Banish!"

Whether Skelton's persistence or the king's sense of obligation to his first tutor played the major part, in the spring of 1512 or 1513 the poet was formally recognized by letters patent as *orator regius,* court poet and rhetorician to Henry VIII. At first he seems to have written court poems natural to that office, including an epigraph for Henry VII ("Eulogium pro suorum temporum conditione") that he used to honor the son – "Noster Honor solus, filius, ecce, suus!" – and which was duly hung in the Chapel of Henry VII in Westminster Abbey, and an "Elegia" for Lady Margaret Buford which, more than a century later, John Weever found still hanging over her tomb. The king's orator also wrote occasional poems on political triumphs. "Contra Gallos" celebrates the Battle of the Spurs in 1513, when Henry VIII invaded France and took Thérouenne and Tournai. A series of other poems honors Skelton's longtime patrons, the Howard family who defeated Scottish forces at Flodden Field in 1513; they include the "Chorus de Dis contra Scottis," the "Ballad of the Scottish King," and, later, a revision of the ballad with added invective, retitled "Against the Scots."

There is some indication that Skelton was part of the large retinue from court that went with Henry VIII to France in 1513, for it was there that Christopher Garnesche, Sergeant of the King's Tent and a partisan of Wolsey, was knighted for his services. Skelton's series of poems "Against Garnesche," some of which are written in Skeltonics, is part of a notable duel of invective, although Skelton remarks at the end of each section of his work that this contest of abuse was actually written "by the King's most noble commandment." Although this highly personal and doubtless occasional work is a minor part of Skelton's canon, it remains important as the first example of a "flyting" in English. He also returned at this time to the mock epitaph in his diatribe against William Bedell, former Treasurer of the Household for Lady Margaret Buford. The Latin poem is based on Psalm 73, but its cause and meaning remain obscure.

Two works of 1516 were aimed at Wolsey. The first one, "Against Venemous Tongues," was occasioned by the elevation in 1515 of the archbishop of York to cardinal of the church (and so chief prelate in all England). Skelton admonishes: "All matters well pondered and well to be regarded, / How should a false lying tongue then be rewarded? / Such tongues should be torn out by the hard roots, / Hoyning [grunting] like hogs that gronis [grunt] and wrotez [root in soil]." The reference to "hogs," alluding to Wolsey as a butcher's son, clearly identifies Skelton's target. But more galling than the cardinal's low birth is his ostentatious display of his new badge of office: "for before on your breast and behind on your back, / In Roman letters I never found lack." "Never found lack" is a turning point in the poem, for while there is a surplus of letters ("T" and "C" for "Thomas Cardinalis") on his livery, there is a "lack," which Skelton finds "In your cross-row nor Christ-cross-you-speed, / Your *Pater noster,* your *Ave,* nor your Creed," for these are the true texts which the cardinal forgets both to speak and to practice.

Although the poem is ostensibly one of denunciation, the poet must find a way to salvage language when it has been all but destroyed by debasement. His means for achieving this is to make an analogy between proper and improper use of language and the good and bad men who are responsible for its corruption; further, he makes good men (such as himself) those who remain responsible to the beliefs of the Church and the lessons of Scripture and the evil ones those who flout their office at the expense of their faith. Thus the poem is really a colloquy between the priest of the Church, who calls on the Church's authority for his credentials, and that Church's prelate, who has apparently forgotten what lessons that Church taught him.

The second work of 1516 is Skelton's only surviving play, the allegorical morality play *Magnificence.* In her 1980 edition of the play, Paula Neuss claims that its title has three meanings: "liberality . . . combined with good taste," or "munificence," as derived from Aristotle's use of the word; "glory," which can lead either to proper dignity or, when misused, pride; and "a title of honor applied

to . . . distinguished persons." The play unfolds simultaneously on at least three levels. On the allegorical level, the title character is a figure for mankind, over whose soul and mind the virtues and vices of measure are warring. On the philosophical level, the play considers the meaning of *magnificence* to be proper balance or moderation: "measure is treasure." On a literal or narrative level, the character named Magnificence ceases to be prudent, invites corrupt conspirators to his court, loses his power, and struggles to regain his authority. Although Skelton seems by this time to have taken sanctuary in Westminster under the auspices of John Islip, Abbot of Westminster Abbey and a member of the king's Privy Council, there is nevertheless in the play a mix of moral debate and tragedy and a constant movement from the abstract to the specific and back to the abstract, which prevents any easy association of Wolsey with the central character.

The theme of the play is the traditional one of virtue versus vice, as in *The Bouge of Court.* The struggle is between prudence and folly, not good and evil, but the play is concerned with worldly success rather than salvation. Although the text is not divided, *Magnificence* clearly falls into five stages or acts: prosperity, conspiracy, delusion, overthrow, and restoration (again resonant of *The Bouge of Court*). But this moral allegory about good and evil is also a political allegory about good and bad rule. The prince is distracted and seduced by six vices which have been associated with Wolsey, such as Counterfeit Countenance, aimed at Wolsey's lower social origins, and Courtly Abusion, aimed at reminding the audience of Wolsey's love for extravagant dress. In the vices there is great wit, and many of the scenes inject a comedy not common to moralities of the time. Nan Cooke Carpenter notes that *Magnificence* is "a mixture of old and new, of seriousness and humor, of traditional religion and practical politics. Its hero is Henry VIII and at the same time any man whom adverse Fortune may cast down at any time. Its vices add up to Thomas Wolsey, or to anyone else motivated by extreme self-love and selfish ambition." Cloaking pointed references in the guise of general wrongs, Skelton is able to write strong satire while never clearly attacking the king's favored adviser.

Magnificence was Skelton's first lengthy attack on Wolsey, followed in the 1520s by three more daring poems which must have been risked only because Skelton had been granted sanctuary and because, urging traditional morality, he could argue that he was a truer priest than Wolsey was a prelate: "Speak, Parrot" (1521), "Colin Clout" (1522), and "Why Come Ye Not to Court?" (late 1522 and 1523), each increasingly direct. "Speak, Parrot" is Skelton's most recalcitrant work. Not only is it obscure in itself, but it exists only in two separate, partial versions (one in manuscript) that must be conflated to establish a full text. It was written at discrete periods and seems layered in its presentation. Even in the opening section, which like *The Bouge of Court* declares the situation on which the poem elaborates, the Parrot feels it necessary to speak figuratively rather than directly, by what he describes as "Confuse distributive": that is, speech that seems confusing because it scatters or distributes its meaning throughout the poem, though its significance grows in the mind of the reader as he progresses through it (as was often the case with the reading of Scripture and its exegesis).

But the poem is hardly the "cryptogram of which we have lost the key" that C. S. Lewis thought it. "Speak, Parrot" is a poem of commentary and instruction in which Parrot does not warn us what will happen so much as tell us what we are to know and how we are to interpret it. About this, Parrot could not be plainer:

> But of that supposition that called is art,
> *Confuse distributive,* as Parrot hath devised,
> Let every man after his merit take his part;
> For in this process, Parrot nothing hath surmised,
> But that *metaphora, alegoria* withall,
> Shall be his protection, his pavys [shield], and his wall.

In constructing a proposition ("supposition") that one would consider well arranged ("art"), Parrot has jumbled together scattered bits of truth ("Confuse distributive") in a way that will allow readers to determine their meaning, each according to his merit, reminiscent of the biblical "every man shall receive his own reward, according to his own labor" (1 Corinthians 3:8). But the "art" is in the "supposition," the controlling idea and the selection, not in the subject matter, which is neither original ("No matter pretended") nor unusually arranged ("nor nothing enterprised").

Parrot employs signs and figures (metaphor, allegory) as his shield ("pavys"). Moreover, he will use the mirror in his cage to see prismatically, as if through a glass darkly: "The mirror that I tote [peer] in *Quasi di phanum, / Vel quasi speculum in engimate*" (1 Corinthians 13:12). But although what he will say is politically dangerous, this is not the reason for his indirection – he is only a parrot and will not flinch in his envois from openly exposing Cardinal Wolsey. Rather, metaphor and allegory are necessary because God's truth is so dazzling. Parrot's truth, like Saint Paul's, must be comprehended indirectly on earth; only in Parrot's home of Paradise would we be able to see it directly, in all its brilliant glory. There, it would be splendidly lucid, neither divided in its grand design nor distributed across human history.

The plainness of Parrot's message, once the parts are connected, is complicated by the narrator, a composite which Skelton expects his readers to take apart. Parrot derives from at least three traditions. Contemporary bestiaries stressed the parrot's exotic origins (in India), its skill at language, and its quick ability to mimic others. Thus Parrot the narrator can change swiftly, gather up varied scraps of wisdom in foreign tongues, and put his bits of knowledge into revealing juxtaposition. This wise fool came from Paradise, and, still trailing clouds of that glory, he will occasionally speak in what seems to be tongues, reminiscent of Pentecost or Whitsunday. A second pedigree comes from Boccaccio's *Decameron* (1353), which assigns to Parrot divinity as a descendant of Prometheus, who breathed life into clay, like God. Parrot, as the son of Deucalion, barely escaped the flood, the apocalyptic memory of which will nearly overcome him at the end of the poem. Finally Parrot has in his cage a special mirror that refracts light and so throws into relief much that is around him. In medieval homiletic literature, the mirror was a figure for the Host, its broken pieces the various communicants who wished to unite their bodies with Christ's. Parrot's comments, then, are divinely inspired.

In part 1, Parrot begins by trying to keep things as whole as possible. He injects stanzas to demonstrate that in Tudor England (where he is presently caged) Henry VIII and Cardinal Wolsey are reenacting typological roles already forewarned in the Old Testament. Three biblical types offer man's basic choice for Parrot: Melchisedech, Moloch, and Gideon. Melchisedech offers Abraham bread and wine (Genesis 14:18), prefiguring the Eucharist. In time Melchisedech came to prefigure Christ as Prince of Peace (Hebrews 6:20), and his name was invoked in each Mass celebrated by the Church during the celebrant's fifth pass over the chalice. Parrot directs his Tudor congregation back through the Mass to Church history beause Melchisedech's law was the continuity of a covenant with Noah, and Parrot identifies his own history with the time of Noah's flood. Parrot even identifies with Melchisedech because neither had any known parents. But speaking in tongues, he joins with Henry VIII, as the King of Peace, in eternal contest with Moloch/Wolsey. Wolsey, however, is identified with Moloch (the Antichrist of Leviticus 18:21). For Moloch, God allows no concessions: "the people of the land shall stone him" (Leviticus 20:2). Moloch's position in the Old Testament prefigures that of Herod in the New Testament, an enemy of God familiar to the viewers in Skelton's day of the cycle of biblical mystery plays. As part 1 progresses, Parrot grows more urgent, even more plainspoken. He first condenses his fears into a single line, "But *moveatur terra,* let the world wag," recalling Psalm 98 ("The Lord hath reigned, let the people be angry: he that sitteth on the cherubims: let the earth be moved") and the *Libera me* from the Office for the Dead ("In that dreadful day, when the heavens and the earth are shaken").

That dreadful day, Doomsday, is brought closer to home in part 2, where the apparent digression concerning the "Grammarians' War" of 1519–1521 enlists humanist educators to testify to the advancing forces of Moloch, because their New Learning provides referential texts that are no longer Scriptural. Parrot's own attempted use of "Such shreds of sentence, strewn in the shop / Of ancient Aristippus and such mother more" leads into rhetorical nonsense that can only suggest the fallen world, and grammatical nonsense that suggests the Tower of Babel.

Part 3 is a single brief interlude in a markedly different tone. Parrot's mistress, Galathea, approaches his cage and "prays" that, "for Mary's sake," he will sing her a love song. Parrot's response is a song at once erotic and so general that it seems to be a song of intercession for all mankind. His song wins Galathea's gratitude and blessing, and their subsequent dialogue suggests that the imminence of the Last Judgment predicted in earlier times is possible again in their own.

Part 4 is a series of four unusually long envois (sequentially dated by an internal system beginning with the year of Skelton's laureateship at Oxford) which details Wolsey's failure at Calais as an index (as Moloch/Wolsey) of his increasingly futile but dangerous power. The envois conclude with a reference to Edward Stafford, third Duke of Buckingham, who was executed in 1521 on trumped-up charges of treason by Wolsey. Wolsey used this event to ruin the spirit of Thomas Howard, Skelton's lifelong patron, and so effectively ended the power of the older aristocracy which both Buckingham and Howard represented.

Early in the poem there are dark hints of such an outcome. The whole work places an increasingly powerful Moloch against a progressively weaker Melchisedech. What is needed is a savior, figured in Gideon. Parrot tried to be that Gideon but failed, and in a sense Skelton tries and fails, too. Warnings fall on deaf ears, and the poem is taken over by the

hulking body of Wolsey. "Speak, Parrot" draws to a close with a portrait of England's chief prelate riding his mule in trappings of gold, a parody of Jesus on his way to Jerusalem where his trial and crucifixion would allow him to harrow hell. The gold associated with Wolsey here is reminiscent of Aaron's golden calf, the story used by Parrot earlier in the poem to begin the history of man's fall.

But Wolsey's thirst for power and greed for wealth knew no bounds that Skelton could discern. As Cardinal and Lord Chancellor, he embodied an unholy wedding of sacred and secular power, of church and state; in his papal appointment in 1518 as *legatus a latere* he threatened the very foundation of the English Catholic Church. This papal appointment enormously extended Wolsey's ecclesiastical powers; acting in the place of the pope in England, he could remit sins, take jurisdiction of wills from English bishops, demand tribute from all levels of the clergy, and (in time) legitimize bastards, chastise the clergy, grant degrees in theology, arts, and religious orders, appoint benefices at will, absolve those excommunicated or under other sentences, and reform the monasteries. Wolsey even undermined these privileges. By simultaneously holding a bishropic and an archbishopric, he introduced episcopal pluralism into England. He made a game out of appointments for himself, trading up the sees by turning in Bath and Wells when Durham fell vacant, and exchanging that for the see at Winchester. Most disastrous of all, he dissolved twenty-nine monasteries on the grounds that they were hopelessly decayed and then took their confiscated property to endow the colleges he was building at Ipswich and Oxford as well as to make extensive alterations to York Place and Hampton Court.

Skelton's next attack on Wolsey, in "Colin Clout," was prompted in part by the dissolution of the nunneries of Lillechurch, Kent, and Bromehall, Berkshire, effected at the cardinal's direction in October 1521. The poem takes the form of a colloquy announced in the epigraph's juxtaposition of passages from the Old and New Testaments: "Quis consurget mihi adversus malignantes, aut quis mecum adversus operantes iniquitatum? Nemo, Deomine!" (Who will rise up with me against evil-doers? Or who will stand up with me against the workers of iniquity? [Psalm 93:16]; No one, O Lord! [John 8:11]). Representative of the common man, Colin is opposed to Wolsey instinctively because he is simple, blunt, and honest. But he does not merely discern and announce the truth; he *is* truth.

The poem spirals outward in a lengthy series of observations that are highly critical of Wolsey's

Title page for an early collection of Skelton's works

spiritual and temporal actions. As Wolsey is both chief prelate and lord chancellor, so this poem, like the opening epitaph as colloquy, keeps splintering and doubling. In the course of Colin's investigation, Wolsey becomes both the origin of evil and simply the worst example of it, both type and prototype. Colin, too, becomes more than simply Colin; he also becomes the spokesman for a whole community of suffering, honest laymen: "I, Colin Clout, / As I go about, / And wandering as I walk, / I hear the people talk." In all of his characteristics – his simplicity, his clear-sightedness, his bluntness, his pain, his anxiety, and his stubborn faith – Colin resembles the anonymous author of Psalm 93 with his cry of tribulation and his prayer for deliverance. Indeed the moving inner drama of "Colin Clout" is Colin's sense of possible complicity and his struggle to maintain the force of the psalmist's lament, alongside the Christian understanding of man's need, from time to time, for charity and divine support. It is this conflict within Colin that makes his poem especially rich and powerful.

Skelton's next poem on Wolsey, "Why Come Ye Not to Court?," is even more direct in its bitter attack than "Colin Clout." It is also far simpler and so more forceful. The structural principle is also plainer, because Skelton announces it in his incipit and repeats it twice in the opening lines: "All noble men, of this take heed, / And believe it as your Creed." His prologue then begins with the general state of the world that produces the need for a new creed to replace the Nicene Creed. Such fundamental and summary charges concerning selfish, negligent, and ignorant leadership cause the speaker to level the damning accusation that the Church creed from the Council of Nicaea, in use since the sixth century when it replaced the Apostles' Creed, has now been overturned by the practices of Wolsey as the new apostle to the devil. "Why Come Ye Not to Court?" thus presents a tripartite argument: (1) it begins with a statement full of interpretive details to give a concrete and comprehensive view of the present condition of men under the dispensation of the new creed; (2) it supplies, through a series of questions and answers, an itinerary of events, often in foreign countries, which are a direct consequence; and, finally, (3) it locates the cause of all these evil conditions and acts in the biography of Dicken (the devil symbolizing Wolsey), who alone is responsible.

Part 2 of the poem, rather than examine the catechumen on the Ten Commandments, asks a series of ten quite different questions, the answers to which (as potential commandments) can only reveal Wolsey's misdeeds and shortcomings – for their focus is on him, not on church belief. When the catechumen is asked the ultimate question under the

New Dispensation, "Why come ye not to court?," he must understand it is not the king's court where God has presumably placed his regent, but Hampton Court where Wolsey in true power and majesty now resides. By sharply juxtaposing the fall of Sodom and Gomorrah, by which God punished blind sinners in the Old Testament (Genesis 19:11), with the current Litany of the Mass, Skelton ends part 2 by triumphantly showing how Wolsey's usurpation of the king's rule and justice has led to a moral blindness by which Wolsey also means to usurp God's teachings to the faithful – and God himself. Truly, Wolsey is the devil incarnate.

Part 3 is an infernal biography, in which Wolsey is compared to Amalek, a chronic enemy of God (Exodus 17:8-16), and condemned as the antitype to Saint Peter from which the true Church descended. The prelate's wild boasts are compared to those of the character Mahomet in the anonymous Corpus Christi plays; tropes make Wolsey analogous to the necromancer at Charlemagne's court and show him descending to hell to harrow it but staying to take over: "he would break the brains / Of Lucifer in his chains, / And rule them each one / In Lucifer's throne." Skelton next portrays Wolsey usurping the archbishop of Canterbury, the lesson from the Confessor Bishop Mass (a movable feast), canon law, and finally the law of the provincial synods of Canterbury and York. Skelton's anger cannot subside: the poem concludes with an epitome and a decasticon, which present another biography of Wolsey, modeled on a debased Nicene Creed. "Why Come Ye Not to Court?" thus argues forcefully, typologically, specifically, and savagely that both for men of corruption and for men of the Holy Spirit, the Holy Bible and the catechism are the only sources of reliable instruction. But Wolsey is seen as blind to what every child of the Church is taught from the beginning.

Skelton creates a more common devil incarnate in the eponymous heroine of what, from Pope's day on, was Skelton's best-known and most notorious poem, *The Tunning of Elinor Rumming*. John Harvey has discovered in the court rolls of the manor of Packenescham what may be an authentic source of the poem: an actual Alianora Romyng, "a common tipellar of ale" who ran the Running Horse tavern that still stands in Leatherhead, Surrey, was fined two pence on 18 August 1525 for selling ale "at excessive price and by small measures." "Tunning" means both "brewing" (the process) and "brew" (the product), and by extension drinking and drink. The poem is a portrait of an early Tudor alehouse and the narrative of Elinor,

an alewife. She makes her own brew with the aid of chicken dung, taking as payment anything her large and degenerate crowd of women will give her. The poem also concentrates on how such corrupt habits contaminate the personalities of her customers and deform them physically as they arrive, one by one, for a drunken melee, until the poet breaks off what appears an endless troping when a particularly fastidious customer, asking for additional credit, catches sight of all the goods that the greedy Elinor has collected and stashed under her bed.

Nearly from the start the poem begins to fill with her customers, who flock to her alehouse for more of her "noppy ale" than they can quite manage. Although "Some have no money / That thither comey, / For their ale to pay," she allows them to barter freely. "Instead of coin and money, / Some brought her a conny [rabbit], / And some a pot with honey, / Some a salt, and some a spoon, / Some their hose, some their shoon [shoes]," and some, things they have stolen, including even sacred things such as rosary beads. In the end, "Such were there many / That had not a penny" that, when they stagger to their feet, Elinor has them chalk up their own indentures on a board hanging in the tavern. Gluttony as one of the seven deadly sins had been a frequent subject of satire in the medieval period – by the goliardic poets, by Geoffrey Chaucer, by William Langland – but Skelton's subject is also deformity, both spiritual and physical.

Following several goliardic predecessors, the poem portrays a topers' Mass or mock Mass: "Now truly, to my thinking, / This is a solemn drinking." Elinor, the high priestess, is a devil or witch practicing *maleficium*: "The devil and she be sib [siblings]." She is dressed like a Turk (infidel) or gypsy (pagan) in "Her huke [cape] of Lincoln green," the devil's color, with "Her kirtle Bristol red" mocking the liturgical color of the vestments for Passion Week and Whitsunday as her brewing mocks Christ's first miracle at Canna (turning the water into wine) and its prefiguration of the Last Supper. Her preparations are clearly meant to mock ablutions and Communion because the real subject of the poem is a portrayal of a witch's coven, and the customers who come perform a mock confessional and perform the Offertory with various goods – some frivolous, some vital, some stolen, and some sacred – holding them up, indiscriminately, "To offer to the alepole" or "To offer to the ale tap." The "tunning" which Elinor serves is, in short, witch's brew, and her "tunning" or celebration is a witch's or devil's Sabbath, a Black Mass.

This poem is, in fact, a deliberate inversion of "Philip Sparrow," which talks of sacrifice instead of self-indulgence; the connection here is more firmly made by Elinor's means of taking over the property of her sisters as they enter her establishment, which is a detailed mockery of the practice at Benedictine abbeys, linked to the priory of Saint Mary at Carrow. The poet thus stops abruptly when the fastidious customer sees her rosary treated like so many worthless trinkets in the mock reliquary under the bed where Elinor and her husband "root like hogs." He stops when Saint Benedict himself is invoked as one who argues for vows of poverty coupled with obedience and, in his case, charity. But the poet does not stop without cause: he stops because he is so outraged at what he has described and because this portrayal of the wages of sin is so total in its condemnation. This is, however, the only poem which Skelton set at Leatherhead; the reason may be that it was a popular alehouse with visitors to Hampton Court. In fact, the alehouse may be an inversion of Wolsey's court, since it consists of all women and not, like Wolsey's court, all men, while it is in full congruence in also being a place absolutist in its power and autocratic (for Skelton) in its immorality and self-indulgence. This may also explain why this poem was written as late as the 1520s, when the actual Alianora Romyng was declared a con artist by the courts.

The Garland of Laurel, Skelton's first major poem, was not published until 1523, incorporating some later incidents in Skelton's life and a mysterious and puzzling envoi that seems to argue a final reconciliation with Wolsey. It has been contended that *The Garland,* which concentrates on happier early days at Sheriff Hutton Castle with the Howard family, was deliberately published at the retirement of Skelton's patron, Thomas Howard, from court in 1522. The newly augmented and completed poem, which traces the incidents in the life of a poet laureated in three universities, thus becomes the record of a poet's life work, the fortunes which a patron helped to produce, and a unique and charming tribute to the family that made Skelton's career possible. But the Latin envoi ("To the Most Serene Royal Majesty, equally with the Lord Cardinal, Most Honored Legate-from-the-side") may still bewilder. Most scholars have thought the poem is meant to establish Skelton's mastery as a poet and the envoi an apology meant to win a prebendary so that he might retire from the sanctuary of Westminster into a pastoral life in his final years. That would not square, however, with the contention that *The Garland* is a tribute to Howard, whose retirement was forced by Wolsey and who remained, until his early death, Wolsey's arch-enemy.

Read more closely, however, the envoi may also be seen to venerate and praise not Wolsey but the king: the reverence due to the cardinal is directly contingent on the fulfillment of a promise already made but one that must come eventually from the king and not the cardinal. Forcing Wolsey's hand in a poem which honors Howard, Henry VIII's Lord Treasurer, is also tantamount to insisting that the prelate make good his patronage while the aging Howard still lives: Skelton will honor his patron in a poem which secures continuing patronage through a new appointment.

This apology, if that is what it is, seems to have been unsuccessful, however, for Skelton remained in Westminster. There is, furthermore, no indication that Thomas Howard II ever provided the support and protection for Skelton that his father had. But in the final years of his life, Skelton suffered no abatement in energy, courage, invention, or invective. His final extant poem, "A Replication Against Certain Young Scholars" (1528), is an attack on two Cambridge students, Thomas Bilney and Thomas Arthur, who were declared guilty of Lutheran heresy and required to abjure publicly and to bear faggots to Paul's Cross in London on the Feast of the Conception, 8 December 1527, as a sign of their recantation. The poem is in three parts – the protestation, proposition, and confutation – and borrows legal terminology and form only to transcend them. Skelton argues that while Bilney and Arthur support *latria,* or the supreme worship of God alone, they deny *dulia,* the veneration of angels and saints, and especially *hyperdulia,* the veneration of the Blessed Virgin. In citing the miracle of the Conception, Skelton intercedes to instruct and save the young heretics, much as the Virgin has interceded for all mankind, as the Sequence for the Mass of the feast day of Conception makes clear. He will, therefore, make his own priestly and poetic responsibilities inseparable.

Part 3 bestows special powers, however, on the poet, and Fish has said it is the basis for his entire poetical career:

> There is a spiritual,
> And a mysterial,
> And a mystical
> Effect energial [*energia*]
> (As Greeks do it call),
> Of such an industry
> And such a pregnancy
> Of heavenly inspiration
> In laureat creation,

Of poet's commendation,
That of divine miseration
God maketh his habitation
In poets which excells,
And sojourns with them and dwells.
By whose inflammation
Of spiritual instigation
And divine inspiration,
We are kindled in such fashion
With heat of the Holy Ghost,
Which is God of mightiness most,
That he our pen doth lead.

Skelton elevates poetry and the poet – deliberately giving himself (because of the inspiration of the Holy Ghost) more authority even than Wolsey, *legate a latere*. In addition, the poem, which begins with what appears to be a note of conciliation, actually begins with subterfuge. In arguing that the young heretics were first supported by gifts of money given toward their education by several prelates, including the cardinal, Skelton indirectly argues that Wolsey is also guilty of promoting this heretical act. This gives a new and quite different meaning to the dedication, in which the poet writes that Wolsey is "assuredly the most excellent promoter of this present treatise" and clarifies why and how the poet means to give "all due reverence proper to so great and so magnificent a prince of ecclesiasts" as one who has aided and abetted the very heretics under examination.

Thomas Howard died in 1524, and his bier, transported with the cortege from Framlingham Castle to burial at Thetford Abbey, paused to spend the night midway at Diss, where the Church of Saint Mary the Virgin was draped in black and where a requiem mass, presumably celebrated by the aging Skelton, was the last holy service celebrating him. Skelton died a few years later, on 21 June 1529, in Westminster. According to his early biographer, Edward Braynewood, he was buried before the high altar of Saint Margaret's Church, his parish church alongside the great Abbey, with this inscription on alabaster: "Joannes Skeltonus vates pierius hic situs est" (Here lies John Skelton, Pierian bard). Both the tomb and its marker have long since disappeared, but records remain in the churchwardens' accounts of Saint Margaret's of the expenses incurred: four tapers were lit and set around his body, and four torches illuminated the funeral procession. Church bells tolled and a sum was paid for a special knell by Our Lady's Brotherhood, a parish guild to which Skelton belonged, along with others attached to the neighboring palace. If his service was not as flamboyant as his best-known poetry, it was as cere-monial and holy as he seems, from his final poem, to have wished.

"If we think that we are not in the presence here of poetic greatness," John Holloway told the British Academy in 1958 regarding Skelton, "it is because there is a kind of poetic greatness which we have not learnt to know." Skelton's medieval conventions, his humanist learning, his rhetorical strategies, his hyperbolic wit, his angry invective, and his liturgical allusions have all served to obscure his poetry in the intervening centuries. But that was not always the case. Surely the very fact that he pursued a lifelong career of figural poetry suggests that he had an audience who appreciated him. Nor did his readers disappear with his death. In the short space between 1545 and 1563 – during the Protestant reign of Edward VI and, more appropriately, the Catholic reign of Mary I – there were twenty-one editions recorded of his work. But even then his reputation was being transformed: under Elizabeth I, increasingly more jests and jestbooks about Skelton emphasize his wit and ingenuity at the expense of his piety, as if for a country becoming more determinedly Protestant, a Catholic priest could only trivialize and mislead – could even become a buffoon. Ben Jonson, who in two of his works seems to have admired Skelton, nevertheless makes him into a clown. And the kind of poetry Skelton forged had to wait until John Donne's "Nocturnal upon S. Lucy's Day" (circa 1620) to find an adequate successor. Yet in recent times his Skeltonics have found their disciples in Robert Graves and W. H. Auden and their champions in E. M. Forster and Lewis. The number of major critical studies that have appeared since Richard Hughes's 1924 edition of Skelton has at last conclusively established him as the premier poet under Henry VII and the first major English poet in the court of Henry VIII.

Bibliographies:

Burton Fishman, "Recent Studies in Skelton," *English Literary Renaissance,* 1, no. 1 (Winter 1971): 89–96;

Robert S. Kinsman, ed., *John Skelton, Early Tudor Laureate: An Annotated Bibliography c. 1488–1977* (Boston: G. K. Hall, 1979).

References:

W. H. Auden, "John Skelton," in *The Great Tudors,* edited by Katharine Garvin (London: Nicholson, 1935);

Nan Cooke Carpenter, *John Skelton* (New York: Twayne, 1967);

Anthony S. G. Edwards, ed., *Skelton: The Critical Heritage* (London: Routledge & Kegan Paul, 1981);

H. L. R. Edwards, *Skelton: The Life and Times of an Early Tudor Poet* (London: Cape, 1949);

Stanley Eugene Fish, *John Skelton's Poetry,* Yale Studies in English, no. 157 (New Haven: Yale University Press, 1965);

Alistair Fox and Gregory White, eds., *A Concordance to the Complete English Poems of John Skelton* (Ithaca: Cornell University Press, 1987);

Ian A. Gordon, *John Skelton: Poet Laureate* (Melbourne: Melbourne University Press, 1943; N.p.: Folcroft Press, 1970);

Peter Green, *John Skelton,* Writers and Their Works, no. 128 (London: Longman Group, for the British Council, 1960; revised and enlarged, 1978);

William O. Harris, *Skelton's "Magnyfycence" and the Cardinal Virtue Tradition* (Chapel Hill: University of North Carolina Press, 1965);

A. R. Heiserman, *Skelton and Satire* (Chicago: University of Chicago Press, 1961);

John Holloway, "Skelton," in his *The Charted Mirror* (London: Routledge & Kegan Paul, 1960), pp. 3–24;

Arthur F. Kinney, *John Skelton, Priest as Poet: Seasons of Discovery* (Chapel Hill: University of North Carolina Press, 1987);

Robert S. Kinsman, "The 'Buck' and the 'Fox' in Skelton's 'Why Come Ye Nat to Courte?' " *Philological Quarterly,* 29 (January 1950): 61–64;

Kinsman, "Phyllyp Sparowe: Titulus," *Studies in Philology,* 47 (July 1950): 473–484;

Kinsman, "Skelton's *Magnyfycence:* The Strategy of the 'Olde Sayde Sawe,' " *Studies in Philology,* 63 (April 1966): 99–125;

Kinsman, "Skelton's 'Uppon a Deedmans Hed': New Light on the Origin of the Skeltonic," *Studies in Philology,* 50 (April 1953): 101–110;

Kinsman, "Voices of Dissonance: Pattern in Skelton's *Colyn Cloute,*" *Huntington Library Quarterly,* 26 (August 1963): 291–313;

Kinsman and Theodore Yonge, eds., *John Skelton: Canon and Census,* Renaissance Society of America Bibliographies and Indexes, 4 (N.p.: Monographic Press, 1967);

L. J. Lloyd, *John Skelton: A Sketch of His Life and Writings* (Oxford: Blackwell, 1938);

William Nelson, *John Skelton, Laureate,* Columbia University Studies in English and Comparative Literature, no. 139 (New York: Columbia University Press, 1939; New York: Russell & Russell, 1964);

Maurice Pollet, *John Skelton: Poet of Tudor England,* translated by John Warrington (London: Dent, 1971);

Greg Walker, *John Skelton and the Politics of the 1520s,* Cambridge Studies in Early Modern British History (Cambridge: Cambridge University Press, 1988).

Papers:
A manuscript attributed to John Skelton, "A Laud and Praise Made for Our Sovereign Lord the King" is in the Public Record Office, London (MS E.36/228); another, the dedication to Henry VIII of the "Chronique de Rains," is at Corpus Christi College, Cambridge (MS 432).

Henry Smith

(circa 1560 – circa June 1591)

Mark E. Bingham
Gettysburg College

SELECTED BOOKS: *The Christians Sacrifice. Seene, and Allowed* (London: Printed by Thomas Orwin for Thomas Man, 1589);

A Preparatiue to Mariage. The Summe Whereof Was Spoken at a Contract, and Inlarged After. Whereunto Is Annexed a Treatise of the Lords Supper, and Another of Vsurie (London: Printed by Thomas Orwin for Thomas Man, 1591);

Seven Godly and Learned Sermons vpon Seven Diuers Textes of Scripture, Containing Necessary and Profitable Doctrine, as well for the Reformation of Our Liues, as for the Comfort of Troubled Consciences in All Distresses. By Henrie Smith. Perused by the Author before His Death (London: Printed by Richard Field for Thomas Man, 1591);

Thirteene Sermons vpon Seuerall Textes of Scripture (London: Printed for Thomas Man, 1592);

The Sermons of Master Henrie Smith, Gathered into One Volume. Printed According to His Corrected Copies in His Life Time (London: Printed by Thomas Orwin for Thomas Man, 1592).

Collections: *The Sermons of Mr. Henry Smith,* edited, with a biography of Smith, by Thomas Fuller (London: Printed for Andrew Kembe, John Wright, John Saywell & George Sawbridge, 1657);

The Works of Henry Smith, Including Sermons, Treatises, Prayers, and Poems, 2 volumes, edited by Thomas Smith (Edinburgh: Nichol, 1866, 1867).

OTHER: *Micro-cosmo-graphia,* translated by Joshua Sylvester, in Guillaume de Salluste Du Bartas's *Du Bartas His Diuine Weekes and Workes with a . . . Collection of All the Other . . . Workes Translated and Written by . . . J. Sylvester* (London: Printed by Humphrey Lownes, 1621).

During his brief career Henry Smith enjoyed the greatest popularity of any Elizabethan preacher. After his death the plain but eloquent style of his prose proved as compelling in print as it had been from the pulpit. His career is distinguished not only by his skill as a preacher and as a prose stylist, but also by the precarious position he occupied in the contentious world of Elizabethan Protestantism.

The date of Smith's birth remains uncertain, as does almost every detail of his short life. The eldest son of Erasmus Smith and his first wife, Anne, he was born about 1560, probably at Withcote, his grandfather's manor in Leicestershire. His home during most of his childhood was Husbands Bosworth, the manor that Desiderius Erasmus purchased in 1565, also in Leicestershire.

The young man was admitted as fellow commoner of Queen's College, Cambridge, in July 1573 but apparently matriculated on 15 March 1576 at Lincoln College, Oxford. He is likely the Henry Smith recorded in Joseph Foster's *Alumni Oxonienses, 1500–1714* (1891) as having graduated B.A. from Lincoln College on 16 February 1579 and M.A. from Saint John's College on 3 May 1583. Though in line as an eldest son to inherit a large patrimony (had he outlived his father), Smith dedicated himself to the ministry, rejecting the advice of wealthy relatives to study law and casting aside a youthful interest in poetry. None of his poetry written in English survives; of the poetry he wrote in Latin, Joshua Sylvester's 1621 English translation of Smith's *Microcosmographia* remains available in *The Works of Henry Smith* (1866, 1867). Thomas Nashe's *Pierce Penniless* (1592), however, cites Smith as an instance of divines who "admirably shine . . . above the common mediocrity," having "tasted the sweet springs of Parnassus!" Nashe's encomium to "Silver-tongued Smith" includes this praise for his verse:

Quaintly couldest thou devise heavenly ditties to Apollo's lute, and teach stately verse to trip it as smoothly as if Ovid and thou had but one soul. Hence alone did it proceed, that thou wert such a plausible pulpit man, that before thou enteredst into the rough

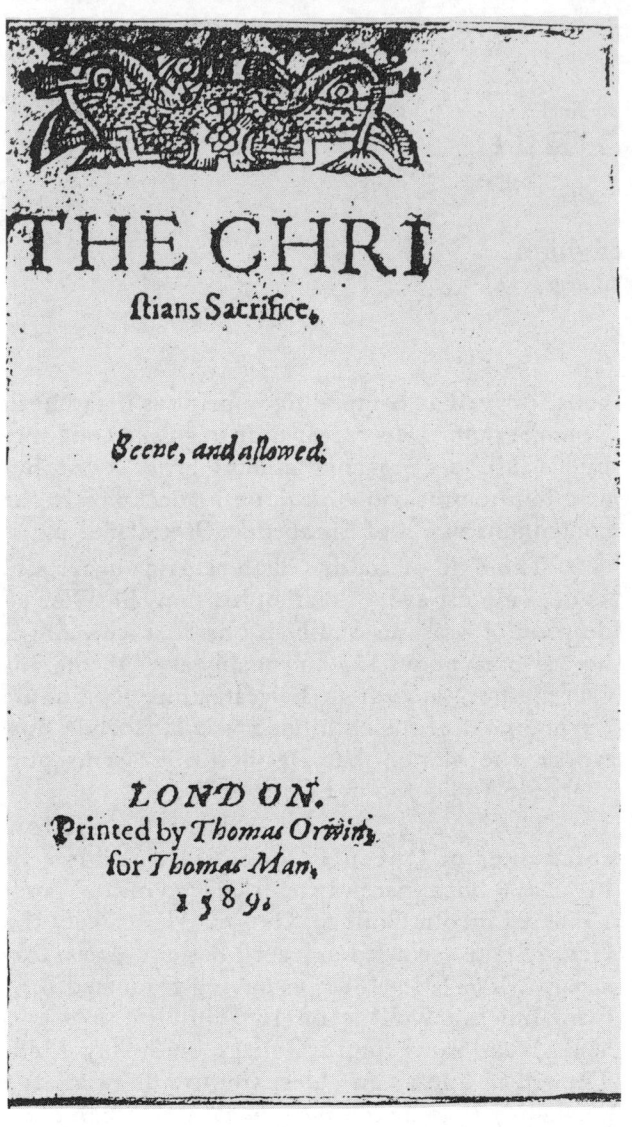

THE CHRI
ſtians Sacrifice.

Seene, and allowed.

LONDON.
Printed by *Thomas Orwin,*
for *Thomas Man,*
1589.

Title page for Henry Smith's first published sermon

ways of theology, thou refinedst, preparedst, and purifiedst thy mind with sweet poetry.

Smith did not remain in continuous residence at Oxford between 1575 and 1583. He spent some time (though how much and when remain uncertain) living and studying with Richard Greenham, rector of Dry Drayton in Cambridgeshire. Greenham seems to have influenced Smith both in his Puritan convictions and in the moderation with which he maintained them. Smith was apparently living at Husbands Bosworth in 1582 when he was called on (perhaps by his uncle Bryant Cave, at the time sheriff of the county) to reclaim a heretic, a Leicestershire youth named Robert Dickons who was claiming to be the prophet Elijah. Smith succeeded in bringing Dickons to recant. The inci-

dent provided the occasion for Smith to preach the sermon later published as "The Lost Sheep Is Found" (Smith's sermons were collected in *The Sermons of Master Henry Smith,* 1592). Whether Smith was at the time rector of the Husbands Bosworth church, of which his father was patron, remains unknown.

Smith's mother died in 1583; three years later his father married Margaret Cave, the widowed sister of William Cecil, Lord Burghley, who would exercise his influence as lord chancellor on behalf of his young stepnephew. In 1587, with the help of Burghley and on the recommendation of Greenham, Smith secured appointment as lecturer, or preacher, in the London parish in which Burghley resided, Saint Clement Danes. Smith achieved prodigious popularity within the first year of this office. In the brief "Life" included in his 1657 compilation of Smith's works, Thomas Fuller describes the preacher's popularity as phenomenal:

[Smith] was commonly called the silver-tongued preacher, and that was but one metal below St. Chrysostom himself. His church was so crowded with auditors, that persons of good quality brought their own pews with them, I mean their legs, to stand thereupon in the alleys. Their ears did so attend to his lips, their hearts to their ears, that he held the rudder of their affections in his hands, so that he could steer them whither he was pleased; and he was pleased to steer them only to God's glory and their own good.

Smith's sermons exemplify the ideal of simple preaching he describes in "The True Trial of the Spirits." Decrying the false simplicity of "a kind of preachers risen up but of late, which shroud and cover every rustical, and unsavory, and childish, and absurd sermon, under the name of the simple kind of teaching, like the popish priests, which make ignorance the mother of devotion," he argues that "to preach simply is not to preach rudely, nor unlearnedly, nor confusedly, but to preach plainly and perspicuously, that the simplest man may understand what is taught, as if he did hear his name." Smith's style is plain, his diction simple; his familiar images tend toward homeliness. His sentences, though sometimes long, consist of short, direct periods that are often organized in parallels and sometimes balanced with antitheses. The periods occasionally expand in a series, swell in emotional force, and test the limits of a listener's patience, but they never lose a sense of control, restraint, measure, and containment. In "The True Trial," for example, having asked why the Apostle Paul, in Philippians

2:29, instructs his readers to "make much of such" as teach them, Smith offers this answer:

> Because they are like lamps, which consume themselves to give light to others; so they consume themselves to give light to you: because they are like a hen, which cluketh her chickens together from the kite; so they cluck you together from the serpent: because they are like the shout, which did beat down the walls of Jericho [Joshua 6:20]; so they beat down the walls of sin: because they are like the fiery pillar, which went before the Israelites to the land of promise; so they go before you to the land of promise: because they are like good Andrew, which called his brother to see the Messias [John 1:41]; so they call upon you to see the Messias, and therefore make much of such.

More typical of Smith's prose style is the sentence that unfolds more loosely, its expansion in the form of smaller series and balances, with syntactically less complicated items requiring less elaborate syntactical parallelism to remain lucid, as in this discussion, from *The Christian's Sacrifice* (1589), of God's right to request the hearts of his children:

> If thou be his son, thou wilt give him thy heart, because thy Father desires it, thy Maker desires it, thy Redeemer desires it, thy Savior desires it [1 Corinthians 4:16]; thy Lord, and thy King, and thy Master desires it, which hath given his Son for a ransom, his Spirit for a pledge, his word for a guide, the world for a walk, and reserves a kingdom for thine inheritance [Romans 8:32]. Canst thou deny him anything, which hath given the heir for the servant, his beloved for his enemy, the best for the worst? Canst thou deny him anything, whose goodness created us, whose favor elected us, whose mercy redeemed us, whose wisdom converteth us, whose grace preserved us, whose glory shall glorify us? Oh! if thou knewest (as Christ said to the woman of Samaria when she huckt [haggled] to give him water [John 4:10]), if thou knewest who it is that saith unto thee, *Give me thy heart,* thou wouldst say unto him as Peter did when Christ would wash his feet, *Lord, not my feet only, but my hands and my head* [John 13:9]; not my heart only, but all my body, and my thoughts, and my words, and my works, and my goods, and my life, take all that thou hast given.

In its allusions to the Samaritan woman and to Peter, this passage also illustrates one of Smith's favorite rhetorical devices: the involvement of biblical narratives in his exposition, not to appeal to their authority or to argue their pertinence to the substance of his point, but to use as dramatic analogues to the responses to which he exhorts his audience.

The climactic series contributes only occasional ballast, however, to Smith's usually light and graceful style. Earlier in *The Christian's Sacrifice,* as he begins to expound Proverbs 23:26 ("My son, give me thy heart") as God's request of all his creatures, Smith writes:

> He which always gave, now craves; and he which craved always, now gives: Christ stands at the door like a poor man, and asks not bread, nor clothes, nor lodgings, which we should give to his members, but our heart; that is, even the continent of all, and governor of man's house, which sits on the bench like a judge to give the charge, and teacheth the tongue to speak, the hand to work, the foot to walk, the ear to attend, the eye to observe, the mind to choose, and the flesh to obey. That we must present to God, like a burnt-sacrifice, wherein all is offered together [Leviticus 1:9, 13], a wise tongue, a diligent hand, a wary foot, a watchful eye, an attentive ear, an humble mind, an obedient flesh, put all together, and it is but the heart; *My son* (saith God) *give me thy heart.*

The periods develop loosely and freely, accumulating images generously and moving in rhythms both natural and unexpected, familiar and fresh.

Smith strikes a precarious balance in his sermons between, on the one hand, his Puritan objections to the forms of Roman Catholicism that had been retained by the established church and, on the other, his loyalty to that church. He concludes "The True Trial of the Spirits" with a discussion of Paul's exhortation in 1 Thessalonians 5:22, "Abstain from all appearance of evil." First he devotes two paragraphs to exposing the appearances of evil characteristic of Dissenters, including these "shows of error":

> Hath it not the show of error to affirm, that the church of Christ was ever invisible before this age, and that it is such a small flock as their number is? and that it hath set foot nowhere but in England? Hath it not the show of error, to hold that for good and sound religion, which is altered every day, adding and detracting, as though a man should make a religion of his own invention, so fast as new conceits come into his brain? . . . Solomon saith, *There is an error upon the right hand, as well as upon the left* [Proverbs 4:27], that is (as I may call it), the zealous error: and if this be not, I know none within this land

He then proceeds to expose the "show of error" among Anglicans themselves:

> Yet, shall I say that we have not the show of error? Nay, I would we were but in the show of error. I may not call evil good, no more than . . . I may call good evil: and therefore let us pull out the beam out of our own eyes, as we would pull the mote out of their eyes. If Paul would have us abstain from every appearance of evil, sure he would have us abstain from heresy and idolatry, for these are the greatest evils. But if we be not idolaters,

yet we have the show of idolatry: if we be not of antichrist's religion, yet we are of antichrist's fashion, so long as we have the same vestures, and the same orders, and the same titles that antichrist knoweth his ministers by.

Smith's outspoken condemnation of Separatists did not suffice, however, to deflect the disapproval of Anglican authorities at his criticisms of the English church. In 1588, in response to allegations that Smith had spoken against the Book of Common Prayer and had not subscribed to the Articles of Faith, John Aylmer, bishop of London, suspended him from preaching. Aylmer further objected that he had never officially licensed Smith to preach in the diocese. The suspension, however, was short-lived. The parishioners of Saint Clement's appealed on Smith's behalf, and he defended himself in a letter to Burghley, whose intervention probably secured reappointment. In his letter Smith protested that he had once been invited by the bishop to preach at Saint Paul's and that the issue of licensing had not been raised either for him on that occasion or at any time for previous lecturers at Saint Clement's. He denied having spoken against the Book of Common Prayer and expressed his willingness to subscribe to the Articles of Faith. One effect of the suspension may well have been to motivate him to commit his preaching to print. His first published sermon, *The Christian's Sacrifice,* appeared in 1589.

After his reinstatement Smith continued as lecturer only until 1589 or 1590. During this time William Harewood, rector of Saint Clement's, became gravely ill. Again the parishioners appealed to Burghley on their lecturer's behalf, this time that Smith might succeed Harewood as rector. Smith was in poor health, however, and it seems likely that he declined the appointment, which went instead to Richard Webster. The ailing Smith retired from preaching and spent his final months preparing his sermons for publication. According to the parish register at Husbands Bosworth, he was buried on 4 July 1591.

A single-volume collection of Smith's sermons, printed "according to his corrected copies in his lifetime" and including his dedication to Burghley, appeared in 1592. The phenomenal popularity of the sermons survived him by many decades. By 1610 his sermons had been published, individually or in collections, in more than eighty-five editions. Their persistent appeal explains Fuller's compilation of 1657, which includes all fifty-six extant sermons in one volume.

Smith's work has received little recent attention; however, it remains a promising site for scholarly exploration. For students of Elizabethan prose style, the distinctive eloquence of the sermons remains to be more fully analyzed. Students of sixteenth-century British cultural history can discover in Smith's life and work a crossroads of popular and literary culture, as well as a battleground in the struggles among Elizabethan Protestant factions.

References:

Charles Henry Cooper and Thompson Cooper, *Athenae Cantabrigienses,* volume 2 (Cambridge: Deighton, Bell, 1861), pp. 103–108;

Walter R. Davis, "Henry Smith: The Preacher as Poet," *English Literary Renaissance,* 12 (Winter 1982): 30–52;

R. B. Jenkins, *Henry Smith: England's Silver-Tongued Preacher* (Macon, Ga.: Mercer University Press, 1983);

James Hisao Kodama, "A Survey of the Data for the Life of Henry Smith," *Annual Collection of Essays and Studies* (Gakushuin University), 31, no. 59 (1984): 31–45;

John L. Lievsay, " 'Silver-tongued Smith,' Paragon of Elizabethan Preachers," *Huntington Library Quarterly,* 11 (November 1947): 13–36;

Thomas Nashe, *The Works of Thomas Nashe,* 5 volumes, edited by Ronald B. McKerrow, revised by F. P. Wilson (Oxford: Blackwell, 1958).

William Smith

(flourished 1595 – 1597)

Lisa Celovsky
University of Toronto

BOOKS: *Chloris, or the Complaint of the Passionate Despised Shepheard* (London: Printed by Edmund Bollifant, 1596).

Collection: *The Poems of William Smith,* edited by Lawrence A. Sasek (Baton Rouge: Louisiana State University Press, 1970).

OTHER: "A notable description of the world," attributed to Smith, in *The Phoenix Nest. Built vp with the Most Rare and Refined Workes of Noble Men. Set foorth by R. S. of the Inner Temple* (London: Printed by John Jackson, 1593), pp. 77–80;

W. S., *The Lamentable Tragedie of Locrine, the Eldest Sonne of King Brutus. Newly Set Foorth, Ouerseene and Corrected,* possibly edited by Smith (London: Printed by Thomas Creede, 1595);

"My thoughts are winged with hopes," attributed to Smith, in *The First Booke of Songes or Ayres of Fowre Partes with Tableture,* by John Dowland (London: Printed by Peter Short, 1597);

"What shall I say of Gold, more than 'tis Gold," attributed to Smith, in *The Wil of Wit, Wits Will, or Wil's Wit, Chuse You Whether. Containing Fiue Discourses,* by Nicholas Breton (London: Printed by Thomas Creede, 1597);

"An Elizabethan Allegory of Time by William Smith," edited by Kent Talbot van den Berg, *English Literary Renaissance,* 6 (Winter 1976): 40–59.

William Smith is the only Elizabethan poet to dedicate a collection of his verse to fellow-poet Edmund Spenser. This dedication and one to Mary Sidney, Countess of Pembroke, seem to place Smith in exalted literary circles. But, as many poets used dedications to attract the attention of influential contemporaries or to gain places in great households, Smith's do not prove acquaintance with Spenser or the Sidneys. Smith's works provide the sole evidence for conjectures about his life, and the only reliable biographical detail that they provide is that

he desired patronage. Smith likely resembled such contemporary poets as Michael Drayton and Nicholas Breton, who wrote to win preferment or at least small monetary gifts. The fathers of these men were merchants, guildsmen, or lesser gentry; their sons had been educated at grammar school and often at university. Like these writers, Smith probably held some position of full-time employment (as civil servant or secretary, for example) but used his literary skills to improve upon it.

The only work Smith published during his life is *Chloris, or The Complaint of the Passionate Despised Shepherd* (1596) — a relatively late contribution to the sonnet tradition consisting of fifty Shakespearean sonnets and two dedications. Though largely unoriginal, mechanical, and perhaps monotonous, Smith's sonnets, like those of other sonneteers, function to display his mastery of established rhetorical techniques, conceits, forms, and metrical exercises. He intersperses lyrics into his sequence, and he produces the requisite galley sonnet, which employs a ship as metaphor; blazon, which catalogues the beloved's attributes; and echo poem, which creates a dialogue between each line and repeated final syllables of that line. Smith also frequently demonstrates the concatenation used by his contemporaries, in which a poem's first line repeats the last line of the preceding poem.

Chloris likewise adheres to the established structural principle of *variatio* and to conventional themes. A static catalog of variations on "despair and hope," *Chloris* describes the futile love of the lowly shepherd Corin for Chloris, a generic "cruel saint" and prescribed "fairest fair" mistress of nondescript but "perfect beauty." As in most sonnet sequences, the mistress is a nonindividualized medium through which the lover creates introspective verse about his predicament and his vocation. Corin is of course also a poet, worried about the reception of his "new-hatched" verse by Chloris and his audience, especially other "shepherds" (that is, contemporary poets). In the opening and closing

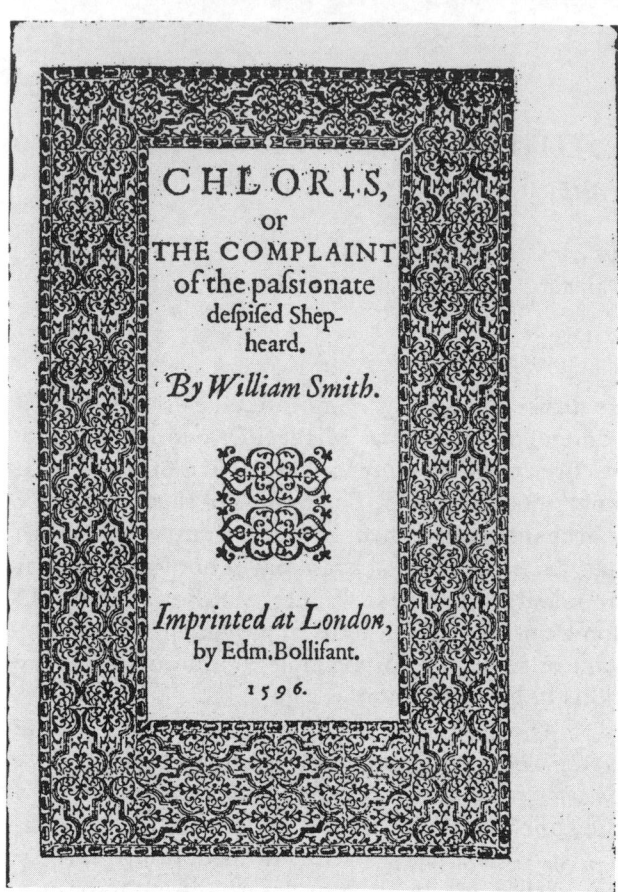

CHLORIS,
or
THE COMPLAINT
of the passionate
despised Shep-
heard.

By William Smith.

Imprinted at London,
by Edm.Bollifant.
1596.

Title page for Smith's 1596 book, the only Elizabethan verse collection dedicated to Edmund Spenser

poems the poet eclipses the lover as Smith blurs distinctions between "Colin Clout" (Spenser), initially Corin's "most entire beloved," and Chloris and even between the figure Chloris and *Chloris,* the sonnet sequence: "now I weigh not who shall Chloris see."

The mostly predictable machinery of *Chloris* contains a few nonconventional features. Corin compares himself to many Ovidian figures – who appear more frequently and with more variety in *Chloris* than in other sequences – and to the aggressor or, alternately, the victim in a relatively large number of allusions to mythical rapes. These comparisons define the speaker's constantly shifting identity as he discards one after another; they consequently enforce the sequence's conventional narcissism.

The pastoral mode of *Chloris* is also anomalous. Most sonneteers ignore physical setting, and though the romance pastoral popularized by Longus's *Daphnis and Chloe* (translated by Angel Day in 1587) pervaded lyrics, few sonneteers wrote pastoral sequences, and none wrote one more sustained than Smith's. By beginning with pastoral poetry, he perhaps attempts, like other Spenserians such as

Drayton, to follow Spenser's Virgilian career model, in which a poet progressed from pastoral to didactic and, finally, to the highest form, epic. Smith imitates Thomas Lodge's *Phillis* (1593) and especially Spenser's *Shepheardes Calender* (1579), in which the "chiefest nymph" bears the name "Chloris."

Chloris begins with praise of Spenser – "The most excellent and learned shepherd Colin Clout" – and a request that Colin accept and protect the poems. Corin's complaint resembles that of Colin in the January eclogue of Spenser's *Shepheardes Calender.* Like Colin, Corin invokes Pan but later breaks his pipe in poetic frustration when unrequited love interferes with the production of art: "my flock all drooping bleats and cries, / Because my pipe . . . All rent and torn, and unrespected lies." Ultimately, the pastoral mode's lack of activity and vocational concerns complement the sonnet sequence's conventional stasis and focus on the poet-lover.

While Smith's conspicuous desire for recognition and patronage is not unusual, *Chloris* is distinguished from other sequences by beginning and ending with poems of praise for and supplication to a patron (Spenser) and other shepherds (contemporary poets). Like Spenser in *The Shepheardes Calender* and *Colin Clouts Come Home Againe* (1595), Smith establishes his shepherd persona in a community of writers. Despite many allusions to *The Shepheardes Calender,* in 1596 he perhaps addresses the Spenser of *Colin Clout,* a poem concerned with the problems a writer must face in securing recognition and patronage. By the time *Chloris* was published, competition for preferment had become intense: many tried; few succeeded. Of the latter, even fewer earned sustained support. The degeneration of the patronage system might explain why Smith ends his sequence complaining about the "raging Envy" around him.

Although verse praise of Spenser was common in the 1590s and although Smith probably imitates the single-poem tributes in Lodge's *Phillis* (1593) and *A Fig for Momus* (1595) and possibly that of Thomas Edwards in *Cephalus and Procris* (1595), only he dedicates his entire collection to Spenser. The poems would be unknown, "But that it pleased thy grave shepherdhood / The Patron of my maiden verse to be." Smith is one of Spenser's earliest followers, yet these words do not necessitate the friendship surmised by early critics: he may have been trying simply to meet Spenser. Spenser's own lack of finances and his position in Ireland make material motives for the dedication unlikely. Rather, Smith may have received or hoped for a valuable connection. Or he

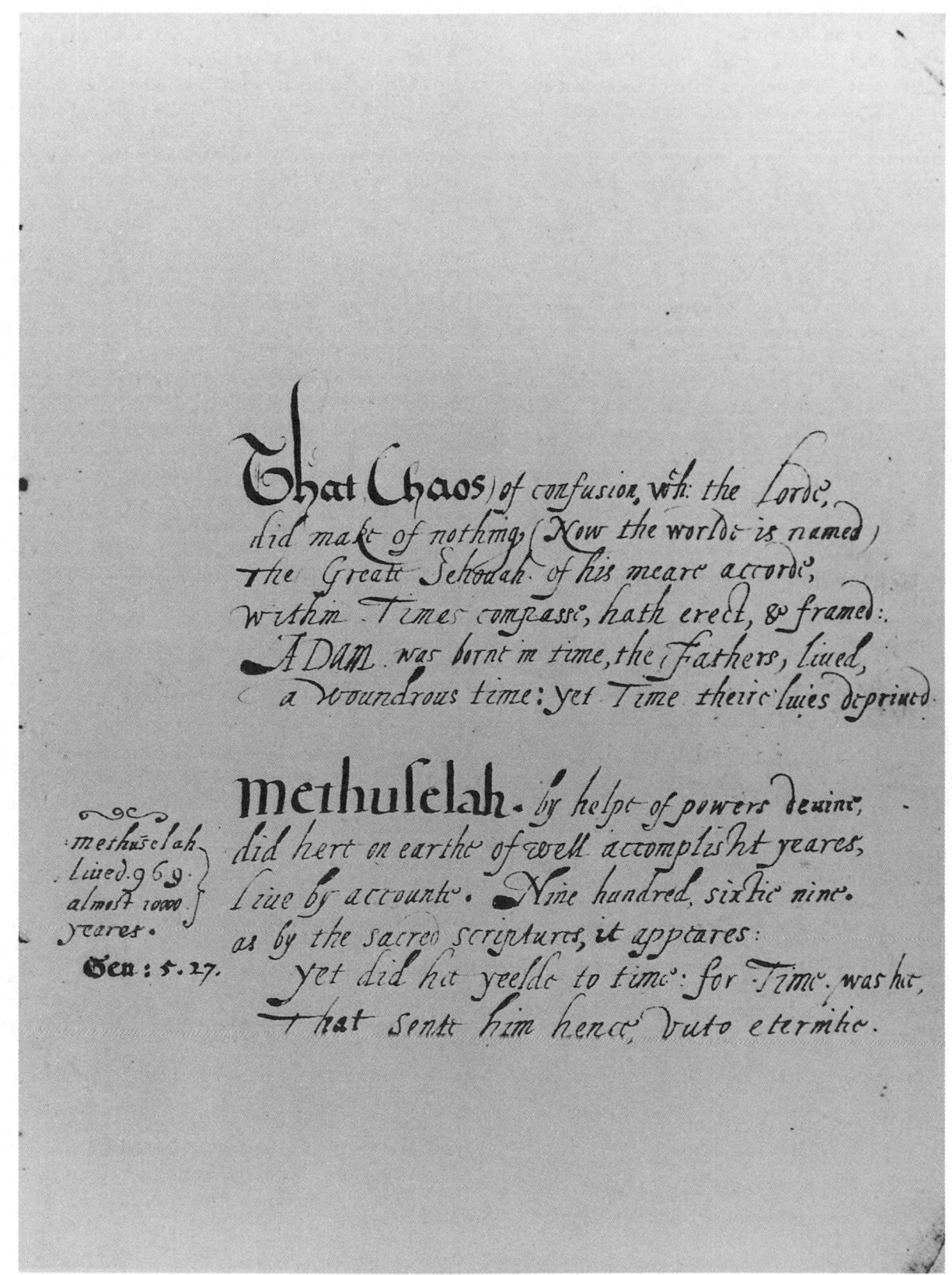

Page from the presentation copy of "An Allegory of Time" that Smith prepared for an unknown lady (James Marshall and Marie-Louise Osborn Collection, Yale University Library)

may have wished to call readers' attention to Spenser's influence on his work.

Although Smith claims that *Chloris* is his "maiden verse," sonneteers often assert that they are fledgling poets. *Chloris* could be predated by one or both of two undated manuscripts which appear to be presentation copies, one to the countess of Pembroke, and the other to an unknown female patron, possibly also the countess, to whom Smith writes "as a stranger." In his dedication of "A New Year's Gift: A Posey Made upon Certain Flowers," he uses the phrase "although unknown," but whether he refers to a lack of acquaintance with her or to his yet-unknown endeavors is unclear. To honor the custom of exchanging New Year's gifts, a poet might give his patron verse; such works are not uncommon in manuscript. Smith may have intended his "New Year's Gift" to be more than a private offering: struggling contemporaries used any holiday to solicit patronage through publication of poetic gifts. The opening poem establishes that Smith owns no land, and throughout the sequence he praises his patron as a representative of the Sidneys (known for their literary patronage) in allusions to her name and references to her wealth.

Smith uses the stanza form of William Shakespeare's *Venus and Adonis* (1593), though with a less rigorously enforced meter. The collection begins with a dedicatory poem and one which introduces the pun on "posies," which can mean "flowers" or "verses." The remaining seven poems hinge on the structural principle of their titular field flowers. Thus the flowers in the collection are the natural creations of the divine maker but also the creations of the poet maker, "divine . . . keeper of the skies," as well as metaphors for the countess and her virtues. He presents her as familiar yet remote by combining the homely with the powerful: like Mary's name, "The cowslip doth cover all the fields / With purpled state, all richly beautified." Similarly, the cyclical structure of "A New Year's Gift" begins with the uncultivated primrose, the "first sweet flower the wealthy earth doth yield," and ends with the garden rose. Near the end of the sequence, Heaven's "fair garden" supplants the natural world of earlier poems: Thyme (spelled *time*), "no flower, but an herb of grace," transcends previous images of birth and death.

Time, "more precious than . . . pearls" in "A New Year's Gift," becomes "a jewel most precious, yet little valued" in Smith's other manuscript poem, "What time all creatures did by joint consent" (published as "An Elizabethan Allegory of Time" in 1976). In this 396–line poem, as in "A New Year's Gift," Smith employs the *Venus and Adonis* stanza form. In the poem the figure of Time harangues a parliament of all creatures and defends his right to join them because of his powers of inevitable, eternal change. Smith adheres to standard medieval and Renaissance concepts of Time. An old man though still "lusty, green, strong," Smith's Time has Occasion's forelock and carries the traditional scythe "To cut down all that on the earth doth stand." His eagle's wings and hind's hooves signify his swift passing, and his lynx's eyes "view . . . Things past, things present, things to come." He is both Ovid's devourer of all he creates (*edax rerum*) and Boethius's providential force: "God's special instrument . . . though before the world I did not live, / Yet with the world, God did me essence give." Unlike Spenser's Mutability, another figure in this tradition, Time recognizes that the Creation, coming of Christ, and judgment occur in time but that time itself ends with eternity. Such apocalyptic visions were common in Renaissance depictions of time.

Time then describes his family: his wife, Opportunity; their children, Patience, Experience, and Truth (traditionally Time's daughter); their servants and neighbors. In his youth, however, Time had formed a liaison with the strumpet Fancy and produced the bastards, Excuse, Protraction, and Deceit, all of whom likewise live with iconographic servants and neighbors. In the background here are perhaps Renaissance art and proverbs in which Time reveals emblematic figures of truth and virtue or exposes figures of worldliness and falsehood. The poem concludes didactically as Time advises the parliament to "use time with care, take heed ere he be spent." Smith does not apply this economic view of time to contemporary figures and events as do other Elizabethan writers such as John Carpenter in *Time Complaining Giveth a Most Godly Admonition to England* (1588), perhaps because he did not intend the work for publication. The poem's dedication and numerous marginal notes on biblical allusions may reflect the religious interests of Smith's patron. Ultimately, the enlightened parliament admits Time and "yield[s] . . . the triumph of the day: a laurel garland." "An Allegory of Time" thus exists in the Petrarchan triumph tradition prevalent in pageants and iconography and present in the works of Stephen Hawes, Sir Thomas More, John Skelton, and Spenser.

Smith's initials led early scholars to confuse him with various other authors: the topographical writer William Smith; the dramatist Wentworth Smith; and Shakespeare. Smith may have written or edited *The Lamentable Tragedy of Locrine* (1595); the Queen's

Men performed this play, which imitates Spenser and Lodge, before 1594, and account books mention an actor named William Smith. Thus Smith's life may have resembled that of George Peele or Lodge.

Some lyrics signed "W. S." may also be Smith's. One such poem is "What shall I say of Gold, more than 'tis Gold," in *The Will of Wit* (1597). Another is "A notable description of the world," a poem about the Creation in *The Phoenix Nest* (1593) – the only poem in this collection with marginal notes, a feature of "An Allegory of Time." Most contributors to this miscellany were at Oxford together; perhaps Smith was among them. John Dowland's *First Book of Songs* (1597) contains an anonymous pastoral celebration of Cynthia attributed in a manuscript version to "W. S.," and *England's Helicon* (1600) reprints this poem as well as sonnet 13 of *Chloris*. But none of these works can be attributed to Smith with certainty. The inclusion of the *Chloris* sonnet in *England's Helicon,* though, may suggest that Smith was not as obscure in 1600 as he is now: most of the poems in this collection had been previously published, and their authors were men of respected literary talent.

The biography Smith's works provide is thus uncertain, obscured by conventions. In his lack of property he differs from courtier poets such as Sir Walter Ralegh who sought political preferment. Conversely, his solicitation of Spenser and lack of bitterness toward the patronage system in works other than *Chloris* distinguish him from professional writers such as Thomas Churchyard or Barnabe Riche, men desperate for any reward. His frank desire for recognition in *Chloris* may only be in imitation of Spenser: the personal nature of "An Allegory of Time" and "A New Year's Gift" and the absence of other surviving publications indicate that, unlike Breton or Drayton, he did not see his career as primarily literary. Perhaps he circulated most of his literary efforts in manuscript, as did many courtiers, in an effort to better an already satisfactory position. His work consequently reveals which conventions, themes, and skills the Elizabethan poet thought would please in courtly circles.

References:

Donald W. Foster, "Appendix A: W. S., 1570–1630," in his *Elegy by W. S.: A Study in Attribution* (Newark: University of Delaware Press, 1989), pp. 263–275;

Lisle C. John, *The Elizabethan Sonnet Sequences: Studies in Conventional Conceits* (New York: Columbia University Press, 1938; New York: Russell & Russell, 1964);

Lu Emily Pearson, *Elizabethan Love Conventions* (London: Allen & Unwin, 1966), pp. 124–125;

Lawrence A. Sasek, "William Smith and *The Shepheardes Calender,*" *Philological Quarterly,* 39 (April 1960): 251–253;

Janet G. Scott, "Minor Elizabethan Sonneteers and Their Greater Predecessors," *Review of English Studies,* 2 (October 1926): 423–427;

Scott, *Les Sonnets Elisabéthains: Les Sources et l'Apport Personnel* (Paris: Honoré Champion, 1929).

Papers:

A manuscript of William Smith's "What time all creatures did by joint consent" is in the James Marshall and Marie-Louise Osborn Collection at Yale University Library, and a manuscript of "A New Year's Gift" (also titled "A Posey Made upon Certain Flowers") is in the British Library (MS. Additional 35,186).

Edmund Tilney

(circa 1536 – 1610)

R. W. Maslen
Glasgow University

BOOKS: *A Briefe and Pleasant Discourse of Duties in Mariage, Called the Flower of Friendshippe* (London: Printed by Henry Denham, 1568);

Topographical Descriptions, Regiments, and Policies, edited by W. R. Streitberger (New York: Garland, 1991).

Edition: *The Flower of Friendship: A Renaissance Dialogue Contesting Marriage,* edited by Valerie Wayne (Ithaca, N.Y. & London: Cornell University Press, 1992).

Edmund Tilney's importance to Elizabethan history has traditionally been held to lie in his influence on the history of drama. He was master of the revels in the latter part of Elizabeth's reign and the early part of James's, and in this capacity he was responsible for the selection and censorship of plays presented at court and in public. He was a man who wielded extraordinary power over the final shape of plays by Christopher Marlowe, William Shakespeare, and their contemporaries. The nature and extent of his power can be judged by his extensive annotations to the manuscript of *Sir Thomas More* (circa 1598), a play by Shakespeare and others which was never performed, probably by reason of the severity of his censorship. A study of Tilney's background and his methods of applying his powers is crucial to any account of the relations between Elizabethan drama and politics.

But Tilney is also significant as the author of one of the most popular early Elizabethan works of prose fiction, *The Flower of Friendship* (1568). This little book's contemporary success is evident by the number of editions it underwent in the two decades after its publication – about six by 1587 – and its influence on some of the most important prose fictions of the 1570s and 1580s. It was the first English prose fiction to imitate the dialogue form as Giovanni Boccaccio and Baldassare Castiglione had practiced it, and so provided a commercially successful English model of the form for Tilney's successors. In addition, it may have initiated a trend

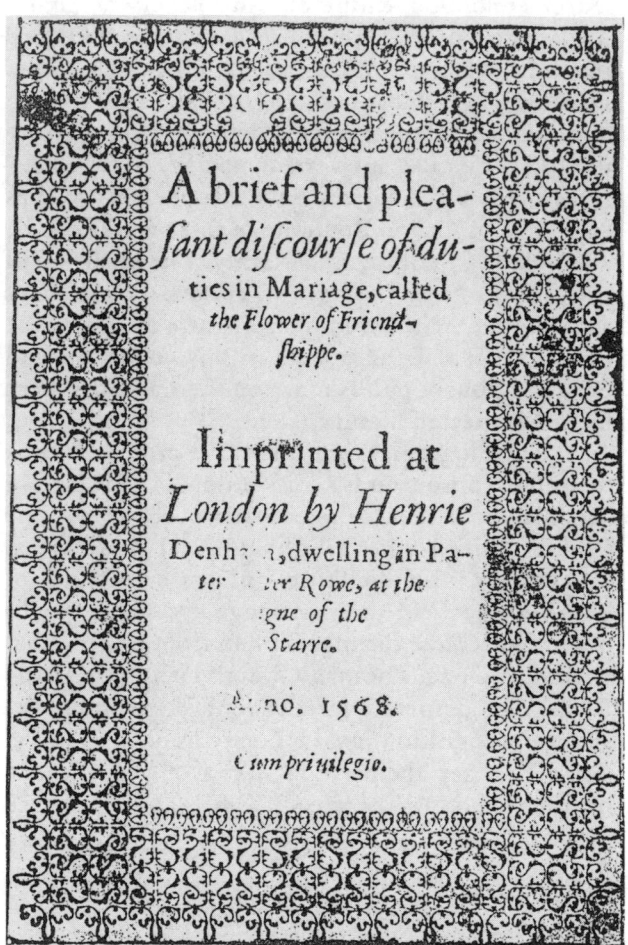

Title page for Tilney's 1568 book, one of the most popular Elizabethan works of prose fiction

for prose fictions having marriage as a prominent theme, ranging from George Pettie's collection *A Petite Palace of Pettie His Pleasure* (1576) and John Grange's *Golden Aphroditis* (1577) to John Lyly's *Euphues and His England* (1580) and George Whetstone's *Heptameron of Civil Discourses* (1582).

Tilney was born circa 1536. His father, Philip Tilney, was usher of the Privy Chamber to Henry VIII, and his mother, Malyn Chambre, was chamber woman to Queen Catherine Howard. Philip died in 1541, leaving Edmund in his mother's care at a time when she was about to become implicated in the scandal surrounding the queen's adultery. She was sentenced to life imprisonment and loss of goods in 1543 but pardoned after the queen's execution. After this pardon it is probable that Tilney and his mother were taken into the household of the dowager duchess Agnes Howard, to whom they were related, and there Edmund may have received private tuition. He may also have traveled with the aid of the Howards. His association with this powerful family continued throughout his life and no doubt supplied him with many of the social and organizational skills which recommended him for the post of master of the revels. Tilney displays some of these skills to advantage in his fiction.

The Flower of Friendship was published soon after the story collections of William Painter (1566) and Geoffrey Fenton (1567) had introduced an immense body of translated fictions into England from the Continent for the first time. Tilney's book made frank use of the vogue for Continental literature, with its dazzling international cast and its Italianate setting. It recounts two after-dinner conversations in the garden of a gentlewoman, Lady Julia, between her family and several distinguished guests on the subject of marriage. The garden itself charmingly invokes the subject of the discourse it should contain, as one of the guests explains:

> And my opinion is, quoth he, forasmuch as everything showeth now a certain natural amity amongst themselves, yea, the trees, sayeth Pliny, hath a natural instinct of friendship, the sweet flowers, the pleasant herbs declares the same also, that we entreat somewhat of friendship; and because no friendship or amity is or ought to be more dear and surer than the love of man and wife, let this treatise be thereof.

The first book describes the duties of the husband, the second those of the wife; together they aim to provide a handbook of instructions for cultivating the "flower of friendship" in marriage. Tilney readily acknowledges the authors to whose works he is indebted. One of the speakers mentions Boccaccio, whose *Filocolo* (1331–1338) had been translated by "H. G." in 1566, as well as Castiglione's treatise *The Courtier* (1528), translated by Thomas Hoby in 1561. From these authors, Tilney derives the custom of courtly conversation which determines the form of his book; the speaker observes "that he well remembered how Boccace and County Balthasar with others recounted many proper devices for exercise, both pleasant and profitable, which, quoth he, were used in the courts of

Italy, and some much like to them are practiced at this day in the English court." No doubt one of the book's attractions for contemporary readers was that it claimed to open a window on the way the governing classes chose to occupy their idle afternoons.

Tilney introduces both himself and the Spanish author Pedro de Lujan into the afternoon's conversation as participants, together with the somewhat anachronistic figures of the Spanish scholar Juan Luis Vives (1492–1540) and Desiderius Erasmus (1467–1536), both of whom had written treatises on women and marriage. Pedro is the principal speaker in the first book, as befits the writer of the *Coloquios Matrimoniales* (1550), from which much of *The Flower of Friendship* is derived.

Castiglione had introduced himself as observer into *The Courtier* alongside historical figures, but Tilney's entry into his own text marks the start of a convention in Elizabethan prose fiction of allowing the author of a tale to take a prominent part in his own narrative. The tradition can be traced back to Geoffrey Chaucer, who rode with his own pilgrims in *The Canterbury Tales* (1386–1394), and Thomas More, who in his *Utopia* (1516) met his fictional narrator. But from the publication of *The Flower of Friendship* onward, authorial intervention became a hallmark of the English form of the Continental novella, to the extent that writers such as Lyly and Robert Greene allowed themselves to become identified with their own protagonists.

In addition, the presence of three eminent humanist scholars in Tilney's text provided the unfamiliar genre of prose fiction with the much-needed endorsement of respectable educationalists, at a time when translations of Boccaccio and other Continental writers on the subject of profane love were about to come under attack from one of the most influential of English educationalists, Roger Ascham, in his *Schoolmaster* (1570). Ascham attacked the sexual mores inculcated by the Italian love story while commending the more restrained, Neoplatonic conception of love in Castiglione; Tilney's book may have provided a necessary counterbalance to Ascham's attack, incorporating the discourse of love into a *Courtier*-style dispute which reinforces the aggressively patriarchal structure of Elizabethan marriage. Soon after its publication in 1573, George Gascoigne's fiction *The Adventures of Master F. J.* was suppressed by the authorities, probably for its bawdy depiction of an adulterous affair. From then on, Elizabethan writers seem to have adopted Tilney's course and ended their love stories with a respectable wedding.

Tilney's influence is particularly evident in Lyly's *Euphues and His England,* published a year

Tilney (far left) and other mourners in the funeral procession of Queen Elizabeth, 28 April 1603 (drawing by an unknown artist, British Library)

after Tilney was appointed master of the revels in 1579. Lyly ends his book with a dispute much like the one in Lady Julia's house. As an author who was to become the most prominent court dramatist of the 1580s, perhaps he hoped to gain the approval of the new master of the revels by composing variations on a theme that Tilney had made popular. If this is the case, then Lyly's subsequent activities at court suggest that his strategy succeeded.

Above all, Tilney's fiction anticipates that of his successors in its treatment of women. The book is predominantly patriarchal, containing careful instructions on the process of subjecting a wife to her husband's rule. Pedro tells his hearers, "In this long and troublesome journey of matrimony, the wise man may not be contented merely with his spouse's virginity, but by little and little must gently procure that he may also steal away her private will and appetite."

At the same time, the women in the book possess a vigorous voice which repeatedly resists the repressive pronouncements of their male interlocutors. Lady Julia's daughter, Isabella, is the strongest spokeswoman for equality between the genders. Throughout the work she engages in a running battle with the misogynist Gualter (Tilney's version of Castiglione's woman hater Gaspar), a battle whose

occasional virulence exposes the underlying seriousness of Pedro's attack on women's freedom. In her most protracted outburst, Isabella argues that

> as meet is it that the husband obey the wife as the wife the husband, or at the least that there be no superiority between them, as the ancient philosophers have defended. For women have souls as well as men, they have wit as well as men, and [are] more apt for procreation of children than men. What reason is it, then, that they should be bound whom nature hath made free? Nay, among the Achaians women had such sovereignty that whatsoever they commanded, their husbands obeyed.

Like some later female protagonists in the fictions of Pettie and Greene, Isabella sees herself as the forerunner of a widespread female insurrection outside the bounds of fiction; her audience agrees. Gualter comments wryly that the women "of this country" have started to act like the inhabitants of Achaia. Although Isabella is silenced soon after her outburst by the interventions of Erasmus and her mother, Tilney ends by suggesting that he wrote the book at her instigation. A small part of the book's function would seem to be to articulate Isabella's objections to contemporary social constrictions of women.

The double vision of women in Tilney's book — as members of an underclass who must be kept firmly in subjection but whose struggle to resist the limitations imposed on them becomes a primary focus of the text — remained one of the chief paradoxes of Elizabethan fiction. This focus led Pettie, Lyly, and others to dedicate their fictions to woman readers and by the seventeenth century seems to have marked out prose fiction as a potential forum in which woman writers such as Lady Mary Wroth, Margaret Lucas Cavendish, and Aphra Behn could articulate women's experiences.

The prominence of dialogue in *The Flower of Friendship* may have recommended Tilney for the office of master of the revels, as a writer with some sense of the dramatic at a time when the quality of drama at court had reached an all-time low. Certainly after his appointment in 1579, Tilney continued to shift the emphasis of entertainment at court from the masque, which had been dominant at the beginning of Elizabeth's reign, to the play. He was responsible for the formation of the Queen's Men, a body of professional players with whom he had worked closely to produce from two to five plays in each season. At the same time, his depiction of Pedro and Julia negotiating between the conflicting opinions of their hearers may have indicated Tilney's aptitude for the most daunting task associated with his office, the task granted him by special commission in 1581: that of acting as chief theatrical censor in England. In this capacity he had to steer his way between the demands of the court for sophisticated entertainment, which necessitated a thriving professional theater, and the strenuous objections to drama mounted by the London City Corporation.

Tilney's success in this tricky task is indicated by his rapid social rise after his appointment. In 1581 he was recommended by the Spanish ambassador as a possible envoy to Spain (his familiarity with Pedro's work suggests an early interest in things Spanish). He married Dame Mary Bray, daughter of Sir Thomas Cotton and widow of Sir Thomas Bray, in 1583. With the help of income from her lands, he purchased the largest house in Leatherhead, Surrey, where the queen visited him in August 1591. For much of the rest of his life he was active in local politics.

His knowledge of European affairs, somewhat self-consciously signaled by the international cast of *The Flower of Friendship,* continued to expand as he sought ways to consolidate his position at court, and found expression in his two manuscript versions of "Topographical Descriptions" (written 1600–1603), an enormous diplomatic manual on Europe. These manuscripts contain a mass of political, geographic, and genealogical information intended for use by those responsible for English foreign policy and provide valuable evidence for what would have been considered sensitive issues while Tilney was acting as censor. He died in 1610, and his monument is at Saint Leonard's Church, Streatham.

As might be expected of a fiction written by the man who became Elizabeth's censor, Tilney's *Flower of Friendship* deserves consideration chiefly as a studiously conventional text, carefully subscribing to cultural values designed to appeal to its dedicatee, Queen Elizabeth. As such it helped to delineate the boundaries within which later fiction writers were forced to enact their more daring interrogations of Elizabethan conventions. A recent article by Valerie Wayne has begun to explore the place of Tilney's book in the development of Elizabethan representations of intelligent and articulate women. More work needs to be done on its position among the neglected prose fictions of the 1560s and earlier, which would provide important evidence of the ways in which Elizabethan authors read and reacted to their Tudor predecessors and of how they adapted their texts to the changing conditions of Elizabeth's reign. Just as no history of the Elizabe-

than drama can ignore Tilney's role as censor, so too no study of early modern fiction can afford to neglect his modest pamphlet.

Biography:

W. R. Streitberger, "On Edmond Tyllney's Biography," *Review of English Studies,* new series 29 (February 1978): 11–35.

References:

Robert Cecil Bald, "The Book of Sir Thomas More and Its Problems," *Shakespeare Survey,* 2 (1949): 44–61;

F. S. Boas, "Queen Elizabeth, the Revels Office and Edmund Tilney," in *Queen Elizabeth in Drama and Related Studies* (London: Allen & Unwin, 1950), pp. 36–55;

Richard Dutton, *Mastering the Revels: The Regulation and Censorship of English Renaissance Drama* (London: Macmillan, 1991);

Ernest J. Moncada, "The Spanish Source of Edmund Tilney's *The Flower of Friendshippe,*" *Modern Language Review,* 65 (April 1970): 241–247;

W. R. Streitberger, *Edmond Tyllney: Master of the Revels and Censor of Plays* (New York: AMS Press, 1986);

Streitberger, ed., *Jacobean and Caroline Revels Accounts, 1603–1642* (Oxford: Malone Society, 1986);

J. G. Tilney-Basset, "Edmund Tilney's *The Flower of Friendshippe,*" *Library,* fourth series 26 (September–December 1945): 175–181;

Valerie Wayne, "Edmund Tilney, *The Flower of Friendshippe* (1568)," in *Channels of Communication,* edited by Philip Hobsbaum, Paddy Lyons, and Jim McGhee (Glasgow: Department of English Literature, University of Glasgow, 1992).

Papers:

Edmund Tilney's manuscript of "The descriptions, regiments, and policies as well general as particularly of Italy, France, Germany, Spain, England, and Scotland, etc., by the several particularities whereof the perfect estate of each one of them may generally be discovered" is in the Folger Shakespeare Library, Washington, D.C. (Di Ricci, 1300.1, MS, V.b. 182). The University of Illinois Library in Urbana has his "The topographical descriptions, regiments, and policies of Italy, France, Germany, England, Spain, Scotland, and Ireland, whereby in some sort the particular estates of every one of those countries may be discovered" (uncatalogued MS).

George Whetstone
(1550 – 1587)

Joseph Black
University of Toronto

BOOKS: *The Rocke of Regard, Diuided into Foure Parts* (London: Printed [by Henry Middleton] for Robert Waley, 1576);

A Remembraunce of the Wel Imployed Life, of George Gaskoigne Esquire, Who Deceased the 7. of October. 1577 (London: Printed for Edward Aggas, [1577]);

The Right Excellent and Famous Historye, of Promos and Cassandra (London: [Printed by John Charlewood for] Richard Jhones, 1578);

A Remembraunce, of the Woorthie Life, of Sir Nicholas Bacon Who Deceased, the 20 Daye of Februarie 1578 (London: Printed [by John Kingston] for Miles Jennyngs, 1579);

An Heptameron of Ciuill Discourses (London: Richard Jones, 1582); republished as *Aurelia. The Paragon of Pleasure and Princely Delights* (London: [Printed by Thomas Orwin for] Richard Johnes, 1593);

A Remembraunce of the Precious Vertues of the Right Honourable Iudge, Sir James Dier, Who Disseased the 24. of Marche, 1582 (London: John Charlewood, [1582]);

A Remembraunce of the Life, Death, and Vertues, of Thomas Late Erle of Sussex (London: John Wolfe & Richard Jones, 1583);

A Mirour for Magestrates of Cyties. Representing the Ordinaunces, of the Emperour, Alexander Severus, to Suppresse Vices. Hereunto, Is Added, a Touchstone for the Time: Containyng: Mischiefes, Bred in London (London: Richard Jones, 1584); republished as *The Enemie to Vnthryftinesse* (London: Richard Jones, 1586);

A Mirror of Treue Honnour and Christian Nobilitie, Exposing: The Life, Death, and Vertues of Frauncis Earle of Bedford (London: Printed by Richard Jones, 1585);

The Honorable Reputation of a Souldier. Drawen out of the Liues, of Romaine, Grecian, and other Martialistes (London: Richard Jones, 1585); enlarged and published with a Dutch translation as *Verduytscht ende by een ghevoecht, door J. Walraven (English Pronounciation: Or a Shorte Introduction to the English Speache [By] J. Walraven)* (Leiden: Jan Paets Jacobszoon & Jan Bouwenszoon, 1586);

The English Myrror. A Regard Wherein Al Estates May Behold the Conquests of Enuy: Containing Ruine of Common Weales, [etc.] (London: Printed by John Windet for Gregory Seton, 1586);

The Censure of a Loyall Subject: Vpon Those Traitors, at the Place of Their Executions, the xx. and xxi. of September (London: Printed by Richard Jones, 1587; enlarged edition, London: Richard Jones, [1587]);

Sir Phillip Sidney, His Honorable Life, His Valiant Death, and His True Vertues. Whereunto Is Adjoyned, One Other Commemoration (London: Printed [by Thomas Orwin] for Thomas Cadman, [1587]).

Editions: *Frondes Caducae*, edited by Alexander Boswell (Auchinleck, Scotland: Auchlinleck Press, 1816);

The Rocke of Regard, Diuided into Foure Parts, edited by John Payne Collier (N.p., n.d. [London, 1868–1870]);

The Right Excellent and Famous Historye, of Promos and Cassandra (London: Tudor Facsimile Texts, 1910);

The Censure of a Loyall Subject (Amsterdam: Theatrum Orbis Terrarum, 1973; New York: Da Capo Press, 1973);

The English Myrror (Amsterdam: Theatrum Orbis Terrarum, 1973; New York: Da Capo Press, 1973);

William Shakespeare, *Measure for Measure,* edited by Mark Eccles, New Variorum Edition (New York: Modern Language Association of America, 1980) – includes Whetstone's *Promos and Cassandra*, pp. 305–369, and a selection from *An Heptameron of Civill Discourses*, pp. 370–378;

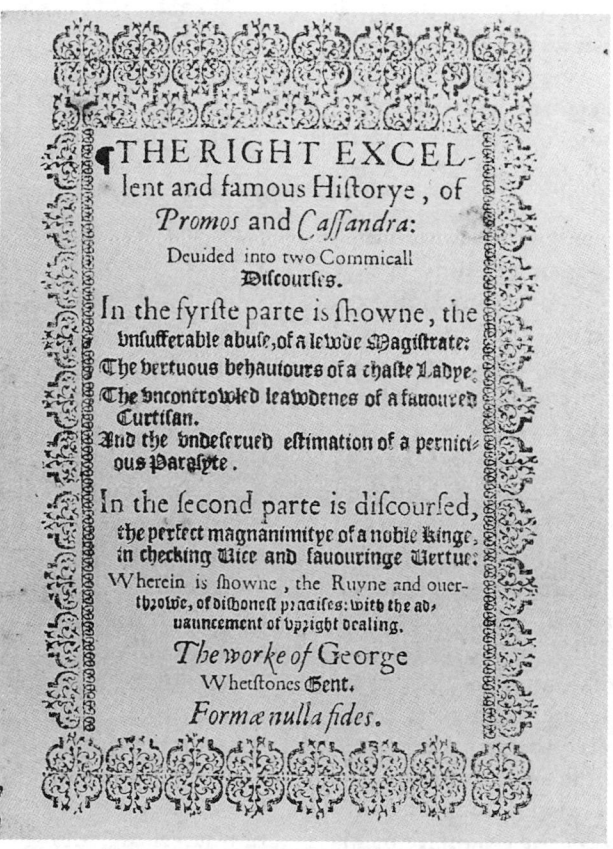

Title page for Whetstone's only play, one of the sources for William
Shakespeare's Measure for Measure (1604)

A Critical Edition of George Whetstone's 1582 "An Heptameron of Civill Discourses," edited by Diana Shklanka (New York: Garland, 1987).

OTHER: "In praise of George Gascoigne and his posies," in *The Posies of George Gascoigne Esquire* (London: Printed by Henry Bynneman for Richard Smith, [1575]);

"George Whetstone, gentleman, in the author's commendation," in *Flowers of Epigrammes, Out of Sundrie the Moste Singular Authors,* by Timothy Kendall (London: [Printed by John Kingston for] John Shepperd, 1577);

"Verses written of twenty good precepts," in *The Paradyse of Daynty Deuises, Aptly Furnished, with Sundry Inuentions: Written for the Most Part, by M. Edwards, the Rest, by Sundry Gentlemen,* by Richard Edwards (London: [Printed by Richard Jones for?] Henry Disle, 1578).

George Whetstone is remembered primarily for *Promos and Cassandra* (1578), his only play and a chief source for William Shakespeare's *Measure for Measure* (1604). But to contemporaries he was better known as an elegist, moralist, and patriotic writer. Whetstone's elegies give him a good claim to the title of first professional biographer in English. His moralistic writings, with their emphasis on the corruptions of the London underworld, offer modern readers a glimpse into the seedier side of Elizabethan England. In his prose, an increasingly explicit patriotism reflects his belief that a reformed and firmly Protestant England could be a first-rate power and role model to the world. While often undistinguished, Whetstone's literary output is deeply characteristic of his era, and his wide range of work illustrates the variety of options available to the professional writer in the 1570s and 1580s.

Whetstone was born in London in 1550. His father, Robert, a wealthy haberdasher, died in 1557, leaving properties in London, as well as Yorkshire and six other counties. Whetstone's share of the inheritance consisted of lands and tenements in London worth one hundred marks a year — a very comfortable income. His mother, Margaret, soon remarried; her second husband, Robert Browne, owned Walcott Hall in Northamptonshire, and the young Whetstone divided his time between London and the country. Country connections would later prove useful: Burghley House was in the neighborhood, and, after dedicating several works to members of the Cecil family, Whetstone was sent to the Netherlands in 1587 as civilian commissary of musters through the patronage of William Cecil, Lord Burghley.

Whetstone did not receive his inheritance until 1573; soon after, he began to study law at Furnivall's Inn, an Inn of Chancery in Holborn. The Inns of Court were nearby, and the area had long been a center of literary activity. Whetstone's first publications were commendatory verses for collections by George Gascoigne (1575) and Timothy Kendall (1577), and he would also have known such writers as Thomas Churchyard, Geoffrey Fenton, and Nicholas Breton. His career as a professional writer consequently had a conventional beginning. Many accounts of his life, however, including that found in the *Dictionary of National Biography,* tell a different, more colorful story. In these versions Whetstone spends a dissipated youth at court unsuccessfully seeking preferment, gambles away his patrimony, and in despair joins the military to fight in the Low Countries. He returns to London in the mid 1570s without means of support or future prospects and, inspired by the examples of his friends Gascoigne and Churchyard, turns as a last resort to literature.

That account is based on a supposedly autobiographical section of Whetstone's first book, *The Rock of Regard* (1576), but is otherwise unsupported; in his *Honorable Reputation of a Soldier* (1585) he in fact states that he has had up to that point no military experience. A different story in *The Rock of Regard,* however, does contain demonstrably autobiographical elements. In "The Invention of P. Plasmos" a youth falls in love with a faithless beauty, spends too much money on her, and falls into debt. He becomes acquainted with a group of "cozeners" (usurers and shady lawyers) who wrap him "in very dangerous and cumbersome bonds." Playing on his inexperience, the cozeners trick Plasmos into signing over his property and then instigate quarrels between him and others in the hope that he will be killed and the properties will revert to them. Plasmos survives the fights, repents his unthrifty ways, and, less wealthy but wiser, has the final revenge of seeing his enemies die horrible deaths. In *Touchstone for the Time* (1584) Whetstone states that Plasmos's fate was his own, and the story was confirmed in most details by the discovery this century of the records of the case Whetstone brought against the cozeners in Star Chamber.

"The Invention of P. Plasmos" adds a personal dimension to the zeal for social and legal reform which characterizes much of Whetstone's work. It also helps lessen the possibility that his moral stance is merely a convention. He dedicates *The Rock of Regard,* for example, to "all the young gentlemen of England" because it "imports necessary matter of direction for unstayed youth." Writers such as Gascoigne and George Turberville had employed similar dedications, and in some cases this nobly purposed didacticism might simply be a ploy to avoid reproof while writing about lowlife. Whetstone's condemnations of the less savory aspects of city life, however, generally ring sincere.

He divided *The Rock of Regard* into four sections. "The Castle of Delight" contains cautionary narratives on the wiles of women and the evils of revenge. "The Garden of Unthriftiness" presents poems in a variety of conventional genres on the troubles attending love. "The Arbor of Virtue" offers a verse tale of a model good woman and poems in praise of various English ladies. "The Orchard of Repentance," which includes the story of young Plasmos, illustrates in verse and prose the evils of life in London: "the miseries of dice, the mischiefs of quarrelling, and the fall of prodigality." The tone is admonitory, and Whetstone emphasizes the role of his own experience in his desire to expose the "deceits of all sorts of people."

Whetstone's preoccupation with civic corruption continues in *Promos and Cassandra.* His source for the story made famous by *Measure for Measure* is a novella in Cinthio's (Giambattista Giraldi's) popular collection *Hecatommithi* (1565). But, in an innovation adopted by Shakespeare, he adds a subplot dealing with the lowlife in the city of the play. Whetstone's dedicatory preface addressed to William Fleetwood — the recorder of London, whose job was to clean up the London underworld — is one of the earliest critical statements in English on drama. Like Sir Philip Sidney, who appears to have read this preface, Whetstone rebukes English dramatists for their indecorous mixing of the tragic with the comic. He stresses the didactic function of drama and to this end insists on realistic presentation and individualized characters. Whetstone's moral concerns have led some critics to label him a Puritan and group his work with that of antistage writers such as Stephen Gosson and Philip Stubbs. But it should be noted that his objection to the stage was not on moral grounds but was due to the bad taste and poor execution exhibited by contemporary productions.

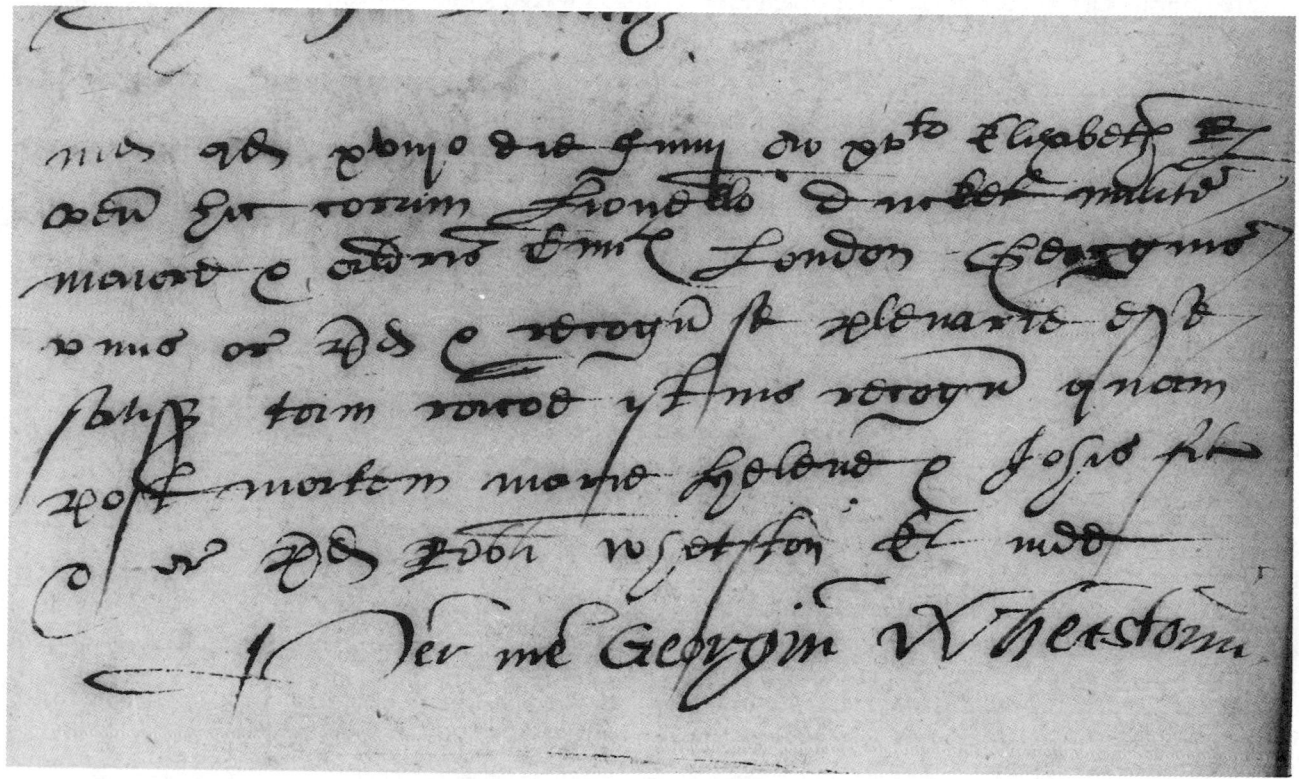

Whetstone's signature on a document acknowledging receipt of his inheritance money from his mother (Corporation of London Records Office, Journal 19, folio 212ʳ)

In the preface to *Promos and Cassandra* Whetstone also notes his intention "to accompany the adventurous captain, Sir Humphrey Gilbert, in his honorable voyage." Gilbert's 1578 expedition set out to combine exploration, colonization, plunder, and harassment of the Spanish. Whetstone was one of many Elizabethan "gentlemen adventurers" who joined expeditions like Gilbert's hoping to make their fortunes. As a means to patronage and preferment, literature was often an uncertain business, and Whetstone was apparently willing to try alternatives. His hopes in this case were disappointed when the ship to which he was attached developed a leak and possibly never even left English waters.

Whetstone did manage to leave England in 1580, when he made a tour through Italy. The principal literary consequence of this trip was the *Heptameron of Civil Discourses* (1582). The novella collection had been a popular genre on the Continent ever since the success of Giovanni Boccaccio's *Decameron* (1350). After Geoffrey Chaucer's *Canterbury Tales* (1386–1394), however, English collections did not appear again until the 1560s, and the *Heptameron* was only the second of these to be structured around a frame story. Motivated as always by his desire to improve English behavior, Whetstone

wanted to present his readers with the models of taste and manners he had encountered in Italy. His frame tale, with its dialogues between the stories, is consequently as important as the stories themselves because his interlocutors illustrate the virtues of civil speech and refinement in action. The subject of both stories and dialogues is marriage, in particular the role of women within marriage; as the collection progresses, the ideals of the frame-tale speakers increasingly coincide with the examples they offer in their stories.

With the combined publication of *A Mirror for Magistrates of Cities* and *A Touchstone for the Time* (1584), Whetstone returned to his moral preoccupations. *Mirror for Magistrates* is an account of the reforms instituted by the Roman Emperor Severus to "suppress and chastise the notorious vices nourished in Rome by the superfluous number of dicing-houses, taverns, and common stews." Pointedly dedicated to the lord mayor, aldermen, and recorder of London, *Mirror for Magistrates* outlines Severus's attempts to regulate gambling, prostitution, usury, taverns, marketplace practices, extravagant lifestyles, idleness, and sanitary conditions.

In *Touchstone* Whetstone turns specifically to London and, "with a care to continue the prosperity of this famous city," suggests a more diligent enforcement of laws on these matters. Tracing the blame for much of London's vice to taverns, dicing houses, "and other like sanctuaries of iniquity," he repeats many of the concerns he voiced when dealing with his own youth in *The Rock of Regard*. Severity is needed, he concludes, because "London is so plentiful of notorious cozeners, cheaters, and dishonest livers, and withal so blemished with heinous cozenages and deceits, as a young man, unless he have an old man's experience, can hardly avoid their snares." Absent, however, are the literary pretensions of the early work: instead of fashionable verse, *Mirror for Magistrates* and *Touchstone* offer practical answers in a solid, didactic prose.

In 1585 Whetstone's brother Barnard accompanied Robert Dudley, Earl of Leicester's expeditionary force to the Low Countries; Whetstone himself would follow in 1587. The concerns of his *Honorable Reputation of a Soldier* (1585) consequently have rather personal implications. *Honorable Reputation* is the only conduct book of its era directed specifically to soldiers. Drawing on classical authors for illustrations, Whetstone stresses the need for courage, temperance, mercy, and proper religious preparation. "The soldier," he argues, "of all men ought to set the fear of God before his eyes, to have a pure conscience, and to be of good conversation, lest in running upon the pikes, he falleth into hell fire." Whetstone leaves questions of strategy to the numerous military handbooks of the period, advising his readers instead on more-personal, practical matters, such as avoiding gluttony because "the soldier must many times endure hunger, thirst, cold, travel, and other sharp miseries, which pampered and delicate bodies cannot endure." He does not glorify war: he concludes by wishing the English forces success but advising clemency and appearing sincerely to wish for a minimum of violence. *Honorable Reputation* was reprinted in Leiden in 1586 with a Dutch translation in parallel columns, and a vocabulary and guide to English pronunciation by the Dutch writer Jacob Walraven. This edition was designed to help Dutch readers learn English and is a useful reminder of the close Anglo-Dutch connections in this period.

To Whetstone, *Mirror for Magistrates*, *Touchstone*, and *Honorable Conduct* were all parts of a larger work called *The English Mirror,* the remainder of which was published under that title in 1586. His most ambitious literary undertaking, and an encyclopedic repository of Elizabethan lore, *The English Mirror* makes explicit the patriotic, Protestant strain which underlies most of Whetstone's books. His

aim was to show England its path to future prosperity. Book 1, dedicated to the nobility, is an eclectic survey of the disruptive role of envy in world history: Whetstone includes chapters on the lives of Muhammad and Tamerlane, the rise of Turkey as a world power, and the decline of Rome. Book 2, dedicated to the clergy, is an extended encomium on the virtues of peace, and it focuses on England. Whetstone presents the calamities that followed the deposition of King Richard II, discusses the reigns of succeeding monarchs, and concludes with a lengthy tribute to Queen Elizabeth I, to whom the work as a whole is dedicated. Book 3, dedicated to magistrates, examines in detail the functioning of the state. Whetstone surveys England's administrative and judicial structure and specifies the duties of each position in producing and maintaining domestic harmony.

Whetstone included in *The English Mirror* a list of the treasonous conspiracies in Elizabeth's reign, a list which is updated by his *Censure of a Loyal Subject* (1587). Presented as a conversation among "Walker, a godly divine; Weston, a discreet gentleman; and Wilcocks, a substantial clothier," *Censure* describes with patriotic fervor the execution of those involved in the Babington conspiracy to assassinate Elizabeth and place Mary on the throne. The tone of *Censure,* unlike that of the courtly dialogues in the *Heptameron,* is informal and colloquial because Whetstone wrote for a popular audience: the title page notes that the book handles "matter of necessary instruction to all dutiful subjects, especially the multitude of ignorant people." The speakers consequently pay frequent tribute to the queen, and their discussion of the executions clearly seeks to shape their readers' response to the event. While the traitors were "clothed in silks and every way furnished to move pity," says Wilcocks, "the odiousness of their treason was so settled in every man's heart, as there appeared no sadness or alteration among the people at the mangling and quartering of their bodies. Yea, the whole multitude, without any sign of lamentation, greedily beheld the spectacle from the first to the last." In this context, Whetstone's message to "the multitude" is slightly threatening: "Please God, be true to thy Prince, and obey the Laws."

Whetstone's last published work was a verse life of Sidney (1587). He had previously written elegies commemorating Gascoigne (1577), Sir Nicholas Bacon (1579), Sir James Dyer (1582), Thomas Radcliffe, Earl of Sussex (1583), and Francis Russell, Earl of Bedford (1585). Whetstone had been present at his friend Gascoigne's death, his brother had and he may have served with Sidney in the Low Countries, and he seems also to have had some acquaintance with Bacon and Bedford. But there is no record that he knew either Dyer or Sussex: these elegies may have been commissioned by their families, or he may have written them in hopes of patronage.

Whetstone was conscious of his reputation as an elegist: in the *Remembrance of Sussex* he writes, "some skill I have on good men's tombs to write." He appears also to have accepted his duties as a biographer seriously, emphasizing at the beginning of each elegy his desire for accuracy. He included in marginal notes information not easily assimilated into the conventions governing the elegy: Sidney, we learn, "was always rich in his martial and decent in his usual apparel," was "much beloved by strangers, especially the Germans," and "spoke the French and Italian languages, but their vices defiled him not." Like all early modern biographers, however, Whetstone did not set out to provide a strict historical record. His primary aim was to present models of living explicitly designed to be emulated. He also hoped that the reformation of the individual would benefit England: in these elegies, he writes in the *Remembrance of Sussex*, "posterity may read / The way to work their own and country's gain."

With his "country's gain" the object, Whetstone attempted to reform English behavior at all levels, from the individual (*The Rock of Regard, Honorable Conduct,* the elegies) to the social (*Heptameron*) to the institutional (the works comprising the *English Mirror* project). His motivation was the fear that corruption and immorality were preventing England from achieving its full potential for greatness. In 1587 Whetstone was killed in a duel while on service in the Low Countries: he was acting, appropriately enough, on the same concerns that dominate his literary work. According to letters by Thomas Digges, the mustermaster under whom he was serving, Whetstone confronted one Captain Edmund Udall about financial abuses connected with the supplies; Whetstone fought and met his death, writes Digges, "no doubt because he could not be corrupted."

References:

Jan A. van Dorsten, *Poets, Patrons, Professors: Sir Philip Sidney, Daniel Rogers, and the Leiden Humanists* (Leiden: Sir Thomas Browne Institute / Leiden University Press, 1962), pp. 139–146;

Mark Eccles, "George Whetstone in Star Chamber," *Review of English Studies,* new series 33 (November 1982): 385–395;

Eccles, "Whetstone's Death," *Times Literary Supplement,* 27 August 1931, p. 648;

Thomas C. Izard, *George Whetstone: Mid-Elizabethan Man of Letters* (New York: Columbia University Press, 1942).

Geoffrey Whitney
(1548 or 1552? – May 1601)

Kenneth Borris
McGill University

BOOK: *A Choice of Emblemes and Other Deuises,* (Leiden: Printed for Christopher Plantin by François Raphelengien, 1586).

Editions: *A Choice of Emblemes,* edited by Henry Green (London: Lowell Reeve, 1866); republished, with an introduction by Frank Fieler (New York: Blom, 1967);

A Choice of Emblemes and Other Deuises, introduction by John Manning (Aldershot, U.K.: Scolar Press, 1989).

OTHER: Janus Dousa (Jan van der Does), Sr., *Odarum Britannicarum Liber,* includes a commendatory poem by Whitney and his translation of a poem by Dousa's son (Leiden: Printed for Christopher Plantin by François Raphelengien, 1586);

George Whetstone, *De eerweerdighe Achtbaerheyt van een Soldener (The Honorable Reputation of a Soldier),* translated by Jacob Walraven, with a commendatory poem by Whitney (Leiden: Jan Paedts Jacobzoon & Jan Bouwenzoon, 1586).

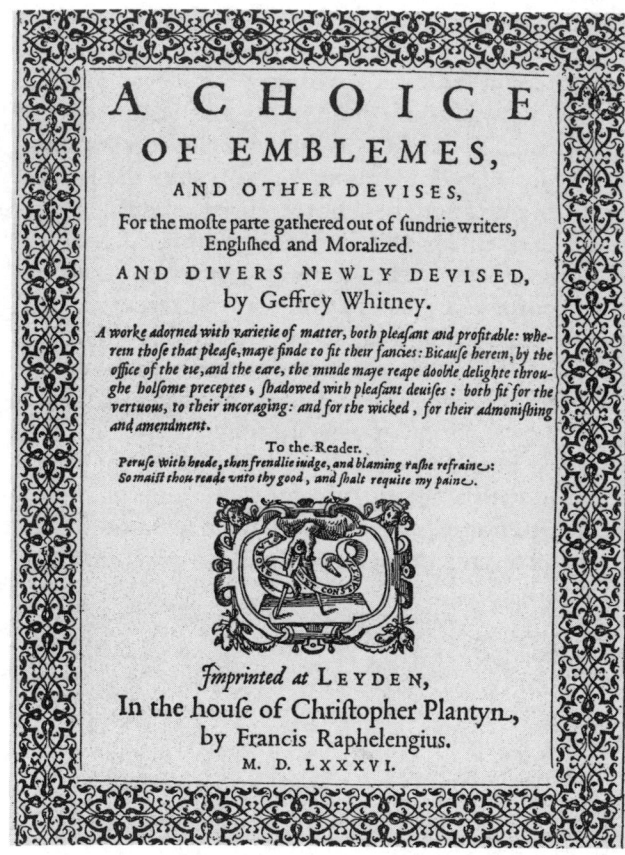

Title page for Whitney's only published book, which established his reputation as the foremost Elizabethan emblematist

The foremost Elizabethan emblematist, Geoffrey Whitney discovered in that genre a means of maximizing his slender capabilities as a poet. Since the form typically supplemented an epigram with a picture and motto, successful use did not depend wholly on poetic accomplishment. Until recently, critics considered Whitney a mere translator and compiler of emblems, thus useful for documenting iconographical and other commonplaces of his culture. Nevertheless, his emblem book evinces its own shaping purposes and artistry through significant alterations and arrangements of borrowed emblems, and some original compositions. Hence Whitney's *Choice of Emblems* (1586) achieves its own significant position as a moralized verbal-visual treatment of human life, especially in the Elizabethan context.

Geoffrey Whitney's obscure origins have been best reconstructed by John F. Leisher, largely according to information included in the poet's *Choice of Emblems* and his sister Isabella's *Sweet Nosegay or, Pleasant Posy* (1573). Most likely born in London around 1552, Whitney was named after his father, was descended from the Whitneys of Herefordshire, and had at least one brother and four sisters. His mother's identity is unknown. The poet was certainly reared near Nantwich in Cheshire, at Combermere, the demesne of Richard Cotton, where his parents obtained a tenancy. Whitneys had been long established at the nearby manor of Coole Pilate. Celebrated in one of Whitney's emblems, Combermere became the poet's final home as well. After attending the school at Audlem (commemorated in another emblem), he probably proceeded to Oxford and then Cambridge but apparently did not earn a degree at either university. Between 1570 and 1574 he likely studied law at Thavies' or Furnivall's Inn in London without completing requirements for being called to the bar.

Whitney probably then obtained a position in the corporation of Great Yarmouth through the patronage of one of his legal instructors, Charles Calthorpe, who was attached to Lincoln's Inn and who became steward of the town in 1573. By 1580 Whitney had become an underbailiff, a burgess, and, in effect, assistant steward. He became acting steward in 1584, and his candidacy for the stewardship itself was supported by Robert Dudley, Earl of Leicester, high steward of Great Yarmouth. When the corporation rejected Whitney because he had not completed legal training, he resigned even his assistantship. A protracted dispute over a promised pension ensued, and Whitney, with Leicester's backing, settled for a lump sum of forty-five pounds in 1588. After spending much of 1586 in the Low Countries while Leicester campaigned there, he returned to England and became an officer of the Crown, most likely through Leicester's influence.

In late November or early December of 1585, just before Leicester assumed command of English forces requested by the provinces of the Low Countries in revolt against Spain, Whitney presented him with a manuscript collection of almost two hundred emblems. They are rendered in sepia, pen and ink, and blue watercolor, probably not in Whitney's own hand. Through this gift he clearly aimed to advance his career by securing further patronage and perhaps also to become involved in Leicester's forthcoming campaign, so as to benefit from its expected success.

Leicester could well have taken special interest in emblems, for Thomas Palmer had already given him a large manuscript collection in the 1560s, apparently the first such endeavor in England. Whitney's dedicatory epistle to Leicester offers the manuscript to requite his "honorable bounty and favor." It is, Whitney insists, an anthology that constitutes a new creation: his own selective "gatherings and gleanings out of other men's harvests," which he himself has "garnished with many histories, with the proper applications and expositions of those emblems . . . found obscure." No one, he claims, has attempted such compilation before, and "divers of the inventions" are his "own . . . workmanship." Whitney avows that Leicester's approbation would encourage him "to assay some matter of more moment," leisure permitting, and he similarly invites his readers' approval in *A Choice of Emblems*. Yet Whitney's literary endeavors apparently ceased with that publication.

Shortly after presenting the manuscript, Whitney moved to Leiden with Janus Dousa, or Jan van der Does, one of the ambassadors sent to Elizabeth I by the Dutch States General, and attended the University of Leiden, where Dousa was curator. Meanwhile, he extensively revised his original collection, and *A Choice of Emblems*, which amounts to a different work, was published in May 1586 by François Raphelengien's Leiden branch of the Christopher Plantin press. Whitney's new address "To the Reader," which supplements the epistle to Leicester, retained from the manuscript, declares that "some" pressed him to publish the manuscript. They included Leicester, a dedicatory poem claims, and probably certain Dutch humanists, such as Dousa.

According to Mason Tung, *A Choice of Emblems* comprises 248 emblems, one "naked," or without picture, including all but 13 from the manuscript, often in revised form, and adding more than 60. Of the 15 emblems apparently invented by Whitney, 10 also appear in the manuscript. Having published many emblem books, the Plantin press readily supplied 207 of the woodblocks for pictures from its own stock; 40 more woodblocks were newly cut, 25 to copy pictures from other sources and 15 for Whitney's invented emblems. As Tung shows, Whitney drew selectively on diverse collections. His sources for the manuscript and the published book were Andrea Alciati, *Emblemata* (1531), 78 emblems in the manuscript and 87 in the book; Joannes Sambucus, *Emblemata* (1564), 44 and 51; Claude Paradin, *Les Devises héroïques* (1551; enlarged 1557), 22 and 32; Hadrianus Junius (Adriaan de Jonge), *Emblemata* (1565), 17 and 21; Guillaume de la Perrière, *Le Théâtre des bons engins* (1539), 9 and 8; and Barthelemy Aneau, *Picta Poesis* (1552), 7 and 8. Whitney had two additional sources for the published book, taking 16 emblems from Gabriello Faerno's *Fabulae Centum* (1563) and 9 from Georgette de Montenay's *Emblèmes, ou devises chrestiennes* (1571). Twenty emblems in the manuscript are apparently original, as opposed to 15 in *A Choice of Emblems*, and Whitney thoroughly rearranged the sequence of emblems from the manuscript while altering many mottoes, verses, or pictures.

Whereas Whitney's manuscript generally takes Leicester's learning for granted, in *A Choice of Emblems* he explains even the emblematic form, drawing on Claude Mignault's essay "Syntagma de Symbolis," first published in Plantin's 1577 edition of Alciati's emblems. Whitney calls the *emblem* "some witty device expressed with cunning workmanship, some-

The Janus emblem that introduces the second part of Whitney's book and the final emblem, dedicated to Whitney's patron, Robert Dudley, Earl of Leicester

thing obscure to be perceived at the first, whereby, when with further consideration it is understood, it may the greater delight the beholder." Emblems comprehend diverse matter, Whitney continues, including exemplary historical events, acts, or persons, or instructive natural phenomena; but primarily they pertain "to virtue and instruction of life.... For all do tend unto discipline, and moral precepts of living." By 1586 the emblem usually consisted of a gnomic motto, a related picture, and a concluding epigram, each with varying capacities for interaction with the other elements and for the concealment or revelation of meaning. Whitney used this model in keeping with his preferred sources. *A Choice of Emblems* also features extensive Latin marginal annotations, the better to accommodate Continental readers, Whitney observes, and also to be more compendious. In any case synthetic commentaries for emblem books had become widespread.

According to Frank Fieler, John F. Leisher, and John Manning, *A Choice of Emblems* was part of the "propaganda" to further Leicester's ambitions and prestige, English imperialism, the Anglo-Dutch alliance, and the Protestant cause. Yet the book includes no directly anti-Spanish or anti-Catholic comments, aside from one antipapal remark, mild for the period, in the epistle to Leicester. None of the polemical or apocalyptic iconography of the Dutch revolt appears. No emblems are based on the Book of Revelation, which was being used in literature and the visual arts to justify the Dutch cause according to Protestant historiography, as in Jan van der Noot's genuinely propagandistic emblem book, *A Theatre for Worldlings* (1569). Though none of Whitney's emblems deals directly with the Anglo-Dutch alliance, the epigrams on friendship and good neighbors could have readily accommodated such political digression. Yet the lack of direct comment on the Low Countries and Protestantism in *A Choice of Emblems* is astonishing, considering the circumstances of its publication.

Rather than being an Anglo-Dutch or Leicestrian "propagandist," Whitney distanced his book somewhat from immediate political and religious exigencies, perhaps deliberately to attract wider and more enduring interest. Unlike the manuscript his *Choice of Emblems* dedicates many emblems to friends, colleagues, relatives, and benefactors; only a minority are Dutch or involved in Leicester's campaign. Some emblems deal with military matters, but few explicitly address topical events.

Though Whitney endorsed the Elizabethan established church, the religious emblems seem studiously uncontentious for his time. *A Choice of Emblems* deals generally with Elizabethan conditions and attainments, such as Sir Francis Drake's circumnavigation, rather than focusing narrowly on the Dutch campaign. Thus Whitney provided a broad-based moral consideration of life that especially focuses on current English experience. To some extent *A Choice of Emblems* endeavors to foster good Anglo-Dutch relations, but other themes, such as Whitney's biography and personal obligations, are at least as prominent. The title page announces a work "adorned with variety of matter," framed for the promotion of pleasure and virtue.

Whitney's revisions of the manuscript for his published book demonstrate this movement toward generality of application. The manuscript includes an emblem that credits Leicester with mastering Fortune herself through God's favor: "In logum et foelicissimum statum illustrissimi comitis Leicestrensis." In a variant copy of *A Choice of Emblems* in the Folger Library, this emblem appears with the new motto *Fato, non fortuna,* detaching it from Leicester; but, indicating Whitney's final decision, most copies exclude the emblem altogether.

For *A Choice of Emblems* Whitney invented a final emblem that is dedicated to Leicester but is far less congratulatory. All things must end, this new emblem stresses, even "princely" labors. It has not been previously recognized that in this emblem the fall of the "greatest oak," a tree symbolic of fortitude and associated with the Roman civic crown in Alciati's *Emblemata,* suggests the end of a great enterprise or career of national service such as Leicester's, more than the end of a "simple book." In keeping with the eschatological themes of the concluding emblems, Whitney indirectly adjures Leicester to recognize and allow for his limitations and mortality, while directly wishing for Leicester's approval and continued accomplishment. This ambiguity makes the final couplet especially pungent, since Leicester had just overreached himself by accepting princely distinctions in the Low Countries, thus enraging Elizabeth. Thereafter, his popularity, prestige, and campaign quickly foundered. Leicester appears to have accepted this indirect admonition, for he continued to assist Whitney – a striking instance of the latitude a poet could assume with a discerning patron.

Far from narrowly propagandistic, this emblem and the book as a whole indicate that all human endeavors, including England's on behalf of the Low Countries, are limited and fallible. Overall, *A Choice of Emblems* encourages readers to look beyond particular circumstances to definitive moral principles and ultimate ends. The book finally aims to offer exemplars for living that are broadly relevant to many situations and lifetimes.

Whitney evinces creative independence not only through his apparently original emblems but also through revision and redeployment of derivative emblems to serve his own structural or thematic purposes. The emblem of Janus introducing the second section of the bipartite *A Choice of Emblems* derives from La Perrière's similar emblem opening his *Théâtre des bons engins;* but Whitney revised the position, motto, and epigram to exploit the structural and self-reflexive potential of the subject more thoroughly. In Whitney's book Janus aptly looks forward and backward through the collection, so that he presides over *A Choice of Emblems* like its tutelary deity, surveying both its parts at once and enjoining readers to do likewise in assessing what they read and how they live. Moreover, as Manning has pointed out, Whitney's version of this emblem metaphorically commends the Dousas, father and son, who were both called Janus in their Latin appellations.

Whitney lost his powerful patron when Leicester died in 1588. The poet's will, written in 1600, indicates that he eventually returned to Combermere to reside under leasehold at Ryles Greene, perhaps his parents' former home. It seems he never married; his emblems tend to portray love as a painful experience best avoided, and they treat females repressively. Whitney probably died in May of 1601, perhaps in London. His will was probated on 28 May of that year. Didactic to the end, he left his library to his nephew Geoffrey Whitney on the condition that he learn Latin.

In his own time Whitney seems to have enjoyed at least some literary succès d'estime, for Francis Meres's *Palladis Tamia* (1598) and Henry Peacham's *Minerva Britannia* (1612) find his *Choice of Emblems* generically exemplary. It functioned also as a pattern book for English decorative arts such as embroidery and architectural ornamentation, and its iconography influenced literary endeavors as well. Yet Whitney's *Choice of Emblems* was not republished until the antiquarian emblematic revival of the mid nineteenth century. Perhaps its many dedications to contemporaries, or the large number of woodblocks required from diverse textual sources, discouraged later editions. But even in 1585 Whitney's verses would have seemed clumsily old-fashioned, and not only because of his Dutch compositors' eccentric punctuation and orthography. Whitney is au courant in applauding the literary accomplishments of Sir Edward Dyer and Sir Philip Sidney. Yet, significantly, one of his favorite verse forms is the outdated, monotonous, and jingling poulter's measure (an iambic rhymed couplet in which a hexameter line with a caesura after the third foot precedes a heptameter with a caesura after the fourth, repeated relentlessly, as in "For, when that barren verse made Muses void of mirth: / Behold, Lucina sweetly sung of Sidney's joyful birth"). Whitney's poetry suffers even in comparison to Richard Barnfield's extremely marginalized work, so that interest in *A Choice of Emblems* has been mostly documentary and antiquarian, rather than critically analytic and appreciative.

Fortunately, Whitney's poems need not stand on their own dubious merits, for the tripartite emblematic form provides them a supportive context. Moreover, while necessarily a miscellany, compendium, or farrago, the emblem collection was yet capable of meaningfully selective arrangement. As Hessel Miedema has explained, the emblem book was generically defined in part by the derivation of the Latin *emblemata* from mosaics composed of diverse selected pieces. Through astute sequencing and careful choice of emblems that occupy important positions, such as beginnings and endings of sections, Whitney exploited this capacity of the emblem collection to accommodate diversely meaningful patterns of organization. Most obviously, he grouped some emblems according to shared themes, topics, sources, or literary kind, such as the Aesopic fable. Yet his structural devices can be far more subtle. Some emblems in the first part of *A Choice of Emblems* significantly correspond to others in the second. In part 1, for example, skulls tumbling down a hill in different ways symbolize the diversity of human viewpoints; but in the second edition a single skull signifies that all must share a common end. Likewise, the whole collection moves toward eschatological concerns in conclusion, so that the moralizing order of the book is constructed as a meaningful reflection of the general course of life.

By strategically drawing on others' assemblages and adding emblems of his own, Whitney creates a unique epitome, analysis, and overview of the genre, developing its possibilities for multiple organizational schemes and options beyond anything envisioned by many Continental emblematists. By far the most insightful analyst of such aspects of Whitney's work to date, Manning, in his 1990 article, enables justly heightened estimation of a writer previously dismissed by Rosemary Freeman and others as almost nothing more than a translator and emblematic magpie. Whitney even elicited new significance in translated emblems by changing their context so that they appear in a different thematic or structural aspect. Within the general framework of Whitney's wittily titled *A Choice of Emblems,* readers are themselves to choose "to fit their fancies," as the title page advises, by focusing on personally relevant elements and patterns of his *emblemata.* The more we take an overview of *A Choice of Emblems,* as Whitney's Janus does, the more rewarding it becomes.

References:

Peter M. Daly and others, eds., *Index Emblematicus: The English Emblem Tradition,* volume 1 (Toronto: University of Toronto Press, 1988);

Jan A. van Dorsten, *Poets, Patrons, and Professors: Sir Philip Sidney, Daniel Rogers, and the Leiden Humanists* (Leiden: Sir Thomas Browne Institute / University of Leiden Press, 1962), pp. 123–127, 131–146;

Rosemary Freeman, *English Emblem Books* (London: Chatto & Windus, 1948), pp. 56–113;

John F. Leisher, *Geoffrey Whitney's "A Choice of Emblemes" and Its Relation to the Emblematic Vogue in Tudor England,* dissertation, Harvard University, 1952 (New York: Garland, 1987);

John Manning, "Unpublished and Unedited Emblems by Geffrey Whitney: Further Evidence of the English Adaptation of Continental Traditions," in *The English Emblem and the Continental Tradition,* edited by Peter M. Daly (New York: AMS Press, 1988), pp. 83–107;

Manning, "Whitney's *Choice of Emblemes:* A Reassessment," *Renaissance Studies,* 4 (June 1990): 155–200;

Hessel Miedema, "The Term *Emblema* in Alciati," *Journal of the Warburg and Courtauld Institutes,* 31 (1968): 234–250;

Mason Tung, "Emblematic Inventions of Alciati and Whitney," *English Miscellany,* 24 (1973–1974): 9–17;

Tung, "Whitney's *A Choice of Emblemes* Revisited: A Comparative Study of the Manuscript and the Printed Versions," *Studies in Bibliography,* 29 (1976): 32–101.

Papers:

The manuscript collection of emblems that Whitney presented to Leicester is now at the Houghton Library of Harvard University (MS Typ 14). The archives of Great Yarmouth preserve a brief Latin account, apparently by Whitney, of a visit to the temporary island of Scratby, near Great Yarmouth, published and translated in the 1866 edition of *A Choice of Emblems.*

Isabella Whitney

(flourished 1566 – 1573)

Betty S. Travitsky
New York Public Library

BOOKS: *The Copy of a Letter, Lately Written in Meeter, by a Youge Gentilwoman: To Her Vnconstant Louer,* as Is. W. (London: Printed by Richard Jones, 1567?);

A Sweet Nosgay, or Pleasant Posye: Contayning a Hundred and Ten Phylosophicall Flowers, as Is. W. (London: Printed by Richard Jones, 1573).

Editions: "The 'Wyll and Testament' of Isabella Whitney," edited by Betty Travitsky, *English Literary Renaissance,* 10 (Winter 1981): 76–94;

The Floures of Philosophie by Sir Hugh Plat. And A Sweet Nosgay and The Copy of a Letter by Isabella Whitney, edited by Richard J. Panofsky (Delmar, N.Y.: Scholars' Facsimiles and Reprints, 1982).

Isabella Whitney claims attention as the first Englishwoman believed to have written original secular poetry for publication. Her established oeuvre consists of two short anthologies of lively materials joined in a winsome, original manner. *The Copy of a Letter* (1567?) includes three robust love poems, with an "admonition" appended to the first, written in the personae of jilted (but unconventional) men and women and playing on the debates on women's nature popular in the sixteenth century; *A Sweet Nosegay* (1573) combines prose and verse in what appears to be an autobiographical narrative. Both works suggest that Whitney was a most unconventional woman, an inference underlined by her seemingly easy publication of breezy, secular verses.

Little is known about Whitney's life. Like most woman writers of her time, she has been neglected by scholars until recently; she is noted only briefly in the *Dictionary of National Biography,* for example, where two sentences are devoted to her in the entry on her brother, Geoffrey, author of *A Choice of Emblems* (1586), a book of no great distinction.

As Geoffrey's sister, Isabella Whitney can be described as the descendant of a Cheshire family that had been settled on a small estate at Coole Pilate, near Nantwich, long before the sixteenth century. Her brother was named after their father; their mother's name is not known. Although styled a "young gentlewoman" on the title page of *The Copy of a Letter,* Whitney may, therefore, more precisely be described as a member of the minor gentry. She was not wealthy: her self-descriptions indicate that she is down on her luck, having lost her post as a servant of an unnamed person; she describes herself in *A Sweet Nosegay* as "whole in body, and in mind, / but very weak in purse." Moreover, the advice on performing menial tasks that she writes to "two of her younger sisters serving in London" in that work seems clearly founded on her own experience. She explains that she has turned to writing as a profession since she is "harvestless, / and serviceless also." The opportunity to write is also related to her single state: "Had I a husband, or a house, / and all that longs thereto / My self could frame about to rouse / as other women do: / But till some household cares me tie, / My books and pen I will apply." Finally, the "Certain Familiar Epistles and Friendly Letters by the Author: With Replies," included in *A Sweet Nosegay* and directed in sprightly verse to a brother, a brother-in-law, and three sisters, indicate that her immediate family was fairly large; these persons are also mentioned in Geoffrey's will of 1600. It cannot, however, be proved that Isabella, who is not otherwise named in that will, is the "Sister Eldershae" to whom Geoffrey left five marks, or even that she was still alive in 1600.

The reasons for Whitney's obscurity and for the general paucity of published writings by women of her period are not far to seek, for even privileged women of the sixteenth century were usually denied training in or exercise of rhetoric, the touchstone of Renaissance culture. In his *Instruction of a Christian Woman* (1523) Joannes

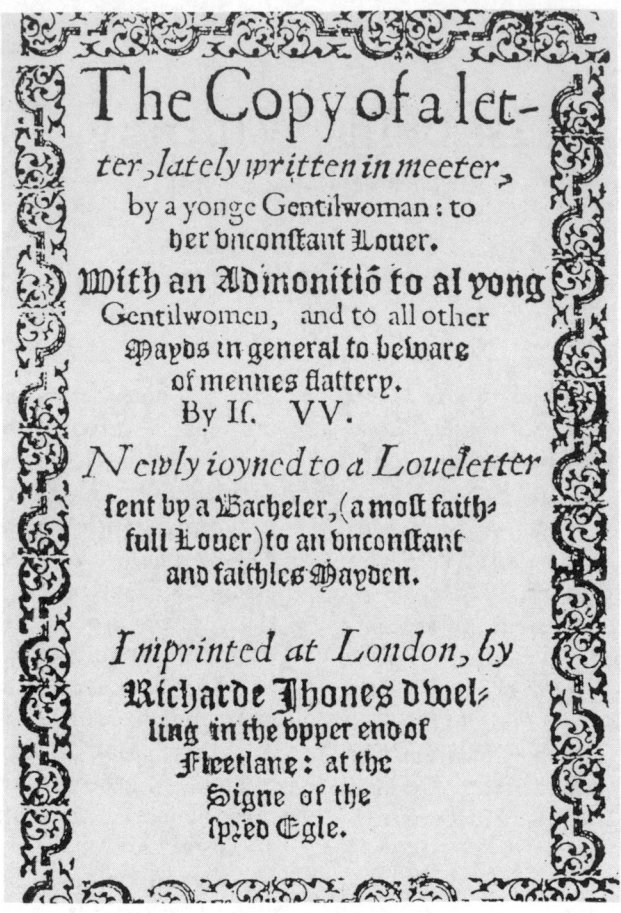

The Copy of a let-
ter, lately written in meeter,
by a yonge Gentilwoman : to
her vnconstant Louer.

With an Admonitió to al yong
Gentilwomen, and to all other
Mayds in general to beware
of mennes flattery.
By Is. VV.

Newly ioyned to a Loueletter
sent by a Bacheler, (a most faithfull Louer) to an vnconstant
and faithles Mayden.

Imprinted at London, by
Richarde Ihones dwel-
ling in the vpper end of
Fleetlane : at the
Signe of the
spred Egle.

*Title page for Isabella Whitney's collection of poems about
unfaithful lovers*

Ludovicus (Juan Luis) Vives, perhaps the most influential author of the sixteenth century on women's education, prescribes an impressive *reading* list for women – impressive relative to earlier centuries, limited relative to the list he prescribes for men in *De Ratione Studii ad Carolum Montjorum* (1524) – but a most limited *writing* program for women. Like other Christian humanists, Vives wanted women to be introduced to sober and pious writers and believed that they would be inspired to live upright lives on the basis of such a program of controlled reading but felt that they had no need to study eloquence or rhetoric. How much Whitney benefited from the Renaissance opening of some education to some women is not known, but such strictures make her effervescent poetry all the more remarkable.

Both of Whitney's collections were printed by Richard Jones, who specialized in popular ephemeral works. "The Copy," the title poem of the earlier anthology, as well as the "Admonition by the Author, to All Young Gentlewomen and to All Other Maids in General to Beware of Men's Flattery," are written in a woman's voice. "The Copy" is a strong-minded retort by a young woman of spirit to a former lover who, she has learned, has married another woman. Her complaint may be imaginative rather than literal, for the statement by "The Printer to the Reader" says that *The Copy of a Letter* is "both false and also true." Whitney's simplicity, unadorned language, commonsensical statements and devices, and realistic point of view have an affinity to "the native plain style of poetry" characteristic of such poets as George Turberville, George Gascoigne, and Barnabe Googe.

The female love lament was popularized by Turberville's translation of Ovid's *Heroides* as *The Heroical Epistles* in the same year that *The Copy of a Letter* probably appeared. Her inclusion of such a lament shows Whitney's familiarity with current literary trends but reflects them with a difference. She identifies with the classical women whom she mentions, and shows her awareness of the passivity expected of women and of the double standard that disadvantaged women. It has been said that she transformed the solitary Ovidian heroine into a more bourgeois figure – that of the marriage counselor – who could write to an inconstant male lover from the vantage point of a superior.

Perhaps most impressive of all, Whitney reduces the devices of unfaithful men to the status of a cruel sport in her "Admonition," in which, after instancing many betrayals of women by men in antiquity, she likens an unlucky woman to an unwary fish caught on a hook. Whitney's jocose tone renders these comments sporting rather than plaintive, and the reader senses that the situation is under control. The two final pieces in *The Copy of a Letter,* "A Loveletter, Sent from a Faithful Lover to an Unconstant Maiden" and "R. W. against the Willful Inconstancy of His Dear Foe E. T.," may have been written by men. All the pieces in the anthology express the hard-won wisdom that could be expected of a relatively free literary spirit.

Whitney's second collection – particularly "The Will and Testament" with which it closes – is arguably her more substantial work. As several scholars have noted, *A Sweet Nosegay,* comprising 110 quatrains of advice, falls within the tradition of such popular literature as Gascoigne's *A Hundred Sundry Flowers* (1573), a work that includes several experiments with narrative, including "The Adventures of Master F. J." – a novella in prose with fourteen interpolated poems – and "The Delectable History of Sundry Adventures Passed by Dan Bartholomew of Bath," with an interpolated mock last will and testament. In writing a narrative composed of diverse parts, Whitney resembles such other mid-Elizabethan poets as Turberville, who ties a series of love poems into a vague love narrative; George Whetstone, who recounts a romantic story about Bohemian knights somewhat similar to *Cymbeline*; and Nicholas Breton, who ties a group of diverse poems together. But the body of *A Sweet Nosegay* is derived particularly from Sir Hugh Plat's *The Flowers of Philosophy* (1572) – in Whitney's own words, from "Plat his Plot . . . / where fragrant flowers abound."

Plat has been remembered until recently as a practical scientist and writer on gardening, domestic economy, and applied science, rather than as a poet. But while neither the first edition of *The Flowers of Philosophy* nor a later edition of 1581 (each preserved in only one copy) was listed in the *Short-Title Catalogue* of 1926, the book, written in the tradition of the plain style, was obviously known to his contemporaries, and its style can be compared with that in poems in such anthologies as *Tottel's Miscellany*

(1557), *A Handful of Pleasant Delights* (1566?), *The Paradise of Dainty Devices* (1576), *The Gorgeous Gallery of Gallant Inventions* (1584), and Robert Allot's *England's Parnassus* (1600). Building on maxims in Plat's collection, Whitney embroiders and points many of his themes, dividing her epigrams into such categories as friendship, love, and dependence, although Plat's collection is more formal and impersonal than hers. She develops a coherent narrative framework for her rhymed adages in the form of an autobiographical account of her troubles and of her need for comfort.

The body of *A Sweet Nosegay* is followed by "Certain Familiar Epistles and Friendly Letters by the Author: With Replies," which provide information on Whitney's family and life. They continue the autobiographical frame and lead to the final poem in the collection, "The Will and Testament," written because Whitney must leave London as a result of her troubles. Certainly the will is tied thematically to the complaints in the earlier part of the Nosegay by the prefatory statement that "the author (though loath to leave the city) upon her friends' procurement, is constrained to depart, wherefore she faineth as she would die and maketh her will and testament, as followeth." Though, as Geoffrey Whitney's sister, Isabella Whitney must have been at least partially bred in Cheshire, she had obviously lived in the London she describes so lovingly in this poem – perhaps as a serving maid, to judge from the evidence of her epistle to her sisters, perhaps with her parents, of whom she says in her "Will and Testament," "To Smithfield I must something leave / my parents there did dwell."

The lively, sometimes even madcap, mock legacy brings contemporary London alive as a place replete with "brave buildings rare," "boots, shoes or pantables," "handsome men," "proper girls," "coggers, and some honest men." Her vividness, perhaps the more remarkable for its presence in a nondramatic poem, reminds one of the London of the city comedies that would be a feature of the early-seventeenth-century stage. Wendy Wall discusses the relationship of Whitney's "Will" to more somber legacy literature by women. It is also useful to consider qualities in the poem that relate it to other popular literary types, including emblem books such as those by Whitney's brother, the vernacular character sketches that were developing throughout the sixteenth century, and other mock testaments – that is, types of popular writing not traditionally associated with *women* writers. For example, her poem can be connected with character sketches embodied in the list of sixteenth-century tradesmen in "Cock Lorell's Boat." It should also be noted that Whitney's occasional descriptions of rogue types is a kind of depiction that was to become popular in the developing contemporary genres of the rogue tract and the cony-catching pamphlet. Some of these works, such as John Awdeley's "Fraternity of Vagabonds ... Whereunto also Is Adjoined the Twenty-five Order of Knaves ... Confirmed for Ever by Cock Lovell" (1575), carry an obvious relationship to the earlier character studies.

The "Will" is also similar to such mock testaments as William Dunbar's "Testament of Mr. Andro Kennedy" (1508), Humphrey Powell's "Will of the Devil and His Last Testament" (circa 1550), "The Testament of the Hawthorn" (in *Tottel's Miscellany*, 1557), and Robert Copland's *Jill of Breyntford's Testament* (circa 1563). Perhaps it most suggestively resembles the most polished of such works, Gascoigne's "Last Will and Testament of Dan Bartholomew of Bath," particularly in being fit into a narrative frame. None of these poems, however, with the possible exception of Gascoigne's much slighter piece, can compare with her "Will" in incisiveness or interest. Gascoigne's testament may even have been written in imitation of Whitney's *A Sweet Nosegay*. The similarities among these pieces and Whitney's "Will" suggest that Isabella Whitney was inexplicably the embodiment of a "Judith Shakespeare," the imaginary Elizabethan woman whom Virginia Woolf conjured up – before Whitney's existence was known – and imagined to have been "as adventurous, as imaginative, as agog to see the world as [William Shakespeare] was."

It remains to note the suggestion by Robert J. Fehrenbach that Whitney may have been the author of several otherwise unassigned poems printed by Jones in two miscellanies: "The Lady Beloved Exclaimeth of the Great Untruth of Her Lover" and "The Lamentation of a Gentlewoman upon the Death of Her Late Deceased Friend William Gruffith, Gent.," in *A Gorgeous Gallery of Gallant Inventions*, and "The Complaint of a Woman Lover," in *A Handful of Pleasant Delights*. Like the earlier hypothesis that Whitney wrote "Another by I. W.," one of the introductory poems in Thomas Morley's *Plain and Easy Introduction to Practical Music* (1597), this is an unprovable, but interesting, possibility.

References:

Elaine V. Beilin, *Redeeming Eve: Women Writers of the English Renaissance* (Princeton: Princeton University Press, 1987);

Robert J. Fehrenbach, "Isabella Whitney (fl. 1655–75) and the Popular Miscellanies of Richard Jones," *Cahiers Elisabéthains,* 19 (April 1981): 85–87;

Fehrenbach, "Isabella Whitney, Sir Hugh Plat, Geoffrey Whitney, and 'Sister Eldershae,' " *English Language Notes,* 21 (September 1983): 7–11;

Rev. Henry Green, *On the Emblems of Geffrey Whitney, of Nantwich, in the Sixteenth Century: A Paper Read before the Architectural, Archeological, and Historic Society of Chester* (Chester, U.K.: Minskill & Hughes, 1865);

Green, *Whitney's "Choice of Emblemes": A Facsimile Reprint with an Introductory Dissertation, Essays Literary and Bibliographical, and Explanatory Notes* (London: Lovell Reeve, 1866);

Ruth Hughey, "Cultural Interests of Women in England, from 1524–1640, Indicated in the Writings of the Women," Ph.D. dissertation, Cornell University, 1932;

Ann Rosalind Jones, *Currency of Eros: Women's Love Lyric in Europe, 1540–1620* (Bloomington: Indiana University Press, 1990);

Ruth Kelso, *Doctrine for the Lady of the Renaissance* (Urbana: University of Illinois Press, 1956);

Charlotte Kohler, "Elizabethan Woman of Letters: The Extent of Her Literary Activities," Ph.D. dissertation, University of Virginia, 1936;

Ellen Moers, *Literary Women: The Great Writers* (New York: Doubleday, 1976);

Betty Travitsky, " 'The Lady Doth Protest': Protest in the Popular Writings of Renaissance Englishwomen," *English Literary Renaissance,* 14 (Autumn 1984): 255–283;

Travitsky, ed., *Paradise of Women: Writings by Englishwomen of the Renaissance* (Westport, Conn.: Greenwood, 1981);

Wendy Wall, "Isabella Whitney and the Female Legacy," *ELH,* 58 (Spring 1991): 35–62;

Yvor Winters, "Aspects of the Short Poem in the English Renaissance," in his *Forms of Discovery: Critical and Historical Essays on the Forms of the Short Poem in English* (Chicago: Swallow, 1967);

Virginia Woolf, *A Room of One's Own* (London: Hogarth Press, 1929; New York: Harcourt, Brace, 1929).

Checklist of Further Readings

Bibliographies and other reference materials:

Arber, Edward, ed. *A Transcript of the Registers of the Company of Stationers of London, 1554–1640* [*Stationers' Register*], 5 volumes. London, 1875–1894.

Bietenholz, Peter G., and Thomas B. Deutscher, eds. *Contemporaries of Erasmus: A Biographical Register of the Renaissance and Reformation,* 3 volumes. Toronto & Buffalo, N.Y.: University of Toronto Press, 1985–1987.

Eccles, Mark. "Brief Lives: Tudor and Stuart Authors," *Studies in Philology: Texts and Studies 1982,* 79 (Fall 1982): 1–135.

"English Literature/1500–1599," *MLA Bibliography of Books and Articles on the Modern Languages and Literatures.* New York: Modern Language Association, annually.

Fédération international des sociétés et instituts pour l'étude de la Renaissance. *Bibliographie internationale de l'humanisme et de la Renaissance.* Geneva: Droz, annually.

Hamilton, A. C., gen. ed. *The Spenser Encyclopedia.* Toronto: University of Toronto Press, 1990.

Harner, James L. *English Renaissance Prose Fiction, 1500–1660: An Annotated Bibliography of Criticism.* Boston: G. K. Hall, 1978.

Harner. *English Renaissance Prose Fiction, 1500–1660: An Annotated Bibliography of Criticism, 1976–1983.* New York: G. K. Hall, 1985.

Harner. *English Renaissance Prose Fiction, 1500–1660: An Annotated Bibliography of Criticism, 1984–1990.* New York: G. K. Hall, 1992.

Hogrefe, Pearl. *Women of Action in Tudor England: Nine Biographical Sketches.* Ames: Iowa State University Press, 1977.

Ijsewijn, Jozef. *Companion to Neo-Latin Studies.* Amsterdam: North-Holland, 1977.

Lanham, Richard A. *A Handlist of Rhetorical Terms,* second edition. Berkeley: University of California Press, 1991.

Lievsay, John L., ed. *The Sixteenth Century: Skelton Through Hooker.* Goldentree Bibliographies. New York: Appleton-Century-Crofts, 1968.

Marcuse, Michael J. "Literature of the Renaissance and Earlier Seventeenth Century," section O in *A Reference Guide for English Studies.* Berkeley: University of California Press, 1990, pp. 323–338.

O'Dell, Sterg, ed. *A Chronological List of Prose Fiction in English Printed in England and Other Countries, 1475–1640.* Cambridge, Mass.: MIT Press, 1954.

Ousby, Ian, ed. *The Cambridge Guide to English Literature.* Cambridge: Cambridge University Press, 1988.

Pollard, A. W., and G. R. Redgrave, eds. *A Short-Title Catalogue of Books Printed in England, Scotland, and Ireland, and of English Books Printed Abroad, 1475–1640* [*STC*], 3 volumes. London: Bibliographical Society, 1926; revised and enlarged by W. A. Jackson, F. S. Ferguson, and Katharine F. Pantzer. London: Bibliographical Society, 1976–1991.

Preminger, Alex, and T. V. F. Brogan, eds. *The New Princeton Encyclopedia of Poetry and Poetics*. Princeton: Princeton University Press, 1993.

"Recent Studies in the English Renaissance," *Studies in English Literature, 1500–1900*. Annually, Winter.

Ruoff, James E. *Crowell's Handbook of Elizabethan and Stuart Literature*. New York: Crowell, 1975.

Schweitzer, Frederick M., and Harry E. Wedeck, eds. *Dictionary of the Renaissance*. New York: Philosophical Library, 1967.

Stephens, Leslie, and Sidney Lee, eds. *The Dictionary of National Biography from the Earliest Times to 1900* [*DNB*]. London: Oxford University Press, 1885–1900; reprinted with supplements, 1967–1968.

Watson, George, ed. *The New Cambridge Bibliography of English Literature* [*NCBEL*], volume 1: *600–1600*. Cambridge: Cambridge University Press, 1974.

Anthologies, collections:

Alexander, Nigel, ed. *Elizabethan Narrative Verse*. Cambridge, Mass.: Harvard University Press, 1968.

Byrne, Muriel St. Clare, ed. *The Lisle Letters*, 6 volumes. Chicago: University of Chicago Press, 1981.

Dodd, A. H., ed. *Life in Elizabethan England*. New York: Putnam, 1961.

Donno, Elizabeth Story, ed. *Elizabethan Minor Epics*. New York: Columbia University Press, 1963.

Ferguson, Moira, ed. *First Feminists: British Women Writers, 1578–1799*. Bloomington: Indiana University Press / Old Westbury, N.Y.: Feminist Press, 1985.

Henderson, Katherine Usher, and Barbara F. McManus, eds. *Half Humankind: Contexts and Texts of the Controversy about Women in England, 1540–1640*. Urbana: University of Illinois Press, 1985.

Hurstfield, Joel, and Alan G. R. Smith, eds. *Elizabethan People: State and Society*. New York: St. Martin's Press, 1972.

Mahl, Mary R., and Helene Koon, eds. *The Female Spectator: English Women Writers before 1800*. Bloomington: Indiana University Press / Old Westbury, N.Y.: Feminist Press, 1977.

Manley, Lawrence, ed. *London in the Age of Shakespeare: An Anthology*. London: Croom Helm, 1986.

May, Steven W., ed. *The Elizabethan Courtier Poets: The Poems and Their Contexts*. Columbia: University of Missouri Press, 1991.

Millward, J. W., ed. *Portraits and Documents: Sixteenth Century*. London: Hutchinson, 1961.

Myers, James P., Jr., ed. *Elizabethan Ireland: A Selection of Writings by Elizabethan Writers on Ireland*. Hamden, Conn.: Archon, 1983.

Otten, Charlotte F., ed. *English Women's Voices, 1540–1700.* Miami: Florida International University Press, 1992.

Rollins, Hyder E., and Herschell Baker, eds. *The Renaissance in England: Non-dramatic Prose and Verse of the Sixteenth Century.* Lexington, Mass.: Heath, 1954; reprinted, Prospect Heights, Ill.: Waveland, 1992.

Shepherd, Simon, ed. *The Women's Sharp Revenge: Five Women Pamphleteers from the Renaissance.* New York: St. Martin's Press, 1985; republished as *The Women's Sharp Revenge: Five Women's Pamphlets from the Renaissance.* London: Fourth Estate, 1985.

Smith, G. Gregory, ed. *Elizabethan Critical Essays,* 2 volumes. Oxford: Oxford University Press, 1904.

Travitsky, Betty, ed. *The Paradise of Women: Writings by Englishwomen of the Renaissance.* Westport, Conn.: Greenwood, 1981; revised edition, New York: Columbia University Press, 1989.

Williams, Penry, ed. *Life in Tudor England.* New York: Putnam, 1964.

Wilson, Katharina M., ed. *Women Writers of the Renaissance and Reformation.* Athens: University of Georgia Press, 1987.

Recommended works:

Allen, Don Cameron. *Mysteriously Meant: The Rediscovery of Pagan Symbolism and Allegorical Interpretation in the Renaissance.* Baltimore: Johns Hopkins University Press, 1970.

Alpers, Paul J., ed. *Elizabethan Poetry: Modern Essays in Criticism.* New York: Oxford University Press, 1967.

Anderson, Judith H. *Biographical Truth: The Representation of Historical Persons in Tudor-Stuart Writing.* New Haven: Yale University Press, 1984.

Bainton, Roland H. *The Reformation of the Sixteenth Century.* Boston: Beacon, 1952.

Bakhtin, Mikhail M. *Rabelais and His World,* translated by Hélène Iswolsky. Cambridge, Mass.: MIT Press, 1984.

Beilin, Elaine V. *Redeeming Eve: Women Writers of the English Renaissance.* Princeton: Princeton University Press, 1987.

Binns, J. W. *Intellectual Culture in Elizabethan and Jacobean England: The Latin Writings of the Age.* Leeds, U.K.: Cairns, 1990.

Black, J. B. *The Reign of Elizabeth, 1558–1603,* second edition, volume 8 of *The Oxford History of England,* edited by George Clark. Oxford: Clarendon, 1959.

Booty, John E., and others, eds. *The Godly Kingdom of Tudor England: Great Books of the English Reformation.* Wilton, Conn.: Morehouse-Barlow, 1981.

Bradner, Leicester. *Musae Anglicanae: A History of Anglo-Latin Poetry, 1500–1925.* New York: Modern Language Association, 1940; republished with supplement in *Library,* fifth series 22 (1967): 93–103.

Briggs, Julia. *This Stage-Play World: English Literature and Its Background, 1580–1625.* Oxford: Oxford University Press, 1983.

Brooke, Tucker, and Matthias A. Shaaber. *The Renaissance (1500–1600),* book 2 of *A Literary History of England,* second edition, edited by Albert C. Baugh. New York: Appleton-Century-Crofts, 1967.

Burckhardt, Jacob. *The Civilization of the Renaissance in Italy,* translated by S. G. C. Middlemore. Oxford: Oxford University Press, 1944.

Bush, Douglas. *The Renaissance and English Humanism.* Toronto: University of Toronto Press, 1939.

Dowling, Maria. *Humanism in the Age of Henry VIII.* London & Dover, N.H.: Croom Helm, 1986.

Dubrow, Heather, and Richard Strier, eds. *Historical Renaissance: New Essays on Tudor and Stuart Culture.* Chicago: University of Chicago Press, 1988.

Eccles, Mark. "A Biographical Dictionary of Elizabethan Authors," *Huntington Library Quarterly,* 5 (April 1942): 281–302.

Ferguson, Margaret, and others, eds. *Rewriting the Renaissance: The Discourse of Sexual Difference in Early Modern Europe.* Chicago: University of Chicago Press, 1986.

Ford, Boris, ed. *Renaissance and Reformation,* volume 3 of *The Cambridge Guide to the Arts in Britain.* Cambridge: Cambridge University Press, 1989; republished as *Sixteenth-century Britain,* volume 3 of *The Cambridge Cultural History of Britain.* Cambridge: Cambridge University Press, 1992.

Foucault, Michel. "What Is an Author?," translated by Josué V. Harari, in *The Foucault Reader,* edited by Paul Rabinow. New York: Pantheon, 1984, pp. 101–120.

Fox, Alistair. *Politics and Literature in the Reigns of Henry VII and Henry VIII.* Oxford: Blackwell, 1989.

Fox and John Guy. *Reassessing the Henrician Age: Humanism, Politics and Reform, 1500–1550.* Oxford: Blackwell, 1986.

Grant, Leonard. *Neo-Latin Literature and the Pastoral.* Chapel Hill: University of North Carolina Press, 1965.

Greenblatt, Stephen Jay. *Renaissance Self-Fashioning from More to Shakespeare.* Chicago: University of Chicago Press, 1980.

Greene, Thomas M. *Light in Troy: Imitation and Discovery in Renaissance Poetry.* New Haven: Yale University Press, 1982.

Guy, John. *Tudor England.* New York: Oxford University Press, 1988.

Hannay, Margaret P., ed. *Silent but for the Word: Tudor Women as Patrons, Translators, and Writers of Religious Works.* Kent, Ohio: Kent State University Press, 1985.

Haugaard, William P. "The Preface," in *The Folger Library Edition of the Works of Richard Hooker,* volume 6, part 1 (Binghampton, N.Y.: Medieval and Renaissance Texts and Studies, 1993), pp. 1–80.

Helgerson, Richard. *Self-Crowned Laureates: Spenser, Jonson, Milton, and the Literary System.* Berkeley: University of California Press, 1983.

Hoffmann, Ann. *Lives of the Tudor Age, 1485–1603.* London: Osprey, 1977; New York: Barnes & Noble, 1977.

Hogrefe, Pearl. *Tudor Women: Commoners and Queens.* Ames: Iowa State University Press, 1975.

Howell, Wilbur Samuel. *Logic and Rhetoric in England, 1500–1700.* Princeton: Princeton University Press, 1956.

Hull, Suzanne W. *Chaste, Silent, and Obedient: English Books for Women, 1475–1640.* San Marino, Cal.: Huntington Library, 1982.

Javitch, Daniel. *Poetry and Courtliness in Renaissance England.* Princeton: Princeton University Press, 1978.

Keach, William. *Elizabethan Erotic Narrative: Irony and Pathos in the Ovidian Poetry of Shakespeare, Marlowe, and Their Contemporaries.* New Brunswick, N.J.: Rutgers University Press, 1977.

Kelley, Donald R. "The Theory of History," in *The Cambridge History of Renaissance Philosophy,* edited by Charles B. Schmidt and others. Cambridge: Cambridge University Press, 1988, pp. 746–761.

Kerrigan, William, and Gordon Braden. *The Idea of the Renaissance.* Baltimore & London: Johns Hopkins University Press, 1989.

King, John N. *English Reformation Literature: The Tudor Origins of the Protestant Tradition.* Princeton: Princeton University Press, 1982.

Kristeller, Paul Otto. "Humanism," in *The Cambridge History of Renaissance Philosophy,* pp. 113–137.

Lathrop, Henry Burrowes. *Translations from the Classics into English from Caxton to Chapman, 1477–1620.* University of Wisconsin Studies in Language and Literature, no. 35. Madison, 1933; New York: Octagon, 1967.

Levin, Harry T. *The Myth of the Golden Age in the Renaissance.* Bloomington: Indiana University Press, 1969.

Lewis, C. S. *The Discarded Image: An Introduction to Medieval and Renaissance Literature.* Cambridge: Cambridge University Press, 1964.

Lewis. *English Literature in the Sixteenth Century, Excluding Drama,* volume 3 of *The Oxford History of English Literature,* edited by F. P. Wilson and Bonamy Dobrée. Oxford: Clarendon, 1954.

Lovejoy, Arthur O. *The Great Chain of Being: A Study of the History of an Idea.* Cambridge, Mass.: Harvard University Press, 1936.

Mackie, J. D. *The Earlier Tudors, 1485–1558,* volume 7 of *The Oxford History of England,* edited by George Clark. Oxford: Clarendon, 1978.

Marcus, Leah S. "Renaissance / Early Modern Studies," in *Redrawing the Boundaries: The Transformation of English and American Literary Studies,* edited by Greenblatt and Giles Gunn. New York: Modern Language Association of America, 1992, pp. 41–63.

Mason, H. A. *Humanism and Poetry in the Early Tudor Period: An Essay.* London: Routledge & Kegan Paul, 1959.

Matthiessen, F. O. *Translation: An Elizabethan Art.* Cambridge, Mass.: Harvard University Press, 1931.

May, Steven W. *The Elizabethan Courtier Poets: The Poems and Their Contexts.* Columbia: University of Missouri Press, 1991.

McLean, Antonia. *Humanism and the Rise of Science in Tudor England.* London: Heinemann Educational, 1972; New York: Watson Academic, 1972.

Mueller, Janel M. *The Native Tongue and the Word: Developments in English Prose Style, 1380–1580*. Chicago: University of Chicago Press, 1984.

Norbrook, David. Introduction to *The Penguin Book of Renaissance Verse, 1509–1659,* selected by Norbrook, edited by H. R. Woudhuysen. London: Penguin, 1992, pp. 1–67.

Norbrook. *Poetry and Politics of the English Renaissance*. London: Routledge & Kegan Paul, 1984.

Parker, Patricia A. *Literary Fat Ladies: Rhetoric, Gender, Property*. Berkeley: University of California Press, 1987.

Parker and David Quint, eds. *Literary Theory / Renaissance Texts*. Baltimore: Johns Hopkins University Press, 1986.

Patterson, Annabel. *Censorship and Interpretation: The Conditions of Writing and Reading in Early Modern England*. Madison: University of Wisconsin Press, 1984.

Peterson, Douglas L. *The English Lyric from Wyatt to Donne: A History of the Plain and Eloquent Styles,* second edition. Princeton: Princeton University Press, 1990.

Pitcher, John. "Tudor Literature (1485–1603)," in *The Oxford Illustrated History of English Literature,* edited by Pat Rogers. Oxford: Oxford University Press, 1987, pp. 59–111.

Ricks, Christopher, ed. *English Poetry and Prose, 1540–1674,* revised edition, volume 2 of *[Sphere] History of Literature in the English Language*. London: Barrie & Jenkins, 1986.

Rivers, Isabel. *Classical and Christian Ideas in English Renaissance Poetry: A Students' Guide*. London: G. Allen & Unwin, 1979.

Rubel, Veré L. *Poetic Diction in the English Renaissance from Skelton through Spenser*. New York: Modern Language Association, 1941.

Salzman, Paul. *English Prose Fiction, 1558–1700: A Critical History*. Oxford: Clarendon, 1985.

Schmitt, Charles B., and others, eds. *The Cambridge History of Renaissance Philosophy*. Cambridge: Cambridge University Press, 1988.

Sloan, Thomas O., and Raymond B. Waddington, eds. *Rhetoric of Renaissance Poetry from Wyatt to Milton*. Berkeley: University of California Press, 1974.

Smith, Hallett. *Elizabethan Poetry: A Study in Conventions, Meaning, and Expression*. Cambridge, Mass.: Harvard University Press, 1952.

Southall, Raymond. *The Courtly Maker: An Essay on the Poetry of Wyatt and His Contemporaries*. Oxford: Blackwell, 1964.

Stauffer, Donald A. *English Biography before 1700*. Cambridge, Mass.: Harvard University Press, 1930.

Stevens, John. *Music and Poetry in the Early Tudor Court*. London: Methuen, 1961.

Stone, Lawrence. *The Crisis of the Aristocracy, 1558–1641*. Oxford: Clarendon, 1965.

Stone. *The Family, Sex and Marriage in England, 1500–1800*. New York: Harper & Row, 1977.

Tillyard, E. M. W. *The Elizabethan World Picture*. New York: Macmillan, 1944.

Tuve, Rosemund. *Allegorical Imagery: Some Medieval Books and Their Posterity.* Princeton: Princeton University Press, 1966.

Tuve. *Elizabethan and Metaphysical Imagery: Renaissance Poetics and Twentieth-Century Critics.* Chicago: University of Chicago Press, 1947.

Vickers, Brian. *In Defence of Rhetoric.* Oxford: Clarendon, 1988.

Vickers, "Rhetoric and Poetics," in *The Cambridge History of Renaissance Philosophy,* pp. 715–745.

Waller, Gary. *English Poetry of the Sixteenth Century.* London: Longman, 1986.

Warnicke, Retha M. *Women of the English Renaissance and Reformation.* Contributions in Women's Studies, no. 38. Westport, Conn.: Greenwood, 1983.

Whigham, Frank. *Ambition and Privilege: The Social Tropes of Elizabethan Courtesy Literature.* Berkeley: University of California Press, 1984.

Wilson, K. J. *Incomplete Fictions: The Formation of English Renaissance Dialogue.* Washington, D.C.: Catholic University of America Press, 1985.

Winters, Yvor. "The 16th Century Lyric in England: A Critical and Historical Reinterpretation," *Poetry,* 53 (1939): 258–272, 320–335; 54 (1939): 35–51; reprinted in his *Forms of Discovery: Critical and Historical Essays on the Forms of the Short Poem in English.* Chicago: Swallow, 1967, pp. 1–120; reprinted in Alpers, ed., *Elizabethan Poetry: Modern Essays in Criticism,* pp. 93–125.

Woodbridge, Linda. *Women and the English Renaissance: Literature and the Nature of Womankind, 1540–1640.* Urbana: University of Illinois Press, 1984.

Wright, Louis B. *Middle-Class Culture in Elizabethan England.* Chapel Hill: University of North Carolina Press, 1935.

Zocca, Louis R. *Elizabethan Narrative Poetry.* New Brunswick, N.J.: Rutgers University Press, 1950.

Contributors

Sheila Ahern...*Victoria University of Wellington*
Donald Beecher ....*Carleton University*
Elaine V. Beilin..*Framingham State College*
Mark E. Bingham ....*Gettysburg College*
Joseph Black ....*University of Toronto*
Kenneth Borris ....*McGill University*
James P. Carley...*York University, Toronto*
D. Allen Carroll..*University of Tennessee, Knoxville*
Lisa Celovsky..*University of Toronto*
Jeanne Costello ....*Fullerton College*
D. H. Craig...*University of Newcastle*
Mary Thomas Crane ....*Boston College*
Edward Doughtie ....*Rice University*
D. S. Dunnan ....*Saint James School*
Juliet Fleming ....*University of Southern California*
Madeleine Forey..*All Souls College, Oxford University*
Alistair Fox ....*University of Otago*
Mary C. Fuller...*Massachusetts Institute of Technology*
David Galbraith...*University of Toronto*
Elizabeth Hanson ....*Queen's University*
Edmund M. Hayes ....*Worcester Polytechnic Institute*
Peter C. Herman ....*Georgia State University*
Victor Houliston..*University of the Witwatersrand*
Seymour Baker House...*University of Otago*
John Jowett ....*University of Birmingham*
Arthur F. Kinney..*University of Massachusetts, Amherst*
Janice Liedl ....*Laurentian University*
A. Lynne Magnusson..*University of Waterloo*
R. W. Maslen ....*Glasgow University*
Steven W. May...*Georgetown College*
Michael McClintock ....*University of Toronto*
Elizabeth McCutcheon ....*University of Hawaii*
Gordon McMullan ....*University of Newcastle upon Tyne*
James Nielson..*University of British Columbia*
G. J. R. Parry...*Victoria University of Wellington*
Renée Pigeon...*California State University, San Bernardino*
Jeffrey Powers-Beck ....*East Tennessee State University*
Julian Roberts...*Bodleian Library, Oxford University*
Mary M. Schmelzer...*Temple University*
William H. Sherman...*University of Maryland at College Park*
Emily E. Stockard...*Florida Atlantic University*
Susan C. Staub...*Appalachian State University*
Alison Taufer ....*California State University, Los Angeles*
Betty S. Travitsky ....*New York Public Library*
Luke Wilson..*Ohio State University*

Cumulative Index

Dictionary of Literary Biography, Volumes 1-136
Dictionary of Literary Biography Yearbook, 1980-1992
Dictionary of Literary Biography Documentary Series, Volumes 1-11

Cumulative Index

DLB before number: *Dictionary of Literary Biography*, Volumes 1-136
Y before number: *Dictionary of Literary Biography Yearbook*, 1980-1992
DS before number: *Dictionary of Literary Biography Documentary Series*, Volumes 1-11

B

G

H

L

M

N

O

Cumulative Index

ISBN 0-8103-5395-4
90000

9 780810 353954